ROUTLEDGE HANDBOOK OF INDIGENOUS WELLBEING

The *Routledge Handbook of Indigenous Wellbeing* consists of five themes, namely, physical, social and emotional, economic, cultural and spiritual, and subjective wellbeing. It fills a substantial gap in the current literature on the wellbeing of Indigenous people and communities around the world.

This handbook sheds new light on understanding Indigenous wellbeing and its determinants, and aids in the development and implementation of more appropriate policies, as better evidence-informed policymaking will lead to better outcomes for Indigenous populations.

This book provides a reliable and convenient source of information for policymakers, academics and students, and allows readers to make informed decisions regarding the wellbeing of Indigenous populations. It is also a useful resource for non-government organizations to gain insight into relevant global factors for the development of stronger and more effective international policies to improve the lives of Indigenous communities.

Christopher Fleming is Professor at Griffith Business School, Griffith University.

Matthew Manning is Associate Professor at the Centre for Social Research and Methods, Australian National University.

ROUTLEDGE HANDBOOK OF INDIGENOUS WELLBEING

*Edited by Christopher Fleming and
Matthew Manning*

LONDON AND NEW YORK

First published 2019
by Routledge
2 Park Square, Milton Park, Abingdon, Oxon OX14 4RN
605 Third Avenue, New York, NY 10017

First issued in paperback 2021

Routledge is an imprint of the Taylor & Francis Group, an informa business

Publisher's Note
The publisher has gone to great lengths to ensure the quality of this reprint
but points out that some imperfections in the original copies may be apparent.

British Library Cataloguing in Publication Data
A catalogue record for this book is available from the British Library

Library of Congress Cataloging in Publication Data
Names: Fleming, Christopher (Christopher M.), editor. |
Manning, Matthew (Microeconomist), editor.
Title: Routledge handbook of indigenous wellbeing / edited by
Christopher Fleming and Matthew Manning.
Description: Abingdon, Oxon ; New York, NY : Routledge, 2019. |
Series: Routledge international handbooks |
Includes bibliographical references.
Identifiers: LCCN 2018060181| ISBN 9781138909175 (hbk) |
ISBN 9781351051262 (ebk)
Subjects: LCSH: Indigenous peoples–Social conditions–Case studies. |
Indigenous peoples–Health and hygiene–Case studies. |
Indigenous peoples–Mental health–Case studies.
Classification: LCC GN380 .R58 2019 | DDC 305.8–dc23
LC record available at https://lccn.loc.gov/2018060181

Typeset in Bembo
by Newgen Publishing UK

ISBN 13: 978-1-03-209279-9 (pbk)
ISBN 13: 978-1-138-90917-5 (hbk)

CONTENTS

Contents

FIGURES

TABLES

CONTRIBUTORS

Annabel Ahuriri-Driscoll is Lecturer in Māori Health in the School of Health Sciences, University of Canterbury, New Zealand.

Christopher L. Ambrey is Research Fellow at the Institute for Social Science Research, The University of Queensland, Australia.

Robert B. Anderson is Professor Emeritus (Entrepreneurship and Management Accounting) within the Hill/Levene Schools of Business at the University of Regina, Saskatchewan, Canada.

Mapuana C.K. Antonio is a faculty member of the Social Sciences Division at Leeward Community College, University of Hawaiʻi Community Colleges, USA.

Lilia Arcos Holzinger is Research Assistant in the Research School of Social Sciences and the Tax and Transfer Policy Institute of The Australian National University.

Per Axelsson is Associate Professor at the Vaartoe – Centre for Sámi Research, The Centre for Population Studies and the Department for Historical Philosophical and Religious Studies, Umeå University, Sweden.

Nicholas Biddle is Associate Director of The Australian National University Centre for Social Research and Methods and Director of the newly created Policy Experiments Lab.

Amohia Boulton is Director of Whakauae Research for Māori Health & Development, Whanganui, New Zealand and is Adjunct Professor for the Faculty of Health and Environmental Sciences, Auckland University of Technology, New Zealand.

Paz Chávez is Graduate Student at the Latin American Faculty of Social Sciences, Mexico City, Mexico.

Rick Colbourne is Professor in the Business department at Capilano University, North Vancouver, British Columbia, Canada. In 2016 Rick was awarded the Fulbright Canada

Scholarship to conduct research in Indigenous entrepreneurship and entrepreneurial ecosystems at the University of Arizona.

Ashlee Cunsolo is Director of the Labrador Institute, Cross-Appointed with Community Health and Humanities, Memorial University, Canada, and Associated Graduate Faculty, University of Guelph, Canada.

Christopher Fleming is Professor at the Griffith Business School, Griffith University, Australia.

Susanne Garvis is Professor of Child and Youth Studies at the Department of Education, Communication and Learning, University of Gothenburg, Sweden.

Joel Gittelsohn is Professor of Human Nutrition within the Department of International Health at the Johns Hopkins Bloomberg School of Public Health, USA.

Joseph P. Gone is Director of Native American Studies, Professor of Psychology and Professor of American Culture at the University of Michigan, Ann Arbor, Michigan, USA.

Matthew Gray is Director of the Centre for Social Research and Methods, The Australian National University.

Cornelis W. Haasnoot is Lecturer in Macroeconomics and International Economics at the Amsterdam School of Economics, University of Amsterdam, the Netherlands.

Sherilee L. Harper is Assistant Professor, Department of Population Medicine, University of Guelph, Canada.

Andrea H. Hermosura is Assistant Professor, Department of Native Hawaiian Health, John A. Burns School of Medicine, University of Hawai'i, USA.

Robert K. Hitchcock is Research Professor, Department of Anthropology, University of New Mexico, Albuquerque, New Mexico, USA.

Belayet Hossain is Associate Professor, School of Business and Economics, Thompson Rivers University, Kamloops, British Columbia, Canada.

Carla A. Houkamau is Senior Lecturer and the Associate Dean for Māori and Pacific Development in the Business School at the University of Auckland, New Zealand.

Boyd Hunter is IZA Research Fellow and Senior Fellow at the Centre for Aboriginal Economic Policy Research, Research School of Social Sciences, The Australian National University.

Shashi Kant is Professor of Forest Resource Economics and Management, Faculty of Forestry, and Director, Master of Science in Sustainability Management, University of Toronto, Canada.

Joseph Keawe'aimoku Kaholokula is Professor and Chair, Department of Native Hawaiian Health, John A. Burns School of Medicine, University of Hawai'i, USA.

Laura Lamb is Associate Professor, School of Business and Economics, Thompson Rivers University, Kamloops, British Columbia, Canada.

Munib Said Mafazy holds a doctorate in Nursing and works at Advocate Neurology in Bloomington, Illinois, USA. He also serves as Executive Director of the Lamu Center of Preventative Health.

Rebecca Gearhart Mafazy is Professor of Anthropology in the Department of Sociology and Anthropology at Illinois Wesleyan University, USA.

Matthew Manning is Associate Professor at the Centre for Social Research and Methods, The Australian National University.

Christina Storm Mienna is Senior Dental Officer, Doctor of Medicine and is affiliated with the Vaartoe – Centre for Sámi Research, at Umeå University, Sweden.

Pelotshweu Moepeng is Chief Executive Officer of the Botswana-based consultancy firm Sustainable Development Research Solution (SDRS) (Pty) Ltd. Pelotshweu holds a PhD in Economics from the University of Queensland, Australia.

Daniel Neff is Research Fellow at the German Institute of Global and Area Studies, Hamburg, Germany.

Lyle J. Noisy Hawk is an enrolled member of the Oglala Lakota Sioux Tribe, and a native speaker of the Lakota language. Lyle holds a PhD in counseling psychology from the University of Minnesota, USA. He consults on Lakota wellness practices with the Medicine Horse Society.

Keitseope Nthomang is Professor and Head of the Department of Social Work at the University of Botswana. Keitseope has consulted for the UNDP, the Botswana Institute for Development Policy Analysis, Government of Botswana, and the African Comprehensive HIV/AIDS Programme.

Lotta Omma is a researcher at the Department of Clinical Sciences Psychiatry, Umeå University, Sweden.

Ana Maria Peredo is Professor in the School of Environmental Studies at Victoria University, Canada. She holds a PhD in Sustainable Development and Environmental Management from the University of Calgary.

Andrew Pomerville is a doctoral candidate in psychology, Clinical Science Area, Department of Psychology, College of Literature, Science, and Arts, University of Michigan, Ann Arbor, Michigan, USA.

Leslie Redmond is Senior Researcher in Human Nutrition within the Department of International Health at the Johns Hopkins Bloomberg School of Public Health, and Nutrition Communications Specialist at the California Strawberry Commission, USA.

Sebastian Renner is Postdoctoral Researcher at the University of Göttingen and research fellow at the German Institute of Global and Area Studies, Hamburg, Germany.

Mariano Rojas is Professor at the Latin American Faculty of Social Sciences, Mexico City and at the Universidad Popular Autónoma del Estado de Puebla, Puebla, Mexico.

Maria Sapignoli is a social anthropologist and a research fellow at the Max Planck Institute for Social Anthropology, Halle, Germany.

Alexandra Sawatzky is PhD candidate in Public Health, Department of Population Medicine, University of Guelph, Canada.

Kunal Sen is Professor of Development Economics in the Global Development Institute, University of Manchester, UK.

Inez Shiwak is Community Research Lead and Coordinator of the "My Word:" Storytelling and Digital Media Lab, Rigolet Inuit Community Government, Canada.

Joseph E. Trimble is Distinguished University Professor and Professor of Psychology at Western Washington University in Bellingham, Washington, USA.

Ilan Vertinsky is Vinod Sood Professor of Strategy and Business Economics, and associate of the Peter Wall Institute of Advanced Studies at the University of British Colombia, Canada.

Isaac Warbrick is Senior Lecturer, Taupua Waiora Centre for Māori Health Research, and the School of Public Health and Psychosocial Studies, Auckland University of Technology, New Zealand.

Denise Wilson is Professor of Māori Health at the Taupua Waiora Centre for Māori Health Research, and the School of Public Health and Psychosocial Studies, Auckland University of Technology, New Zealand.

Michele Wood is Health Researcher/Evaluator at the Nunatsiavut Government Department of Health and Social Development, Canada.

Mandy Yap is Research Scholar at The Australian National University's Centre for Aboriginal Economic Policy Research.

Eunice Yu is a Yawuru person currently employed by the Yawuru Jarndu Aboriginal Corporation in Broome, Western Australia.

Bin Zheng is Assistant Professor at the Faculty of Economics and Management, Nanjing Forestry University, Nanjing, People's Republic of China.

1

THE COMPLEXITY OF MEASURING INDIGENOUS WELLBEING

Matthew Manning and Christopher Fleming

Improving the lives of Indigenous people irrespective of location is one of our most important priorities. Moreover, working toward reducing the gap between non-Indigenous and Indigenous people across all domains of life is critical. This includes domains related to Indigenous peoples' physical, social and emotional, economic, cultural and spiritual, and subjective wellbeing. Also important is ensuring that we provide Indigenous children with a healthy start to life that will give them the best chance of success in school and future employment opportunities.

So, what do we mean by wellbeing in this book? Wellbeing, sometimes referred to as wellness, describes the condition of an individual or group. It includes choices and activities aimed at achieving physical vitality, mental alacrity, social satisfaction, a sense of accomplishment, and personal fulfilment. We understand a high level of wellbeing to mean that in some sense the individual's or group's condition is positive.

Wellbeing has diverse and interconnected dimensions that extend beyond the traditional definition of health; such diversity must be captured and understood before substantive and sustainable choices and change can be made. However, it is important to recognize that one group's conceptualization of the dimensions of wellbeing and their respective indicators may be different from another's, and as such, a 'one size fits all' approach will be limited. A useful first step is to disaggregate wellbeing into a range of domains and go to those who have substantive expertise and knowledge within those domains. These experts can then refine the definition of these domains within particular contexts, and inform us of how best to measure wellbeing within this domain, what the evidence tells us about currents states and trends, and offer some suggestions of how wellbeing can be improved. That is the goal of this handbook.

By no means do we claim that this handbook will represent all Indigenous populations, or provide definitive solutions to all of the injustices or inequities that Indigenous people have experienced and continue to face. Rather, our goals are more modest. When we initially spoke with numerous Indigenous people and Indigenous researchers from around the world about this book, support was incredibly strong. They assisted us in shaping our goals and the best way of achieving them. The consensus was that we provide an opportunity for those researchers, many of whom are Indigenous or have worked and lived within Indigenous communities, to share their unique knowledge and the lessons they have learnt over the years. But importantly, not to do this in isolation – hence a handbook. Very few individuals disagreed with the domain classifications we proposed. Rather, they helped us shape the domains so they – to the best of our ability – drill down to what aspects of an individual's life matter and in a context that truly represents the communities they describe. Of course, there will always be those who vehemently disagree with the choices we made. But, in spite of their disagreement we pushed on with the knowledge that our intentions are good and we did all we could to be informed by the majority on how we best describe the wellbeing of Indigenous people from various parts of the world. This is not the end: we hope in the future to bring together more research from other Indigenous populations around the world in order to get a greater understanding of how all Indigenous people fare and what governments can do to make real sustainable change.

Why the handbook

Policies, programmes and initiatives aimed at improving the lives of Indigenous peoples and communities must be informed by current evidence regarding the physical, social and emotional, economic, cultural and spiritual, and subjective domains of wellbeing. Moreover, Indigenous policy must incorporate an understanding of factors central to Indigenous peoples' concept of wellbeing. With a clearer understanding of Indigenous wellbeing and its determinants, more appropriate policy can be developed and implemented. Ultimately, evidence-informed policy-making will lead to better outcomes for Indigenous populations.

Currently there is no readily accessible source of information that identifies and discusses the important factors that are relevant to the wellbeing of various Indigenous cultures. There is also no source of information that appreciates the diversity of Indigenous cultures around the world. The objective of this handbook, therefore, is to fill a substantial gap in the current literature on the wellbeing of Indigenous peoples and communities across the world. The handbook provides a reliable and convenient source of information for policymakers, academics and students. This will allow readers to make informed choices when making decisions regarding the wellbeing of Indigenous populations. The handbook will also assist non-government organizations such as the World Health Organization, the World Bank and the Organisation for Economic Co-operation and Development to gain a global perspective of factors that are relevant to the development of stronger and more effective international policy aimed at improving the lives of Indigenous communities. In addition, this handbook will also assist the United Nations (UN) Permanent Forum on Indigenous Issues to achieve its objective of providing expert advice and recommendations on Indigenous issues to the UN Economic and Social Council, as well as to programmes, funds and agencies of the UN.

Handbook structure

The handbook contains twenty-four substantive chapters, encompassing six regions (Europe and the Circumpolar North, North America, South and Central America, Africa, Asia/Pacific and Oceania) and structured around five domains: physical wellbeing (Chapters 3–8); social and emotional wellbeing (Chapters 9–12); economic wellbeing (Chapters 13–18); cultural and spiritual wellbeing (Chapters 19–22) and subjective wellbeing (Chapters 23–26).

2

UNDERSTANDING WELLBEING

Matthew Manning and Christopher Fleming

The importance of wellbeing

The concept of 'wellbeing' underpins our institutions of morality, politics, law and economics. Theologians and philosophers continue to inquire how best to understand wellbeing, its measurement, and its place in moral and political thought. In more recent times, scholars from areas as diverse as economics, anthropology, sociology and psychology have focused their attention on what it means to live well, with many earlier preconceptions being challenged.

The Organisation of Economic Co-operation and Development (OECD) has led the way with regards to instilling the importance of the measurement of wellbeing as a policy instrument. For example, following the second OECD World Forum in 2007, the Istanbul Declaration was ratified between the OECD, the European Commission, the Organisation of the Islamic Conference, the United Nations, the UN Development Programme and the World Bank. The aim of the declaration was to reaffirm a commitment to accurately measuring – across all relevant dimensions – the progress of societies so as to improve policy and enhance democracy and citizens' wellbeing (OECD, 2007).

Alongside the OECD's agenda, a vast and growing body of literature has developed with the explicit aim of developing and empirically validating alternative measures of the standard of living using data collection frameworks and national surveys (Pink, Taylor, & Wetzler, 2014; Stiglitz, Sen, & Fitoussi, 2009). Examples of such surveys include the National Aboriginal and Torres Strait Islander Social Survey (NATSISS) in Australia (Australian Bureau of Statistics, 2017) and the Aboriginal Peoples Survey Canada (Statistics Canada, 2017). The aim of such highly specific surveys is an attempt to expel our reliance on indicators of societal development that may be flawed – a movement that is occurring in both developed and developing countries (Bache & Reardon, 2016). As highlighted by Stiglitz et al. (2009), national level statistics that reflect societal progress need, first, to reflect on the ways in which progress is measured. Such a statement is part of the wave of movement questioning the ability of measures such as GDP per capita to accurately reflect individual and societal wellbeing.

The recognized importance of wellbeing, which gained momentum from the 1970s, underpins the policy agenda in most countries, which has, in turn, led to a proliferation of research efforts toward measuring wellbeing. However, in order to meaningfully implant a notion of wellbeing into policy, one must first gain a deep understanding of the concept of wellbeing from all perspectives, its measurement – both quantitatively and qualitatively – and the tools used to evaluate and compare. As stated by Sen (1987b), the necessary tasks include deciding on "what are the objects [and] how valuable are they?" (p. 4). Although these questions appear simple, the answers are dependent upon how wellbeing is conceptualized by an individual and the theory that one subscribes.

Theories of wellbeing

Theories of wellbeing traditionally fall into three categories, which in part mirror long established divisions between contrasting schools of thought in normative ethics. These theories are complex and require significant discussion to fully comprehend their meaning. Such an exercise, however, is not the purpose of this chapter. Rather, the paragraphs that follow introduce the main schools of thought, providing the reader with links to writings that fully unpack these theories.

Hedonistic theories of wellbeing

Hedonistic theories focus on the intrinsic value of certain psychological states, highlighting that what is good for a person overall is the greatest 'achievable' balance in terms of the calculus of pleasure over pain (Crisp, 2006). On the other hand, desire-satisfaction theories propose that wellbeing reflects the satisfaction of a person's desires or preferences (Olsaretti & Arneson, 2006). In short, both hedonistic and desire-satisfaction theories of wellbeing are founded on the utilitarian ethical tradition, and together dominate the evaluative foundations of contemporary research on this topic.

Objective list theories of wellbeing

Objective list theories of wellbeing propose that certain objective conditions define personal wellbeing, and that these conditions do not necessarily reject the inclusion of happiness and desire satisfaction. Objective list theories typically owe their evaluative origins to varieties of deontology (i.e. the science of the determination of duties within social circumstances or the theory of moral norms), and especially to the natural law and human rights traditions in moral and political philosophy (Finnis, 2011). Contemporary virtue ethical accounts of wellbeing which trace their origins to Aristotelian ethics also establish an objective list rather than a hedonistic or desire-satisfaction theory (Hursthouse, 1999).

The capabilities approach

More recently an approach to understanding individual wellbeing has emerged that has moved the discussion away from the traditional theoretical presumption of foundational monism, towards a more flexible pluralist approach. The most prominent and philosophically sophisticated of pluralist accounts is the freedom-based 'capabilities' approach (Nussbaum, 2000; Sen, 1985, 1987a, 1992, 1999a, 1999b, 2008).

The approach concerns the distinction between capabilities and functionings. Sen (1999b) refers to functionings as achievements and capabilities – the ability to achieve – which is inextricably linked to freedom and the real opportunities to live the life one has reason to value. Advocates of this approach call for an evaluative space to understand an individual's command of their resources, their ability and freedom to achieve wellbeing and the structures that promote or constrain their individual pursuit of wellbeing (Alkire, 2002, 2015; Clark, 2005; Deneulin, 2008; Robeyns, 2005; Stewart, 2005). It is important to note that this approach, however, does not advocate the privileging of objective or subjective measures. Here, Sen (2004) chooses not to recommend a list of functionings and capabilities to which society should ascribe. Rather, he chooses to leave that process to be dependent on context and reason, favouring deliberative participation. Nussbaum (2000), on the other hand, provides a list of ten central human capabilities (yet to be challenged; Clark, 2005) – these include life expectancy, bodily health, bodily integrity, sense imagination and thought, emotions, practical reason, affiliation, other species, play and control over the environment – as substantive capabilities, which she subscribes as being universally critical dimensions of wellbeing. Irrespective of list or no list, the UNDP Human Development reports and associated Human Development Indices are the key products stemming from this approach (McGillivray & Clarke, 2006; United Nations Development Programme, 1990).

Wellbeing and its multidimensionality

Wellbeing is a multidimensional construct. It incorporates both subjective and objective elements that are context and population-specific. However, in light of this now obvious fact, there remains a tendency, in international discourse, to establish common criteria and indicators for the measurement of societal progress with the common ambition of comparing between individuals from different backgrounds (OECD, 2015). The main problem with such an approach is that different people hold different meanings and understanding of what constitutes wellbeing and these can sometimes be misinterpreted within the dominant universalist model (White & Blackmore, 2016). Indigenous meaning and understanding of wellbeing is certainly subject to such distortions by the dominant paradigm (Jordan, Bullock, & Buchanan, 2010).

In part, this may be due to a lack of informed information on what constitutes wellbeing from an Indigenous perspective. Yap (2017) proposes that this may stem from a power imbalance between Indigenous peoples and their nation-states, and a lack of informed data of what constitutes wellbeing from an Indigenous perspective. Why is this? Yap states:

> The first [reason] is the difference in worldviews and priorities of indigenous peoples and government reporting frameworks around conceptions of wellbeing. Second, there is a lack of effort towards developing culturally appropriate methodologies to elicit indigenous indicators of wellbeing. In particular, there is a need for methodologies which are emancipatory, which potentially transform current research paradigms so that those on the ground meaningfully participate in the research process.
>
> (p. 5)

Empirical approaches to measuring wellbeing

Both qualitative and quantitative approaches have been used to explore individual wellbeing. Qualitative approaches (such as those used in anthropological research) have been traditionally employed in this space as it is argued that they enable a more nuanced understanding of wellbeing across different locations (Adelson, 2009; Izquierdo, 2009). Interviews and focus groups are often employed to identify and generate themes of Indigenous wellbeing. Alexandra Sawatzky and colleagues (Chapter 19 in this book), for example, drew data from

106 interviews conducted through a community-led participatory project in the Inuit region of Nunatsiavut, Labrador, Canada to explore perspectives on land-based activities and connections to wellbeing.

Quantitative approaches (such as those used by economists and political scientists) are also employed in this space to take advantage of data drawn from surveys such as the NATSISS in Australia (Australian Bureau of Statistics, 2017) and the Aboriginal Peoples Survey Canada (Statistics Canada, 2017). For example, Easterlin (1974), building on the work of Veblen (1899) and Duesenberry (1949) provided an economic perspective on how absolute and relative incomes affect subjective wellbeing (Grimes, 2015). Ambrey, Fleming, and Manning (Chapter 27 in this book), for example, employ a quantitative approach to explore the subjective wellbeing of Indigenous Australians. Evidence is provided on: (1) mean levels of self-reported life satisfaction; (2) trends in these means; and (3) differences in the determinants of life satisfaction between Indigenous and non-Indigenous Australians.

Understanding Indigenous wellbeing

McCubbin, McCubbin, Zhang, Kehl, and Strom (2013) propose that Indigenous wellbeing begins from a relational perspective, with a focus on the collective rather than the individual. It is tied around notions or domains such as culture and spirituality, social and emotional, physical, subjective (Dockery, 2012; Ganesharajah, 2009; Greiner, Larson, Herr, & Bligh, 2005; Grieves, 2007; Merino, 2016; Watene, 2016) and finally economic wellbeing (Altman, 2004; Godoy, Reyes-García, Byron, Leonard, & Vadez, 2005).

To date, efforts to measure Indigenous wellbeing have tended to be built upon theories of wellbeing which stem from non-Indigenous values. Further, national policies aimed at improving the lives of Indigenous populations tend to be top-down, with a narrow conceptualization of wellbeing and little input from those affected. This may be, in part, due to: (1) a lack of engagement with the Indigenous population; (2) poor research on the part of those who undertake empirical research; (3) a lack of research by qualified researchers who know how to engage with the population under investigation; and (4) a lack of knowledge and lessons learnt from other studies conducted on the wellbeing of Indigenous populations from other parts of the world.

Indigenous context

Perceptions of wellbeing cannot be separated from context, which includes 'place'. Place moves beyond the physical geographical space to incorporate a spiritual connection that many Indigenous people have to their ancestral land (Panelli & Tipa, 2007). Context, from an Indigenous perspective, also requires an understanding of how a history of colonization and marginalization has affected Indigenous health and wellbeing (Axelsson, Kukutai, & Kippen, 2016; Gee, Dudgeon, Schultz, Hart, & Kelly, 2015). In addition, understanding context also requires a familiarization of the social and political circumstances and struggles of Indigenous peoples (Deneulin, 2008).

Domains of wellbeing

In order to insert wellbeing into policy, one requires an understanding of wellbeing concepts, measures and evaluation tools. The fundamental task here includes deciding 'what objects (domains and indicators) are of value' and the 'importance attached to the object or objects' (Sen, 1987a). Deceptively straightforward, this task is critically dependent on how wellbeing is conceptualized, by whom and through what process.

In this handbook, we attempt to draw together researchers from around the world, who have extensive knowledge of one of five domains of Indigenous wellbeing – physical, social and emotional, economic, cultural and spiritual and subjective. We do this to not only understand and learn how Indigenous populations fare with respect to one of the domains, but also what we can learn from their attempts to measure it and how policy can be shaped to improve the lives of Indigenous peoples in their population.

Physical wellbeing

Physical wellbeing is one dimension contributing to your holistic health. It involves a range of lifestyle behavioural choices that an individual makes to "ensure health, avoid preventable diseases and conditions, and live in a balanced state of body, mind and spirit" (American Association of Nurse Anesthetists, 2016).

Social and emotional wellbeing

Social and emotional wellbeing refers to the way a person thinks and feels about themselves and others. Good social and emotional wellbeing involves being able to adapt and manage challenges (through resilience and employing a range of coping skills) – often on a daily basis – while leading a fulfilling life (Australian Institute of Health and Welfare, 2012).

Economic wellbeing

Economic wellbeing of individuals, families or households relates to the economic resources they have available to support their material living conditions and their control over these resources and conditions. Typically, economic wellbeing has three key interrelated components: income, consumption and wealth (Australian Bureau of Statistics, 2015).

Cultural and spiritual wellbeing

Cultural wellbeing refers to the freedom to practise or 'live' your own culture, and importantly feel belonging to your cultural group. Cultural wellbeing emanates from being valued for our unique differences and beliefs that define us, our beliefs, our history and our origins. This domain of wellbeing assists us to define who we are as individuals (Reid, Varona, Fisher, & Smith, 2016). Spiritual wellbeing defines an ability to experience and integrate meaning and purpose in life through individual connectedness with one's self, others, art, music, literature, nature or a power greater than oneself (Fisher, Francis, & Johnson, 2000).

Subjective wellbeing

Subjective wellbeing is defined as an individual's cognitive and affective evaluations of his or her life (Diener, Oishi, & Lucas, 2002). The cognitive component refers to how one thinks about his/her life satisfaction in global terms (i.e. life as a whole) and in domain terms (i.e. in specific areas of life such as work, relationships, etc.). The affective component refers to emotions, moods and feelings. Affect is considered positive when the emotions, moods and feelings experienced are pleasant (e.g. joy, elation, affection, etc.) and negative when the emotions, moods and feelings experienced are unpleasant (e.g. guilt, anger, shame, etc.).

References

Adelson, N. (2009). The shifting landscape of Cree well-being. In G. Mathews & C. Izquierdo (Eds.), *Pursuits of happiness: Well-being in anthropological perspective.* London: Berghahn.

Alkire, S. (2002). *Valuing freedoms: Sen's capability approach and poverty reduction.* Oxford: Oxford University Press.

Alkire, S. (2015). *The capability approach and well-being measurement for public policy.* OPHI working paper no. 94, University of Oxford. Retrieved from https://ora.ox.ac.uk/objects/uuid:d1f98a31-d549-4dc1-a7b1-1352f9ac46fe.

Altman, J. (2004). *The economic status of Indigenous Australians.* ANU Centre for Aboriginal Economic Policy Research (CAEPR) discussion papers, The Australian National University, Canberra.

American Association of Nurse Anesthetists. (2016). *Physical well-being.* Retrieved from www.aana.com/resources2/health-wellness/Pages/Physical-Well-Being.aspx.

Australian Bureau of Statistics. (2015). *Economic wellbeing.* Retrieved from www.abs.gov.au/ausstats/abs@.nsf/Lookup/by%20Subject 4160.0.55.001~Jun%202015~Main%20Features~Economic%20wellbeing~10015.

Australian Bureau of Statistics. (2017). *National Aboriginal and Torres Strait Islander Social Survey, 2014–15.* Retrieved from www.abs.gov.au/ausstats/abs@.nsf/mf/4714.0.

Australian Institute of Health and Welfare. (2012). *Social and emotional wellbeing: Development of a children's headline indicator.* Retrieved from www.aihw.gov.au/reports/children-youth/social-emotional-wellbeing-development-of-chi/contents/table-of-contents.

Axelsson, P., Kukutai, T., & Kippen, R. (2016). The field of Indigenous health and the role of colonisation and history. *Journal of Population Research, 33*(1), 1–7.

Bache, I., & Reardon, L. (2016). *The politics and policy of wellbeing: Understanding the rise and significance of a new agenda.* Cheltenham: Edward Elgar Publishing.

Clark, D. (2005). *The capability approach: Its development, critiques and recent advances.* GPRG working paper series no. 32. Retrieved from www.gprg.org/pubs/workingpapers/pdfs/gprg-wps-032.pdf.

Crisp, R. (2006). Pleasure and the good life: Concerning the nature, varieties and plausibility of hedonism. *The Philosophical Quarterly, 56*(222), 152–154.

Deneulin, S. (2008). Beyond individual freedom and agency: Structures of living together in the capability approach. In F. Comim, M. Qizilbash, & S. Alkire (Eds.), *Capability approach: Concepts, measures and applications* (pp. 105–124). New York: Cambridge University Press.

Diener, E., Oishi, S., & Lucas, R. (2002). Subjective well-being: The science of happiness and life satisfaction. In C. Snyder & S. Lopez (Eds.), *Handbook of positive psychology.* Oxford and New York: Oxford University Press.

Dockery, A.M. (2012). Do traditional culture and identity promote the wellbeing of Indigenous Australians? Evidence from the 2008 NATSISS. In B. Hunter & N. Biddle (Eds.), *Survey analysis for Indigenous policy in Australia: Social science perspectives* (pp. 281–305). Canberra: ANU E Press.

Duesenberry, J. (1949). *Income, savings, and the theory of consumer behaviour.* Cambridge, MA: Harvard University Press.

Easterlin, R. (1974). Does economic growth improve the human lot? Some empirical evidence. In P. David & M. Reder (Eds.), *Nations and households in economic growth* (pp. 89–125). New York: Academic Press.

Finnis, J. (2011). *Natural law and natural rights.* Oxford: Oxford University Press.

Fisher, J., Francis, L., & Johnson, P. (2000). Assessing spiritual health via four domains of spiritual well-being: The SH4DI. *Pastoral Psychology, 49*(2), 133–145.

Ganesharajah, C. (2009). *Indigenous health and wellbeing: The importance of country.* Retrieved from https://aiatsis.gov.au/publications/products/indigenous-health-and-wellbeing-importance-country.

Gee, G., Dudgeon, P., Schultz, C., Hart, A., & Kelly, K. (2015). Aboriginal and Torres Strait Islander social and emotional wellbeing. In P. Dudgeon, H. Milroy, & R. Walker (Eds.), *Working together: Aboriginal and Torres Strait Islander mental health and wellbeing principles and practice* (pp. 55–68). Canberra: Department of The Prime Minister and Cabinet.

Godoy, R., Reyes-García, V., Byron, E., Leonard, W., & Vadez, V. (2005). The effect of market economies on the well-being of indigenous peoples and on their use of renewable natural resources. *Annual Review of Anthropology, 34*(1), 121–138.

Greiner, R., Larson, S., Herr, A., & Bligh, V. (2005). *Wellbeing of Nywaigi Traditional Owners: The contribution of country to wellbeing and the role of natural resource management.* Retrieved from https://publications.csiro.au/rpr/pub?pid=procite:a3fd9102-b143-4058-a1c0-2972b017c60a.

Grieves, V. (2007). *Indigenous well-being: A framework for governments' Aboriginal cultural heritage activities.* Retrieved from www.environment.nsw.gov.au/conservation/IndigenousWellbeingFramework.htm.

Grimes, A. (2015). Recent quantitative approaches to measuring wellbeing in New Zealand. *New Zealand Sociology, 30*(3), 112.

Hursthouse, R. (1999). *On virtue ethics.* Oxford: Oxford University Press.

Izquierdo, C. (2009). Well-being among the Matsigenka of the Peruvian Amazon: Health, missions, oil, and progress. In G. Mathews & C. Izquierdo (Eds.), *Pursuits of happiness: Well-Being in anthropological perspective.* London: Berghahn.

Jordan, K., Bullock, H., & Buchanan, G. (2010). Exploring the tensions between statistical equality and cultural difference in Indigenous wellbeing frameworks: A new expression of an enduring debate. *Australian Journal of Social Issues, 45*(3), 333–362.

McCubbin, L., McCubbin, H., Zhang, W., Kehl, L., & Strom, I. (2013). Relational well-being: An Indigenous perspective and measure. *Family Relations, 62*(2), 354–365.

McGillivray, M., & Clarke, M. (2006). Human well-being: Concepts and measures. In M. McGillivray & M. Clarke (Eds.), *Understanding human well-being.* New York: United Nations University Press.

Merino, R. (2016). An alternative to 'alternative development'? Buen vivir and human development in Andean countries. *Oxford Development Studies, 44*(3), 271–286.

Nussbaum, M. (2000). *Women and human development: The capabilities approach.* Cambridge: Cambridge University Press.

OECD. (2007). *Measuring and fostering the progress of societies.* Paper presented at the OECD World Forum – Instanbul 2007, Istanbul. Retrieved from www.oecd.org/site/worldforum06/.

OECD. (2015). *How's life? 2015.* Retrieved from www.oecd-ilibrary.org/economics/how-s-life-2015_how_life-2015-en.

Olsaretti, S., & Arneson, R. (2006). *Preferences and well-being.* Cambridge: Cambridge University Press.

Panelli, R., & Tipa, G. (2007). Placing well-being: A Maori case study of cultural and environmental specificity. *EcoHealth, 4*(4), 445–460.

Pink, B., Taylor, S., & Wetzler, H. (2014). The international context. In A. Podger & D. Trewin (Eds.), *Measuring and promoting wellbeing: How important is economic growth?* (pp. 163–189). Canberra: ANU Press.

Reid, J., Varona, G., Fisher, M., & Smith, C. (2016). Understanding Maori 'lived' culture to determine cultural connectedness and wellbeing. *Journal of Population Research, 33*(1), 31–49.

Robeyns, I. (2005). The capability approach: A theoretical survey. *Journal of Human Development, 61*(1), 93–117.

Sen, A. (1985). Wellbeing, agency and freedom: The Dewey Lectures 1984. *The Journal of Philosophy, 82*(4), 169–221.

Sen, A. (1987a). *On ethics and economics.* Oxford: Basil Blackwell.

Sen, A. (1987b). *The standard of living: The Tanner lectures on human values.* Cambridge: Cambridge University Press.

Sen, A. (1992). *Inequality reexamined.* Oxford: Clarendon Press.

Sen, A. (1999a). *Commodities and capabilities.* New Delhi: Oxford University Press.

Sen, A. (1999b). *Development as freedom.* New York: Alfred A. Knopf.

Sen, A. (2004). Capabilities, lists and public reason: Continuing the conversation. *Feminist Economics, 10*(3), 77–80.

Sen, A. (2008). Capability and wellbeing. In D. Hausman (Ed.), *The philosophy of economics: An anthology.* Cambridge: Cambridge University Press.

Statistics Canada. (2017). *Aboriginal Peoples Survey (APS).* Retrieved from www.statcan.gc.ca/eng/survey/household/3250.

Stewart, F. (2005). Groups and capabilities. *Journal of Human Development and Capabilities, 6*(1), 182–204.

Stiglitz, J., Sen, A., & Fitoussi, J. (2009). Report by the Commission on the Measurement of Economic Performance and Social Progress. *Sustainable Development, 12*(1), 292.

United Nations Development Programme. (1990). *Human development report.* New York: UNDP.

Veblen, T. (1899). *The theory of the leisure class: An economic study in the evolution of institutions.* New York: The Macmillan Company.

Watene, K. (2016). Valuing nature: Māori philosophy and the capability approach. *Oxford Development Studies, 44*(3), 287–296.

White, S., & Blackmore, C. (2016). *Culture of wellbeing: Method, place and policy.* Basingstoke: Palgrave Macmillan.

Yap, M. (2017). *In pursuit of culturally relevant indicators of Indigenous wellbeing: Operationalising the 'recognition space'.* PhD thesis, Australian National University, Canberra.

PART I

Physical wellbeing

3

HEALTH AND PHYSICAL WELLBEING OF THE SÁMI PEOPLE

Per Axelsson and Christina Storm Mienna

Introduction

The first attempt to create a global overview of Indigenous peoples' health and wellbeing against benchmark populations was undertaken by Anderson et al. (2016). A total of twenty-eight Indigenous populations in twenty-three countries were studied, with infant mortality, maternal mortality, high or low birthweight, obesity and life expectancy among the health indicators measured, alongside educational attainment, relative poverty and unemployment rates; the aim was to understand social outcomes. The overall conclusion of the study stated that Indigenous peoples' health and social outcomes were poorer than those of non-Indigenous peoples living in the same country.

There were, however, two Indigenous peoples that had almost the same outcomes as the majority benchmark populations – the Sámi people of Scandinavia and the Mon of Myanmar. In Norway for example, Sámi life-expectancy was 1.6 years shorter than the benchmark non-Sámi population, while in Sweden Sámi life-expectancy was approximately 0.3 years shorter than non-Sámi. However, Anderson et al. (2016) emphasized that the Swedish numbers were built on geographical proxies not individual-level data, further stressing that "we have concerns about the accuracy of this [Sweden's] picture of Sámi health status, in view of reports due to suicide, accident and injury" (p. 22). Sámi people in Finland and Russia were not included in the study as data were unavailable (Anderson et al., 2016).

The uncertainty of reliable official statistics is one of the recurring themes in the literature pertaining to Sámi health and demography over the past century. This has been addressed by several reports and studies (Axelsson, 2015; AHDR-II, 2014; Madden et al., 2016). The Centre for Sámi Health Research at the University of Tromsö in Arctic Norway is responsible for a large population-based study of the health and living conditions in areas with mixed Sámi and non-Sámi populations (the SAMINOR study). This study has been conducted twice (2003–04 and 2012–14) and has been crucial in measuring the health status of participants and establishing preventive measures to combat lifestyle diseases (Lund et al., 2007; Brustad et al., 2014). Unfortunately, this important Sámi-led contribution to our understanding of Sámi health is unique in Scandinavia. As the Sámi People's traditional lands – Sápmi – extend into four countries (Norway, Sweden, Finland and the Kola Peninsula of Russia; Figure 3.1), presenting a

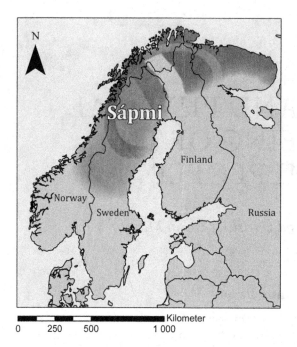

Figure 3.1　Map of Sápmi (with credit to Isabelle Brännlund)

coherent picture of the health and wellbeing of the only recognized Indigenous people in the north of Europe is challenging to say the least, and in many cases impossible.

Given this, the current chapter will outline the health and physical wellbeing of the Sámi people living in Sápmi. Knowing that the effects of colonization are crucial for an understanding of the present-day health and wellbeing status of the Sámi people, we begin by outlining the historical background to the present situation.

History and health

The Sámi have lived in northern Fennoscandia since time immemorial. They were hunters and gatherers, but coinciding with external colonial pressure, full-scale reindeer husbandry developed in the early seventeenth century. The Sámi economy has long been tied to a specific form of social organization: the *siida*. Even though it is not believed that these institutions developed simultaneously in all areas of Sápmi, and even though researchers do not agree about the collective character of the *siida*, it is understood that they played a decisive role in resource management and the regulation of relationships between individual households. Within the *siida*, distribution of resource areas was decided and the common use of wild reindeer, fish and beaver was established. Family rights to hunting and fishing sites were passed down the generations, and confirmed by the *siida*, which also negotiated with other groups concerning the use of the wider land system (Sara, 2009; Brännlund & Axelsson, 2013). From the sixteenth and seventeenth centuries onwards, the Sámi people began to be Christianized by the Orthodox church in the eastern part of their traditional lands, while the Lutheran church forced many Sámi to abandon their traditional religion in what later became Finland, Norway and Sweden. Alongside Christianization, the state introduced taxes from the early seventeenth century; these, the Sámi paid collectively. Alongside the building of churches, courts were also established in the north. It is recognized that up until the early nineteenth century, Sámi land rights were legally protected in court decisions, but a more repressive state policy replaced the Sámi traditional division and use of land with a national administrative system. In Sweden particularly, the state partitioning of land (*avvittringen*) was a process in which the state claimed ownership of the land and 'gave' Sámi rights to use their traditional land for reindeer herding. This had detrimental impacts on Sámi society. Sámi rights were enacted through customary law with little resonance in other parts of state legislation and traditional Sámi ways of living were not taken into account (Lundmark, 2006; Allard, 2006). Rights to fishing, hunting and forestry on what had become Crown land became tied to how the state defined reindeer herding, which ultimately affected a large group of Sámi people. Sámi who did not fit the Swedish state's description of a reindeer herder lost their right to use their traditional lands and waters (Lantto & Mörkenstam, 2008). Adding to this, from the late nineteenth and into the early part of the twentieth century there was a growing focus on the 'purity' of races and the Swedish state set up the world's first institute for racial biology in 1922 in Uppsala, Sweden. Their main focus was on the 'degeneration' of races. They regarded the Sámi as a 'primitive race' that would soon succumb to the influence of 'civilization'. Meanwhile state officials thought that the Sámi needed protection and as reindeer herding was seen as the livelihood most fit for the Sámi, protecting reindeer herding was considered to equate to protection of the state-defined Sámi people.

In Norway, Sámi were exposed to profound state assimilation – Norwegianization – that justified paternalistic policies and laws in which Sámi were not permitted to speak their native language. The Sámi on the Russian Kola peninsula have been strongly influenced by the administration of Russia and the Soviet Union. For instance, as a group they were, in the 1950s and 1960s, forced to move to live in Lovozero (Sergejeva, 2000). As in Sweden and Norway, the Sámi people in Finland were forced to learn Finnish in school and their culture was repressed (Juutilainen et al., 2014; Lehtola, 2015).

During the second half of the nineteenth century, in many traditional areas, the Sámi went from being a majority population to being a minority (Figure 3.2). This occurred around the 1870s in Sámi core areas such as Gällivare and Jukkasjärvi in Sweden.

A strong political Sámi movement began in the early twentieth century, which led to the Sámi in Norway, Finland and Sweden being acknowledged as the original inhabitants of northern Scandinavia. In addition, a National Sámi Parliament was established in each of these three countries. In Russia (since 2010), a Kola Sámi Assembly, modeled after the Scandinavian parliaments, was established. However, this assembly is yet to be recognized by the Russian government.

The Sámi people have also long been actively engaged in the international Indigenous political arena and were a core part of the first step towards what is now the United Nations Permanent Forum for Indigenous Issues. The Sámi further strengthened their identity as a people with the introduction of the Sámi flag (in 1986) and use of the Sámi anthem (first used on 6 February 1993 – Sámi National Day – celebrating the first Sámi congress in Tråante/Trondheim in 1917). The United Nations Declaration on the Rights of Indigenous Peoples, was signed by Finland, Sweden and Norway in 2007, while the Russian Federation abstained from voting and has yet to sign (Rohr, 2014).

Depending on terms and definitions, there are three different Sámi languages (East Sámi, Central Sámi and South Sámi) and within these languages there are nine Sámi language dialects (or varieties) spoken today; six of them are written languages. In Norway, Finland and Sweden, Sámi languages are protected by language acts, but Russia has not conferred official status on the Sámi languages (Svonni, 1998).

The latest official count of the Sámi population took place in the 2002 Russian census, when a total of 1,991 Sámi people were listed as residing on the Kola Peninsula. In Norway, Sweden and

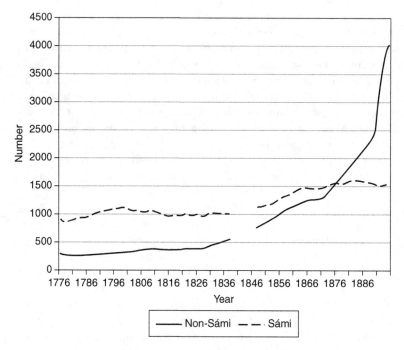

Figure 3.2   Population trends in Gällivare, 1776–1895

Source: Demographic Data Base, Gällivare parish.

Finland there is a lack of demographic data on Sámi identity in official statistics. Consequently, we do not have an accurate estimate of the number of Sámi people living in traditional Sámi areas. Estimates, however, of the number of Sámi people range from 80,000 to 140,000, with the majority of Sámi living in the northern part of the four countries (Axelsson, 2015).

Current health issues and physical wellbeing in Sápmi

During the eighteenth and nineteenth centuries, deaths due to accidents in the cold climate, drowning and complicated childbirths were reported more commonly among Sámi than among the non-Sámi population. Infant and childhood mortality rates were often three times higher among the Sámi compared with the non-Sámi population in the same area. This affected crude mortality rates, indicating that Sámi life expectancy was considerably shorter. However, the period of risk was childhood, and when the Sámi reached adulthood, their life expectancy often exceeded that of the non-Sámi settlers.

Today we have a picture showing more similarities than differences in mortality between the Sámi and non-Sámi populations in the traditional Sápmi area (Hassler et al., 2005; Tynes & Haldorsen, 2007; Soininen & Pukkola, 2008; Brustad et al., 2009). However, as stated in the introduction, one of the major challenges is being able to monitor the general health trends in Sápmi. This is due to laws around data registers, which forbid ethnic identification, thus rendering official statistics useless as regards to understanding health and living conditions in Sápmi. Health surveys are consequently few and far between. Efforts such as the Survey of Living Conditions in the Arctic (SLiCA) (Poppel, 2015) study and the Arctic Human Development Report (AHDR) (Nordic Council of Ministers, 2014) can only highlight the vast gap in knowledge relating to this area. One rare example of a successful health investigation, however, is the SAMINOR study. The study is led by the Sámi Center for Health research at the Arctic University of Norway (UIT). The SAMINOR is both a questionnaire and a clinical study and has run twice (2003–04 and 2012–14) in selected municipalities in the traditional Sámi area of Norway. The SAMINOR study has mainly focused on adults (+18 years) and the clinical studies in the last SAMINOR involved individuals 40–79 years of age. Participants self-identify their ethnic affiliations and answer questions regarding, for example, psychosocial health, discrimination and trust in healthcare systems. The 2012–14 study involved 11,600 participants and the 2003–04 version 16,865 participants. This is a very valuable health survey for understanding some of the current health issues in Norwegian Sápmi.

Based on the literature we find that mortality in the Sámi population of north Norway between 1970 and 1998 was slightly higher in total compared to the non-Sámi in the same area. This is in accordance with more recent findings from the SAMINOR study based on data from 2013 (Tynes & Haldorsen, 2007; Anderson et al., 2016). Certain causes of death exhibited a higher standardized mortality rate (SMR) in Sámi populations; these included cerebrovascular disease and violent deaths. However, mortality from malignant neoplasms and chronic liver disease were lower among Sámi than in the reference population (Tynes & Haldorsen, 2007).

Studies conducted in Sweden, where data ended in the year 2000, reveal that differences in mortality and life expectancy between the Sámi and a reference population were small. Sámi men had a lower SMR for cancer but a higher SMR for injuries with external causes. Among Sámi women, higher SMRs for diseases of the circulatory and respiratory systems were found (Hassler et al., 2005). An increased risk of dying from subarchnoid hemorrhage was also reported among both Sámi men and women. Life expectancy at birth was 74.9 years for Sámi men and 80.0 years for Sámi women. The most common causes of death were diseases of the circulatory system, followed by cancer and injuries with external causes. Accidents related to vehicles were reported as common causes of unnatural deaths among reindeer-herding Sámi families in Sweden between 1961 and 2001: road traffic accidents contributed to 16 percent of deaths and 11 percent were due to snowmobile fatalities. Half of the victims were involved in alcohol-related incidents. Suicides accounted for 23 percent of deaths (Ahlm et al., 2010). Deaths caused by vehicle accidents were also common in Finland. Suicide mortality among Sámi men was elevated compared to non-Sámi men. However, lower disease-related mortality among Sámi men compared to the general population in Finland was observed, attributable to the low mortality from cancer but possibly also related to diet, physical activity and genetics (Soininen & Pukkola, 2008).

Cancer

Cancer is one of the diseases that has been thoroughly studied in the Sámi population. A major reason for this interest was the fear of increased cancer risk due to nuclear fallout contamination in areas within Sápmi as a result of the Chernobyl nuclear reactor accident in 1986, and also from nuclear weapons testing on the island of Novaya Zemlya in the 1950s and 1960s. Studies from Norway, Sweden and Finland reveal a generally lower risk of cancer for Sámi than for non-Sámi people living in the same regions. However, cancers of the stomach in these regions are more prevalent than the national average. In all countries, Sámi show a lower risk of prostate cancer (Hassler et al., 2008b). In Sweden, the risk of stomach cancer in Sámi men and for cancers of the stomach and ovaries among Sámi women seemed to be higher than for the non-Sámi population. In addition, lower risks of cancer of the colon (this is also true for Norway), malignant melanoma and non-Hodgkin lymphoma were found among Sámi men in Sweden.

Among Sámi women in Sweden, a lower risk of bladder cancer has been reported (Hassler et al., 2008a; Haldorsen & Tynes, 2005). Significantly lower standardized incidence ratios for bladder cancer were reported for Sámi men in both Finland and Norway. In Finland, breast cancer was less common among Sámi than non-Sámi people. To date, no detectable excess of the radiation-sensitive cancers such as leukemia and thyroid cancer has been observed in either of the countries (Hassler et al., 2008b).

In conclusion, reports indicate a low risk in developing and dying from cancer among Sámi people. Suggested explanations for the low cancer risk are factors related to traditional Sámi life-style, such as dietary components (high intake of antioxidants and unsaturated fatty acids) and high levels of physical activity that may be protective factors from developing cancer. Genetic factors have also been suggested as an explanation for the lower risk of developing cancer.

Cardiovascular diseases

In Sweden, only small differences between Sámi and non-Sámi people with respect to the risk of developing cardiovascular diseases have been reported. The differences in risk factors are mostly related to working conditions and lifestyle factors associated with reindeer herding, lower blood pressure, higher job demands and physically active lifestyles. Higher incidences of stroke and subarachnoid hemorrhage (SAH) for Sámi men and women compared to a non-Sámi control population were found, but there was no increase in the risk of acute myocardial infarction (AMI) (Sjölander et al., 2008a; Edin-Liljegren et al., 2004). In Norway, marginalized Sámi living in areas dominated by non-Sámi people were more likely to report CVD than non-marginalized Sámi living in Sámi majority areas. No gender differences were found. The exposure to chronic stress following marginalization has been suggested as a plausible explanation (Eliassen et al., 2013). The prevalence of self-reported myocardial infarction is similar between Sámi and non-Sámi people in rural areas in Norway (Eliassen et al., 2015). Similar living conditions and close interactions between ethnic groups have been suggested as plausible explanations. Self-reported angina pectoris, on the other hand, was found to be more prevalent in Sámi compared to non-Sámi people (Eliassen et al., 2014).

Other somatic diseases

Metabolic syndrome refers to a cluster of risk factors associated with adverse health effects, for example cardiovascular disease or type 2 diabetes mellitus. Results from the SAMINOR study show a high prevalence of metabolic syndrome in both Sámi and non-Sámi populations and no ethnic differences were found in the prevalence of diabetes mellitus (c. 5%); however, ethnicity seemed to affect treatment. A combined treatment involving insulin and tablets was used more frequently among Sámi men than among non-Sámi men, and treatment with tablets was more commonly used among Sámi women than among non-Sámi women (Broderstad & Melhus, 2016). Naseribafrouei et al. (2016) found that pre-diabetes was reported by 2.8 percent and that the prevalence for both diabetes and pre-diabetes increased with age. They did not observe any ethnic differences.

Multiple sclerosis (MS) occurs among $100/10^5$ inhabitants in northern Europe, and among Norwegians the prevalence is in the range $73–164/10^5$ inhabitants. A low prevalence of MS among Sámi in Norway has been reported, but there are no data on MS prevalence among Sámi in Finland, Sweden or Russia. However, prevalence estimates of MS from the general population in Sweden and Finland are in the same range as in Norway; estimates from Russia are somewhat lower. It has been suggested that a low frequency of the MS-associated haplotype is related to the low prevalence among Sámi, together with other reduced genetic and environmental risk factors associated with the disease (Harbo et al., 2007).

In a study from northern Norway an association between Sámi ethnicity and asthma and allergy among schoolchildren has been found. Asthma and allergies are more prevalent among schoolchildren (7–13 years of age) from a Sámi origin compared to non-Sámi children of the same age and in the same geographic area. A greater increase in the cumulative incidence of asthma and allergy prevalence among Sámi children was also found over a ten-year period (Selnes et al., 1999; Selnes et al., 2002).

Musculoskeletal disorders

Chronic pain conditions are common in the general population. Around 20 percent of the European population suffers from chronic pain (Breivik et al., 2006). Markedly higher prevalences of musculoskeletal pain have been reported among 15–16-year-old adolescents Sámi in Norway (Table 3.1). No differences in the prevalence of musculoskeletal pain between Sámi and non-Sámi young people were found. The most common causes of pain in the orofacial area are temporomandibular disorders (TMD), which exhibit comorbidity with other pain symptoms such as headache and neck/shoulder pain (Storm & Wänman, 2006). High prevalences have been found among adult Sámi women in Sweden.

A strong association was found between musculoskeletal pain sites and psychosocial problems and studies have also linked childhood violence to chronic pain in adulthood. In the first study comparing Indigenous and non-Indigenous populations (based on the SAMINOR study) chest and stomach pain were more frequently reported by Sámi men than non-Sámi men. Sámi women reported stomach and pelvic pain more frequently than non-Sámi women (Eckoff & Kvernmo, 2014; Eriksen et al., 2016). Musculoskeletal symptoms are also reported to be common in reindeer-herding families in Sweden (Sjölander et al., 2008b). No current studies on musculoskeletal disorders among Sámi are available from either Finland or Russia.

Discussion

Sjölander (2011) stated in his review of Sámi health that "[i]n comparison with other Indigenous people in the circumpolar region, the health and living conditions are exceptionally good" (p. 9). He also, however, pointed out the general population's lack of knowledge about Sámi people and understanding of Sámi issues, which creates marginalization. This chapter illustrates a rather fragmented picture of Sámi health. Since Sjölander's study, three reports including references

Table 3.1 Prevalence of musculoskeletal disorders among Sámi

Symptoms	Country	Women (%)	Men (%)
Headache	Norway	65.6	42.7
	Sweden	61.1	–
Neck/shoulder pain	Norway	45.5	29.0
	Sweden	56	–
Back pain	Norway	31.1	28.8
Arm/knee/leg pain	Norway	31.6	32.9
TMD pain	Sweden	31.8	–

to Sámi health and wellbeing have been published. The AHDR-II (2014) and SLiCA** study (Poppel, 2015) show differences in health and mortality between the four countries where Sámi people live. In Russia, the decrease in mortality rates did not start until the 1960s, and infant mortality rates are still considerably higher than in the Scandinavian countries. On the other hand, the Sámi of the Murmansk region have the highest life expectancy of all Indigenous peoples of Arctic Russia. Norway, Sweden and Finland share a more consistent picture of health where life expectancies are among the best in the world.

Our chapter reveals that at present there are no or very minor differences in life expectancy between Sámi and non-Sámi people in the northern region. The specific causes of death are also similar. The similarities between the Sámi and non-Sámi are probably due to centuries of close interaction and equal access to healthcare services and the social security system. *The Lancet*-Lowitja Institute global collaboration (Anderson et al., 2016) highlighted that Sámi people are, in general, living longer and healthier lives than most other Indigenous people worldwide.

Nevertheless, there are pronounced challenges and threats to Sámi people and their health. In recent years there have been increasing reports of suicide, depression and anxiety among young Sámi reindeer herders; these are rooted in a complex web of factors connected with ongoing colonization, cumulative effects of resource exploitation, climate and conflicts with the majority society (Stoor, 2016). These health disparities are difficult to examine further due to the fact Sámi people are not recognized in official statistics. This means that Norway, Finland and Sweden lack a system that continuously documents, analyzes and provides information to ensure that the countries are delivering services to ensure the health and wellbeing of Sámi society. This has hampered studies such as SLiCA (Poppel, 2015) and *The Lancet*-Lowitja Institute global collaboration (Anderson et al., 2016) and means that Finland and Sweden have been unable to undertake robust research. Furthermore, it is difficult to make comparisons between different studies, regions and countries because Sámi people are defined differently (Pettersen & Brustad, 2013).

Despite signing the UNDRIP and other international declarations, the Nordic countries lack a long-term strategy and commitment for supporting Sámi health research. As previously mentioned, Norway with its SAMINOR study is unique in the four countries where Sámi people live, but is also dependent on securing project funding to ensure that future studies can be carried out. It is also Norway that leads discussions on ethical guidelines for Sámi health research, which are important in further supporting relevant research in the field (Stordahl et al., 2015).

One of the future challenges for Sámi health, as well as Indigenous health generally, is connected to understanding the effects of colonization on the people affected. Colonization is a process that is considered to be the 'cause of the causes' explaining why Indigenous peoples experience worse health than non-Indigenous populations. Colonization is often poorly articulated in health research (King et al., 2009; Axelsson, Kukutai, & Kippen, 2016). In Finland, Juutilainen et al. (2014) suggest intergenerational effects of the repression of language and culture, but the effects on morbidity and mortality have yet to be addressed. Finally, we can conclude that, at present, most studies regarding health and wellbeing among Sámi originate from Norway. Knowledge gaps are extensive, particularly in Finland and Russia.

References

Ahlm, K., Hassler, S., Sjölander, P., & Eriksson A. (2010). Unnatural deaths in reindeer-herding Sámi families in Sweden, 1961–2001. *International Journal of Circumpolar Health, 69*(2), 129–137.

Allard, C. (2006). *Two sides of the coin-rights and duties: The interface between environmental law and Saami law based on a comparison with Aoteoaroa/New Zealand and Canada.* Doctoral dissertation, Luleå tekniska universitet.

AHDR-II. Nordic Council of Ministers. (2014). *Arctic Human Development Report: Regional processes and global linkages.* Copenhagen: Nordic Council of Ministers.

Anderson, I., Robson, B., Connolly, M., Al-Yaman, F., Bjertness, E., King, A., & Pesantes, M.A. (2016). Indigenous and tribal peoples' health (*The Lancet*-Lowitja Institute Global Collaboration): A population study. *The Lancet, 388*(10040), 131–157.

Axelsson, P. (2015). Urfolkshälsa: Eftersatt och efterfrågat. *Socialmedicinsk Tidskrift, 6,* 726–739.

Axelsson, P., Kukutai, T., & Kippen, R. (2016). Indigenous wellbeing and colonisation: Editorial. *Journal of Northern Studies, 10*(2), 7–18.

Breivik, H., Collet, B., Ventafridda, V., Cohen, R., & Gallacher, D. (2006). Survey of chronic pain in Europe: Prevalence, impact on daily life, and treatment. *European Journal of Pain, 10*(4), 287–287.

Broderstad, A.R., & Melhus, M. (2016). Prevalence of metabolic syndrome and diabetes mellitus in Sámi and Norwegian populations. The SAMINOR – a cross-sectional study. *BMJ Open, 6*(4), e009474.

Brustad, M., Pettersen, T., Melhus, M., & Lund, E. (2009). Mortality patterns in geographical areas with a high vs. low Sámi population density in Arctic Norway. *Scandinavian Journal of Public Health, 37*(5), 475–480.

Brustad, M. Hansen, K.L., Broderstad, A.R., Hansen, S., & Melhus, M. (2014). A population-based study on health and living conditions in areas with mixed Sámi and Norwegian settlements – the SAMINOR 2 questionnaire study. *International Journal of Circumpolar Health, 73*(1), 23147.

Brännlund, I., & Axelsson, P. (2013). Representation of Swedish Sámi households at the turn of the nineteenth century. In *About the hearth: Perspectives on the home, hearth and household in the circumpolar North* (pp. 103–122). New York and Oxford: Berghahn Books.

Eckhoff, C., & Kvernmo, S. (2014). Musculoskeletal pain in Arctic indigenous and non-indigenous adolescents, prevalence and associations with psychosocial factors: A population-based study. *BMC Public Health, 14*(1), 617.

Edin-Liljegren, A., Hassler, S., Sjölander, P., & Daerga, L. (2004). Risk factors for cardiovascular diseases among Swedish Sámi – a controlled cohort study. *International Journal of Circumpolar Health, 63*(Suppl. 2), 292–297.

Eliassen, B.M., Melhus, M., Hansen, K.L., & Broderstad, A.R. (2013). Marginalisation and cardiovascular disease among rural Sámi in northern Norway: a population-based cross-sectional study. *BMC Public Health, 13*(1), 522.

Eliassen, B.M., Graff-Iversen, S., Melhus, M., Løchen, M.L., & Broderstad, A.R. (2014). Ethnic difference in the prevalence of angina pectoris in Sámi and non-Sámi populations: The SAMINOR study. *International Journal of Circumpolar Health, 73*(1), 21310.

Eliassen, B.M., Graff-Iversen, S., Braaten, T., Melhus, M., & Broderstad, A.R. (2015). Prevalence of self-reported myocardial infarction in Sámi and non-Sámi populations: The SAMINOR study. *International Journal of Circumpolar Health, 74*(1), 24424.

Eriksen, A.M., Schei, B., Hansen, K.L., Sørlie, T., Fleten, N., & Javo, C. (2016). Childhood violence and adult chronic pain among indigenous Sámi and non-Sámi populations in Norway: A SAMINOR 2 questionnaire study. *International Journal of Circumpolar Health, 75*(1), 32798.

Haldorsen, T., & Tynes, T. (2005). Cancer in the Sámi population of north Norway, 1970–1997. *European Journal of Cancer Prevention, 14*(1), 63–68.

Harbo, H.F., Utsi, E., Lorentzen, A.R., Kampman, M.T., Celius, E.G., Myhr, K.M., & Thorsby, E. (2007). Low frequency of the disease-associated DRB1*15-DQB1*06 haplotype may contribute to the low prevalence of multiple sclerosis in Sámi. *Tissue Antigens, 69*(4), 299–304.

Hassler, S., Johansson, R., Sjölander, P., Gronberg, H., & Damber, L. (2005). Causes of death in the Sámi population of Sweden, 1961–2000. *International Journal of Epidemiology, 34*(3), 623–629.

Hassler, S., Soininen, L., Sjölander, P., & Eero, P. (2008a). Cancer among the Sámi – a review on the Norwegian, Swedish and Finnish Sámi populations. *International Journal of Circumpolar Health, 67*(5), 421–432.

Hassler, S., Sjölander, P., Grönberg, H., Johansson, R., & Damber, L. (2008b). Cancer in the Sámi population of Sweden in relation to lifestyle and genetic factors. *European Journal of Epidemiology, 23*(4), 273–280.

Juutilainen, S.A., Miller, R., Heikkilä, L., & Rautio, A. (2014). Structural racism and indigenous health: What Indigenous perspectives of residential school and boarding school tell us? A case study of Canada and Finland. *The International Indigenous Policy Journal, 5*(3), 3.

King, M., Smith, A., & Gracey, M. (2009). Indigenous health part 2: The underlying causes of the health gap. *The Lancet, 374*(9683), 76–85.

Lantto, P., & Mörkenstam, U. (2008). Sámi rights and Sámi challenges: The modernization process and the Swedish Sámi movement, 1886–2006. *Scandinavian Journal of History, 33*(1), 26–51.

Lehtola, V. (2015). Sámi histories, colonialism, and Finland. *Arctic Anthropology, 52*(2), 22–36. http://doi.org/10.3368/aa.52.2.22.

Lund, E., Melhus, M., Hansen, K.L., Nystad, T., Broderstad, A.R., Selmer, R., & Lund-Larsen, P.G. (2007). Population based study of health and living conditions in areas with both Sámi and Norwegian populations – The SAMINOR study. *International Journal of Circumpolar Health, 66*(2), 113–128.

Lundmark, L. (2006). *Samernas skatteland i Norr-och Västerbotten under 300 år.* Institutet för rättshistorisk forskning.

Madden, R., Axelsson, P., Kukutai, T., Griffiths, K., Mienna, C., Brown, N., Coleman, C., & Ring, I. (2016). Statistics on indigenous peoples: International effort needed. *Statistical Journal of the IAOS, 32*(1), 37–41.

Naseribafrouei, A., Eliassen, B.M., Melhus, M., & Broderstad, A.R. (2016). Ethnic difference in the prevalence of pre-diabetes and diabetes mellitus in regions with Sámi and non-Sámi populations in Norway – the SAMINOR1 study. *International Journal of Circumpolar Health, 75*(1), 31697.

Pettersen, T., & Brustad, M. (2013). Which Sámi? Sámi inclusion criteria in population-based studies of Sámi health and living conditions in Norway: An exploratory study exemplified with data from the SAMINOR study. *International Journal of Circumpolar Health, 72,* 21813. http://doi.org/10.3402/ijch.v72i0.21813.

Poppel, B. (Ed.). (2015). *SLiCA: Arctic living conditions: Living conditions and quality of life among Inuit, Saami and Indigenous peoples of Chukotka and the Kola Peninsula.* Copenhagen: Nordic Council of Ministers.

Rohr, J. (2014). *Indigenous peoples in the Russian Federation.* IWGIA Report 18, IWGIA, Copenhagen.

Sara, M.N. (2009). Siida and traditional Sámi reindeer herding knowledge. *Northern Review, 30,* 153–178.

Selnes, A., Bolle, R., Holt, J., & Lund, E. (1999). Atopic diseases in Sámi and Norse schoolchildren living in northern Norway. *Pediatric Allergy and Immunology, 10*(3), 216–220.

Selnes, A., Bolle, R., Holt, J., & Lund, E. (2002). Cumulative incidence of asthma and allergy in north-Norwegian schoolchildren in 1985 and 1995. *Pediatric Allergy and Immunology, 13*(1), 58–63.

Sergejeva, J. (2000). The Eastern Sámi: A short account of their history and identity. *Acta Borealia, 17*(2), 5–37.

Sjölander, P., Hassler, S., & Janlert, U. (2008a). Stroke and acute myocardial infarction in the Swedish Sámi population: Incidence and mortality in relation to income and level of education. *Scandinavian Journal of Public Health, 36*(1), 84–91.

Sjölander, P., Daerga, L., Edin-Liljegren, A., & Jacobsson, L. (2008b). Musculoskeletal symptoms and perceived work strain among reindeer herders in Sweden. *Occupational Medicine, 58*(8), 572–579.

Sjölander, P. (2011). What is known about the health and living conditions of the indigenous people of northern Scandinavia, the Sámi? *Global Health Action, 4*(1), 8457. http://doi.org/10.3402/gha.v4i0.8457.

Soininen, L., & Pukkola, E. (2008). Mortality of the Sámi in northern Finland 1979–2005. *International Journal of Circumpolar Health, 67*(1), 43–55.

Stoor, J.P.A. (2016). *Kunskapssammanställning om psykosocial ohälsa bland samer.* Kiruna: Sametinget Sverige.

Stordahl, V., Tørres, G., Møllersen, S., & Eira-Åhren, I.-M. (2015). Ethical guidelines for Sámi research: The issue that disappeared from the Norwegian Sámi Parliament's agenda? *International Journal of Circumpolar Health, 74,* 10.3402/ijch.v74.27024. http://doi.org/10.3402/ijch.v74.27024.

Storm, C., & Wänman, A. (2006). Temporomandibular disorders, headaches, and cervical pain among females in a Sámi population. *Acta Odontologica Scandinavica, 64*(5), 319–325.

Svonni, M. (1998). Sámi. In A. Ó Corráin & S. Mac Mathuna (Eds.), *Minority languages in Scandinavia, Britain and Ireland. Acta Universitatis Upsaliensis* (pp. 21–49) (Studia Celtica Upsaliensia 3).

Tynes, T., & Haldorsen, T. (2007). Mortality in the Sámi population of north Norway, 1970–98. *Scandinavian Journal of Public Health, 35*(3), 306–322.

4

CHRONIC DISEASE AMONG NATIVE NORTH AMERICANS

Leslie Redmond and Joel Gittelsohn

Introduction

The earliest evidence of human inhabitance of North America has been estimated prior to 50,000 years ago (University of South Carolina, 2004). Today, these first inhabitants include American Indian (AI), Alaska Native (AN) (together AIAN) and First Nations (FN) populations – collectively known Native North Americans (NNA). As of 2012, 5.2 million individuals identify as AIAN alone or in combination with one or more other races (Norris, Vines, & Hoeffel, 2012). There are 567 federally recognized tribal nations in urban areas and 326 reservations in thirty-four states across the United States (US) (Bureau of Indian Affairs, n.d.). In Canada, there are over 1.8 million individuals reporting Aboriginal ancestry, with about 900,000 Registered Indians belonging to 617 FN communities (Aboriginal Affairs and Northern Development Canada, 2014). At 2 percent of the total US population and 5.6 percent of the Canadian population, AIAN and FN peoples are important populations in North America.

Unfortunately, NNA suffer disproportionately from several chronic health conditions, including type 2 diabetes (Schiller, Lucas, Ward, & Peregov, 2012a; Shaw, Brown, Khan, Mau, & Dillard, 2012), obesity and heart disease (Barnes, Adams, & Powell-Griner, 2010), stroke, some cancers, and high blood pressure (Schiller, 2012a). The prevalence of chronic health conditions among NNA is a relatively new phenomenon. In fact, evidence of chronic disease in NNA was a rare occurrence until the mid-twentieth century. Medical surveys noted rare cases of obesity in the AI population of the Southwestern US between 1898 and 1905, with increases first being noted around 1940 (Sievers & Fisher, 1981). High prevalence of obesity and related chronic disease (e.g. diabetes) was being reported in some tribes by the 1960s (Henry, Burch, Bennett, & Miller, 1969; Mayberry & Lindeman, 1963; Stein, West, Robey, Tirador, & McDonald, 1965; Westfall & Rosenbloom, 1971). This raises the question of what led to today's health disparities experienced by NNA populations and what efforts have been made to reverse this trend? In this chapter we will address the historical, cultural and economic context of today's NNA peoples, the prevalence and epidemiology of chronic disease within NNA, and discuss strategies for chronic disease prevention.

Historical context

Traditional lifestyle and culture

By the time European explorers began to arrive in the fifteenth century, an estimated 50 million people were already living in North America, with about 10 million in what is the present-day US (*History*, 2009). These Indigenous peoples can be grouped into ten separate cultural/linguistic areas: Arctic, Subarctic, Northeast, Southeast, Plains, Southwest, Great Basin, California, Northwest Coast and Plateau (*History*, 2009). Lifestyle varied drastically from area to area, ranging from nomadic fishermen in the Arctic, to organized farming communities along the east coast, to family-based bands of hunter-gatherers in what is now California (*History*, 2009). Although the language, family and community structure, and diet differed between groups, there were many similarities. All peoples shared a lifestyle that demanded physical fitness and high energy output for survival, and had a similar holistic, collectively oriented view of nature and the place of human beings. Historical accounts of tribal structure and lifestyle give the overall impression of advanced, organized and healthy tribal communities. A common thread among nearly all AIAN and FN peoples was an intimate relationship with the earth, and the understanding that people were placed on the earth as caretakers with the responsibility to care for the earth and preserve its resources to ensure the survival of the seventh generation (Clarkson, Morrissette, & Régallet, 1992). The understanding that decisions must be made to guarantee survival for at least the next seven generations led to the concepts of social responsibility and obligation to the group as necessary for survival, which were maintained and fulfilled within a clan system (Clarkson et al., 1992). Political organization tended to be egalitarian and democratic in nature, without strict social classes or autocratic leaders and with community members working together to make decisions that would benefit all (Pauls, n.d.).

Colonial period to present day

The arrival of European explorers to North America brought about many changes for NNA. Spanish explorers began pushing north from Mexico, establishing missions, forts and pueblos (communities) in an attempt to evangelize the Native peoples and turn them into 'productive' members of society loyal to the Spanish crown. Between 1492 and 1828, European colonies along the east coast acquired Indian lands under the doctrine of discovery as well as through signed treaties with tribes, setting the precedent for treating tribes as foreign governments (National Congress of American Indians (NCAI), n.d.). As the US population grew, settlers began to push west into Indian Territory. This lead to the Indian Removal Act of 1830, which began a period of forced relocation of AI to reservations established through treaties that guaranteed the right of self-governance under the protection of the US in exchange for the forfeiture of large tracts of land (NCAI, n.d.). Unfortunately, these treaties were repeatedly ignored and abused, and over the next several decades more than 90 million acres of tribal land were forcefully acquired (NCAI, n.d.).

In addition to dislocation due to the expanding colonial population, further population shifts occurred as a result of disease and war. The introduction of diseases such as smallpox and tuberculosis wreaked havoc on Indigenous populations, with mortality rates during these pandemics estimated to be as high as 95 percent (Pauls, n.d.). European conflicts including Queen Anne's War (1702–1713), the French and Indian War (1754–1763), the American Revolution (1775–1783), and the War of 1812 (1812–1814) often forced tribal nations to choose sides and engage in combat, which inevitably would lead to loss of native life and land. During the same era, tribes in the West and Southwest US continued to clash with Spanish forces and Arctic peoples dealt with Russian occupation (Pauls, n.d.).

The 1930s began a new period of relations between the US government and tribal governments with the Indian Reorganization Act of 1934, which attempted to restore Indian land to tribes, reestablish tribal governments and stimulate economic growth on reservations (*Encyclopaedia Britannica*, n.d.). This period was followed by the Termination Era, during which the US Congress attempted to terminate federal recognition and assistance to tribes. This was accomplished through relocation programs, termination of tribes and the extension of state juris- diction into Indian Country (NCAI, n.d.). With the growing civil rights movement of the 1960s, the fight for AI rights also gained momentum, resulting in a period of self-determination that carries through to present day (NCAI, n.d.). Key policies during this period included the Indian Civil Rights Act of 1968 and the Self-Determination and Education Act of 1975, enabling the government to contract with Indian tribes for the implementation of programs and distribution of funds (NCAI, n.d.). Today, federally recognized AI tribes control their own land and resources and continue to make strides towards revitalizing their unique cultures and societies.

Historical trauma

Unfortunately, decades of colonization and paternalism took its toll on NNA populations, leading to what many refer to as historical trauma, defined as complex collective trauma inflicted on a group of people sharing a specific identity or affiliation, such as ethnicity, reli- gion or nationality (Evans-Campbell, 2008). Effects of historically traumatic events are trans- mitted intergenerationally and descendants continue to identify emotionally with suffering experienced by previous generations. For NNA, these events might include forced relocation and boarding school attendance, banning of religious practices, flooding of homelands or pro- hibition of traditional hunting practices such as whaling (Evans-Campbell, 2008). Historical trauma is linked to several consequences, including loss of ethnic identity, economic hardship and increased health disparities.

Present-day barriers impacting health and wellbeing

Poverty

AI populations have the highest poverty rates of any race or ethnicity in the US, with 27 per- cent of the population living in poverty (Macartney, Bisaw, & Fontenot, 2013). In 2000, in the Navajo Nation alone, 43 percent of the population lived below the poverty line (Choudhary, 2004). Poverty is associated with unemployment and is related to poor quality diet, physical inactivity, overcrowded or poor living conditions, psychosocial stress and an increased burden of chronic illness (Moore, 2010).

Health insurance

All AIAN individuals are eligible for healthcare via Indian Health Service and tribal-contract healthcare facilities, which are funded by the US Congress (Indian Health Service (IHS), n.d.). However, current annual funds provided by the US Congress only cover approximately 60 percent of the healthcare needs of eligible AIAN individuals (IHS, n.d.). The Federal Government spends less per capita on AIAN healthcare than on any other group, including individuals receiving Medicaid, prisoners, veterans and military personnel (US Commission on

Civil Rights, 2003). Many AIAN obtain private insurance, however approximately 27 percent still lack adequate insurance, compared to 14.5 percent of non-Hispanic whites (US Census Bureau, 2015).

Access to medical care

AIANs are also limited in their ability to access health facilities and professionals. According to a 2011 IHS report, only 17 percent of IHS health facilities were adequately staffed and the average vacancy rate for physicians at IHS facilities was 22 percent, substantially higher than the vacancy rates in the private sector (Miller, 2011). Further, 54 percent of IHS facility administrators noted that the shortage of primary care physicians compromised access to healthcare in their service areas, with care also compromised (to a lesser degree) by a shortage of dentists, physician assistants, registered nurses and pharmacists (Miller, 2011). Decreased access to medical care can make a significant impact on disease prevalence, treatment and leading causes of death in AIAN communities, as medical issues that may otherwise be easily diagnosed and treated are instead left to persist and worsen. Staff shortages and decreased access to diagnostic tools at remote locations can increase wait times, disrupt continuity of care and delay diagnosis and treatment, resulting in increased mortality rates for health conditions that are otherwise treatable.

Access to healthy food

High food insecurity is linked to poor nutritional, physical and mental health (Larson & Story, 2010; Seligman, Bindman, Vittinghoff, Kanaya, & Kushel, 2007; Stuff et al., 2004; Walker, Holben, Kropf, Holcomb, & Anderson, 2007; Weigel, Armijos, Hall, Ramirez, & Orozco, 2007). The connection between food insecurity and obesity in particular is still being explored, as some experts suggest that the least expensive foods, and therefore the foods more commonly purchased by individuals on a low or fixed income, are typically high in calories and fat (Drewnowski & Specter, 2004; Larson & Story, 2010; Ludwig & Pollack, 2009), although at least one study has found no such association (Pardilla, Prasad, Suratkar, & Gittelsohn, 2013).

The Healthy Food Financing Initiative defines a food desert as a community in which residents do not live in close proximity to affordable and healthy food retailers (US Department of Health and Human Services, 2017). According to the US Department of Agriculture (USDA), nearly all AIAN reservations are in food deserts (USDA Economic Research Service, n.d.). These reservations tend to be rural, difficult to access and spread over several hundred acres. The Navajo Nation, for example, spans 27,000 square miles, yet has only ten full grocery stores in operation (Landry, 2015). The Diné Community Advocacy Alliance found that up to 80 percent of the foods stocked in these grocery stores qualifies as junk food, and that more than half of Navajo Nation residents travel off-reservation and up to 240 miles in a round trip to purchase fresh fruits, vegetables and meats (Landry, 2015). Food insecurity, or the state of being without reliable access to a sufficient quantity of affordable, nutritious food, affects approximately 22 percent of AI households with children and 16.3 percent of AI households without children (Gundersen, 2006). A study published in 2013 found even higher reported rates in the Navajo Nation of almost 77 percent, more than five times the US national rate (Pardilla et al., 2013).

It should be acknowledged, however that government food assistance programs have a longstanding presence within AIAN communities. Food assistance began in the 1930s, as commodity foods such as cheese, butter and flour were distributed to low-income and needy families while supporting farm prices. This evolved into several food distribution programs, such as the Supplemental Nutrition Assistance Program, the Special Supplemental Nutrition Program for Women, Infants and Children, the National School Lunch Program and the Food Distribution Program on Indian Reservations (FDPIR). Many efforts have been made by the USDA to make food assistance programs such as FDPIR as accessible and culturally appropriate as possible. One such recent effort is the availability of bison in FDPIR packages, supplied by KivaSun™ Foods, a Native-owned all-natural food company (Butler, 2016). Eligibility for food assistance is based on income, nutritional risk, or both. In 2011, FDPIR served about 80,000 individuals per month (Hipp, Romero, & Racine, n.d.).

Lifestyle, health and wellbeing

The current lifestyle of AIAN is drastically different from that of their ancestors. These populations have undergone a rapid transition in nutritional intake and physical activity patterns, influencing lifestyle habits and health.

Epidemiologic transition

The epidemiologic transition is a model used to explain shifts in population patterns of health and disease, and their interactions with economic, demographic and sociologic determinants (Katzmarzyk & Mason, 2009; Omran, 1971). It is characterized by a shift from mortality rates driven by infectious disease to mortality rates driven by degenerative disease (Omran, 1971). The model is described in four stages: (1) pestilence and famine; (2) receding pandemics; (3) degenerative and man-made diseases; and (4) delayed degenerative diseases (Katzmarzyk & Mason, 2009). Mortality rates due to a number infectious disease in AIAN populations are higher than the US average, including influenza (1.6 times higher) and septicemia (1.6 times higher) (IHS, 2017). While these numbers remain high, mortality rates tied to degenerative disease are also high, in keeping with Stage 3 of the epidemiologic transition.

Nutrition transition

The nutrition transition, first described by Popkin and Gordon-Larsen in 2004, is defined as a shift in nutritional concerns from malnutrition and starvation to the nutrition-related non-communicable diseases such as obesity (Compher, 2006; Popkin & Gordon-Larsen, 2004). This model is described in five stages: (1) collection of food; (2) famine; (3) receding famine; (4) degenerative disease; and (5) behavioral change (Popkin, 1993, 1994). The transition characterizes a shift away from traditional diets based on grains, legumes, fruits and vegetables, and limited animal sources, to a diet based on more animal sources and processed foods high in saturated fats and sugars (Katzmarzyk & Mason, 2009). This typically results in a dietary pattern of increased energy intake, as traditional foods are replaced by processed and energy-dense convenience foods (Compher, 2006). Primary nutritional concerns for AIAN in the early twentieth century were focused on malnutrition resulting from poor diet quantity and quality (Compher, 2006; Story et al., 2003).

Dietary intake in Native North Americans today

The dietary intake of NNA today is varied, but there are some common trends (Table 4.1). The Strong Heart Dietary Study (SHDS) Phase II found that AI adults aged 45 or older from

Table 4.1 Summary of evidence on nutrient intake in American Indian and Alaska Native communities

High intake	Low intake
Carbohydrates	Folate
Fat	Vitamin A
Sodium	Vitamin C
	Vitamin B6
	Vitamin E

Arizona, North and South Dakota and Oklahoma consumed higher amounts of carbohydrates and sodium compared with National Health and Nutrition Examination Survey (NHANES) III estimates, conducted at about the same time (Stang et al., 2005; Wiedman, 2005). Researchers also found that AI adults in general consumed lower amounts of folate, AI adult women consumed lower amounts of vitamins A and C, and AI adult men consumed lower amounts of vitamins A, B6 and E (Stang et al., 2005; Wiedman, 2005). Less than half of the participants in the SHDS study met US Department of Agriculture guidelines for reduction of risk of chronic disease (Zephier, Himes, Story, & Zhou, 2006). Several studies have revealed that AI diets tend to be high in fat, and they rarely meet recommendations for fruit and vegetable intake (Berg et al., 2011). Two separate studies have estimated that only 24–37 percent of AI adults meet the recommended intake of five fruits and vegetables per day (Berg et al., 2011; Centers for Disease Control and Prevention, 2007). The Navajo Health and Nutrition Survey (1991–1992) found intake of fruit and vegetables was less than once per day, whereas intake of fats and energy from foods such as fried bread, home-fried potatoes, bacon, sausage and soft drinks was high, providing 41 percent of total energy intake (Ballew et al., 1997).

Physical activity transition

Just as there has been a rapid nutrition transition among AIANs, their physical activity patterns have transitioned as well. Today, engagement in physical activity differs dramatically in AIAN compared to non-Hispanic whites. Approximately 52 percent of AIAN adults 18 years or older do not meet federal physical activity guidelines compared to approximately 43 percent of non-Hispanic whites (Schiller, 2012a). Other studies have also found low physical activity and decreased leisure time in AI populations (Ho et al., 2008; Yurgalevitch et al., 1998), with the Centers for Disease Control and Prevention estimating that AIAN adults are 30 percent less likely than white adults to engage in regular leisure-time activity (Schiller, 2012a).

Chronic disease

Obesity and metabolic syndrome

Today, the primary nutritional concern is the proportion of the population who are overweight or obese. The National Health Interview Survey estimated that in 2011 the age-adjusted prevalence of obesity in AIAN adults 18 years or older was 40.8 percent, versus 27.2 percent for non-Hispanic white adults (Schiller, Lucas, & Peregoy, 2012b). Obesity is associated with much comorbidity. According to NHANES III data, prevalence of metabolic syndrome in AIAN men age 45–59 was 43.6 percent compared to an national average of 20 percent, whereas prevalence in AIAN women age 45–59 years of age was 56.7 percent compared to 23.1 percent compared to an national average of (Ford, Giles, & Dietz, 2002; Resnick, 2002; Resnick et al., 2003).

Cardiovascular disease

AIAN are more than twice as likely to be diagnosed with cardiovascular disease as non-Hispanic white adults (Barnes et al., 2010). The age-adjusted prevalence of cardiovascular disease for adults 18 years or older between the years 2004–2008 was estimated at 14.7 percent in AIAN and 12.2 percent in non-Hispanic whites (Barnes et al., 2010). Additionally, AIAN are more than twice as likely to be diagnosed with coronary artery disease and 1.3 times more likely to have high blood pressure than non-Hispanic white adults (Schiller, 2012b). Finally, AIAN adults 18 years or older are also 2.4 times more likely to suffer a stroke than non-Hispanic whites (Schiller, 2012b).

Type 2 diabetes

The Centers for Disease Control and Prevention estimates that AIAN are 2.1 times more likely to be diagnosed with type 2 diabetes than non-Hispanic whites (Shaw et al., 2012). Results from the SHDS estimated prevalence to be four to five times higher than the national estimates for the general adult population at the time of the study (M.I. Harris et al., 1998; Stang et al., 2005; Welty et al., 2002). Estimates from the National Health Interview Survey in 2010 found that the average rate of type 2 diabetes AIAN adults years or older was 16.3 percent, compared to the average national rate of 7.6 percent (Schiller, 2012b). Prevalence of type 2 diabetes in AIAN has been estimated to be as high as 50 percent in some tribes (IHS, 2009). Data from the Centers for Disease Control and Prevention show that estimates also vary by region, from 5.5 percent among Alaska Native adults to 33.5 percent among AI adults in the Southwest (Centers for Disease Control and Prevention, 2011). Such high prevalence of type 2 diabetes leads to several comorbidities. Among all US adults, type 2 diabetes is the leading cause of kidney failure, amputation and new cases of blindness (Centers for Disease Control and Prevention, 2011). American Indian and Alaska Native populations suffer from the highest rates of these diabetes-related complications and comorbidities, in addition to heart disease and depression (Howard et al., 1999; IHS, 2009; Jiang, Beals, Whitesell, Roubideaux, & Manson, 2008; Sahmoun, Markland, & Helgerson, 2007). Moreover, an IHS report on AIAN health disparities in 2008 reported that the mortality rate due to type 2 diabetes is 2.8 times higher in AIAN as compared to all races in the US (IHS, 2017).

Cancer

There is a high prevalence of cancer among AIAN and while cancer rates have declined among non-Hispanic whites within the last two decades, the same trend has not been observed among AIAN populations (M.C. White et al., 2014). Espey, Wingo, and Lee (2008) report that, compared to non-Hispanic whites, cervical cancer is up to 69 percent higher, lung cancer is up to 83 percent higher, colon cancer is up to 162 percent higher, liver cancer is up to 198 percent higher, stomach cancer is up to 490 percent higher and gall bladder cancer is up to 691 percent higher. Reasons for this higher rate of cancer include a high burden of cancer risk factors such as tobacco use, alcohol abuse, unhealthy diets, obesity, lack of physical activity and barriers to prevention and care. As discussed earlier, access to medical care can be limited, resulting in fewer individuals seeking healthcare services, which could include routine cancer screenings and/or treatment.

Interventions, programs and policies

Because of the numerous health disparities present within NNA populations, partnerships between tribal communities and public health organizations have been formed in attempts to improve current health conditions as well as to prevent future development of chronic disease. Many national health organizations provide funding opportunities for collaborative research between tribal governments and academic institutions. The National Institute of Health provides funding to develop, adapt and test the effectiveness of health promotion and disease prevention interventions in NNA populations. The USDA also offers multiple grant opportunities, ranging from support for projects that aim to reduce food insecurity to strengthening small businesses and creating jobs.

A number of health promotion programs and chronic disease interventions have been implemented within NNA populations in partnership with academic institutions. Earlier intervention efforts tended to operate at selected levels and institutions within the communities, and did not utilize a comprehensive multi-level, multi-component approach to influence the overall food and physical activity environment, nor attempt to address the more ingrained influencers of chronic disease such as poverty and intergenerational trauma. More recent efforts seek to address this limitation by taking a more comprehensive approach; for example, where earlier interventions may have been limited to schools, current interventions are implemented in schools, food stores and worksites, and incorporate strategies to empower community members to create and sustain healthy environmental changes. Examples of such programs include Zhiwaapenewin Akino'maagewin (Ho, Gittelsohn, Harris, & Ford, 2006), Apache Healthy Stores (Gittelsohn et al., 2013a), Navajo Healthy Stores (Gittelsohn, Kim, He, & Pardilla, 2013b), Healthy Foods North (Kolahdooz et al., 2014) and OPREVENT 1 and 2 (Gittelsohn et al., 2017). Such research depends on the establishment of collaborative relationships with tribal leaders and representatives, stakeholders and by having tribal members involved throughout each stage of the research, from proposal and development to implementation and evaluation.

Further, tribal nations are taking it upon themselves to develop and implement policies in support of healthy food and physical activity environments, as mainstream political strategies do not always reach or have an effect in separate, reservation-based sovereign communities. A notable example of such policy implementation is the sugar sweetened beverage and junk food tax implemented in the Navajo Nation in 2013, known as the Healthy Diné Nation Act. At the time, the tribe was the first community in the US besides Berkeley, California to enact such a tax, and the only nation besides Mexico to approve a tax specifically targeting nutritionally related health problems (Ahtone, 2013). The act adds a 2 percent tax to unhealthy foods, like potato chips and sugar sweetened beverages, and eliminates taxes on healthy items, like fruits and vegetables. Enacted as a way for the Navajo Nation to take ownership of their health, the tax is nevertheless controversial. While proponents argue that the tax will decrease purchases of unhealthy foods and encourage purchases of healthy foods, thereby improving dietary intake and ultimately diet-related chronic disease, others claim that the tax just raises prices in food stores where there is a complete lack of healthy alternatives.

Other health policy approaches utilized in Native communities are not necessarily implemented at the government level. The OPREVENT 2 intervention, a multi-level, multi-component obesity intervention being implemented within six AI communities, is structured to include a policy component that supports structural and environmental changes to the food and physical activity environment in partnership with community partners (Gittelsohn et al., 2017). This component will function to form relationships between stakeholders and align existing health programs to support environmental changes and develop health policies, leading to increased sustainability of the OPREVENT 2 program (Gittelsohn et al., 2017). Example policies might include a ban on sugar sweetened beverages in on-reservation schools, or incentive programs to encourage employees to walk or bike to work.

Conclusion

AIAN and First Nations peoples make up a culturally rich and diverse Indigenous population of North America. Rich histories of tradition and legend, yet also marked by colonialism and historical trauma, have contributed to the health and characteristics of these groups today. The health status of NNA continues to lag behind that of all other population groups in North America, as poverty, food insecurity and chronic disease are experienced at much greater levels than in any other minority group. However, despite this suffering, there is also hope. Indigenous peoples of North America are resilient and strong, and many are motivated to make positive changes to their own health and that of their communities. Grassroots movements to take ownership over societal and health issues are gaining momentum, and the needs of these populations are beginning to be recognized at the national level. One of the goals of the USDA Healthy People 2010 is to eliminate health disparities (US Department of Health and Human Services, 2000). The pervasiveness of social media has also provided a platform to spread knowledge and educate the public, serving to make more people aware not only of the burdens suffered by Native communities but of the fact that these communities are still here and still thriving despite the challenges of the past. It is important that the health disparities and other struggles suffered by these peoples take precedence as a public health priority. Moving forward, it will be necessary to address the social, cultural and structural barriers that affect the overall health status of NNA.

References

Aboriginal Affairs and Northern Development Canada. (2014). *First Nations People in Canada*. Retrieved from www.aadnc-aandc.gc.ca/eng/1303134042666/1303134337338.

Ahtone, T. (2013). *The Navajo Nation just passed a junk food tax. Too bad junk food is all you can buy*. Retrieved from http://talkingpointsmemo.com/theslice/navajo-nation-junk-food-tax.

Bureau of Indian Affairs. (n.d.). *Frequently asked questions*. Retrieved from www.bia.gov/frequently-asked-questions.

Ballew, C., White, L.L., Strauss, K.F., Benson, L.J., Mendlein, J.M., & Mokdad, A. H. (1997). Intake of nutrients and food sources of nutrients among the Navajo: Findings from the Navajo Health and Nutrition Survey. *Journal of Nutrition, 127*, 2085S–2093S.

Barnes, P.M., Adams, P.F., & Powell-Griner, E. (2010). *Health characteristics of the American Indian or Alaska Native adult population: United States, 2004–2008* (No. 20) (pp. 1–23). US Department of Health and Human Services, Centers for Disease Control and Prevention.

Berg, C.J., Daley, C.M., Nazir, N., Kinlacheeny, J.B., Ashley, A., Ahluwalia, J.S., et al. (2011). Physical activity and fruit and vegetable intake among American Indians. *Journal of Community Health, 37*(1), 65–71. http://doi.org/10.1007/s10900-011-9417-z.

Butler, K. (2016). *KivaSun Foods distributes all-natural bison to Natives through FDPIR*. Retrieved from http://indiancountrytodaymedianetwork.com/2016/02/09/kivasun-foods-distributes-all-natural-bison-natives-through-fdpir-163347.

Centers for Disease Control and Prevention. (2007). Prevalence of fruit and vegetable consumption and physical activity by race/ethnicity – United States, 2005. (2007). *Morbidity & Mortality Weekly, 56*(13), 301–304.

Centers for Disease Control and Prevention. (2011). *National diabetes fact sheet: National estimates and general information on diabetes and prediabetes in the United States, 2011* (pp. 1–12). Atlanta, GA: US Department of Health and Human Services, Centers for Disease Control and Prevention.

Choudhary, T. (2004). *Navajo Nation data*. Retrieved from www.navajobusiness.com/pdf/NNCensus/Census2000.pdf.

Clarkson, L., Morrissette, V., & Régallet, G. (1992). *Our responsibility to the seventh generation indigenous peoples and sustainable development*. Retrieved from www.iisd.org/pdf/seventhgen.pdf.

Compher, C. (2006). The nutrition transition in American Indians. *Journal of Transcultural Nursing, 17*(3), 217–223. http://doi.org/10.1177/1043659606288376.

Drewnowski, A., & Specter, S.E. (2004). Poverty and obesity: The role of energy density and energy costs. *American Journal of Clinical Nutrition, 79*, 6–16.

Encyclopaedia Britannica. (n.d.). *Indian Reorganization Act*. Retrieved from www.britannica.com/topic/Indian-Reorganization-Act.

Espey, D.K., Wingo, P.A., & Lee, N.C. (Eds.). (2008). An update on cancer in American Indians and Alaska Natives, 1999–2004. *Cancer*, 1113–1273.

Evans-Campbell, T. (2008). Historical trauma in American Indian/Native Alaska communities: A multi-level framework for exploring impacts on individuals, families, and communities. *Journal of Interpersonal Violence, 23*(3), 316–338. http://doi.org/10.1177/0886260507312290.

Ford, E.S., Giles, W.H., & Dietz, W.H. (2002). Prevalence of the metabolic syndrome among US adults. *Journal of the American Medical Association, 287*(3), 356–359.

Gittelsohn, J., Anliker, J., Ethelbah, B., et al. (2013a). A food store intervention to reduce obesity in two American Indian communities: Impact of food choices and psychosocial indicators. *Journal of Nutrition, 143*, 1495–1500.

Gittelsohn, J., Kim, E.M., He, S., & Pardilla, M. (2013b). A food store-based environmental intervention is associated with reduced BMI and improved psychosocial factors and food-related behaviors on the Navajo Nation. *Journal of Nutrition, 143*(9), 1494–1500. http://doi.org/10.3945/jn.112.165266.

Gittelsohn, J., Jock, B., Redmond, L., Fleischhacker, S., Eckmann, T., Bleich, S.N., Loh, H., Ogburn, E., Gadhoke, P., Swartz, J., Pardilla, M., & Caballero, B. (2017). OPREVENT2: Design of a multi-institutional intervention for obesity prevention and control for American Indian adults. *BMC Public Health, 17*(105), 1–9.

Gundersen, C. (2006). Measuring the extent and depth of food insecurity: An application to American Indians in the United States. *Journal of Population Economics, 21*, 191–215.

Harris, M.I., Flegal, K.M., Cowie, C.C., Eberhardt, M.S., Goldstein, D.E., Little, R. R., et al. (1998). Prevalence of diabetes, impaired fasting glucose, and impaired glucose tolerance in US adults. *Diabetes Care, 21*(4), 518–524.

Henry, R.E., Burch, A., Bennett, P.H., & Miller, M. (1969). Diabetes in the Cocopah Indians. *Diabetes, 18*(1), 33–37.

Hipp, J.S., Romero, V.A., & Racine, R. (n.d.). *Sovereignty impaired: Tribal food security*. Retrieved from www.iactechhelp.com/2013/10/sovereignty-impaired-tribal-food-security/.

History. (2009). *Native American cultures*. Retrieved from www.history.com/topics/native-american-history/native-american-cultures.

Ho, L.S., Gittelsohn, J., Harris, S.B., & Ford, E. (2006). Development of an integrated diabetes prevention program with First Nations in Canada. *Health Promotion Interventions, 21*, 88–97.

Ho, L., Gittelsohn, J., Sharma, S., Cao, X., Treuth, M., Rimal, R., et al. (2008). Food-related behavior, physical activity, and dietary intake in First Nations – a population at high risk for diabetes. *Ethnicity & Health, 13*(4), 335–349. http://doi.org/10.1080/13557850701882936.

Howard, B.V., Lee, E.T., Cowan, L.D., Devereux, R.B., Galloway, J.M., Go, O.T., et al. (1999). Rising tide of cardiovascular disease in American Indians: The Strong Heart study. *Circulation, 99*(18), 2389–2395. http://doi.org/10.1161/01.CIR.99.18.2389.

Indian Health Services. (n.d.). *Frequently asked questions*. Retrieved from www.ihs.gov/GeneralWeb/HelpCenter/CustomerServices/FAQ/.

Indian Health Service. (2009). *Indian Health Service trends in Indian health, 2002–2003 edition*. Retrieved from www.ihs.gov/dps/includes/themes/responsive2017/display_objects/documents/Trends_02-03_Entire%20Book%20(508).pdf.

Indian Health Service. (2017). *Indian health disparities*. Retrieved from www.ihs.gov/newsroom/includes/themes/responsive2017/display_objects/documents/factsheets/Disparities.pdf.

Jiang, L., Beals, J., Whitesell, N.R., Roubideaux, Y., & Manson, S.M. (2008). Stress burden and diabetes in two American Indian reservation communities. *Diabetes Care, 31*, 427–429. http://doi.org/10.2337/dc07.

Katzmarzyk, P.T., & Mason, C. (2009). The physical activity transition. *Journal of Physical Activity and Health, 6*, 269–280.

Kolahdooz, F., Pakseresht, M., Mead, E., Beck, L., Corriveau, A., & Sharma, S. (2014). Impact of the Healthy Foods North nutrition intervention program on Inuit and Inuvialuit food consumption and preparation methods in Canadian Arctic communities. *Nutrition Journal, 13*(68), 1–10. http://doi.org/10.1186/1475-2891-13-68.

Landry, A. (2015). *A junk food tax in a food desert: Navajo Nation tries to curb unhealthy snacking.* Retrieved from http://indiancountrytodaymedianetwork.com/2015/04/02/junk-food-tax-food-desert-navajo-nation-tries-curb-unhealthy-snacking-159865.

Larson, N., & Story, M. (2010). *Food insecurity and risk for obesity among children and families: Is there a relationship?* Retrieved from www.banpac.org/pdfs/resources_food_security/2010/rwj_obesity_food_insecurity_12_2_10.pdf.

Ludwig, D.S., & Pollack, H.A. (2009). Obesity and the economy. *Journal of the American Medical Association, 301*(5), 533–535.

Macartney, S., Bisaw, A., & Fontenot, K. (2013). *Poverty rates for selected detailed race and Hispanic groups by state and place: 2007–2011.* Retrieved from www.census.gov/prod/2013pubs/acsbr11-17.pdf.

Mayberry, R.H., & Lindeman, R.D. (1963). A survey of chronic disease and diet in Seminole Indians in Oklahoma. *American Journal of Clinical Nutrition, 13*(3), 127–134.

Miller, P. (2011). 2011 *clinical staffing and recruiting survey.* Retrieved from www.npaihb.org/images/resources_docs/QBM%20Handouts/2013/April/8A%20-%20IHS%20Administrative%20Survey%20Final.pdf.

Moore, K.R. (2010). Youth-onset type 2 diabetes among American Indians and Alaska Natives. *Journal of Public Health Management and Practice, 16*(5), 388–393.

National Congress of American Indians. (n.d.). *An introduction to Indian Nations in the United States.* Retrieved from www.ncai.org/about-tribes/indians101.pdf.

Norris, T., Vines, P.L., & Hoeffel, E.M. (2012). *The American Indian and Alaska Native Population: 2010.* Retrieved from www.census.gov/prod/cen2010/briefs/c2010br-10.pdf.

Omran, A.R. (1971). The epidemiologic transition: A theory of the epidemiology of population change. *The Milbank Memorial Fund Quarterly, 49*(4), 509–538.

Pardilla, M., Prasad, D., Suratkar, S., & Gittelsohn, J. (2013). High levels of household food insecurity on the Navajo Nation. *Public Health Nutrition, 17*(1), 58–65. http://doi.org/10.1017/S1368980012005630.

Pauls, E.P. (n.d.). *Native American.* Retrieved from www.britannica.com/topic/Native-American/Prehistory.

Popkin, B.M. (1993). Nutritional patterns and transitions. *Population and Development Review, 19*, 138–157.

Popkin, B.M. (1994). The nutrition transition in low-income countries: An emerging crisis. *Nutrition Reviews, 52*(9), 285–298.

Popkin, B.M., & Gordon-Larsen, P. (2004). The nutrition transition: Worldwide obesity dynamics and their determinants. *International Journal of Obesity, 28*, S2–S9. http://doi.org/10.1038/sj.ijo.0802804.

Resnick, H.E. (2002). Metabolic syndrome in American Indians. *Diabetes Care, 25*(7), 1246–1247.

Resnick, H.E., Jones, K., Ruotolo, G., Jain, A. K., Henderson, J., Lu, W., & Howard, B.V. (2003). Insulin resistance, the metabolic syndrome, and risk of incident cardiovascular disease in nondiabetic American Indians. *Diabetes Care, 26*, 861–867.

Sahmoun, A.E., Markland, M.J., & Helgerson, S.D. (2007). Mental health status and diabetes among whites and Native Americans: Is race an effect modifier? *Journal of Health Care for the Poor and Underserved, 18*, 599–608.

Schiller, J.S., Lucas, J.W., Ward, B.W., & Peregoy, J.A. (2012a). Summary health statistics for US adults: National Health Interview Survey, 2010 National Center for Health Statistics. *Vital Health Statistics, 10*(252). Retrieved from www.cdc.gov/nchs/data/series/sr_10/sr10_252.pdf.

Schiller, J.S., Lucas, J.W., & Peregoy, J.A. (2012b). Summary health statistics for US adults: National Health Interview Survey, 2011 National Center for Health Statistics. *Vital Health Statistics, 10*(256).

Seligman, H.K., Bindman, A.B., Vittinghoff, E., Kanaya, A.M., & Kushel, M.B. (2007). Food insecurity is associated with diabetes mellitus: Results from the National Health Examination and Nutrition Examination Survey (NHANES) 1999–2002. *Journal of General Internal Medicine, 22*(7), 1018–1023. http://doi.org/10.1007/s11606-007-0192-6.

Shaw, H., Brown, J., Khan, B., Mau, M.K., & Dillard, D. (2012). Resources, roadblocks and turning points: A qualitative study of American Indian/Alaska Native adults with type 2 diabetes. *Journal of Community Health, 38*(1), 86–94. http://doi.org/10.1007/s10900-012-9585-5.

Sievers, M.L., & Fisher, J.R. (1981). Diseases of North American Indians. In H.R. Rothschild (Ed.), *Biocultural aspects of disease* (pp. 191–252). New York: Academic Press.

Stang, J., Zephier, E.M., Story, M., Himes, J.H., Yeh, J.L., Welty, T., & Howard, B.V. (2005). Dietary intakes of nutrients thought to modify cardiovascular risk from three groups of American Indians: The Strong

Heart Dietary Study, Phase II. *Journal of the American Dietetic Association, 105*(12), 1895–1903. http://doi.org/10.1016/j.jada.2005.09.003.

Stein, J.H., West, K.M., Robey, J.M., Tirador, D.F., & McDonald, G.W. (1965). The high prevalence of abnormal glucose tolerance in the Cherokee Indians of North Carolina. *Archives of Internal Medicine, 116,* 842–845.

Story, M., Stevens, J., Himes, J., Stone, E., Rock, B.H., Ethelbah, B., & Davis, S. (2003). Obesity in American-Indian children: Prevalence, consequences, and prevention. *Preventative Medicine, 37,* 1–10. http://doi.org/10.1016/S0091-7435(03)00192-0.

Stuff, J.E., Casey, P.H., Szeto, K.L., Gossett, J.M., Robbins, J.M., Simpson, P.M., et al. (2004). Household food insecurity is associated with adult health status. *Journal of Nutrition, 134,* 2330–2335.

United States Census Bureau. (2015). *Facts for features: American Indian and Alaska Native Heritage Month: November 2015.* Retrieved from www.census.gov/newsroom/facts-for-features/2015/cb15-ff22.html.

United States Commission on Civil Rights. (2003). *A quiet crisis: Federal funding and unmet needs in Indian Country.* Retrieved from www.usccr.gov/pubs/na0703/na0204.pdf.

United States Department of Health and Human Services. (2000). *Healthy people 2010.* Retrieved from www.cdc.gov/nchs/healthy_people/hp2010.htm.

United States Department of Health and Human Services. (2017). *Healthy food financing initiative.* Retrieved from www.acf.hhs.gov/programs/ocs/programs/community-economic-development/healthy-food-financing.

University of South Carolina. (2004). *New evidence puts man in North America 50,000 years ago.* Retrieved from www.sciencedaily.com/releases/2004/11/041118104010.htm.

Walker, J.L., Holben, D.H., Kropf, M.L., Holcomb, J.P., Jr, & Anderson, H. (2007). Household food insecurity is inversely associated with social capital and health in females from special supplemental nutrition program for women, infants, and children households in Appalachian Ohio. *Journal of the American Dietetic Association, 107*(11), 1989–1993. http://doi.org/10.1016/j.jada.2007.08.004.

Weigel, M.M., Armijos, R.X., Hall, T., Ramirez, Y., & Orozco, R. (2007). The household food insecurity and health outcomes of US–Mexico border migrant and seasonal farmworkers. *Journal of Immigrant and Minority Health, 9*(3), 157–169. http://doi.org/10.1007/s10903-006-9026-6.

Welty, T.K., Rhoades, D.A., Yeh, F., Lee, E.T., Cowan, L.D., Fabsitz, R.R., et al. (2002). Changes in cardiovascular disease risk factors among American Indians: The Strong Heart Study. *Annals of Epidemiology, 12*(2), 97–106.

Westfall, D.N., & Rosenbloom, A.L. (1971). Diabetes mellitus among the Florida Seminoles. *HSMHA Health Reports, 86*(11), 1037–1041.

White, M.C., Espey, D.K., Swan, J., Wiggins, C.L., Eheman, C., & Kaur, J.S. (2014). Disparities in cancer mortality and incidence among American Indians and Alaska Natives in the United States. *American Journal of Public Health, 104,* S377–S387. http://doi.org/10.2105/AJPH.

Wiedman, D. (2005). American Indian diets and nutritional research: Implications of the Strong Heart Dietary Study, Phase II, for cardiovascular disease and diabetes. *Journal of the American Dietetic Association, 105*(12), 1874–1880. http://doi.org/10.1016/j.jada.2005.10.016.

Yurgalevitch, S.M., Kriska, A.M., Welty, T.K., Go, O., Robbins, D.C., & Howard, B.V. (1998). Physical activity and lipids and lipoproteins in American Indians ages 45–74. *Medical Science in Sports and Exercise, 30*(4), 543–549.

Zephier, E., Himes, J. H., Story, M., & Zhou, X. (2006). Increasing prevalences of overweight and obesity in Northern Plains American Indian children. *Archives of Pediatric and Adolescent Medicine, 160,* 34–39.

5

CHANGING CONCEPTS OF WELLNESS AMONG THE SWAHILI OF LAMU TOWN, KENYA

Rebecca Gearhart Mafazy and Munib Said Mafazy

Introduction

Maintaining a state of spiritual purity is vital to wellbeing among the Swahili peoples of Lamu Town, a Muslim community of roughly 30,000 inhabitants, who live on Lamu Island in the Lamu archipelago, off the northern Kenya coast (Gearhart & Abdulrehman, 2012, 2014). The daily quest for wellness begins around 4.00 am, when men and women awake with the call to early morning (*alfajiri* <Sw.; *fajr* <Ar.) prayers, performed as the first petition for Divine protection against the ill will of others known as *husuda*, a malevolent force that has the power to bring illness and misfortune to a person or an entire household. As Lamu Town awakens, children about to leave home for school are reminded to recite specific versus from the Qur'an (e.g. *Yasin, Aytul-Qursi, Alam Nashrah*) to add another layer of defense, a habit also kept by shopkeepers opening their doors for the day. Recorded Qur'anic recitation (*uradi*) can be heard softly streaming from the windows of homes and businesses, and gentle wafts of smoke from burning frankincense (*ubani*), believed to usher away negative energy and welcome propitious guests, perfume the serpentine corridors filled with children on their way to school and shoppers on their way to the market. Donkeys and their riders navigate through the town's narrow passageways, avoiding pedestrians and open water drains carrying soapy bathwater from houses to the bay that separates Lamu from a neighboring island. Though the absence of motorized traffic makes Lamu Town quieter than many urban communities, the distant whine of a boat engine, the hammer and buzz of carpentry workshops, roosters crowing and donkeys braying combine to create a familiar soundtrack for the day's activities.

In this chapter, we reflect on a range of ethnographic and clinical experiences we have had living among, working with and caring for the Swahili of Lamu Town. As co-founders of a free clinic in Lamu Town that focuses on preventative health, we also reflect on the changes we have observed in how patients identify, conceptualize and treat chronic illnesses such as diabetes and hypertension, and how these changes fit into the paradigm of Swahili wellbeing.

Achieving wellness

Understanding how the Swahili of Lamu Town manipulate the natural and social environments in which they live to augment their family's moral integrity, economic status and social standing in their community is critical to understanding how the Swahili conceptualize and attempt to enhance wellbeing. One critical element of wellbeing is avoiding the jealousy of others, who because of their own spiritual shortfalls have not been blessed with the things that are most important to the Swahili: maintaining social respect (*heshima*), being economically secure, marrying well and bearing healthy children. Yet rather than simply considering calamity to be the product of a curse (*fitna*) imposed by the envy of another, a victim considers her/his own recent behavior that may have opened him/her up to spiritual attack. Examples of such behavior include not performing the five required daily prayers, not properly bathing after sex, not showing modesty of wealth (e.g. by covering food) in front of the poor. That illness and other misfortune are associated with *not doing* something properly (e.g. spiritually protecting oneself) rather than with *doing* anything particularly egregious highlights the importance of the rituals associated with maintaining spiritual purity – a prevention strategy the Swahili of Lamu Town believe to enhance health and wellbeing.

A case study of medical pluralism

A case in point is a fisherman we will call Hamidi, who after a series of misfortunes with his boat, his boat crew, his fishing equipment and his own health decided to seek guidance from a well-regarded Islamic healer (*mwalimu*) in Lamu Town. During the diagnosis phase, Hamidi was asked to consider his own recent behavior and that of his close family members, as curses as well as the evil eye are often misdirected to a relative rather than the intended person. After careful self-reflection, Hamidi disclosed in the second consultation that he had secretly married a woman who lived in one of the mainland villages he frequented during his fishing expeditions. Secret marriage (by men), though sanctioned by Islam if performed by a Muslim cleric, is relatively uncommon among the Swahili of the Lamu archipelago because it is so difficult to maintain secrecy in such a close-knit community, and like polygyny generally, is challenging to maintain economically (Keefe, 2015). Hamidi had only been married two months before his first wife suspected his infidelity, and his sons stopped speaking to him. Since then, a member of his fishing crew had moved to another place, one of his best fishing nets had been stolen and he began suffering from a leg ache that prevented him from getting enough sleep.

Once Hamidi confessed to the *mwalimu* about his second wife, the healer began questioning him about his daily habits to assess whether or not he had made himself vulnerable to the curses (intentional or unintentional) of his first wife and children. What the healer learned was that Hamidi had not properly blessed the new fishing boat he had purchased six months earlier and had begun using regularly. To amend the situation, the healer told Hamidi to immediately go and invite a teacher at one of the Islamic schools in town to come with a group of his male students to sit in the boat and recite special versus of the Qur'an, thereby protecting it against harm, be it caused by humans of wicked intention or supernatural entities such as the evil eye or *vibengwa* (water spirits). Hamidi was told to purchase high-quality frankincense for the purification ritual as well as to prepare a nice lunch of chicken and rice (*pilau*), including sodas, for the group who would dine at his house after the ceremony. The healer also suggested that Hamidi ask the teacher and his students to recite an additional set of verses well known in Lamu Town for praising the Prophet Muhammad, which they did immediately after the lunch. By garnering the blessings of an Islamic teacher and his students, and ritually cleansing his boat and the home of his first wife and children, the healer believed that the evil that had befallen Hamidi would be driven out. Rather than ask Hamidi to divorce the second wife to appease the first one, whose jealousy had presumably attracted the evil eye, the healer prescribed a series of rituals that bolstered Hamidi's defenses from further spiritual attack.

Hamidi also sought care for his leg with a well-known local herbalist, who owns a popular plant medicine store in Lamu Town. After Hamidi described the pain he was having in his knee, the herbalist prepared a mixture of herbs for Hamidi to brew and drink as a tea, and a paste to apply to the kneecap and back of the knee, every day for seven days. In addition, Hamidi was instructed to avoid foods known to produce heat in the body, a recommendation based on the Swahili's own humoral theory (Beckerleg, 1994; Gearhart & Abdulrehman, 2014; Parkin, 2000). He was asked to return to the herbalist for a second week of treatment even if the pain had subsided. Hamidi did so, and received two weeks of the herbalist's medicine.

Though the herbalist's treatment did offer some relief, Hamidi's pain continued to prevent him from sleeping so he decided to visit the Lamu Center of Preventative Health, a free healthcare clinic in Lamu Town. The clinical officer (equivalent to a nurse practitioner) who Hamidi consulted there diagnosed his leg pain to be caused by osteoarthritis of the knee. During the consultation, Hamidi also revealed that his insomnia was related to frequent urination. The practitioner tested Hamidi's blood sugar levels and found them to be elevated, leading to a discussion about diabetes (*sukari*) and its prevalence among members of his immediate family. After a consultation regarding how to avoid eating foods that elevate blood sugar levels in the carbohydrate-rich Swahili diet, the clinical officer asked Hamidi to return in a week to check his blood sugar again. Hamidi was also advised to stay off his legs for a few days, to take two ibuprofen (*prufin* < Sw.) tablets thrice a day (morning, noon, before bed) to reduce the inflammation and the pain, and take a mild sleep aid before bed so he could get some much-needed rest.

Epidemiological change and genetic and dietary influences

Hamidi's health scenario illustrates the rise in chronic illnesses among sub-Saharan Africans, including hypertension, chronic obstructive pulmonary disease (COPD) and diabetes mellitus (Aikins et al., 2010; Ganu, Fletcher, & Caleb, 2016; Werfalli et al., 2016). The rapid growth of urban populations and the impact of globalization over the past fifty years have transformed the way the majority of Africans now live; their sedentary lifestyle and access to foreign foods and recreational drugs (e.g. tobacco and alcohol) have promoted chronic diseases such as diabetes, obesity and hypertension that are common in high- and middle-income countries (Maiyaki & Garbati, 2014). The prior assertion that type 2 diabetes primarily impacts the wealthy is no longer valid. There is a clear association between members of low-income households and increased prevalence of type 2 diabetes (Ross, Gilmour, & Dasgupta, 2010). This is true in Lamu Town, where many people who have type 2 diabetes are struggling financially. Like other communities in sub-Saharan Africa, where there has been an increase in complications associated with type 2 diabetes that have significantly impacted the healthcare system (Brown et al., 2014; Folb et al., 2015; Jaffiol, 2010; Ovbiagele, 2015), we have observed peripheral neuropathy, diabetic retinopathy, diabetic foot ulcers, chronic renal disease and brain strokes among the Lamu Town population.

When genetic risks are coupled with environmental/epigenetic factors such as a sedentary lifestyle, obesity and maternal factors (malnutrition, hyperglycemia, obesity, smoking, drinking and stress) the predisposition to type 2 diabetes increases substantially (Jiang, Ma, Wang, & Liu, 2013). In Kenya, we see increased risk for diabetes among those who have a first degree relative with type 2 diabetes and among those who suffered from malnutrition and/or childhood starvation (Chege, 2010). Research has shown that chronic illnesses may favor certain ethnic groups (Abate & Chandalia, 2001, 2003; Christensen et al., 2009; Mathenge, Foster, & Kuper, 2010). For example, people of Asian descent appear to have higher predictive risk for diabetes compared to those of European descent (Abate & Chandalia, 2001, 2003; Rosella et al., 2012). In Kenya, one study suggests that there is more prevalence of hypertension, obesity, diabetes and high cholesterol among Kikuyus compared to Kalenjins (Mathenge, Foster, & Kuper, 2010).

No research to date has determined the influence of ethnicity on the risk of diabetes among the Swahili peoples of Lamu Town compared to neighboring groups. What Abdulrehman et al. (2016) found among this population is that half of the sample (N=30) reported a first degree relative with type 2 diabetes, and two thirds of the sample had either a first or second degree relative with type 2 diabetes. This is an intriguing area of future research, especially given the unique genetic and cultural heritage of the Swahili, stemming from centuries of interaction with traders from Africa, South Asia, Persia and Arabia. The Swahili co-author (Munib) and his sister recently received DNA test results that confirm their mixed ancestry of African, South West Indian, Persian and Arab descent. A more complete genetic profile of the Swahili would help researchers better predict the risks of various chronic diseases such as type 2 diabetes among the population.

The unique fusion of cultural influences, including dietary preferences, is another line of inquiry into Swahili health. Indian dishes such as *biriyani*, *sambusa* and *chapatti*, and delicacies from Arabia such as *halua* (*halva* <Ar.) have been modified to make use of local ingredients and to satisfy Swahili tastes. Many of these dishes are high in saturated fats, salt, spices and sugar, and have contributed to a rise in obesity and related complications (heart disease, hypertension, type 2 diabetes, chronic orthopedic pain including leg and back pain) among the Swahili, especially women. Dishes known to be traditional Swahili recipes are often much healthier than those integrated through contact with foreigners. A sourdough bread made with sorghum flour known as *mofa* and baked in an underground oven, grilled fish with tamarind sauce (*samaki wa ukwaju*) and fresh coconut water (*maji ya madafu*) have generally been replaced by sliced white bread (*bufflo*), fried fish (*samaki wa kukanga*) and soda pop, respectively. Modern kitchen appliances allow Swahili women (the primary cooks) to quickly make foods that would otherwise take all day to prepare. For example, coconut bread (*mkati wa nazi*) wrapped in banana leaves and baked over charcoal is now prepared in minutes with the help of a sandwich maker. And processing fresh fruit juice is now done with high-speed blenders.

The strategies family members and friends are using to treat their chronic illnesses are frequently discussed during large gatherings such as weddings, when people avoiding foods high in saturated fats and carbohydrates express their frustrations with being surrounded by foods they have been advised to avoid (Abdulrehman, 2015). We have noticed that some of the upper-class families in Lamu Town now provide plain white rice along with rice dishes such as *biriyani*, which are higher in salt and saturated fats, as well as fresh vegetables for guests on special diets. As new culinary influences are incorporated into Swahili cuisine, items such as guacamole, salads made with fresh greens and fresh fruit desserts are appearing on Swahili menus. With increasing awareness of the important role that diet plays in avoiding chronic illness and in reducing the symptoms associated with them, the Swahili of Lamu Town may reintroduce recipes of old as well as incorporate new recipes that help them manage new chronic diseases.

Access to healthcare in Lamu Town

Another important factor in maintaining wellness among the Swahili of Lamu Town is access to qualified medical professionals, be they of spiritual, herbal or biomedical background. The notion that medicine from outside the culture is more capable of combating illnesses that originate outside the society has been well documented in many East African societies (Feierman & Janzen, 1992; Rekdal, 1999; Whyte, 1988) and explains why the Swahili of Lamu Town are prepared to travel great distances for medical treatment, including psychiatric care, if they have the financial means to do so. Over the past decade, it has become more common for people with life-threatening illnesses such as cancer to raise funds from family members and travel to India for treatment. Those who cannot afford the costs associated with travel abroad or even to other towns along the coast must seek medical attention from local healers at local facilities. In the biomedical arena, the Lamu County Hospital offers government subsidized care that is affordable to most people but is generally lacking in cutting-edge diagnostic equipment and treatment options. Specialized medicine is limited to short-term clinics set up annually by medical teams that offer specific kinds of treatment such as cataract surgery. The temporary nature of these clinics, the patients' unfamiliarity with the healthcare providers (typically outsiders from Nairobi or abroad), and the lack of follow-up care have led to skepticism in free surgeries from mobile health clinics in Kenya generally (Briesen et al., 2010) and in Lamu Town in particular (Henderson & Gearhart, 2013). A perceived inadequacy of care has led to distrust in the proficiency of the biomedical services provided locally, leading to a continuation of the pluralistic healthcare model among the Swahili of Lamu Town (Abdulrehman et al., 2016) that is common throughout the continent (Aikins, 2005; Kolling, Winkley, & Deden, 2010; Murphy et al., 2015; Nagata et al., 2011).

The perception that the biomedical care available in Lamu County is generally inadequate is related to the history of marginalization of the Swahili and other coastal peoples (the Mijikenda, Orma, Pokomo and Boni) by the Kenyan government since the country's independence in 1963. Since then, the central government has failed to acknowledge the Swahili as a distinct ethnic group, preferring to identify the Swahili as Arab foreigners with little claim to coastal lands or the high-quality education, development programs, transportation infrastructure or healthcare facilities made available to upcountry ethnic groups that have benefitted from stronger government representation (Wolf, Muthoka, & Ireri, 2013). Though Kenya's nationally recognized lingua franca is Swahili, the Swahili people's first language and the language associated with Indian Ocean trade with Swahili middlemen, the Swahili are not listed among the fifty plus ethnic groups with which one might associate on the national population census. Even Lamu Town's designation by UNESCO as a World Heritage Site, due to its continuous occupation by Swahili people for over 700 years, has not convinced the Kenyan government of the Swahili people's unique ethnic identity. And perhaps most ironic is the Swahili Cultural Festival, sponsored annually in Lamu Town by the Kenyan government since 2000. Indeed, it is this festival that draws thousands of Kenyans to the historic town to witness Swahili music and dance (*ngoma*) competitions, Swahili boat (*mashua*) races and Swahili wedding festivities such as the stick dance (*Kirumbizi*) (Gearhart, 2005, 2015).

The high rates of poverty and unemployment, low levels of education (including public health education) (Maulana, Krumeich, & van den Borne, 2012), and inability to meet basic needs (food, clean water, medical treatment, school fees) among the Swahili compared to upcountry Kenyans (Wolf, Muthoka, & Ireri, 2013; Kenya National Bureau of Statistics, 2015) can be traced to this persistent neglect. It is within this context that the Swahili of Lamu Town continue to consult a range of healers in addition to biomedical professionals, including Islamic healers, midwives and herbalists, who would fall under the 'complementary and alternative medicine' (CAM) category.

Herbal use for chronic disease management: the case of type 2 diabetes mellitus

There is a plethora of evidence to suggest that CAM use for chronic disease management, and in diabetes management in particular, is prevalent in Africa (Balde et al., 2006; Kibiti & Afolayan, 2015; Ogbera, Dada, Adeleya, & Jewo, 2010; Singh, Raidoo, & Harries, 2004). In Kenya, there is wide use of herbal remedies in the management of disease states (Geissler & Prince, 2009; Odhiambo, Lukhoba, & Dossaji, 2011), even in urban areas such as Nairobi (Furukawa et al., 2016). This is also true in coastal Kenya (Gathirwa et al., 2011; Muthaura et al., 2015; Nguta et al., 2010; Pakia, 2000). The use of herbal remedies for lowering blood glucose levels has been found in a variety of Kenyan communities (Chege et al., 2015; Kamau et al., 2016; Keter & Mutiso, 2012), including Lamu Town (Abdulrehman et al., 2016). While examining diabetes self-management, Abdulrehman and colleagues (2016) reported that half of their research participants (*N*=30) regularly used herbal remedies to manage diabetes. This was primarily due to the affordability of herbal medicines compared to pills, and the lack of other pharmaceuticals such as injectable insulin due to the unavailability of refrigeration among many Lamu Town residents.

Due to the pervasive use of herbal remedies among the Lamu Town population, we urge local healthcare providers to initiate open dialogue with their patients about the herbal medicines they may be using, often concurrently with pharmaceuticals, to manage their health. We have noticed a general disregard for the role of CAM in chronic disease management such as diabetes among biomedically trained providers in Lamu Town. In such environments, patients fear being scolded for seeking advice from so-called 'alternative healers' and undergoing treatments considered 'backward.' We believe that open communication between healthcare providers and their patients in Lamu Town will ultimately lead to safer care, as adverse reactions associated with pharmaceutical-herbal contraindications will be avoided.

Conclusion

The increased prevalence of chronic diseases and improved access to biomedically trained healthcare providers have changed the way the Swahili of Lamu Town conceptualize and manage these diseases. Exposure to new medical theories such as the role genetics plays in diabetes, the deleterious effects of change in diet and the sustained use of plant medicines continue to transform the health of Swahili peoples of Lamu Town. The Swahili have remained pluralistic in their wellness strategies by employing herbal remedies, biomedicine and ritual to treat the new challenges associated with diseases such as diabetes.

Understanding the cultural framework within which African societies such as the Swahili conceptualize illness and wellness, treat symptoms and manage chronic diseases in medically dynamic and pluralistic contexts is important for guiding healthcare providers, researchers and policymakers toward the delivery of healthcare that makes sense within specific cultural frameworks, and that ultimately better serves those seeking to improve their wellbeing.

References

Abate, N., & Chandalia, M. (2003). The impact of ethnicity on type 2 diabetes. *Journal of Diabetes and Its Complications, 17*(1), 39–58.

Abate, N., & Chandalia, M. (2001). Ethnicity and type 2 diabetes: Focus on Asian Indians. *Journal of Diabetes and Its Complications, 15*(6), 320–327.

Abdulrehman, M.S. (2015). Reflections on native ethnography by a nurse researcher. *Journal of Transcultural Nursing, 28*(2), 152–158, doi:10.1177/1043659615620658.

Abdulrehman, M.S., Woith, W., Jenkins, S., Kossman, S., & Hunter, G.L. (2016). Exploring cultural influences of self-management of diabetes in coastal Kenya: An ethnography. *Global Qualitative Nursing Research, 3*, 1–13.

Aikins, A. (2005). Healer shopping in Africa: New evidence from rural-urban qualitative study of Ghanaian diabetes experiences. *BMJ: British Medical Journal, 331*(7519), 737–742.

Aikins, A., Unwin, N., Agyemang, C., Allotey, P., Campbell, C., & Arhinful, D. (2010). Tackling Africa's chronic disease burden: From the local to the global. *Globalization and Health, 6*(5), 1–7.

Balde, N.M., Youla, A., Balde, M.D., Kake, A., Diallo, M.M., Balde, M.A., & Maugendre, D. (2006). Herbal medicine and treatment of diabetes in Africa: An example from Guinea. *Diabetes & Metabolism, 32*(2), 171–175.

Beckerleg, S. (1994). Medical pluralism and Islam in Swahili communities in Kenya. *Medical Anthropology Quarterly, 8*(3), 299–313.

Briesen, S., Geneau, R., Roberts, H., Opiyo, J., & Courtright, P. (2010). Understanding why patients with cataract refuse free surgery: The influence of rumours in Kenya. *Tropical Medicine & International Health, 15*(5), 534–539.

Brown, J.B., Ramaiya, K., Besançon, S., Rheeder, P., Tassou, C.M., Mbanya, J., & Schneider, E. (2014). Use of medical services and medicines attributable to diabetes in sub-Saharan Africa. *Plos ONE, 9*(9), 1–13. doi:10.1371/journal.pone.0106716.

Chege, I.N., Okalebo, F.A., Guantai, A.N., Karanja, S., & Derese, S. (2015). Management of type 2 diabetes mellitus by traditional medicine practitioners in Kenya: Key informant interviews. *Pan African Medical Journal, 22*, 1–8.

Chege, M.P. (2010). Risks factors for type 2 diabetes mellitus among patients attending a rural Kenyan hospital. *African Journal of Primary Healthcare Family Medicine, 2*(1), 1–5.

Christensen, D., Friis, H., Mwaniki, D., Kilonzo, B., Tetens, I., Boit, M., & Borch-Johnsen, K. (2009). Prevalence of glucose intolerance and associated risk factors in rural and urban populations of different ethnic groups in Kenya. *Diabetes Research & Clinical Practice, 84*(3), 303–310.

Feierman, S., & Janzen, J.M. (1992). *The social basis of health and healing in Africa*. Berkeley, CA: University of California Press.

Folb, N., Timmerman, V., Levitt, N.S., Steyn, K., Bachmann, M.O., Lund, C., & Fairall, L.R. (2015). Multimorbidity, control and treatment of noncommunicable diseases among primary healthcare attenders in the Western Cape, South Africa. *South African Medical Journal = Suid-Afrikaanse Tydskrif Vir Geneeskunde, 105*(8), 642–647.

Furukawa, T., Kiboi, S.K., Mutiso, P.C., & Fujiwara, K. (2016). Multiple use patterns of medicinal trees in an urban forest in Nairobi, Kenya. *Urban Forestry & Urban Greening, 18*, 34–40.

Ganu, D., Fletcher, N., & Caleb, N.K. (2016). Physical disability and functional impairment resulting from type 2 diabetes in sub-Saharan Africa: A systematic review. *African Journal of Diabetes Medicine, 24*(1), 10–14.

Gathirwa, J., Rukunga, G., Mwitari, P., Mwikwabe, N., Kimani, C., Muthaura, C., & Omar, S. (2011). Traditional herbal antimalarial therapy in Kilifi district, Kenya. *Journal of Ethnopharmacology, 134*(2), 434–442.

Gearhart, R. (2015). Forming and performing Swahili manhood: Wedding rituals of a groom in Lamu Town. In K. Thompson & E. Stiles (Eds.), *Gendered lives in the western Indian Ocean: Islam, marriage, and sexuality on the Swahili coast* (pp. 269–290). Athens, OH: Ohio University Press.

Gearhart, R. (2005). Ngoma memories: How ritual music and dance shaped the northern Kenya coast. *African Studies Review, 48*(3), 21–47.

Gearhart, R., & Abdulrehman, M.S. (2014). Concepts of illness among the Swahili of Lamu, Kenya. *Journal of Transcultural Nursing, 25*(3), 218–222.

Gearhart, R., & Abdulrehman, M.S. (2012). Purity, balance and wellness among the Swahili of Lamu, Kenya. *The Journal of Global Health, 2*(1), 42–44.

Geissler, P.W., & Prince, R.J. (2009). Active compounds and atoms of society: Plants, bodies, minds and cultures in the work of Kenyan ethnobotanical knowledge. *Social Studies of Science, 39*(4), 599–634.

Henderson, E., & Gearhart, R. (2013). Observations on eye care in Lamu, Kenya: Overlooked needs and proposed interventions. *The Journal of Global Health, 3*(1), 36–39.

Jaffiol, C. (2010). The burden of diabetes in Africa: A major public health problem. *Bulletin de L'Academie Nationale de Medecine, 195*(6), 1239–1253.

Jiang, X., Ma, H., Wang, Y., & Liu, Y. (2013). Early life factors and type 2 diabetes mellitus. *Journal of Diabetes Research, 485082*, 1–11.

Kamau, L.N., Mbaabu, M.P., Mbaria, J.M., Karuri, G.P., & Kiama, S.G. (2016). Knowledge and demand for medicinal plants used in the treatment and management of diabetes in Nyeri County, Kenya. *Journal of Ethnopharmacology, 189*, 218–229.

Keefe, S.K. (2015). Being a good Muslim man: Modern aspirations and polygynous intentions in a Swahili Muslim village. In K. Thompson & E. Stiles (Eds.), *Gendered lives in the western Indian Ocean: Islam, marriage, and sexuality on the Swahili coast* (pp. 321–353). Athens, OH: Ohio University Press.

Kenya National Bureau of Statistics. (2015). *Kenya Demographic and Health Survey 2014: Key indicators.* Nairobi: Kenya National Bureau of Statistics. Retrieved from https://dhsprogram.com/pubs/pdf/FR308/FR308.pdf.

Keter, L.K., & Mutiso, P.C. (2012). Ethnobotanical studies of medicinal plants used by traditional health practitioners in the management of diabetes in lower Eastern Province, Kenya. *Journal of Ethnopharmacology, 139*(1), 74–80.

Kibiti, C.M., & Afolayan, A.J. (2015). Herbal therapy: A review of emerging pharmacological tools in the management of diabetes mellitus in Africa. *Pharmacognosy Magazine, 11*(44), 258–274.

Kolling, M., Winkley, K., & Deden, M. v. (2010). "For someone who's rich, it's not a problem". Insights from Tanzania on diabetes health-seeking and medical pluralism among Dar es Salaam's urban poor. *Globalization and Health, 6*(8), 1–9.

Maiyaki, M.B., & Garbati, M.A. (2014). The burden of non-communicable diseases in Nigeria; in the context of globalization. *Annals of African Medicine, 13*(1), 1–10.

Mathenge, W., Foster, A., & Kuper, H. (2010). Urbanization, ethnicity and cardiovascular risk in a population in transition in Nakuru, Kenya: A population-based survey. *BMC Public Health, 10*(569), 1–12.

Maulana, A.O., Krumeich, A., & van den Borne, B. (2012). In their eyes: HIV prevention from an Islamic perspective in Lamu, Kenya. *Health, Culture, and Society, 2*(1), 89–102.

Murphy, K., Chuma, T., Mathews, C., Steyn, K., & Levitt, N. (2015). A qualitative study of the experiences of care and motivation for effective self-management among diabetic and hypertensive patients attending public sector primary health care services in South Africa. *BMC Health Services Research, 15*, 303. doi:10.1186/s12913-015-0969-y.

Muthaura, C., Keriko, J., Mutai, C., Yenesew, A., Gathirwa, J., Irungu, B., & Derese, S. (2015). Antiplasmodial potential of traditional antimalarial phytotherapy remedies used by the Kwale community of the Kenyan coast. *Journal of Ethnopharmacology, 170*, 148–157.

Nagata, J.M., Jew, A.R., Kimeu, J.M., Salmen, C.R., Bukusi, E.A., & Cohen, C.R. (2011). Medical pluralism on Mfangano Island: Use of medicinal plants among persons living with HIV/AIDS in Suba District, Kenya. *Journal of Ethnopharmacology, 135*(2), 501–509.

Nguta, J., Mbaria, J., Gakuya, D., Gathumbi, P., & Kiama, S. (2010). Traditional antimalarial phytotherapy remedies used by the South coast community, Kenya. *Journal of Ethnopharmacology, 131*(2), 256–267.

Odhiambo, J.A., Lukhoba, C.W., & Dossaji, S.F. (2011). Evaluation of herbs as potential drugs/medicines. *African Journal of Traditional, Complementary, and Alternative Medicines: AJTCAM / African Networks on Ethnomedicines, 8*(5), 144–151.

Ogbera, A.O., Dada, O., Adeleya, O., & Jewo, P.I. (2010). Complementary and alternative medicine use in diabetes mellitus. *West African Journal of Medicine, 29*(3), 158–162.

Ovbiagele, B. (2015). Tackling the growing diabetes burden in sub-Saharan Africa: A framework for enhancing outcomes in stroke patients. *Journal of the Neurological Sciences, 348*, 136–141. doi:10.1016/j.jns.2014.11.023.

Pakia, M. (2000). *Plant ecology and ethnobotany of two sacred forests (kayas) at the Kenya coast.* Master's thesis, University of Natal, Durban, South Africa. Retrieved from http://hdl.handle.net/10413/3829.

Parkin, D. (2000). Islam among the humors: Destiny and agency among the Swahili. In I. Karp & D. Masolo (Eds.), *African philosophy as cultural inquiry* (pp. 50–65). Bloomington, IN: Indiana University Press.

Rekdal, O.B. (1999). Cross-cultural healing in East African ethnography. *Medical Anthropology Quarterly, 13*(4), 458–482.

Rosella, L.C., Mustard, C.A., Stukel, T.A., Corey, P., Hux, J., Roos, L., & Manuel, D.G. (2012). The role of ethnicity in predicting diabetes risk at the population level. *Ethnicity & Health, 17*(4), 419–437.

Ross, N.A., Gilmour, H., & Dasgupta, K. (2010). 14-year diabetes incidence: The role of socio-economic status. *Health Reports, 21*(3), 19–28.

Singh, V., Raidoo, D., & Harries, C. (2004). The prevalence, patterns of usage, and people's attitude towards complementary and alternative medicine (CAM) among the Indian community in Chatsworth, South Africa. *BMC Complementary and Alternative Medicine, 4*(1), 1–7.

Werfalli, M., Engel, M.E., Musekiwa, A., Kengne, A.P., & Levitt, N.S. (2016). Review: The prevalence of type 2 diabetes among older people in Africa: A systematic review. *The Lancet Diabetes & Endocrinology, 4*, 72–84. doi:10.1016/S2213-8587(15)00363-0.

Wolf, T., Muthoka, S., & Ireri, M. (2013). *Kenya coast survey: Development, marginalization, security, and partici-pation.* Ipsos Public Affairs, The Social Research and Corporate Reputation Specialists. Retrieved from www.google.com/?gws_rd=ssl#q=Kenya+coast+survey:+development%2C+marginalization%2C+s ecurity%2C+and+participation.

Whyte, S.R. (1988). The power of medicines in East Africa. In S. van der Geest & S.R. Whyte, *The context of medicines in developing countries: Studies in pharmaceutical anthropology* (pp. 217–233). Norwell, MA: Kluwer Academic Publishers.

Ziyyat, A., Legssyer, A., Mekhfi, H., Dassouli, A., Serhrouchni, M., & Benjelloun, W. (1997). Phytotherapy of hypertension and diabetes in oriental Morocco. *Journal of Ethnopharmacology, 58*(1), 45–54.

6

PHYSICAL WELLBEING OF NATIVE HAWAIIANS, THE INDIGENOUS PEOPLE OF HAWAI'I

Joseph Keawe'aimoku Kaholokula, Andrea H. Hermosura and Mapuana C.K. Antonio

Introduction

Native Hawaiians are descendants of the original inhabitants from the islands of the Hawaiian archipelago in Northern Polynesia, collectively known as Hawai'i. The ancestors of contemporary Native Hawaiians settled in Hawai'i 1,200 years ago. They developed a sophisticated socio-religious system of rule and resource management that sustained a population close to 700,000 in 1778 – the year Captain James Cook's expedition came upon the Hawaiian Islands. Cook and his men observed a healthy and robust Indigenous population in which disease and illness were uncommon. In relation to physical wellbeing, they observed that the natives were "above middle size, strong, well made… a fine handsome set of people" (Beaglehole, 1967, p. 1178).

The relatively excellent physical health status enjoyed by the Indigenous population of Hawai'i at the time of contact with Cook's expedition soon changed. European and American settlers introduced infectious diseases to the Indigenous population – diseases toward which they had no natural immunity. The venereal diseases of gonorrhea and syphilis started the decimation of the Indigenous population followed by epidemics of cholera, influenza, whooping cough, Hansen's disease, measles, small pox, mumps, diphtheria and tuberculosis between the 1800s and early 1900s (Bushnell, 1993). Consequently, the native population dwindled to roughly 30,000 by the end of the 1800s, a 95 percent decline in a matter of a century.

Since the development of antiviral treatments and immunizations in the early 1900s, deaths due to infectious diseases abated leading to a rebound in the Native Hawaiian population. The 2010 United States (US) Census indicated roughly 530,000 Native Hawaiians living in the US, with 289,970 living in Hawai'i (about 25 percent of the population). The population of Native Hawaiians across the US are estimated to nearly double by 2045, with an increase to 512,000 in Hawai'i alone (State of Hawai'i Department of Business, Economic Development and Tourism, 2012). Although infectious diseases are no longer a serious threat to Native Hawaiians, their physical wellbeing is threatened by higher rates of chronic diseases, such as diabetes and cardiovascular disease (CVD) when compared to other ethnic groups (Mau, Sinclair, Saito,

Baumhofer & Kaholokula, 2009), resulting in higher mortality rates (Panapasa, Mau, Williams, & McNally, 2010).

Because of the disproportionate burden of chronic diseases and other health inequities among Native Hawaiians, the Native Hawaiian Health Care Act was authorized in 1988 and reauthorized under the Native Hawaiian Health Care Improvement Act in 1992 and 2009 by the US Congress. The Act requires the US Department of Health and Human Services to make funding available to support community-based and culturally meaningful health promotion initiatives and healthcare workforce development for Native Hawaiians. The intent of the Act was to close the gap between Native Hawaiians and other ethnic groups in terms of chronic disease incidence and prevalence. At the time the Act was first promulgated, Native Hawaiians were 44 percent more likely to have CVD, 31 percent more likely to have cerebrovascular disease, 39 percent more likely to have cancer and two times more likely to have diabetes than the US national average and their overall death rate was 34 percent higher (Native Hawaiian Health Research Consortium & Alu Like, 1985).

In this chapter, we examine the current physical wellbeing of Native Hawaiians, with a focus on chronic diseases and their impact on morbidity and mortality. We also examine the subjective impact of these chronic diseases on their sense of physical wellbeing, their social and cultural determinants of physical wellbeing and community-based health promotion programs that offer the promise of achieving health equity. We conclude with an analysis of policies and efforts since the promulgation of the Native Hawaiian Health Care Act of 1988.

Chronic diseases and their risk factors

Excess body weight

Excess body weight is defined as having a body mass index (BMI) of 25 or greater and it is a risk factor for chronic diseases, such as diabetes, hypertension, CVD and certain types of cancer (WHO, 2017). Seventy-three percent of Native Hawaiian adults in Hawai'i have excess body weight, with 37 percent in the overweight (BMI=25–29.9) and 39 percent in the obese (BMI≥30) category (Nguyen & Salvail, 2016).

Figure 6.1 summarizes the trends in overweight and obesity from 2011–2014 across the four largest ethnic groups in Hawai'i – Native Hawaiians, Japanese, Filipinos, Caucasians and the general population. Native Hawaiians had a prevalence of overweight that varied between 34 and 37 percent, which was comparable to Japanese (33% to 36%), Filipinos (33% to 39%), Caucasians (34% to 36%) and Hawai'i at large (33% to 36%) (Hawai'i Health Data Warehouse [HHDW], 2016). However, the prevalence of obesity was two times greater in Native Hawaiians (varying between 39% and 44%) compared to those other ethnic groups and the general population during the same period (HHDW, 2016).

Despite the high prevalence of obesity, 81.2 percent of Native Hawaiians report participating in physical activities outside of their regular job. Thirty-two percent of Native Hawaiian adults report engaging in physical activity levels that meet US National recommendations for both aerobic (i.e. 150 minutes of moderate exercise each week) and muscle strengthening (i.e. 2 or more days) activities, which is higher than the general adult population in Hawai'i at 27 percent (HHDW, 2016). Aside from a possible reporting bias (i.e. overestimating physical activity levels), this paradoxical pattern may indicate other risk factors for excess body weight, such as excessive alcohol consumption and caloric intake (McEligot et al., 2012; Kim, Park, Grandinetti, Holck, & Waslien, 2008). As seen in other Indigenous communities, the drastic change from traditional dietary patterns based on subsistence living to Western dietary patterns (e.g. calorie and

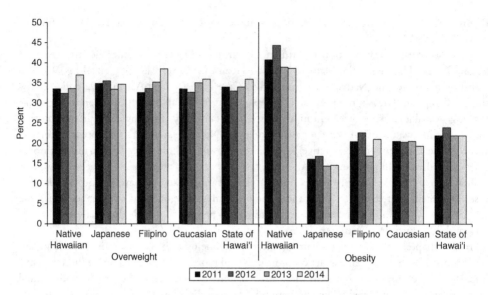

Figure 6.1 Prevalence of overweight and obesity by ethnicity in the state of Hawai'i, 2011–2014

fat-dense foods) are believed to contribute to this obesity epidemic (Inda, Washburn, Beckham, Talisayan, & Hikuroa, 2011).

Cardiovascular and cerebrovascular disease

CVD, which includes coronary heart disease (CHD), and cerebrovascular disease, which includes stroke, are the first and third leading causes of death in Native Hawaiians, respectively. As Figure 6.2 indicates, the age-adjusted prevalence of CHD and stroke between 2011 and 2013 were higher for Native Hawaiians and trending upwards compared to other ethnic groups in Hawai'i and the general population. The CHD and stroke prevalence for Native Hawaiians increased from 2.9 percent and 2.7 percent, respectively, in 2011 to almost 5 percent for both in 2012 and 2013, which are higher than those for Japanese, Caucasians and Filipinos during this period (HHDW, 2016). In 2014, the crude prevalence of CHD and stroke remained higher for Native Hawaiians compared to other ethnic groups at 4.2 percent and 3.7 percent (except for Japanese at 4.2%), respectively (Nguyen & Salvail, 2016).

Native Hawaiians develop cerebrovascular disease a decade sooner than other ethnic groups in Hawai'i. Nakagawa and colleagues (2013, 2015), in cross-sectional studies of Asians, Native Hawaiians and Pacific Islanders hospitalized for ischemic stroke found that Native Hawaiians and Pacific Islanders presented with stroke an average of 10 years younger than Asians and Caucasians. They attributed these ethnic differences in stroke onset to differences in biological (e.g. genetic variations) and social determinants (e.g. access to care) of the disease (Nakagawa, Koenig, Asai, Chang, & Seto, 2013).

Overall, the age-adjusted mortality rate due to CVD is 313.1 per 100,000 for Native Hawaiians, which is higher than the CVD rates of 205.3 per 100,000 for the general population of Hawai'i and 287.0 per 100,000 for the entire US (Balabis, Pobutsky, Kromer Baker, Tottori, & Salvail, 2007). In a study of 855 Native Hawaiians who were followed for fifteen years, it was found that 56 percent of deaths in men and 54 percent of deaths in women were due to CVD (Aluli et al., 2010), with a majority due to CHD and myocardial infarctions. The

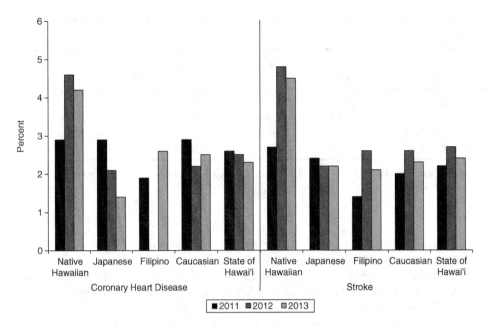

Figure 6.2   Age-adjusted prevalence (%) of CHD and stroke by ethnicity in the state of Hawai'i, 2011–2013

average age of CVD-related deaths in Native Hawaiians is 65.2 for males and 72.3 for females compared to 73.1 and 79.6, respectively, for the general population of Hawai'i (Balabis et al., 2007). High rates of CVD-related deaths and earlier age of onset for Native Hawaiians could be associated with various factors, such as their lower average socioeconomic status and higher rates of obesity, diabetes and hypertension (Aluli, Reyes, & Tsark 2007; Aluli et al., 2010).

Hypertension is the leading cause of CVD and cerebrovascular disease related morbidity and mortality. Native Hawaiians had a higher age-adjusted prevalence of hypertension than the other major ethnic groups in Hawai'i in 2011 and 2013 (HHDW, 2016). Their prevalence was 34.7 percent and 34.1 percent in 2011 and 2013, respectively, compared to Filipinos at 30.4 percent and 29.0 percent, Japanese at 26.8 percent and 28.1 percent, and Caucasians at 22.1 percent and 20.9 percent (HHDW, 2016).

Cancer

Cancer is the second leading cause of death in Native Hawaiians. Native Hawaiian males and females have greater mortality rates due to cancer compared to other ethnic groups in Hawai'i. Table 6.1 summarizes the incidence and mortality rates of certain cancer cases by ethnicity and gender in Hawai'i between 2000 and 2005 (Green, 2010). Cancer tends to occur at younger ages and is detected at later stages, often resulting in lower survival rates compared to others (Braun, Fong, Gotay, & Chong, 2004; Mokuau, Braun, Wong, Higuchi, & Gotay, 2008). Specifically, Native Hawaiians are more likely to be diagnosed with late-stage breast, cervix, lung and bronchus, prostate, and colon and rectum cancers compared to other ethnic groups (Green, 2010).

With the exception of Filipinos, cancer screening behaviors are lower for Native Hawaiians than other ethnic groups. The percentage of Native Hawaiian males ages 40 and up who had a Prostate-Specific Antigen (PSA) test was lower (27%) than for Japanese (51.4%) and Caucasian (54.6%) males of the same ages (Nguyen & Salvail, 2016). The percentage of women ages 40

Table 6.1 Incidence and mortality rates of cancer cases (per 100,000) by ethnicity and gender in Hawai'i, 2000–2005

	Native Hawaiian	Caucasian	Chinese	Filipino	Japanese
Male incidence rate	479.6	542.4	423.5	466.8	476.3
Female incidence rate	447.8	413.6	317.3	341.4	363.9
Male mortality rate	231.7	198.2	154.4	178.7	187.1
Female mortality rate	171.0	133.6	107.2	98.3	109.9

Source: Table modified from Green (2010). Original source: Hawai'i Tumor Registry, Cancer Research Center of Hawaii, University of Hawai'i.

and up who received a mammogram was also lower in Native Hawaiians (92.5%) than Japanese (96.2%) and Caucasians (94%) (Nguyen & Salvail, 2016).

Based on the 2014 Hawai'i Behavioral Risk Factor Surveillance System (BRFSS), the prevalence of current smokers for Native Hawaiian adults (27%) was higher than for Japanese (8.8%), Filipinos (11.5%) and Caucasians (12%). According to the 2013 Youth Tobacco Survey, Native Hawaiian youth also have higher tobacco use (13.4%) than Japanese (10.8%), Filipinos (9.2%) and Caucasians (11.8%) (HHDW, 2016). The prevalence of current smokers across Hawai'i is 14.1 percent for adults and 11.8 percent for youth.

Diabetes

Diabetes is an emerging public health concern as the fourth leading cause of death in Native Hawaiians. Based on the 2014 BRFSS, 13 percent of Native Hawaiians self-reported having diabetes, which is comparable to Japanese at 14 percent and Filipinos at 13 percent, but considerably higher than Caucasians at 5 percent and Hawai'i's general population at 9.8 percent. As shown in Figure 6.3, the prevalence of diabetes in Native Hawaiians has increased by 3 percent over the past four years compared to a steady prevalence of roughly 5 percent for Caucasians and 8 percent for the general population of Hawai'i.

The prevalence of diabetes in Native Hawaiians is considerably higher when based on its actual diagnosis. Grandinetti et al. (2007) found the prevalence of diabetes to be 19 percent for adult Native Hawaiians, of which 11 percent reported knowing they had diabetes and 8 percent were newly diagnosed (i.e. those who had diabetes but were unaware of it). They also found that the prevalence of diabetes was nearly two times greater than Caucasians, adjusting for socio-demographics, BMI, waist-to-hip ratio, and caloric, fiber and carbohydrate intake. The age-adjusted mortality rate due to diabetes for Native Hawaiians is two times greater (38.0 per 100,000) than for Hawai'i overall (16.3 per 100,000) (Johnson, Oyama, LeMarchand, & Wilkens, 2004).

Subjective physical wellbeing

Physical wellbeing goes beyond the mere absence or presence of disease. For Native Hawaiians, spiritual and social wellbeing can mitigate the adverse effects of having a chronic physical disease on their overall sense of wellbeing. Studies find that spiritual and social wellbeing are important to the overall wellbeing of Native Hawaiians living with a chronic disease (Kaholokula, Saito, Mau, Latimer, & Seto, 2008; Ka'opua, Mitschke, & Kloezeman, 2008).

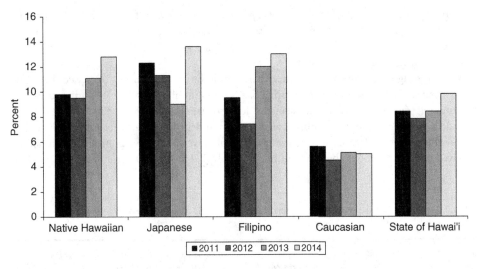

Figure 6.3 Prevalence of diabetes by ethnicity in the state of Hawai'i, 2011–2014

To further examine the subjective physical wellbeing of Native Hawaiians, we conducted secondary analysis of data from the Kohala Health Research Project[1] (KHRP), which was an epidemiological study of diabetes and CVD risk in a multiethnic cohort of over 1,400 people from 1997 to 2000. For more details about KHRP's methods and participants' characteristics, see Kaholokula, Braun, Kana'iaupuni, Grandinetti, and Chang (2006). The database includes 526 Native Hawaiians, 190 Japanese, 186 Filipinos, and 295 Caucasians for distinct ethnic comparisons.

Among the biological, behavioral and psychosocial measures taken, the participants' medical history (i.e. diagnosis of various medical conditions) and their health-related quality of life (HRQL) as measured by the SF-36 Health Survey (Ware, Snow, Kosinski, & Gandek, 1993) were analyzed for our purpose here. The SF-36 measures eight aspects of HRQL, three of which directly pertain to physical wellbeing: (1) physical functioning; (2) role-physical functioning (e.g. role limitations due to physical health problems); and (3) bodily pain. A summary measure was calculated combining these three subscales of the SF-36 to yield a score ranging from 0 to 100, with higher scores indicating better physical wellbeing.

Table 6.2 summarizes the descriptive data for age and SF-36 summary scores and number of participants with chronic medical conditions ranging from 0 to ≥ 3 by ethnic group and combined sample. The conditions included were respiratory (e.g. asthma, bronchitis), cancer, endocrine and metabolic (e.g. diabetes), hyperlipidemia and circulatory diseases (e.g. hypertension and heart disease) and obesity. There were significant differences between ethnic groups in mean age and in number of medical conditions linked to individuals. Native Hawaiians were younger and Japanese were older than the other ethnic groups. Caucasians had more persons with no chronic medical condition while Native Hawaiians had more persons living with three or more co-morbid medical conditions. There was no significant difference between ethnic groups in SF-36 mean scores.

With the SF-36 as our measure of physical wellbeing, we first sought to determine if perceptions of physical wellbeing would differ significantly across Native Hawaiians who vary from not having any medical condition to upwards of three or more co-morbid conditions. Based on one-way analysis of variance (ANOVA), we found that Native Hawaiians without any medical condition had the highest mean SF-36 score at 86.2 followed by those with one condition at 82.3 and two conditions at 79.1, with the lowest for those with three or more co-morbid conditions at 78 [$F(3, 492)=4.35, p<.01$]. After adjusting for age, the differences in SF-36 scores were mainly between those without any medical condition and those with three or more conditions. Summary statistics for the SF-36 are summarized in Table 6.3 for Native Hawaiians and the other ethnic groups.

We then sought to determine whether there would be any significant differences between ethnic groups in SF-36 scores after adjusting for age and number of medical conditions. Based on a multiple regression analysis (i.e. standard least squares method) with SF-36 scores as the dependent variable and ethnic group category as the independent variable, and age (in years) and number of medical conditions as control variables, we found no significant difference in perceived physical wellbeing between ethnic groups [$F(7, 1159)=10.01, p<.0001$].

Table 6.2 Descriptive statistics by ethnicity and combined sample and analysis of differences between ethnic groups on study characteristics

Characteristics	Native Hawaiian (n=526)	Filipino (n=186)	Japanese (n=190)	Caucasian (n=295)	Combined (N=1,197)
Age (years)*	44.7 ± 14.6	53.7 ±16.2	58.9 ± 16.4	49.4 ± 12.4	49.5 ± 15.5
SF-36 scores	81.5 ± 18.3	77.7 ± 22.5	80.2 ± 18.7	79.7 ± 21.8	81.7 ± 3.0
Number of medical conditions**					
0	124 (23%)	43 (23%)	48 (25%)	105 (35%)	320 (27%)
1	183 (35%)	75 (40%)	67 (35%)	112 (38%)	437 (37%)
2	107 (20%)	35 (19%)	41 (22%)	49 (17%)	232 (19%)
≥ 3	112 (22%)	33 (18%)	34 (18%)	29 (10%)	208 (17%)

Notes: Data shown as mean ± standard deviation or number (%). Higher scores on the SF-36 (range is 0 to 100) indicate better physical wellbeing. Combined = combined sample.

*indicates significant differences between ethnic groups based on Analysis of Variance [$F(3, 1194) = 49.17, p<.0001$].

**indicates significant difference between ethnic groups based on likelihood ratio test [$\chi^2 = (9, N=1,197) = 30.2, p<.001$].

Table 6.3 Descriptive statistics for SF-36 scores by number of medical conditions across ethnic groups

Number of medical conditions	Native Hawaiian	Filipino	Japanese	Caucasian
	SF-36 physical summary score			
	M ± SD	M ± SD	M ± SD	M ± SD
0	86.2 ± 17.4	83.6 ± 16.5	82.3 ± 17.8	81.4 ± 22.1
1	82.1 ± 18.1	81.7 ± 21.8	79.6 ± 18.4	80.7 ± 20.4
2	79.1 ± 18.5	68.3 ± 23.6	80.9 ± 16.0	78.9 ± 18.8
≥ 3	78.0 ± 20.7	70.8 ± 25.3	77.7 ± 23.1	70.7 ± 28.5

Notes: Data shown as mean ± standard deviation. Higher scores on the SF-36 (range is 0 to 100) indicate better physical wellbeing. No significant ethnic differences in SF-36 scores across medical condition category after adjusting for age [$F(7, 1159) = 10.0, p<.0001$].

What these findings suggest is that, despite living with chronic diseases at younger ages, Native Hawaiians' perceptions of their physical wellbeing are relatively good on average and comparable to people of other ethnic groups in Hawai'i. Even among Native Hawaiians who are living with three or more medical conditions, their perceptions of physical wellbeing, as measured by the SF-36, was on the higher end. Aside from possible reporting biases, it could be that the adverse physical effects (e.g. bodily pain and decreased mobility) of a chronic disease are tempered by other aspects of wellbeing that remain strong for Native Hawaiians, such as cultural, social and spiritual wellbeing. These other aspects of wellbeing could be the key to the resilience of Native Hawaiians in overcoming the adverse effects of chronic diseases.

Social and cultural determinants of physical wellbeing

The biological (e.g. genetic predispositions) and behavioral (e.g. lifestyle choices) determinants of health are often the focus in explaining health inequities and in informing strategies for interventions. However, increasing attention is being paid to the social and cultural determinants of health. The former refers to the societal, political and economic forces that influence the social structure and hierarchy and the distribution of power, resources and opportunities across society that differentially impact the wellbeing of people (Braveman, Egerter, & Williams, 2011). Cultural determinants of health for Indigenous Peoples refer to the same aforementioned forces that influence the degree to which they can revive, maintain and/or pass on their cultural traditions (e.g. native language, values and practices), and to protect and access their sacred places and ancestral lands (Kaholokula, 2016).

Among the social determinants of health, Native Hawaiians are more likely to live in obesogenic environments; that is, environments that promote obesity and makes achieving and maintaining a healthy weight challenging within the home or workplace (Swinburn, Egger, & Raza, 1999). Communities with less access to, or availability of, healthy eating and physical activity options are associated with higher rates of obesity for Native Hawaiians, and communities with a larger Native Hawaiian population are more likely to have inadequate access to these resources (Mau et al., 2008).

Among the cultural determinants of health, acculturative stressors and ethnic discrimination are associated with chronic disease risk and indices of physical wellbeing in Native Hawaiians (Kaholokula, Nacapoy, & Dang, 2009). Large within group differences in the risk for diabetes have been found in Native Hawaiians based on their acculturation mode. Native Hawaiians who have a traditional mode of acculturation (i.e. identify strongly with their native culture but not with the American culture) have a diabetes prevalence nearly double (27.9% versus 15.4%) that of Native Hawaiians who have a bicultural mode of acculturation (i.e. identify strongly with both their native and the American culture) (Kaholokula, Nacapoy, Grandinetti, & Chang, 2008). An explanation for this finding is that Native Hawaiians with a traditional mode experience more acculturative stress, such as racism and a greater sense of social injustices toward them, which could be part of a complex stress-related causal pathway leading to higher diabetes risk (Kaholokula, 2007).

Subsequent studies have found a positive correlation between Hawaiian cultural identity and perceptions of racism in Native Hawaiians but that perceived racism, not Hawaiian cultural identity, is associated with disease risk and indices of physiological health. Higher levels of perceived racism have been found to be associated with hypertension (Kaholokula, Iwane, & Nacapoy, 2010) and obesity (McCubbin & Antonio, 2012) in Native Hawaiians. Higher levels of perceived racism have been found to be associated with lower diurnal cortisol output in Native Hawaiians, which persisted after adjusting for sociodemographic, biological and other psychosocial factors (Kaholokula, Grandinetti et al., 2012). Cortisol is a hormone that usually increases in response to stress. However, cortisol may behave differently in regards to a chronic stressor, such as racism. Prolonged sympathetic–adrenal–medullary and hypothalamic–pituitary–adrenal axis activation due to chronic psychological stress may lead to abnormal physical responses, such as metabolic dysregulation, hypertension and changes in cortisol homeostasis (DeSantis et al., 2007; Miller, Chen, & Zhou, 2007).

Promising health promotion programs

The Partnership for Improving Lifestyle Interventions (PILI) 'Ohana Project[2]

Because excess body weight is a major risk factor for diabetes and CVD, the community and academic researchers of the PILI 'Ohana Project (POP) developed the PILI Lifestyle Program (PLP). It was designed to be delivered by community peer educators in group format across various community settings (e.g. community health centers as well as Hawaiian homestead communities) to help Native Hawaiians and Pacific Islanders lose excess body weight and keep it off. It was designed with input from over 300 Native Hawaiians and Pacific Islanders, community leaders and health professionals to ensure both its clinical and cultural relevance (see Kaholokula et al., 2014).

The PLP curriculum entails culturally relevant behavioral strategies and strategies for soliciting family and community support to promote healthy eating and physical activity and problem-solving to sustain those efforts. The PLP is delivered in two phases: a three-month phase (eight lessons spread over twelve weeks) to initiate weight loss, which is based on the Diabetes Prevention Program's Lifestyle Intervention, followed by a six-month weight-loss maintenance phase. The latter phase was designed to build on the healthy lifestyle strategies learned from the first phase by incorporating family and community activities to build and maintain a supportive environment (see Kaholokula, Mau et al., 2012; Mau et al., 2010).

When compared to a standard behavioral weight-loss maintenance program (SBMP), via a randomized controlled trial, the PLP was found superior in achieving ≥3 percent weight loss in 144 Native Hawaiians and Pacific Islanders over nine months (Kaholokula, Mau et al., 2012). Fifty-one percent of PLP participants met the ≥3 percent weight-loss goal (mean weight loss of 2.54kg) compared to 31.4 percent of those in a SBMP (mean weight loss of 0.45kg). To place the findings of the POP in perspective, researchers of the Diabetes Prevention Program found that a person's risk for diabetes is reduced by 16 percent for every 1.0 kg of weight-loss achieved (Hamman et al., 2006). Modest weight loss can improve high-density lipoproteins, glucose metabolism, triglycerides and other risk factors for CVD (Donnelly et al., 2009).

The researchers of the POP also developed Partners in Care (PIC) for Native Hawaiians and Pacific Islanders living with diabetes (Sinclair et al., 2013). PIC is a three-month (one-hour lesson each week) diabetes self-care program originally developed for African-Americans and Latinos (Spencer et al., 2011). PIC was designed to be delivered by community peer educators with familiarity of Pacific Islander cultures and delivered in a group setting. It is based on the American Diabetes Association's (2005) clinical guideline goals for effective diabetes management and the self-care behavioral strategies were situated within a culturally relevant context.

The adapted PIC was found effective in achieving significant reductions in hemoglobin A1c (HbA1c; i.e. average blood sugar levels) and improvements in diabetes self-management knowledge and behaviors compared to a waitlist-control (Sinclair et al., 2013) in Native Hawaiians and Pacific Islanders. Those who completed the PIC achieved an average HbA1c reduction of 1.6 percent compared to a reduction of 0.3 percent for those randomized to waitlist. It is estimated that a 1 percent reduction in HbA1c corresponds to a risk reduction of 21 percent for deaths related to diabetes, 14 percent for myocardial infarction and 37 percent for micro-vascular complications (Welschen et al., 2005).

The Hula Enhancing Lifestyle Adaptation (HELA) project

Because hypertension is a major risk factor for CVD, community and academic researchers of the HELA Project developed a culturally grounded hypertension management intervention called Ola Hou i ka Hula (translates as "regaining life through hula"; referred to as Ola Hou from here on). Ola Hou uses hula, the traditional dance of Native Hawaiians, as its primary physical activity component coupled with four brief, one-hour lessons on signs and symptoms of hypertension, medication management, sodium reduction, physical activity and managing negative emotions.

The participants of Ola Hou engage in hula lessons over three months (two one-hour lessons per week) delivered by a Kumu Hula (Hula expert and teacher) in a group format similar to actual hula lessons delivered at traditional hula schools. Hula is the hallmark of Hawaiian culture today, and its practice has spread beyond Hawai'i to places such as Japan, Mexico and Europe. Hula conveys historical events and persons, spiritual beliefs and one's connection to the natural world. It is now practiced as both a form of cultural and creative expression. It involves controlled rhythmic movements that illustrate the meaning or poetry of the accompanying songs or chants. The dances can vary in intensity and duration depending on their choreography and tempo of the music, and modified to accommodate people who have physical limitations (see Look, Kaholokula, Carvhalo, Seto, & de Silva, 2012).

The Ola Hou program was tested against a waitlist-control with fifty-five Native Hawaiians and Pacific Islanders with physician-diagnosed hypertension and a systolic blood pressure (SBP) ≥ 140 mmHg. Participants who were randomized to Ola Hou had reduced their SBP by an average of 18.3 mmHg compared to 7.6 mmHg for those randomized to the waitlist (Kaholokula et al., 2015). The SBP improvements for Ola Hou participants were associated with improvements in their reports of bodily pain and social functioning. Studies find that a 5 mmHg reduction in SBP can lower a person's risk of ischemic heart disease by 21 percent, stroke by 34 percent and all cause-mortality by 7 percent (Whelton, Chin, Xin, & He 2002; Law, Wald, & Morris, 2005).

Final comments

The higher prevalence of chronic diseases and resulting mortality rates among Native Hawaiians compared to most other ethnic groups and the general population of Hawai'i and the continental US continue to persist since the enactment of US Federal legislation in 1988 to 'close the gap' (Mau et al., 2009; Panapasa et al., 2010). Their subjective reports of physical wellbeing, however, are relatively good, even among those with co-morbid medical conditions, which suggest that other aspects of wellbeing may be mitigating the adverse effects of a medical condition. Despite bearing a disproportionate burden of chronic diseases, Native Hawaiians continue to flourish, which is evident in their population growth, expected population-doubling by 2045, and the growing Native Hawaiian cultural revitalization movement (Goodyear-Kaopua, Hussey, & Wright, 2014).

The Native Hawaiian Health Care Improvement Act is a necessary and important piece of US federal legislation that offers the mechanism by which to address the health inequities experienced by Native Hawaiians. However, several issues need to be addressed to fully realize the potential of this Act. First, the funding made available through this Act is not enough to adequately address the health concerns of Native Hawaiians. In 2015, the funding made available was US$13.6 million, which equates to about US$39 per a Native Hawaiian living in Hawai'i. Second, unlike American Indians/Alaskan Natives who have the Indian Health Services (IHS), there is no such federal agency for Native Hawaiians to engage in consultation with the federal government over budgetary issues and types of services to provide. IHS received US$5.989 billion in 2015, which equates to about US$2,700 per an American Indian/Alaskan Native. Third, there is no companion State of Hawai'i legislation to the Native Hawaiian Health Care Improvement Act, despite the fact that a majority of Native Hawaiians reside in Hawai'i – their ancestral home – and they make up 25 percent of the state's population. In the Hawai'i State Department of Health there are no programs or units specifically tasked with addressing the health inequities experienced by Native Hawaiians.

Perhaps another reason that the gap has not closed between Native Hawaiians and other ethnic groups has to do with the overemphasis placed on biomedical and behavioral-focused solutions when resources are available, such as increasing access to healthcare and focusing on the lifestyle choices of individuals. Indeed, they are important to achieving health equity, but they are often dealing with disease management rather than disease prevention. Thus, an equal amount of emphasis needs to be placed on the social and cultural determinants of health, such as in developing safer and well-resourced communities, providing livable wages, investing in high-quality public education and supporting cultural revitalization for Native Hawaiians. If we can turn our attention to the forces that contribute to disease development (e.g. obesogenic environments) in Native Hawaiians, perhaps we can more effectively close the gap.

Notes

1 This project was supported by grants (G12RR003061, P20RR011091) from the National Center for Research Resources of the National Institutes of Health (NIH). The views here do not necessarily represent the official views of NIH.
2 *Pili* is a Hawaiian word meaning "to join" or "close relationship" and *'ohana* means "family."

References

Aluli, N.E., Reyes, P.W., Brady, S.K., Tsark, J.U., Jones, K.L., Mau, M., & Howard, B.V. (2010). All-cause and CVD mortality in Native Hawaiians. *Diabetes Research & Clinical Practice, 89*(1), 65–71. doi: 10.1016/j.diabres.2010.03.003.

Aluli, N.E., Reyes, P.W., & Tsark, J. U. (2007). Cardiovascular disease disparities in Native Hawaiians. *Journal of the Cardiometabolic Syndrome, 2*(4), 250–253. doi: 10.1111/j.1559-4564.2007.07560.

American Diabetes Association. (2005). Standards of medical care in diabetes. *Diabetes Care, 28,* 154–536. doi: 10.2337/diacare.28.suppl_1.54.

Balabis, J., Pobutsky, A., Kromer, K., Tottori, C., & Salvail, F. (2007). *The burden of cardiovascular disease in Hawai'i 2007.* Honolulu, HI: Hawai'i State Department of Health.

Beaglehole, J. (Ed.) (1967). *The journals of Captain James Cook on his voyage of discovery, Vol. III: The voyage of the resolution and the discovery, 1776–80.* London: Cambridge University.

Braun, K.L., Fong, M., Gotay, C.C., & Chong, C.D.K. (2004). Ethnic differences in breast cancer in Hawai'i: Age, state, hormone receptor status, and survival. *Pacific Health Dialogue, 11*(2), 146–153. Retrieved from http://pacifichealthdialog.co.nz/wp-content/themes/dialog/old-issues/Volume2011/no2/PHD1120220p1462015320Braun20orig.pdf.

Braveman, P., Egerter, S., & Williams, D.R. (2011). The social determinants of health: Coming of age. *Annual Review of Public Health, 32*, 381–398. doi: 10.1146/annurev-publhealth-031210-101218.

Bushnell, O. (1993). *The gift of civilization: Germs and genocide in Hawai'i.* Honolulu, HI: University of Hawai'i Press.

DeSantis, A.S., Adam, E.K., Doane, L.D., Mineka, S., Zinbarg, R.E., & Craske, M.G. (2007). Racial/ethnic differences in cortisol diurnal rhythms in a community sample of adolescents. *The Journal of Adolescent Health, 41*(1), 3–13. doi: 10.1016/j.jadohealth.2007.03.006.

Donnelly, J.E., Blair, S.N., Jakicic, J.M., Manore, M.M., Rankin, J.W., & Smith, B.K. (2009). American College of Sports Medicine Position Stand. Appropriate physical activity intervention strategies for weight loss and prevention of weight regain for adults. *Medicine & Science in Sports & Exercise, 41*(2), 459. doi: 10.1249/MSS.0b013e3181949333.

Goodyear-Kaopua, N., Hussey, I., & Wright, E.K. (2014). *A nation rising: Hawaiian movements for life, land, and sovereignty.* Durham, NC: Duke University Press.

Grandinetti, A., Kaholokula, J., Theriault, A., Mor, J., Chang, H., & Waslien, C. (2007). Prevalence of diabetes and glucose intolerance in an ethnically diverse rural community of Hawai'i. *Ethnicity & Disease, 17*(2), 250–255.

Green, M.D. (Ed.). (2010). *Hawai'i cancer facts & figures 2010: A sourcebook for planning & implementing programs for cancer prevention & control.* Honolulu, HI: American Cancer Society, Cancer Research Center of Hawaii & Hawaii State Department of Health.

Hamman, R.F., Wing, R.R., Edelstein, S.L., Lachin, J.M., Bray, G.A., Delahanty, L., & Wylie-Rosett, J. (2006). Effect of weight loss with lifestyle intervention on risk of diabetes. *Diabetes Care, 29*(9), 2102–2107. doi: 10.2337/dc06-0560.

Hawaii Health Data Warehouse; Hawaii State Department of Health, Behavioral Risk Factor Surveillance System. (2016). Retrieved from http://hhdw.org/health-reports-data/.

Inda, C., Washburn, A., Beckham, S., Talisayan, B., & Hikuroa, D. (2011). Home grown: The trials and triumphs of starting up a farmers' market in Waianae, Hawaii. *Community Development, 42*(2), 181–192. doi: 10.1080/15575330.2011.520327.

Johnson, D.B., Oyama, N., LeMarchand, L., & Wilkens, L. (2004). Native Hawaiians mortality, morbidity, and lifestyle: Comparing data from 1982, 1990, and 2000. *Pacific Health Dialog, 11*(2), 120–130.

Kaholokula, J.K. (2007). Colonialism, acculturation and depression among känaka maoli of Hawai'i. In P. Culbertson, M. Agee, & C. Makasiale (Eds.), *Penina uliuli: Confronting challenges in mental health for pacific peoples.* Honolulu, HI: University of Hawai'i Press.

Kaholokula, J.K. (2016). Mauli ola: Pathways to optimal Kanaka 'Öiwi health. In M. Look & W. Mesiona-Lee (Eds), *Mauli Ola: Hawai'inuiākea monograph* (Vol. 5). Honolulu, HI: University of Hawai'i Press.

Kaholokula, J.K., Braun, K.L., Kana'iaupuni, S., Grandinetti, A., & Chang, H.K. (2006). Ethnic-by-gender differences in cigarette smoking among Asian and Pacific Islanders. *Nicotine & Tobacco Research, 8*, 275–286. doi: 10.1080/14622200500484600.

Kaholokula, J.K., Grandinetti, A., Keller, S., Nacapoy, A.H., Kingi, T.K., & Mau, M. K. (2012). Association between perceived racism and physiological stress indices in Native Hawaiians. *Journal of Behavioral Medicine, 35*(1), 27–37. doi: 10.1007/s10865-011-9330-z.

Kaholokula, J.K., Iwane, M.K., & Nacapoy, A.H. (2010). Effects of perceived racism and acculturation on hypertension in Native Hawaiians. *Hawaii Medical Journal, 69*, 11–15.

Kaholokula, J.K., Kekauoha, B.P., Dillard, A.Y., Yoshimura, S., Palakiko, D.M., Hughes, C., & Townsend, C.K.M. (2014). The PILI 'Ohana Project: A community-academic partnership to achieve metabolic health equity in Hawai'i. *Hawai'i Journal of Medicine and Public Health, 73*(12; Suppl. 3), 29–33.

Kaholokula, J.K., Look, M., Mabellos, T., Zhang, G., de Silva, M., Yoshimura, S., & Sinclair, K.A. (2015). Cultural dance program improves hypertension management for Native Hawaiians and Pacific Islanders: A pilot randomized trial. *Journal of Racial and Ethnic Health Disparities.* Advance online publication. doi: 10.1007/s40615-015-0198-4.

Kaholokula, J.K., Mau, M.K., Efird, J.T., Leake, A., West, M., Palakiko, D.M., & Gomes, H. (2012). A family and community focused lifestyle program prevents weight regain in Pacific Islanders: A pilot randomized control trial. *Health Education & Behavior, 39*(4), 386–395. doi: 10.1177/1090198110394174.

Kaholokula, J.K., Nacapoy, A.H., & Dang, K.L. (2009). Social justice as a public health imperative for Känaka Maoli. *AlterNative: An International Journal of Indigenous Peoples, 5*, 117–137.

Kaholokula, J.K., Nacapoy, A., Grandinetti, A., & Chang, H. (2008). Association between acculturation modes and type 2 diabetes among Native Hawaiians. *Diabetes Care, 31*(4), 698–700. doi: 10.2337/dc07-1560.

Kaholokula, J.K., Saito, E., Mau, M., Latimer, R., & Seto, T. (2008). Pacific Islanders' perspectives on heart failure management. *Patient Education and Counseling, 70*(2), 281–291. doi: 10.1016/j.pec.2007.10.015.

Kim, H.S., Park, S.Y., Grandinetti, A., Holck, P.S., & Waslien, C. (2008). Major dietary patterns, ethnicity, and prevalence of type 2 diabetes in rural Hawaii. *Nutrition, 24*(11–12), 1065–1072. doi: 10.1016/j.nut.2008.05.008.

Law, M., Wald, N., & Morris, J. (2005). Lowering blood pressure to prevent myocardial infarction and stroke: A new preventive strategy. *International Journal of Technology Assessment in Health Care, 21*(1), 145. doi: 10.1017/S0266462305220196.

Look, M.A., Kaholokula, J.K., Carvhalo, A., Seto, T., & de Silva, M. (2012). Developing a culturally based cardiac rehabilitation program: The HELA study. *Progress in Community Health Partnerships: Research, Education, & Action, 6*(1), 103–110. doi: 10.1353/cpr.2012.0012.

Mau, M.K., Kaholokula, J.K., West, M.R., Leake, A., Efird, J.T., Rose, C., & Gomes, H. (2010). Translating diabetes prevention into native Hawaiian and Pacific Islander communities: The PILI 'Ohana Project. *Progress in Community Health Partnerships, 4*(1), 7–16. doi: 10.1353/cpr.0.0111.

Mau, M.K., Sinclair, K., Saito, E.P., Baumhofer, K.N., & Kaholokula, J.K. (2009). Cardiometabolic health disparities in native Hawaiians and other Pacific Islanders. *Epidemiologic Reviews, 31*, 113–129. doi: 10.1093/ajerev/mxp004.

Mau, M.K., Wong, K.N., Efird, J., West, M., Saito, E.P., & Maddock, J. (2008). Environmental factors of obesity in communities with Native Hawaiians. *Hawaii Medical Journal, 67*(9), 233–236.

McCubbin, L., & Antonio, M. (2012). Discrimination and obesity among Native Hawaiians. *Hawaii Medical Journal, 71*(12), 346–352.

McEligot, A.J., McMullin, J., Pang, K.A., Bone, M., Winston, S., Ngewa, R., & Tanjasiri, S.P. (2012). Dietary intakes, obesity and health behaviors in Native Hawaiians residing in southern California. *Hawai'i Journal of Medicine & Public Health: A Journal of Asia Pacific Medicine & Public Health, 71*(5), 124.

Miller, G.E., Chen, E., & Zhou, E.S. (2007). If it goes up, must it come down? Chronic stress and the hypothalamic-pituitary-adrenocortical axis in humans. *Psychological Bulletin, 133*(1), 25–45. doi: 10.1037/0033-2909.133.1.25.

Mokuau, N., Braun, K.L., Wong, L.K., Higuchi, P., & Gotay, C. (2008). Development of a family intervention for Native Hawaiian women with cancer: A pilot study. *Social Work, 53*(1), 9–19. doi: 10.1093/sw/53.1.9.

Nakagawa, K., Koenig, M.A., Asai, S.N., Chang, C.W., & Seto, T.B. (2013). Disparities among Asians and Native Hawaiians and Pacific Islanders with ischemic stroke. *Neurology, 80*(9): 839–43. doi: 10.1212/WNL.0b013e3182840797.

Nakagawa, K., MacDonald, P.R., & Asai, S.M. (2015). Stroke disparities: Disaggregating Native Hawaiians from other Pacific Islanders. *Ethnicity & Disease, 25*(2), 157–161.

Native Hawaiian Health Research Consortium & Alu Like. (1985). *E ola mau: The Native Hawaiian health needs study: A preliminary plan for improving Native Hawaiian health through health promotion, disease prevention and health protection.* Honolulu, HI: The Consortium.

Nguyen, D.H., & Salvail, F.R. (2016). *The Hawaii behavioral risk factor surveillance system: 2014 results.* Retrieved from: http://health.hawaii.gov/brfss/files/2015/08/HBRFSS_2014_results.pdf.

Panapasa, S.V., Mau, M.K., Williams, D.R., & McNally, J.W. (2010). Mortality patterns of Native Hawaiians across their lifespan: 1990–2000. *American Journal of Public Health, 100*(11), 2304–2310. doi: 10.2105/AJPH.2009.183541.

Sinclair, K.I., Makahi, E., Shea-Solatorio, C., Yoshimura, S., Townsend, C., & Kaholokula, J.K. (2013). Outcomes from a diabetes self-management intervention for Native Hawaiians and Pacific people: Partners in care. *Annals of Behavioral Medicine, 45*(1), 24–32. doi: 10.1007/s12160-012-9422-1.

Spencer, M.S., Rosland, A.M., Kieffer, E.C., Sinco, B.R., Valerio, M., Palmisano, G., & Heisler, M. (2011). Effectiveness of a community health worker intervention among African American and Latino adults with type 2 diabetes: a randomized controlled trial. *American Journal of Public Health, 101*(12), 2253–2260. doi: 10.2105/AJPH.2010.300106.

State of Hawai'i Department of Business, Economic Development and Tourism. (2012). *2012 State of Hawai'i data book.* Retrieved from http://dbedt.hawaii.gov/economic/databook/db2012/.

Swinburn, B., Egger, G., & Raza, F. (1999). Dissecting obesogenic environments: The development and application of a framework for identifying and prioritizing environmental interventions for obesity. *Preventive Medicine, 29*, 563–570.

Ware, J.E., Snow, K.K., Kosinski, M., & Gandek, B. (1993). *SF-36 health survey manual & interpretation guide.* Boston, MA: The Health Institute.

Welschen, L.M., Bloemendal, E., Nijpels, G., Dekker, J.M., Heine, R.J., Stalman, W. A., & Bouter, L.M. (2005). Self-monitoring of blood glucose in patients with type 2 diabetes who are not using insulin: A systematic review. *Diabetes Care, 28,* 1510–1517. doi: 10.2337/diacare.28.6.1510.

Whelton, S.P., Chin, A., Xin, X., & He, J. (2002). Effects of aerobic exercise on blood pressure: A meta-analysis of randomized, controlled trials. *Annals of Internal Medicine, 136*(7), 493–503.

World Health Organization. (2017). *Obesity and overweight: Fact sheet.* Retrieved from: www.who.int/mediacentre/factsheets/fs311/en/.

7

TRADITIONAL HEALING AND INDIGENOUS WELLBEING IN AOTEAROA/NEW ZEALAND

Annabel Ahuriri-Driscoll and Amohia Boulton

Introduction

Traditional healing or traditional medicine has been practised to some degree in all cultures and societies as a means to maintain health and treat disease or illness (World Health Organization [WHO], 2000). However, the retention of traditional healing following the introduction of modern/allopathic medicine has varied across countries and regions, according to the extent of formalization, contact with Western culture and population access to 'mainstream' health services (Bodeker, Kronenberg, & Burford, 2007; Western Pacific Regional Office/WHO, 2002; Montenegro & Stephens, 2006). In colonial settings such as New Zealand, traditional health systems were frequently outlawed by authorities, which in turn led to the large-scale adoption of introduced approaches and a monopolistic situation in which medical doctors had the sole right to practise medicine (Bodeker, 2001). Despite these obstructions, as Bodeker (2001) has described them, traditional medicine and healing practices have been maintained in all regions of the developing world, and their use is spreading rapidly in industrialized countries and among urban populations (WHO, 2003).

Traditional healing and wellbeing

Emerging from a worldview that emphasizes interconnection, interdependence and balance (Royal, 2009), wellbeing is conceptualized by Indigenous communities as existing within a web of relationships, benefit and obligation, a holistic and spiritual attribute (Pitama, Ririnui, & Mikaere, 2002). Traditional healing practices are those "designed to promote mental, physical and spiritual wellbeing... based on [such] beliefs, which go back to the time before the spread of western 'scientific' bio-medicine" (Royal Commission on Aboriginal Peoples [RCAP], 1996, p. 325). As an extension of and vehicle for traditional/Indigenous knowledge (Robbins & Dewar, 2011), traditional healing is culturally concordant and offers benefits to Indigenous health/wellbeing in a number of ways – specific methods and therapies are valuable in their own right for efficacy in treatment; and as a whole, these approaches incorporate thinking that may be utilized to restore holistic health to Indigenous peoples (RCAP, 1996, p. 193).

Rongoā Māori is a holistic system of healing derived from Māori philosophy and customs (Ahuriri-Driscoll et al., 2008; Mark & Lyons, 2010) which has endured in spite of significant challenges post-colonization (including the Tohunga Suppression Act 1907 and declining use of the Māori language). Durie et al. (1993) observe that rongoā Māori encompasses five different categories of Māori healing including *ritenga* (rituals) and *karakia* (prayers), *rongoā rākau* (remedies derived from plant material, for application and ingestion), *mirimiri* (massage), *wai* (water) and surgical interventions. Healers may use one or more categories of healing in any one healing intervention. Arguably then, the provision of *rongoā Māori* within New Zealand's contemporary health system supports Māori wellbeing at two levels: providing holistic, culturally consistent assessment and treatment of individual symptoms/conditions (Jones, 2000), while maintaining and revitalizing Māori knowledge, traditions and language (Ahuriri-Driscoll et al., 2008). Thus, beyond its development as an approach to health, is its intrinsic value as a cultural healing tradition.

The public funding of *rongoā* services in New Zealand

Although there were clear attempts by government early in the twentieth century to suppress healing practice and deny its legitimacy, *rongoā Māori* endured and in recent years has experienced something of a revival (Jones, 2000). Several reasons are cited for this, including:

- the removal of any legal barrier to healing practice with the repeal of the Tohunga Suppression Act in 1964;
- a resurgence of interest in all aspects of Māori culture, in conjunction with a call by Māori for greater autonomy and self-determination;
- some loss of confidence in 'Western' methods of treatment;
- disparities in Māori access to primary medical services; and
- the identification of a 'missing link' in health services, the *taha wairua* or spiritual dimension.
(Durie et al., 1993)

In the midst of health reforms in the 1990s, movements were made towards formalizing the funding and delivery of *rongoā Māori* services (Jones, 2000). Following several consultation *hui* (gatherings or meetings), a background paper (Durie et al., 1993) and a policy advice paper from a national network of Māori traditional healers (Ngā Ringa Whakahaere o te Iwi Māori), the National Advisory Committee on Core Health and Disability Support Services recommended, on the basis of potential improvements in Māori access to effective services and improved health outcomes, that Regional Health Authorities purchase aspects of Māori traditional healing in conjunction with other primary care services. Two small-scale services were subsequently contracted in 1995.

Following the development of a framework for purchasing traditional healing services (Durie, 1996) and Māori traditional healing standards (Ministry of Health (MoH), 1999), ten new services were then funded at a more substantial level (MoH, 2006). Funding for *rongoā* has steadily increased to the point where the MoH administers fifteen *rongoā* contracts with providers throughout the country, of which a small number (three) have also been funded to deliver accident treatment and rehabilitation services. Funding of a *rongoā* training programme to support practising and emerging healers is also provided by the Clinical Training Agency, delivered through a Māori tertiary institution.

A number of policy documents present high-level principles for the delivery of rongoā and confirm its status as a health service option. The document *Taonga Tuku Iho: Treasures of our heritage* (MoH, 2006) aligns *rongoā* development with the Māori health strategy, *He Korowai Oranga* (MoH, 2002a) through its overall aim of *whānau ora* (family wellbeing) and its key threads of *rangatiratanga* (self-determination), building on gains and reducing inequalities. Through

Whakatātaka, the Māori Health Action Plan 2002–2005 (MoH, 2002b), the actions to progress *He Korowai Oranga* are outlined, and within them, traditional healing is specifically noted as needing to be recognized and valued by the health and disability sector, alongside Māori models of health. Furthermore, *Taonga Tuku Iho* offers a framework for strengthening the provision of quality *rongoā* services throughout the country in four main areas: (1) improving the quality of *rongoā* services; (2) creating leadership to strengthen safe practice through networking and quality assurance; (3) increasing the capacity and capability of *rongoā* services; and (4) constructing a workplan for research and evaluation activities (MoH, 2006).

Furthering the MoH's focus on the development of *rongoā*, a national trust, Te Kāhui Rongoā, was established in 2011. Te Kāhui Rongoā (TKR) is an amalgamation of two 'peak bodies' – Ngā Ringa Whakahaere o te Iwi Māori (NRW) and Te Paepae Matua mō te Rongoā (TPM), following a ministerial directive for both to merge into one overarching body responsible for "the proper governance of rongoā" (Te Kāhui Rongoā, 2011, p. 2). A key first task for TKR has been to develop 'sector-driven' or healer-led *tikanga* standards to replace the earlier MoH-authored standards – standards for the practice of *rongoā Māori* according to cultural customs and traditions (Boulton, Hudson, Ahuriri-Driscoll, & Stewart, 2014).

Investment in the development of policy documents and the allocation of dedicated government funding for services (albeit to only a small number of providers) has served to confer a certain degree of respectability on traditional Māori healing services. However, *rongoā Māori* remains relatively marginal within the broader New Zealand health system, possibly as a consequence of the MoH's incomplete advocacy (Waitangi Tribunal, 2011, p. 655), misunderstanding about what *rongoā* entails, or a lack of 'scientific' evidence as to the efficacy of the various healing modalities that comprise *rongoā*. A key barrier to more comprehensive inclusion of *rongoā* within the formal health system involves the requirement that *rongoā Māori* services meet various criteria on the basis of needing to be accountable for use of public funds. This includes the fulfilment of administrative and reporting functions, and the standardization of delivery and products. A number of healers and practices currently deliver care successfully according to prescribed *rongoā* service specifications, although the constraints of working to such criteria are noted (Ahuriri-Driscoll et al., 2008, 2012).

Practice and service – a key distinction

Originating from a Māori value system and base, *rongoā* has been embedded traditionally in communities, practised by those identified as having a gift for healing and nurtured by senior healers through apprenticeship. This *practice-focused* approach entails a more organic model of development that is locality-specific, funded by *koha* (gifts or donations) and based on oral transmission of knowledge (Ahuriri-Driscoll et al., 2008; Reinfeld & Pihama; 2010). Conversely, publicly funded health services place emphasis on standardized practice, delivered by formally trained health professionals within contracted organizations. Beyond the administrative and compliance requirements which must be met by those who hold service contracts (Lavoie, Boulton, & Dwyer, 2010), a *service-focused* approach may see increased professionalization of healers, the development and implementation of practice standards and funding more explicitly linked to outcomes of *rongoā* care. Thus, both practice-focused and service-focused approaches seek to support the development of *rongoā*, but in markedly different ways. Underpinning this distinction is the assumption that the delivery of *rongoā* is at all times bound by tensions between the *practice* of *rongoā* and its delivery as a funded health *service*. Arguably, the tensions which exist between these dual functions are not only played out in the health sector, they are in fact exacerbated by the funding and contracting environment itself.

A number of studies have been conducted with the *rongoā* sector which have highlighted the challenges to the sector posed by the current funding and contracting environment. In this chapter, we draw upon the findings and our analysis of three studies in order to highlight the impact of *service contracts* on the practice of *rongoā*. Two challenges in particular have been highlighted by healers, health stakeholders and researchers: the exclusion of core aspects of *rongoā* from funding; and the limited *rongoā*-specific funding that is currently provided by the MoH. First however, we briefly present the projects from which we have drawn our discussion.

Drawing on evidence: three research projects

The findings from two studies conducted by the lead author elucidated a number of issues regarding the sustainability of *rongoā Māori* in New Zealand, which then informed a third, more recent, study. *The future of Rongoā* (FoRM) project was commissioned research conducted on behalf of the MoH between 2006 and 2008. The study identified the contribution of *rongoā* to Māori wellbeing and outlined the issues, as well as a vision, for the sustainability of healing practice (Ahuriri-Driscoll et al., 2008). The study was undertaken by a team of Māori researchers from two research entities, the Institute of Environmental Science and Research Ltd and Te Whare Wānanga o Awanuiārangi, in partnership with Ngā Ringawhakahaere o te Iwi Māori (an organization representing Māori healers). Qualitative data were collected from participants at four focus groups and five workshops, held in five different communities (Auckland, Whakatāne, Taumarunui, Wellington and Christchurch). Participants comprised healers and their associates (*n*=51), as well as health and local authority stakeholders (*n*=61). All participants were Māori.

The study concluded that despite increased demand for Māori healing services, integrating traditional healing into the mainstream, publicly funded, health system presents many challenges, not the least of which being how to appropriately fund, monitor and account for those services within a system that is driven by a need for 'evidence-based' results (Ahuriri-Driscoll et al., 2008). It was in the conduct of this project that the distinction between a 'practice-focused' approach and a 'service-focused' approach was first identified.

The Ngā Tohu o te Ora – Traditional Māori healing and wellness outcomes study followed on from the FoRM project and was conducted between 2008 and 2010 by a team of Māori researchers. This study focused on the wellness outcomes pursued by healers in their practice with individual patients (Ahuriri-Driscoll et al., 2012). The study was undertaken in two stages, with the first stage comprising key informant interviews and hui with healers and the members of the study's working group. In the second stage group interviews were conducted with healers and staff from four individual *whare oranga* (health services) comprising between three and seven staff each. All participants were Māori. Key findings from this project confirmed those of the FoRM study, indicating a clear desire on the part of Māori communities to continue to access *rongoā Māori*. However, once again, issues of integration with the publicly funded system were highlighted as barriers to the sustainability of *rongoā Māori*.

The concerns expressed by the sector regarding the practice/service distinction and indeed the long-term viability of *rongoā Māori* given in the contemporary funding environment prompted the conduct of the third study. *The supporting traditional Rongoā practice in contemporary health care settings* project was a three-year study conducted between 2012 and 2015 aimed at identifying the contractual environments and service delivery elements that would best contribute to the long-term sustainability of *rongoā Māori* (Boulton, Ahuriri-Driscoll, Potaka Osborne, & Stewart, 2015). The study employed a theoretical and analytical approach grounded in Māori epistemology and ontology (Mahuika, 2008), involving three discrete phases of data collection and cycles of iterative data analysis. In the first phase of data collection, thirteen semi-structured key informant interviews were conducted with health policy- and decision-makers, funders of *rongoā* services at national and regional level, fund-holders, managers of *rongoā* services and sector advocates. In the second phase of the project, a nationwide survey to gather data regarding existing *rongoā* practice and service delivery was undertaken specifically with healers, but also with those who ran *rongoā* clinics or were allied to the *rongoā* sector. The survey achieved a 79 per cent response rate (Ahuriri-Driscoll, Boulton, Stewart, Potaka-Osborne, & Hudson, 2015). Finally, the study examined the experiences of three funded and contracted *rongoā* clinics in greater depth, using a case study approach (Yin, 2003) in order to understand the complexities and dynamics of contracting for *rongoā* services, and the accountability, regulatory, legislative and human resource aspects of service provision. This chapter draws on our expertise, knowledge and experiences of the sector, as well as the findings from the three studies identified above. Views expressed by study key informants in particular are employed to illustrate key points. Some survey data from *The supporting traditional Rongoā practice in contemporary health care settings* project are also reported in this chapter.

The exclusion of core aspects of *rongoā* from funding

One of the most significant issues for the *rongoā* sector is that only some of the many *rongoā* modalities are currently funded within MoH contracts. In its research of Crown support of traditional healing as part of WAI 262 (a claim concerned with the effects of New Zealand law and policy upon Māori culture and identity), the Waitangi Tribunal notes the exclusion of *rongoā rākau* in 2004 by mutual agreement between the MoH and a meeting of healers. MoH officials instigated this change because they were "not... able to monitor safety or quality control or ensure other protection mechanisms for consumers and providers" (Wi Keelan, cited in Waitangi Tribunal, 2011, p. 631). Providers' funding remained the same despite this fairly significant change in service specifications. The response by MoH officials implies that this is only a temporary situation, which will be resolved ultimately by the generation of new (*tikanga*) standards by the newly endorsed national collective of healers. In other words, the onus is on healers to address the health and safety concerns associated with *rongoā rākau*.

An informant in the *Supporting traditional Rongoā practice in contemporary health care settings* project confirmed this change to the *rongoā* contracts, perceiving it as an inappropriate application of Western scientific standards to *rongoā*, demonstrating the disjuncture between what the Crown funds and what *ought* to be funded:

> When the contract first started it was for the collection, preparation and provision of rongoā... and over time they took out the preparation and the collection component which kind of, it, it didn't sit well with the provider because actually collecting and preparing is very much part of the role... One of the problems was that they were trying to fund a traditional healing service but make it fit some standards that applied to Western scientific medicine. And, and so there was quite a tension there in terms of expecting a rongoā healer to do what a rongoā healer would do but contracting for something else and, and that continued to be a tension the whole time that we held this contract.
>
> (KI 11)

Counsel for WAI 262 claimants stated that the non-funding of *rongoā rākau* "fundamentally [broke] rongoā apart" (Waitangi Tribunal, 2011, p. 631), as to exclude one modality from a suite of healing therapies was seen to conflict with the holistic nature of the healing process.

This is a point that O'Connor (2007), in his consideration of the impacts arising from the public funding of *rongoā Māori* services, also speaks to. O'Connor identifies that spiritual aspects of healing (apart from *karakia*) are also omitted from service specifications and that this has marginalized healers who work primarily in the *wairua* (spiritual) domain, according them less legitimacy and support. He argues that the service specifications place bureaucratic limits on what *rongoā* knowledge and practice the Crown will protect, and through funding, which aspects may prosper and which may decline. O'Connor observes that it is those healers and healing traditions *complementary* to and not too different from Western biomedicine that are privileged in the contracting process. However, this negative impact extends beyond spiritual healers: McGowan (2000, p. 115) argues that te taha wairua (the spiritual dimension) is *the* core element of traditional healing, and failure to include this in the Standards dismisses *rongoā Māori* in its essential form, encouraging a view of "a list of criteria drawn up to provide a means of assessment for funding purposes".

The concerns cited by O'Connor and McGowan are certainly supported by the first-hand reports of healers in our research. Healers reported financial and practice consequences of the 'reductionist' service specification exclusions. Due to the dwindling and degraded supply of native forest/bush in many areas of the country, healers are finding that they have to travel significant distances to gather healthy *rongoā rākau*, with no financial assistance to support this necessary activity. A recent survey of healers found the use of plant-based remedies or preparations were utilized by just under two-thirds (64%) of practices (Ahuriri-Driscoll, Boulton, Potaka-Osborne, Stewart, & Hudson, 2015), a marked change from the observations by McGowan (2000) and Jones (2000) of its universality among healers. Several providers felt compelled to 'hide' their specialist modalities (specifically *matakite* or second sight) as a protective mechanism. Other healers separated *wairākau* (plant fluid and materials) from other modalities so that "recompense was not given for the infusion of wairua into rongoā", ensuring adherence to the terms of the service specifications (Ahuriri-Driscoll et al., 2008). Overall, healers perceived that the restricted definition of *rongoā* within MoH contracts devalues their practice.

Limited *rongoā*-specific funding

Rongoā Māori services are currently delivered nationwide, contracted by a number of funders. As noted previously, the MoH administers fifteen contracts, which cover some twenty-two individual providers. The sum total of these contracts is approximately NZ$1.9 million. In addition, two District Health Boards (DHBs) contract *rongoā* services, and several other DHBs fund *rongoā* services indirectly through their contracts with Primary Health Organisations which employ traditional healers (Waitangi Tribunal, 2011, p. 630). In considering whether this level of *rongoā* funding is sufficient, the Waitangi Tribunal estimates current *rongoā* expenditure to be just 0.02 per cent of the country's total annual health expenditure, an amount it considers "wholly inadequate" to address the burden of disease and poor health experienced by Māori and indicative of the Crown's "lack of commitment to the idea that rongoā can make a difference" (Waitangi Tribunal, 2011, p. 649).

Policymaker, funder and service manager informants in the *Supporting traditional Rongoā practice* project commended the advocacy by Māori that resulted in the first *rongoā* contracts: "I think it was directly related to Māori staff within the Health Funding Authority who moved across to the Ministry actually wanting to put a mark in the ground and say 'there are some things that are valuable to Māori and we should fund them'" (KI 11). However, there was some concern that the amount of funding allocated to *rongoā* is not based on identified need or any costings of how much it takes to run a clinic but rather "largely it's a historic thing" (KI 11).

Two informants talked about the need for more sophisticated costings and better analysis to work out the exact costs associated with running a healing clinic, with one informant observing that the only work that had been done in this area had been initiated by the sector itself. In addition to the lack of a logical rationale for the determination and allocation of funding quantum to the sector, informants agreed that the amount contracted providers received was insufficient: "Not enough money – only receive a pittance, $120–130k which barely pays to keep a clinic running" (KI 02). Another informant added that "I don't think any additional funding has ever been put into it from that initial… funding… and I don't believe that it's anywhere near a priority going forward. So I would say it's probably stagnated or stalled if not gone backwards" (KI 03). One healer stated that funding is insufficient to keep up both with compliance and demand, particularly given the intensive nature of the work. Several participants referred to the high administrative and infrastructural requirements of contracts. In some cases, this has resource implications, for instance, ensuring telecommunication capability for remote database access and data entry. Furthermore, as some healers find they need to engage with multiple contracts to sustain their practice, the extent of their compliance and reporting requirements also multiplies (Ahuriri-Driscoll et al., 2008, 2012).

A further complication in the sector is that in at least two instances MoH *rongoā* contracts are administered by Māori Development Organisations, local level fund-holders that then subcontract out for services, within their community. Whereas the concept of fundholding was meant to reduce the administrative burden upon small providers, in both cases the fund-holding concept seems simply to result in dividing a small amount of funding into even smaller parcels of funding:

> In 2001 the Collective received funding from MoH to deliver Traditional Rongoā Maori Services. The contract was administered by [name] Trust, a Māori Development Organisation. Funding at this stage was $100k. [The Trust] took 10 percent which left $90k split between the 6 *rongoā* healers in the area ($15k per annum each). This amount really only covered administration costs, power, telephone costs and petrol for travel to *marae* and private homes for healing sessions.
>
> (KI 02)

Healers in our previous research have spoken of the 'sense of powerlessness' felt when their inability to access funding has limited their potential to work with Māori. Attendees at one focus group talked openly about financial difficulties that saw them resort to using funds allocated for one task to pay for another. Although traditionally surrounding communities would support healers through *koha*, participants reported that *koha* could no longer be relied upon to cover their costs associated with travel, resources and rent. And in the absence of an easily accessible funding stream, considerable time (a full-time job in itself) can be spent on locating and applying for funding, detracting from core business (Ahuriri-Driscoll et al., 2008). As one attendee at a workshop of health stakeholders noted: "it's good to have a primary source, otherwise you spend time chasing bits and pieces of funding, tying up resources and time in trying to get it".

Due to the finite number of *rongoā* contracts and limited scope for growth, many healers are not contracted for *rongoā* per se. One *rongoā* provider reported holding Māori health promotion (injury prevention, reducing family violence and Māori language resources), mental health community transport and training/workforce development contracts from various funders, in addition to working with clients in their clinic (Ahuriri-Driscoll et al., 2012). Although this provider noted several constraints of *rongoā* contracts (prescriptive standards, recognized healing activities limited to *mirimiri*), they reported feeling similarly constrained by other service area contracts: "we have to go the mental health route because we don't have *rongoā* contracts, it feels like we have no choice". Classification as a non-clinical Kaupapa Māori (for Māori, by Māori) provider restricts the contracts that the provider is eligible for, and geographically bounded service delivery limits responsiveness to need within the immediate region. In addition, while this provider opts for contracts which they perceive pose least threat to the *mauri* (life force or essence) of *rongoā*, they then find that "we're not really growing, we're just fighting to hold onto existing contracts". The principal healer lamented the lack of recognition accorded specifically to *rongoā* within these contracts, which do not reflect the clinic's central focus, expertise or, indeed, identity as healing practitioners.

Health sector informants identified a number of problems associated with the contracts held by *rongoā* providers. The main concerns centred around misunderstanding of the nature of healing and where healing might take place; the prescriptive nature of the contracts; and concerns around performance monitoring and in particular how outcomes were reported and understood. Whereas traditionally *rongoā* practitioners worked from their homes, taking as long as required to perform a healing and using a multiplicity of techniques and therapies as required, *rongoā* as a modern-day health service faces a number of constraints in terms of where a healing may take place, how long it should take, and what therapies in particular may or may not be used. One informant noted that the contracts are a "direct conflict of the way we do sessions" (KI 02), while another observed that:

> in terms of the contract stuff, the concept of 'oh, we're buying healing for a hundred people' is totally isolated from what [healers] actually did, you know? The idea that there's a clinic. There's no clinic. There's her house… It's not a clinic like a medical centre which is open from nine till five, you know? So we've gotta make sure that our, our service spec[ification] recognises it's delivered in a very different cultural way.
>
> (KI 11)

Because *rongoā* contracts comprise one part of a suite of contracts which go to make up the National Service Schedule, the contracts themselves are very prescriptive and regarded by many as limiting not only the work that healers can do but the flexibility of the DHB to better recognize the work that healers do, as this informant noted:

> the service schedules are again fed from the national template from the Ministry… and then there's a few things that you can do differently that you can add in at a DHB level… but not a lot. You're supposed to stay within the national framework… [The service schedules] talk about how many clients you have to see each year. They talk about the *rohe* (area). They talk about the types of services that you provide. That you can't provide… Even the way that they describe rongoā is quite limited.
>
> (KI 08)

Health stakeholder participants were agreed on the need to resolve these funding issues in the interests of healers: "Whatever it is, we need to find the function to support what [healers] do, because what they do is no less than what anyone else does" (focus group participant, Ahuriri-Driscoll et al., 2008). Specific suggestions included increasing healers' understanding of funding allocation tools and a voucher mechanism to subsidize healing services. Ultimately however, stakeholders saw healers and health providers working together to develop service arrangements as most beneficial for the development of *rongoā* in the longer term (Ahuriri-Driscoll et al., 2008).

Approaches for the future

Rongoā *in the context of* iwi *development*

Throughout our research the call has been made for increased support of *rongoā* by *iwi*, primarily because in the post-Treaty of Waitangi settlement era, *iwi* entities possess both influence and resources, and are a key part of Māori social, political and cultural landscapes. Engagement between healing organizations and *iwi* authorities varies across the country, but is generally limited. At one workshop, two reasons cited for this: a lack of interest on the part of *iwi* authorities due to preoccupation with Treaty settlement and resource issues, and a lack of certainty regarding what types of relationships were possible. One attendee remarked on the general belief held by *iwi* authorities that health, and therefore healing, falls within the government's remit (Ahuriri-Driscoll et al., 2008). However, participants felt that *rongoā* would fit well within a cultural revitalization focus, worthy of preservation and sustenance similarly to other *taonga*, other aspects of Māori knowledge and traditions (e.g. Māori language, genealogy, food-gathering practices).

The improved status of *rongoā* within the Māori world was deemed important, providing a more solid foundation for strengthening *rongoā* in non-Māori settings:

> But actually, we need to heal ourselves first within and part of that is getting to the point where there is an acceptance of the importance of rongoā within Māoridom itself. But let's face it, a lot of Māori don't use rongoā services… so I think we need to look inside ourselves first and, um, you know, push our own tribal leaders who understand the importance of rongoā, um, and to accept that they need to support, protect, nurture, grow rongoā services themselves… so it must be within a Māori structure, which upholds a Māori worldview.
>
> (KI 08)

Non-reliance on non-Māori or Crown entities was another important motivation for seeking support from within the Māori world: "Maybe the steps that we're taking, that we're putting it back to the rohe [regional areas] and, and back to the people might be a good step. I'm hoping that's a good step. You know, so you're not reliant on the government" (KI 05). It was felt that *iwi* entities' economic savvy would also be valuable: "Part of the answer is to, um, not look to non-Māori organisations for funding… so part of the answer is to look to our iwi authorities… cos they all know how to put up economic models, you know?" (KI 08).

Rongoā *within the health sector*

A number of informants expressed concern about the sector's reliance on the Crown, or central government, in the form of the Ministry of Health for their ongoing funding. Instead, they mooted the possibility of funding and contracting relationships with DHBs rather than with central government/MoH. For these informants, regionally based DHBs, the entities responsible for providing, or funding the provision of, health services in their district, were regarding as being a more 'natural' partner to regionally based healers. However, one informant felt that in order to be able to engage effectively with DHBs, healers would need to bolster their regional presence:

> And the… big challenge for rongoā in the primary healthcare setting that we're working with now and in the immediate future is that the DHBs are being increasingly

pushed to regionalise their services… How do they have a profile that will allow them to be heard in a regional setting?… But they haven't got their act together enough to make a loud enough impact in a regional setting let alone some of the DHBs.

(KI 08)

It was perceived that flexibility might be more likely at a DHB level (a supportive contract manager or General Manager Māori permitting), for instance with additions to service schedules. Considering the limited funding available, informants felt that openness and flexibility were much needed: "I think it's really small pots of money, eh?… I don't know how the Ministry funds their rongoā services but certainly the ones that we've funded we've tried to be as open and flexible as possible so they can do their thing" (KI 01). Similarly, another informant noted that:

you can always have contractual obligations and then people would deliver the service how they want to do it, yeah… For myself I always say to our providers, you know, 70 per cent of the time you do your contractual thing, 30 per cent of the time you could do anything else that you want to do.

(KI 13)

A 'consensus' model of contracting was favoured by one informant, where flexibility would be enabled through negotiation of parameters of service delivery, but these specific parameters would be stated explicitly: "If you write your service specification with the contractor then you can write what they're actually going to do, and what they say they're going to do. And if you don't like what they say they're gonna do then don't contract with them" (K1 11).

Informants perceived a host of opportunities for *rongoā* in the health sector related to integration. Collaboration with General Practitioners and in primary care were noted as possibilities, but it was agreed that further clarity regarding the mechanisms involved (for instance, cross-referrals) and the specific contribution of *rongoā* was required. Furthermore, informants were reticent about placing *rongoā* contracts in a developing area even though these might be promising (for instance, Whānau Ora; see discussion in Dwyer, Boulton, Lavoie, Tenbensel, & Cumming, 2014), because of the potential risks of instability. It was clear from informants' aspirations, that the safety and security of *rongoā* contracts was paramount; retaining the gains made was a prerequisite for any further developments.

Rongoā *as a Crown responsibility*

In their findings relating to the WAI 262 claim, the Waitangi Tribunal makes a series of recommendations regarding the Crown's responsibilities with respect to *rongoā* Māori:

- **Continue to support contracts through direct funding**: the Tribunal suggests that the Crown may need to continue funding of *rongoā* contracts from MoH funds for some time, because of the risks that a devolved model may pose to *rongoā* providers.
- **Give more comprehensive support to *rongoā***: in addition to providing more substantive funding, the Tribunal surmises that the Crown must openly accept *rongoā* and demonstrate willingness to "genuinely allow rongoā to make a difference to health in New Zealand".
- **Accord *rongoā* active protection due to its *taonga* status**: given that *rongoā* is a *taonga* guaranteed protection under Article 2 of the Treaty of Waitangi, the Tribunal

considers that the Crown has a duty to not only "respect and encourage", but actively mitigate threats to *rongoā* (for example, environmental degradation and negativity associated with Māori knowledge), and therefore expand state support.

- **In summary, work in genuine partnership**: invoking Article 1 of the Treaty, the Tribunal calls for the Crown to recognize the significant potential of *rongoā Māori* to improve Māori health, incentivize the health system to expand *rongoā* services, adequately support peak bodies to play a quality-control role, and to gather data about the extent of current Māori use of services and the likely ongoing extent of demand.

(Waitangi Tribunal, 2011, pp. 648–657)

Final comments

Despite developments in support of *rongoā* since the 1990s, the resounding message from healers, health managers/stakeholders and policymakers is that improvements must be made in order to enable *rongoā Māori* practitioners the autonomy and resourcing to sustain their practice adequately and appropriately. While a supportive policy infrastructure exists, funding remains limited, and inflexible contracting and service specifications compromise both service delivery and practice; with regards to the latter, it is notable that *rongoā Māori* has not benefitted from some of the recent integrated contracting developments in health and social service delivery (Dwyer et al., 2014).

Going forward, iwi, health sector stakeholders and government each have distinct but complementary responsibilities relating to *rongoā Māori* and Māori health more broadly. However, ambivalence must be supplanted by advocacy. As the account in this chapter has shown, certain gains have been realized in both areas from high-level responsiveness and acknowledgment of the unique status of Māori as *tangata whenua* (people of the land) and Treaty partners. However, the insistence on a universal accountability framework positions Māori healers primarily as 'contract-takers', with no recourse to negotiate or tailor the terms and conditions of their service delivery to their unique community and cultural accountabilities. Reform needed is at once basic and substantive: (1) challenging the assumption of contractual accountability as a universal, culture-free and therefore unchangeable construct; (2) ensuring consistency throughout the health system, and that the principles set in policy are enacted at all levels; and (3) cultivating trust between funders and providers that might enable progress towards relational contracting or reciprocal accountability.

Holding the following four essential characteristics (RCAP, 1996, pp. 203–204) might also underpin and support reform:

- Pursuit of **equity** in access to health *and* healing services and in Indigenous health status outcomes, which may entail unequal mechanisms or measures and justify increased resourcing.
- **Holism** in approaches to Indigenous health problems and their treatment and prevention, including collaboration across government sectors and community, and funding healing practice in its entirety.
- Indigenous **authority** over health systems and, where feasible, community control over services; support of communities' grassroots initiatives; enabling Indigenous communities to define traditional healing.
- **Diversity** in the design of systems and services to accommodate differences in culture and community realities; and allowing flexibility in service specifications to support diversity of traditional healing practice.

References

Ahuriri-Driscoll, A., Baker, V., Hepi, M., Hudson, M., Mika, C., & Tiakiwai, S-J. (2008). *The future of rongoā Māori: Wellbeing and sustainability.* Christchurch, New Zealand: Institute of Environmental Science and Research (ESR) Ltd/Ministry of Health.

Ahuriri-Driscoll, A., Boulton, A., Stewart, A., Potaka-Osborne, G., & Hudson, M. (2015). Mā mahi, ka ora: By work we prosper – traditional healers and workforce development. *New Zealand Medical Journal, 128*(1420), 34–44.

Ahuriri-Driscoll, A., Hudson, M., Bishara, I., Milne, M., & Stewart, M. (2012). *Ngā tohu o te ora: Traditional Māori healing and wellness outcomes.* Porirua, New Zealand: ESR Ltd.

Bodeker, G.C. (2001). *Traditional health systems and national policy.* Retrieved 3 April 2007 from www.rccm.org.uk/static/Article_Gerry_Bodeker.aspx.

Bodeker, G., Kronenberg, F., & Burford, G. (2007). Policy and public health perspectives on traditional, complementary and alternative medicine: An overview. In G. Bodeker & G. Burford (Eds.), *Traditional, complementary and alternative medicine: Policy and public health perspectives* (pp. 9–40). London: Imperial College Press.

Boulton, A., Hudson, M., Ahuriri Driscoll, A., & Stewart, A. (2014). Enacting kaitiakitanga: Challenges and complexities in the governance and ownership of rongoā research information. *International Indigenous Policy Journal, 5*(2). doi: 10.18584/iipj.2014.5.2.1.

Boulton, A., Ahuriri-Driscoll, A., Potaka Osborne, G., & Stewart, A. (2015). Tatauranga Rongoā: Reflections on a survey of rongoā practitioners. *Proceedings of the International Indigenous Development Research Conference, Auckland 25–28 November 2014* (pp. 114–120). Auckland, New Zealand: Ngā Pae o Te Māramatanga.

Durie, M.H. (1996). *A framework for purchasing Māori traditional healing services: A report for the Ministry of Health.* Palmerston North, New Zealand: Massey University.

Durie, M.H., Potaka, U.K., Ratima, K.H., & Ratima, M.M. (1993). *Traditional Māori healing: A paper prepared for the National Advisory Committee on Core Health & Disability Support Services.* Palmerston North, New Zealand: Massey University.

Dwyer, J., Boulton, A., Lavoie, J.G., Tenbensel, T., & Cumming, J. (2014). Indigenous peoples' health care: New approaches to contracting and accountability at the public administration frontier. *Public Management Review, 16*(8), 1091–1112.

Jones, R. (2000). *Rongoā Māori and primary health care.* Unpublished Master's thesis, University of Auckland, New Zealand.

Lavoie, J., Boulton, A., & Dwyer, J. (2010). Analysing contractual environments: Lessons from indigenous health in Canada, Australia and New Zealand. *Public Administration, 88*, 665–679.

Mahuika, R. (2008). Kaupapa Maori theory is critical and anti-colonial. *MAI Review, 3*(Article 4), 1–16.

Mark, G.T., & Lyons, A.C. (2010). Māori healers' views on wellbeing: The importance of mind, body, spirit, family and land. *Social Science & Medicine, 70*, 1756–1764.

McGowan, R. (2000). *The contemporary use of rongoā Māori: Traditional Māori medicine.* Unpublished Master's thesis, University of Waikato, Hamilton, New Zealand.

Ministry of Health. (1999). *Standards for traditional Māori healing.* Wellington, New Zealand: Ministry of Health.

Ministry of Health. (2002a). *He korowai oranga: Māori health strategy.* Wellington: MoH.

Ministry of Health. (2002b). *Whakatātaka – Māori health action plan 2002–2005.* Wellington: MoH.

Ministry of Health. (2006). *Taonga tuku iho – treasures of our heritage: Rongoā development plan.* Wellington: MoH.

Montenegro, R.A., & Stephens, C. (2006). Indigenous health 2: Indigenous health in Latin America and the Caribbean. *Lancet, 367*, 3 June, 1859–1869.

O'Connor, T. (2007). *Governing bodies: A Māori healing tradition in a bicultural state.* Unpublished doctoral thesis, University of Auckland, New Zealand.

Pitama, D., Ririnui, G., & Mikaere, A. (2002). *Guardianship, custody and access: Māori perspectives and experiences.* Wellington, New Zealand: Ministry of Justice.

Reinfeld, M., & Pihama, L. (2010). *Matarākau: Ngā kōrero mō ngā rongoā o Taranaki.* New Plymouth/Auckland, New Zealand: Karangaora Inc/Māori and Indigenous Analysis Ltd.

Robbins, J.A., & Dewar, J. (2011). Traditional indigenous approaches to healing and the modern welfare of traditional knowledge, spirituality and lands: A critical reflection on practices and policies taken from the Canadian indigenous example. *International Indigenous Policy Journal, 2*(4), 2–17.

Royal, C. (2009). *Let the world speak: Towards indigenous epistemology.* Monograph 2. Porirua, New Zealand: Mauriora-ki-te-Ao/Living Universe Ltd.

Royal Commission on Aboriginal Peoples. (1996). *Report of the Royal Commission on Aboriginal Peoples,*Vol. 3. Retrieved 2 January 2016 from http://caid.ca/Vol_3_RepRoyCommAborigPple.html.

Te Kāhui Rongoā. (2011). *Trust deed relating to the Te Kāhui Rongoā Trust.* Retrieved 2 November 2015 from www.rongoamaori.org.nz/data/_uploaded/file/Signed%20Trust%20Deed.pdf.

Waitangi Tribunal. (2011). *Ko Aotearoa tēnei: A report into claims concerning New Zealand law and policy affecting Māori culture and identity, Vol. 2.* Wellington, New Zealand: Waitangi Tribunal.

World Health Organization. (2000). *Traditional and modern medicine: Harmonising the two approaches.* Manila, Philippines: WHO – Regional Office for the Western Pacific Publications Unit.

World Health Organization. (2002). *Traditional medicine strategy 2002–2005.* Retrieved 21 November 2006 from http://whqlibdoc.who.int/hq/2002/WHO_EDM_TRM_2002.1.pdf.

World Health Organization. (2003). *Factsheet No. 134: Traditional medicine.* Retrieved 21 November 2006 from www.who.int/mediacentre/factsheets/fs134/en/.

Yin, R.K. (2003). *Case study research: Design and methods.* Thousand Oaks, CA: Sage Publications.

8

PHYSICAL WELLBEING OF MĀORI

Denise Wilson, Amohia Boulton and Isaac Warbrick

Introduction

Ngā hiahia kia titiro ki te timata, a ka kite ai tātou te mutunga.

We must understand the beginning, if we wish to see the end.

Māori (Indigenous peoples of Aotearoa New Zealand) experience notable inequities in access to and use of health services, and in health outcomes. As with most colonized Indigenous people, Māori suffer disproportionately from so-called 'first world' diseases such as diabetes, heart disease, stroke, gout and particular cancers when compared to non-Māori. Poor physical health is not new to Māori as a population however. Combined with inequities of access and deferential treatment patterns, poor health can lead to chronic illness and premature mortality. Mainstream approaches to enhancing Māori physical wellbeing have proven to be inadequate in eliminating these inequities, in part because of the differences in viewing, assessing and defining physical wellbeing.

Indigenous views of wellbeing contrast starkly with the dominant biomedical approach that informs how healthcare services are structured, organized, funded and delivered. The biomedical approach focuses primarily on individuals, on personal responsibility, and places a disproportionate emphasis on the physical components of health above all others. An Indigenous Māori worldview, in contrast, positions physical health as merely one factor influenced by and influencing one's environment, *whānau* (family), *whakapapa* (genealogy and histories) and *wairua* (spiritual element). Nevertheless, the privileging of mainstream approaches overlooks these key tenets of Māori physical wellbeing.

In this chapter we provide an overview of the current status of physical wellbeing for Māori. We introduce the reader to Māori values, beliefs and practices underpinning concepts of physical wellbeing, contrasting an Indigenous worldview of *hauora* (integrated and holistic health and wellbeing) with commonly accepted mainstream approaches. We discuss the historical and contemporary influences that have, and continue to have a negative impact on Māori health including perspectives taken from the field of epigenetics. Drawing on *whakataukī* (traditional sayings) to illustrate our narrative, we discuss ways forward for promoting Māori physical wellbeing.

A traditional approach to Māori physical wellbeing

Tama tu, tama ora, tama noho, tama mate.

The working person flourishes, the idle one suffers.

A Māori worldview

A traditional Māori perspective of health differs markedly from that of Western (non-Māori) approaches. Māori, in common with Indigenous peoples globally, take a holistic view of health and wellbeing where each component is inseparable from each other. Hence, while this chapter is titled 'Physical wellbeing of Māori' it is important to note that for Māori distinguishing between physical health and all other aspects of wellbeing is counterintuitive. Health is regarded as all-embracing, encompassing not only the physical wellness of the body (*tinana*), the mind (*hinengaro*), one's spirit (*wairua*) as well as the health of the wider family (*whānau*) (Pomare, 1986), but also includes one's relationships with the land, language (Durie, 1985) and the wider environment.

A leading Māori scholar, Sir Professor Mason Durie, argued that optimal wellbeing for Māori was founded on the three principal institutions of land (*whenua*), family (*whānau*) and the language (*reo*). Although Durie was referring to psychological aspects of health, these 'institutions of health', whenua, whānau and reo, are embedded in Māori culture (Durie, 1985, p. 65). They underpin views and values relating to 'health', and pre-date colonization and the understandings of health and illness that colonists brought with them. Understanding these concepts which underpin traditional Māori society, alongside others such as *tapu* (sacred, restricted) and *noa* (without restriction), assist our understanding of how Māori maintained their health and wellbeing in one of the most isolated countries in the world for hundreds of years (Durie, 1998).

Environment and whenua

Māori, in common with other Indigenous peoples, have an enduring link with the land in which they were born, raised and died. As a tribal people, the connections to the land occur from birth, when the placenta is buried in ancestral land (a practice that continues to this day) through to death, when the dead are interred in this same land. Interestingly, '*whenua*' is the word for both placenta and land in Māori, as both provide support, nourishment, security and anchorage (Durie, 1985). Mead (2003) observed that the associations between the words *whenua* (meaning placenta *and also* the ground, and land) inextricably link Māori identity and culture to the land – the mountains which rise above it, the rivers that flow through it, and the oceans that surround it (Mead, 2003, p. 270). This is further evident, for instance, in the words of *iwi* (tribes) from the Whanganui River and Waikato regions:

> *Ko au ko te awa, Ko te awa ko au*
> I am the river and the river is me.

It should come as no surprise many Māori, the majority of whom have been living in urban environments for the sake of employment and 'opportunities' for many generations, have become detached from ancestral lands and practices, and are struggling to adapt to an environment which is foreign to their genetic and cultural make up. Accordingly, Durie (1985) argued that the loss of land through dispossession, war or ill fortune would bring about despondency and grief, which in turn could lead to poor health of not only the immediate family but the wider *hapū* (sub-tribe) and *iwi* (tribe).

Whakapapa and whānau

Related to the concepts of land as *whenua* is the principle of *whakapapa. Whakapapa* forms the foundation of Māori society and the relationships and interactions Māori have with the world around them (Brannelly, Boulton, & Te Hiini, 2013), while providing a person's identity within a tribal structure (Mead, 2003). *Whakapapa* has often been translated as, and used synonymously with, the Western idea of genealogy. However, *whakapapa* is far more than just genealogy, it is a structure of interconnected relationships that extend beyond those within a *whānau, hapū* or *iwi* to encompass the wider physical and meta-physical environment (Ratima, Durie, & Hond, 2015). Māori are able to trace their lineage not only to their forebears but also to their lands and other physical elements such as mountains, flora, fauna and water (Ratima et al., 2015). Ratima and colleagues argued from a population perspective that once *whakapapa* is understood as a "system of relationships" (p. 45), then Māori wellbeing can also be understood in terms of the links between the immediate *whānau* and the wider tribe; between the physical and the social environments; between a community's potential and its ability to draw upon the land, and the resources contained within that land. Ultimately, *whakapapa* acknowledges that the health (or sickness) of the environment is embodied within each individual, their *whānau* and tribe.

Whakapapa highlights the place of Māori within a wider ecological system, linking individuals both to their environment and to deities, who are in turn their ancestors. The health of people is literally tied to *maunga* (mountains) where *awa* (rivers) originate. As *awa* flow down the mountains they feed the *ngahere* (forests); a source of food. *Awa* themselves provide fish and drinking water for the *iwi* (tribe) that resides within that ecosystem. The health and wellbeing of these landforms and bodies of water influence not only the spiritual wellbeing of Māori but also their physical wellbeing. Accordingly, when Māori introduce themselves in formal settings, we start by introducing our *maunga*, then our *awa*, our *iwi*, our *hapū* (sub-tribe/extended family). It is only at the very end of the recitation people mention their name. This purposefully ordered introduction is just one example of our acknowledgement of how vital the environment is to our survival.

While the *whenua* provided for the needs of Māori, *whānau* are regarded as the primary building block upon which the entire Māori social system was based (Mead, 2003, p. 212). Traditionally, *whānau* embodied a wide and often complex set of relationships, and far from being nuclear, may encompass many generations. As a collective, *whānau* operated to support and assist one another, caring for the young, the elderly and the infirm. Mead (2003) noted that "one must be born into the fundamental building block of the system in order to be a member of right" (pp. 212–213). A person's *whānau* and *whakapapa*, their link to particular family and tribal groupings, their birth order and relationship to their siblings all impact upon that person's role in the collective that is their immediate *whānau*, and thus their contribution, responsibilities and accountabilities to the wider collective, be it *hapū* or *iwi*. A dominant mainstream paradigm, on the other hand, focuses primarily on the responsibility and choices of the individual so that obesity or diabetes for example is blamed on an individual lack of willpower to resist unhealthy foods and motivate oneself to overcome laziness and exercise. The concept of individualism, of an individual identity is not one which sits well with Māori. Durie (1985) observed that, for Māori, being "a person in one's own right" is considered unhealthy, as it assumes a distance from one's primary cultural support structures, i.e. *whānau, hapū* and *iwi*.

Tapu *and* noa

Two further concepts are intrinsic to understanding a Māori worldview of health, illness and sickness behaviour: *tapu* and *noa*. *Tapu* refers to something that is sacred or restricted (Ryan, 1999) and any person, object or place designated as being *tapu* requires dignity and respect. A person of *mana* (someone with prestige and great power) could deem a certain location, a person, or any item such as a cloak, tool or ornament *tapu* by placing restrictions on that person or for use or an item, for example. This *tapu* is usually upheld by a higher spiritual power. Thus, *tapu* was used as an 'effective social sanction', guiding behaviours and the relationships between people and their surrounding environment (Durie, 1995, p. 2).

Noa, on the other hand, is the condition or state that balances *tapu*. While objects or places that are *noa* (or free from *tapu*) may be approached, and used freely, care needs to be taken to keep these separate from *tapu* objects (Ryan, 1999). Food, for example, is *noa* and can contaminate anything that is *tapu*. Those indigenous people who believe in the values of *tapu* and *noa* will avoid 'breaching' *tapu*. They believe if *tapu* is breached, this could lead to 'mate Māori' – that is, a form of sickness, which can in extreme instances, lead to death. For Māori, wellbeing and balance in one's life is, in part, managed by avoiding behaviours that breach the sanctity of *tapu* (Mead, 2003).

Language

Again, as with other Indigenous peoples, language is central to Māori culture. Those without the language are not able to fully understand and enjoy the depth and richness of the culture. For that reason, the loss of language is equated with "incomplete personal development" (Durie, 1985, p. 67). Embedded within language is important *mātauranga* (knowledge) and messages about protective strategies that kept Māori well and healthy – this *mātauranga* cannot simply be translated into English. Without having *te reo Māori* (Māori language) this *mātauranga* remains inaccessible to many.

Physical health

The *whakataukī* (proverb) at the start of this section sums up the traditional perspective on physical wellbeing. Literally, the man that stands, and is active lives, the man that sits, idle, dies. The proverb conveys the importance of being physically active, industrious, working hard and generally contributing to the *whānau* or *hapū*. These are characteristics that were highly valued in traditional Māori society. Given the collective nature of traditional Māori society, where everyone had a role to play and a function to perform to ensure the tribe's survival, those who were not physically active or who were weak and lazy would have been a burden on the tribe, thus held in low regard. Thus, physical wellbeing is crucial to fulfilling the obligations Māori have to one another and to ensuring the survival and functioning of the *whānau* as a whole.

More importantly perhaps, traditional Māori, males and females alike, would have been expected to gather, hunt and harvest food supplies throughout the summer months to ensure the tribes survival during winter. Men would have been also expected to be able to wage war for new land or defend the existing villages and landholdings of an *iwi* or *hapū*. This all required the dexterity, strength and fitness to travel to battles, to wield weapons and engage in warfare, and hunt and gather food as necessary, and for as long as necessary. Traditional games and pastimes that have survived to the present time, for example, *kapa haka* (perform haka and dance), *mau rakau* (wielding weapons), *ki-o-rahi* (traditional ball game), indicate that time was specifically set aside during times of peace to ensure the physical robustness and fitness of the people.

Historical and contemporary impacts on health and wellbeing

Tokotoko tao, kotahi te tūranga
Tokotoko rangi, ka ngaro te kai, ka ngaro te tangata

The spear of wood, one at a thrust
The spear of heaven, food disappears, people disappear

Māori were described in early historical documents as being fit and healthy, active, strong and physically intimidating. Today, a little under 200 years later, many Māori experience chronic health conditions, suffer inequities in health outcomes, and die before they reach the age of 65 years of diseases that are essentially preventable. Dr Maui Pomare in 1909 stated:

> The Māori of old was lean, sinewy, tough and mentally active. He lived the natural, open, out-of-door life, and thus was always in the best of physical condition. Those who reached maturity were literally the fittest of their race, for no weakling could survive the hardships and exposure of their primitive life.
>
> (Cited in Lange, 1999, p. 1)

This depiction of Māori pre-colonization is very different from the physical health and wellbeing of many contemporary Māori. Without question, colonization has had deleterious impacts on Māori, similar to Indigenous peoples elsewhere (Paradies, 2016; Sherwood, 2013). In this section, we explore the impact external forces, both historical and contemporary, have made, and continue to make, on the physical health of Māori.

Colonization

With the advent of colonization came a change to the way of life for Māori and other Indigenous peoples, which altered the basic requirements of survival. This new way of life devalued the traditional knowledge gained from generations of experience, observation and experimentation – knowledge that enabled Indigenous peoples to thrive in their environment. Survival for Māori was guided by *mātauranga* (Māori knowledge) about *rongoā* (traditional healing methods), concepts of *tapu* and *noa* and *tikanga* (cultural processes). These ensured Māori sustainability and survival as they interacted with the environment and spiritual world (Durie, 2005).

The arrival of settlers and later colonizers brought infectious diseases to which Indigenous peoples had not been previously exposed. The geographical isolation of Aotearoa New Zealand meant that Māori had not acquired immunity to these diseases (Durie, 2005). In most cases, this led to widespread epidemics that resulted in drastic depopulation of Indigenous populations globally. The *whakataukī* at the start of this section refers to the devastating affect infectious diseases such as measles had upon a people who had no natural immunity.

Mātauranga Māori (Māori knowledge and customary practices), which prior to colonization had kept Māori safe and well, was systematically invalidated and replaced by introduced Euro-Western ideologies. This was aided by legislation such as the Tohunga Suppression Act 1907 that banned *tohunga* and cultural healing practices (Māori healers) (Ahuriri-Driscoll et al., 2008). In addition to legislation, assimilation of Māori was also expedited by policies aimed at removing Māori culture. This meant that the protective factors embedded in traditional know-ledge and practices became lost to most Indigenous people and not valued (Lange, 1999).

In Aotearoa New Zealand, increased interest in 'exotic' lands led to growing numbers of colonizing immigrants excited to stake a claim to vast amounts of seemingly 'unused' land. As the immigrant population grew, tribal lands begun to shrink, much of which was illegally confiscated. A comprehensive history of land confiscation and destruction is beyond the scope of this chapter. Briefly, within just a few generations forests which were traditionally hunted for birds were cleared for farming, fishing grounds were left depleted of life, waterways polluted and many *wahi tapu* (mountains, rivers and other locations with cultural and spiritual significance) were desecrated to build roadways or for other ventures. A loss of land led to a direct loss of traditional food and water sources. This process, in addition to deliberate policies of urban-ization, compelled Māori to move into urban centres. In these urban centres, access to natural and traditional foods was difficult and expensive. The loss of traditional food sources, in add-ition to Māori living a 'Western' lifestyle has over time led to the situation where many Māori *whānau* have diets high in processed food, in refined sugar, in low-nutrient foods, and with few vegetables primarily because such food is cheap and readily available.

Historical trauma

Te toto o te tangata, he kai, te oranga o te tanagata, he whenua.

Food supplies the blood of man, his welfare depends on land.

Remembering that Indigenous peoples are defined by the land from which they were born and raised, the loss of land not only affected the health of Indigenous people through access to food, it also impacted on their identity in very real and devastating ways. As we noted earlier in this chapter, the identity of Indigenous people is intertwined with the land from which they come. People are tied to the land, belong to the land, and their histories are framed by the land and their connection to (or disconnection from) the land (Durie, 1998; Smith, 2012). Ngaruru (2008) highlights the importance of land or the *whenua*:

> From a Maori world view, whenua is a significant part of our well-being. We have a physical (environmental), spiritual (mauri), psychological (ora) and cultural attachment similar to that of any other country's aboriginal people. Land gives identity and iden-tifies cultural and customary difference.

(p. 2)

Thus, for Māori if the land is sick, so too is our wellbeing impacted on a spiritual and phys-ical level. The dispossession of Māori from their land through the processes of colonization and assimilation, particularly those *hapū* and *iwi* whose land was forcibly taken through confiscation and land wars has resulted in what is now recognized as historical trauma.

Historical trauma is described as "an event or set of events perpetrated on a group of people (including their environment) who share a specific identity (e.g. nationality, tribal affiliation, ethnicity, religious affiliation) with genocidal or ethnocidal intent (i.e. annihilation or disruption to traditional lifeways, culture and identity)" (Walters et al., 2011, p. 181).

In addition to historical trauma being referred to as a 'soul wound' and unresolved grieving (Duran, 2006; Pihama et al., 2014; Walters et al., 2011), it has also contributed to the neuro-biological, physiological and epigenetic changes (see Table 8.1) in response to ongoing stress and trauma that people experience when they were forcibly, or by other means, dispossessed of

Table 8.1 Definitions for neurobiological, physiological and epigenetic changes

Changes	What is affected
Neurobiological	Changes in the pathways in our brains that lead to long-term changes in psychological functioning, causing heightened anxiety, poor impulse control or posttraumatic stress disorder, for example.[a]
Physiological	Chronic stress that causes the body to alter the stress hormone levels in the body and elevate blood pressure. This alters the hypothalamus-pituitary-adrenal axis that regulates the stress hormones in our bodies.[b]
Epigenetic	Epigenetics is about how genes are expressed, that is turned on or off in the body in response to environmental conditions.[b]

Sources: [a] Sherin & Nemeroff (2011); [b] Walters et al. (2011).

their land (Whitbeck, Adams, Hoyt, & Chen, 2004) – their *tūrangawaewae* (a place to stand in the world).

Wirihana and Smith (2014) made it clear that the historical and contemporary trauma Māori have been exposed to over the generations is "chronic and complex" (p. 201). As part of the colonization and assimilation processes Māori were subjected to, racism became a tool to paint Indigenous people as inferior. Racism has contributed to Māori being exposed to interpersonal and institutional trauma, and they continue to be treated inequitably in education, health, the workplace, the judicial system and almost every other aspect of society (Came, 2014; Jones, 2000). Without doubt racism effects not only the psychological and spiritual wellbeing of Māori, it impacts people's overall wellbeing and is a cause of chronic stress. This stress in turn contributes to negative physical (spiritual and psychological) health outcomes and is associated with cardiovascular disease and health risk activities such as smoking and hazardous drinking (Harris et al., 2012).

Socioeconomic deprivation

Many Māori now live in neighbourhoods with high socioeconomic deprivation (influenced by factors such as income, being on a welfare benefit, and access to transport and the internet), which in turn influences their abilities to access the necessary determinants of health. The impacts of socioeconomic deprivation spill over into the ability to access quality health services (Reid & Robson, 2007). This is an issue because high levels of deprivation, commonly referred to as poverty, affects the health of both adults and children – people have more physical health problems and are more likely to have chronic disease and illness leading to premature mortality (Bethell, Newacheck, Hawes, & Halfon, 2014). Poverty is an adverse childhood experience, known to set children onto a lifelong pathway of social and physical health problems (Poulton et al., 2002). Both the New Zealand Dunedin Longitudinal and the USA Adverse Childhood Experiences studies have demonstrated how poverty (sometimes referred to as deprivation) in the first decade of a child's life, along with other factors such as exposure to smoking, lead to poor physical, social and health outcomes that increase the burdens on their health and wellbeing as adults (Brown et al., 2009; Caspi et al., 2016).

Current status of Māori physical wellbeing

Having canvassed both traditional understandings of what constitutes optimum wellbeing for Māori and the many impacts on, and drivers of, physical wellbeing, it is timely to turn our attention to the current state of Māori physical wellbeing, and how Māori health fares in comparison to other citizens of Aotearoa.

According to the New Zealand Health Survey, which surveyed 13,781 adults and 4,721 children, Māori remain over-represented in activities associated with increased health risk and poor health outcomes (Ministry of Health, 2015). Despite the appreciable gains in Māori health status and life expectancy, Māori continue to experience persistent health and social inequities when compared to others living in Aotearoa New Zealand (see for example, Ministry of Health, 2015; Reid & Robson, 2007). This section provides an overview of the immense burdens associated with health risks, non-communicable and communicable diseases Māori and their *whānau* face. The high prevalence of these often long-term health conditions reduces both their life expectancy and quality of life. For example, the high prevalence of type 2 diabetes among Māori is associated with complications such as lower limb amputations and or renal failure that reduces their quality of life. Other threats to their wellbeing include, for instance, violence within communities and *whānau* (Family Violence Death Review Committee, 2014), and inequities in accessing necessary determinants of health (for example, education, housing and income) (Ministry of Health, 2015). Furthermore, Māori children living in some areas of Aotearoa are also affected by rheumatic fever, which if left undiagnosed leads to rheumatic heart disease in their adulthood (Mardini, Calder, Haydon-Carr, Purdie, & Jones, 2011). These threats to wellbeing are compounded by difficulties with accessing timely and appropriate health services together with receiving quality healthcare.

According to Statistics New Zealand, Māori are a youthful population, with the median age being 14.1 years younger than the total population, one third of Māori are 15 years of age or younger (Table 8.2). While life expectancy continues to increase for those living in Aotearoa New Zealand, Māori still die on average 7.2 years younger than non-Māori (Statistics New Zealand, 2014b). This lower life expectancy highlights the compromised physical wellbeing for many Māori that is caused mostly by non-communicable diseases, intentional and non-intentional injury, and the inequities they encounter when accessing health services for ill health.

Non-communicable diseases and illness

Non-communicable diseases (NCDs) pose significant threats to the physical wellbeing of Māori. Ischaemic heart disease, lung cancer and diabetes are key causes of Māori mortality. In addition to those already listed, Māori men also die of suicide and motor vehicle accidents, while Māori women also die of obstructive pulmonary disease and stroke, and die prematurely

Table 8.2 Māori and non-Māori age profile

		Māori	Non-Māori	Difference
Median age		23.9 years	38.0 years	−14.1 years
Percentage of population under 15 years		33.8%	20.4%	
Percentage of population over 65 years		5.4%	14.3%	
Life expectancy	Males	72.8 years	80.2 years	−7.4 years
	Females	76.5 years	83.7 years	−7.2 years

Source: Ministry of Health; Statistics NZ (2014b).

from breast cancer compared with other women living in Aotearoa (Ministry of Health, 2015). Compared to others living in Aotearoa New Zealand, Māori are more likely to die and be hospitalized from:

- cardiovascular disease;
- stroke;
- heart failure;
- rheumatic heart disease.

Table 8.3 shows the higher rate ratios Māori have for communicable diseases that are either avoidable or amenable to equitable access to determinants of health along with access to timely and quality healthcare. Of notable interest, is the higher rate ratios for hospitalization Māori women are likely to experience, particularly for heart failure (more than two times greater), rheumatic heart disease (more than five times greater), and for chronic obstructive pulmonary disorder (COPD) (almost 3.5 times greater). The higher rate for COPD for Māori women is possibly related to their higher smoking rates (Ministry of Health, 2016). Furthermore, Māori also endure a higher health burden related to type 2 diabetes and its related complications compared to the non-Māori population; for instance, high rates of renal failure (five times greater) and lower limb amputations (3.5 times greater for Māori) that compromise quality of life and longevity (Ministry of Health, 2015).

The greater burden of ill-health for many Māori is not only confined to the adult population. Māori infants have a higher prevalence for low birthweight that is associated with 1.5 times greater likelihood of death. Moreover, Māori babies are five times more likely to die of sudden unexplained death in infancy (SUDI) and is greater (5.5 times) for Māori girls. They are also three times more likely to die of sudden infant death syndrome (SIDS), although for Māori boys they have a fourfold likelihood of death related to SIDS (Ministry of Health, 2015).

'Risky' lifestyle activities

A number of so-called 'lifestyle' activities also negatively impact Māori physical wellbeing. Smoking is a commonly known to cause a range of non-communicable diseases such as cardiovascular disease, cancers and chronic obstructive pulmonary disease. Although there have been improvements in smoking rates, Māori continue to have the highest rate of smoking in Aotearoa New Zealand – 38.6 per cent of Māori over the age of 15 years smoke, with Māori women

Table 8.3 Rate ratios for Māori mortality and hospitalization compared to non-Māori*

	Mortality	*Hospitalization*
Cardiovascular disease	2.17	1.64
Stroke	1.56	1.76
Heart failure	2.36	4.01
Rheumatic heart disease	5.23	4.82
Asthma	–	1.96
Chronic obstructive pulmonary disease	2.94	3.59

Source: Ministry of Health (2015).

* These age standardized rate ratios are for both Māori men and women.

having a slightly higher prevalence of smoking. However, smoking is a particular issue for young Māori women aged 14–15 years, who have five times the prevalence for tobacco smoking than their non-Māori counterparts.

Māori have similar alcohol consumption profiles to the general population and are less likely to drink more than four times per week. However, when Māori do drink, they are twice as likely to drink large amounts in short periods of time. These 'binge' drinking patterns are hazardous and are often associated with injury, motor vehicle accidents and violence (Ministry of Health, 2016).

According to the body mass index categories used in the New Zealand Health Survey, almost half (47%) of Māori adults are obese, while Māori children are 1.6 times more likely to be obese than non-Pacific non-Māori children. While neighbourhood deprivation is associated with negative impacts on the nature of people's physical wellbeing, some of the weight gain observed over time in both adults and children has been attributed to the consumption of diets lacking in optimal nutrition that include high sugar drinks and fast food (Ministry of Health, 2016). For example, Māori are less likely to have the recommended more than three servings of vegetables and more than two servings of fruit per day. Despite this tendency toward obesity and nutritionally lacking diets, half of Māori adults undertake the recommended physical activity of 30 minutes five days per week (Ministry of Health, 2016).

Unintentional and intentional injury

Injury, whether unintentional or intentional, cause harm to people's physical wellbeing and is quite often avoidable, and in many cases, leads to disability. Unintentional injury is an area Māori experience greater rates of hospitalization – Māori children aged 0–14 years are 3.5 times more likely to have unintentional injuries than non-Māori children, and are significantly more likely to be hospitalized as a result. This disparity also exists for 15–64-year-olds, who are 1.5 times more likely to have an unintentional injury and are 30 per cent more likely to be hospitalized. However, unintentional injury for Māori women is significantly lower than non-Māori women (Ministry of Health, 2015). Motor vehicle accidents, accidental poisoning and falls are the main causes of unintentional injury across the age groups.

Intentional injury occurs in the forms of suicide, intentional self-harm and interpersonal violence. Suicide rates are almost twice that of non-Māori, with 15–24-year-olds having the highest rate among all age groups. Intentional self-harm results in significantly more hospitalizations for Māori, with the rates twice that for women compared to men, although Māori men are 1.5 times more likely to be hospitalized compared to non-Māori men. Those especially at risk of hospitalization are 15–24-year-olds and 25–64-year-olds (Ministry of Health, 2015).

Interpersonal violence in the form of assault and homicide is more prevalent for Māori, with Māori women having nearly four times the rate than non-Māori men. Māori are three times more likely to be hospitalized for assault, while Māori women are six times more likely than non-Māori women to be hospitalized (Ministry of Health, 2015). Māori are over-represented in deaths resulting from violence in their *whānau* – half of the homicides in Aotearoa are family violence-related, and half of the family violence homicides involve Māori as the deceased or the offender. This over-representation is reflective of the high likelihoods of death. For instance, Māori children are 5.5 times more likely to die of child abuse and neglect, Māori women are three times more likely to be victims of intimate partner violence homicide, and Māori men are almost five times more likely to be offenders. Family violence-related homicide extends beyond partners and children to include wider *whānau* members. Māori are 5.5 times more likely to be a victim of intrafamilial family violence, and 13 times more likely to be an offender (Family Violence Death Review Committee, 2014).

Disability

The most common causes of disability for Māori adults are accident and injury, disease and illness, and ageing. Māori adults have on average higher disability rates than non-Māori – 32 per cent compared to 24 per cent (adjusted for the age profile of total population). Māori with disability are younger (40 years) than New Zealand European (57 years) and Asian peoples (45 years). A similar pattern exists for Māori children (15% compared to 9%). More than half of Māori children had a single impairment and Māori boys were more likely to experience disability than Māori girls. More than 60 per cent of Māori adults aged 45 years or more have multiple impairments of which the most common impairments affected people's mobility, hearing and agility. Māori also reported higher rates of unmet health and disability support needs (Statistics New Zealand, 2014a). In terms of physical activity, disability impacts personal care, shopping and undertaking heavy and household activities (Ministry of Health, 2015).

Access to health services

The New Zealand Health Survey found Māori children and adults are more likely to report unmet need for healthcare (Ministry of Health, 2016). There are a number of reasons a person may experience an unmet need including being unable to get an appointment with a medical practitioner within 24 hours; being unable to attend a general practitioner due to the cost of the appointment; not having childcare; or lacking transport to a healthcare service. Cost was also cited as a reason for not collecting prescriptions for Māori children and adults, especially for Māori women (Ministry of Health, 2016). Not accessing primary healthcare services in a timely manner is reflected in the higher amenable mortality (2.5 times higher than non-Māori) and ambulatory sensitive hospitalization rates (1.5 times higher than non-Māori) (Ministry of Health, 2015). This lack of timely access to health services also impacts physical wellbeing for Māori children and adults.

When Māori do access health services, they are more likely to experience differences in the quality of care they receive. Māori are three times more likely to report unfair treatment attributable to ethnicity (Ministry of Health, 2015). They are also more likely to experience racism (Harris et al., 2012; Harris et al., 2006), along with adverse events such as avoidable complications or errors in a person's healthcare by healthcare professionals either doing something wrong or not providing usual or expected care (Davis et al., 2006; Rumball-Smith, Sarfati, Hider, & Blakely, 2013). Such actions impact on physical wellbeing resulting in the need for hospitalization, and in some cases, can lead to long-term impairment or even death.

Promoting Māori physical wellbeing

He kai kei aku ringa.

There is food at the end of my hands.

This *whakataukī* speaks directly to the value of having the skills to provide for yourself and *whānau*. At another level however, the *whakataukī* also implies that the answers to many of the problems that affect Māori today are best answered by Māori themselves. In the process of colonization, many Indigenous people have lost the ability to determine their own health and success. It is only through determining our own solutions that we will truly overcome the many obstacles and challenges that prevent us from leading a healthy, active and vital lifestyle. Durie (2005) reminds us that over time, endurance and resilience in adapting to adversity aided Māori survival. This ability to adapt and the resilience of Māori indicates their potential to become self-determining and reclaim their physical wellbeing.

During the 1980s, Māori leaders held a series of summits focusing on aspects of Māori development, from the economic to the social realm. At the health summit, Whakaoranga, Māori doctors expressed concerned about the health system's focus on illness (Boulton, 2005). In 1984 the Hui Taumata, or Māori Economic Summit, concluded that:

> Māori have the knowledge, skills and foresights to create a future where younger generations and generations yet to come can prosper in the world, and at the same time live as Māori.
>
> (Cited in Durie, 2011)

But it was not until the 1990s health reforms that the environment for greater Māori input into health service delivery was created. These reforms changed the way in which health services were purchased and delivered (commonly referred to as the funder–provider split), enabling Māori to construct *iwi* health plans and the opportunity arose for Māori health service provision (Boulton, Tamehana, & Brannelly, 2013). It was within this environment that Māori health promotion activities emerged, reinforced by the New Zealand Health Strategy (King, 2000) and He Korowai Oranga – the Māori Health Strategy (King & Turia, 2002; Ministry of Health, 2014).

In the early twenty-first century, government policies such as Healthy Eating Healthy Action contributed to the proliferation of Māori health promotion programmes. More recently, despite a shift in government policy direction that places more responsibility on individuals regarding physical activity, Māori themselves as *whānau, hapū, iwi*, have embraced health promotion messages and driven their own, very distinct programmes. Initiatives such as Iron Māori and Tri Māori, *whānau*-based, triathlon events, have emerged as a consequence (Pohatu, 2015).

Māori have a collective orientation, and while current health policy is heavily focused on individual's physical wellbeing, He Korowai Oranga – the Māori Health Strategy (Ministry of Health, 2014) highlights the importance of a *whānau*- or family-centred approach to improving Māori health and wellbeing. The pathways in which to achieve *pae ora* (healthy futures) include *mauri ora* (healthy individuals); *whānau ora* (healthy families); and *wai ora* (healthy environments) that require supporting *whānau, hapū, iwi* and community development, Māori participation and the need for cross-sectoral collaboration. These pathways reinforce the platform for future health promotion activities based on Māori health models, such as Te Pae Mahutonga (Durie, 1999). Te Pae Mahutonga is the Māori name for the constellation of stars that is now more widely known as the Southern Cross. In our history, this constellation was the main navigational aide for the peoples on the first voyaging *waka* that came from Hawai'iki-nui to Aotearoa. Adopted as a model for Māori health promotion, the various stars comprising Te Pae Mahutonga represent the foundations for health: Mauriora (cultural identity), Waiora (physical environment), Toiora (healthy lifestyles) and Te Oranga (participation in society). Two pointers indicate the essential abilities needed for progress: Ngā Manukura (community leadership) and Te Mana Whakahaere (autonomy).

Ratima et al. (2015) maintain that "health is inseparable from Māori realities and perspectives" (p. 43), of which having a secure cultural identity is important. The processes of colonization and the associated factors like deculturation, dispossession of land and dislocation from

Māori cultural ties all impact on Māori wellbeing, and consequently Māori physical wellbeing. Therefore, as Ratima et al. (2015) indicate, Māori health promotion, including the promotion of physical health and wellbeing, must be positioned within a Māori worldview and incorporate activities that promote secure cultural identities and a collective orientation (including *whānau, hapū, iwi* and diverse Māori communities) and incorporate the diverse realities of contemporary Māori. Importantly, Māori health promotion approaches are underpinned by collective autonomy to promote Māori control and identifies the collective's aspirations and needs for their health and wellbeing (Ratima et al., 2015).

While this chapter has shown that Māori bear a disproportionate burden of ill health and premature mortality, Māori-led solutions and programmes to reverse these statistics are growing. Examples of strengths-based, community- and *whānau*-led, culturally grounded programmes aimed at improving Māori physical wellbeing are making an impact on the lives of many Māori *whānau*. Recently, for example, Warbrick, Wilson, and Boulton (2016) reported how Māori men who were sedentary recognized the value of being physically active while undertaking daily activities for the *whānau* and *marae*, such as gathering *kaimoana* (food from the sea) when they were younger. The answers for addressing the contemporary health status of Māori lie within our *mātauranga* Māori (traditional knowledge) and ways of life.

Final comments

The irony of writing a chapter on physical wellbeing, is that for Māori there is no differentiation between physical, psychological, spiritual and social wellbeing – all must be well and in balance for optimal wellbeing to exist. Separating out physical wellbeing from all other aspects which go into the wellbeing of the whole person is in direct contradiction to our Indigenous viewpoint of *hauora*. The dire health status of much of the Māori population today and the growing levels of disparity between Māori and non-Māori health status compels us to look at more culturally embedded ways of promoting health and wellbeing. The lines between the various aspects of mainstream views of health make it difficult to address physical wellbeing on its own. Underpinning health plans that promote wellbeing with *mātauranga* Māori are essential, and therefore, Indigenous approaches and strategies based on traditional and innovative ways of undertaking Māori health promotion are needed. Drawing on the words of our ancestors:

> *Waiho i te toipoto, kaua i te toiroa.*
>
> Let us keep close together, not wide apart.

References

Ahuriri-Driscoll, A., Baker, V., Hepi, M., Hudson, M., Mika, C., & Tiakiwai, S.J. (2008). *The future of rongoā: Wellbeing and sustainability*. Christchurch, New Zealand: ESR.

Bethell, C.D., Newacheck, P., Hawes, E., & Halfon, N. (2014). Adverse childhood experiences: Assessing the impact on health and school engagement and the mitigating role of resilience. *Health Affairs, 33*(12), 2106–2115.

Boulton, A. (2005). *Provision at the interface: The Māori mental health contracting experience*. PhD in Māori Health, Massey University – Turitea Campus, Palmerston North, New Zealand.

Boulton, A., Tamehana, J., & Brannelly, P.M. (2013). Whānau-centred health and social service delivery in NZ: The challenges to, and opportunities for, innovation. *MAI Journal, 2*(1), 18–32.

Brannelly, T., Boulton, A., & Te Hiini, A. (2013). A relationship between the ethics of care and Māori worldview: The place of relationality and care in Maori mental health service provision. *Ethics and Social Welfare, 7*(4), 410–422.

Brown, D.W., Anda, R.F., Tiemeier, H., Felitti, V.J., Edwards, V.J., Croft, J.B., & Giles, W.H. (2009). Adverse childhood experiences and the risk of premature mortality. *American Journal of Preventive Medicine, 37*(5), 389–396.

Came, H. (2014). Sites of institutional racism in public health policy making in New Zealand. *Social Science & Medicine, 106*, 214–220.

Caspi, A., Houts, R.M., Belsky, D.W., Harrington, H., Hogan, S., Ramrakha, S., & Moffitt, T.E. (2016). Childhood forecasting of a small segment of the population with large economic burden. *Nature Human Behaviour, 1*, 0005. doi:10.1038/s41562-016-0005.

Davis, P., Lay-Yee, R., Dyall, L., Briant, R., Sporle, A., Brunt, D., & Scott, A. (2006). Quality of hospital care for Maori patients in New Zealand: Retrospective cross-sectional assessment. *The Lancet, 367*(9526), 1920–1925.

Duran, E. (2006). *Healing the soul wound: Counselling with American Indians and other native peoples.* New York: Teachers College Press.

Durie, M. (1985). Māori health institutions. *Community and Mental Health in New Zealand, 2*(1), 63–69.

Durie, M. (1995). Culture, mental illness and the Māori of New Zealand. In I. Al-Issa (Ed.), *Handbook of culture and mental illness: An international perspective.* Calgary: University of Calgary.

Durie, M. (1998). *Whaiora: Maori health development* (2nd ed.). Auckland: Oxford University Press.

Durie, M. (1999). Te Pae Mahutonga: A model for Māori health promotion. *Health Promotion Forum of New Zealand Newsletter, 49*, 2–5.

Durie, M. (2005). *Ngā tai matatū: Tides of Māori endurance.* Melbourne: Oxford University Press.

Durie, M. (2011). *Ngā tini whetū: Navigating Māori futures.* Wellington: Huia.

Family Violence Death Review Committee (FVDRC). (2014). *Fourth annual report: January 2013 to December 2013.* Retrieved from www.hqsc.govt.nz/assets/FVDRC/Publications/FVDRC-4th-report-June-2014.pdf.

Harris, R., Cormack, D., Tobias, M., Yeh, L.-C., Talamaivao, N., Minster, J., & Timutimu, R. (2012). The pervasive effects of racism: Experiences of racial discrimination in New Zealand over time and associations with multiple health domains. *Social Science & Medicine, 74*(3), 408–415.

Harris, R., Tobias, M., Jeffreys, M., Waldegrave, K., Karlsen, S., & Nazroo, J. (2006). Racism and health: The relationship between experience of racial discrimination and health in New Zealand. *Social Science & Medicine, 63*(6), 1428–1441.

Jones, C.P. (2000). Levels of racism: A theoretic framework and a gardener's tale. *American Journal of Public Health, 90*, 1212–1215.

King, A. (2000). *New Zealand Health Strategy.* Retrieved from www.moh.govt.nz/publications/nzhs.

King, A., & Turia, T. (2002). *He korowai oranga: Māori health strategy.* Wellington: Ministry of Health.

Lange, R. (1999). *May the people live: A history of Māori health development 1900–1920.* Auckland: Auckland University Press.

Mardani, J., Calder, L., Haydon-Carr, J., Purdie, G., & Jones, N.F. (2011). Throat swabbing for primary prevention of rheumatic fever following health information. *New Zealand Medical Journal, 124*(1333), 46–51. Retrieved from www.nzma.org.nz/journal/read-the-journal/all-issues/2010–2019/2011/vol-124-no-1334.

Mead, H.M. (2003). *Tikanga Māori: Living by Māori values.* Wellington: Huia.

Ministry of Health. (2016). *Annual update of key results 2015/16: New Zealand Health Survey.* Retrieved from www.health.govt.nz/system/files/documents/publications/annual-update-key-results-2015-16-nzhs-dec16-v2.pdf.

Ministry of Health. (2014). He Korowai Oranga: Māori health strategy 2014. Retrieved from www.health.govt.nz/publication/guide-he-korowai-oranga-maori-health-strategy.

Ministry of Health. (2015). *Tatau Kahukura Māori health chart book 2015* (3rd ed.). Wellington: Ministry of Health.

Ngaruru, D.C.T. (2008). Whenua: The key to Maori health and well-being. *Kai Tiaki Nursing New Zealand, 14*(5), 2.

Paradies, Y. (2016). Colonisation, racism and indigenous health. *Journal of Population Research, 33*(1), 83–96.

Pihama, L., Reynolds, P., Smith, C., Reid, J., Smith, L.T., & Rihi, T.N. (2014). Positioning historical trauma theory within Aotearoa New Zealand. *AlterNative, 10*(3), 248–261.

Pohatu, L. (2015). *Iron Maori: A kaupapa Māori driven hauora initiative.* Thesis, Master of Public Health, University of Otago. Retrieved from http://hdl.handle.net/10523/5811.

Pomare, E. (1986). Māori health: New concepts and initiatives. *New Zealand Medical Journal, 99*, 410–411.

Poulton, R., Caspi, A., Milne, B., Thomson, W., Taylor, A., & Sears, M. (2002). Association between children's experience of socioeconomic disadvantage and adult health: A life-course study. *Lancet, 360*(9346), 1640–1645.

Ratima, M., Durie, M., & Hond, R. (2015). Māori health promotion. In L. Signal & M. Ratima (Eds.), *Promoting health in Aotearoa New Zealand* (pp. 42–63). Dunedin: University of Otago Press.

Reid, P., & Robson, B. (2007). Understanding health inequities. In B. Robson & R. Harris (Eds.), *Hauora: Maori health standards IV. A study of the years 2000–2005* (pp. 3–10). Wellington: Te Ropu Rangahau Hauora a Eru Pomare.

Rumball-Smith, J., Sarfati, D., Hider, P., & Blakely, T. (2013). Ethnic disparities in the quality of hospital care in New Zealand, as measured by 30-day rate of unplanned readmission/death. *International Journal of Quality in Health Care, 25*(3), 248–254.

Ryan, P.M. (1999). *The Reed pocket dictionary of modern Māori.* Auckland: Reed Publishing.

Sherin, J.E., & Nemeroff, C.B. (2011). Post-traumatic stress disorder: The neurobiological impact of psychological trauma. *Dialogues in Clinical Neuroscience, 13*(3), 263–278.

Sherwood, J. (2013). Colonisation – it's bad for your health: The context of Aboriginal health. *Contemp Nurse, 46*(1), 28–40.

Smith, L.T. (2012). *Decolonizing methodologies: Research and indigenous peoples* (2nd ed.). London: Zed Books.

Statistics New Zealand. (2014a). *Disability survey: 2013.* Retrieved from www.stats.govt.nz/browse_for_stats/health/disabilities/DisabilitySurvey_HOTP2013.aspx.

Statistics New Zealand. (2014b). *Quick stats: About culture and identity.* Retrieved from www.stats.govt.nz/Census/2013-census/profile-and-summary-reports/quickstats-culture-identity.aspx.

Walters, K.L., Mohammed, S.A., Evans-Campbell, T., Beltrán, R.E., Chae, D.H., & Duran, B. (2011). Bodies don't just tell stories, they tell histories: Embodiment of historical trauma among American Indians and Alaska Natives. *Du Bois Review: Social Science Research on Race, 8*(1), 179–189.

Warbrick, I., Wilson, D., & Boulton, A. (2016). Provider, father, and bro: Sedentary Māori men and their thoughts on physical activity. *International Journal for Equity in Health, 15*(1), 1–11.

Whitbeck, L.B., Adams, G.W., Hoyt, D.R., & Chen, X. (2004). Conceptualizing and measuring historical trauma among American Indian people. *American Journal of Community Psychology, 33*(3–4), 119–130.

Wirihana, R., & Smith, C. (2014). Historical trauma, healing and well-being in Māori communities. *MAI Journal, 3*(3), 197–210.

PART II

Social and emotional wellbeing

9

WELLBEING IN SWEDISH INDIGENOUS SÁMI CHILDREN AND YOUNG PEOPLE

Looking back and looking forward

Susanne Garvis and Lotta Omma

Introduction

The land of the Sámi, known as Sápmi, stretches across four countries: Sweden, Norway, Finland and Russia. Today, according to official records there are around 20,000 to 25,000 Sámi in Sweden. However, Hassler et al. (2004) suggest that the number may be closer to 40,000 to 50,000, depending on how Sámi identity is defined. Throughout history, the Sámi have been subject to discrimination, with implications such as loss of landholdings and the suppression of political and cultural ways of being. Pikkarainen and Brodin (2008) suggest that this has led to a weakening of the Indigenous peoples' economy and culture. Such prejudices have also led to members of the Sámi population suppressing their ethnicity and adjusting to the dominant society around them in order to be accepted (Blind, 2006).

This chapter summarizes the existing literature regarding Swedish Indigenous Sámi children and young people to provide a snapshot of the current context. Two perspectives will be explored: (1) mental health; and (2) education. By exploring these perspectives, we highlight where support and further research is needed. We also provide important considerations in health and education for Sweden to enhance the wellbeing of Sámi people today.

Who are the Sámi people in Sweden?

The Swedish government officially recognized the Sámi as Indigenous people in 1977 (SÖ, 2002, p. 2). In 2010, they were recognized as a people within the Swedish constitution, giving them to have the right to self-determination. Sámi identity, however, is complex on both an individual and group level (Amft, 2000) and is also dependent on where the Sámi person lives and where they were raised (Åhren, 2008). Sámi identity is made up of a range of attributes, including language, clothing, 'duodji' (Sámi handicraft), working with reindeer and ethnic cuisine (Amft, 2000). To Sámi, the north region in Sweden is also important. The north of Sweden provides a sense of history, physical connection to a geographic area and connection with the future (Cocq, 2014).

Today, about 10–15 per cent of Sámi are reindeer herders. Reindeer herding is restricted by Swedish law and is organized into 'Sameby'. A *Sameby* is both a geographical area for reindeer herding and an economic organization. In Sweden, there are fifty-one *Samebyar* (plural form).

A brief history of the Sámi in Sweden

To understand the Sámi and their situation today, it is important to understand historical ideas and values. Up until the eighteenth century, Sweden was a state that wanted to expand territory in the north in order to create boundaries with other countries (such as Russia). Government policy supported Swedes who settled in the north. These Swedes were able to take over the land for agriculture. The land, however, was already occupied by the Sámi who had lived there for thousands of years, living on reindeer herding, hunting and fishing.

During the 1800s, the Sámi's situation was difficult, with exceptionally cold winters leading to a lack of food and increased starvation. At the same time there were conflicts over ownership of land and the Sámi population found it difficult to access grazing areas for their reindeer. As a consequence, the Sámi population decreased significantly during this period.

At the beginning of the twentieth century, there was a strong belief that Sámi culture would become extinct, based on the emerging Darwinian concept of 'survival of the fittest'. The Sámi culture based on a nomadic lifestyle could not compete with Swedish agriculture. The Swedish government created two distinct paths for the Sámi people depending on whether or not they owned reindeer. Sámi with reindeer could maintain their nomadic way of living and be protected from 'civilization'. Sámi who did not have reindeer were expected to assimilate into Swedish society. The Sámi people thus became divided. The first group became isolated with no self-determination. They were ruled by 'outsiders' who had no knowledge about Sámi culture and did not understand the importance of reindeer herding. The second group became invisible and, in many respects, became indistinct from the mainstream population. During this time, there was also a belief in a race-based biological hierarchy that considered Sámi people of lower maturity and intelligence, thus portraying the Sámi as incapable of managing their own interests.

Following the Second World War, the situation for the Sámi began to improve as a result of a strong international Indigenous movement (Lantto & Mörkenstam, 2008). During this period there was a radical change in how Sámi policy and the system of rights were explained and justified, with previous arguments about race-based biological hierarchy now considered obsolete in the public discourse. Since 1993 there has been a Sámi parliament in Sweden. However, the Sámi parliament acts in a counselling function and does not have real power to make decisions for issues important to Sámi people.

Human rights

The International Covenant on Civil and Political Rights (United Nations, 1966) suggests that within Sweden the Sámi have the right to self-determination, the right to determine their political status, and the right to develop their own economy, society and culture (Article 1). According to Anaya (2004), self-determination requires both autonomy for Indigenous institutions and a higher political mandate for Indigenous participation. Further, the Indigenous and Tribal Peoples Convention (ILO 169) states that Indigenous people have rights to both education and health.

The Convention on the Rights of the Child (United Nations, 1989) provides specific direction for the treatment and protection of Indigenous children. Sweden ratified the Convention in 1990 without any reservation (Prop, 1990, p. 107). Article 29.1.c states that education shall be directed to: "The development of respect for the child's parents, his or her own cultural identity, language and values, for the national values of the country in which the child is living, the country from which he or she may originate, and for civilizations different from his or her own." In a similar vein, Article 30 states: "In those States in which ethnic, religious or linguistic minorities or persons of indigenous origin exist, a child belonging to such a minority or who is indigenous shall not be denied the right, in community with other members of his or her group, to enjoy his or her own culture, to profess and practise his or her own religion, or to use his or her own language."

Another right for consideration specific to the European region is the Council of Europe's Framework Convention for the Protection of National Minorities (Council of Europe, 1998). The documents state that: "Parties shall, where appropriate, take measures in the fields of education and research to foster knowledge of the culture, history, language and religion of their national minorities and of the majority" (Article, 12, p.1). The Convention also states that minorities' language and culture should be protected from assimilation (Article 5.12, p. 2). According to Swedish legislation, the Sámi as a national minority group have the right to learn and use their own language. In addition, the language is to be protected and promoted. As such, the public has a responsibility to encourage the Sámi people to preserve and develop their culture, and a child has the right to develop a cultural identity (SFS, 2009, p. 600).

From the Covenant and Conventions, it can be argued that the health and education of the Sámi need to be supported by the Swedish people and the Swedish government. Strong provision is required for health and education, and this requires adequate advocacy, funding and implementation by organizations. The next section, however, discusses gaps between policy and practice. In particular, there appears to be large gaps between policy and practice in the implementation of support and advocacy for the health and education of Sámi children and young people.

Health and wellbeing

In the beginning of the twenty-first century, a number of suicides occurred by young Sámi reindeer herding men in the south of Sápmi, which led to concern and despair among the Sámi community. This resulted in great concern about the mental health and wellbeing of young Sámi people and a need for further research to understand the problem. During this time the lack of data about Sámi people's mental health was also discovered, leading some researchers to specifically focus on the health and wellbeing of Sámi children and young people.

In the last decade, research on the status of Sámi health has started to grow. In 2011, Omma et al. explored the perspectives of 876 Sámi young people (aged (18–28 years) about their own health and wellbeing, and what it meant to be Sámi. The study reported that many of the participants did not think it was easy to live as a Sámi person in Sweden. Close to half of the young adults had perceived bad treatment by others because of their Sámi background (♂42%, ♀48%) and 25 percent had heard teachers saying something bad about the Sámi or had been unfairly treated by a teacher due to their Sámi background (♂23%, ♀27%). Those young Sámi who reported having experienced bad treatment were more likely to be irritated and worried, and less likely to feel calm and relaxed (Omma et al., 2011). These experiences were equally common in Sámi males and Sámi females. Sámi young people were also worried that their culture would disappear in the future. They felt it was their personal responsibility to save the Sámi language from extinction.

In another Study, Omma et al. (2015) explored the perspectives of 121 young Sámi children (aged 12–18 years) with the use of a Kidscreen questionnaire. The questionnaire attempted to measure ten domains pertaining to health-related quality of life (HRQL): physical wellbeing, psychological wellbeing, moods and emotions, self-perception, autonomy (free time), parent relation and home life, social support and peers, school environment, social acceptance (not being bullied) and financial resources (Bisegger et al., 2005).

In general, the Sámi children reported a high degree of social acceptance, were not afraid of peers and did not feel bullied (Omma et al. 2015). All of the children attended a Sámi educational programme and participated in traditional Sámi activities such as working with reindeer, hunting, fishing and handicrafts. The majority of children also spoke or understood the Sámi language (65%).

Treatment at school however was not as positive for Sámi children. One in four children reported being unfairly treated by teachers because of their ethnicity. Fifteen percent of the children had also experienced the teacher saying negative things about the Sámi culture. This suggests the school environment may not be inclusive of all children.

Differences also emerged in the overall HRQL satisfaction of Sámi children based on age. Younger Sámi children (aged 12–13 years) ranked their health-related quality of life higher than Sámi children aged over 15 years. Findings from the study were also compared to the HRQL of Swedish children of similar age from geographically similar areas. The Sámi children reported lower levels of social support from peers, difficult relationships with parents and lower physical wellbeing. No differences between Sámi children and Swedish children were found for self-perception, psychological well-being, moods and emotions and social acceptance (bullying).

Suicide behavior

A cross-sectional study of 516 Sámi young people (aged 18–28) was conducted to investigate the experience of suicidal expressions (death wishes, life weariness, ideation, plans and attempts) (Omma, Sandlund, & Jacobsson, 2013). The sample was geographically matched with a reference group of Swedish young people ($n=218$). The results showed that while both groups reported suicidal ideation, life weariness and death wishes (30–50%), findings were slightly higher in Sámi young people (for example, suicidal ideation had 45% of Sámi young people vs 37% of Swedish young people). One hypothesis for the difference may be because of the ability to access suicide programs and support services.

Alcohol use

Employing the same sample, Omma et al. (2015) explore the use of alcohol by Sámi young people. Results showed no difference in the use of alcohol in both groups. However, approximately 45 percent of males in both groups were classified as 'binge drinkers' (six glasses or more consumed at one occasion every month). Ethnicity-related bad treatment was found to be a risk factor of hazardous/harmful drinking. Sámi with experience of ethnicity-related bad treatment had about 1.5 times higher risk of hazardous/harmful drinking compared to Sámi without this experience.

Conclusions of health and wellbeing

Young Sámi people and children are proud to be Sámi; they have great respect for their culture and take an active responsibility to ensure the preservation of their language and traditions.

However, Sámi young people and children still experience discrimination at school leading to increased stress and worry (influencing mental health and wellbeing). Education is an important area for consideration in supporting all Sámi people. Overall, more research is needed to develop the current understanding of the mental health and wellbeing of Sámi children and young people in Sweden.

Education provision

Education has been identified as one of the important institutions for socializing and leading to change within society (Ledman, 2015). The Swedish curriculum is the steering document for what should be taught within Swedish schools. The Swedish curriculum states that the role of education is "to transfer and develop a cultural heritage – values, traditions, language, knowledge – from one generation to the next" and that "school should impart the more resistant skills that constitute the common frame of reference all in society need" (Lpo 11, National Compulsory School Curricula, 2011). Education is, therefore, important for all Swedish children in regards to their culture, identity and knowledge. The curriculum, therefore, provides an opportunity as a "mighty tool of social justice for the marginalised" (Kovach, 2009, p. 6). However, like any institution, education can also "reproduce and preserve differences among ethnicities" (Tallberg, Rubenstein, & Hägerstöm, 2002, p. 105).

In Sweden, compulsory school education starts when a child reaches 7 years. There are nine grades of schools. There is a national school curriculum consisting of three parts: (1) the schools' values and assignment; (2) the general goals and guidelines; and (3) the syllabi for all school subjects. Within the syllabus, there are a further three parts consisting of aims, central content and knowledge requirements guiding the grades. Sámi have the right to choose their own educational system (Parliamentary Resolution 1962) and there are five Sámi schools (year 1 to 6) located in the northwest part of Sweden (Svonni, 2015). Sámi students can attend any compulsory school and are supported by the Lpo 11 regulation, an important document that enables the Sámi to exercise their right to decide over their own education. The document also "guides teachers to provide a correct picture of the Sámi people, their history and culture to avoid further discrimination and stereotypic misconceptions and to make the content about the Sámi people from the Sámi perspective" (Svonni, 2015, p. 899). This document is based on important concepts of rights to self-determination.

Prior to 1962, schooling for Sámi, however, was different with little choice. Sámi who were connected to the mountain reindeer husbandry attended a Sámi school (boarding school), while other Sámi children attended Swedish schools (SFS, 1938) The change in policy allowed Sámi to be given a choice about their own education.

Today's Sámi schools are run by the government (Lpo, 2011, Lpo for the Sámi School), with an emphasis on Sámi culture and language. The Sámi thematic is also implemented across all subject areas. The Sámi school has a national curriculum, with the emphasis on mother tongue, allowing all children to learn the Sámi language.

Limited information is available within Sweden on the educational achievement between Sámi and Swedes. However, on a health-related quality of life scale, the education situation was one area where Sámi children scored lower compared to Swedish children (Omma, 2013).

In a review of the Swedish National Curriculum (2011) in regards to Sámi provision, Svonni (2015) reported a large gap within the curriculum in regards to Sámi provision. In her review of the 279-page document, she found that the word 'Sámi' did not feature in the school values and assignment section. It did feature as one of the sixteen requirements of knowledge within the general goals and guidelines section. As part of the required knowledge students, "each student completing the school… have gotten knowledge about the national minorities (Jews, Romanize, the Indigenous people Sámi's, Sweden Finish's, and Tornedalingars) culture, language, religion and history".

Within the Syllabi component, Svonni (2015) found that the word 'Sámi' was mentioned four times, corresponding to 0.5 percent of the central content. The central contents where Sámi thematic was found covered historical perspectives on the Sámi situation in Sweden (history syllabus, central content grades 7–9) as well as their rights today. Other representations included the positioning of the Indigenous people of Sweden within the social science syllabus (grades 4–6 and grades 7–9) and the use of stories from old Sámi religion that should be known (religion syllabus, grades 4–6).

The syllabi in Lpo 11 that explicitly addresses minorities are history, social science and Swedish language. The low degree of visibility and knowledge requirements of minority topics can't possibly live up to the expectations of providing and evolving their cultural identity, learning and evolving their language, nor getting knowledge about their culture, history and religion. The schools' values articulate respect and tolerance for other peoples, but it also guides into Swedish norms and values, which means it is an area where minorities do get assimilated into Swedish society.

What appears within the perspective of education is tensions between international covenants and conventions, steering documents for compulsory schooling as well as the formulations of the curriculum and guidelines. From the curriculum level, there is a lack of the Sámi peoples' thematic within the syllabi and no evaluable knowledge goals in the knowledge requirements about Sámi culture, history and living condition. As such, Sámi people may have not real influence over the compulsory Swedish curriculum, further exposing the marginalization of a minority group and a power balance. Svonni (2015) calls for an immediate policy reform to support the Sámi peoples' influence over education and also to customize the curriculum to both Swedish and Sámi children. Curriculum writers do not only require a knowledge of international and national laws, but they also require a working understanding of Sámi history, culture and the contemporary related situation of today.

Conclusion

Overall, this chapter has provided a snapshot of the current situation for Sámi children and young people's wellbeing in Sweden. The challenges in regards to health and education have identified some problems with government policy, leading to negative perceptions of identity and culture. This has also been extended to elements within the Swedish national curriculum and the absence of Sámi representation within the document. If the Swedish government is dedicated to supporting the rights and provision for Sámi children and young people as a minority group, change and reform are needed within health and education. This includes policy development and support to implement new policies. Given the number of international policies regarding minority groups and Indigenous populations that Sweden is familiar with, a revision of these documents and the role of the government is the first step in bringing change. We would like, therefore, to make the following six considerations for the future development of policy and provision in regards to health and education: (1) the development of health programmes to support the health and wellbeing of Sámi people in Sweden. This includes support for the provision of mother tongue as well as a focus on identity and Sámi culture. (2) Health and wellbeing programmes that educate all people on the importance of stopping discrimination for all people in society.

(3) Revision of the Swedish National Curriculum to provide adequate representation and knowledge of Sámi people, together with resources that are able to support the implementation of the curriculum surrounding the provision of Sámi people. (4) Teacher education that has courses focused on Sámi culture and perspectives. (5) Professional learning of current teachers to support Sámi children and young people. This also includes social and emotional wellbeing of Sámi children and young people. And (6) a review of Sámi language provision, and adequate steps taken to ensure people who ask for education in Sámi can receive an education in Sámi.

We hope that as this chapter is read and re-read, action can be implemented to bring about real change in the situation. Health and education are the starting point to bring such reform to the wellbeing of Sámi people in Sweden.

References

Amft, A. (2000). *Sápmi I förändringens tid. En studie av svenska samers levnadsvillkor under 1900-talet ur ett genusouch etnicitetsperspektiv.* PhD thesis, Umeå University.

Anaya, J. (2004). *Indigenous people's international law.* Oxford: Oxford University Press.

Åhren, C. (2008). *Är jag en riktig same? En ethnologisk studie av unga samers identitetsarbete.* PhD thesis, Umeå University.

Bisegger, C., Cloetta, B., von Bisegger, U., Abel, T., & Ravens-Sieberer, U. (2005). Health-related quality of life: Gender differences in childhood and adolescence. *Soscial and Preventative Medicine, 50*(5), 281–291.

Blind, E. (2006). Att förlora sitt språk. *Att åtgerta mitt språk. Åtgärder för att stärka det samiska språket. SOU, 19, Slutbetänkande från utredningen om finska och sydsamiska språken.* Stockholm: Statens Offentliga Utredningar.

Cocq, C. (2014). *Platsskapande och synliggörande in Kulturella perspektiv, Svensk ethnologisk tidskrift.* Umeå: Umeå University.

Council of Europe. (1998). *Framework Convention for the Protection of National Minorities.* Strasbourg: Council of Europe.

Hassler, S., Sjölander, P., & Erikcsson, A.J. (2004). Construction of a database on health and living conditions of the Swedish Sámi population. In P. Lantto & P. Sköld (Eds.), *Befolkning och bosättning I norr. Ethnicitet, identitet och gränser I historiens sken* (pp. 107–124). Umeå: Umeå University.

Kovach, M. (2009). *Indigenous methodologies. Characteristics, conversations and context.* Toronto: University of Toronto Press.

Lantto, P., & Mörkenstam, U. (2008). Sámi rights and Sámi challenges. *Scandinavian Journal of History, 33*(1), 26–51.

Ledman, K. (2015). *Historia för yrkesprogrammen. Innehåll och betydelse I policy och praktik.* PhD thesis, Umeå University.

Lpo 11 (2011). *Läroplan för grundskolan, förskoleklassen och fritidhemmet 2011.* Stockholm: Skolverket.

Omma, L.M. (2013). *Ung same I Sverige- Livsvillkor, självvärdering och hälsa.* PhD thesis, Umeå University.

Omma, L.M., Holmgren, L.E., & Jacobsson, L.H. (2011). Being a young Sámi in Sweden: Living conditions, identity and life satisfaction. *Journal of Northern Studies, 5*(1), 9–28.

Omma, L., & Petersen, S. (2015). Health related quality of life in Sámi schoolchildren. *Acta Paediatrica, 104*(1), 75–84.

Omma, L., Sandlund, M., & Jacobsson, L. (2013). Suicide expressions in young Swedish Sámi, a cross-sectional study. *International Journal of Circumpolar Health, 72*(1), 19862.

Pikkarainen, H., & Brodin, B. (2008). *Discrimination of national minorities in the education system.* DO's Report No. 2008: 2. Stockholm: Ombudsmannen mot etnisk diskriminering.

Prop. (1990). *Regeringens proposition om godkännande av FN-konventionen om barns rättigherer.* Stockholm: Statens Offentliga Utredningar.

SFS (1938). *Swedish Code of Statutes 1938:400.* Stockholm: Sveriges Riksdag.

SFS (2009). *Språklagen [Language act] 2009:600.* Stockholm: Sveriges Riksdag.

SÖ (2002). *Sveriges internationaella Överenskommelser, Ramkonvention om skydd för nationella minoriteter 2002:2.* Stockholm: Sveriges Riksdag.

Svonni, C. (2015). At the margin of educational policy: Sámi/Indigenous peoples in the Swedish National Curriculum 2011. *Creative Education, 6*(9), 898–906.

Tallberg, B. I. Rubenstein, R.L., & Hägerström, J. (2002). *Likvärdighet I en skola för alla- Historisk bakgrund och kritisk granskning.* Stockholm: Statens skolverk.

United Nations. (1966). *International Covenant on Civil and Political Rights.* Geneva: United Nations.

United Nations. (1989). *Convention on the Rights of the Child.* Retrieved 15 February 2017 from www. ohchr.org/EN/ProfessionalInterest/Pages/CRC.aspx.

10

WELLBEING CONSIDERATIONS AMONG SELECTED NORTH AMERICAN INDIAN POPULATIONS

Relationships, spirits and connections

Lyle J. Noisy Hawk and Joseph E. Trimble

Introduction

In this study, seven traditional Lakota healers were interviewed using a three-question semi-structured interview guide. The interviews were recorded on video, transcribed into the Lakota language, and then translated from Lakota to English. This method was undertaken to preserve syntactical and thematic emphasis of the Lakota speakers. The interview transcripts were then analyzed inductively using a grounded theory method. From the data, a central theme emerged: when questioned about mental health, all of the interviewees focused on the traditional Lakota concept of wellbeing (Wicozani). The healers identified six distinct ways that wellbeing (Wicozani) may be achieved. These are: (1) wellbeing is the result of lifelong practice; (2) wellbeing is attained and maintained through awareness of the sacred (Wakan); (3) wellbeing is attained and maintained through healthy relationships; (4) wellbeing is attained and maintained through consistent practice of prayer; (5) wellbeing is attained and maintained through successful recovery from traumatic experiences; and (6) wellbeing is attained and maintained through enacting Lakota values.

This chapter offers a preliminary exploration into the possibility that the treatment of mental health issues in American Indian/Alaskan Native racial/ethnic groups could be improved with the use of traditional healing practices.

Background

Few psychological studies of American Indian/Alaska Native (AI/AN) people that pertain to their specific history of mental health problems, including prevalence, assessment and treatment, have yielded outcomes that help professionals improve treatment. Some reasons include their relatively small population size as an ethnic/racial minority, their particular historical relationship with US government structures, and the history of psychological academic research of AI/AN populations since their contact with European Americans.

The US Census Bureau has estimated that 4.1 million American Indians/Alaskan Natives live in the US, which is about 1.5 percent of the US population (US Census Bureau, 2002). Within this group are more than 561 federally recognized tribes who speak more than 220 tribal languages. This large number of tribal groups scattered throughout the US makes it difficult to generalize across tribal groups. Each group has unique circumstances along with differing cultural viewpoints. Therefore, researchers have argued that psychological interventions should be individually constructed for each American Indian/Alaskan Native group (Alcántara & Gone, 2007).

AI/AN people have tolerated centuries of colonialism. Since contact, the history of interactions between AI and European Americans in the United States has been shaped by military conflicts, federal policies of reservation captivity, assimilation efforts, and theft of lands along with other cultural and natural resources (Gone & Alcántara, 2007). This is also reflected in the greater attention that is now being paid to the psychology, psychological wellbeing and mental health of American Indians. For example, Trimble and Clearing-Sky (2009) found that the American Psychological Association's PsycINFO electronic database references for AI/AN in the 1960s amounted to 203 entries. In the 1990s, the number had increased to 1,434. As of 2011, the number of articles on AI/AN psychological issues cited in PsycINFO are 4,741. However, there have been few studies published on the psychological wellbeing of AI people.

Evaluating traditional healing as a psychological resource

The research related to AI/AN mental health, substance use and suicide issues has not taken into account traditional healing approaches and practices, nor does it take into account psychological wellbeing as a preventative factor or healing force. In particular, Manson's (2000) review of service-related literature found the following topics in need of more research: culturally sensitive assessment and care, local AI/AN's contribution to the planning of treatments, and the role for traditional healing approaches that have been empirically examined.

The AI-SUPERPFP study by Beals et al. (2005) mentioned earlier, reported the estimates of lifetime help-seeking from mental health professionals, medical professionals, traditional healers, and other help sought from AI/ANs. Comparing the rates of specific help-seeking behaviors of participants with lifetime depressive and/or anxiety disorders between the AI/ANs from the Southwest tribe and those from the Northern Plains tribe, 48.9 percent of the participants from the Southwest tribe sought help from a traditional healer, while 33.7 percent of the participants from the Northern Plains tribe did. Those with lifetime substance use disorders only and those with lifetime comorbid depressive and/or anxiety and substance disorders who sought help from a traditional healer were reported as 37.7 percent and 61.0 percent respectively among Southwest tribe participants, and 16.9 percent and 37.4 percent respectively among the Northern Plains tribe.

Other studies have found that AI/AN utilize alternate therapies, specifically the use of traditional healing. In these studies, most AI/ANs utilized both Western and AI/AN traditional forms of healing (Buchwald, Beals, & Manson, 2000; Kim & Kwok, 1998; Marbella, Harris, & Diehr, 1998; Moodley, Sutherland, & Oulanova, 2008). While rates of the use of traditional healing are variable, taken together these studies do show that many American Indians depend on traditional healers and traditional healing practices to assist them with managing those psychological issues that can curtail their sense of wellbeing.

Understanding the historical and current roles of traditional Lakota healers in AI/AN communities

Historically, traditional healers were central to AI/AN cultural healing practices. Many tribal members, "who after centuries of struggle, resurrected and liberated their cultural healing practices from the repression of Colonialism" (Moodley et al., 2008, p. 155), and many today continue to integrate traditional healing with contemporary Western healing practices.

For Oglala Lakota people, or Oglala Sioux tribal people, who currently reside in southwestern South Dakota, the generic term 'sacred man or sacred woman' was used to designate a healer or medicine person. The Lakota term for sacred man was *wicasa wakan* while for women the term was *winyan wakan*. The sacred healers' functions include, to heal people from illnesses including somatic and psychosomatic, find items that have been lost or stolen, functions as an advisor to the people regarding family matters, finances, educational aspirations, "and other exigencies confronted by people growing up in a modern reservation community" (Powers, 1986, pp. 179–180). Other scholars used the term 'shaman' or 'medicine man' to designate a traditional healer or *wicasa wakan*.

Walker (1917) states that shaman were endowed with the comprehension of the laws, doctrines, ceremonies and customs of Lakota people and were the keepers of supernatural wisdom, which they practiced through the cultural interpretation of the messages and will of supernatural beings. Furthermore, as guardians of myth and rituals, shamans hid much of their knowledge in an esoteric language that was known only to them. In performing their rituals, their formal words and ritualistic movements referenced a vast orally transmitted body of Lakota mythology (Walker, 1917).

Traditional healers understand the milieu of their patients and affirm the idea that the cultural meaning of illness and healing is embedded in the patients' particular cultural paradigm. As stated by Moodley et al. (2008),

> illness does not simply refer to the problems associated with the body and mind, but also the spirit, where the ancestors, gods, spirits, deities and the environment are all legitimate points of reference for understanding causation and treatment...
>
> (p. 156)

The traditional healer's knowledge and understanding of the community's history, language, religious beliefs, cultural beliefs, values and the behavior of its individual members were used to guide their work in curing illnesses and healing physical and emotional wounds.

Traditional healers play an integral part in the wellbeing of their families, communities and tribes. They interpret the external and internal causes of disease/illness, and offer diagnoses and treatment to promote wellbeing. This wellbeing exists within a prescribed cultural paradigm that relies heavily on its own mythology. Individuals learn that the mythic foundation is attached to the healing process (Dow, 1986).

All schemes of symbolic healing refer to a culturally established mythical world. Those systems are differentiated from each other by where they place symbolic healing. Some cultures, like the Oglala Lakota and other AI/AN, locate it in the supernatural realm, while others see symbolic healing as part of everyday reality or as scientific knowledge. Those cultural mythic worlds include experiential knowledge that is considered, although not necessarily empirically, true. A healer and patient make use of a part of their cultural mythical world for symbolic healing (Dow, 1986).

In simplest terms, everyday cultural life impacted human development and the *wicasa wakan* was the principal source of information and advice regarding how to apply cultural mythical knowledge in order to heal from disruptive life moments. They taught that all beings are sacred or *wakan*, which is the key and significant difference between Western psychological thought and Lakota psychological thought. Traditional Lakota people believe in the concept of animism or that objects in the physical world have consciousness or a soul and as such all life is held in reverence. The belief in animism originates in the Lakota mythical stories beginning with the creation story. The creation story along with other Lakota mythical stories explain the origins of how a people came into existence, and how they should live or be in world. Mythical stories give meaning to people's behavior, and meaning to how they should strive to develop their thoughts, feelings and actions and their reference groups.

For the Native American, including the Oglala Lakota people, traditional healing was based on the idea of conducting a healthy way of life by mitigating the effects from behavior or activity that caused disease, and heeding the spiritual laws that were used to restore balance (Cohen, 1998, p. 47). Unhealthy or immoral behavior was viewed as causes for some illnesses/conditions that have been inherited. Disease was considered in terms of its spiritual significance, "morality, balance, and the action of spiritual power rather than specific, measurable causes… rather than a materialistic or Cartesian view of life" (Cohen, 1998, p. 47). Within Native American traditional healing traditions, "The binary divide of the Cartesian body-mind split is interrogated, brought to consciousness and integrated" (Moodley et al., 2008, p. 154).

Traditional healers were an integral component in aiding individual development, and they continued prospering within their cultural universe, community, and tribe through facilitating the establishment, cultivation and maintenance of existential relationships that tied all together. Healers fulfill a traditional role of mediating wellbeing through rituals and the affirmation of beliefs to help people attain wellbeing.

Rationale for using grounded theory as a research design

Ponterotto (2005) and Morrow and Smith (2000) (as noted by Fassinger, 2005) locate the current construction of grounded theory inside the paradigm of constructivist/interpretative research, although there is debate as to where to place the home for the paradigm of grounded theory. Ontologically, constructivist-interpretivist scholars assert that there are multiple constructed realities, which are subjective and influenced by the situational context. Specifically, the dimensions of the context are thought to influence the subjectivity of individual experience and perception, the social milieu, and the interaction between the researcher and subjects.

People construct multiple meanings of experience and multiple interpretations of realities. The research seeks to identify multiple common themes both within and across a sample group, and not single truths. This is achieved epistemologically by the concentrated interaction between the research participant and researcher. This type of interaction allows, "for the examination of the lived experience (Erlebnis) of the participants and the hermeneutic (interpretive) understanding of these experiences" (Ponterotto, 2005, p. 134).

The goal of the grounded theory method is to produce a theory that is grounded in the interviewees' experiences living in their particular social context, which in this case is traditional Lakota healers living and practicing their cultural lifeways on their respective reservations. Inductive analysis of participants' construal of their phenomenological reality is a technique of analysis recommended by Fassinger (2005). Other techniques used for data analysis have also been identified by Chesler (1987), Strauss and Corbin (1990) in Eaves (2001), and particularly Charmez (1983), which are rooted in the traditional framework of Glaser and Strauss (1967) and Glaser (1978). The process identified by these theorists is recursive. It involves simultaneously collecting and analyzing data to generate a theory that is grounded in the context where inquiry takes place. This process entails, "data collection, coding, conceptualizing, and theorizing, wherein new data are constantly compared to emerging concepts until no new themes, categories, or relationships are being discovered…" (Fassinger, 2005, p. 157). The process is also reflexive in that it is captured by writing memos about evolving ideas, concepts, and questions pertaining to, "conceptual, procedural, and analytic questions and decisions" (Fassinger, 2005, p. 163).

In this study we have chosen the paradigm constructivism-interpretivism and the grounded theory of qualitative research because they coincide with the Lakota understanding that individuals continually construct their own personal reality based on their experience, which is continually in the process of development. The research design selected entails gathering each traditional healer's distinct understanding of wellbeing and utilizing inductive analysis that is both recursive and reflexive for the purpose of providing a clearer understanding of traditional Lakota wellbeing.

Participant selection, recruitment and interview

Purposive sampling was used to select as participants for the study traditional Lakota healers with the most experience in the roles of guiding people towards wellbeing. The traditional healers speak the Lakota language, which is the primary purveyor of the cultural understandings necessary to function effectively in the traditional healing role. Thus, in order to be qualified to participate in this study, participants had to be recognized as traditional healers by their respective communities, and they further had to be speakers of the Lakota language.

Due to the ongoing resurgence of Lakota cultural practices, elders who speak Lakota who serve as leaders and healers function today as sources of cultural knowledge. In particular, they have been defined as leaders and healers by their fellow traditional Lakota relatives. Those healers and leaders lead by example and they take care of oneself, family and their communities. Older relatives continually give advice and encouragement, "and they watched that the social system provided respect for relatives. The social system and the political leadership system were intertwined" (Young Bear & Theisz, 1994, p. 121). The healers selected for this study have watched the lead researcher grow and develop and each is considered a relative. Therefore, in a sense, those interviewed provide sufficient cultural and behavioral homogeneity to warrant few respondents.

Procedures

Participants were contacted and interviewed at a mutually agreed upon location at the convenience of the participant. Six interviews were conducted in the interviewees' home while one was conducted inside a house designated only for the purpose of the yuwipi ceremony (i.e. a one room small house with only a wood stove and one window to allow minimal light to enter that is set aside for ceremonial use). All locations were favorable for video-taping. Interviews were conducted at individual locations free of noise, interruptions and without the presence of other individuals. The goal of the interviews was to gain information about the research subject that required the researcher's ability "to form an accepting relationship, skill in active listening, and focus on the other's experiential world" (Polkinghorne, 2005, p. 142).

The interviews were conducted using a semi-structured interview design with three open-ended questions developed prior to the study that were utilized throughout. The interviewees were asked these open-ended questions with follow-up questions used to explore each interviewee's responses further. The follow-up questions thus varied between interviewees based on their interview content. This is consistent with standard practice in that in qualitative research using semi-structured interviews, the researcher probes below the surface to bring forth accounts that are refined, rich descriptions of the phenomenon under study (Polkinghorne, 2005). Participants were interviewed only once, and each interview lasted from 55 to 75 minutes.

The researchers prior work with traditional healers, who developed a Lakota mental health program, gave me valuable experience and insight into working with them. Because one of the authors of this chapter is a member of the Pine Ridge Indian Reservation community, we were able to identify those traditional healers who conduct their rituals in the Lakota language. The healers who were interviewed were (1) A. White Hat, (2) R. Two Dogs, (3) R. Broken Nose, (4) W. Mesteth, (5) R. Stone, (6) A. Looking Horse, and (7) B. Kills Straight.

The interviews were video-recorded, transcribed into Lakota, and then translated into English, which was the primary language used for data analysis. Lyle M. Noisy Hawk, Sr reviewed the accuracy of the translated text from Lakota to English.

Findings

Theme 1: wellbeing is the result of lifelong practice

For traditional Lakota people, wellbeing is a philosophical way of life. Reverence is bestowed to the world because all life and creation possesses the sanctity of its creator (*wakan*), God. Lakota cultural lifeway requires a persistent routine of ongoing evaluation or awareness of thoughts, feelings and actions and the relationships with the outside world. The goal is to live in peaceful equilibrium with the 'self' and its relations to the outside world and with God. Proficient understanding of Lakota teaching, virtues and customs throughout successive life stages is required to live well. Knowledge and wisdom are gleaned from myths, historical and contemporary stories such as accounts of journeys (*ozuye*). The development of character begins from birth and continues throughout the child-rearing years when ongoing counseling and teaching about appropriate conduct are the focus. Coinciding with development are the Lakota customs that occur both secularly and ceremonially that likewise guide individuals along their development throughout the stages of life.

The healers state that wellbeing is continual striving to be mentally and physically healthy through putting back into accord the mind and body thereby becoming content, satisfied and happy. Achieving the state of wellbeing entails enduring suffering, difficulties, adverse experiences and maltreatment through resiliency; quickly recovering from those experiences to become strong, healthy, happy and move forward in life again.

Regarding defining wellbeing (*wicozani*), A. White Hat stated that the "ni" in "zani" (from *wicozani*) means:

> something (*za*) that is alive (*ni*)... a living being that has a spirit and is in living movement... weakened from something... that has come back to life (*zani*)... It is not things you acquired but bringing back to life your thoughts (*nitawacin*) and body and not living sickly...

Theme 2: well-being is attained and maintained through awareness of the sacred (wakan)

According to the healers' interviews in this study, attaining and maintaining wellness means being mindful of one's spirituality or the *wakan*. *Wakan* means potentiality or spiritual potency, which is the power of life. A. White Hat explained what *wakan* means "as related to the creation story". He stated:

> Now this term wakan has the power of life. Wakan can give life or give death. It can create something or take apart something. And whatever is bad and good it is within... so every creation has those three things.

A. White Hat states that Lakota people have historically lived through the concept of *wolakota* or peace and harmony. Through taking care of themselves and where they lived, they prevented anything bad coming into their area. Because of *wolakota*, "they don't want anything bad coming in there, long ago Lakota people lived that way... we didn't want negative energy..."

Theme 3: wellbeing is attained and maintained through healthy relationships

A third theme that arose from interviewing the Lakota healers was that wellbeing is attained and maintained through continuing to have healthy relationships with oneself, family, the tribe and all of creation. How to relate to each of these entities is guided by Lakota values.

Values themselves come from God and are understood and applied according to the situation at hand. As stated by R. Broken Nose, "each value could be taken apart and translated many ways depending on the intended function within a specific context that it is utilized".

According to B. Kills Straight, there are seven values concerning how families and tribes should function together interpersonally. His verbatim comments are summarized in Table 10.1.

The healers stated that to attain and maintain wellbeing, individuals are expected to be aware that they are *quadra-parte* beings whose beings consist of interrelated components (body, spirit, mind, emotions); and that they should critically evaluate the impact of various situations or circumstances on their lives through that lens. An example of this is a statement made by R. Two Dogs, in which he said:

Table 10.1 Lakota values or laws

Woope sakowin (seven laws)		
Wacante Ognanake	Generosity	Someone who is kind-hearted, good minded, good feelings and helps, shares, gives.
Wowaunsila	Compassion	Demonstrated honor, to respect, have compassion for everything around you.
Wowauonihan	Honor, respect	To respect, to honor people and everything.
Wowacintanka	Fortitude	Patience, control of self, tolerance.
Wowahwala	Humility	Conducting oneself in a subtle, delicate manner, to be humble, being happy, honoring, respecting people and everything, compassionate.
Woohitike	Courage/Bravery	Guided through principles, disciplined, brave and courageous.
Woksape	Wisdom	Wisdom and understanding.

> If someone is startled or suddenly encounters a negative experience then it is the spirit that is first distressed by it… if you continue to carry the negative encounter then it will manifest itself in the body or your thoughts, in that manner.

Next, the individual evaluates oneself in relation to the world around. R. Two Dogs explains that four constituents are evaluated first beginning with; how you conduct yourself within yourself. How you evaluate your own self. Another is being with the people around you how you will conduct yourself within that context. And the third one is how you will conduct yourself before the animal nations and those living on this earth, which they call spirits, spiritual entities, how you conduct yourself before them. And the fourth one is your conduct on this earth is being witnessed and therefore known by your relatives who have completed their life on this earth. So, there are four ways of being/conducting oneself but one that has the most power is your own self because you're always with yourself. So that is what the term wellbeing means: "my manner of being/*mi'ohan* is the first, yourself… individually… And how you feel about yourself."

Theme 4: wellbeing is attained and maintained through consistent practice of prayer

Participants identified several ritual and traditions that are connected to attaining and maintaining wellbeing. Those rituals and traditions function to facilitate the establishment and maintenance of all those corporeal and spiritual relationships, including meditation on and prayerful communication with God, Grandmother Earth and the manifestation of God in the four directions and with the ancestors.

The healers specifically discussed how the purification (*inipi*, renewal of oneself), vision quest, sun dance rituals and the *zuye* custom facilitated the process of introspection, self-reflection and prayerful communication to attain a balanced sense of wellbeing.

Participating in purification/renewal ritual (inipi)

The *inipi* is utilized to wake and bring oneself back to life beginning with formulating an understanding of one's self, including identifying strengths and weakness. Each individual utilizes his/her power to understand and assess themselves to take care of their 'self'. For instance, through the ritual and with sincerity, negative thoughts are understood followed by developing a plan to cure that condition. Prayer is made, appealing for aid and grace from all of one's relations and God, thereby addressing those negative thoughts. The process strengthens the individual as life continues (White Hat).

Using the vision quest to guide one's life

The vision quest also functioned as a rite of passage transitioning children to become young adults. After receiving instruction and meaning of the custom, an individual is left alone directed to not eat or drink water for a period up to four days. The individual sits in prayerful contemplation with his/her pipe and with faith to comprehend what he/she had been taught. The purpose of the ritual is to connect meaningfully with God, who through divine intervention will allow one's spirit to understand, acknowledge, and connect with one's relatives or all of creation he/she is surrounded with, thereby cultivating one's faith. In the continual process of generating realizations with divine assistance, the individual will evaluate one's life and begin to realize the task set forth for his/her life, which is to be completed while living on the earth, and he/she will understand life and death (W. Mesteth).

Using the vision quest and the sun dance to make sacrifice for others

An individual may also pledge to undergo the vision quest ritual if they or another suffers from something such as an illness. If through the various healing ceremonies, the suffering or illness has been alleviated or healed, then the vision quest is initiated as a form of payment or to say thank you for the return of one's own or another's health. Similarly, an individual will participate in the sun dance ritual in order to bring health (*zani*), wellbeing (*wicozani*) and life (*wiconi*) for oneself, another, and/or all of creation (White Hat).

Attending to the stories of the elders (ozuye)

Both *ozuye* or stories of journeys long ago and the *zuya* custom or embarking on an adventurous journey also are used to attain and maintain wellbeing. When the group returned home and after a type of cleansing ritual had been performed, the men shared the knowledge acquired along with what they have come to learn, understand, demonstrating that they have engaged in serious thought becoming mature, responsible and strong men (White Hat).

R. Two Dogs states that the term *ozuye* or journey means to encounter a situation and entering into that situation without knowing the outcome with a strong heart. The deeper structure for the term *zuya* means to put the 'other' before oneself (R. Two Dogs).

Theme 5: wellbeing is attained and maintained through successful recovery from traumatic experiences

The healers explained that to attain and maintain wellbeing, individuals need to understand the effect of the relationship of one's mind, body and spirit on one's wellbeing. They state that injury to one's spirit by an adverse experience, traumatic event, being inappropriately treated, or not living well or the good life causes the spirit to move away from its body.

Furthermore, if an individual has an adverse experience(s), traumatic experience(s), or has not put effort into living appropriately, then these instances cause the sprit to move away from the remaining *quadra-parte* being. That being seeks to reunite the spirit by manifesting symptoms outwardly, such as depression, negative feeling/thoughts or relationships, using alcohol and drugs, and suicidal intent, attempt or completion. The detached spirit is reunited by attending to one's emotions through the various rituals. The experiences that led to this detachment may include the commission of an offense toward another spirit, whether living on earth or among the star nation above, which is addressed through a cleansing ritual along with the purification ritual. The goals are to determine the cause of a spirit's detachment and to treat those illnesses that have caused the spirit to detach through rituals, such as calling one's spirit back into their entire self, purification/cleansing ritual or other types of rituals. The traumatic event is acknowledged and dealt with, bringing cathartic relief and recovery from its effects (Two Dogs).

Theme 6: wellbeing is attained and maintained through enacting Lakota values

Two Dogs states that practicing the Lakota laws or values particularly increases fortitude to endure. Such fortitude today has not been fully enacted that tasks in life are not accomplished.

Essentially, he states, not attending to the emotional effects of life struggles through the knowledge of some system to have wellbeing causes maladaptive lifeway patterns, "many of the people do not know… so they would utilize other things maybe alcohol, marijuana, or drugs in such a manner to take care of themselves".

As stated before, rituals and traditions functioned to strengthen the connection or love that ties the individual to the 'other' in order to keep the individual connected to the Eternal or *wakan*. Beauty is experienced both aesthetically and emotionally. For instance, in Lakota ceremonies songs create a vocal harmony, beauty, to which one responds first emotionally through their spirit. It is understood that beginning with the emotions or the spirit the individual begins healing oneself; mind and body. Ritual and customs function by focusing the encounter with the self, the 'other' comprising all creation and God and they function to facilitate the reencounter of traumatic experiences to successfully recover from them. The cultural rituals and mythical stories functioned to establish, cultivate and maintain relationships with the self, people and the all of creation.

Furthermore, the healers understood the mind, body and spiritual conceptual framework in which their patients present and represent their illness and psychological distress, which is grounded in their cultural philosophy of wellbeing and illness (Moodley et al., 2008). The healing processes they utilize rely on guiding individuals to construct meaning through culturally based metaphors rooted in their cultural paradigm, including language, myth, folk knowledge, rituals, customs, song, dance and stories.

Interpretation

Levi-Strauss (1967) and Dow (1986) (in Kirmayer, 2004) explain how the process associated with symbolic interpretation or symbolic representation transforms an individual's bodily experience or structure. Levi-Strauss (in Kirmayer, 2004) contends, "that the transformations of healing involve a symbolic mapping of bodily experience onto a metaphoric space represented in myth and ritual" (p. 36). The structure of ritual and its accompanying connoted account moves the individual seeking healing to a representational space; movement to this space affects personal bodily thoughts and feelings, along with current situation within the community. Building on Levi-Strauss's explanation, Dow (in Kirmayer, 2004) alludes that symbols used in healing stimulate emotions because they map personal problems onto a collective mythological world.

Kirmayer (2004) continues to explain that metaphor theory places abstract interpretation of concepts within the progression of sensory-affective imagery and corporeal activity. Metaphors change and move individual perceptions and representations between the sensory, emotional and abstract conceptual spaces (Kirmayer, 2004). Similarly, healing rituals create and change the illness experience through their context, symbols and symbolic action. Metaphorically, afflicted individuals ascribe a different meaning to their illness experience. "Elaborating implications of the metaphorical representation or the adoption of new metaphors yield new ways of thinking about and experiencing illness" (p. 37).

The effectiveness of traditional healing practices is contingent on the "grounding of symbolic in core values, well-learned and lived daily in local worlds that reflect a coherent and well-integrated social system" (Kirmayer, 2004, p. 44). The healers spoke about living through ethical principles or the Lakota values to have an integrated sense of wellbeing, which consists of having *wolakota* or peace and harmony with all of creation, which possesses a spirit comprising the *wakan* nature, and having a relationship with Taku Wakan (God). Those values are further developed and they are relied upon in the context of rituals and traditions where self-evaluation occurs followed by the (re)establishment and maintenance of relationships. Traditional Lakota hold in high regard their relatives on earth and of the spiritual realm who they petition for aid, forgiveness, and/or thanksgiving including Taku Wakan and its various manifestations.

The traditional healers (*wicasa wakan*) or men who understand the Wakan through having been endowed with the command of the Lakota language and of its spiritual and natural laws/ values, ceremonies and customs have imparted a portion of their uncanny wisdom in relation to the question of what wellbeing means and how it is attained and maintained. For traditional Lakota's, wellbeing (*wicozani*) is a psychological state of being at peace and harmony (*wolakota*) with oneself and with all of creation (*mitakuye oyasin*); the good happy life.

Conclusion

The lack of harmony-wellbeing or lack of success in AI/AN counseling strategies could be improved by more research to discern how AI/AN conceptualize and process cultural determinants of psychological illness and wellness and by incorporating aspects of the traditional Lakota path to wellbeing. Wellbeing for AI/AN could be strengthened by providing a cultural context for healing programs and research that incorporates and emphasizes the importance of language, mythology and ritual. Those components of a culturally specific context mediate the self-identification of the path to healing/wellbeing. The healers have identified wellbeing as the result of living in context with cultural laws, family and the tribe. The application of Western psychology's principles, such as positive psychology into a culturally appropriate counseling paradigm will improve results.

Clearly, much more theoretical research in diverse fields, including cultural anthropology, linguistics, internal medicine and clinical and counseling psychology will be required to gain an accurate picture for the way contemporary Western mental health research can be most effectively applied to AI/AN populations that have preserved traditional cultural frameworks. The conversation must begin somewhere, and we believe that the results of this study along with the review of past research and the additional analysis from future research will show how wellbeing fits in a specific AI/AN worldview that will allow us to move the conversation forward with the intent of creating better, more effective frameworks for treating the mental health challenges experienced by AI/AN peoples.

Acknowledgments

The senior author wishes to extend his deepest gratitude to his dissertation committee at the University of Minnesota, Sheri Turner, Susan Rose, Geoffrey Maruyama, Jeylan Mortimer, and Michael Goh, for their guidance, support, insights and encouragement; Sheri Turner was especially helpful in assisting him with the design of the study and various drafts of his dissertation. He also wants to express his gratitude for the financial support he received from the RUTH LANDES MEMORIAL RESEARCH FUND, a program of The Reed Foundation for the conduct of his research.

References

Alcántara, C., & Gone, J.P. (2007). Reviewing suicide in Native American communities. Situating risk and protective factors within a transactional-ecological framework. *Death Studies, 31*, 457–477.

Beals, J., Manson, S.M., Whitesell, N.R., Spicer, P., Novins, D.K., & Mitchell, C.M. (2005). Prevalence of DSM-IV disorders and attendant help-seeking I 2 American Indian reservation populations. *Archives of General Psychiatry, 62*, 99–108.

Buchwald, D., Beals, J., & Manson, S.M. (2000) Use of traditional health practices among Native Americans in a primary care setting. *Medical Care, 38*, 1191–1199.

Charmaz, K. (1983) The grounded theory method: An explication and interpretation. In R.M. Emerson (Ed.), *Contemporary field research: A collection of readings* (pp. 109–128). Boston, MA: Little, Brown.

Chesler, M.A. (1987). *Professionals' views of the dangers of self-help groups.* Center for Research on Social Organization, Working Paper Series # 345. Retrieved 10 March 2011 from University of Michigan, Center for Research on Social Organization website: http://deepblue.lib.umich.edu/bitstream/2027.42/51113/1/345.pdf.

Cohen, K.B.H. (1998). Native American medicine. *Alternative Therapies, 4*, 45–57.

Dow, J. (1986). Universal aspects of symbolic healing: A theoretical synthesis. *American Anthropologist, 88*, 56–69.

Eaves, Y.D. (2001). A synthesis technique for grounded theory data analysis. *Journal of Advanced Nursing, 35*, 654–663.

Fassinger, R.E. (2005). Paradigms, praxis, problems, and promise: Grounded theory in counseling psychology research. *Journal of Counseling Psychology, 52*, 156–166.

Glaser, B.G. (1978). *Theoretical sensitivity: Advances in the methodology of grounded theory.* Mill Valley, CA: Sociology Press.

Glaser, B.G., & Strauss, A.L. (1967). *The discovery of grounded theory: Strategies for qualitative research.* Chicago, IL: Aldine.

Gone, J.P., & Alcántara, C. (2007). Identifying effective mental health interventions for American Indians and Alaska Natives: A review of the literature. *Cultural Diversity & Ethnic Minority Psychology, 13*, 356–363.

Kim, C., & Kwok, Y. S. (1998). Navajo use of native healers. *Archives of Internal Medicine, 158*, 2245–2249.

Kirmayer, L.J. (2004). The cultural diversity of healing: Meaning, metaphor and mechanism. *British Medical Bulletin, 69*, 33–48.

Levi-Strauss, C. (1967). *Structural anthropology.* New York: Basic Books.

Manson, S.M. (2000). Mental health services for American Indian and Alaska Natives: Need, use, and barriers to effective care. *Canadian Journal of Psychiatry, 45*, 617–626.

Marbella, A.M., Harris, M.C., & Diehr, S. (1998). Use of Native American healers among Native American patients in an urban Native American health center. *Archives of Family Medicine, 7*, 182–185.

Moodley, R., Sutherland, P., & Oulanova, O. (2008). Traditional healing, the body and mind in psychotherapy. *Counseling Psychology Quarterly, 21*, 153–165, 617–626.

Morrow, S.L., & Smith, M.L. (2000). Qualitative research for counseling psychology. In S. Brown & R. Lent (Eds.), *Handbook of counseling psychology* (3rd ed., pp. 199–230). New York: Wiley.

Polkinghorne, D.E. (2005). Language and meaning: Data collection in qualitative research. *Journal of Counseling Psychology, 52*, 137–145.

Ponterotto, J.G. (2005). Qualitative research in counseling psychology: A primer on research paradigms and philosophy of science. *Journal of Counseling Psychology, 52*, 126–136.

Powers, W.K. (1986). *Sacred language: The nature of supernatural discourse in Lakota.* Norman, OK: University of Oklahoma Press.

Strauss, A., & Corbin J. (1990). *Basic of qualitative research: Grounded theory procedures and techniques.* Newbury Park, CA: Sage.

Trimble, J.E., & Clearing-Sky, M. (2009). An historical profile of American Indians and Alaska Natives in psychology. *Cultural Diversity & Ethnic Minority Psychology, 15*, 338–351.

US Census Bureau. (2002). *American Indian and Alaska Native Population: 2000.* Census 2000 Brief. Retrieved 19 August 2009, from www.census.gov/prod/2002pubs/c2kbr01-15.pdf.

Young Bear, S. & Theisz, R.D. (1994). *Standing in the light: A Lakota way of seeing.* Lincoln, NE: University of Nebraska Press.

Walker, J.R. (1917). The sun dance and other ceremonies of the Oglala division of the Teton Dakota. *Anthropological Papers of the American Museum of Natural History, 16*, part 2, 51–221.

11

SOCIOECONOMIC WELLBEING OF THE BASARWA PEOPLE OF BOTSWANA

A forgotten generation

Keitseope Nthomang and Pelotshweu Moepeng

Introduction

The situation of Basarwa in Botswana has attracted much attention over the years, mainly as an underserved population group. Numerous studies have been conducted on Basarwa on a wide range of social and economic issues. History books, academic journal articles and documentaries on their lives have been written, published and widely distributed by professional researchers, including anthropologists, sociologists, human rights activists and development practitioners. The researchers generally find that Basarwa are highly marginalized, suffer from extreme poverty, persecution by more powerful groups and are dependent on government welfare programmes (Hitchcock, 1999; Saugestad, 2001; Taylor, 2000; Nthomang, 2004).

The Basarwa in Botswana, for example those who inhabited the Central Kalahari Game Reserve (CKGR), were forcibly removed by the government of Botswana from their ancestral lands in 1997, 2002 and 2005 and relocated to newly created settlements under the Remote Area Development Programme (RADP). Relocation resulted in the destruction of homes, closure of schools, health posts (first level of primary healthcare in Botswana for settlements with a population of less than 100 people) and the disconnection of water. Currently, Basarwa live in settlements under the RADP where they are not permitted to continue their traditional hunting and gathering lifestyle. Being dislodged from their traditional mode of existence, they now live a life of squalor and boredom. They suffer from alcoholism, malnutrition and chronic diseases such as tuberculosis (TB), human immuno virus (HIV) and acquired immune deficiency syndrome (AIDS). The Botswana government has sought to respond to some of these challenges. For example, in 1977 a programme to deal with the plight of Basarwa was initiated. The RADP was formally adopted in 1978 as a chief strategy for Basarwa development. This initiative recognized that Basarwa (a culturally, ethnically and linguistically distinct group in Botswana) were excluded from developments enjoyed by other citizens and needed assistance with regards to, for example, socioeconomic development.

However, there have been increasing concerns that the RADP has not fully delivered on its mandate to improve the socioeconomic wellbeing of Basarwa. Several evaluation studies (e.g. NORAD, 1986, 1997; Kann, 1990; MLG, 2009) have found that the RADP is ineffective in addressing many of the challenges faced by Basarwa. Hitchcock (1990), for example, blame this on, among other things: (i) lack of material and financial resources; (ii) lack of land rights and access to natural resources and other sources of livelihood; (iii) human resources problems, exacerbated by social prejudice at a variety of levels in government structures; (iv) a top-down, non-consultative and paternalistic approach to development that effectively disempowers its intended beneficiaries at a variety of levels and actively discourage their participation in decision-making processes; and (v) limited government commitment to expand or protect Basarwa land rights and access to natural resources. These challenges, in particular, lack of land rights, access to natural resources and other sources of livelihood, weak leadership, poor governance structures and management capacity have resulted in high levels of poverty and marginalization (Le Roux, 1996; Saugestad, 2001; Taylor, 2000).

To fully understand the above-mentioned issues, this chapter explores in detail the socioeconomic wellbeing of Basarwa in Botswana for the reader. Specifically, we examine programme responses meant to improve their socioeconomic wellbeing. This chapter shares the findings of studies conducted over the years on the socioeconomic wellbeing of Basarwa in Botswana. It provides empirical evidence to demonstrate Basarwa's deteriorating socioeconomic wellbeing in the face of development interventions by government. It argues that the RADP is not the only answer to Basarwa development challenges and that more innovative approaches are required.

Background and context: the Basarwa in Botswana

The Basarwa are recognized by the African Commission on Human and Peoples' Rights (2005) as an Indigenous people. Basarwa also self-identify as Indigenous people in terms of the international understanding of the term (ILO, 1989; IWIGIA, 1999–2000). The population of Basarwa is estimated to be between 50,000 and 60,000 people, which is approximately 3 percent of the country's population. Following Botswana's policy on non-racialism, which de-emphasizes ethnicity, no specific reference is made to people by their ethnic group. As a result, the official population census makes no reference to ethnicity, primarily because of the belief that all Batswana (citizens of Botswana irrespective of their ethnic origin) are Indigenous to Botswana and no Motswana (a citizen of Botswana by birth or naturalization) can claim to be more Indigenous than others.

Traditionally, Basarwa depended on hunting and the gathering of wild animals and plants for their livelihood. Politically, they tended to be nomadic and organized in small groups or bands, therefore generally less centralized than their Tswana (a dominant ethnic group in Botswana who speak Setswana language and after whom the country was named) counterparts. However, under the RADP policy on 'villagization' the situation has changed. Basarwa have become sedentary and many are now assimilated into mainstream Tswana society.

Socioeconomic wellbeing of Basarwa: a brief historical overview

To understand the socioeconomic wellbeing of Basarwa, it is important to briefly reflect on the history of the relationship between Basarwa and dominant Tswana groups. Two critical questions arise. Who are the Basarwa? And what is their relation with Tswana groups? While there are many definitions of Basarwa, the authors have chosen to use Saugestad's (2001) definition. According to Saugestad, Basarwa are culturally different, they have had a tradition of using resources and territories in ways that differ from the social and economic arrangements of the present Batswana. They also perceive themselves as different from the Batswana and define themselves as Indigenous. Like the Bushman, they are considered to be the oldest inhabitants of southern Africa, where they have lived for centuries. The Bushman, San or Basarwa, are the hunter and gatherers Indigenous to southern Africa (Hays, 2002). Their home is the vast expanse of the Kalahari Desert. Historically, they are known as the remnants of Africa's oldest cultural group, genetically the closest surviving people to the original *Homo sapiens*, from which the negroid people of Africa emerged (Tlou & Campbell, 1984).

Historical sources have claimed that Basarwa were the first to inhabit present-day Botswana. By the end of the nineteenth century, they were in control of valuable natural resources such as land and were skilled artists, hunters and gatherers (Wilmsen, 1989). These claims have been supported by archaeological excavation evidence that have identified a number of sites inhabited by Basarwa in the Kalahari dating from AD 700. European travellers, such as William Burchell (1824) and David Livingstone (1858), also provided eyewitness accounts of the Basarwa presence in the Kalahari. This situation changed when Basarwa came into contact with other settler groups (Bantu and European colonialists). The recorded history of contact between Basarwa and the different settler groups in southern Africa indicates that, for centuries, Basarwa were in direct conflict with other groups resulting in their dispossession, dislodgement, enslavement, suppression and exploitation by stronger and more sedentary tribes (see Kuper, 1970; Schapera, 1943; Silberbauer, 1965). Subsequent to this, the socioeconomic situation of Basarwa deteriorated to a point where they now generally live in landless poverty (Perrot, 1999; Ministry of Local Government [MLG], 1978a). There is evidence to suggest that Basarwa are the poorest of the poor in Botswana. This phenomenon has continued to date and manifests itself in what has been referred to as relentless colonialism (Nthomang, 2004; MLG, 1978b).

The RADP and socioeconomic wellbeing of Basarwa, 1978–2016

For many years Botswana's economy was among the world's fastest growing, with real GDP growth averaging 8 percent per annum. As a result of this growth, Botswana has gone from being one of the poorest countries in the world at the time it attained independence in 1966 to become a middle-income country. Despite sustained levels of economic growth and physical development over the past five decades, however, abject poverty, unemployment and inequalities remain high (IMF, 2012; Government of Botswana, 2016). For example, nearly 20 percent of the population live below the poverty datum line (US$1.25 a day) and the distribution of income is seriously skewed, with a very wide gap between the rich and the poor (Statistics Botswana, 2011, 2013; Government of Botswana, 2016). Since independence, the government has initiated development programmes geared towards the elimination of poverty, specifically singling out Basarwa as the target group. The RADP was launched in 1978 to develop what is often referred to as Remote Area Dwellers (RADs), the majority of whom are acknowledged to be Basarwa. The RADP acknowledged that, relative to other population groups, Basarwa were underdeveloped, marginalized and therefore in need of special attention in respect of development assistance (MLG, 1978b).

To this end, the RADP sought to respond directly to the problems the Basarwa face as an ethnic group with a view to improve their socioeconomic wellbeing, livelihoods and quality of life. This is an integrated programme co-ordinated by the Ministry of Local Government, which aimed at assisting all those who live in remote areas far removed from settled villages or urban centres. The government's basic premise is that RADs constitute a socioeconomically marginalized group requiring special development attention. The broad goal of RADP is to promote the social, cultural and economic development of RADs through the establishment of organized settlements, provision of basic social services and allocation of land. Other aspects of the RADP include income-generating activities, access to land, community leadership and active participation, as well as the preservation of Basarwa's unique culture and tradition. Such noble aims could indeed ensure the socioeconomic development of Basarwa.

Realization of the above aims involves settling Basarwa into Tswana-type settlements so that they can live a life comparable to that of other Batswana. The government, in setting up settlement schemes, provide several arguments for this approach. First, it is easier to provide water and social services such as education and health if people are concentrated in one area. Second, settlements are viewed as a means of encouraging Basarwa to settle, develop and promote Indigenous leadership, and integrate into the national economy and society. Third, the settlement approach provides a focal point for targeted economic development assistance, such as the Economic Promotion Fund (EPF) which focuses on promoting income-generating activities such as carpentry, bakery, weaving and other related small businesses (Hitchcock, 1999).

The major advantage of the RADP is that the programme has brought obvious social provisions to most Basarwa settlements. Basarwa have now moved into a more sedentary mode of life, which is no longer based on hunting and gathering but on agriculture and generation of cash income (Nthomang, 2004). To further strengthen the RADP, several initiatives were undertaken by the government in recent years, including the review of the RADP in 2009 and establishment of an RADP Task Force to develop a set of recommendations. The review pointed out many challenges that require affirmative action. The Affirmative Action Framework for Remote Area Communities was launched in 2014. This was yet another government initiative to address the Basarwa problem (Ministry of Local Government and Rural Development [MLG & RD], 2014). While these efforts would ordinarily be commendable, a number of challenges were experienced. These are briefly discussed below.

RADP shortcomings: implications for Basarwa socioeconomic wellbeing

The shortcomings of the RADP programme are extensively documented in the literature on the Basarwa in Botswana (Kann, 1990; NORAD, 1997; Hitchcock, 1999; Nthomang, 2003; Saugestad, 2001; MLG & RD, 2014). To begin, the RADP has existed for almost four decades. During this time, the programme has been evaluated four times. The first evaluation was undertaken by NORAD (1986), followed by Kann (1990), NORAD (1997) and, most recent, Government of Botswana (2009). All of the evaluations concluded that the RADP has greatly disadvantaged Basarwa. The RADP, though successfully implemented in terms of relocating Basarwa from their ancestral lands and settling them as RADs, has had devastating socioeconomic outcomes and impacts. Socioeconomic programmes promoted under RADP which were meant to improve the wellbeing of Basarwa such as education, health, and income-generating projects have not produced the desired results. They have been criticized and blamed for reinforcing, rather than redressing, forms of poverty, deprivation and marginalization of Basarwa. Sedentarization of Basarwa and their integration into the mainstream Tswana way of life, with little regard to their culture and economic wellbeing condemned them to poverty of immense proportions (Nthomang, 2004). According to Saugestad (2001), the design of the RADP as a welfare programme, which provided services and economic undertakings meant to address poverty among Basarwa, has only succeeded in creating social welfare clients at the expense of improved socioeconomic wellbeing and empowerment. This assessment remains valid today as it was four decades ago.

Saugestad's (2001) observations support earlier assertions by Hitchcock (1999), who argued that the RADP has failed to improve quality of life for the Basarwa. First, RADP has the effect of denying Basarwa their ethnic and cultural identity by focusing primarily on the economic aspect of development. Second, RADP assumed that the mainstream model of economic development will work for all groups. Regrettably, this model did not recognize the right of Basarwa to freely determine their political status and pursue economic, social and cultural development of their choosing (Nthomang, 2004). For example, under the RADP, Basarwa were expected to settle and become agro-pastoralists. Since Basarwa were traditionally non agro-pastoralist, this objective predictably failed.

The evidence presented above supports the central theme of this chapter – that implementation of the RADP resulted in a deterioration of the socioeconomic wellbeing of Basarwa. In the same vein, Nthomang (2004) concluded that RADP successes were far outweighed by its failures. The socioeconomic needs of Basarwa were continually undermined, leading to a deterioration of socioeconomic wellbeing. Thus, despite the RADP intervention, both empirical and documentary evidence suggests worsening socioeconomic wellbeing of Basarwa (MLG & RD, 2014; Nthomang, 2003; Bojosi, 2009). Available literature shows that Basarwa have fared badly in all the international human development indices used to measure quality of life. This includes deficiencies in food security, health, education, housing and general socioeconomic wellbeing (Government of Botswana, 2010); BIDPA & World Bank, 2013). These quality of life indicators are briefly discussed below.

Food security

Evidence gleaned from the various official reports suggests that in all the sixty-nine remote area dweller settlements that exist in Botswana, Basarwa communities depend to a large extent on food rations they receive from the government under the RADP and other social protection programmes such as the Destitute Programme. Basarwa are disproportionately poor and experience all of the problems associated with poverty, such as poor nutrition, poor housing and inadequate healthcare. They also depend on *Ipelegeng* (drought relief), government-sponsored agricultural development schemes, and engage in temporary low-paying jobs such as working at the lands and cattle posts owned by dominant Tswana groups (Nthomang, 2003; Ipelegeng Evaluation Report, 2012). Given the lack of employment opportunities and limited opportunities to generate income, Basarwa are left with no choice but to rely on government food handouts and *Ipelegeng*, if available. Thus, the majority of Basarwa settlements are food insecure.

Healthcare

With respect to health, the situation is also concerning. Lack of access to medication places Basarwa at the risk of serious illness or even death. It is important to point out that although Basarwa communities have lived and survived under these conditions for a long time, such standards can no longer be tolerated given high levels of HIV and AIDS, and high rates of maternal and child mortality (MDG Status Report, 2010).

Education

Education for Basarwa has also fared badly. Basarwa children have limited or no access to education. Literacy levels are extremely low. Thus, the majority of Basarwa adults and children are illiterate and very few children can barely read and write because they drop out early from school. The rate of school dropout is very high. According to Mazonde (2002), 88 percent of the non-enrolled children commonly referred to as the 'missing children' are in areas inhabited by Basarwa. He observed that within this sub-group non-enrolment, drop-out, repetition and poor academic performance rates are very high. This has been blamed on a number of factors, including maltreatment by Tswana teachers, corporal punishment, mother tongue (language) issues, lack of funds for equipment, uniforms and other school requirements.

The situation is worsened by debilitating poverty, low regard for education and lack of parental involvement in the education of Basarwa children. Coupled with low value placed on education by Basarwa parents (given their illiteracy), cultural factors that do not promote the value of education and distance from schools conspire to undermine Basarwa education and push many out of the school system. Thus, poor levels of education exclude Basarwa from the realization of their rights and access to services – driving them deeper into poverty and deprivation (Kann et al., 1989; Tshireletso, 1995; Motshabi, 2006).

Similar observations were made by Hitchcock (2000). In describing the educational situation of Basarwa, he gave seven primary reasons, including an emphasis in schools on the dominant Tswana culture; teachers with cultural backgrounds different from the Basarwa, teaching and corporal punishment methods which are contraru to Baarwa culture, the separation of parents from their families, insufficient financial support and the need for parents to have their children working at home. A study conducted by Polelo and Molefe (2006) in primary and junior schools in Basarwa communities on the relationship between drop-out rates, gender and other socioeconomic and cultural processes, concluded that almost all measures taken by government in terms of policy and programmes meant to increase Basarwa access to the education system – like other Batswana such as RADP, provision of hostel accommodation, school uniforms, meals – have not been very successful in achieving set objectives. It was also found that the main causes of school dropout are desertion (57.3%) and teenage pregnancy (31.5%). Although the figures may well have improved since then, evidence, both empirical and anecdotal, still shows continued problems with regards to school dropout and non-enrolment in school among children in Basarwa communities.

Summary of RADP

It is clear from the quality of life indicators briefly discussed above that the objectives of RADP have not been totally achieved. An assessment of the quality of life indicators revealed that most social and economic services provided under the RADP such as infrastructural developments like schools, clinics, hostels, boreholes, small-scale agricultural schemes and income generating projects have hitherto failed to improve their quality of life. Instead, Basarwa's socioeconomic wellbeing continues to deteriorate as reflected by their level of poverty, marginalization and dependency on the government for survival (Nthomang, 2003; MLG & RD, 2014). Failure has been blamed on projects that do not reflect Basarwa's culture, self-identity and way of life as well as their understanding and aspirations for development (Nthomang, 2003). Current programmes implemented under the RADP, not only represent a typical top-down approach to social and economic development, but also involve the imposition of alien economic activities on Basarwa communities, thus worsening or deteriorating socioeconomic wellbeing.

Recent research

In this section we report on a qualitative multi-method research study undertaken in 2000, during the months of January to November, to understand experiences of the RADP – as felt by the Basarwa – and its impact on their socioeconomic wellbeing. Data were collected from

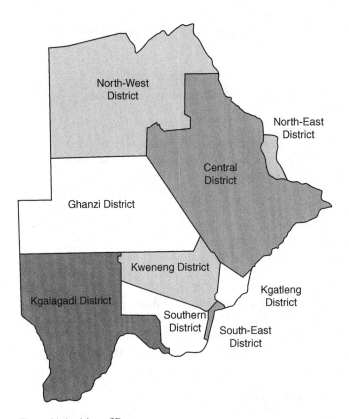

Figure 11.1   Map of Botswana

ninety-seven Basarwa residents in the Kanaku settlement in the southern district of Botswana (see Figure 11.1).

The data collection method involved focus group discussions, in-depth interviews, informal conversations and field observations. Kanaku participants engaged either directly or indirectly in one or more of the four stages of data collection. Focus group discussions, complemented by in-depth interviews, was the primary data collection method. The method was founded on the notion that the Basarwa have a unique knowledge base derived from their personal experiences, understandings and aspirations of development in their communities. Over the course of field-work, the researchers were able to immerse themselves into the lives of Basarwa and develop a detailed understanding of Basarwa development. The method also gave Basarwa the space to articulate their understanding and aspirations of development. Through this process, the researchers were able to draw evidence-based conclusions on the impact of development policies and programmes, in particular, the RADP, on the socioeconomic wellbeing of Basarwa. Qualitative data obtained from fieldwork narratives was analysed and key results are presented and discussed below.

Results

An expression was repeated in almost all the interviews held with residents of Kanaku. This expression characterized everyday life and interactions with Kanaku residents. An expression that signifies poor quality of life among Basarwa is not only unique to the residents of Kanaku but to other Basarwa settlements elsewhere in the country (see for example, Hitchcock, 1990; Saugestad, 2001). The expression is:

> *Hee sodega heri… Hee sodwa ke Bagkhweni le horomente wa bone.*

> We are suffering too much… suffering at the hands of Tswana-speaking groups (Bagkhweni) and their government.

The above expression was repeated almost every day during the ten months of fieldwork. The expression, *hee sodega heri*, therefore appears to have become a symbol of distinctiveness and an expression of the suffering endured by Kanaku residents. Poverty, which seems to affects everyone the same way, is increasing rather than decreasing despite development interventions to address the problem. We observed that food was generally inadequate and, in some cases, not available. Evidently, people were poor and hungry. Children and the elderly were visibly mal-nourished and some people looked older than their biological age.

The level of poverty and suffering is clearly captured in the quotes provided below.

An elderly woman said:

> In the olden days, we had plenty to eat. We hunted and gathered wild fruits and berries and did not depend on government mealie-meal for survival. Our traditional lifestyles have all disappeared and we are now hungry and suffering… *"hee sodega heri"*. We need food. We want to grow our own food because we cannot depend on the government forever.

Similar sentiments were expressed by older men in Kanaku:

> *Re a sotlega… Re sotlwa ke goromente wa lona le badirela puso ba gagwe* [we are suffering too much… suffering at the hands of your government and public officers] we have nothing to eat and we are suffering since we were moved from our land which provided the animals and plants we needed for survival. Life here is nothing but suffering. Life was much better when we lived on our own not under the RADP.

Other residents expressed similar concerns, and linked their suffering to loss of land, culture and self-identity, and the RADP approach to development of their communities:

> You cannot steal our land and put us in matchboxes – called settlements and then deny us hunting and gathering rights. This is killing people because we now depend on mealie-meal provided by government, which only comes once a month. Surely, this is not development. We think government should give us back our land and culture. The government should listen to us. We will tell you the type of development we want and what will work for us. We want development that will recognize us as a different people from Batswana.

Kanaku residents also complained about condescending attitudes displayed by government employees who routinely came to the settlement to provide services:

> They despise us. We have been told many times that we are useless; *jaanong re itlhobogile* [we have given up], to the extent that some of us would refuse to work even for Ipelegeng. Instead, we prefer to wait for food handouts from the social workers. This

is not good… he asked rhetorically… for how long are we going to be dependent on the government?

A Village Development Committee (VDC) member expressed her opinion about the failure of income-generating projects:

I think these projects failed because the government did not have much interest in them. They neglected them and did not motivate people to work hard and educate residents on the importance of such projects and the benefits to be derived. These projects should generate income to sustain our lives.

A focus group discussion with unemployed youth noted:

Government takes the youth for granted. This is clear from the way they conduct themselves. Decisions on various youth programmes are taken without consulting us. Government seems to know everything and wants to fix it all. This is clear from the way they impose programmes without listening to what young people have to say. They have little regard to the views and opinions of the youth.

During an in-depth interview in Kanaku, an official of the RADP summed up the dilemma that many residents in Kanaku and other Basarwa settlements face:

The government is trying its best to provide for the people here but there seems to be disconnect between government intentions and the expectations of the people. Under the RADP, government provide food and other basic needs, including eco-nomic opportunities. People say it is not enough but government expects people to engage in income-generating activities to augment what they get from government. These expectations need to be reconciled for effective delivery of services.

It is clear from the quotes presented above that Basarwa were not happy with development in their settlement. Some of the major concerns expressed revolve around the high failure rate of government programmes. Basarwa's major contention is that projects implemented under the RADP do not take into account their culture and self-identity, and therefore work against their best interests and aspirations for development. A number of factors gleaned from the narratives provided above are instructive; Basarwa's deteriorating socioeconomic wellbeing can be attributed to the following.

Social exclusion

Basarwa encounter greater challenges with respect to lack of access to land, productive resources and entrepreneurial skills. By the government's own admission, and in comparison to Batswana in major villages, Basarwa settlements often lack access to social services and economic oppor-tunities and are, therefore, vulnerable to poverty. Driven into and trapped by poverty they become exposed to systematic exclusion, discrimination and stigmatization which worsens their socioeconomic wellbeing (MLG & RD, 2014). Basarwa's marginality is often exacerbated by location. They inhabit remote and inaccessible areas far away from public services, jobs, markets, roads, transportation and other resources (Thapelo, 2002).

Denial of human rights

Human rights are fundamental to all human beings, including Basarwa. However, given conditions of extreme poverty and marginalization, Basarwa often face considerable interrelated and mutually reinforcing deprivations that prevent them from realizing their human rights. In particular, the right to enjoy basic human needs such as food, education, water and shelter. Denial of human rights often manifests itself in exposure to vulnerability, as associated with ill health, illiteracy, inhuman working conditions and limited access to nutritious food. The result is a vicious cycle of social and economic disadvantage undermining an improvement in socio-economic wellbeing.

Basarwa-centred development: an alternative development framework

Our documentary analysis suggests that the attitude of RADP towards Basarwa development is misguided and wrong. RADP ignores the culture and identity of Basarwa. Basarwa problems and challenges are unique therefore their solutions should be home grown, relevant and appropriate to local conditions. Basarwa-centred development offers Basarwa and the government a unique opportunity to develop and implement alternative solutions that best address the present challenges in the most sustainable way as compared to sourcing solutions from outside and imposing them under the RADP. This approach is an alternative to current approaches and seeks to affirm Basarwa's aspirations for development. The Basarwa-centred development approach recognizes the shortcomings of RADP while building upon its strengths. When well executed, this approach promotes the principle of dialogue, democracy, mutual decision-making and equal benefits. To this end, the proposed approach provides a framework to address, in a more positive way, the shortcomings of RADP and suggests possible ways to make development more meaningful, appropriate, inclusive and responsive to the needs, problems and aspirations of Basarwa (Smith, 1999).

In recommending the adoption of Basarwa-centred development, Le Roux's (1996) definition of people-centred development is useful and consistent with the overall aims of a Basarwa-centred development paradigm. Le Roux strongly advocated for a people-centred development, which is in favour of 'bottom-up' approaches to social development. He asserts that for communities to attain desired development outcomes, the community must be involved in the design, planning and execution of local development processes. A people-centred development is, therefore, appropriate because it recognizes Basarwa's disadvantaged position in society and places them at the centre of development. This represents a departure from the top-down approach, to a holistic development strategy which recognizes the centrality of people in the development processes (Le Roux, 1996). Basarwa-centred development emphasizes the process rather than the outcomes of development and its focus is on personal growth and institutional capacity. It embodies the principles of justice, human rights, empowerment, sustainability and inclusiveness. Thus, the approach acknowledges that people themselves can define what they consider to be improvements in the quality of their lives.

Discussion

This chapter explored the socioeconomic wellbeing of Basarwa in Botswana. Basarwa present socioeconomic wellbeing is a cause for concern. Existing policies and programmes meant to improve Basarwa socioeconomic wellbeing, in particular the RADP, have not effectively responded to some of the pressing socioeconomic challenges facing this population group.

The latest government initiatives such as the Revised Remote Area Development Programme (2009), The Recommendations of the Report of the Task Force on the Review of the Impact of the RADP on Livelihoods of the Remote Area Dwellers (2010) and the Affirmative Action Framework for Remote Area Communities (2014) do not appear to be successful. Within the RADP and, ironically, the Affirmative Action Framework, development experiences and aspirations of Basarwa such as preservation of culture, land rights and self-identity have largely been ignored. Failure to incorporate these important aspects may increase vulnerability and marginalization of Basarwa leading to a deterioration in socioeconomic wellbeing (Hitchcock, 1987; Saugestad, 2001).

It is important to note that the literature is replete with examples of Basarwa as being underdeveloped, abused, neglected, underserved and discriminated against. Furthermore, evidence gleaned from the literature review, in-depth interviews and FGDs shows that Basarwa's socioeconomic wellbeing has deteriorated over the years despite RADP interventions. By the government's own admission, Basarwa communities in all RADP settlements:

> face challenges caused by historical cultural practices, inadequate infrastructural development, low levels of education, unemployment, poverty, malnutrition and inadequate availability of social amenities.
>
> (Government of Botswana, 2014, p. 1)

Evidence from the narratives identifies similar challenges, in particular poverty, inadequate social amenities and lack of economic opportunities. This suggests a deterioration in the socioeconomic wellbeing of Basarwa, despite more than four decades of government development policy and programming (Nthomang, 2003, 2004).

We found that the RADP has brought very few positive results. It is still not achieving the goal of sustainable livelihood of Basarwa (Ministry of Local Government, 2010). It has brought misery as manifested in poverty, lack of food, unemployment, poor healthcare and education, limited economic opportunities and failed income generating projects. All these stand as a symbol of RADP failure to develop Basarwa communities and conspire to undermine Basarwa's socioeconomic wellbeing. As a result, Basarwa remain vulnerable and desperate. Perhaps the most surprising result is that despite the fact that various studies and reviews of the RADP have identified culture and self-identity as an impediment to Basarwa development, the government continues to ignore and deprioritize Basarwa's unique culture in development. Instead of promoting development that is compatible with the traditional structures and cultures of Basarwa, the government promotes mainstream development agendas focusing on outcomes rather than the process of development. A Basarwa-centred development is recommended to address this gap. Future research should focus on the search for, and development of, such frameworks with a view to addressing the present challenges in a sustainable manner.

Final comments and recommendations

Basarwa have a unique culture and, as such, development approaches meant to help them should take this into account. They should be relevant and appropriate. It is argued in this chapter that Basarwa can integrate better in the development process when development policies and programmes recognize them not as objects to be developed but as subjects who are actively involved in development decisions that affect their socioeconomic wellbeing. Their unique cultural disposition, self-identity and skills can be used to foster local development leading to improved socioeconomic wellbeing. Basarwa are more likely to become actively engaged in local development when they are more able to achieve what makes their lives valuable to them (Nthomang, 2003; Le Roux, 1996).

Basarwa's development in Botswana is mortgaged to the RADP. This makes it impossible for them to chart a development approach they consider relevant and appropriate in their contexts. This chapter, therefore, calls for reorientation of current development approaches to Basarwa development. It argues for the adoption of a Basarwa-centred development approach that respects Basarwa as people who are capable of determining their destiny and survival. When their development needs and aspirations are listened to, they can integrate with the rest of the population and participate effectively in national development. The development framework presented in this chapter is a call for the government of Botswana, development agencies, NGOs and society at large to unite and support Basarwa with a view to promoting and improving their socioeconomic wellbeing.

References

African Commission on Human and Peoples' Rights. (2005). *Botswana*. Mission Working Group Indigenous Populations/Communities, Banjul, The Gambia.

Bojosi, K. (2009). *The rights of indigenous peoples in Botswana: Country report of the research project by ILO and the African Commission on Human and Peoples Rights*. Gaborone: Ditshwanelo – Centre for Human Rights.

Botswana Institute for Development Policy Analysis & World Bank (BIDPA & WB). (2013). *Botswana Social Protection Assessment Report*. Gaborone: World Bank & BIDPA.

Government of Botswana. (2009). *Revised Remote Area Development Programme (RADP)*. MLG, Gaborone.

Government of Botswana. (2010). *Botswana Millennium Development Goals*. The Government of Botswana and The United Nations in Botswana.

Government of Botswana. (2014). *Affirmative Action Report 2014*. Minister of Local Government and Rural Development, Gaborone, Botswana.

Government of Botswana. (2016). *Vision 2036*. Gaborone: Government Printer.

Hays, J. (2002). Education and the San of southern Africa: The search for alternatives. In I. Mazonde (Ed.), *Minorities in the millennium: Perspectives from Botswana*. Gaborone: Light Books.

Hitchcock, R. (1987). Anthropological research and Remote Area Development among Botswana Basarwa. In R. Hitchcock, N. Parson, & J. Taylor (Eds.), *Research for development in Botswana: Proceedings of a symposium of the Botswana Society (August 19–21, 1985)*. Gaborone: Botswana Society.

Hitchcock, R.K. (1990). Land reform, ethnicity, and compensation in Botswana. *Cultural Survival Quarterly*, *14*(4), 52–55.

Hitchcock, R. (1999). Resource rights and re-settlement among the San of Botswana. *Cultural Survival Quarterly*, *22*(4), 51–55.

Hitchcock, R. (2000). *Education, language, and cultural rights in Southern Africa*. James E. Smith Midwest Conference on World Affairs, Kearney, University of Nebraska.

International Labour Organization (ILO). (1989). *Convention No. 169: Convention concerning Indigenous and tribal peoples in independent countries*. Geneva: International Labour Office.

International Monetary Fund (IMF). (2012). *Botswana country report no. 12/235*. Washington, DC: IMF.

International Work Group for Indigenous Affairs (IWGIA). (1999–2000). *Indigenous world*. Copenhagen: IWGIA.

Kann, U., Mapolelo, D., & Nleya, P. (1989). *The missing children: Achieving universal basic education in Botswana: The barriers and some suggestions for overcoming them*. Gaborone: National Institute for Research and Documentation.

Kann, U., Hitchcock, R., & Mbere, N. (1990). *Let them talk: A review of the accelerated Remote Area Development Programme*. Gaborone: Ministry of Local Government Lands and Housing/NORAD.

Kuper, A. (1970). *Kalahari village politics*. Cambridge: Cambridge University Press.

Le Roux, B. (1996). *Community-owned development: Exploring and alternative rural development support programme*. Discussion paper, D'Kar, Kuru Development Trust.

Mazonde, I. (2002). *Minorities in the millennium: Perspectives from Botswana*. Gaborone: Lightbooks, Lentswe la Lesedi.

Millennium Development Goals (MDG). (2010). *Botswana status report.* Gaborone: UNDP.

Ministry of Local Government. (1978a). *Remote Area Development Programme.* Gaborone: Ministry of Local Government and Lands.

Ministry of Local Government. (1978b). *Remote Area Development Programme: File No 2/1/1.* Gaborone: Ministry of Local Government and Lands.

Ministry of Local Government. (2009). *Revised Remote Area Development Programme.* Gaborone: Government Printer.

Ministry of Local Government. (2010). *Task force on the review of the impact of the Remote Area Development Programme on the livelihood of Remote Area Dwellers.* Gaborone: Government Printer.

Ministry of Local Government and Rural Development. (2014). *The Affirmative Action for Remote Area Communities.* Gaborone: MLGRD.

Motshabi, K.W. (2006). English language and learning achievement in the Remote Area Dweller Settlement and rural Setswana medium schools in Botswana. *Pula: Journal of Modern African Studies, 20*(34), 18–31.

Nthomang, K. (2003). *Understanding the development experience and aspirations of a Basarwa settlement in Botswana: Failed implementation or relentless colonialism.* Unpublished PhD thesis, Brisbane.

Nthomang, K. (2004). Relentless colonialism: The case of the Remote Area Development Programme (RADP) and the Basarwa in Botswana. *Pula: Journal of Modern African Studies, 42*(3), 415–435.

Nthomang, K. (2012). Basic social services and poverty reduction in Botswana. In O. Selolwane (Eds.), *Poverty reduction and changing policy regimes in Botswana.* London: Palgrave Macmillan/United Nations Institute for Social Development (UNRISD).

Norwegian Ministry of Foreign Affairs. (1986). *NORAD support of the Remote Area Development Programme (RADP) in Botswana. An evaluation report.* Oslo: Chr. Michelsen Institute.

Norwegian Ministry of Foreign Affairs. (1997). *NORAD support of the Remote Area Development Programme (RADP) in Botswana. An evaluation report.* Oslo: Chr. Michelsen Institute.

Perrot, G. (1999). South African San Institute, 1996: A service and support organisation to the San. In V.T. Ruud & O. Oussoren (Eds.), *Report on an Indigenous peoples consultation on empowerment, culture, and spirituality in community development.* Shakawe: Kuru Development Trust and WIMSA.

Polelo, M.M., & Molefe, D.B. (2006). Minorities on the margins: Gendered school drop-out in Remote Area Dweller Settlement schools in Botswana. *Pula: Journal of Modern African Studies, 20*(2), 126–139.

Saugestad, S. (2001). *The inconvenient Indigenous: Remote area development in Botswana, donor assistance, and the first people of the Kalahari.* Stockholm: Nordic Africa Institute.

Schapera, I. (1943). *Native land tenure in Bechunaland Protectorate.* Pretoria: Lovedale.

Silberbauer, G. (1965). *Report to government of Bechunaland on the Bushman survey.* Gaberone: Bechunaland Government.

Smith, L.T. (1999). *Decolonising research methodologies: Research and Indigenous peoples.* London: Zed Books.

Statistics Botswana. (2011). *Botswana population and housing census.* Gaborone: Government Printer.

Statistics Botswana. (2013). *Botswana core welfare indicator survey, 2009/10.* Gaborone: Statistics Botswana.

Taylor, M. (2000). *Life, land and power: Contesting development in northern Botswana.* Unpublished PhD thesis, University of Edinburgh.

Thapelo, T.D. (2002). Markets and social exclusion: postcolony and San deprivation in Botswana. *Pula: Botswana Journal of African Studies, 16*(27), 135–146.

Tlou, T., & Campbell, A. (1984). *History of Botswana.* Gaborone: Macmillan.

Tshireletso, L. (1995). *They are the Government children: School and community relations in remote area dweller (Basarwa) settlements in Kweneng district- Botswana.* Unpublished MeD thesis.

Wilmsen, E.N. (1989). *Land filled with flies: A political economy of the Kalahari.* Chicago, IL: University of Chicago Press.

12

THE COMPARATIVE WELLBEING OF THE NEW ZEALAND MĀORI AND INDIGENOUS AUSTRALIAN POPULATIONS SINCE 2000

Matthew Gray and Boyd Hunter

Introduction

This chapter examines trends in the wellbeing of Indigenous Australians and New Zealand Māori since the year 2000. This comparison is of interest because, despite the many similarities in the design of social security, criminal justice and health system institutions in the two countries, Māori have significant higher levels of wellbeing than Indigenous Australians.[1] Notwithstanding the significant differences in the colonial histories and contemporary economic, social, institutional and political circumstances, comparison of the trends in Māori and Indigenous Australian wellbeing can provide insights into how the wellbeing of the Australian Indigenous population might be improved.

The period since 2000 is also of interest because it covers a period of strong economic growth (until 2007) and then following the Global Financial Crisis (GFC) of 2007–2008, an economic slowdown in both countries (Figure 12.1). There are good reasons for expecting that business cycle fluctuations have a greater impact on the economic position of the Indigenous population than the non-Indigenous population in settler societies such as Australia and New Zealand. For example, Indigenous people are more likely to be marginally attached to the labour force or discouraged workers than other Australians, and are likely to engage with the labour market during periods of sustained national employment growth (Hunter & Gray, 2012). Also, some empirical evidence supports the hypothesis that Indigenous labour market outcomes are adversely affected in period of relatively poor macroeconomic outcomes (e.g. Gray & Hunter, 2016; New Zealand Ministry of Business, Innovation and Employment, 2015; Perry 2016).

The negative economic consequences of economic downturns can have flow-on effects on a range of aspects of wellbeing, including financial hardship, criminal justice outcomes, and mental and physical health (Rehkopf & Buka, 2006; Weatherburn et al., 2008; Cole et al., 2009).[2] The impact of economic downturns on the wellbeing of Indigenous populations has received little research attention; indeed, we could not identify any cross-country comparisons of changes in Indigenous wellbeing over the business cycle. The GFC negatively affected

Figure 12.1 Real gross domestic product (annual average % change), New Zealand and Australia, 2000–2016

Source: Reserve Bank of New Zealand, www.rbnz.govt.nz/statistics/key-graphs/key-graph-real-gdp.

economic growth in New Zealand in the two years after 2009 whereas the Australian economy, while also experiencing a reduction on economic growth, did not enter recession. It is possible that these differences in the macroeconomic circumstances resulted in differential trends in Indigenous wellbeing in the two countries, at least for those indicators that are sensitive to economic factors. If macroeconomic factors affect Indigenous and non-Indigenous wellbeing in a similar manner (and there are no other major changes that impact on Indigenous outcomes), then there should be no observable differences in the trends relative measures of wellbeing in the aftermath of the GFC.

We conceptualize wellbeing as being multifaceted and including economic measures, health and criminal justice outcomes. Although similar information may be available for each country, comparing measures of wellbeing across countries can be challenging because of differences in survey questions and definitions, methods of data collection and the nature of administrative collections, which are used to construct measures of wellbeing (such as incarceration rates). The difficulties are magnified when comparing the wellbeing of Indigenous populations across countries because of differences in how Indigenous status is defined and measured in various statistical collections.

The approach taken in this chapter is to compare the wellbeing of the Indigenous population to that of the non-Indigenous populations. Where there are a sufficient number of observations, the trends in relative wellbeing are presented as a 'line of best fit' to represent longer run trends.[3] This approach was adopted for two reasons. First, by focusing on the ratio of Indigenous to non-Indigenous wellbeing, differences in the underlying wellbeing between countries are controlled for. Second, to the extent to there are subtle changes in the various measures over time within a country, the ratio of Indigenous to non-Indigenous wellbeing is likely to provide a more robust measure of changes in the relative wellbeing of the Indigenous population.[4]

Western and Tomaszewski (2016) distinguish between objective and subjective measures of wellbeing. This chapter focuses on objective measures of wellbeing, which are less likely to be influenced by the social and cultural contexts in the respective countries. The specific measures of wellbeing examined are employment, equivalized household income, psychological distress, incarceration and suicide. These measures have been chosen in part because they capture a range of complementary aspects of wellbeing and in part because they are available in a form that is comparable for both Australia and New Zealand, and across time.

The measures of wellbeing used in this chapter can be interpreted as either an improvement or a worsening in Indigenous wellbeing, depending on the direction of change relative to the respective non-Indigenous populations. We do not consider Indigenous specific measures of wellbeing. Although this might be considered a limitation of our work if we were analysing subjective measures of wellbeing, it is less of an issue for more objective measures where there is more agreement about relevant outcomes or there has been some clinical validation.

The remainder of the chapter describes the measures of Indigenous wellbeing used and identifies the trends in relative wellbeing. The chapter concludes by reflecting briefly on the interpretation of the observed trends. The main conclusion is that, while there is evidence of broader macroeconomic factors affecting the measures of economic wellbeing, such as employment and income, and institutional and policy differences, cultural contexts and other societal factors are probably more important for explaining country-specific difference in other observed trends in wellbeing.

Measures of wellbeing

This section provides an overview of the details of the measures of wellbeing used in this chapter. Māori data are based on self-reported ethnicity by the survey respondents.[5] Indigenous Australians are identified in most official data using the self-report for the Australian Bureau of Statistics (ABS) standard Indigenous identification question: 'Are you of Aboriginal or Torres Strait Islander origin?' This question also allows respondents to report that they are both 'Aboriginal' and 'Torres Strait Islander', if that is how they identify.

The decision needs to be made as to whether to age-standardize the estimates of wellbeing. Age-standardization is particularly important for measures that show a strong age pattern, where there is a different age structure between the groups being compared, or where age structure is changing significantly over the period being considered. It is conventional to age-standardize measures of psychological distress, incarceration and suicide; therefore, we report age-standardized estimates except for incarceration rates because we were unable, with available data, to estimate age-standardized incarceration rates for Māori. As is conventional in the economics literature, employment rates are not age-standardized. However, these estimates are provided only for the working age population. Equivalized household income is not age-standardized because it is a household measure.

Paid employment

Employment rates are reported for the population aged 20–64 years. Those aged 15–19 years are excluded in order to avoid the impact of period of the transition period from secondary school. For Australia, Community Development Employment Program (CDEP) participants are classified as being not employed.[6] The New Zealand estimates are based on census data. The Australian estimates are based on data from the National Aboriginal and Torres Strait Islander

Social Survey (NATSISS), to produce estimates of employment that accurately classifies CDEP participants as being not employed (the census data does not provide good identification of all CDEP participants). The CDEP scheme was replaced with the Remote Jobs and Communities Program (RJCP), which was operating in 2014. RJCP participants are classified as being not-employed. Employment estimates for the total Australian population are used as the measure for the non-Indigenous population. Given that the Indigenous population is only a small proportion of the Australian population, the use of the estimate for the total population will have only a very small effect on the estimates of the ratio of Indigenous to non-Indigenous employment rates.

Equivalized household income

Financial living standards are captured using data on real (adjusted for inflation) equivalized median household income. Equivalized household income is total household income adjusted for differences in living costs for households of different sizes and composition, in order to allow the relative material wellbeing of different households to be compared. For the New Zealand data, the Jensen equivalence scale has been used. For the Australian data, the modified Organisation for Economic Co-operation and Development (OECD) equivalence scale has been used (OECD, n.d.). Perry (2016, p. 192) shows that, for New Zealand, the modified OECD scale and the revised Jensen equivalence scale produce very similar estimates of mean equivalized household incomes.

The New Zealand measure is taken from Perry (2016), who uses Household Economic Survey (various years) data to calculate real median equivalized disposable household income (i.e. after-tax cash income before housing costs are deducted, adjusted for household size and composition) for persons aged 15 years and over.[7] Ethnicity is based upon self-report of the survey respondent.[8] The household's equivalized income is attributed to the individual (Perry, 2016).

The Australian equivalized median household income is very similar and is measured for persons aged 18 years and over. The estimates for New Zealand report the ratio of Māori equivalized median household income to European/Pakeha equivalized median household income. We have not been able to locate published data on Māori to non-Māori equivalized household income. However, this appears to have a relatively small impact on the changes in the ratio of income over time.[9]

The Australian equivalized median household income data are taken from NATSISS and various National Health Surveys. The measure used is real equivalized gross household income, since there is no reliable measure of tax in these surveys to estimate disposable income (Howlett et al., 2016). The estimates for Australia report the ratio of Indigenous to non-Indigenous incomes.

Readers should not attempt to directly compare the levels of the measured household income in Australia and New Zealand. However, we argue that there is substantive information on how Indigenous and Māori households fare relative to other residents in their respective countries.

Psychological distress

Mental health is measured using the Kessler Psychological Distress Scale, which is a non-specific, clinically validated psychological distress scale designed to measure levels of negative emotional states experienced by respondents in the four weeks prior to the interview (Kessler et al., 2002; ABS, 2012). According to responses to the questions, respondents are classified as having 'low', 'moderate', 'high' or 'very high' psychological distress. 'High' or 'very high' psychological distress is an indicator of current psychological distress and may indicate a need for professional help.

In this chapter the measure used is the proportion of the adult population that experience high or very high psychological distress.[10] Data are taken from various editions of the New Zealand Health Survey, NATSISS and ABS National Health surveys. The estimates are age-standardized.

Incarceration

Incarceration rates are the product of the interaction between rates of criminality, policing and the operation of the criminal justice system. Higher rates of imprisonment are an indicator of relatively poor outcomes for a population group. Following convention, we report incarceration as a rate per 100,000 adult population. Data are taken from the New Zealand Department of Corrections Prison facts and statistics (June quarter) data reports and Offender Population Reports, and the ABS publication *Prisoners in Australia* (ABS, various years c).

Suicide

Caution needs to be exercised when comparing suicide rates across countries, because a number of factors affect the recording and classification of suicide. Comparison of the relative rates of suicide between the Indigenous and non-Indigenous population mitigates many of the difficulties associated with cross-country comparisons of suicide rates.

In this chapter, age-standardized suicide rates are presented per 100,000 adult population. Data for New Zealand are sourced from the New Zealand Mortality Collection.[11] A death is only classified as suicide by the coroner following a coronial inquiry. In Australia, data limitations mean that reliable data on suicide rates by Indigenous status are only available for New South Wales, the Northern Territory, Queensland, South Australia and Western Australia (ABS, various years a,b). Data for Victoria, Tasmania and the Australian Capital Territory are not available.

Trends in wellbeing

Employment rates

Figure 12.2 shows the employment to population ratio by Indigenous status for New Zealand and Australia, and Figure 12.3 presents this information as the ratio of the Indigenous to non-Indigenous rate for each country. The key points to take from these figures are as follows:

- The Māori employment rate is substantially higher than that of Indigenous Australians. For example, the employment rate of the working age Māori population was 65 per cent in 2013 and for Indigenous Australians it was 51 per cent in 2014.
- Employment rates for Māori and Indigenous Australians increased substantially before the GFC. The Māori employment rate increased from 63 per cent in 2001 to 69 per cent in 2006, and the Indigenous Australian employment rate increased from 39 per cent to 51 per cent over this period.
- Following the GFC, increases in Indigenous Australian employment rates stalled, and in New Zealand Māori employment rates fell substantially.

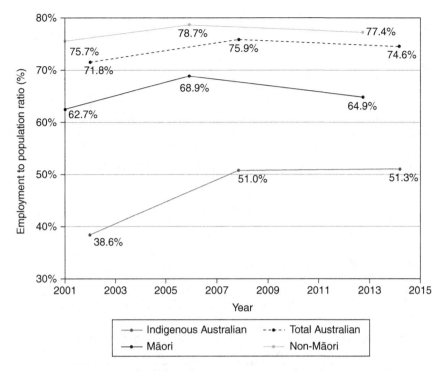

Figure 12.2 Employment to population ratio by Indigenous status, 20–64 years, Australia and New Zealand, 2001–2014

Sources: Estimates for New Zealand use the 2001, 2006 and 2013 censuses. Estimates for Indigenous Australians are from the 2002, 2008 and 2014–2015 National Aboriginal and Torres Strait Islander Social Survey. Estimates for the total Australian population are from the Labour Force Survey for June.

- During the first half of the 2000s, the Māori/non-Māori and Indigenous/non-Indigenous Australian employment gaps narrowed.

Taken together, these trends are suggestive of the importance of macroeconomic conditions for Indigenous Australian and Māori employment rates. The economic slowdown was greater in New Zealand than in Australia (Figure 12.1) and the negative impact on Indigenous employment greater in New Zealand than in Australia.

Median equivalized household income

Figures 12.4 and 12.5 show the median equivalized household incomes since the early 2000s by Indigenous status for New Zealand and Australia, respectively. Figure 12.6 presents the ratio of Indigenous household income to non-Indigenous Australian household income, and of Māori to European/Pakeha household incomes. The key points to take from these figures are as follows:

- Māori and Indigenous Australian households have much lower equivalized household incomes than European/Pakeha and non-Indigenous Australian households. The gap

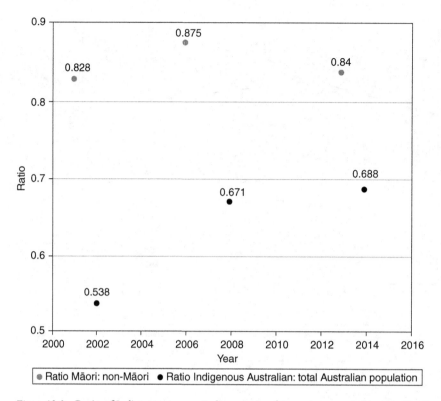

Figure 12.3 Ratio of Indigenous to non-Indigenous employment to population rate, 20–64 years, Australia and New Zealand, 2001–2014

Notes: We argue that 'lines of best fit' are not very useful when there are only three estimates available. Readers can draw lines between the estimates in this figure to get a sense of trends.

Sources: See Figure 12.2.

in household incomes is much larger in Australia than New Zealand; the ratio ranges from 0.70 to 0.81 for New Zealand and 0.54 and 0.64 for Australia.

- Growth in real equivalized household incomes for all groups was quite strong from 2001 to 2015 in New Zealand and Australia, although the increase was larger in New Zealand than in Australia.
- In Australia, the household income gap narrowed slightly between 2002 and 2006, reflecting the strong increases in employment; increased slightly between 2008 and 2012; and then narrowed very substantially between 2012 and 2014–2015 to be 0.64. This increase in the ratio of 0.1 is surprising given that there was not a big increase in Indigenous employment over this period, but it was in the context of falling non-Indigenous household incomes. Indigenous Australians may well be employed in lower paid jobs and thus the potential for falls in equivalized household incomes may be smaller.
- Overall, there is a slight downward trend in the ratio of Māori to European/Pakeha household equivalized incomes, whereas the Australian estimates indicate little or no trend in the equivalized household incomes for Indigenous Australians relative

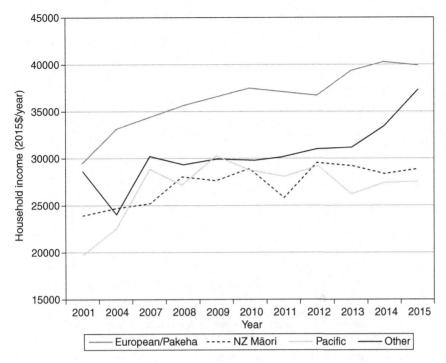

Figure 12.4 Median equivalized household income by Indigenous status, New Zealand, 2001–2015
Notes: Estimates for population aged 15 years and over. The Jensen equivalence scale is used.
Source: Derived from Perry (2016).

to non-Indigenous Australians. These trends in relative income are also broadly consistent with the relatively poor macroeconomic conditions in New Zealand compared to Australia. However, the relationship is weaker than observed in employment data because income is also affected by changes in transfer payments and demographic changes.

Imprisonment rates

Figure 12.7 shows the imprisonment rates for New Zealand and Australia by Indigenous status, and Figure 12.8 shows the ratio or the Māori to non-Māori and Indigenous to non-Indigenous Australian imprisonment rates.[12] The key points to take from these figures are as follows:

- Indigenous Australians have a higher imprisonment rate than Māori and the difference has increased very substantially since the year 2000. In 2000, the imprisonment rate per 100,000 population was 897 for Māori and 1,434 for Indigenous Australians. By 2014, this rate had increased to 2,175 for Indigenous Australians, while the Māori rate had increased to 992.
- In both New Zealand and Australia, the Indigenous imprisonment rate is many times higher than the non-Indigenous imprisonment rate. For Māori, the imprisonment rate declined slightly from around eight times that of non-Māori in 2000 to be about

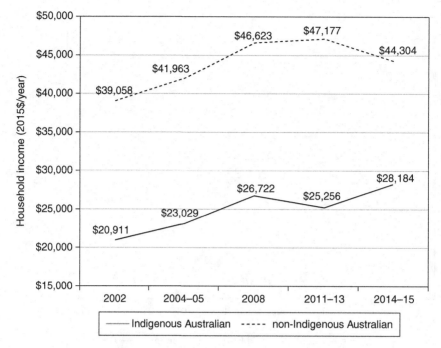

Figure 12.5   Median equivalized household income by Indigenous status, Australia, 2002–2015

Notes: Population aged 18 years and over. Modified Organisation for Economic Co-operation and Development equivalence scale is used.

Sources: Derived from the Steering Committee for the Review of Government Service Provision (2016) based on data from the 2002, 2008 and 2014–2015 National Aboriginal and Torres Strait Islander Social Survey; the 2004–2005 National Aboriginal and Torres Strait Islander Health Survey; the 2012–2013 Australian Aboriginal and Torres Strait Islander Health Survey; the 2002 General Social Survey; the 2004–2005, 2007–2008 and 2014–2015 National Health Survey; and the 2011–2013 Australian Health Survey.

seven times as high in 2014. For Indigenous Australians, the imprisonment rate relative to the rate for the non-Indigenous population is higher than in New Zealand, and increased rapidly over the period from 11.7 times to 15.8 times as high by 2013.

Psychological distress

This section reports the data on rates of psychological distress. For both New Zealand and Australia, data from the Kessler questions are available. Unfortunately, some differences in the implementation of the Kessler questions in the two countries may make the estimates not directly comparable. For this reason, we present only the ratio of Indigenous to non-Indigenous rates of experiencing high or very high psychological distress (Figure 12.9), which, in our judgement, provides a valid cross-country comparisons over time. The key points from Figure 12.9 are as follows:

- Indigenous Australians are much more likely to be experiencing high or very high psychological distress compared to non-Indigenous Australians, and, since 2004, this has become worse.

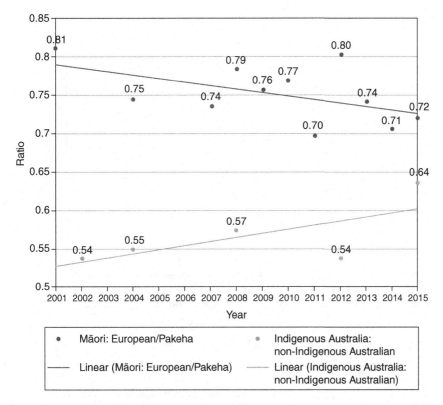

Figure 12.6 Ratio of Indigenous to non-Indigenous equivalized household incomes, Australia and New Zealand, 2001–2015

Notes: See Figures 12.4 and 12.5.

Sources: See Figures 12.4 and 12.5.

- Māori are also more likely to experience high or very high psychological distress than are the non-Māori population, but the difference is smaller than between Indigenous and non-Indigenous Australians. From 2006 to 2014, the difference between Māori and non-Māori rates of experiencing high or very high psychological distress fell.

Suicide rates

Figure 12.10 shows the suicide rate (per 100,000 population) by Indigenous status, and Figure 12.11 shows the ratio of Indigenous to non-Indigenous Australians rates and Māori to non-Māori rates. Because suicide is relatively rare, the suicide rate can vary quite substantially year to year and therefore should be interpreted with caution. The key points from these figures are as follows:

- Indigenous Australians have a substantially higher suicide rate than their non-Indigenous counterparts; the rate has fluctuated between 1.7 times as high in 2003 and 2.7 times as high in 2011.

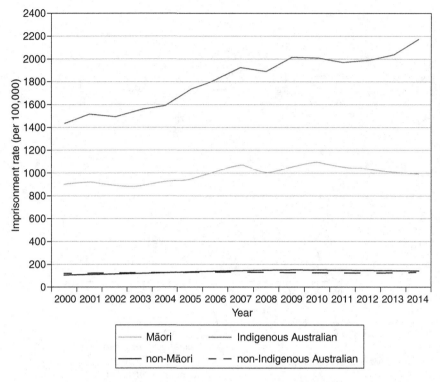

Figure 12.7 Imprisonment rates (per 100,000 adult population) by Indigenous status, Australia and New Zealand, 2000–2014

Sources: New Zealand data are derived from the New Zealand Department of Corrections Prison facts and statistics (June quarter) data reports (www.corrections.govt.nz/resources/research_and_statistics/quarterly_prison_statistics.html), Offender Population Report (www.corrections.govt.nz/resources/research_and_statistics/offender-volumes-report.html), and the estimated resident population from New Zealand Statistics. Australian data are sourced from Steering Committee for the Review of Government Service Provision (2016) and ABS (various years c).

- The Māori suicide rate is also higher than that of the non-Māori population, increasing from close to 1 in 2001 to being 1.5 or more times from 2010.
- Both Māori and Indigenous Australian suicide rates have increased substantially relative to the non-Indigenous populations in the respective countries. These long-run trends are a result of factors that are only affecting Indigenous populations as both non-Māori and non-Indigenous suicide rates have generally declined.

Concluding comments

This chapter has examined the relative wellbeing of Indigenous and non-Indigenous Australians, and Māori and non-Māori New Zealanders using several important measures of wellbeing: employment, income, health and incarceration. Indigenous Australians fare worse relative to the non-Indigenous Australian population than Māori fare relative to the non-Māori population for all the wellbeing measures considered.

However, some improvement for Indigenous Australians was seen in employment and income in absolute terms and relative to the non-Indigenous population, potentially because

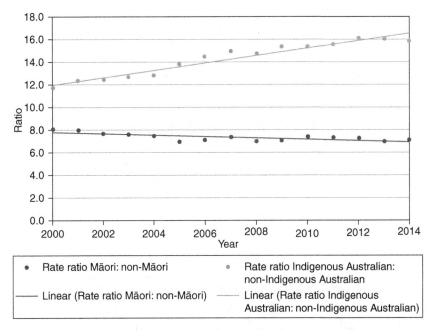

Figure 12.8 Ratio of Indigenous to non-Indigenous imprisonment rates (per 100,000 adult population), 2000–2014

Sources: See Figure 12.7.

the Australian economy was much more robust than the New Zealand economy during the latter part of the period under analysis. For Māori, there were improvements in employment and income relative to the non-Māori population while the economy was growing strongly, and then some relative worsening once economic growth slowed. It appears that macroeconomic factors are affecting these 'economic' measures of wellbeing.

For all other measure of wellbeing measured in this chapter, outcomes for Indigenous Australians have significantly worsened. This is not necessarily the case for Māori, for whom there was some improvement in rates of incarceration and psychological distress relative to non-Māori. However, suicide rates increased for Māori but actually decreased for the non-Māori population. The remarkable increase in Australian Indigenous imprisonment rates, relative to both the rates for non-Indigenous Australians and the New Zealand estimates, may be indicative of a policy failure that requires urgent attention to identify new approaches to address and reverse the trend.

This presents something of a conundrum because, if employment and household incomes are improving, then all else being equal, one might expect this to translate into better outcomes for other wellbeing measures. However, economic factors arguably affect incarceration, psychological distress and suicide indirectly as the resources available to individuals and households do not necessarily affect interactions with the criminal justice system and psychological health.

One possible explanation for the lack of correlation between economic and other wellbeing in Australia is that we have not captured changes in the distribution of economic outcomes across society. There may be substantial groups of Indigenous Australians and Māori who are missing out even when the economic opportunities are enhanced, on average. It appears that in New Zealand there is less tension between the economic and non-economic wellbeing

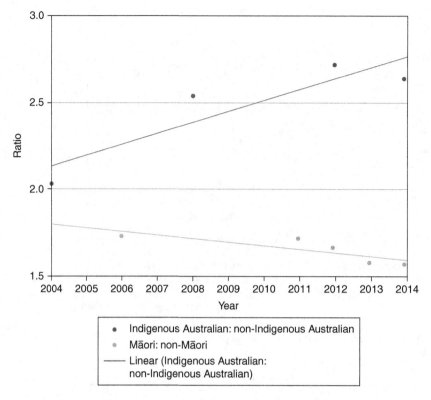

Figure 12.9 Ratio of Indigenous to non-Indigenous high/very high psychological distress rates, adult population, age-standardized, New Zealand and Australia, 2004–2014

Notes: Estimates for New Zealand are for the Kessler 10-item questionnaire (K10) and are for the population aged 14 years and over. Estimates for Australia are from the Kessler K5, which has been specifically developed for the Australian Indigenous population. The Australian estimates are for the population aged 18 years or older, and have been age-standardized to the 2001 Australian estimated resident population.

Sources: Estimates for New Zealand are from New Zealand Ministry of Health (2008, 2012, 2013, 2014, 2015) and are based on the 2006–2007, 2011–2012, 2012–2013, 2013–2014 and 2014–2015 New Zealand Health Survey. Estimates for Australia are from ABS (2014) and ABS (2016), and are based on the 2002, 2008 and 2014–2015 National Aboriginal and Torres Strait Islander Social Survey; the 2012–2013 Australian Aboriginal and Torres Strait Islander Health Survey; the 2001 and 2004–2005 National Health Survey; the 2011–2013 Australian Health Survey; and the 2014–2015 National Health Survey.

outcomes for Māori, because relative incarceration and suicide rates increased when employment and income outcomes declined, especially after the GFC.

Another explanation is that the Australian governments approach to the Indigenous population has increasingly focused on Indigenous people competing in the market economy which means that for those who can (or want to) compete in the market economy do very well, but many of those who do not face falling government benefits as measured relative to market incomes (e.g. Whiteford, 2015) and increasing work requirements for benefit recipients (e.g. Mendes, Katz, & Marston, 2016) result in worsening outcomes for these groups. It appears that in New Zealand there is less tension between the economic and non-economic wellbeing

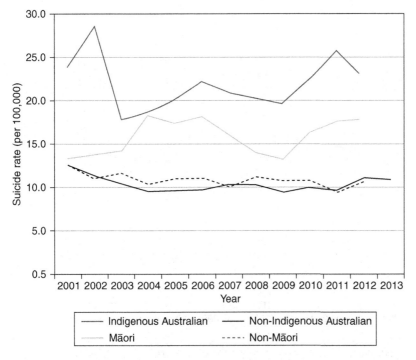

Figure 12.10 Suicide rates (per 100,000 adult population) by Indigenous status, age-standardized, New Zealand and Australia, 2001–2013

Notes: The Australian data are only for New South Wales, the Northern Territory, Queensland, South Australia and Western Australia. Suicide rates by Indigenous status are not available for the Australian Capital Territory, Tasmania or Victoria because of concerns about the data quality of the Indigenous identifier.

Sources: Estimates for New Zealand are from New Zealand Ministry of Health (2016). Estimates for Australia are from ABS (various years a,b).

outcomes for Māori as relative incarceration and suicide rates increased when employment and income outcomes declined, especially after the GFC.

In summary, economic wellbeing can be partially enhanced by addressing broader macro-economic factors. However, institutional differences, cultural contexts and other societal factors are probably more important for explaining country-specific differences in observed trends in other measures of wellbeing. There is no room for complacency among policymakers who need to involve Indigenous peoples in designing policies to address some distressing trends and to identify the groups who are missing out in both growing and stagnant economies.

Acknowledgements

We are grateful to Matthew Manning, Nicholas Biddle, Danielle Venn, Hubert Wu and staff from the Australian Government Department of the Prime Minister and Cabinet for comments on this chapter. The chapter is based upon research funded by the Department of the Prime Minister and Cabinet. The views expressed in it are those of the authors and may not reflect those of the department or the Australian Government. A version of this chapter has been published as a Centre for Aboriginal Economic Policy Research Working Paper.

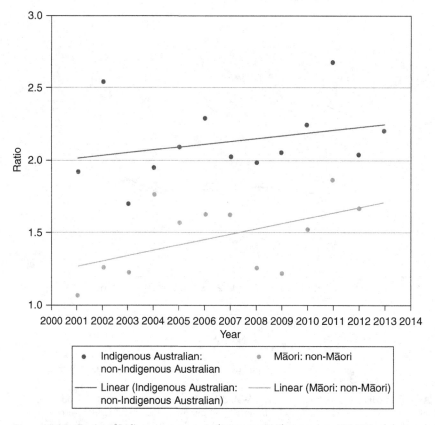

Figure 12.11 Ratio of Indigenous to non-Indigenous suicide rates (per 100,000 adult population), age-standardized, New Zealand and Australia, 2001–2013

Notes: See Figure 12.10.

Sources: See Figure 12.10.

Notes

1 See, for example, Australian Institute of Health and Welfare (2011); Cooke et al. (2007); Hunter and Daly (2013).

2 The correlation of wellbeing with these outcomes is probably strongest for sub-populations and individual-level data. For example, Rehkopf and Buka (2006) present meta-analysis evidence that suicide is inversely correlated with socioeconomic outcomes measured at the macro- or national level; however, more of the correlations between these outcomes are significant when measured at a neighbourhood level.

3 These linear trends or 'lines of best fit' arguably minimize the effect of sampling error in underlying survey/administrative data on observed trends.

4 For example, an earlier study by Borland and Hunter (2000) constructed international measures of arrest and labour market outcomes for Indigenous and non-Indigenous populations in four English-speaking former colonies. However, the substantial differences in the institutional structures meant that the differences in absolute levels were more difficult to interpret than wellbeing indicators measured relative to non-Indigenous populations in their respective countries.

5 If a respondent reports more than one ethnicity, then ethnicity is attributed according to a prioritized classification of Māori, Pacific Islander, Other and then European/Pakeha.

6 The CDEP scheme has been an important institutional feature of the Australian Indigenous labour market over the past three decades (Gray & Hunter, 2011). Recipients are expected to work at least

part-time for their benefit entitlements. However, the reforms since 2008 have meant that CDEP has increasingly become more like the mainstream work-for-the-dole scheme, or even a standard labour market program, than a community development scheme. The number of CDEP participants fell from around 35,000 in 2002–2003 to around 2,200 'grandfathered' participants in 2015 (Hunter, 2016).

7 Median income is a robust summary measure of income that is not sensitive to changes in the extremes of the distribution. If inequality was increasing substantially, then median income trends will be a more reliable measure than the trends in mean income.

8 If a respondent reports more than one ethnicity, then ethnicity is attributed according to a prioritized classification of Māori, Pacific Islander, Other and then European/Pakeha.

9 For example in 2001, the ratio of Māori to European median equivalized household income was 0.813 and the ratio of Māori to the total population median equivalized household income was 0.863. In 2015, the ratio of Māori to European median equivalized household income was 0.722 and the ratio of Māori to the total population equivalized household income was 0.787.

10 There are several versions of the Kessler Psychological Distress Scale. In the New Zealand Health Survey a ten-question version is used (K-10). The Australian Bureau of Statistics (ABS) uses both the K-10 version and a six-question version (K6) and for the National Aboriginal and Torres Strait Islander Health Survey and the National Aboriginal and Torres Strait Islander Social Survey a five-question version is used (K-5). Comparisons of the performance of the K-6 and K-10: K-10 performed marginally better than the K-6 in screening for Composite International Diagnostics Interview (CIDI) and *Diagnostic and statistical manual for mental disorders*, fourth edition (DSM-IV) mood and anxiety disorders. However, the K-6 is preferred in screening for DSM-IV mood or anxiety disorders because of its brevity and consistency across subsamples (Furukawa et al., 2003). The K-5 is a subset of questions derived from the K-10 and there are minor wording changes. For the ABS report, Professor Kessler was consulted and indicated that the K-5 provided a useful measure of psychological distress (ABS, 2012).

11 See www.health.govt.nz/nz-health-statistics/national-collections-and-surveys/collections/mortality-collection.

12 It was not possible, with available data, to estimate age-standardized incarceration rates for Māori, and so non-age-standardized data are reported. However, when the trends in age-standardized Indigenous and non-Indigenous incarceration rates for Australia are examined, the conclusion of a large increase in the relative rate of incarceration holds. Of course, age standardization reduces somewhat the difference in incarceration rates between the Indigenous and non-Indigenous populations.

References

ABS. (2012). *Information paper: Use of the Kessler Psychological Distress Scale in ABS Health Surveys, Australia, 2007–08*. Catalogue No. 4817.0.55.001, ABS, Canberra.

ABS. (2014). *Australian Aboriginal and Torres Strait Islander Health Survey: First Results, Australia, 2012–13*. ABS Catalogue No. 4727.0, ABS, Canberra.

ABS. (2016). *National Aboriginal and Torres Strait Islander Social Survey, Australia, 2014–15*. ABS Catalogue No. 4714.0, ABS, Canberra.

ABS. (various years a). *Suicides, Australia*. Catalogue No. 3309.0, ABS, Canberra.

ABS. (various years b). *Causes of Death, Australia*. Catalogue No. 3303.0, ABS, Canberra.

ABS. (various years c). *Prisoners in Australia*. Catalogue No. 4517.0, ABS, Canberra.

Australian Institute of Health and Welfare. (2011). *Comparing life expectancy of indigenous people in Australia, New Zealand, Canada and the United States: Conceptual, methodological and data issues*. Catalogue No. IHW 47, AIHW, Canberra.

Borland, J., & Hunter, B. (2000). Does crime affect employment status? The case of Indigenous Australians. *Economica*, 67(1), 123–144.

Cole, K., Daly, A., & Mak, A. (2009). Good for the soul: The relationship between work, wellbeing and psychological capital. *Journal of Socio-Economics*, 38(3), 464–474.

Cooke, M., Mitrou, F., Lawrence, D., Guimond, E., & Beavon, D. (2007). Indigenous well-being in four countries: An application of the UNDP's Human Development Index to Indigenous peoples in Australia, Canada, New Zealand and the United States. *BMC International Health and Human Rights*, 7(9). doi:10.1186/1472-698X-7-9.

Furukawa, T.A., Kessler, R.C., Slade, T., & Andrews, G. (2003). The performance of the K6 and K10 screening scales for psychological distress in the Australian National Survey of Mental Health and Well-Being. *Psychological Medicine*, 33, 357–362. doi:10.1017/S0033291702006700.

Gray, M., & Hunter, B. (2011). *Changes in Indigenous labour force status: Establishing employment as a social norm?* Topical Issue 7/2011, Centre for Aboriginal Economic Policy Research, Australian National University, Canberra.

Gray, M., & Hunter, B. (2016). *Indigenous employment after the boom.* CAEPR Topical Issue 1/2016, CAEPR, The Australian National University, Canberra.

Howlett, M., Gray, M., & Hunter, B. (2016). Wages, government payments and other income of Indigenous and non-Indigenous Australians. *Australian Journal of Labour Economics, 19*(2), 53–76.

Hunter, B. (2016). Some statistical context for analysis of CDEP. In K. Jordan (Ed.), *Better than welfare: Work and livelihoods for Indigenous Australians after CDEP.* CAEPR Research Monograph No. 26. Canberra: AUE Press, The Australian National University.

Hunter, B., & Daly, A. (2013). The labour supply of Indigenous Australian females: The effects of fertility and interactions with the justice system. *Journal of Population Research, 30*(1), 1–18.

Hunter, B., & Gray, M. (2012). Indigenous labour supply following a period of strong economic growth. *Australian Journal of Labour Economics, 15*(2), 141–159.

Kessler, R.C., Andrews, G., Colpe, L., Hiripi, E., Mroczek, D.K., Normand, S.L.T., Walters, E.E., & Zaslavsky, A.M. (2002). Short screening scales to monitor population prevalence and trends in non-specific psychological distress. *Psychological Medicine, 32*, 959–976.

Mendes, P., Katz, I.B., & Marston, G. (2016). Introduction for special issue on income management. *Australian Journal of Social Issues, 51*(4), 393–397.

New Zealand Ministry of Business, Innovation and Employment. (2015). *Māori in the labour market.* Wellington: New Zealand Government.

New Zealand Ministry of Health. (2008). *A portrait of health: Key results of the 2006/07 New Zealand Health Survey.* Wellington: Ministry of Health.

New Zealand Ministry of Health. (2012). *The health of New Zealand adults 2011/12: Key findings of the New Zealand Health Survey.* Wellington: Ministry of Health.

New Zealand Ministry of Health. (2013). *Annual update of key results: 2012–13: New Zealand Health Survey.* Wellington: Ministry of Health.

New Zealand Ministry of Health. (2014). *Annual update of key results: 2013/14: New Zealand Health Survey.* Wellington: Ministry of Health.

New Zealand Ministry of Health. (2015). *Annual update of key results: 2014/15: New Zealand Health Survey.* Wellington: Ministry of Health.

New Zealand Ministry of Health. (2016). *Suicide facts: 2014 data.* Wellington: Ministry of Health.

OECD (Organisation for Economic Co-operation and Development). (n.d.). *What are equivalence scales?* Paris: OECD, www.oecd.org/eco/growth/OECD-Note-EquivalenceScales.pdf.

Perry, B. (2016). *Household incomes in New Zealand: Trends in indicators of inequality and hardship 1982 to 2015.* Wellington: Ministry of Social Development.

Rehkopf, D., & Buka, S (2006). The association between suicide and socioeconomic characteristics of geographic areas: A systematic review. *Psychological Medicine, 36*(2), 145–157.

Steering Committee for the Review of Government Service Provision. (2016). *Overcoming Indigenous disadvantage 2016.* Canberra: Productivity Commission.

Weatherburn, D., Snowball, L., & Hunter B. (2008). Predictors of Indigenous arrest: An exploratory study. *Australian and New Zealand Journal of Criminology, 41*(2), 307–322.

Western, M., & Tomaszewski, W. (2016). Subjective wellbeing, objective wellbeing and inequality in Australia. *PLoS ONE, 11*(10), e0163345. doi:10.1371/journal.pone.0163345.

Whiteford, P. (2015). *Adequacy of social security benefits for working age households: A comparative assessment.* Paper presented to the International Conference on Welfare Reform Conference, The Australian National University, Canberra.

PART III

Economic wellbeing

13

ECONOMIC WELLBEING OF CANADA'S INDIGENOUS PEOPLE

Belayet Hossain and Laura Lamb

Introduction

In Canada, as in many countries, the Indigenous population continues to live in an inferior state of economic development and overall wellbeing compared to the non-Indigenous population. While many socioeconomic and institutional factors have been identified as contributing to the wellbeing of Indigenous Canadians, this chapter focuses on the economic wellbeing of Canada's three main Indigenous peoples, the First Nations, the Métis and the Inuit.

According to the OECD (2013), components of economic wellbeing such as income, wealth and consumption are essential to overall wellbeing. Income and wealth determine material living conditions by allowing people to satisfy their consumption needs and to pursue other goals that they deem important. In short, income and wealth enhance peoples' freedom to choose the life they want to live (OECD, 2013). It is common for many countries and organizations to incorporate income into measures of wellbeing (Office of National Statistics UK, 2016; New Economics Foundation: Michealson, Abdallah, Steuer, Thompson, & Marks, 2009), and the United Nation's well-known Human Development Index includes a measure of per capita income. Measures developed specifically to assess the wellbeing of Indigenous communities also incorporate measures of income, such as Beavon and Cooke's (2003) index.[1] At the same time, it is acknowledged that the relationship between income and overall wellbeing is not always direct, particularly when observing wellbeing over time. This is exemplified by the Easterlin Paradox, based on Easterlin's (1995) findings that average happiness levels do not tend to rise over time in spite of substantial increases in per capita income.

To narrow the focus of this chapter, the analysis and discussion restricts itself to the economic wellbeing component of employment income based on the contention that higher employment income is associated with a higher level of wellbeing. In this chapter, we study employment income as a measure of the economic wellbeing of Indigenous peoples in Canada with attention given to explaining differences among the three main groups of Canadian Indigenous peoples, First Nations, Métis and Inuit. Data from the 2012 Aboriginal Peoples Survey (APS) is analysed with an IV-ordered probit model to examine the factors affecting employment income. A set of explanatory variables includes measures of social capital and human capital, assessed via education and health status, as well as other socio-demographic variables.

The focus on employment income suggests a connection between not only income and wellbeing but also labour force participation and wellbeing (Hossain & Lamb, 2014). Employment is one of the most fundamental ways people participate in society, and the basis of self-respect and autonomy, leading to greater life satisfaction (Latif, 2015; Binder & Coad, 2013; Mendelson, 2004).

According to 2011 census data, 1.4 million Canadians self-identify as Aboriginal, or Indigenous, making up approximately 4.3 per cent of the Canadian population. Canada's Indigenous population has grown by 20 per cent between 2006 and 2011, much faster than the non-Indigenous population, which has grown by 5.2 per cent over the same period (Statistics Canada, 2013a). Given the relatively high growth rate of the Indigenous population, the proportion of Indigenous Canadians is expected to continue to rise, thus highlighting the importance of studying Indigenous wellbeing with the intention of providing valuable information for policymakers intent on closing the wellbeing gaps.

Approximately 61 per cent (851,560) of Canada's Indigenous population self-identify as First Nation, the largest component of Canada's Indigenous population. First Nations peoples includes both the Indian peoples registered and not registered under the Indian Act. The Métis comprise close to 32 per cent (451,795) of the Indigenous population and are a people of mixed First Nation and European ancestry. The Inuit, making up 4 per cent (59,445) of the Indigenous population, are Indigenous people of the Arctic, with close to 75 per cent of Canada's Inuit living in fifty-three communities across the northern regions of Canada (Indigenous and Northern Affairs Canada, 2015). The remainder self-identify as either another Indigenous identity or more than one identity (Statistics Canada, 2013a).

This chapter is organized as follows. The next section is a short literature review of the determinants of Indigenous employment income, followed by descriptive statistics on employment income and labour force trends. The empirical analysis of the determinants of employment income of Canada's Indigenous peoples is then explained, followed by a discussion of policy implications. Finally, some concluding comments are made.

Determinants of employment income of Canada's Indigenous peoples

The most common socioeconomic and demographic factors affecting employment income examined in past research on Canada's Indigenous population include educational attainment, marital status, age, gender, children, household size, language, intermarriage, place of residence and parental education (Hossain & Lamb, 2012; Pendakur & Pendakur, 2011; Hull, 2005; Walters, White, & Maxim, 2004; Drost & Richards, 2003; Kuhn & Sweetman, 2002).

Further, Hossain and Lamb (2012) found health status to be a positive significant determinant of employment income for Indigenous Canadians with data from the 2006 Aboriginal Peoples Survey. The human capital literature describes the relevance of including health by explaining its effect on labour productivity and subsequently on earnings (Mankiw & Scarth, 2011; Grossman, 1972).

Past research on the association between social capital and economic outcomes contends that the networks and social relations indicative of social capital are instrumental for labour market success (Grenier & Li Xue, 2009; Matthews, Pendakur, & Young, 2009; Woolcock, 2001). On the macroeconomic level, past research has found positive relationships between social capital and per capita GDP and the growth rate of GDP (Helliwell, 2001). Hossain and Lamb (2012) found social capital to be a positive and significant factor affecting Indigenous employment income with 2006 data.

Statistics on employment income and unemployment trends

To provide context, this section outlines trends in employment income and unemployment rates for Canada's Indigenous and non-Indigenous populations, as well as for the three Indigenous groups over a fifteen-year period based on data from three census years and the 2011 National Household Survey.[2] Figure 13.1 presents trends in median employment income of Indigenous and non-Indigenous Canadians and the three main Indigenous groups. The median incomes of all groups have risen over the fifteen-year period with that of the non-Indigenous population maintaining a clear lead, although the gap has declined from $12,530 in 1996 to $7,427 in 2011. Among Indigenous groups, the Métis have the highest median income rising from $17,513 in 1996 to $28,075 in 2011. For First Nations people, median employment income rose from $15,950 to $22,217 over the fifteen-year period. The Inuit people have the lowest median employment income, rising from $12,753 in 1996 to $19,905 in 2011. In 2010, Wilson and Macdonald estimated that under the current rate of diminishment, the income gap would not be eliminated for another sixty-three years. The social and economic costs of the gap between the Indigenous and non-Indigenous populations are high for Canada.

The unemployment data shown in Figure 13.2 illustrate declining unemployment rates for both the Indigenous and non-Indigenous populations from 1996 to 2006, with a small rise from 2006 to 2011 due to the 2009 financial crisis and subsequent recession. There exists a clear gap between the unemployment rates of Indigenous Canadians and non-Indigenous Canadians with the latter being substantially lower throughout the fifteen-year period. On the positive side, the gap has declined from a 10 per cent spread in 1996 to 8.5 per cent in 2006 and 7.5 per cent in 2011. While the overall unemployment rate rose in Canada, as it did for most countries after the onset of global economic downturn that began in 2008, it rose further and for a longer duration for Canada's Indigenous population than it did for the non-Indigenous population. Within the Indigenous population, the unemployment rate is highest for the Inuit and First Nations peoples and lowest for the Métis. The gap between the Métis and non-Indigenous population has declined the greatest, from 10 per cent in 1996 to 2.9 per cent in 2011. The Inuit unemployment rate has declined the least, likely a factor of the remote economic environment of Canada's northern territories where most Inuit people reside.

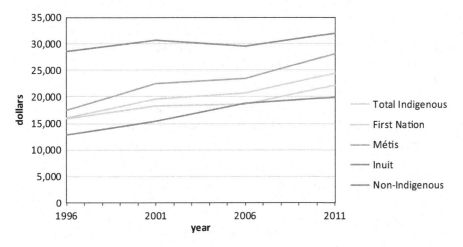

Figure 13.1   Median employment income, by Aboriginal identity (2010 constant $)

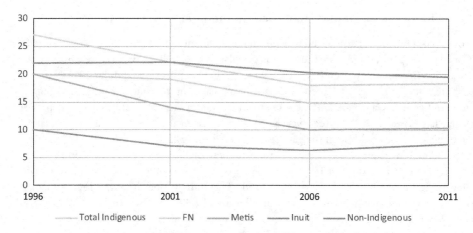

Figure 13.2 Unemployment rate, by Indigenous identity

Exploring the determinants of employment income of Canada's Indigenous peoples

The methodology and results of the econometric analysis of the determinants of employment income of Canada's Indigenous peoples is explained in this section. As discussed in the introduction, employment income is considered an indicator of economic wellbeing, which varies widely among Canada's Indigenous peoples. The analysis is restricted to examining the differences among the three Indigenous groups and not between the Indigenous and non-Indigenous populations.

Methodology

The econometric analysis employs an IV-ordered probit model to explore the factors influencing Indigenous peoples' employment income, which is appropriate given that the dependent variable is measured as an ordinal categorical variable in the survey data (Jang, Park, Chung, & Song, 2010; Kasteridis, Munkin, & Yen, 2010).[3]

Employment income is categorized into the following five levels: (1) no employment income (2) between $1 and $9,999; (3) between $10,000 and $29,999; (4) between $30,000 and $49,999 and (5) $50,000 and above. Let Y_i, the dependent variable, be the level of earned income for respondent i, where

$$Y_i = \begin{cases} 1 \text{ if respondent's employment income is equal to } \$0 \\ 2 \text{ if respondent's employment income is between } \$1 \text{ and } \$9,999 \\ 3 \text{ if respondent's employment income is between } \$10,000 \text{ and } \$29,999 \\ 4 \text{ if respondent's employment income is between } \$30,000 \text{ and } \$49,999 \\ 5 \text{ if respondent's employment income is } \$50,000 \text{ or more} \end{cases} \quad (1)$$

To relate the level of income with the observed explanatory variables, a relationship between a latent variable and the explanatory variables is defined as follows:

$$Y_i^* = X'\beta + \varepsilon \quad (2)$$

where Y_i^* is a latent variable representing unobserved employment income, X is the vector of explanatory variables, β is the vector of parameters to be estimated, and ε is a standard normal residual. The latent variable, Y_i^* relates to the observed level of income Y_i as follows:

$$Y_i = \begin{cases} 1 \text{ if } Y_i^* \le k_1 \\ 2 \text{ if } k_1 < Y_i^* \le k_2 \\ 3 \text{ if } k_2 < Y_i^* \le k_3 \\ 4 \text{ if } k_3 < Y_i^* \le k_4 \\ 5 \text{ if } k_4 < Y_i^* \le \infty \end{cases} \tag{3}$$

where k_1, k_2, k_3, k_4 are estimated threshold points. The probability that a respondent falls into a particular income category is given by

$$\text{Prob } (Y_i = j) = \begin{cases} \text{Prob}\left(X'\beta + \varepsilon \le k_1\right) \text{ if } j = 1 \\ \text{Prob}(k_1 < X'\beta + \varepsilon \le k_2) \text{ if } j = 2 \\ \text{Prob}(k_2 < X'\beta + \varepsilon \le k_3) \text{ if } j = 3 \\ \text{Prob}(k_3 < X'\beta + \varepsilon \le k_4) \text{ if } j = 4 \\ \text{Prob}\left(X'\beta + \varepsilon \le \infty\right) \text{ if } j = 5 \end{cases} \tag{4}$$

where thresholds k_1, k_2, k_3, k_4 are unknown parameters to be estimated by the maximum likelihood method along with β such that all observations are weighted to correct for different sampling probabilities.

Data and explanatory variables

This study uses data from the public use micro-file for the 2012 Aboriginal Peoples Survey (APS), conducted by Statistics Canada during February to July 2012.[4] The Aboriginal Peoples Survey provides data on the social and economic conditions of First Nations people, over the age of 6 years, living off reserve, Métis and Inuit.[5] Only the data for those in the age range of 19 and older are used for the current analysis. After the variables for the model are identified, 14,226 observations are used in the analysis.

The dependent variable, as outlined above, is individual employment income with five ordinal categories, including zero income for those without employment income. The employment income variable measures total individual income received during 2011 as employment and self-employment income including wages and salaries, tips, taxable benefits, research grants, royalties, commissions and gratuities (Statistics Canada, 2013a).

This analysis focuses on assessing the impact of human and social capital, among other variables, on employment income of Indigenous Canadians. As previously mentioned, human capital consists of educational attainment and health status. Four categorical variables are specified to measure the impact of five levels of education (Edu2, Edu3, Edu4 and Edu5), as described in Table 13.1. Following Stephens (2010) and Deschryvere (2005), the status of health is specified using a self-reported index. If a respondent reports good or excellent health, the health variable (Health) is coded 1, if fair or poor health, the variable is coded 0.

An indicator variable is developed to measure social capital (Sock), employing the principal component technique of factor analysis, using responses to three questions about social networks and relations on the APS survey. The questions cover the following aspects of social relations: (i) the strength of family ties; (ii) availability of non-relatives you can turn to for support when in need; and (iii) number of years living in the community.[6]

Other socio-demographic factors that might influence employment income are gender, age, marital status, geographical location and Aboriginal[7]/Indigenous identity. Age can be considered a proxy for work experience. All these factors, except for Indigenous identity, have been examined in previous research (Hossain & Lamb, 2012; Pendakur & Pendakur, 2011; Latif, 2015; Hull, 2005; Walters, White, & Maxim, 2004; Drost & Richards, 2003; Kuhn & Sweetman, 2002). Two categorical variables have been specified to represent the three Indigenous groups (Ai1, Ai2): First Nations, Métis and Inuit. The measurement and description of these variables are presented in Table 13.1.

The econometric problem of endogeneity arises with the health status variable given the possibility of reverse causation between health status and income, which may result in inconsistent estimates of the model (Economou & Theodossious, 2011). For example, those with higher incomes are, on average, more likely to enjoy better health because of their greater ability to attain healthier lifestyles including but not limited to diet. The endogeneity issue is overcome with use of the IV-ordered probit model with three instrument variables. The instruments are smoker status (respondent currently smokes cigarettes), diabetes status (respondent has been told by a healthcare professional that they have diabetes) and obesity status (respondent is obese of type I or II or III). Being diabetic and obese are considered to be appropriate instruments given that Indigenous Canadians appear more likely to be predisposed to diabetes and obesity

Table 13.1 Description and specification of explanatory variables

Variable	Measurement and description
Edu2	If respondent has completed high school then 1; otherwise 0. Default is less than high school.
Edu3	If respondent has some post-secondary then 1; otherwise 0.
Edu4	If respondent has completed post-secondary certificate, diploma or degree (below Bachelor) then 1; otherwise 0.
Edu5	If respondent has bachelor or above Bachelor degree then 1; otherwise 0.
Health	If respondent self-reports good or excellent health then 1; otherwise 0.
Sock	Ranges from −2.445 to 0.9765; continuous variable generated using factor analysis based on strength of family ties, years living in the community and availability of the non-relatives to turn for support.
Gender	If the respondent is male then 1; if female then zero.
Age2	If respondent's age is in the range of 25 to 34 years then 1; otherwise 0. Default is age 19–24.
Age3	If respondent's age is in the range of 35 to 44 years then 1; otherwise 0.
Age4	If respondent's age is in the range of 45 to 54 years then 1; otherwise 0.
Age5	If respondent's age is over 54 years then 1; otherwise 0.
Marital	If respondent is married/living with common law then 1; otherwise 0.
Geo	If respondent resides in CMA then 1; otherwise zero.
Hsmo	If respondent smokes daily then 1; otherwise 0.
Hdib	If respondent has diabetes then 1; otherwise zero.
Hr2	If respondent is obese under class I (high risk) and class II (very high risk) then 1; otherwise 0
Ai1	If Aboriginal single identity is Métis then 1; otherwise 0
Ai2	If Aboriginal single identity is Inuit then 1; otherwise 0

compared to non-Indigenous Canadians (Gionet & Roshanafshar, 2013; University of Ottawa, 2012) and complications related to diabetes and obesity are more frequent among Indigenous Canadians than non-Indigenous Canadians (Public Health Agency of Canada, 2011). Both instruments are valid according to the criteria that they are significantly correlated with the health status variable and are not correlated with the error term of the model outlined above in Equation (4).

Table 13.2 illustrates frequency distributions of all the variables by employment income level. The distribution shows that 29 per cent did not have any earned income, 12 per cent earned between $1 and $9,999, 20 per cent earned between $10,000 and $29,999, 17 per cent earned between $30,000 and 49,999 and 23 per cent earned $50,000 or more. The largest portion of sample members (60%) who did not complete high school earn less than $10,000, while only 10 per cent earn $50,000 or more. Comparatively, only 39 per cent of those who

Table 13.2 Frequency distributions of variables by level of employment income

		Less than $1	$1–9,999	$10,000–29,999	$30,000–49,000	50,000
Total sample		28.61	12.18	20.21	16.52	22.49
Education	< High school	47.28	12.22	19.32	10.80	10.38
	High school	25.37	13.92	23.24	18.24	19.23
	Some post.sec. (non-univ)	22.43	17.37	26.59	16.01	17.60
	Complete post.sec. (non-univ)	18.64	10.02	18.50	22.42	30.42
	Bachelor degree and above	10.63	06.61	14.41	15.51	52.83
Health	Good/excellent	22.40	12.49	21.29	18.34	25.48
	Fair/poor	53.96	10.98	15.83	09.06	10.17
Gender	Male	22.79	09.94	18.85	17.12	31.30
	Female	33.58	14.08	21.37	16.00	14.96
Age	19–24	23.94	26.44	32.79	10.49	06.35
	25–34	21.94	11.99	22.02	20.88	23.16
	35–44	20.52	08.24	16.85	19.69	34.70
	45–54	23.21	06.73	17.72	20.03	32.31
	55+	58.63	06.57	10.61	09.86	14.36
Marital	Married/common law partner	24.93	09.34	17.72	18.17	29.83
	Non-married, widow and divorcee	32.94	15.52	23.14	14.55	13.86
Geolocation	Large urban (CMA)	25.56	10.99	19.94	18.95	24.56
	Small city/rural areas	30.67	12.98	20.40	14.87	21.08
Indigenous single identity	Métis	25.20	10.79	20.21	18.29	25.51
	First Nations	31.50	11.96	20.38	15.41	20.76
	Inuit	30.19	17.09	19.62	14.18	18.92
Social capital	mean	−0.001	−0.134	−0.074	0.052	0.076
	(St. Dev.)	(1.004)	(1.042)	(1.008)	(0.968)	(0.988)

completed high school earn less than $10,000 and close to 20 per cent earn more than $50,000. The frequency statistics show that 30 per cent and 53 per cent of those who have completed non-university post-secondary and university, respectively, earn at least $50,000. Over 25 per cent of sample members reporting good or excellent health earn over $50,000 while almost 65 per cent of those reporting fair or poor health earn less than $10,000. The distribution of earnings by social capital shows that the level of earned income increases systematically with the increase in the mean of the social capital index. Refer to Table 13.2 for frequency statistics of the other socio-demographic variables.

Results

Overall, the specifications of the model are robust, as evidenced by the Wald statistic. The IV-ordered probit estimates, reported in Table 13.3, suggest that all explanatory variables are statistically significant at the 5 per cent level. The estimated threshold values, k_1 to k_4, indicate that the probabilities of earning income in each of the five categories approximately matches the percentage distribution of frequencies in Table 13.2.[8]

The marginal effects of the estimates of the five income groups are presented in Table 13.4.[9] The results indicate that human capital, measured by educational attainment and health status,

Table 13.3 IV-ordered probit estimates of Indigenous employment income

Variables	Coefficient	Robust St. Error	Z-value	P|Z|
Human capital				
Edu2	0.397	0.049	8.07	0.000
Edu3	0.425	0.051	8.37	0.000
Edu4	0.675	0.045	15.08	0.000
Edu5	1.181	0.070	16.92	0.000
Health	0.937	0.111	8.48	0.000
Social capital	0.049	0.016	3.08	0.002
Socio-demographic				
Gender	0.578	0.032	17.86	0.000
Age2	0.238	0.042	5.73	0.000
Age3	0.457	0.044	10.41	0.000
Age4	0.471	0.051	9.31	0.000
Age5	−0.305	0.055	−5.55	0.000
Marital	0.237	0.034	6.94	0.000
Geo	0.112	0.032	3.47	0.001
Ai1	0.145	0.033	4.41	0.000
Ai2	0.111	0.046	2.43	0.015
Thresholds				
k1	1.247	0.097	12.82	0.000
k2	1.595	0.097	16.48	0.000
k3	2.204	0.096	22.97	0.000
k4	2.813	0.097	28.97	0.000
Summary statistics				
Log likelihood at zero	−1158125.7			
Log likelihood at conv.	−1157851.4			
Wald statistic	1708.20			

Table 13.4 Marginal effects of estimates of Indigenous employment income

	Less than $1	$1–9,999	$10,000–29,999	$30,000–49,999	$50,000 and over
Human capital					
Edu2	−0.105	−0.014	−0.004	0.023	0.100
	(0.013)	(0.002)	(0.001)	(0.003)	(0.012)
Edu3	−0.113	−0.015	−0.005	0.024	0.108
	(0.013)	(0.002)	(0.001)	(0.003)	(0.013)
Edu4	−0.179	−0.023	−0.007	0.039	0.171
	(0.012)	(0.002)	(0.002)	(0.004)	(0.011)
Edu5	−0.314	−0.040	−0.013	0.067	0.300
	(0.019)	(0.003)	(0.003)	(0.006)	(0.017)
Health	−0.249	−0.032	−0.010	0.053	0.238
	(0.026)	(0.004)	(0.003)	(0.004)	(0.029)
Social capital	−0.013	−0.002	−0.0005	0.003	0.013
	(0.004)	(0.0005)	(0.0002)	(0.001)	(0.004)
Socio-demographic					
Gender	−0.154	−0.020	−0.006	0.033	0.147
	(0.009)	(0.001)	(0.002)	(0.003)	(0.008)
Age2	−0.063	−0.008	−0.003	0.014	0.060
	(0.011)	(0.002)	(0.001)	(0.003)	(0.011)
Age3	−0.121	−0.016	−0.005	0.026	0.116
	(0.012)	(0.002)	(0.001)	(0.003)	(0.011)
Age4	−0.125	−0.016	−0.005	0.027	0.120
	(0.013)	(0.002)	(0.001)	(0.003)	(0.013)
Age5	0.081	0.010	0.003	−0.017	−0.077
	(0.015)	(0.002)	(0.001)	(0.003)	(0.014)
Marital	−0.063	−0.008	−0.003	0.014	0.060
	(0.009)	(0.001)	(0.001)	(0.002)	(0.009)
Geo	−0.030	−0.004	−0.001	0.006	0.029
	(0.009)	(0.001)	(0.0005)	(0.002)	(0.008)
Ai1	−0.039	−0.005	−0.002	0.008	0.037
	(0.009)	(0.001)	(0.0005)	(0.002)	(0.008)
Ai2	−0.029	−0.004	−0.001	0.006	0.028
	(0.012)	(0.002)	(0.0005)	(0.003)	(0.012)

significantly impacts the employment income of the Canadian Indigenous population. The marginal effects of all five education variables are negative for the first three income groups (up to $29,999) and positive for the last two income groups ($30,000 and over). The signs indicate that respondents with a minimum of high school completion are more likely to earn income of $30,000 or greater and less likely to earn income less than $30,000 compared to those who have not completed high school. The magnitude of the marginal effect for each level of education increases with income level, suggesting that each additional level of education increases the probability of earning $30,000 or greater.

Completion of high school education (Edu2) increases the marginal effect from -0.105 in the lowest income category to 0.10 in the highest income category. That is, sample members with high school education are 11 per cent less likely to earn no income, and are 10 per cent more likely to earn $50,000 or greater compared to those who did not complete high school.

For completion of university education (Edu5), the marginal effect increases from -0.31 for the lowest income category to 0.3 for the highest income category, suggesting that the completion of university decreases the probability of earning zero income by 31 per cent and increases the probability of earning at least $50,000 by 30 per cent, compared to a sample member without high school. The results imply that completion of university education (Edu5) is the most financially rewarding, followed by the completion of non-university post-secondary education (Edu4).

The results suggest a positive relationship between health status and employment income. Sample members reporting excellent or good health are more likely to earn higher levels of employment income. The marginal effect of health status implies that those with excellent or good health have a 25 per cent lower probability of earning zero income than those with fair to poor health. On the other hand, sample members with good or excellent health have a 24 per cent higher probability of earning $50,000 or greater, compared to those with fair to poor health.

The marginal effects of social capital suggest that it has a significant and positive effect on employment income. Marginal effect estimates indicate that the likelihood of earning $50,000 or more increases by 1 per cent for every unit increase in the social capital index.

The results imply that most of the socioeconomic and demographic variables included in the model significantly impact the employment earnings of Canada's Indigenous peoples. Male sample members are less likely to be in the lower three income groups (<$29,000) and are more likely to be in the two highest income groups (≥$30,000) compared to female respondents. For example, males have a 15 per cent higher expected probability of earning $50,000 or greater than females.

The marginal effects of age imply that it has a significant impact on employment income. The marginal effects of those in the age brackets of 25 to 34 (Age2), 35 to 44 (Age3), and 45 to 54 (Age4) are negative for the three lower income groups and positive for the two higher income groups. The signs are reversed for sample members over the age of 54 (Age5), who include retirees without earned income. The results suggest that those in the age range of 24 and 54 are less likely to have employment income under $30,000 and more likely to have employment income of at least $30,000, compared to the younger age range of 19 to 24. On the other hand, respondents over the age of 54 years are less likely to earn $50,000 and over. The marginal effects of Age3 and Age4 are the greatest for the income category of $50,000 and over, implying that people in these age groups have the highest expected probability of earning at least $50,000. For instance, sample members in the age range of 35 to 44 have a 12 per cent higher likelihood of earning at least $50,000 compared to those in the 19 and 24 year range. It may be the case that those in the age group 35 to 44 have more work experience leading to higher earnings.

Those who are married, or living common law, have a higher probability of earning at least $50,000 compared to those who are not married. The marginal effects of Indigenous identity show that being Métis and Inuit increases the likelihood of having higher earned income compared to First Nations. For example, the probability earning $50,000 or more is close to 4 per cent higher for the Métis compared to First Nations. Likewise, it is almost 3 per cent higher for Inuit compared to that of First Nations. The estimated marginal effects of the geographical variables imply that living in a large urban centre (census metropolitan areas) increases the likelihood of earning at least $50,000 compared to living in a rural area or a small city (Geo).

In sum, completion of at least a bachelor's degree has the largest statistically significant marginal impact on employment income, followed by good health. Social capital has a statistically significant positive but small marginal impact on employment income.

Discussion and policy implications

The results provide support for the contention that Canada's Indigenous peoples with higher levels of human capital, as indicated by educational attainment and good health status, and a higher level of social capital, are more likely to earn higher employment income. The importance of education as a determinant of employment income is reinforced by the current results and is in line with findings reported in past research on the Canadian Indigenous population, as well as the general employment income literature (Hossain & Lamb, 2012; Pendakur & Pendakur, 2011; Mendelson, 2004; Hull, 2005; Walters et al., 2004).

The inclusion of health status and social capital have only recently been considered as determinants of Indigenous employment income with the first results reported by Hossain and Lamb (2012), who found both factors to have positive and significant effects. The results imply that Indigenous people with good health are more likely to earn higher incomes than those with poor health. In the context of economic theory, the link between health and earnings may be explained by the causation between labour productivity and wages.

The positive and statistically significant results for the social capital index confirm previous results found by Hossain and Lamb (2012). However, the relationship between social capital and employment income requires further analysis due to the challenges involved in measuring social capital with the limited availability of appropriate variables in the APS 2012 data. Similar results were reported by Hossain and Lamb (2012) using APS 2006 data, with responses to three questions about the availability of someone to ask for advice, to confide in, to listen when you need to talk; similar but different from the measures used in the current analysis.

The analysis reveals differences in economic wellbeing among the three groups of Canadian Indigenous peoples. When other relevant variables, such as education, health and social capital are controlled for, self-identification as Métis suggests greater economic wellbeing compared to First Nations. This result is not surprising given that Métis people generally have a higher degree of interaction with the non-Indigenous population, by nature of their mixed ancestry. The Inuit also appear to have a higher level of economic wellbeing than the First Nations people, measured by employment income. This result for Inuit status is contrary to the descriptive data shown in Figure 13.1 where median employment income for First Nations people is greater than for Inuit people. However, the median employment income data illustrated in the figure does not control for the other variables such as education. For instance, when education is considered, only 55 per cent of the Inuit sample have a minimum of high school completion compared to 70 per cent of the First Nation sample. Thus, the difference in educational attainment levels may explain the difference between the median incomes in Figure 13.1. In addition, it is vital to point out that the cost of living for most Inuit people, who mainly reside in remote northern communities, is much higher than for most First Nations and Métis peoples who mainly reside in cities. As a result, a higher employment income is required for an Inuit person living in a northern remote community than for a First Nations or Métis person living in a city to maintain the same level of consumption or economic wellbeing.

It is important for policymakers to be cognizant of the differences among Canada's Indigenous peoples in terms of their state of economic wellbeing reflecting different needs. It is noteworthy to mention that the First Nations people, who appear to have the lowest level of economic wellbeing, are the largest group making up 61 per cent of Canada's Indigenous population.

The results suggest that future policy development aimed at improving the economic wellbeing of Indigenous Canadians should include initiatives to increase social capital and good health as well as further initiatives to increase levels of educational attainment. While it is acknowledged that improvement in health outcomes has already been identified as a policy objective for Indigenous Canadians, the link between health and employment income has only very recently been identified. Thus, there may now be an additional reason to devote resources to programs for improving health outcomes.

In regard to education, the gap between Indigenous and non-Indigenous attainment levels has fallen overtime, but unfortunately still persists. The most recent data reports that 48 per cent of Indigenous people had a postsecondary credential compared to 65 per cent for non-Indigenous Canadians (Statistics Canada, 2013b). This persistent, albeit decreasing, gap reveals the need for further policy initiatives targeted at increasing education levels.

Social capital is not a clearly defined or understood concept as there is no universally accepted definition, thus policy development towards this goal is somewhat nebulous. Social capital in the current analysis represents networks and social relations, suggesting that any policy designed to increase the quantity and quality of such networks and social relations may have a positive impact on economic wellbeing. For instance, a greater degree of inclusion and interaction between the Indigenous population and the non-Indigenous population may lead to higher levels of social capital, leading to the creation of networks and social relations necessary to improve economic welling being indicators such as employment earnings.

There are four main limitations to the results of the analysis that need to be mentioned. The first is that only those living outside of First Nations reserves are included in the sample of the Aboriginal Peoples Survey. It is expected that those First Nations People living on reserve will have different experiences and levels of economic wellbeing, which must be considered when interpreting the results. Second, it is acknowledged that panel data is more appropriate to examine the factors affecting employment income, but unfortunately no such data exists for Canada's Indigenous population. Third, other variables such as intermarriage and remoteness of residence may be relevant but are not available in the current dataset. Fourth, employment income has not been adjusted to compensate for differences in costs of living due to geographical location because of a lack of required data.

Final comments

The analysis in this chapter reveals that both human and social capital play a significant role in explaining differences in employment income among Canada's Indigenous peoples. Given that employment income, as a measure of wellbeing, is lower for Canada's Indigenous peoples than for the non-Indigenous population, the results provide valuable information for policymakers intent on closing the wellbeing gaps. In addition, Canada's Indigenous population is relatively fast growing compared to the non-Indigenous population (Statistics Canada, 2013a), highlighting the need to address the discrepancy in a timely fashion.

The subject of Indigenous wellbeing is far from an isolated issue affecting only a fraction of Canada's population. Improving the wellbeing of Canada's Indigenous peoples will not only benefit the Indigenous population, but will improve the wellbeing of all Canadians. For instance, two of Canada's major economic challenges include mediocre labour productivity growth (Conference Board of Canada, 2016) and slow labour force growth (Reza & Sarker, 2015). Improvements in Indigenous health, education and social capital measures will lead to greater participation in the labour force, a more skilled labour force and higher employment income. Thus, increasing the economic wellbeing of Indigenous Canadians will contribute to a stronger and healthier Canadian economy.

Notes

1 The other four indicators are education, labour force participation and employment rates, housing and life expectancy.
2 When comparing estimates of education and employment income from the 1996, 2001 and 2006 Census long forms with the 2011 National Household Survey, take into account that the two sources represent different populations (Statistics Canada, 2012, 2014, 2015, 2016). Whereas census long-form data includes usual residents in collective dwellings and persons living abroad, the NHS excludes them. In addition, the NHS is a voluntary survey and thus the estimates are subject to potentially higher response rate error than the estimates derived from the Census long-forms (Statistics Canada, 2013). Also, note that Statistics Canada acknowledges that survey data for Canada's Aboriginal population are incomplete as many reserves are not included or refuse to participate.
3 The ordered logit model is also suitable for analysing ordered categorical dependent variable. The ordered logit and probit models differ in their assumptions about the distribution of errors, such that the ordered logit model uses a logistic distribution while the ordered probit uses a standard normal distribution.
4 The sample for the Aboriginal Peoples Survey is drawn from the 2011 National Household Survey (NHS) according to those reporting Aboriginal ancestry. The public use micro-file, used for this study, contains 377 variables, providing data from various sections of the APS questionnaires.
5 In Canada, Indigenous or Aboriginal people consist of First Nations, Inuit and Métis peoples.
6 Endogeneity could potentially be a problem with social capital because those with stronger social capital are generally better networked and more able to find jobs paying higher salaries. However, the method used to measure social capital in this study addresses the social relations aspect of social capital rather than the extent of networks, thus it is not considered a serious problem.
7 Statistics Canada uses the term Aboriginal rather than Indigenous.
8 The probabilities of earning income in each of the five categories can be calculated using the estimated threshold values and the cumulative normal distribution function, as per the methodology set out in Yang and Raehsler (2005).
9 Note that the marginal effects for each variable sum to zero, by definition, across the five income categories.

References

Beavon, D., & Cooke, M. (2003). An application of the United Nations Human Development Index to registered Indians in Canada. In J. White, D. Beavon, & P. Maxim (Eds), *Aboriginal conditions* (pp. 201–221). Vancouver: UBC Press.

Conference Board of Canada. (2016). *How Canada performs*. Retrieved from www.conferenceboard.ca/hcp/details/economy/measuring-productivity-canada.aspx.

Deschryvere, M.K. (2005). *Health and retirement decisions: An update of the literature*. ENEPRI Research Report 6, Social Science Research Network.

Binder, M., & Coad, A. (2013). Life satisfaction and self-employment: A matching approach. *Small Business Economics, 40*(4), 1009–1033.

Drost, H., & Richards, J. (2003). *Income on – and off-reserve: How Aboriginals are faring*. C.D. Howe Institute, No. 175, ISSN 8001–824.

Easterlin, R.A. (1995). Will raising the incomes of all increase the happiness of all? *Journal of Economic Behavior & Organization, 27*(1), 35–47.

Economou, A., & Theodossiou, I. (2011). Poor and sick: Estimating the relationship between household income and health. *Review of Income and Wealth, 57*(3), 395–411.

Gionet, L., & Roshanafshar, S. (2013). *Select health indicators of First Nations people living off reserve, Métis and Inuit*. Ottawa: Statistics Canada.

Grenier, G., & Li Xue (2009). *Duration of access of Canadian immigrants to the first job in intended occupation*. University of Ottawa, Department of Economics, Working Papers: 0908E.

Grossman, M. (1972). On the concept of health capital and the demand for health. *Journal of Political Economy, 80*(2), 223–255.

Helliwell, J. (2001). Social capital, the economy and well-being. *The Review of Economic Performance and Social Progress, 1*(1), 43–60.

Hossain, B., & Lamb, L. (2012). The impact of human and social capital on Aboriginal employment income in Canada. *Economic Papers: A Journal of Applied Economics and Policy, 31*(4), 440–450.

Hossain, B., & Lamb, L. (2014). Aboriginal labour force participation in Canada: Consideration of a broader definition of capital. *Journal of International Business and Economics, 14*(3), 7–18.

Hull, J. (2005). *Post-secondary education and labour market outcomes Canada, 2001.* Ottawa: Minister of Indian Affairs and Northern Development.

Indigenous and Northern Affairs Canada. (2015). *Aboriginal peoples and communities.* Retrieved from www.aadnc-aandc.gc.ca/eng/1100100013785/1304467449155.

Jang, Kitae, Park, S.H., Chung, S. and Song, K.H. (2010). *Influential factors on level of injury in pedestrian crashes: Applications of ordered probit model with robust standard errors.* UC Berkeley, Safe Transport Research & Education Centre, Institute of Transportation Studies.

Kasteridis, P., Munkin, M.K., & Yen, S. (2010). Demand for cigarettes: A mixed binary-ordered probit approach. *Applied Economics, 42*(4), 413–426.

Kuhn, P., & Sweetman, A. (2002). Aboriginals as unwilling immigrants: Contact, assimilation and labour market outcomes. *Journal of Population Economics, 15*(2), 331–355.

Latif, E. (2015). Happiness and comparison income: Evidence from Canada. *Social Indicators Research, 128*(1), 161–177.

Mankiw, N.G., & Scarth, W. (2011). *Macroeconomics* (4th ed.). New York: Worth Publishers.

Matthews, R., Pendakur, R., & Young, N. (2009). Social capital, labour markets, and job-finding in urban and rural regions: Comparing paths to employment in prosperous cities and stressed rural communities in Canada. *The Sociological Review, 57*(2), 306–330.

Mendelson, M. (2004). Aboriginal *people* in Canada's *labour market:* Work and *unemployment, today and tomorrow.* Caledon Institute of Social Policy, ISBM 1-55382-090-8.

Michaelson, J., Abdallah, S., Steuer, N., Thompson, S., Marks, N., Aked, J., & Potts, R. (2009). *National accounts of well-being: Bringing real wealth onto the balance sheet.* London: New Economics Foundation. Retrieved from www.unicef.org/lac/National_Accounts_of_Well-being(1).pdf.

OECD. (2013). *OECD framework for statistics on the distribution of household income, consumption and wealth.* Retrieved from http://dx.doi.org/10.1787/9789264194830-en.

UK Office for National Statistics. (2016). *Personal well-being in the UK: 2015–2016.* Retrieved from www.ons.gov.uk/peoplepopulationandcommunity/wellbeing/bulletins/measuringnationalwellbeing/2015to2016.

Pendakur, K., & Pendakur, R. (2011). Aboriginal income disparity in Canada. *Canadian Public Policy, 37*(1), 61–83.

Public Health Agency of Canada. (2011). *Diabetes in Canada: Facts and figures from a public health perspective.* Retrieved from www.canada.ca/en/public-health/services/chronic-diseases/reports-publications/diabetes/diabetes-canada-facts-figures-a-public-health-perspective.html.

Reza, A., & Sarker, S. (2015). Is slower growth the new normal in advanced economies? *Bank of Canada Review, 2015*(Autumn), 1–13.

Statistics Canada. (2012). *2001 Census of Canada. Census topic-based tabulations.* Retrieved from www12.statcan.ca/english/census01/home/Index.cfm.

Statistics Canada. (2013a). *Aboriginal peoples in Canada: First Nations people, Métis and Inuit.* Catalogue no. 99-011-201100.

Statistics Canada. (2013b). *The educational attainment of Aboriginal peoples in Canada.* Catalogue no. 99-012-X2011003.

Statistics Canada. (2013c). *Aboriginal peoples survey, 2012.* Data dictionary – public use microdata file.

Statistics Canada. (2013d). *Aboriginal peoples survey, 2012.* Public use microdata file (Adult).

Statistics Canada. (2014). *2006 census of Canada.* Census topic-based tabulations. Retrieved from www12.statcan.gc.ca/census-recensement/2006/dp-pd/tbt/index-eng.cfm.

Statistics Canada. (2015). *1996 census of Canada.* Retrieved from www12.statcan.gc.ca/english/census01/info/census96.cfm.

Statistics Canada. (2016). *2011 National Household Survey: Data tables.* Retrieved from: www12.statcan.gc.ca/nhs-enm/2011/dp-pd/dt-td/Index-eng.cfm.

Stephens, B. (2010). The determinants of labour force status among Indigenous Australians. *Australian Journal of Labour Economics, 13*(3), 287–312.

University of Ottawa. (2012). *Society, the individual, and medicine.* Retrieved from www.medicine.uottawa.ca/sim.

Walters, D., White, J., & Maxim, P. (2004). Does postsecondary education benefit Aboriginal Canadians? An examination of earnings and employment outcomes for recent Aboriginal graduates. *Canadian Public Policy/Analyse de Politiques, 30*(3), 283–301.

Wilson, D., & Macdonald, D. (2010). *The income gap between Aboriginal peoples and the rest of Canada.* Ottawa: Canadian Centre for Policy Alternatives.

Woolcock, M. (2001). The place of social capital in understanding social and economic outcomes. *Canadian Journal of Policy Research, 2*(1), 11–17.

Yang, C., & Raehsler, R. (2005). An economic analysis on intermediate microeconomics: An ordered probit model. *Journal for Economic Educators, 5*(3), 1–11.

14

EL BUEN VIVIR

Notions of wellbeing among Indigenous peoples of South America

Ana Maria Peredo

Introduction

'Development,' the intended blessing for the world's poorest populations, has not delivered well on its promises. Among those whom it has not blessed, and perhaps even cursed, are the Indigenous peoples of South America. In this chapter, I would like to pay some attention to who these people are, spotlighting their traditions of reciprocity and collective action; to consider briefly the trajectory that 'development' has taken in dealing with them along with the rest of the 'underdeveloped' world; and to explore how their evolving practices, such as community-based enterprises (CBEs), may contribute to a *buen vivir* that may be seen as an alternative to 'development.'

Who are the Indigenous of South America?

The Indigenous population of South America is estimated at anywhere from 30 to 36 million. The breadth in estimates stems partly from the variety of criteria used by governments and agencies in estimating the numbers, but also from cultural, political and social discrimination associated with self-identification, which is a commonly used criterion (Canessa, 2007; Layton, Patrinos, & Shapiro, 2006). Nevertheless, it seems clear that the Indigenous may account for as much as 14 percent of the total population, but – significantly – for as much as 40 percent of the rural populace (International Work Group for Indigenous Affairs, 2015).

The distribution of Indigenous peoples is highly varied. Bolivia (about 41%), Peru (about 30%),[1] Ecuador (8%) and Chile (8%)[2] have the largest populations of Indigenous peoples. Most of the Indigenous population are the Quechua and Aymara peoples who live mainly in the Andean mountain region. The Amazon rainforest is another region with significant Indigenous population and ethnic groups, with a smaller number living in the coastal region. These countries (except for Chile) all have a large number of *mestizos* (mix of Spanish and Indigenous and in some regions black peoples), populations that are not represented in these percentages.

In Colombia (3.5%), Argentina (1.5%), Venezuela (2.0%), Paraguay (1.7%), Brazil (0.4%) and Uruguay ('practically non-existent'), the Indigenous population has been considerably more reduced than in the above countries. The Indigenous populations of these countries live mainly in the Amazon and in the Gran Chaco region and to a lesser extent in the Andes.

While the Andes host most of the Indigenous population in South America – mainly Quechua and Aymara peoples – the Amazon region concentrates the largest number of distinct Indigenous groups and languages: more than 400 of them (Greenpeace International, 2015). Among the largest known groups are the Guarani, Shipibo, Yanomamo, Yaruro, Jirabos and Aguaruna. Many Amazonian ethnic groups remain 'uncontacted,' i.e. living in voluntary isolation. Of these, Brazil has the largest number (seventy-seven) (Butler, 2006).

Poverty has long been deeply entrenched in the Indigenous populations of South America, with the average income of the Indigenous poor significantly lower than that of the non-Indigenous poor (Psacharopoulos & Patrinos, 1994). Since the 1990s, poverty in the region has seen some general decline, but among Indigenous people there has, with few exceptions, been either a negligible decrease or a descent into even greater need (Hall & Patrinos, 2006; Ñopo, 2012; World Bank, 2011, p. 105). The evidence is that economic crises, which are not uncommon in South America, affect the Indigenous quite disproportionately, with a lower initial impact but a much slower recovery and a harsher net effect. Researchers conclude that these crises can be particularly detrimental to Indigenous wellbeing, and that policies successful in reducing poverty for the general population are less effective in addressing the plight of the Indigenous (Hall & Patrinos, 2006, p. 222).

The disadvantage of the Indigenous persists in the area of education. Years of schooling average two or more years, less for South American Indigenous in comparison with their non-Indigenous fellow citizens (World Bank, 2011, p. 107). This education gap shrank during the 1990s, but the poverty gap did not. The return on added education is smaller for the Indigenous than non-Indigenous, which may reflect on the quality of education received by the Indigenous and/or racial discrimination.

The disadvantage is similar with respect to healthcare. In general, Indigenous people make less use of medical services even though their needs may be greater (WHO, 2010, p. 8). South American Indigenous women, for instance, are much less likely than their non-Indigenous counterparts to receive antenatal care or give birth in a healthcare facility (World Bank, 2011, p. 108). In general, health indicators such as maternal mortality, life expectancy and vaccination are systematically worse for the Indigenous peoples. Particularly worrying are the very high rates of Indigenous childhood malnutrition in these populations (Hall & Patrinos, 2006, p. 228).

Despite public declarations and legal agreements, the access of Indigenous peoples to their own land and resources has been increasingly threatened by government initiatives, spurred by a neoliberal agenda, to secure investment in industrial agriculture and extractive industry (International Work Group for Indigenous Affairs, 2015). In the last twenty years, there has been a marked increase in South American Indigenous peoples' mass mobilizations aimed at defending their rights to land and other resources that are being affected by these policies.

Traditions of solidarity and reciprocity in the Andes

Twenty-five years ago, as a graduate student of anthropology, I went to Acara, an Aymara community in the southern Peru. My intention was to study the impact of rural credit in a rural Indigenous community. Traditionally, the national Agrarian Bank had given subsidized agricultural loans to the large *haciendas* in the coast areas, which produced sugar cane and cotton for external markets. A year before my arrival in the Aymara community, the new government of Peru met with thousands of Indigenous leaders in regional meetings called *Rimanakuy* ('Let's talk'). There, President Alan Garcia promised to end social injustice in the treatment of the Indigenous peoples of Peru. The young president eloquently read a few passages from the *El Mundo es ancho y ajeno* [*Broad and alien is the world*] (1983) by Indigenist Ciro Alegria. Indigenous leaders focused intently on every word of the young president. They were hearing the story of their everyday life.

Acara was the first Indigenous community to receive communal credit, loans given to communities which then distribute the funds among their members. The community is located in the highest part of the Andes, the Altiplano, 4,500 metres above sea level, far from the oft-portrayed Andean highlands with their beautiful and colorful mountains. Surrounding Acara, there was mainly thick, brown grass and bitter cold, with houses scattered here and there through the hills. From far away, they looked close together, but they were not. The distance between them increases when you are pursued by dogs with an intense sense of territory, as I was. During my first day, I was unable to get close to anyone's house. I knew it was harvest season, so I expected it would not be hard to get something to eat. As the day went on, I asked several people I encountered on the road if they would sell me something to eat. All were courteous, but told me something like 'I am sorry, I do not have anything; maybe the next one has.' No one would sell me anything, even if I offered money. 'What is happening?,' I wondered. Were they not poor? My friends from the NGOs and the university talked about 'development' for these people: increasing their income. Here I was offering – according to my *mestizo* and urban view – an opportunity for profit, for development. Why were there no sellers?

A month later, I was working with the families harvesting potatoes. The situation was quite different. They provided me with potato, *chuño* (dry potato) and cheese, but would not accept money in exchange. I was being introduced to the most important concept in understanding how Andean Indigenous people survive. Initially, I called it 'the Andean insurance.' Acara was, in its own way, a wealthy community, with complex ways of sharing work and its fruits, and ways of taking care of each other.

I had come with the idea of studying the impact and functioning of credit programs in Andean communities, but I soon realized that there was a much richer system, consisting of large networks of reciprocity and exchange where monetary and non-monetary goods and services circulated and enriched lives of people in the community. In their economic dimension, these systems constituted a way to organize production, redistribution and consumption. These different forms of exchange are embedded in social networks and rituals, and they are hidden from the view of somebody who is just looking for market activity.

At the heart of these systems is the institution of reciprocity (Argumedo & Pimbert, 2010; Rist, 2000) – exchange for mutual benefit and typically based on rates established by something other than forces of supply and demand. 'The economic and cultural analysis of reciprocity allows us to highlight, or at least get a sense of, the whole world in which the Andean peasant[3] moves: his habitat, resources, customs, traditions and worldviews' (Alberti & Mayer, 1974, my translation).

Life and wellbeing in the Andean rural highlands depend fundamentally on cooperation. The land tends to be poor; and agriculture, which forms the backbone of the economy, is risky and uncertain. Most families, in order to diversify crops and minimize risk, possess a number of small plots in different areas. The nature of agricultural activity requires most families to depend on outside labor at certain times. Mechanisms of cooperation in this highly risky environment, where there is no state support, diminish overall insecurity and provide a level of food security.

Practices of reciprocity allow Indigenous families to achieve diversification in their diet even if the harvest of one product or another fails. Village commoners – members of the community 18 years and older – live in a context where even better off families depend on cooperative relations. To survive in the highlands, each Indigenous family must develop the ability to mobilize a social network through the careful cultivation of social ties. Individual and family wellbeing are thus secured in the context of community.

The Andean networks of reciprocal practices and exchanges form an historical, socio-cultural and economic system that continues to evolve. There are variations in its practices and the names by which it is known, as well as the extent of practice and the processes of adaptation in response to internal and external challenges that affect Indigenous communities.

In general, we can identify three levels of reciprocal exchange: (a) between families, (b) between families and community, and (c) between humans and other beings. Internally, Indigenous communities are non-homogenous in their access to resources, and there are symmetrical and non-symmetrical modes of exchange. There is also a temporal dimension. Some actions are reciprocated within a short time span, while others take much longer and may even require generations to be fulfilled.

At the family level, there are many mechanisms of cooperation. *Ayni* is a form of reciprocity among families and neighbours with similar access to land and other resources (Argumedo & Pimbert, 2010, p. 344). What is received is returned in a similar form, and the basis of expectation is not a formal agreement but an understood moral requirement. There are asymmetrical reciprocal relations, in which families with not enough land or resources earn their way through *mingas*, or collective work parties. Generally, a *minga* involves a gathering of two or more families working in exchange for a portion of the harvest they help reap (Rist, 2000).

There are many variations of *ayni* and *minga* modalities, and these forms of reciprocity do not apply only to agriculture. Families build a number of work relationships to reciprocate, barter and/or exchange goods and services, including such things as the erection of a dwelling (Peredo, 1995).

Ceremony and ritual are an essential aspect of Andean reciprocity, through which, for example, spiritual kinship is created. Kinship brings with it an obligation to both parties: to well-off families the responsibility to provide work and goods, and to the not so well-off the duty to provide labor in exchange for goods. Spiritual kinship is linked to life cycles of individuals-in-community. For example, when the first haircut of a child takes place at about the age of five, godparents are formally designated in a public ceremony that involves most of the community (Graham, 1999; Peredo, 1995). During the ceremony, the godparents make public promises to support the wellbeing of the child. All those present give a small amount of money to the child and this acts as an economic support fund, which the community will preserve over the years. Godparents' gifts are expected to be larger than anyone else's. Mutual obligations are formed between the godparents and the child and his or her family. The ceremonial kinship thus formed acts as 'insurance' for the child, as the godparents are expected to look after the wellbeing not only of the child but also of his or her family. The standing of godparent and godson or goddaughter is a very important cultural dimension for the social and economic life of the community. Similar ceremonies and promises are made for newlyweds.

At the community level, the community provides commoners access to common land, water and other resources. It also provides entertainment and enjoyment through the *fiestas* and ceremonial celebrations. In exchange, commoners have an obligation to protect the community, serve the community through occupying *cargos* – community leadership positions – and working in the *faenas*. The *faena* is among the most interesting mechanisms contributing to the wellbeing of all commoners. Every head of a household is obliged to participate in *faenas* from time to time, contributing work toward public services such as bridge-repair, construction of schools, cleaning of rivers, etc. *Faenas* often include a celebratory aspect, in which families are working together, women bring food, coca and liquor, and there is a general sense of conviviality.

Relations of reciprocity extend beyond human beings. Celebrations of a sense of reciprocity and gratitude that include a relationship with the *Pachamama* – Mother Earth – and the

Wamanis – the mountains – are major events in Indigenous Andean communities. In those cere-monies, goods such as potatoes, corn, coca and other products are offered as well as sacrifices of animals, in reciprocity for the benefits received from *Pachamama* and the *Wamanis*.

This system of reciprocity may be seen as an 'umbilical cord' (Alberti & Mayer, 1974), from which families can draw resources in times of need and to which they contribute in times of relative prosperity. It is common that after the harvest, Indigenous families select and distribute the products: some for their own consumption, some for barter, for gifts, *minga*, others for the market, bearing in mind their multiple relationships.

Beside reciprocal exchanges, there are other exchanges of goods through *trueque* – barter exchanges. Goods in those markets have historically established standards of value and tend to happen among individuals and families from different communities and in regional markets (Argumedo & Pimbert, 2010). It is interesting to note that in times of inflation, Andean Indigenous peoples have protected themselves by increasing barter exchanges rather than cash.

These ancestral systems of exchange and reciprocity continue to be transformed and adapted in response to factors such as increased migration to the city, especially of men. Increased production of cash products is changing the nature of *ayni* and *minga* and the reciprocity rela-tionship among families and community. For example, if women with absent husbands find it difficult to engage in *ayni*, they can participate in *ayni* with another family in the same situation, and/or work for *minga* in exchange for part of the harvest and or salary (Peredo, 1995). A family engaged in cash-cropping might find it difficult to receive labor from *ayni* and or *minga*, and consequently have to pay salaries for the help they receive. Situations certainly arise where reciprocity arrangements are exploited. A well-off family, for example, may manipulate its rela-tionship with blood kin to gain cheap access to products. I once met a well-off man who had more than 100 godchildren, and used those relationships to access alpaca fiber to sell to a large factory in the city. In communities with increased out-migration, the level of participation of young people in the *faenas* is decreasing. Some families begin to pay poor commoners to fulfill their *faena* obligations. At the same time, for working in some communal lands, rules of com-pulsory *faenas* have been relaxed, as commoners can do *faena* voluntarily in exchange for a share in the harvest.

Despite its adaptation and transformation, the Andean system of reciprocity remains a mech-anism that facilitates and provides for the economic, social, cultural and spiritual needs and wellbeing of families and community.

The trajectory of 'development'

US President Harry S. Truman is widely credited with launching the discourse of 'development' and an era devoted to its pursuit (Truman, 2009 [1949]). His commitment was enthusiastically seconded by much of the industrialized world and eagerly adopted by the new international organizations emerging from the post-war dynamic: the United Nations, the World Bank and the International Monetary Fund. In the more than half-century since Truman's declaration, international commitment to the development project has only intensified. The understanding of development – both what it is aimed at and the means by which it is pursued – has, however, undergone major shifts.

'Underdevelopment' was clearly seen by Truman to be an economic disorder: a 'primi-tive and stagnant' economic life. This view of the problem shaped the means of addressing it. For Truman, and for generations of development advocates, the solution for poverty and its associated conditions lay in addressing the underlying condition by means of economic growth, and that meant industrialization. Modernization theory built on this assumption with a model outlining a linear sequence of stages through which developing countries must progress on their way to development as defined by industrialized, consumer societies such as the US (see Rostow, 1960). The agents of development in this model are nation-states. Their role is to create a policy framework encouraging savings and investment, which will be enriched by foreign trade and used to promote progress through the required stages of industrialization, which was identified as development.

By the 1960s, it had become clear to many that the hoped-for progression through stages of development was not taking place in many poor countries; indeed conditions were worsening in many (Halperin, 2015). Argentinian economist Raúl Prebisch (1950) launched the view that the economies of 'developing' countries are structurally different from those of industrialized nations, and that the differences in structure place the former at systemic disadvantage in relation to the latter. The structural differences arise from a difference between the industrialized 'centre' of the world economy, which draws on food and raw materials produced elsewhere, and the 'periphery' of the world economy – including Latin America, which produces and exports that food and those raw materials and imports processed outputs from the center. Technological development and the ability to set prices mean that industrialized countries are able to retain a much greater share of the value created in these exchanges. This approach, and the 'structuralist/dependency theory' that grew out of it (Halperin, 2015; Knutsson, 2009), retained the assumptions maintained that economic development was the goal, that industrialization was the means, and the state was the primary agent of development. It rejected modernization's program of free trade and foreign investment, instead focusing inward within nations and regions, developing internally the industry and technology that could allow them to add value that they could retain. 'Import substitution industrialization' was a central pillar of this approach.

Though it generated a spirited challenge to modernization theory and influenced policy in several countries, the structuralist/dependency approach to development failed to produce large-scale improvement (Hettne, 1982). Theorists and policymakers began a shift toward export-driven strategies in an effort to secure a place in world markets, taking advantage of low wages and low levels of domestic consumption to improve competitiveness (Halperin, 2015). The result for many poor countries, however, was spiralling national debt.

Against this backdrop, a dramatic shift began in the early 1980s. The election of prime minister Margaret Thatcher in the UK and President Ronald Reagan in the USA signaled the beginning of a social and political transformation that soon spread worldwide (Harvey, 2005). Neoliberalism, grounded in advocacy of free market capitalism, produced an approach to 'development' that followed modernization theory in equating development with economic growth. Where it differed was in seeing the nation-state as more often an impediment to development than its agent. In neoliberal thinking, the market replaced the state as the agent of development (Knutsson, 2009, p. 27). Markets need to be free from government control and regulation, which is argued to inhibit the ability of free trade to produce economic wealth, and look to the unfettered movement of capital, goods and services to deliver prosperity.

The World Bank and the International Monetary Fund became mechanisms to disseminate, implement and enforce neoliberal strategies (Stiglitz, 2002, p. 14). The World Bank/IMF approach to national indebtedness and underdevelopment is a system of conditional loans known as Structural Adjustment Programs that required such things as reduced social spending, privatization of publicly owned enterprises, reduced economic regulations, reduced trade barriers and so on, to provide a welcome environment to foreign direct investment (Greenberg, 1997). The rise of neoliberalism is coupled with the rise of corporate power to the point that this approach to development could be seen as not really based on free markets but the interests of powerful corporate forces from the industrialized West (Crouch, 2011; Korten, 1995).

It is hard to deny that the result of neoliberal development policy has been devastating for the poor, including and perhaps especially Indigenous peoples. Structural Adjustment Programs pursued during the 1990s and into the early twenty-first century did not have the desired outcomes. Indeed, what seemed aggravated conditions of poverty and maldevelopment attracted a storm of criticism (see Knutsson, 2009, p. 25). The results in most 'developing' countries was actually slower growth, increased inequality of income and greater economic instability (Chang, 2007, pp. 26–31; Stiglitz, 2002, p. 18). Perhaps more significantly, the social fallout in terms of unemployment, reduced social services and rising prices, which were meant to be short-term prices worth paying, turned out to be lasting hardships, especially among the rural poor caught in a cycle of export induced mono-cropping, higher input costs and fluctuating world demand (Greenberg, 1997, p. 85).

An influential approach that captured much of the existing dissatisfaction of the previous three decades came to be known as the 'Human Development' outlook: a shift from the view that development concerns just economic factors such as income and wealth, to a multidimensional consideration of 'wellbeing.' A leading proponent of this point of view, Amartya Sen (1999), sees the goal of development as the "expansion of the 'capabilities' of persons to lead the kind of lives they value – and have reason to value" (1999, p. 18). Poverty is seen as a lack of basic freedoms; and while it is often related to low income, that is only one variable and contingent factor in relation to the freedoms that development aims at (Sen, 1999, pp. 87–88). An exclusive attention to income, and economic measures to improve it, are therefore shortsighted and likely to miss much of what is important.

This approach has influenced the United Nations Development Programme in producing a Human Development Index to measure development using comparative rates of life expectancy, literacy and school enrolment as well as income per capita to publish report cards on how well nations were faring in attempts at development.

'Post-development' thinking and the buen vivir

'Post-development' scholars argue that mainstream notions of underdevelopment and poverty are based on ethnocentric and industrialized assumptions about the good life that simply fail to fit the 'Third World' created by this discourse. Even reformed approaches to development, which reduce the emphasis on economic growth and industrialization and embrace human development as the goal, nevertheless continue to apply a single cultural model to the whole world. The development discourse in general is seen as "a regime of representation" (Escobar, 1995, pp. 6, 10, 12, 15, 19), in which the identities of the poor and 'underdeveloped' are constructed in terms of Western primacy.

Post-development advocates do not deny that there are social and material disadvantages in the majority of the world's population, though they would say that many of these are actually created by the joint projects of development and globalization. As a response, however, 'they are interested,' as Escobar strikingly puts it, 'not in development alternatives but in alternatives to development' (1995, p. 215). Those alternatives are rooted in a rejection of the absolutes of "Western modernity" that ignore the multitude of distinct local realities and cultures that shape the realities in which people live (Esteva & Prakash, 1998, pp. 292–294). What needs to be remedied, and what the remedies might be, must be determined at that level. Escobar observes, 'A relatively coherent body of work has emerged which highlights the role of grassroots movements, local knowledge, and popular power…' This approach, he writes, is grounded in "an interest in in local culture and knowledge; a critical stance with respect to established scientific discourses; and the defense and promotion of localized, pluralistic grassroots movements" (1995, p. 215).

The post-development proposal to find alternatives to development finds an application in a Latin American movement built on the concept of *buen vivir*. The movement arose independently of the post-development program, but its approach is deeply resonant with the post-development outlook (Gudynas, 2011, p. 442). The *buen vivir* perspective gained prominence in the late twentieth and early twenty-first centuries as a Latin American response to neoliberal pressures and classical 'Western' development programs, but it is deeply rooted in the traditional worldviews of the South American Indigenous.

The Spanish *buen vivir* is in fact a rendering of several different Indigenous expressions: *sumak kawsay* in the kichwa language of Ecuador, *suma qamaña* in the Aymara of Bolivia, *kuome mongen* in the Mapuche tongue of Chile, and similar expressions from other Andean Indigenous languages (Gudynas, 2011). Each of these conceptions that have evolved into the concept of *buen vivir* is embedded in its own cultural, historical and political context, and the Spanish concept inherits that variety of nuance. Underlying that variety, however, is a worldview, a *cosmovision*, that sees human life poised at the intersection of material, spiritual and social reality (Rist, 2000). The good life consists in finding a balance that combines these realities into an integrated whole.

The concepts of *buen vivir* that entered Latin America discourse in the late 1990s and early 2000s took shape in current political and social dialogue, including the dissatisfaction with neoliberal ideology and the forms of 'development' identified with Western hegemony. But they inherited from their Indigenous and related antecedents this idea of a harmonious balance, which places human life in a specific community with its accompanying spiritual and material realities (Cerdán, 2013; Gudynas, 2011; Rist, 2000; Walsh, 2010). This approach is fundamentally opposed, therefore, to an individualistic understanding of development and incorporates a sensitivity to ecology that goes beyond seeing it as a resource, even one to be protected. 'Nature becomes part of the social world, and political communities could extend in some cases to the non-human' (Gudynas, 2011, p. 445). Translating *buen vivir* into the English 'wellbeing' fails to capture the enlarged sense of reality that the Spanish expression and its antecedents embody.

Buen vivir is not a single concept, but a fluid conception that allows for different understanding in different settings. The recent inclusion of *buen vivir* in the constitutions of Ecuador and Bolivia reflects the appeal this idea has, but also different ways in which it may be conceived (Gudynas, 2011). It serves as a kind of platform from which a number of alternatives to development may be launched.

In our own way: collective action and wellbeing in the Andes

Faced with environmental, social, economic and political crisis, the Indigenous of South America have found ways of enlisting practices of reciprocity and exchange at the community level to re-energize and rebuild Indigenous ways of life. In the following, I look at five Indigenous communities in the Andean region of Peru that have created self-managed collective enterprises, and through them responded to the negative forces that confront them. Contrary to conventional community development – interventions that focus primarily on outside inputs (e.g. financing, infrastructure building, education, health, advocacy, mass mobilization, training, education, etc.) – the development happening in the Indigenous communities builds upon community strengths.

I have pointed out how the interrelated system of reciprocity is a mechanism that not only provides basic material being and fosters social relationships, but also forms the backbone for nourishing cultural needs through rituals, ceremonies and community *fiestas*. Community cohesiveness and the use of ancestral cooperative practices and values have been the driving force behind the creation of 'community-based enterprises' (CBEs) in Colcas, Accas, Quchu and Achumba.[4] They have been built on the foundation of the capacity of local people to pool and mobilize all kinds of resources – human, natural and, to a lesser extent, monetary – to improve their lives collectively.

The roots of community entrepreneurship

CBE is a mechanism for change and an adaptive response to pressing macro-economic, social and political factors that affect impoverished Indigenous communities. It occurs where communities, acting as communities, form an enterprise of some sort that they operate as a community. In effect, they become, collectively, both entrepreneur and enterprise (Peredo & Chrisman, 2006).

CBE arises in response to economic crisis and a lack of opportunities in the countryside, processes of social disintegration, social alienation, environmental degradation and postwar disruption. The factors are interrelated, and many communities suffer from more than one at the same time.

Lack of economic opportunity arises not only from rural isolation but also from social and cultural marginalization as reflected in the deficiency of services in rural areas of the Andes where the Indigenous peoples live. The lack of economic opportunity allies with marginalization to create a catalyst for the creation of CBE. Indigenous peoples living in the rural communities do not seek full-time employment. Rather, they look for opportunities to generate income that complement their agricultural activities, serving as a source of diversification that softens the consequences of uncertain and high-risk agricultural activity. The weekly regional market in Colca – a community initiated and operated enterprise – and the collective *granjas* – collective stockyards – have created income that supports the community's school. It also provides income for individual families who can now sell their products in the main plaza of their community, and allows the Mothers' Club to support itself by selling prepared foods. In Accas, 130 direct part-time jobs have been created by CBEs in the community-owned mine, the bottled water factory, the school, dining center and other enterprises that have flourished there. Commoners welcome these jobs especially for the way they accommodate the agricultural cycles of Indigenous families farming their parcels.

Andean Indigenous communities have long faced diverse forms of social disintegration, especially as a result of migration and increased social stratification. These demographic changes affect traditional cooperative relations and amplify poverty, especially among the most vulnerable: the elderly, women and children. The community of Colcas, in an attempt to overcome its poverty, adopted a process of land redistribution for the purpose of increasing food security, reducing social polarization and strengthening solidarity. In Accas, Colcas and other communities, many young men have returned to their families and to their communities because of the existence of the CBE. One of the benefits of CBE is its potential to reduce the forces promoting migration and strengthen practices of solidarity.

As mentioned earlier, in South America and in the Andean area in particular, there is a close connection between poverty and alienation due to ethnicity. Their ethnic origin places the Indigenous at the bottom of a social, economic, political and cultural ladder.[5] Alienation and marginalization is reflected not only in macroeconomic terms and policies such as lack of major investment in the area, but also in everyday life. Overall, there is a desire among the Indigenous to gain control over their own lives, especially in Peru where the Indigenous lack political power or voice in national life.

In many communities, men and women tell stories of abuse while living in the city because of their ethnic background. For example, in 1994 I interviewed twenty-two male immigrants from the Quechua community of Cuzno, who were living in the city capital of Lima. Three of them were working as servants for *mestizo* or white families. All of them complained about the treatment they were receiving from their employers, and the constant references to their origins. Although I did not interview women, it is well known that female servants are often the targets of physical abuse including rape. In spite of this treatment, Indigenous working in the city may consider themselves the lucky ones, as servants at least have a place to sleep and something to eat. Most migrants I encountered were wandering from city to city, begging and self-employed, selling handicrafts such as palm mats, which the family in the village produced during the agricultural off-season. All of them lived in precarious and often violent conditions in shantytowns.

In the communities of Colcas, Accas and Quichu personal experiences of social alienation have drawn people to return and work for the CBEs. In the assemblies convened to discuss the enterprise, they often talked about the painful experiences living in the city. In Colcas, during a special assembly to discuss the CBE, a young man related with tears:

> I wanted to be someone. I worked as a servant and I managed to convince my boss to let me go to school at night. So, I decided to go and sign up in spite of the fact that I was so tired. When I was on my way on the bus, my documents were stolen. Shortly after that the police came to check documents and I was arrested. After spending some time in jail, I continued on to the school, but no one would help me since I didn't have the other documents. The person at the front desk told me: "Get out of here, *cholo.*"[6]

He wiped away his tears and said:

> I lost everything and now I am here. The community has given me land. I have some sheep and my little grocery store. The cities look good from a distance when one is curious. But when we are there, the city doesn't offer anything to people like us. Here the community protects us.

Stories like this are abundant in these communities.

Environmental degradation is a concern in many Andean communities, and appears as an important factor in the emergence of CBEs among the cases studied. It was, for example, clearly a motivating force in the community of Colcas. Severe erosion of the land moved the commoners to restructure their entire communal lands arrangement. The measure was introduced collectively with a view to avoiding future damage to the physical base of their already precarious economy by adding community monitoring of use and degradation, but had the effect as well of reviving and reinforcing traditional forms of collective work that had been disappearing. The restructuring of the land stimulated the creation of a regional market and other communal enterprises as a way of economic diversification beyond exploitation of natural resources.

From 1979 to 1992, Peru was the scene of a bitter guerrilla war. Terror drove many to flee their communities, among them the citizens of Quichu. During the early period of the war, families often escaped to the mountains. "It was cold," said Toribio Quispe, "but we were afraid to stay in our huts, because we never knew when the *Senderistas* [Shining Path guerrilla group] or the military would come." Now, people in Quichu are proud. "We have a soccer field and other facilities. Now the community has been reborn..." A number of young people live there, including a large number of single abandoned mothers. In Quichu, the need to rebuild their community drove the people to organize themselves. During the war years, "We had come to the point where the community had only six families still here – mostly old people determined to die in their own place." These experiences led to the cohesion that enabled the community to organize its communal *granjas*. Thus, the formation of CBEs addresses poverty not only as scarcity of material resources, but also as a multifaceted phenomenon including social and political insecurity.

In the communities studied, the population expressed the need to gain control over their lives and over their communities as important dimensions of their wellbeing. The community of Accas lodged protests over *Cerro de Pasco* Corporation's despoliation of the environment. In creating its own enterprises, they aimed not only to create jobs, but also to control environmental damage, to build economic alternatives, and to generate dividends that will promote social development. The community has challenges in achieving this economic diversification, but the commoners believe at least that they are controlling their own destiny. In other cases studied, the communities similarly tried to achieve a degree of control, and – rather than waiting for the government to step in – to facilitate the establishment of social services and opportunities. It is precisely for this reason that enterprise creation in these communities has been a political as much as an economic process.

Wellbeing and poverty alleviation entail the control of resources, and this requires an organization. The formation of these organizations is as much a political as an economic process. The communities where I observed CBEs arising share a common patrimony, a common history of mobilization and ancestral cooperative traditions that were converted through collective action into the organizational forms that I refer to as self-managed community-based enterprises.

Previous skills in economically productive activities, such as livestock, cheese making, mining, trade, etc. are closely related to the type of CBE that emerges. Some of those skills are based on ancestral Indigenous knowledge, such as livestock and crop management, while others have been developed through working in areas outside of normal agricultural activities. For example, many commoners in Accas prior to the establishment of the Accas Self-Managed Community Enterprise worked for an American mining company, Cerro de Pasco Copper Corporation.

It is evident that not every community possessing the above-mentioned assets is capable of maintaining a CBE of the magnitude referred here (e.g. selling minerals and creating schools, pharmacies, and so on); but the ancestral reciprocal relations and common lands that exist to some extent in most if not all communities give an indication of a level of community management, even if the commoners do not call the result a 'self-managed community enterprise' and the community does not, as a community, produce goods for the market.

CBE has emerged as a mechanism to boost the wellbeing and health of the community through market participation. Wealth creation in these cases is not the goal in and of itself. Rather, self-reliance and improvement of life in the community through income opportunities, access to social services and support for cultural activities are the aims. These in turn reduce the drive for migration due to economic circumstances. The formation and functioning of CBEs is affected by the ability of a community to combine and adapt in an innovative way – ancestral and new skills, experiences, cooperative practices and values to meet the challenges and engage in a global market.

In sum, typically CBEs are triggered by social, economic and political stress. They draw on cultural heritage, experience of collective action, values toward protection of common patrimony for the common good. In these ways, communities that have engaged the market economy in their own collective ways have been able to gain some control over their lives. They have been able to increase food security, create and direct jobs, build a social infrastructure, increase security and achieve civic democracy. The cases studied reinforce the possibilities of Indigenous, endogenous forms of development that have potential to generate a multifaceted wellbeing.

Challenges: "broad and alien is the world"

CBEs are an instrument rich with potential for improving the lot of Indigenous peoples in South America, but they face significant challenges.

One internal and ongoing task is the need to balance the needs of families with those of their communities. Another is to achieve a balance among the multiple goals characteristic of CBEs, in particular their social and commercial goals. One emerging challenge is a product of management education. Several commercially successfully CBEs have created scholarships enabling their young people to study business in regional universities. The mainstream private business models are not adapted or supplemented to deal with the collective enterprises operating in communities. Young people return, then, with convictions that enterprises should be privatized, and question the pursuit of social, political and cultural goals in the operation of community enterprises.

CBEs face external challenges as well. Commercial competition is a challenge for any enterprise, though CBEs are able to compete by using 'Indigenous strategy,' combining non-market with market approaches in order to remain flexible (Peredo, 2012).

Dealing with governments has been difficult. The individualist development model favored by governments clashes with the collective Andean models embodied in such activities as CBEs. The Peruvian government has neither understood nor supported the important role that CBEs play in creating local development. The explosive growth of extractive industry in the last ten years, combined with other projects embodying neoliberal conventions of development threatens the wellbeing and even the existence of Andean Indigenous communities (Bebbington, 2007; Bebbington & Williams, 2008; Bury, 2005). The reports that began more than a decade ago of Indigenous peoples killed or injured as they protest the presence of mining exploration in their territories (Bury, 2002) have only grown more frequent and more alarming (BBC News, 2015a, 2015b; *The Economist*, 2007; Slack, 2009).

In 2007, the Peruvian president's newspaper article, "*El síndrome del perro del hortelano*" ("The syndrome of the dog in the manger," Perez, 2007), asserted that the Indigenous communities are "incapable" of using their natural resources "productively." "They only wait," he wrote, for "handouts from the State, rather than putting a commercial value on the mountains and lands that are unproductive for them, but if rented or sold could produce the high level of investments and technology that a buyer could bring" [my translation]. The president's contention that the Indigenous people of Peru are obstructing their own development has only become more strident and widespread in the years since, with little consideration of what the communities might be developing themselves, that they value more than cash and technology. This outlook places CBEs and other forms of endogenous development in Indigenous communities at serious risk. Yes, *broad and alien is the world*. Let us see how *buen vivir* might find its own way nevertheless.

Notes

1 Lima: CVR, 2003.
2 Except for Peru and Uruguay, data come from (International Work Group for Indigenous Affairs, 2015)
3 In Peru, Indigenous peoples in the Andes are called *campesinos*, 'peasants'. This reflects a transition outlined by Ferrari (1984) and Spalding (1974).
4 The names of these communities have been changed to respect their privacy.
5 Ethnic discrimination is part of everyday life in Peru. I remember that when I was at school other *mestizo* children seized an Indian girl and cut off her hair. The schoolteacher said: "She should be thankful because now she can look decent." 'Decent' is a term used commonly to describe whites or *mestizos*. Ethnic discrimination against Indigenous people is part of Peruvian mestizo-white society. During my trips through the Andes, especially during the insurgency period (1979–1992), I witnessed how the lives

of the Indigenous were considered of little value. The police harassed them on the road or in buses, often beating them for little or no reason and without any restraint.

6 *Cholo* is a derogatory term applied to Andean Indigenous living in the city.

References

Alberti, G., & Mayer, E. (1974). *Reciprocidad andina: ayer y hoy*. In G. Alberti & E. Mayer (Eds.), *Reciprocidad e intercambio en los Andes peruanos* (pp. 13–37). Lima, Peru: Instituto de Estudios Peruanos.

Alegria, C. (1983). *Broad and alien is the world*. Chester Springs, PA: Dufour Editions.

Argumedo, A., & Pimbert, M. (2010). Bypassing globalization: Barter markets as a new indigenous economy in Peru. *Development, 53*(3), 343–349.

BBC News. (2015a). *Peru anti-mining protest sees deadly clashes*. Retrieved 20 January 2016 from www.bbc.com/news/world-latin-america-34389803.

BBC News. (2015b). *Peru: Troops deployed after deaths in Tia Maria mine protests*. Retrieved 20 January 2016 from www.bbc.com/news/world-latin-america-32677410.

Bebbington, A. (2007). *Mining and development in Peru: With special reference to the Rio Blanco Project, Piura: A delegation report*. Peru Support Group.

Bebbington, A., & Williams, M. (2008). Water and mining conflicts in Peru. *Mountain Research and Development, 28*(3), 190–195.

Bury, J.T. (2002). Livelihoods, mining and peasant protests in the Peruvian Andes. *Journal of Latin American Geography, 1*(1), 1–19.

Bury, J.T. (2005). Mining mountains: Neoliberalism, land tenure, livelihoods, and the new Peruvian mining industry in Cajamarca. *Environment and Planning A, 37*(2), 221–239.

Butler, R.A. (2006). People in the Amazon rain forest. *A place out of time: Tropical rainforests and the perils they face*. Retrieved 19 January 2016 from http://rainforests.mongabay.com/amazon/amazon_people.html.

Canessa, A. (2007). Who is Indigenous? Self-identification, indigeneity, and claims to justice in contemporary Bolivia. *Urban Anthropology, 36*(3), 195–237.

Cerdán, P. (2013). Post-development and buenvivir: An approach to development from Latin-America. *International Letters of Social and Humanistic Sciences, 10*, 15–24.

Chang, H.-J. (2007). *Bad samaritans: Rich nations, poor policies and the threat to the developing world*. London: Random House Business Books.

Crouch, C. (2011). *The strange non-death of neoliberalism*. Cambridge: Polity.

Escobar, A. (1995). *Encountering development: The making and unmaking of the Third World*. Princeton, NJ: Princeton University Press.

Esteva, G., & Prakash, M.S. (1998). Beyond development, what? *Development in Practice, 8*(3), 280–296. doi: 10.1080/09614529853585.

Ferrari, A. (1984). El concepto de indio y la cuestión racial en el Perú en los "Siete ensayos" de José Carlos Mariátegui. *Revista Iberoamericana, 50*(127), 395–409.

Graham, M.A. (1999). *Child nutrition and seasonal hunger in an Andean community (Department of Puno, Peru)*. Department of Anthropology and Sociology, San Clara, CA 95053.

Greenberg, J.B. (1997). A political ecology of Structural-Adjustment Policies: The case of the Dominican Republic. *Culture & Agriculture, 19*(3), 85–93.

Greenpeace International. (2015). *People of the Amazon*. Retrieved 19 January 2016 from www.greenpeace.org/international/en/campaigns/forests/amazon/people-of-the-amazon/.

Gudynas, E. (2011). Buen Vivir: Today's tomorrow. *Development, 54*(4), 441–447.

Hall, G., & Patrinos, H.A. (Eds.). (2006). *Indigenous peoples, poverty, and human development in Latin America*. New York: Palgrave Macmillan.

Halperin, S. (2015). Development theory. *Encyclopædia Britannica Online*. Retrieved 11 January 2016 from www.britannica.com/topic/development-theory.

Harvey, D. (2005). *A brief history of neoliberalism*. Oxford: Oxford University Press.

Hettne, B. (1982). *Development theory and the Third World*. SAREC Report No. 2, Stockholm.

International Work Group for Indigenous Affairs. (2015). *Indigenous peoples in Latin America – a general overview*. Retrieved 7 January 2016 from www.iwgia.org/regions/latin-america/indigenous-peoples-in-latin-america.

Knutsson, B. (2009). *The intellectual history of development: Towards a widening potential repertoire*. University of Gothenburg.

Korten, D.C. (1995). *When corporations rule the world.* West Hartford, CT: Kumarian Press; San Francisco, CA: Berrett-Koehler Publishers.

Layton, H.M., Patrinos, H.A., & Shapiro, J. (2006). Estimating the number of Indigenous peoples in Latin America. In G. Hall & H. A. Patrinos (Eds.), *Indigenous peoples, poverty, and human development in Latin America.* New York: Palgrave Macmillan.

Ñopo, H. (2012). Overlapping disadvantages: Ethnicity and earnings gaps in Latin America. In *New century, old disparities: Gender and ethnic earnings gaps in Latin America and the Caribbean .* Washington, DC: World Bank Publications.

Peredo, A.M. (1995). *The 'Devil' entering our lives: Andean peasant women in Otuzco, Peru.* MA thesis, University of Calgary.

Peredo, A.M. (2012). The difference culture makes: The competitive advantage of reciprocal, non-monetary exchange. In L. Mook, J. Quarter, & S. Ryan (Eds.), *Businesses with a difference: Balancing the social and economic* (pp. 87–110). Toronto: University of Toronto Press.

Peredo, A.M., & Chrisman, J.J. (2006). Toward a theory of community-based enterprise. *Academy of Management Review, 31*(2), 309–328.

Perez, A.G. (2007). El síndrome del perro del hortelano. *El Comercio,* 28, a4.

Prebisch, R. (1950). *The economic development of Latin America and its principal problems.* Lake Success, NY: Economic Commission for Latin America, United Nations Department of Economic Affairs.

Psacharopoulos, G., & Patrinos, H.A. (1994). *Indigenous people and poverty in Latin America: An empirical analysis.* Washington, DC: World Bank.

Rist, S. (2000). Linking ethics and the market: Campesino economic strategies in the Bolivian Andes. *Mountain Research and Development, 20*(4), 310–315.

Rostow, W.W. (1960). *The stages of economic growth: A non-communist manifesto.* Cambridge: Cambridge University Press.

Sen, A. (1999). *Development as freedom.* New York: Alfred A. Knopf.

Slack, K. (2009). *Mining conflicts in Peru: Condition critical.* Oxfam America, Washington, DC.

Spalding, K. (1974). *De indio a campesino: cambios en la estructura social del Perú colonial.* Lima: Instituto de Estudios Peruanos.

Stiglitz, J.E. (2002). *Globalization and its discontents.* New York: WW Norton & Company.

The Economist. (2007). Revolt in the Andes: A vote of sorts against big mines. *The Economist.*

Truman, H.S. (2009 [1949]). Inaugural address. In *Inaugural addresses of the presidents of the United States: From George Washington to Barack Obama.* Washington, DC: Joint Congressional Committee on Inaugural Ceremonies.

Walsh, C. (2010). Development as buen vivir: Institutional arrangements and (de) colonial entanglements. *Development, 53*(1), 15–21.

WHO. (2010). *World Health Report 2010: Health systems financing: The path to universal coverage.* Geneva, Switzerland: World Health Organization.

World Bank. (2011). Assisting Indigenous and socially excluded populations. *Improving the odds of achieving the MDGs: Global Monitoring Report 2011.* Washington, DC: The World Bank Group.

15

THE ECONOMIC WELLBEING OF THE SAN OF THE WESTERN, CENTRAL AND EASTERN KALAHARI REGIONS OF BOTSWANA

Robert K. Hitchcock and Maria Sapignoli

Introduction

The San in the Kalahari Desert region of southern Africa traditionally self-identify as hunter-gatherers but today the vast majority are small-scale agro-pastoralists, cattle post workers, free-hold ranch residents, and people with mixed economies who reside in both rural and urban areas (Cassidy et al., 2001; Barnard, 2007; Sapignoli, 2018). The San of Botswana in general can be described as an underprivileged minority who have some of the highest rates of poverty, the lowest rates of employment, the lowest nutritional and health standards, and the least access to land and resources of various groups in the country (Egner & Klausen, 1980; Christian Michelsen Institute 1996; Nteta, Hermans, & Jeskova, 1996; Botswana Institute for Development Policy Analysis, 1997, 2003; LeRoux, 1999; Ingstad & Fugelli, 2006; Pagiwa, 2013; United Nations Childrens Fund, 2014). The various indicators of wellbeing among Botswana San reveal that they are among the lowest in the country.

The Republic of Botswana is the country with the largest population of San in southern Africa, supporting approximately 63,500, some 2.8 percent of the country's 2017 population of 2,214,858. While the San see themselves as indigenous to Botswana, the government of Botswana does not view them that way, arguing that all of the people in the country are indigenous (Saugestad, 2001; Anaya, 2010; Sapignoli, 2015, 2018). The San are subdivided into a large number of named groups, most of whom speak their own mother tongues in addition to other languages (Güldemann, 2014). There is a significant degree of diversity among the San of Botswana, with some San being highly urbanized and well-educated, while others live in remote areas where they depend, to at least a limited extent, on wild natural resources and sometimes have relatively limited access to social services. There is a government program that covers the San and other groups residing in remote areas of the country which provides assistance of various kinds to those people who are living outside of government-recognized villages (Government of Botswana, 2009).

In the course of the work on San indigenous wellbeing, a set of indicators was used to reflect wellbeing, in line with recommendations from the United Nations Permanent Forum on Indigenous Issues (UNPFII) and governments such as Australia (see Taylor, 2008; Manning, Ambry, & Fleming, 2015). We looked specifically at livelihood security, income, employment, education, nutrition, demography, culture, health, quality of life, and, to a limited extent, at life satisfaction (see Nussbaum & Sen, 1993; Dockery, 2010, 2014; Ambrey & Fleming, 2014; White & Abeyasekera, 2014; Manning, Ambrey, & Fleming, 2015a, 2015b; Singh et al., 2015). Botswana, it should be noted, does not have statistics on populations broken down according to ethnicity, nor does the government maintain data on 'Remote Area Dwellers', those groups who reside outside of gazetted (government-recognized) settlements. As a result, we have relied largely on anthropological and socioeconomic data obtained either by us or by some of our colleagues working in Botswana.

For purposes of this chapter, we consider those San groups occupying areas along a transect from the Ghanzi Farms region in the western Kalahari across the central Kalahari (now a game reserve) to the east-central Kalahari, which is a region dominated by cattle posts and commercial leasehold ranches (see Figure 15.1). The western area includes a town that is a district capital, Ghanzi (Gantsi), a municipality that supported a population of some 13,500 in 2017. Ghanzi District is 117,910 km² in size. Part of Ghanzi District is made up of freehold farms, while there are approximately a dozen largely San settlements in communal (tribal) areas that were created in the 1970s and 1980s in order to provide places for people who were living previously on farms (Childers, 1976; Wily, 1979; Guenther, 1986). There are small, scattered settlements in the Central Kalahari Game Reserve, which is 52,313 km² in size (44.36% of the district) ranging in size from 85 to 140 people (Remote Area Development Office, Ghanzi District Council, 2017). Removals of people from the Central Kalahari at the hands of the government took place in 1997 and 2002 (Ikeya, 2001; Good, 2009, pp. 129–141). Some of the Central Kalahari communities were re-established after 2007, having won a major legal case against the government which restored their occupancy rights in the reserve (see Sapignoli, 2015, 2018).

The east-central Kalahari is largely made up of communal (tribal) land, some of which has been leased out under government land policies as leasehold ranches. Some parts of the east-central Kalahari comprise cattle posts (*meraka*), where people keep livestock (cattle and horses) and small stock (sheep and goats). Individuals and small groups either manage the cattle posts themselves or they hire local people to oversee the animals (Hitchcock, 1978, 1980; Campbell, Main, & Hitchcock, 2006). Cattle post populations in the east-central Kalahari range in size from twelve per location to as many as 200 people, many of them family members of workers (Hitchcock & Ebert, 2011). In the eastern Kalahari, cattle posts average 64 km² in size (6,400 hectares) while some are smaller, averaging 4 km by 4 km in size (Hitchcock, 1978; Motlopi, 2006). There is one so-called communal service center in the east-central Kalahari, Malatswae, which had a population of over 800 people in 2017. The largest town in the eastern Kalahari is Serowe, the district capital of Central District, which in 2017 had a population of about 60,000, a small proportion of whom (some 4%) are San. The straight-line distance along the transect from Ghanzi to Serowe is 527 km, while driving distance is 832 km. The San groups in this region of Botswana include, from west to east, the Naro, ‡X'ao-ǁ'aen, G/ui, G//ana, Tsasi, Tsila, Kua and Tshwa (Barnard, 1992; Valiente-Noailles, 1993; Kiema, 2010; Hitchcock & Sapignoli, 2016; Sapignoli, 2018).

The San on freehold farms and cattle posts are among the most underprivileged people in Botswana, with a high percentage living below the poverty line (World Bank, 2015, pp. 5, 140–142, 146; Hitchcock et al., 2016). In general, the San in these places have the highest

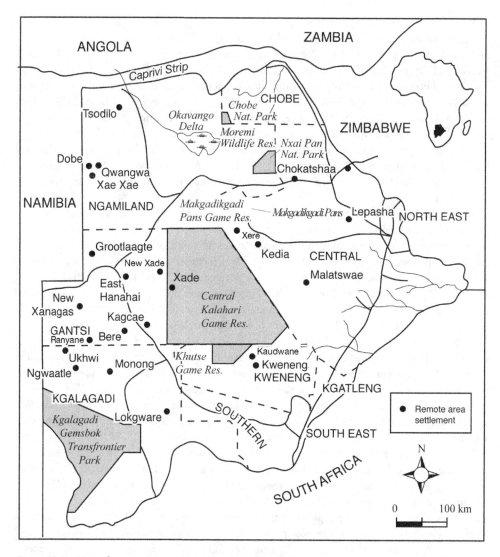

Figure 15.1 Map of remote area settlements and districts in Botswana

levels of unemployment, the lowest levels of education, and some of the poorest health of all of the people in Botswana (Christian Michelsen, 1996; Sapignoli & Hitchcock, 2013a, 2013b; World Bank, 2015). Child poverty is an issue in Botswana, as is undernutrition and stunting (UNICEF, 2014). Botswana today is considered an upper middle-income country (World Bank, 2018, p. 9). The Botswana government social safety net supports many, if not most, of its poor people, including those classified as 'Remote Area Dwellers' (Seleka et al., 2007; World Bank, 2015, 2018).

In the late nineteenth and early twentieth centuries, a substantial portion of the Ghanzi San population became what in effect were landless laborers on land that was in the hands of other people (Wily, 1979; Russell & Russell, 1979). San men worked as cattle herders and farm laborers and did other livestock-related labor such as *kraal* (corral) and fence construction. San women and sometimes children engaged in domestic labor, firewood and water collection, and they did other jobs around the farmsteads. At first, they were paid in kind, usually in the form of food, clothing and tobacco, but later, by the early to the mid-twentieth century, they began to be paid in cash. There were sizable numbers of San, however, who essentially were squatters on the farms belonging to other people, and they were constantly at risk of losing their homes. Their livelihoods were precarious, particularly those who did not have jobs on the farms.

The Central Kalahari Game Reserve, the Ghanzi Farms region and the east-central Kalahari all have substantial symbolic significance for the people who call these areas their home. Some people say, "This is my land." Kiema (2010, p. 11) points out that the name for the Central Kalahari Game Reserve is Tc'amnqoe. Each group from Tc'amnqoo claims a specific territory, which they see as their home area (Kiema, 2010, p. 24). Groups were known to visit other groups' territories for purposes of social and economic interaction and for seeking marriage partners. They also visited what they considered 'sacred places' including the graves of their ancestors.

A culturally significant customary activity of the population in the western, central and eastern Kalahari was the establishment of graves for loved ones, some of which were visited on a regular basis by relatives or friends of the deceased. There were differences of opinion about the ways that local people deal with graves, with some people admitting that they preferred not to spend much time around graves because of what Guenther (1986, p. 282) refers to as 'a vague sense of dread' about them. Graves have become an important reference point for San on the Ghanzi farms, nearly all of which were protected in some way, usually by acacia thorn fences to keep domestic or wild animals from disturbing them. Some of these graves were marked with stones that were erected or laid on them or sticks that were placed in the ground. Many of the graves were located close to trees that provided shade for the grave. As Guenther (1986, p. 282) points out, "It is the location of their relatives' graves, rather than where they work or live that defines //ai (home) for the Naro." Having access to the graves of loved ones was a substantial factor in people's sense of wellbeing. The proximity of graves to the homes of some San was seen as a key reason for why people were happy or unhappy.

Government-sponsored settlements and other communities

Remote area dweller settlements were established in various places in rural Botswana and scattered groups of San living in remote areas were encouraged to move into the settlements, now known as remote area communities (Hitchcock, 1978; Wily, 1979). By the early part of the new millennium, there were sixty-seven government-sponsored settlements which generally were made up of a variety of ethnic groups, the majority of whom were San. The settlements were provided with social and physical infrastructure, much of it supported through inter-national donor funds (Wily, 1979; Saugestad, 2001; Botswana Institute for Development Policy Analysis, 2003).

The Remote Area Development Program (RADP) was housed in the then Ministry of Local Government and Lands; today, it is in the Ministry of Local Government and Rural Development. The RADP had funds under a government program known as LG 32 (later called LG 127), part of the government's national development planning process. Funds were allocated to the seven districts that had remote area dwellers, including Ghanzi, Central and Kweneng Districts. Assistance was provided to people in the settlements but not, it should be noted, in the Central Kalahari Game Reserve after 2002 (Sapignoli, 2015; Hitchcock, Sapignoli, & Babchuk, 2011; Sapignoli, 2018). Most of the support from the RADP went to the sixty-seven remote area settlements and to the three Central Kalahari Game Reserve resettlement sites of New Xade, Kaudwane and Xere, which by 2017 had over 3,800 people in them, many of whom were wondering what their futures were going to be like, especially as social support systems and services such as water and health were being cut back.

The Botswana government and various non-government organizations sought to provide assistance to the people in the settlements in the form of food, livestock and cash-for-work schemes (e.g. road building and brush clearing) (Seleka et al., 2007). In general, these schemes served primarily to provide a buffer against hunger, which is on the increase among some segments of the population, especially vulnerable groups such as pregnant and lactating women, children, the elderly and those with HIV/AIDS and tuberculosis. This was particularly true in the remote area settlements as the numbers of people in them increased and livelihood and social support programs were cut back as part of government and NGO austerity efforts in recent years.

In terms of the land tenure arrangements in the three areas of concern here, the Ghanzi District, the Central Kalahari Game Reserve and the east-central Kalahari in Central District, district council officers provided assistance to people living in settlements but not to those living on freehold farms in Ghanzi or on leasehold farms and cattle posts in the east-central Kalahari (Ghanzi and Central District Council data, 2017). After 2002, it was only the only government personnel living and working in the Central Kalahari Game Reserve (game scouts from the Department of Wildlife and National Parks and, periodically, members of the Botswana police, including the Special Support Group, a paramilitary unit that was tasked with 'stopping poaching' in the reserve) who received water, salaries and rations. Those people who remained in the reserve were provided with nothing, and their nutritional and health statuses declined substantially. It is important to note that in fact there was relatively little poaching in the reserve itself; those groups and individuals that did get arrested were generally from outside of the reserve. The presence of the game scouts and the police did, however, serve to intimidate, leading people in the reserve to be extremely careful about their foraging activities (Sapignoli, 2018). The livelihood security issues resulted in Central Kalahari residents expressing major concerns about their wellbeing.

For purposes of our analysis, we measured an individual's self-reported life satisfaction where 0 is totally dissatisfied and 10 is totally satisfied (using the index reported by Manning, Ambrey, & Fleming, 2015a, pp. 1–6). The life satisfaction indices for Molapo were 4/10, Metsiamonong, 5/10, Mothomelo, 5/10, Gugamma 6/10 and Gope 3/10. Life satisfaction levels in the three resettlement sites were higher: New Xade 6/10, Kaudwane, 7/10 and Xere, 5/10 (data obtained in 2011, 2012 and 2015). When examined over time, it is apparent that the life satisfaction levels in the reserve were higher before the police incursions in 2014, while the levels in the resettlement sites were steady through time.

Analysis of the economic wellbeing of San in Ghanzi, the central Kalahari and the eastern Kalahari

In order to assess the economic wellbeing of San in the various land tenure zones across the Kalahari, we undertook surveys in the region during the period from 2011 to 2017 (Sapignoli & Hitchcock, 2011; Hitchcock & Sapignoli, 2016; Sapignoli, 2018). Five principal forms of data collection were used: (1) participant observation, (2) focus group discussions, (3) key-informant interviews, (4) archival work and (5) analyses of legal cases. The participant observation, interviews and focus group discussions took place at the national, district, community and individual levels. Key-informants were defined as individuals with intimate knowledge of specific subjects. The legal analysis was done using the founding affidavits of the legal cases and the judgments of the Botswana High Court and the Court of Appeal (see, for example, High Court of Botswana, 2002; Sapignoli, 2015, 2018).

It should be noted at the outset that the government of Botswana does not obtain and manage census, administrative or socioeconomic data on populations broken down by ethnicity. The RADP also does not keep statistics on Remote Area Dwellers nor does it track the status of people in the settlements with which it works. Virtually all of the data on San and other remote, rural and peri-urban populations are found in anthropological, sociological, non-government organization and research unit publications and reports (see, for example, Childers, 1976; Hitchcock, 1978, 1988; Wily, 1979; English et al., 1980; Mogalakwe, 1986; Campbell & Main, 1991; Toteng, 1991; Hitchcock & Masilo, 1995). It is difficult, therefore, to do comparative analyses of specific ethnic groups, in this case, San, with aggregated data on populations at the national level. Nevertheless, I drew on existing data, some of which I obtained myself during the course of fieldwork and interviews in the region.

There are a number of different sources of employment, income and subsistence for San residing in the western, central and eastern Kalahari regions of Botswana. For employment, these include working for government, non-government organizations, churches, private sector companies (including those engaged in tourism, mining and safari hunting), freehold farm owners and livestock owners. In most cases, people who are employed receive wages on a monthly or weekly basis. In the case of working for livestock owners, individuals may receive wages but are also given food (including milk as much as 20 or more liters per day, and sometimes maize meal), clothing and other goods. Cash payments for work have increased over time and tend today to be given more often than payments in kind.

Informal sector work includes craft production and sale (e.g. ostrich eggshell bead necklaces and bracelets, skin bags), which are sold to buyers such as Gantsicraft and Botswanacraft, tourism companies and individuals. Some individuals obtain high value plants such as grapple plant (Devil's claw, *Harpagophytum procumbens*) which are sold to buyers. Government social support systems that provide cash or food or both to individuals include payment for 'destitutes' (those people who are defined as having insufficient means to sustain themselves; Republic of Botswana, 2002; Seleka et al., 2007), pensions for the elderly, cash and food-for-work programs (one of which is known as *Ipelegeng*), drought relief programs, and assistance to pregnant and lactating mothers, school-going children, and individuals with HIV/AIDS and or tuberculosis (Seleka et al., 2007).

Subsistence hunting and gathering made up part of the diet of many of the people who were interviewed. I was able to obtain some data on hunting, but it was not easy, since game scouts and police were on the lookout for people with wild animal meat, skins and ostrich eggshell products which required licenses to possess. It turned out to be easier to get hunting data on freehold farms than it was in either the Central Kalahari Game Reserve or the east-central Kalahari. Most people that I interviewed said that they did not hunt. As for gathering of wild plant foods and medicines, I did see people engaged in these activities but generally was not able to get detailed data on amounts obtained or consumed. Some people collected high value plants including Devil's claw and Hoodia and sold them to middlemen and women who operated as buyers for pharmaceutical and other companies. A compilation of the data obtained is presented in Table 15.1. We did not attempt to monetize the subsistence category since virtually all of the people interviewed (*N*=36) said that they consumed the wild plants and meat either at the household or community level.

In the analysis, we considered six different land tenure categories: (1) freehold farms in Ghanzi District (10,405 km²), (2) the Central Kalahari Game Reserve (52,347 km²), which is considered state land, (3) the communal areas (17,619 km²) and remote area dweller settlements of Ghanzi District (2,415 km²), (4) the three resettlement sites related to the Central Kalahari Game Reserve relocations (1,200 km²) and (6) the east-central Kalahari Tribal Grazing Land

Table 15.1 Employment, cash income and subsistence returns for people in the western, central and eastern Kalahari in 2012

	No. of employees			Income	%
	Full-time	Part-time	Total		
Government employees	11	6	17	P318,450	19
Government pensions	22	N/A	22	P153,000	9
Destitute payments (cash)	46	N/A	46	P33,672	2
Farm workers	21	4	25	P360,000	22
Safari hunting	8	1	9	P92,000	6
Mining	26	4	30	P288,000	16
Miscellaneous jobs	3	7	10	P97,000	6
Crafts	–	56	56	P260,000	15
Tourism	3	3	6	P32,600	2
Devil's claw collection	–	7	7	P12,000	1
Cattle-post workers	15	–	15	P16,200	2
Subsistence foraging	–	36	36	N/A	N/A
Total	155	124	279	P1,662,922	100

Notes: A comparable table is presented by Wiessner (2003, p. 154, table 4) on the Nyae Nyae region of Namibia, where the Ju/'hoansi reside. Note that in the calculations shown here for the destitute payments, only the amounts paid in cash were included. Most of the funds for Devil's claw collection went to middlemen rather than the collectors.

Policy leasehold ranches and cattle posts (28,000 km²). Freehold farm owners could, and sometimes did, require residents on the farms to leave, meaning that land tenure security for farm workers and their families was insecure. All of the other land tenure categories allowed free access of people from outside of the settlements, leasehold ranches or cattle posts to enter, although admittedly leasehold ranch owners began pressuring people to move out of them in the early part of the new millennium, a process which increased after the passage of a new land policy in Botswana in 2015 (Republic of Botswana, 2015; see Sapignoli & Hitchcock, 2013a; Hitchcock & Sapignoli, 2016; Isaacs & Manatsha, 2016). Those people who were resettled away from their homes after 2015, as occurred, for example, in places such as Ranyane in Ghanzi District tended to express their dissatisfaction with government land policies either through filing formal complaints with the district councils, the Ministry of Local Government and Rural Development, and the office of the State President, or they obtained the services of lawyers and filed cases in the High Court.

The topics examined in the western, central and eastern Kalahari were as follows: (1) mobility, (2) demography, (3) employment, (4) income, (5) access to government support programs, (6) occupation(s), (7) education, (8) health, (9) housing and (10) experience, if any, with the legal and criminal justice systems. Virtually all San were now settled and residing in units ranging in size from five to 200. Some of the San on the farms have permission to hunt and gather on them, while others do not. Life satisfaction levels varied in part with the attitudes and behavior of the farm owners and leaseholders in western Botswana. Most San had mixed production and subsistence systems, combining employment and income-generating activities with a certain amount of dependence on the state and, in some cases, non-government organizations, exchanges and transfers from kin and friends, and asking other people for food or cash. It is largely an economy that can be seen as semi-dependent or totally dependent on the state.

Economic wellbeing was correlated in part with a combination of employment and labor that generated cash, supplemented with foraging and craft production. People who had returned to the Central Kalahari and were living independently from other groups and had little contact with government had the highest levels of life satisfaction, while those living in the remote area dweller settlements and resettlement sites had the lowest levels of life satisfaction. Those who had the option of engaging in hunting and gathering had the highest levels of satisfaction, while those who were unemployed and living in settlements had the lowest levels of satisfaction. San who worked on cattle posts had moderate levels of life satisfaction, depending on wages that they earned, ability to drink milk from the cattle they cared for, the quantity and quality of food handouts provided by the livestock owner, and the ability to hunt and gather. None of the people who foraged had Special Game Licenses, subsistence hunting licenses, in spite of the High Court judgment that people from the Central Kalahari had the right to get them from the Department of Wildlife and National Parks (Sapignoli, 2015, 2018; Hitchcock & Sapignoli, 2016).

From a demographic perspective, completed family size ranged between five and seven children. Infant mortality was low to moderate except in some of the settlements. Mortality rates were moderate relative to the national average (13.39/1,000 deaths). Migration rates were relatively low except in those cases on cattle posts where herders were replaced by members of other groups. Maternal mortality rate of San was above the national average (129/100,000), in part because of lack of access to clinics and medicines in some areas.

The vast majority of San households were living below the poverty line. Only those individuals who had jobs with government, NGOs or private companies, or who were working on freehold farms or on leasehold ranches and cattle posts in the western and eastern Kalahari had regular incomes. The incomes generally were below P150 per month or P1,800 per annum, well below the national average income of P16,600 (US $1,705.24; the exchange rate in April 2018 was P1/US$0.10). Data obtained on wages paid to cattle post employees over the period from 1975 to 2017 reveal that the average monthly wage rose from P10 in 1975 to P130 in 2017 (Campbell, Main, & Hitchcock, 2006; authors' field data, 2011–2015, 2017). Wages have not kept pace with inflation. At the same time, the number of employees per location dropped from seven in 1975–1977 to three in 2017 as livestock owners reduced the numbers of workers in order to save money. There is not a minimum wage in the agricultural sector in Botswana, unlike in neighboring Namibia. The result is that people in the livestock and agricultural economies who are employees are in positions where they do not get pay increases, unlike those people working for government or ones living in urban areas.

Conclusions

Botswana has instituted social safety net programs that are supposed to ensure that the poorest and most disadvantaged people in the population are protected (Republic of Botswana, 2002; Seleka et al., 2007; World Bank, 2015, 2018). A problem with these programs is that many people in remote, rural and peri-urban areas miss out. Another problem is that there are places in the country where government decisions were made that no such programs be implemented, notably the Central Kalahari Game Reserve, leaving people who are sick, disabled or elderly at a severe disadvantage. This was the case in spite of Botswana High Court decisions to restore services to the people in the Central Kalahari, something that had not been done as of April 2018.

San generally had lower levels of employment and lower incomes than did members of neighboring groups in the western and eastern Kalahari. Approximately a quarter of the San households were receiving cash and or food from government social support programs. Older people living in the Central Kalahari had to leave the Central Kalahari Game Reserve in order to obtain their pensions in the peripheral settlements, something that they said was a major imposition and very difficult for them. This situation added to their unhappiness and dissatisfaction levels.

Health statuses were poor to moderate on the farms, in the settlements and in the cattle post areas of Botswana. People in the Central Kalahari who had accidents or needed to see a nurse or physician because of illness sometimes had to walk or be carried on donkey-back as much as 200 km to get to a clinic (Sapignoli, 2018). In many cases, there were insufficient medicines at the clinics to meet the needs of patients. All too often, there were no medical personnel there to provide assistance to patients. Government's monitoring of the health facilities in remote and rural areas can only be described as inadequate.

Education levels for San were well below the national average and many San adults had never been to school. San children from the communal areas and from the Central Kalahari were transported to schools by the RADP where they stayed in hostels (boarding facilities). Schools were found only in remote area dweller settlements and towns, not on freehold farms or in cattle post areas. There were no schools in the Central Kalahari Game Reserve, only ones in the three resettlement sites. Dropout rates were higher than those for children of other groups and much higher than the national average (LeRoux, 1999). Children on freehold farms only went to school if the farm owner was willing to build a school and cover the costs of the teachers and school books and other materials. Farm schools usually were not provided with food for the children who attended them. Interviews of children attending schools indicated that they liked going there on the condition that the teachers and other students did not beat them and they were fed regularly.

Few people lived in government or NGO-provided houses. Most San built their own houses out of materials they either purchased or collected themselves. Many of the houses were made of mud, sticks and thatching grass. It was unusual for a house to be made of brick and to have a tin roof. It is interesting to note, however, that housing was rarely mentioned as an issue in interviews regarding life quality and satisfaction. Happiness levels appeared to correlate with people's sense of social, economic and political security. It is also important to point out that there is no single word that means happiness in G/ui. A common expression relevant to it is *!aĩ ja ǂao* which means 'fine in the heart.' The word *!aĩ* means 'good, fine, comfortable, tasty', then *ja*, which is linked with the meaning of the locative, and *ǂao* 'heart'. This phrase is used as follows: *cire !aĩ ja ǂao*, I am comfortable in the heart, or 'I am happy/glad/pleased' (Hirosaki Nakagawa, personal communication, 2017).

There were few data on self-harm such as suicide among San other than anecdotal. It was apparent that the reported frequency of suicide and serious drug and alcohol use was much greater in the resettlement sites around the Central Kalahari than it was inside of the Central Kalahari Game Reserve itself. Alcohol and drug abuse and related domestic abuse were serious problems in many communities in rural and urban Botswana and were independent of the ethnic backgrounds of the members of those communities. Based on anecdotal reports, alcoholism and drug abuse rates were much lower in the Central Kalahari than was the case on the freehold farms and cattle posts and in urban areas.

In conclusion, there was a direct correlation between life satisfaction levels and remoteness in Botswana; the more remote that people were, the greater sense that people had of a good quality of life. It is also important to note that assessments of quality of life were related in part to livelihood security. If people were able to obtain sufficient food and income to meet their needs, they said that they had a good to excellent quality of life. Economic wellbeing generally was low to moderate for San households as compared to those people living in towns and urban areas, but life satisfaction was higher for people in rural and remote places, including freehold farms and the Central Kalahari Game Reserve.

One of the greatest fears of many of the people in the Kalahari was that they would be evicted and thus they would lose access to the land and natural resources where they lived. This fear of dispossession increased when the government of Botswana decided to relocate the people of the Central Kalahari out of the reserve in 1997 and 2002 and moved people from Ranyane in Ghanzi District to another place, Bere in 2010. Additional evictions were threatened in the Okavango Delta in 2017. The fact that the former residents of the reserve took the government of Botswana to court and won the right to return to their land and resources turned out to be an important factor in life satisfaction estimations and in the attitudes of San in the western, central and eastern Kalahari regarding their hopes for the future.

The problem now is that the government of Botswana aims to relocate people out of other conservation areas in the country, and people living in what were community-controlled areas with community trusts are finding themselves in situations where their community-based organizations have been taken over by private companies, many with the full support of the Botswana government (Hitchcock & Babchuk, 2018; Sapignoli, 2018). If these processes continue, the social, economic and spiritual wellbeing of the San will continue to decline. It is clear that the Botswana government will have to ensure that it is in fact committed to human rights and social justice for all, as it claims frequently in its statements to the international community.

Acknowledgments

Support for the fieldwork and archival research upon which this chapter is based was provided by the government of Botswana's Remote Area Development Program, the US National Science Foundation (grants SOC75-02253 and BNS76-20676), the International Work Group for Indigenous Affairs (IWGIA), Social Impact Assessment and Policy Analysis (SIAPAC), the US Agency for International Development (USAID), the Max Planck Institute for Social Anthropology and the Norwegian Agency for International Development (NORAD). We thank Matthew Manning and Christopher Fleming for their comments on an earlier draft of this chapter. We also want to thank our field assistants for their hard work on the data collection, and the people of the Kalahari in Botswana for the information that they so willingly provided.

Bibliography

Albertson, A. (2000). *Traditional land-use systems of selected traditional territories in the Central Kalahari Game Reserve.* Report to First People of the Kalahari, Ghanzi, Botswana.

Ambrey, C.L., & Fleming, C.M. (2014). Life satisfaction in Australia: Evidence from ten years of the HILDA survey. *Social Indicators Research, 115*(2), 691–714.

Anaya, S.J. (2010). *Twelfth Session, Agenda Item 3, Human Rights Council. Promotion and protection of human rights, civil, political, economic, social and cultural rights, including the right to development. Report of the Special Rapporteur on the situation of human rights and fundamental freedoms of indigenous people, James Anaya, Addendum: The situation of Indigenous peoples in Botswana.* Geneva: Human Rights Council. A/HRC/ 13, 22 February.

Barnard, A. (1992). *Hunters and herders of southern Africa: A comparative ethnography of the Khoisan peoples.* Cambridge: Cambridge University Press.

Barnard, A. (2007). *Anthropology and the Bushmen.* Oxford: Berg.

Bennett, G., & Hitchcock, R. (2017). Depositions and dilemmas: Anthropological collaborations with lawyers on indigenous legal cases in Botswana. In A.-M. Foblets, M. Sapignoli, & B. Danahoe (Eds.), *Anthropological expertise in legal practice.* Halle: Max Planck Institute for Social Anthropology & London: Routledge.

Botswana Institute of Development Policy Analysis. (1997). *Study of poverty and poverty alleviation in Botswana, volumes I and II.* Gaborone: Ministry of Finance and Development Planning.

Botswana Institute of Development Policy Analysis. (2003). *Review of the Remote Area Development Program.* Gaborone: Ministry of Local Government.

Campbell, A.C. (1964). A few notes on the Gcwi Bushmen of the Central Kalahari Desert, Bechuanaland. *Nada, 9*(1), 39–47.

Campbell, A.C., & Main, M. (1991). *Western Sandveld Remote Area Dwellers: Socio-economic survey, Remote Area Development.* Serowe: Central District Administration and Gaborone: Remote Area Development Program, Ministry of Local Government and Lands.

Campbell, A., Main, M., & Hitchcock, R.K. (2006). Land, livestock, and labor in rural Botswana: The Western Sandveld Region of Central District as a case study. In R.K. Hitchcock, K. Ikeya, M. Biesele, & R.B. Lee (Eds.), *Updating the San: Image and reality of an African people in the 21st century* (pp. 183–288). Osaka, Japan: National Museum of Ethnology.

Cassidy, L., Good, K., Mazonde, I., & Rivers, R. (2001) *An assessment of the status of San in Botswana.* Windhoek, Namibia: Legal Assistance Center.

Childers, G.W. (1976). *Report on the survey/investigation of the Ghanzi Farm Basarwa Situation.* Gaborone: Government Printer.

Christian Michelsen Institute. (1996). *NORAD's Support of the Remote Area Development Programme in Botswana (RADP) in Botswana.* Bergen, Norway: Chr. Michelsen Institute, University of Bergen/Oslo, Norway: Royal Norwegian Ministry of Foreign Affairs and Gaborone/Botswana: Ministry of Local Government, Lands, and Housing.

Dockery, A.M. (2010). *Culture and wellbeing: The case of Indigenous Australians.* Perth, WA: Centre for Labour Market Research.

Dockery, A.M. (2014). *A wellbeing approach to mobility and its application to Aboriginal and Torres Strait Islander Australians.* New York: Springer.

Egner, B., & Klausen, A.L. (1980). *Poverty in Botswana.* Gaborone: National Institute of Development and Cultural Research.

English, M., Clauss, B., Swartz, W., & Xhari, J. (1980). *"We, the people of the short blanket": Development proposals based on the needs and aspirations of the Central Kalahari Game Reserve populations.* Ghanzi, Botswana: Remote Area Development Office, Ghanzi District Council.

Good, K. (2009). *Diamonds, dispossession and democracy in Botswana.* Johannesburg: James Currey and Jacana Media.

Government of Botswana. (2009). *Revised Remote Area Development Programme (RADP).* Gaborone: Ministry of Local Government.

Guenther, M.G. (1986). *The Nharo Bushmen of Botswana: Tradition and change.* Hamburg: Helmut Buske Verlag.

Güldemann, Tom (2014). 'Khoisan' linguistic classification today. In T. Güldemann & A.-M. Fehn (Eds.), *Beyond 'Khoisan': Historical relations in the Kalahari Basin* (pp. 1–44). Amsterdam: John Benjamins.

High Court of Botswana. (2002). *Central Kalahari Legal Case No. MISCA 52/2002 in the Matter between Roy Sesana, First Applicant, Keiwa Setlhobogwa and 241 others, Second and Further Applicants, and the Attorney General (in his capacity as the recognized agent of the Government of the Republic of Botswana).* Lobatse: High Court of Botswana.

Hitchcock, R.K. (1978). *Kalahari cattle posts: A regional study of hunter-gatherers, pastoralists and agriculturalists in the Western Sandveld Region, Central District, Botswana* (2 Vols.). Gaborone: Government Printer.

Hitchcock, R.K. (1980). Tradition, social justice, and land reform in central Botswana. *Journal of African Law, 24*(1), 1–34.

Hitchcock, R.K. (1988). *Monitoring, research, and development in the remote areas of Botswana.* Gaborone: Ministry of Local Government, Lands, and Housing, and Oslo, Norway: Norwegian Agency for Development Cooperation.

Hitchcock, R.K., & Babchuk, W.A. (2018). *Tourism, heritage preservation, and sustainable development: Kalahari San perspectives.* Paper presented at the 78th annual meetings of the Society for Applied Anthropology (SfAA), Philadelphia, PA, USA, 3–7 April.

Hitchcock, R.K., & Ebert, J.I. (2011). Where is that job? Hunter-gatherer information systems in complex social environments in the Eastern Kalahari Desert, Botswana. In R. Whallon, W.A. Lovis, & R.K.

Hitchcock (Eds.), *Information and its role in hunter-gatherer bands* (pp. 133–166). Los Angeles, CA: The Cotsen Institute of Archaeology Press.

Hitchcock, R.K., & Masilo, R.R.B. (1995). *Subsistence hunting and resource rights in Botswana*. Gaborone: Department of Wildlife and National Parks.

Hitchcock, R.K., & Sapignoli, M. (2016). 21st century foraging among Western and Central Kalahari San. In B.S. Codding & K.L. Kramer (Eds.), *Why forage? Hunting and gathering in the 21st century* (pp. 89–111). Santa Fe, NM: School for Advanced Research Press/Albuquerque, NM: University of New Mexico Press.

Hitchcock, R.K., Sapignoli, M., & Babchuk, W.A. (2011). "What about our rights"? Settlements, subsistence, and livelihood security among Central Kalahari San and Bakgalagadi. *The International Journal of Human Rights, 15*(1), 62–88.

Hitchcock, R.K., Sapignoli, M., Frost, J., & Babchuk, W.A. (2016). Botswana. In C. Mikkelsen (Ed.), *The Indigenous world 2016* (pp. 456–463). Copenhagen: International Work Group for Indigenous Affairs (IWGIA).

Hitchcock, R.K., Ikeya, K., Biesele, M., & Lee, R.B. (Eds.) (2006). *Updating the San: Image and reality of an African people in the 21st century*. Senri Ethnological Studies 70. Osaka, Japan: National Museum of Ethnology.

Ikeya, K. (2001). Some changes among the San under the influence of relocation plan in Botswana. In D.G. Anderson & K. Ikeya (Eds.), *Parks, property, and power: Managing hunting practice and identity within state policy regimes* (pp. 183–198). Senri Ethnological Studies No. 59. Osaka, Japan: National Museum of Ethnology.

Ingstad, B., & Fugelli, P. (2006). 'Our health was better in the time of Queen Elizabeth': The importance of land to the health perception of the Botswana San. In R.K. Hitchcock, K. Ikeya, M. Biesele, & R.B. Lee (Eds.), *Updating the San: Image and reality of an African people in the 21st century* (pp. 61–79). Osaka, Japan: National Museum of Ethnology.

Isaacs, S.M., & Manatsha, B.T. (2016). Will the dreaded 'Yellow Monster' stop roaring again? An appraisal of Botswana's 2015 land policy. *Botswana Notes and Records, 48*(1), 383–395.

Kiema, K. (2010). *Tears for my land: A social history of the Kua of the Central Kalahari Game Reserve, Tc'amnqo*. Gaborone: Mmegi Publishing House.

LeRoux, W. (1999). *Torn apart: San children as change agents in a process of acculturation: A comprehensive report on the educational situation of San children throughout southern Africa*. Ghanzi, Botswana: Kuru Development Trust/Windhoek, Namibia: Working Group of Indigenous Minorities in Southern Africa.

Manning, M., Ambrey, C.L., & Fleming, C.M. (2015a). *Subjective wellbeing of the Aboriginal and Torres Strait Islander people of Australia*. Canberra: Center for Aboriginal Economic Policy Research, Australian National University.

Manning, M., Ambrey, C.L., & Fleming, C.M. (2015b). *Indigenous wellbeing in Australia: Evidence from HILDA*. Center for Aboriginal Economic Policy Research Working Paper No. 101. Canberra: Center for Aboriginal Economic Policy Research, Australian National University.

Ministry of Commerce and Industry. (1986). *Report of the Central Kalahari Game Reserve fact finding mission*. MCI Circular No. 1 of 1986. Gaborone: Ministry of Commerce and Industry.

Mogalakwe, M. (1986). *Inside Ghanzi freehold farms: A look at the conditions of Basarwa farm workers*. Gaborone: Applied Research Unit, Ministry of Local Government and Lands.

Motlopi, K. (2006). *Privatization of rangelands, ranch development, management, and equity: The case of Area 4B, Botswana*. MA thesis, Norwegian University of Life Sciences Department of International Environmental and Development Studies.

Nteta, D., & Hermans, J. (Eds.), with Jeskova, P. (1996). *Poverty and plenty: The Botswana experience. Proceedings of a symposium organized by the Botswana Society, October 15–18, 1996*. Gaborone: Botswana Society.

Nussbaum, M., & Sen, A. (Eds.). (1993). *The quality of life*. Oxford: Clarendon Press.

Osaki, M. (1984). The social influence of change in hunting technique among the Central Kalahari San. *African Study Monographs, 5*(1), 49–62.

Pagiwa, V. (2013). *High incidence and prevalence rates of pulmonary TB among nomadic Basarwa in Gantsi sub-district, Botswana*. MSc. thesis, Ritsumeikan Asia Pacific University, Oita, Japan.

Republic of Botswana. (1975). *National policy on tribal grazing land*. Government Paper No. 2. Gaborone: Government Printer.

Republic of Botswana. (1986). *Wildlife conservation policy*. Government Paper No. 1 of 1986. Gaborone: Government Printer.

Republic of Botswana. (2002). *Revised national policy on destitute persons*. Gaborone: Government Printer.

Republic of Botswana. (2014). *Supplement C. wildlife conservation and national parks (prohibition of hunting, capturing, or removal of animals order, 2014). Statutory instrument No. 2 of 2014. Botswana Government Gazette, Volume LII, No. 2, 10 January, 2014.* Gaborone: Botswana Government Gazette.

Republic of Botswana. (2015). *Botswana land policy.* Government Paper No. 4 of 2015. Gaborone: Botswana Government Printer.

Russell, M. (1976). Slaves or workers? Relations between Bushmen, Tswana and Boers in the Kalahari. *Journal of Southern African Studies, 2*(2), 178–197.

Russell, M., & Russell, M. (1979). *Afrikaners of the Kalahari: White minority in a Black state.* Cambridge: Cambridge University Press.

Sapignoli, M. (2015). Dispossession in the age of humanity: Human rights, citizenship, and indigeneity in the Central Kalahari. *Anthropological Forum: A Journal of Social Anthropology and Comparative Sociology, 25*(3), 285–305.

Sapignoli, M. (2018). *Hunting justice: Displacement, law and activism in the Kalahari.* Cambridge: Cambridge University Press.

Sapignoli, M., & Hitchcock, R.K. (2011). *Social impact assessment anthropological analysis of the Ghanzi copper mine area, Western Botswana.* Gaborone, Botswana: Loci Environmental/Windhoek, Namibia: SIAPAC.

Sapignoli, M., & Hitchcock, R.K. (2013a). Development and dispossession: Land reform in Botswana. In S. Evers, C. Seagle, & F. Krijten (Eds.), *Africa for sale: Analyzing and theorizing foreign land claims and acquisitions* (pp. 217–246). Leiden: Brill Academic Publishers.

Sapignoli, M., & Hitchcock, R. (2013b). Indigenous peoples in southern Africa. *The Round Table: The Commonwealth Journal of International Affairs, 102*(4), 355–365.

Saugestad, S. (2001). *The inconvenient Indigenous: Remote area development in Botswana, donor assistance, and the first people of the Kalahari.* Uppsala, Sweden: Nordic Africa Institute.

Seleka, T., Siphambe, H., Ntseana, D., Mbere, N., Kerapeletswe, C., & Sharp, C. (2007). *Social safety nets in Botswana: Administration, targeting, and sustainability.* Gaborone: Lightbooks.

Sheller, P. (1977). *The people of the Central Kalahari Game Reserve: A report on the reconnaissance of the Reserve, July–September, 1976.* Report to the Ministry of Local Government and Lands, Gaborone, Botswana.

Silberbauer, G.B. (1965). *Report to the Government of Bechuanaland on the Bushman Survey.* Gaberone: Bechuanaland Government.

Silberbauer, G.B. (1981). *Hunter and habitat in the Central Kalahari Desert.* New York: Cambridge University Press.

Silberbauer, G.B. (2012). Why the Central Kalahari Game Reserve? *Botswana Notes and Records, 44*(1), 201–203.

Singh, K.K., Le Brocque, A., Costanza, R., & Cadet-James, Y. (2015). Ecosystems and Indigenous wellbeing: An integrated framework. *Global Ecology and Conservation, 4*(1), 197–206.

Takada, A. (Ed.). (2016). *Natural history of communication among the Central Kalahari San.* African Study Monographs Supplementary Issue 52. Kyoto: African Study Monographs.

Takada, A. (2016). Unfolding cultural meanings: Way finding practices among the San of the Central Kalahari. In W.A. Lovis & R. Whallon (Eds.), *Marking the land: Hunter-gatherers creation of meaning in their environment* (pp. 180–205). New York: Routledge.

Tanaka, J. (1980). *The San, hunter-gatherers of the Kalahari. A study in ecological anthropology.* Tokyo: Tokyo University Press.

Tanaka, J. (2014). *The Bushmen: A half-century chronicle of transformation in hunter-gatherer life and ecology.* Kyoto: Kyoto University Press/Melbourne: Trans Pacific Press.

Taylor, J. (2008). Indigenous peoples and indicators of well-being: Australian perspectives on United Nations Global Framework. *Social Indicators Research, 87*(1), 111–126.

Toteng, E.N. (1991). *Socio-economic population and land-use survey – Kweneng District and Central Kalahari Game Reserve.* Gaborone: Applied Research Unit, Ministry of Local Government and Lands.

United Nations Childrens Fund. (2014). *UNICEF Annual Report 2014: Botswana.* New York: United Nations Childrens Fund (UNICEF).

United Nations Development Program. (2015). *Human Development Report 2015: Work for human development.* New York: United Nations Development Program (UNDP).

Valiente-Noailles, C. (1993). *The Kua: Life and soul of the Central Kalahari Bushmen.* Amsterdam: A.A. Balkema.

White, S.C. with Abeyasekera, A. (2014). *Wellbeing and quality of life assessment: A practical guide.* Rugby: Practical Action Publishing.

Wiessner, P. (2003). Owners of the future? Calories, cash, casualties, and self-sufficiency in the Nyae Nyae Area between 1996–2003. *Visual Anthropology Review, 19*(1–2), 149–159.

Wily, E.A. (1979). *Official policy towards San (Bushmen) hunter-gatherers in modern Botswana: 1966–1978.* Gaborone: National Institute of Development and Cultural Research.

Wily, E.A. (1982). A strategy of self-determination for the Kalahari San (The Botswana government's programme of action in the Ghanzi farms). *Development and Change, 13*(2), 291–308.

World Bank. (2015). *Botswana poverty assessment.* Washington, DC: The World Bank.

World Bank. (2018). *The state of social safety nets 2018.* Washington, DC: World Bank.

16

ECONOMIC WELLBEING OF THE INDIGENOUS PEOPLE IN THE ASIA PACIFIC REGION

The role of entrepreneurship in sustainable development

Rick Colbourne and Robert B. Anderson

Introduction

The United Nations Permanent Forum on Indigenous Issues (2015, p. 1) estimates that there are more than 370 million Indigenous people spread across seventy countries worldwide practicing unique traditions and retaining social, cultural, economic and political characteristics that are distinct from those of the dominant societies within which they live. The Indigenous peoples living in the Asia Pacific region represent approximately 70 percent of the world's Indigenous population (UNDP, 2012) and almost 15 percent of the world's poor, facing many challenges such as poor health, discrimination, substandard education, the loss of traditional livelihoods and restricted access to work and other socioeconomic opportunities (Dhir, 2015; UNDP, 2012). Despite broad efforts over the past four decades to improve the wellbeing of Indigenous peoples and increase their recognition, many Asian countries have not yet recognized and/or acted on Indigenous rights (Dhir, 2015). This, coupled with weak frameworks for the protection of human rights evident in some Asia Pacific countries, poses severe challenges to improving the prospects for promoting economic development and wellbeing for Indigenous peoples in the Asia Pacific (Dhir, 2015, pp. 3–4). Asia Pacific's Indigenous peoples are responding to these issues and challenges by working to preserve and sustain traditional cultural and linguistic practices, addressing complex land rights, ownership and exploitation issues, managing demands on natural resources, asserting political self-determination and autonomy, coping with environmental degradation and globalization (Dhir, 2015; UNDP, 2012). Permanent self-determination over the natural resources within their traditional territories is necessary for these efforts to be successful and sustainable (Corntassel, 2008).

The sections that follow in this chapter explore the importance of economic wellbeing and entrepreneurship in the Asia Pacific region through introducing and exploring the concepts of Indigenous self-determination and economic wellbeing. The chapter ends with three case studies which examine Indigenous entrepreneurship and the potential that it holds for promoting self-determination, sustainability and economic wellbeing by, and for the benefit of, Indigenous peoples.

Indigenous self-determination, economic wellbeing and entrepreneurship

Self-determination and recognition as distinct peoples in Asia Pacific

Historically, Indigenous peoples suffered colonization, subjugation, integration and assimilation by merchants, traders, states and churches aimed at diminishing or eradicating Indigenous cultures, practices and identities (Russell, 2009). The effects of colonization deprived Indigenous peoples in Asia Pacific of access to and collective ownership of the natural resources of their traditional territories and undermined unique cultures, languages and religions. Post-colonial governments exacerbated these negative effects by supporting and advancing non-Indigenous interests over those of their Indigenous peoples (Russell, 2009).

In response to ongoing challenges faced by the world's Indigenous people and their long-standing struggle for redress, the United Nations adopted the United Nations Declaration on the Rights of Indigenous Peoples (UNDRIP) on 13 September 2007 to enshrine those rights that "constitute the minimum standards for the survival, dignity and wellbeing of the indigenous peoples of the world" (Article 43) (Amnesty International Canada, 2016; Blackstock, 2013). The most relevant concepts that relate to the economic wellbeing of Indigenous peoples in the Asia Pacific are: (a) the right to self-determination; (b) the right to be recognized as distinct peoples; and (c) the right to free, prior and informed consent.

The right to self-determination is the right for Indigenous peoples to freely determine their political status and freely pursue their economic, social and cultural development while being respectful of the human rights of their community members and other peoples (Blackstock, 2013, p. 12; United Nations General Assembly, 2008). This includes the right to autonomy or self-government in matters relating to their internal and local affairs, as well as the ways and means for financing their governance and economic development activities (United Nations General Assembly, 2008). Indigenous peoples have the right to be recognized as distinct peoples. They have a collective right to live in freedom, peace and security as distinct peoples and maintain and strengthen their distinct political, legal, economic, social and cultural institutions, while retaining their rights to participate fully in the political, economic, social and cultural life of their country (United Nations General Assembly, 2008). They have the right to manifest, practice, develop and teach their spiritual and religious traditions, customs and ceremonies; the right to maintain, protect, and have access in privacy to their religious and cultural sites; the right to the use and control of their ceremonial objects; and the right to the repatriation of their human remains (United Nations General Assembly, 2008). Finally, the right to free, prior and informed consent (FPIC) obliges governments to obtain the consent of Indigenous peoples before making decisions that impact them within their traditional territories (United Nations General Assembly, 2008). FPIC does not supersede a sovereign country's law with respect to its legislative and decision-making responsibilities. The principle that Indigenous peoples have the right to give or withhold their free, prior and informed consent is not only recognized by and strengthened as a legal right by the UNDRIP (Anderson, 2011) but is reinforced by other international bodies as well.

A number of countries in the Asia Pacific still struggle with the definition of 'indigenous' and with determining who their Indigenous peoples are and this has resulted in a variety of designations being used (Lama, 2013, p. 34). Some Asian Pacific countries refer to Indigenous peoples as minority nationalities, schedule tribes, ethnic minorities, hill tribes, cultural communities, adivasi, or janajati among other designations (Lama, 2013, p. 34) and this has resulted in increased confusion and complexity related to engagement processes. Asian Pacific countries such as the Philippines, Taiwan, Malaysia, Nepal and Japan have officially recognized the term 'Indigenous peoples', in accordance with the UNDRIP and the International Labour

Organization Convention No. 169 on Indigenous and Tribal Peoples, to identify those peoples they regard as having a distinct cultural tradition and history (Lama, 2013). Finally, due to internal socio-political issues surrounding the notion of defining 'indigenous', Asia Pacific countries such as China, India and Bangladesh have resisted designating and identifying peoples as 'indigenous', opting instead to adopt country and context-specific monikers (Lama, 2013).

Indigenous wellbeing

Indigenous wellbeing is premised on sustainable self-determination that is in turn dependent on a community's evolving model for economic development, its cultural traditions, relationship to its traditional territories and its particular spiritual practices to enable the transmission of these traditions and practices to future generations (Corntassel, 2008). In this context, Indigenous leaders have consistently and repeatedly declared their desire to participate in the Asia Pacific economy, capitalize on the abundance of resources on their traditional lands and create long-term sustainable and distributional social and economic development opportunities within their communities. They believe that enhanced control of their lands and resources will enable them to develop a mode of social regulation that will end dependency and foster development without sacrificing distinct Indigenous cultures, values and practices. Sustainable self-determination, then, operates at the community level as a process to promote wellbeing through the creation of economic development opportunities via the regeneration of cultural traditions, renewal of its relationship to its traditional territories and through practicing its particular spiritual practices (Corntassel, 2008). Through participating in the global economy and that of their country and by exercising effective control over and use of their traditional lands and resources, Indigenous leaders are confident that they can achieve economic wellbeing through attaining the particular socioeconomic objectives valued by their communities (see Table 16.1). This, in turn, represents a strong potential for Indigenous peoples in the Asia Pacific to re-establish larger regional economic networks with each that facilitate the formation alliances that might lead to sustainable futures and greater community wellbeing (Corntassel, 2008).

Historically, effective participation by Indigenous peoples in their country's mainstream economy has been difficult due to political indifference, government policy, archaic legislation, narrow interpretations of Indigenous rights to land and resources, and a reluctance to acknowledge the validity of traditional Indigenous approaches to the exercise of these rights. Indeed, Indigenous peoples choosing to opt in to the Asia Pacific economy find themselves at the beginning of a long process of interaction with representatives of the state(s) which encompass their lands, supranational organizations and actors in global economy, principally multinational corporations. Key to this interaction is recognition and assertion of their rights

Table 16.1 Indigenous socioeconomic objectives

Indigenous socioeconomic objectives	• Greater control of activities on their traditional lands • Self-determination and an end to dependency through economic self-sufficiency • The preservation and strengthening of traditional values and their application in economic development and business activities • Improved socioeconomic circumstance for individuals, families and communities

Source: Anderson, Dana, and Dana (2006, p. 47).

with all parties accountable for respecting the UNDRIP's directive of free, prior and informed consent (Anderson, Wingham, Giberson, & Gibson, 2014). With increased recognition of rights comes increased opportunities to address Indigenous wellbeing through a renewed focus on Indigenous economic development for and by Indigenous peoples. Economic wellbeing involves building capacity across three main dimensions: human, financial and physical. The recognition of Indigenous rights provides both financial and physical capacity. People must know *how to do* entrepreneurship, broadly defined, to realize the potential in the capacity inherent in these rights, an aspect of human capital if they are to improve individual and community wellbeing (Anderson, 2001; Colbourne, 2012).

Indigenous entrepreneurship

Indigenous entrepreneurship is a distinctive activity that operates at the intersection of social and economic entrepreneurship whereby entrepreneurship is tempered by a community's particular social, cultural and economic objectives, its rights and access to assets and resources (Anderson, Honig, & Peredo, 2006). For Indigenous peoples in the Asia Pacific, entrepreneurship represents an opportunity to build a vibrant Indigenous-led economy that can support sustainable economic wellbeing (Anderson, Giberson, Hindle, & Kayseas, 2004). It is also a means by which they can exercise and sustain their rights to design, develop and maintain political, economic and social systems or institutions, to be secure in the enjoyment of their own means of subsistence and development, and to engage freely in traditional and economic activities occurring on or near their traditional territories (Peredo, Anderson, Galbraith, & Honig, 2004; United Nations General Assembly, 2008, p. 8). Although the evidence suggests that the circumstances of Indigenous peoples in the Asia Pacific provide strong incentives for entrepreneurship, their non-mainstream status carries a number of liabilities that challenge them as they attempt to realize their entrepreneurial potential.

For Indigenous entrepreneurship and, therefore, economic wellbeing to thrive there needs to be a supportive infrastructure in place that is responsive to the particular issues and challenges faced by Indigenous peoples. While Indigenous peoples in the Asia Pacific region value the potential that entrepreneurial activities hold for rebuilding and redeveloping their communities, they also recognize the need to consider traditional knowledge and understandings and their particular histories, cultures and values in entrepreneurial decision-making (see Table 16.2) (Anderson et al., 2006).

Indigenous peoples in the Asia Pacific region do not share common values or approaches to economic development. Therefore, while they value the potential that entrepreneurial activities hold for rebuilding and redeveloping their communities, they also recognize the need to consider traditional knowledge and understandings and their particular histories, cultures and values in entrepreneurial decision-making (Anderson et al., 2006). Decisions are made to participate in particular entrepreneurial opportunities based on an Indigenous community's access to resources, proximity to markets, social needs in context of traditional knowledge values and culture (Anderson et al., 2014). Indigenous economic development and wellbeing initiatives are more successful when the rights of Indigenous peoples are addressed and when these initiatives are led by or engage Indigenous communities. In combination with holistic and dynamic notions of sustainable self-determination, Indigenous entrepreneurship holds the potential for increasing the wellbeing of Indigenous peoples through restoring both their cultural and ecological ecosystems (Corntassel, 2008).

The case studies that follow focus on the economic wellbeing of Indigenous people in the Asia Pacific. The studies highlight that economic wellbeing is not just about money, it is about

Table 16.2 Characteristics of indigenous entrepreneurship

Collective	• Predominantly collective-centered approach that supports and builds on the specific values, resources and needs of the particular Indigenous community
Economic self-sufficiency	• Attainment of economic self-sufficiency as a necessary condition for the realization of Indigenous self-government
Socioeconomic development	• Improvement of the socioeconomic conditions of the people of the Indigenous community
Traditional cultures, values and languages	• Preservation and strengthening of particular traditional values, culture language and knowledge of importance to particular Indigenous community
Business ownership	• Creation of Indigenous businesses to exercise the control over the economic development process
Global competition	• Creation of Indigenous businesses to compete profitably over the long term in the global economy and to build an Indigenous-based economy that supports self-government and improves socioeconomic conditions
Alliances and joint ventures	• Formation of alliances and joint ventures between Indigenous communities and with non-Indigenous partners to create businesses that compete profitably in the global economy

Source: Anderson (1997).

history, tradition, culture and language embedded in time and traditional territory. It is sustainable self-determination – the creation, management and development of new ventures by Indigenous peoples for the benefit of Indigenous peoples (Hindle & Lansdowne, 2005, p. 132). These ventures can be private, public or non-profit that can benefit individual Indigenous entrepreneurs or more broadly provide multiple social and economic advantages for entire communities and non-Indigenous enterprise partners and stakeholders (Hindle & Lansdowne, 2005, p. 132).

Asia Pacific Indigenous entrepreneurship and economic wellbeing case studies

Indonesia: Lembah Mukti Village and Talaga Village

In the Asia Pacific region, the right of Indigenous peoples to give or withhold their free, prior and informed consent is central to the United Nations' collaborative initiative on Reducing Emissions from Deforestation and forest Degradation (REDD+) in developing countries. REDD+ was launched in 2008 to promote informed and meaningful involvement of all partners, including Indigenous peoples and other forest-dependent communities, in national and international REDD+ implementation processes (Ogle, 2012, p. i). FPIC in this context involves the collective right of Indigenous peoples and communities to informed participation through understanding the full range of issues in discussions and decision-making related to proposed changes in resource management activities that might affect their lands, traditional territories, resources or other rights (Anderson, 2011; Ogle, 2012).

Indonesia, with a population of approximately 250 million, is home to up to 70 million Indigenous peoples (Erni & Nilsson, 2015, p. 262). While the Ministry of Social Affairs identifies some Indigenous communities as *komunitas adat terpencil* (geographically isolated Indigenous communities), many other peoples self-identify, or are considered by others, as Indigenous. Recent government legislation uses the term *masyarakat adat* to refer to Indigenous peoples. Most recently, Indonesia has worked to clarify land rights and the solving of land disputes related to its Indigenous peoples (Erni & Nilsson, 2015). Central Sulawesi, for example, was chosen as a pilot province for Indonesia's UN-REDD National Programme due to the high deforestation rate of 118,744 hectares per year between 2003 and 2006 attributed to planned and unplanned forest conversions caused by plantations, mining, cocoa production, illegal logging and forest fires (Ogle, 2012, p. 8). During 2012, draft FPIC guidelines were piloted with two villages: Lembah Mukti Village (includes five sub-villages) and Talaga Village to assist the local Forestry Management Unit (FMU) in implementing a forest rehabilitation program. This involved promoting opportunities for creating socioeconomic wellbeing by replanting areas of degraded forest with species valued by the local community (rubber and /or jabon). In exchange the village was expected to take responsibility for carrying out forest conserva-tion activities (Ogle, 2012). The FPIC process for Lembah Mukti Village and the Talaga Village began similarly and involved:

1. the design, development, testing and revision of communication materials that included banners, posters, brochures and calendars;
2. the recruitment and training (trained on climate change, REDD+, and the FPIC process negation and facilitation skills) of twenty facilitators from the two main villages and nearby villages;
3. initial visits to each village to explain the REDD+ forest rehabilitation proposal by the FMU; and
4. return visits by facilitators two weeks later to Lembah Mukti Village to hold workshops on the forest rehabilitation program (they did not return to Talaga Village).

While the FMU's FPIC process was the same for both villages, it resulted in two very different outcomes.

Lembah Mukti Village: the villagers of Lembah Mukti agreed to implement the forest rehabilitation program as proposed by the FMU but requested that changes such as assistance to resolve boundary disputes, forest management training and the provision of nutmeg and durian seedlings be made. The result was that negotiators representing the village and the FMU signed a Letter of Agreement, formal assistance was provided to address boundary disputes and work was undertaken to delineate and clarify the status of private land owned by the village and that owned by the FMU. In addition, rubber and janbon were replanted, nutmeg and durian seeds were provided to the villages, training on replanting and social forestry was provided, and a formal process was developed for managing complaints and feedback (Ogle, 2012, pp. 9, 10). Lembah Mukti villagers agreed to address forest conservation and management through halting illegal logging activities, establishing regulations to prohibit poaching, planting trees on steep slopes to reduce natural disasters and through permitting the FMU to carry out its rubber and janbon replanting program (Ogle, 2012, pp. 9, 10).

Talaga Village: in contrast, the villagers of Talaga did not wish to consult with the FMU on the REDD+ forest rehabilitation program. Pokja Pantau, an NGO, had informed them that the REDD+ process would impact their engagement with the forest and destroy the socio-cultural values of the community. As a result, the FPIC process was discontinued by the FMU. Pokja Pantau requested further consultation with the FMU and the UN-REDD Programme in order to exchange information and to clarify any misunderstandings about the role of the UN-REDD Programme (Ogle, 2012, pp. 9, 10). The result was that Indonesia's UN-REDD

National Programme facilitated meetings between Pokja Pantau and other interested parties during which they presented their concerns that adequate safeguards be put in place and argued for the need to provide sufficient information to the affected villages before the REDD+ activities were implemented (Ogle, 2012, pp. 9, 10).

The experience of the FMU in engaging the two villages in central Sulawesi in the pilot for Indonesia's UN-REDD National Programme demonstrates a central tenet of FPIC in context of Indigenous peoples' right to choose how they participate or not participate in activities related to the global economy – primarily, that a community may refuse permission to engage in consultations and/or participate, as happened with Talaga Village and that, where this occurs, this decision must be respected. It also reinforces that, due to the issues and challenges related to complex interactions between Indigenous peoples, language, culture, territories, globalization and corporate and governmental interests, FPIC processes require adequate time to be set aside to facilitate awareness building. More specifically, first, a single awareness raising event for local communities and Indigenous peoples is insufficient to address and fully inform community members. The inherent complexity of FPIC engagement activities requires repeated communications across different modes and channels to facilitate discussions that raise awareness, inform community members and ensure that key messages and issues are clearly understood (UNDP, 2012). Second, local facilitators are essential for building awareness and facilitating informed discussions in an Indigenous people's first or common language. While local facilitators require training and development in REDD+ issues as well as in community facilitation, negotiation and engagement processes, they represent significant potential for accelerating community understanding and trust (Ogle, 2012). Finally, FPIC is a right of Indigenous peoples to be treated as owners and/or stewards of their traditional territories with full and equal participation guaranteed in all stages of decision-making, development, planning and implementation for projects (i.e. REDD+) that affect them.

FPIC must be viewed as an ongoing commitment to ensuring transparency, understanding and greater participation and engagement by Indigenous peoples and communities. Promoting social and economic wellbeing for Indigenous peoples hinges on the right to self-determination, the right to be recognized as distinct peoples and the fundamental right to free, prior and informed consent (Anderson, 2011).

Japan: Ainu museums and heritage sites

The Ainu are Indigenous peoples of Japan whose traditional territory primarily encompassed the inhabited part of Hokkaido, southern Sakhalin and Kuril islands and the far-eastern region of Russia (Pennewiss, 2007; Tanabe, 2014). Traditionally, they were involved in hunting, fishing and subsistence farming while also acting as intermediaries among the Japanese, Dutch, Chinese, Russian and Korean traders among others (Espiritu, 2005). For over a century, the Japanese government denied that the Ainu were an Indigenous peoples and it was only with the ratification of the UNDRIP and a court ruling of the Sapporo District Court recognizing and protecting of Ainu culture in 1997 that the they were formally recognized as an Indigenous peoples by Japan in 2008 (Okada, 2012; Pennewiss, 2007). Recognition, however, could not reverse the loss of traditional territory and the erosion and displacement of their traditional names, language and culture over the past century. While the Japanese government has made concessions in the form of funding teaching, promoting and researching Ainu culture and promoting coexistence with the Ainu peoples, they have not addressed any of the political, economic and other traditional rights of the Ainu as Indigenous peoples. Subsequently, they have been denied the rights to use and control the land which anchors Ainu culture (Morris-Suzuki, 1999).

Historically, the Ainu appropriated local, regional and international tourism as a political instrument in the constitution of their identity (see for example, Friedman, 1990). In 1916, for example, the Kawamura Ainu Memorial Museum in Hokkaido and in 1972 the Nibutani Ainu Culture Information Centre were established to preserve and promote Ainu culture. More recently, the Ainu have developed heritage sites modeled on traditional Aiun villages at Lake Akan and Shiraoi and other museums at Shizunai, Obihiro, Abashiri, Hakodate, Kushiro and Sapporo. All of these ventures feature performances of traditional dance, cultural practices and handicrafts related to the Aiun peoples and focus on Ainu history, traditional lifestyle, and culture related to that particular region (Savage & Hindle, 2008). While the sales of carvings, fabrics, recordings of oral stories, contemporary plays, musical performances and cultural teaching materials, etc. provide some Ainu with an income, entrepreneurial activities related to tourism are motivated by the need of the Ainu to reinforce their identities as Indigenous peoples in the minds and sensibilities of the Japanese, to strengthen claims to traditional territories and to preserve and revitalize their traditional culture and language for future generations (Savage & Hindle, 2008). In contrast to the previous cases, Ainu wellbeing, sustainability and entrepreneurship collide in the peoples' continued struggle for recognition of traditional rights and for self-determination. Through rebuilding, revitalizing and reasserting their cultural practices, the Japan's Ainu peoples are slowly working towards full recognition and self-determination over the land and resources of their traditional territories (Corntassel, 2008).

Final comments

Asia Pacific's Indigenous peoples continue to work to improve their communities' economic wellbeing through actively seeking recognition as distinct peoples and through demanding that governments, corporations and international agencies recognize and act with respect to their basic human rights and their rights as Indigenous peoples as framed by the United Nations Declaration of the Rights of Indigenous Peoples and other international agencies. The central Sulawesi, Indonesia draft FPIC guidelines pilot with Lembah Mukti Village and Talaga Village for the UN-REDD National Programme discussed above demonstrated that Indigenous peoples have a right to choose how they participate or not participate in engagement activities related to the global economy. That Indigenous communities may refuse permission to engagement activities and where this occurs, this decision must be respected. It also reinforced the need to consider the complexity of FPIC processes inherent in engagement interactions between Indigenous peoples and corporate and governmental interests. In this manner, Asia Pacific's Indigenous peoples are managing increased demands being placed on their lands and resources by growing populations, industrialization and multinational corporations. With weak frameworks for protecting these rights in the Asia Pacific, Indigenous peoples are addressing challenges and considering opportunities to improve economic development and wellbeing in their communities that do not infringe on their rights to preserve and sustain traditional cultures and linguistic practices and to political self-determination and autonomy.

Indigenous economic wellbeing is not just about money, it is about history, tradition, culture and language embedded in time and traditional territory. It is the creation, management and development of new ventures by Indigenous peoples for the benefit of Indigenous peoples. For Japan's Ainu peoples, entrepreneurship is motivated by the need to reinforce their identities, strengthen their claims to traditional territories and preserve and revitalize their traditional culture and language for future generations in Japan – it supports their efforts at reclaiming their right to self-determination.

These examples demonstrate that Indigenous entrepreneurship represents a real opportunity for Indigenous communities to build vibrant Indigenous-led economies that support sustainable economic development and wellbeing as well as a means by which they can assert their rights to design, develop and maintain Indigenous-centric political, economic and social systems and institutions. Ultimately, Asia Pacific's Indigenous peoples have the right to engage freely on their own terms in traditional and economic activities occurring on or near their traditional territories. Self-determination, to be sustainable in practice, has to come with the right of self-determination over natural resources within traditional territories (Corntassel, 2008). Indigenous economic development and wellbeing initiatives are more successful when the rights of Indigenous peoples are addressed and when these initiatives are led by or engage Indigenous communities.

References

Amnesty International Canada. (2016). The United Nations Declaration on the Rights of Indigenous Peoples.

Anderson, P. (2011). *Free, prior, and informed consent in REDD+: Principles and approaches for policy and project development*. Bangkok, Thailand: Deutsche Gesellschaft für Internationale Zusammenarbeit (GIZ) GmbH Sector Network Natural Resources and Rural Development – Asia.

Anderson, R., Honig, B., & Peredo, A. (2006). Communities in the global economy: Where social and indigenous entrepreneurship meet. In C. Steyaert & D. Hjorth (Eds.), Entrepreneurship as social change: A third new movements in entrepreneurship book. Cheltenham: Edward Elgar Publishing.

Anderson, R.B. (1997). Corporate/Indigenous partnerships in economic development: The First Nations in Canada. *World Development, 25*(9), 1483–1503.

Anderson, R.B. (2001). Aboriginal people, economic development and entrepreneurship. *Journal of Aboriginal Economic Development, 2*(1) 231–242.

Anderson, R.B., Giberson, R.J., Hindle, K., & Kayseas, B. (2004). Understanding success in indigenous entrepreneurship: An exploratory investigation. In *Proceedings of the AGSE-Babson Regional Entrepreneurship Research Exchange*. Hawthorn, Victoria: Swinburne University of Technology.

Anderson, R.B., Wingham, D., Giberson, R.J., & Gibson, B. (2014). Indigenous economic development: A tale of two wineries. In G. Campbell & N. Guibert (Eds.), *Wine, society and globalization: Multidisciplinary perspectives on the wine industry* (pp. 201–220). New York: Palgrave Macmillan.

Blackstock, C. (2013). *Know your rights! United Nations Declaration on the Rights of Indigenous Peoples for Indigenous Adolescents*. Retrieved from http://files.unicef.org/policyanalysis/rights/files/HRBAP_UN_Rights_Indig_Peoples.pdf.

Colbourne, R. (2012). Ch'nook Indigenous business education initiative. *Journal of Aboriginal Economic Development, 8*(1), 73–80.

Corntassel, J. (2008). Toward sustainable self-determination: Rethinking the contemporary Indigenous-rights discourse. *Alternatives: Global, Local, Political, 33*(1), 105–132.

Dhir, R.K. (2015). *Indigenous peoples in the world of work in Asia and the Pacific: A Status Report*. Geneva, Switzerland: International Labour Organization.

Erni, C., & Nilsson, C. (2015). East and Southeast Asia. In C. Mikkelsen & S. Stidsen (Eds.), *The Indigenous world 2015* (pp. 218–232). Copenhagen, Denmark: International Work Group for Indigenous Affairs (IWGIA).

Espiritu, A.A. (2005). Ainu. In M. Nuttall (Ed.), *Encyclopedia of the Arctic*. New York: Routledge.

Friedman, J. (1990). Being in the world: Globalization and localization. *Theory, Culture and Society, 7*(2), 311–328.

Hindle, K., & Lansdowne, M. (2005). Brave spirits on new paths: Toward a globally relevant paradigm of indigenous entrepreneurship research. *Journal of Small Business & Entrepreneurship, 18*(2), 131–141.

Lama, M. (2013). Access to health services by Indigenous peoples in Asia. In J. Reading (Ed.), *State of the world's Indigenous peoples: Indigenous people's access to health services* (Vol. 2, pp. 33–57). New York: United Nations Department of Social and Economic Affairs.

Morris-Suzuki, T. (1999). The Ainu: Beyond the politics of cultural coexistence. *Cultural Survival Quarterly, 23*(4), 19–23.

Ogle, L. (2012). *Free, prior and informed consent for REDD+ in the Asia-Pacific Region: Lessons learned.*

Okada, M.V. (2012). The plight of Ainu, Indigenous people of Japan. *Journal of Indigenous Social Development*, 1(1).

Pennewiss, S. (2007). The Ainu of Japan and the land given by the river. In L.-P. Dana & R.B. Anderson (Eds.), *International handbook of research on indigenous entrepreneurship* (p. 175). Cheltenham: Edward Elgar Publishing.

Peredo, A.M., Anderson, R.B., Galbraith, C.S., & Honig, B. (2004). Towards a theory of indigenous entrepreneurship. *International Journal of Entrepreneurship and Small Business*, 1(1), 1–20.

Russell, G. (2009). *The Indigenous Peoples' declaration.* Chiang Mai, Thailand.

Savage, T., & Hindle, K. (2008). *Indigenous entrepreneurs: Ainu museums.* AGSE.

Tanabe, Y. (2014). The UN Declaration of the Rights of Indigenous Peoples and the Ainu of Japan: Development and challenges. *Indigenous Policy Journal*, 24(4).

UNDP. (2012). *Indigenous Voices in the Asia Pacific: Identifying the Information and Communication Needs of Indigenous Peoples.* Bangkok, Thailand: UNDP.

United Nations. (2015). *Indigenous peoples, Indigenous voices: Who are Indigenous peoples?* United Nations Permanent Forum on Indigenous Issues, United Nations, New York.

United Nations General Assembly. (2008). *United Nations Declaration on the Rights of Indigenous Peoples.* United Nations, New York.

17

THE SOCIAL AND ECONOMIC SITUATION OF SCHEDULED TRIBES IN INDIA

Daniel Neff, Cornelis W. Haasnoot,
Sebastian Renner and Kunal Sen

Introduction

India is home to more than 700 tribal groups (Census of India, 2013), which refer to themselves as Adivasi – a term commonly translated as 'original (*adi*) inhabitant (*vasi*)' (Rycroft & Dasgupta, 2011 p. xiv). The tribal groups are believed to be the first inhabitants of India; although this is difficult to prove given the waves of settlers and invaders that have arrived in India throughout its history (see Xaxa, 1999). In contrast to the Untouchables (Dalits/Scheduled Castes [SC]) – which are situated at the bottom of the Indian four-fold caste system (Varna) – Scheduled Tribes (STs) are not an integral part of the Hindu social hierarchy and are thus often considered to be non-Hindu (Xaxa, 2005; Das, Hall, Kapoor, & Niktin, 2014).

Since independence, India has constitutionally recognized the need for special protection of the Adivasi, which has seen the government use scheduling to identify these tribal communities.[1] To date, however, there is no clear official government definition of what constitutes a tribe. The full list of STs, which formed the basis of the 1950 Constitution (Scheduled Tribes) Order, was based on the list of 'backward tribes' that originated from a list prepared under British rule in 1936 (Maharatna, 2011). The official practice is to classify communities as STs if they demonstrate 'primitive traits, distinctive culture, geographical isolation, shyness of contact with the community at large, and backwardness' (Government of India, 2014). Obviously, such a vague definition is not able (and does not aim) to accommodate all Adivasi groups in India.

The granting of ST status for administrative, policymaking and developmental purposes is an ongoing and often highly political process, in which distinct social groups are classified as STs or lose ST status. Thus, since the 1951 census the number of groups classified as STs has risen from 212 to 705.[2] However, some Adivasi groups are not classified as STs, while others have lost their ST status (see Rathva, Rai, & Rajaram, 2014). Other non-ST groups – like the Gujjar community in Rajasthan or the Meitei – have started to demand ST status in order to get access to the associated privileges granted by their respective states and the central government (e.g. Nongkynrih, 2010; Piang, 2014). Furthermore, ST categorization is state specific, which means that some communities are classified as STs in one state but not in another (Ministry of Tribal Affairs, 2014, p. 56). Some tribal groups for example, migrated from central India to work in the tea plantations in Assam, but have to date not been granted ST status there, which they had in their respective places of origin (Ananthanarayanan, 2010). Hence, the overall picture of the situation of tribal groups in India is less than complete.[3] Despite this and the problems associated with the official definition of 'ST' in the census (see Nongkynrih, 2010), the aggregate data still provide a meaningful picture of the situation of STs over time (Maharatna, 2011).[4]

Current social and economic situation of ST

Demographics

According to official figures, India's tribal population constitutes, percentage-wise, a fairly small minority of about 8.6 percent (Census of India, 2013). However, in terms of total numbers (approx. 104.3 million) it is the single largest tribal population in the world. Tribes can be found throughout India, but the majority of Adivasi (around 67.3%) are concentrated in the seven states of Chhattisgarh, Gujarat, Jharkhand, Madhya Pradesh, Maharashtra, Rajasthan and Odisha; according to official data, there is no ST population in the three states of Delhi NCR, Punjab and Haryana or the two union territories of Puducherry and Chandigarh (see Table 17.1). The largest proportion of STs (around 53%) is situated in the central-eastern belt, which covers the states of Andhra Pradesh, Bihar, Jharkhand, Madhya Pradesh, Chhattisgarh, Odisha and West Bengal. In some of the smaller states or union territories – such as Lakshadweep, Mizoram, Nagaland and Meghalaya – STs account for over 86 percent of the population, whereas in larger states like Uttar Pradesh, Tamil Nadu, Bihar and Kerala STs make up less than 2 percent of the population. The vast majority of STs (around 90%) reside in rural areas and make up around 11.3 percent of the total rural population (Ministry of Tribal Affairs, 2013a).

According to the latest census, carried out in 2011, there are 705 groups which are classified as STs (Census of India, 2013). These groups are by no means homogeneous and differ with respect to their size, language, cultural practices and mode of livelihood (see Vidyarthi & Rai, 1976). Some tribes have large populations (such as the Bhil, 12.7 million; Gond, 10.9 million; and Santhal, 5.8 million); others, very small populations of less than 100 people (such as the Andamanese Islanders, 43; Sentinelese, 39; and Birija, 17). The larger tribes are often spread out over a number of states. For example, the Gond and Bhil can be found in ten states; the Santhal in five states. Adivasi can be found in 590 of India's 640 districts (Ministry of Tribal Affairs, 2013a, p. 7). In fact, in 152 districts tribal populations account for more than 25 percent of the total population; in ninety districts, more than 50 percent.

Poverty

Improving the living conditions of the underprivileged, particularly of the tribes and lower castes, has always been a focus of the Indian government. Although India has seen a tremendous reduction in poverty in recent decades, STs are still the most deprived social group in India. Between 2004/05 and 2011/12 there was an overall decrease of 13.5 percentage points (see Table 17.2). Interestingly, both STs and SCs exhibit above average declines in poverty although their poverty levels remain significantly higher than the average. While urban STs and SCs are generally less poor than their rural counterparts, they are still considerably poorer than the rest of the urban population.

In addition to a decrease in the absolute number of poor people, there was also a decline in the poverty gap index for all social groups, reflecting a general reduction in poverty depth (see Table 17.2). From 2004/05 to 2011/12 the average decline for the whole population was about 44 percent. Rural and urban STs and SCs experienced large decreases of poverty, but coming

Table 17.1 Demographic characteristics of ST population in India, 2011

State/UT	Total population	Total ST population	% of ST in state	% of nat. ST population	No. of districts in state	No. of districts >25% ST	No. of tribes in state
Andaman & Nicobar Islands	380,581	28,530	7.49	0.02	3	1	6
Andhra Pradesh (undivided)	84,580,777	5,918,073	6.99	5.67	23	1	25
Arunachal Pradesh	1,383,727	951,821	68.78	0.91	19	16	16
Assam	31,205,576	3,884,371	12.44	3.72	32	7	29
Bihar	104,099,542	1,336,573	1.28	1.28	38	0	33
Chhattisgarh	25,545,198	7,822,902	30.62	7.50	27	15	42
Dadra & Nagar Haveli	343,709	178,564	51.95	0.17	1	1	7
Damman & Diu	243,247	15,363	6.31	0.01	2	0	5
Goa	1,458,545	149,275	10.23	0.14	2	0	8
Gujarat	60,439,692	8,917,174	14.75	8.55	33	9	29
Himanchal Pradesh	6,864,602	392,126	5.71	0.37	12	3	10
Jammu & Kashmir	12,541,302	1,493,299	11.90	1.43	22	5	12
Jharkhand	32,988,134	8,645,042	26.20	8.29	24	11	32
Karnataka	61,095,297	4,248,987	6.95	4.07	30	0	50
Kerala	33,406,061	484,839	1.45	0.46	14	0	36
Lakshadweep	64,473	61,120	94.79	0.05	1	1	1
Madhya Pradesh	72,626,809	15,316,784	21.08	14.68	51	19	43
Maharashtra	112,374,333	10,510,213	9.35	10.07	36	4	45
Manipur	2,570,390	902,740	35.12	0.86	9	5	34
Meghalaya	2,966,889	2,555,861	86.14	2.45	11	7	17
Mizoram	1,097,206	1,036,115	94.43	0.99	8	8	15
Nagaland	1,978,502	1,710,973	86.47	1.64	11	11	5
Odisha	41,974,218	9,590,756	22.84	9.19	30	14	62
Rajasthan	68,548,437	9,238,534	13.47	8.85	33	6	12
Sikkim	610,577	206,360	33.79	0.19	4	4	04
Tamil Nadu	72,147,030	794,697	1.10	0.76	32	0	36
Tripura	3,673,917	1,166,813	31.75	1.11	8	4	19
Uttar Pradesh	199,812,341	1,134,273	0.56	1.08	75	0	15
Uttarakhand	10,086,292	291,903	2.89	0.27	13	0	5
West Bengal	91,276,115	5,296,953	5.80	5.07	20	0	40
India	1,210,569,573	104,281,034	8.61	–	640	152	693

Source: Census 2011. According to the census there are no STs in the states of Punjab and Haryana or the union territories of Delhi (NCT), Puducherry and Chandigarh.

Table 17.2 Poverty headcount, gap and severity of population groups, 2004/05–2011/12

	Population group	Poverty headcount index			Poverty gap index			Poverty severity index		
		2004/05	2011/12	Change	2004/05	2011/12	Change	2004/05	2011/12	Change
Urban	ST	35.52	24.44	−11.07	9.92	4.97	−4.95	3.80	1.53	−2.27
	SC	40.53	23.06	−17.46	9.85	4.74	−5.11	3.38	1.43	−1.95
	Other	22.46	13.15	−9.31	4.84	2.54	−2.30	1.52	0.74	−0.78
	All	25.67	14.99	−10.68	5.77	2.95	−2.82	1.88	0.87	−1.01
Rural	ST	62.24	45.39	−16.85	16.98	10.04	−6.93	6.33	3.33	−3.00
	SC	53.53	34.87	−18.65	12.26	7.07	−5.19	3.96	2.09	−1.87
	Other	35.03	22.83	−12.20	7.12	4.06	−3.07	2.10	1.11	−0.99
	All	41.79	27.84	−13.95	9.24	5.35	−3.89	2.94	1.56	−1.38
Total	ST	59.95	43.06	−16.89	16.37	9.48	−6.89	6.11	3.13	−2.98
	SC	50.90	32.28	−18.62	11.77	6.56	−5.21	3.84	1.94	−1.90
	Other	31.42	19.69	−11.74	6.47	3.56	−2.90	1.93	0.99	−0.94
	All	37.71	24.17	−13.54	8.36	4.66	−3.70	2.67	1.36	−1.31

Source: NSS 2004/05 and 2011/12, own calculations.

from higher initial poverty levels still remain deeper in poverty than the average population. As in the poverty headcount index, we find that urban STs and SCs are better situated than their rural counterparts, but within their urban and rural areas they are still deeper in poverty than the rest of the respective population. The poverty severity index, which takes inequality into account, also shows an average decline. In percentage terms urban STs and SCs experienced the greatest decreases in poverty severity and decreases for the rural ST and SC that are within the general trend. Again, starting from a higher initial poverty level, the absolute changes for rural ST and SC are considerable.

Within the different social groups, recent economic growth has not been equally distributed. Average annual growth rates from 2004/05 to 2011/12 per expenditure percentile are displayed as growth incidence curves in Figure 17.1. On average, we find that households between the 50th and 80th percentile have experienced higher expenditure gains than average. Strikingly, economic growth rates for STs have been about 1 percent lower than average growth rates, while we find the opposite effect for the growth rates for SC. The poorest 20 percent of STs and households between the 55th and 85th percentile had above-average economic growth rates than the top 15 percent. We find higher economic growth rates for SCs than for STs over the entire distribution. Here, the relatively richer households between the 75th and 95th per-centile exhibit above-average growth compared to the average SC population. Because STs and SCs are mainly in rural areas, they dominate the overall results.[5]

Education and health

In India there have been substantial improvements in education in recent decades, which are well documented (see Barakat, 2015). The share of the population with no education at all dropped from 38 percent in 2004/05 to 30 percent in 2011/12 (see Table 17.3). Despite STs and SCs in both rural and urban areas still generally having lower education levels than the total popu-lation, their educational attainment levels generally followed this trend. There were, however, differences between groups and between rural and urban areas. For instance, urban STs generally have higher education levels than rural STs. Furthermore, both urban STs and SCs are more likely than rural STs and SCs to have higher than primary education. Although we see fewer persons with no education among urban ST and SC groups, rural STs and SCs have disproportionally climbed the education ladder from no education to having some education but still below primary level. We find substantial increases in the shares of those with secondary education and above, with the largest increase occurring among urban STs. However, because urban

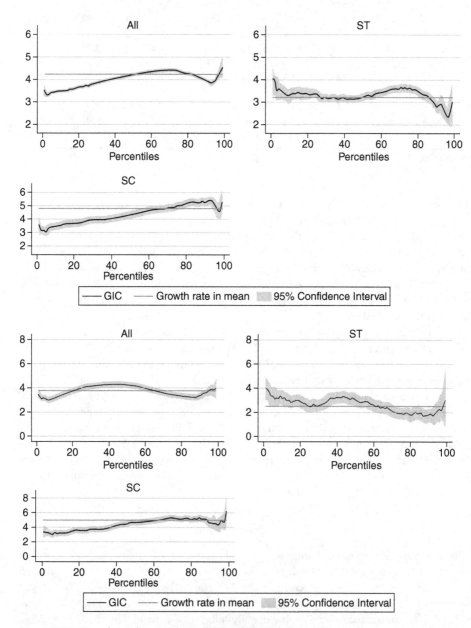

Figure 17.1   Growth incidence curve India, 2004/05–2011/12

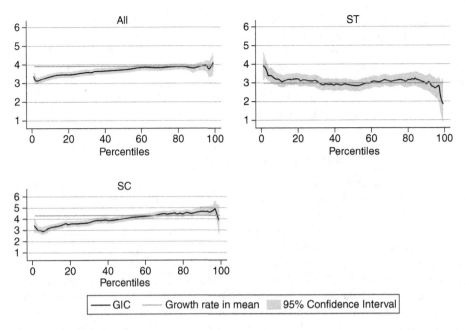

Figure 17.1   (Continued)

Table 17.3 Education by social group, 2004/05–2011/12

Education status		Urban			Rural			Total		
		ST	SC	All	ST	SC	All	ST	SC	All
No education	2004–2005	28.5	31.6	19.4	59.0	54.2	44.9	56.1	49.3	37.9
	2011–2012	22.5	23.9	16.0	44.4	43.4	35.8	41.9	38.8	29.8
Below primary	2004–2005	5.9	7.4	6.0	9.0	7.6	8.0	8.7	7.6	7.4
	2011–2012	6.8	7.9	6.7	11.7	10.6	10.5	11.1	10.0	9.4
Primary	2004–2005	12.3	14.8	12.0	11.5	12.7	13.7	11.6	13.2	13.3
	2011–2012	9.8	11.9	9.9	12.6	12.8	12.1	12.3	12.6	11.5
Middle	2004–2005	21.0	20.4	19.5	12.3	14.3	16.9	13.1	15.6	17.6
	2011–2012	17.2	18.6	15.8	15.1	15.8	16.8	15.4	16.4	16.5
Secondary	2004–2005	12.9	11.9	16.2	4.4	6.2	9.0	5.2	7.4	11.0
	2011–2012	14.2	15.7	17.8	8.8	9.5	12.7	9.5	10.9	14.2
Higher secondary and above	2004–2005	19.5	13.8	27.0	3.7	4.9	7.5	5.2	6.9	12.9
	2011–2012	29.4	21.9	33.8	7.3	8.0	12.1	9.9	11.2	18.6

Source: NSS 2004/05 and 2011/12, own calculations.

STs and SCs are the minority within their groups, the significant improvements they have made have only had a small positive effect on the overall education levels of STs and SCs. Thus, lower education rates continue to be a major issue for STs and SCs despite significant improvements.

Along with general improvements in living conditions over the last decades, India has also witnessed improvements in the health status of the population. Early childhood mortality rates decreased significantly from 1992/1993 to 2005/2006 (IIPS, 2007).[6] Despite this improvement, SCs and STs had significantly higher under-5 mortality rates than the average population in 2005/2006.[7] ST children aged between 1 and 5 have about twice the risk of dying than the average child. Moreover, malnutrition levels (which have a direct effect on mortality rates) among SC and particularly ST children are absolutely and relatively high compared to national averages. In 2004/2005 48 percent and 55 percent of SC and ST children, respectively, were underweight compared 34 percent of non-ST/SC children.

Patterns of occupational segregation

In this section we look at the relationship between social groups and rural occupational structure to see if it has changed over time. We compare changes in the occupational segregation of both ST and SC households. Figure 17.2 shows occupational categories by social group for 1983 and 2009. Dalits and Adivasis are still significantly represented in the agricultural-labourer class, which have the highest incidence of poverty in India (Gang, Sen, & Yun, 2008). They are also under-represented in the 'miscellaneous' occupational category, which has the lowest incidence of poverty. We also observe that there are clear differences in occupational distribution between ST households and SC households. For example, a far larger proportion of ST households are self-employed as agricultural cultivators (44.7% in 1983/84 and 39.1% in 2009/10) than are SC households (20.1 in 1983/84 and 17.1 percent in 2009/10). In fact, in 2009/10 the number of ST households engaged as cultivators exceeded the number of ST households working as agricultural labourers. It should be noted that the 'self-employed, agriculture' category is the occupational type with the second-lowest incidence of poverty. Furthermore, a larger proportion of SC households are non-agricultural self-employed (14.8% in 2009/10) than are ST households (6.8% in 2009/10) (Gang, Sen, & Yun, 2017).

A convenient measure that highlights occupational segregation is the Duncan dissimilarity index, which is defined as:

$$D = 0.5 \sum_{c=1}^{C} | A_c - B_c |,$$

where A_c is the proportion of households in occupational category c among social group A, and B_c is the proportion of households in occupational category c among social group B ($\neq A$).

The Duncan index captures in a simple way the degree of dissimilarity in occupational structure between SC and ST households, on one hand, and non-SC/ST households, on the other. The index (D) ranges from 0 to 1, revealing the proportion of either social group that would have to shift occupations to generate identical occupational distributions. If D is 0, we have complete integration, which indicates that the distribution of one social group across occupations is identical to that of the other social group. However, if D is 1, we have complete occupational segregation, which means one social group is distributed across occupations that are not at all held by members of the other social group (Blau & Hendricks, 1979; Spriggs & Williams, 1996).

Based on the Duncan index, there was less occupational dissimilarity between ST and non-SC/ST households (0.162) than there was between SC and non-SC/ST households (0.341) in 1983 (see Table 17.4). However, in the period 1983–2009 occupational dissimilarity increased from 0.162 to 0.171 between ST and non-SC/ST households and decreased from 0.341 to 0.255 between SC and non-SC/ST households, suggesting greater occupational similarity between SC and non-SC/ST during this period. As already observed, occupational similarity

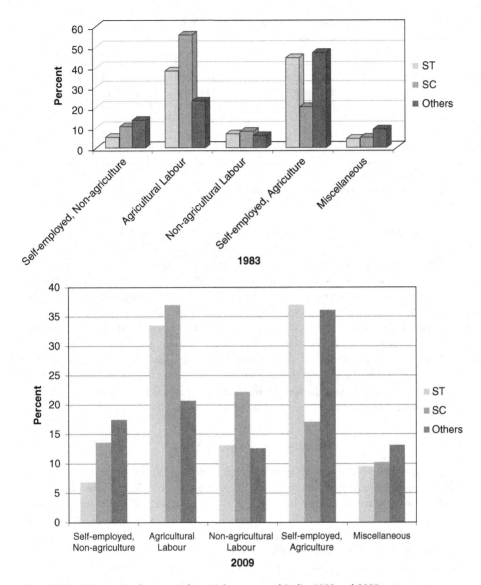

Figure 17.2   Occupational structure by social group, rural India, 1983 and 2009

between ST and SC social groups is not high. A 1983 Duncan index of occupational dissimilarity for these two groups was 0.238, though this had dropped to 0.202 in 2009, suggesting occupational similarity between these two groups has grown over time.

In a systematic examination of the relationship between social group identity and occupational segregation during the period 1983–2009, Gang et al. (2017) find that there has been a significant movement of SC households from agricultural employment to non-agricultural employment. However, they find no such movement for ST households, which also have a large proportion of agricultural labourers. This implies that ST households still remain occupationally segregated from SC households in occupations with the highest incidences of poverty. The authors suggest that this is linked to geographical differences

Table 17.4 Duncan index of occupational dissimilarity between ST, SC and non-SC/ST households

Year	ST–SC	ST–Non-SC/ST	SC–Non-SC/ST	*Number of observations*
1983	0.238	0.162	0.341	*65,552*
1987	0.195	0.206	0.323	*67,173*
1993	0.182	0.206	0.329	*55,835*
1999	0.188	0.198	0.300	*59,840*
2004	0.191	0.194	0.283	*63,612*
2009	0.202	0.171	0.255	*45,106*

Notes: Male-headed households only. An increase in the Duncan index suggests greater occupational dissimilarity, while a decrease in the index suggests greater occupational similarity.

Source: NSS.

between SC households and ST households. The villages in which SC households are predominantly based are close to large towns or in agriculturally dynamic regions and are populated by other castes and social groups. Whereas these villages enjoyed a significant degree of occupational mobility due to the increasing commercialization and mechanization of agriculture brought about by the Green Revolution and the growth of non-farm rural employment evident in post-1980 India (such as in Punjab; see Jodhka, 2004), the isolated, homogenous villages (often adjacent to or in forests) populated by ST groups had poor agricultural potential, which limited their possibilities to mechanize and commercialize. Ultimately, this prevented ST households from taking part in this process of rural change (von Fürer-Haimendorf, 1982). Gang et al. (2017) argue that as a consequence, ST households were also constrained in their ability to move out of agricultural labour and into non-farm employment and more diversified income-earning.

Heterogeneity among STs

Research and government policy tends to treat STs as a single group. However, this is a flawed approach as it ignores the massive heterogeneity that exists between STs in terms of both culture and development. In this section we highlight two main aspects of heterogeneity among STs: inter-tribal differences within states and intra-tribal differences across states. We will also discuss some potential ways of categorizing different tribes to account for this heterogeneity, focusing on the Particularly Vulnerable Tribal Groups (PVTGs).

Inter-tribal heterogeneity within the same state can be illustrated by literacy and urbanization rates. For instance, in the state of Chhattisgarh the Saonta had a 26 percent literacy rate and a 3 percent urbanization rate in 2011, while the Andh had an 81 percent literacy rate and a 95 percent urbanization rate (see left scatter plot in Figure 17.3). During the same year in Jharkhand the Parhaiya and the Oraon had literacy rates of 26 percent and 56 percent, respectively, whereas the Sauria Paharia and the Banjara had urbanization rates of almost 0 percent and 55 percent, respectively (see right scatter plot in Figure 17.3).

Intra-tribal heterogeneity across states can be revealed by comparing a tribe's literacy rates across states. Every dot in Figure 17.4 represents a tribe's performance in two states, Bihar and Jharkhand or Chhattisgarh and Madhya Pradesh. There is a statistically significant relationship between the literacy rate in Bihar and Jharkhand, but only at the 10 percent level.[8] There is no statistically significant relationship between the literacy rate in Madhya Pradesh and Chhattisgarh, which shows that STs are heterogeneous across states as well. Just because a tribe is well developed in one state does not mean that it is well developed in another state.

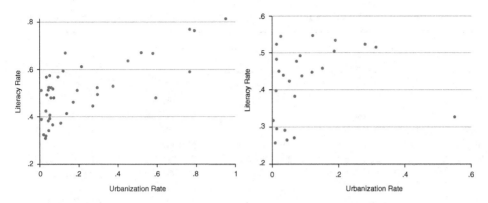

Figure 17.3   Literacy and urbanization rates of ST in Chhattisgarh and Jharkhand, 2011

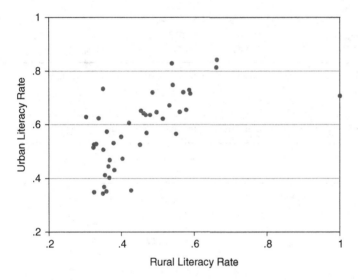

Figure 17.4   ST literacy rates in urban and rural Madhya Pradesh, 2011

Implications for research

The Indian government does sometimes make the distinction between different kinds of STs. For example, 3 percent of all STs are members of a PVTG (Planning Commission, 2013). And a number of ST development schemes put extra focus on these PVTGs. However, the concept of PVTGs is problematic. The PVTG classification – having been created in 1973 – represents a limited and static concept of tribal development, which makes it a bit outdated. The distinction between PVTGs and 'normal' STs is strict and, much like the general term of 'Scheduled Tribes', belies the massive variation between the different tribes. It is also a political construct, at least in part. Tables 17.5 and 17.6 show the literacy rates, urbanization rates and status of all PVTGs in Bihar, Chhattisgarh, Jharkhand and Madhya Pradesh compared to those of all STs in the same states. Figure 17.5 provides a comparison of literacy rates by tribes and state in 2011. The important thing to note here is that some tribes with PVTG status are actually

Table 17.5 Literacy rates of PVTGs in Bihar, Chhattisgarh, Jharkhand and Madhya Pradesh

Tribe	Madhya Pradesh/ Chhattisgarh	Lit_{Chh}	Lit_{MP}	Bihar/Jharkhand	Lit_{Bih}	Lit_{Jha}
Average		50%	41%		42%	47%
Abujh Maria	PVTG			Not present		
Asur	Not present			PVTG	33%	37%
Baiga	PVTG	32%	38%	Not PVTG	46%	29%
Bharia	PVTG	39%	39%	Not present		
Birhor	PVTG	32%	77%	PVTG	24%	26%
Birjia	PVTG			PVTG	31%	40%
Kamar	PVTG	39%	61%	Not present		
Hill Kharia	Not PVTG	48%	52%	PVTG	44%	56%
Korwa	Not PVTG	31%	49%	PVTG	25%	29%
Mal Paharia	Not present			PVTG	51%	31%
Parhaiya	Not present			PVTG	25%	26%
Sahariya	PVTG	67%	33%	Not present		
Sauria Paharia	Not present			PVTG	37%	32%
Savar	Not PVTG	57%	45%	PVTG	54%	27%

Note: If cells are empty, it is because there were no data or the tribes are not present in those states.

Source: Census 2011.

Table 17.6 Urbanization rates of PVTGs in Bihar, Chhattisgarh, Jharkhand and Madhya Pradesh

Tribe	Madhya Pradesh/ Chhattisgarh	Urb_{Chh}	Urb_{MP}	Bihar/Jharkhand	Urb_{Bih}	Urb_{Jha}
Average		8%	7%		5%	9%
Abujh Maria	PVTG			Not present		
Asur	Not present			PVTG	3%	5%
Baiga	PVTG	2%	5%	Not PVTG	11%	4%
Bharia	PVTG	5%	5%	Not present		
Birhor	PVTG	3%	79%	PVTG	14%	5%
Birjia	PVTG			PVTG	3%	1%
Kamar	PVTG	1%	35%	Not present		
Hill Kharia	Not PVTG	6%	29%	PVTG	11%	8%
Korwa	Not PVTG	3%	51%	PVTG	13%	2%
Mal Paharia	Not present			PVTG	3%	1%
Parhaiya	Not present			PVTG	2%	1%
Sahariya	PVTG	58%	4%	Not present		
Sauria Paharia	Not present			PVTG	5%	<1%
Savar	Not PVTG	10%	15%	PVTG	1%	7%

Source: Census 2011.

more literate or more urban than the average ST in that state. In some cases, tribes that do not have the PVTG status in one state, such as the Baiga tribe in Jharkhand, are actually less literate than their counterparts in other states where they do have PVTG status. It could well be that this was not the case when these groups were first classified as PVTGs, especially considering the fact that one of the criteria for being classified as such was a low level of literacy (Ministry

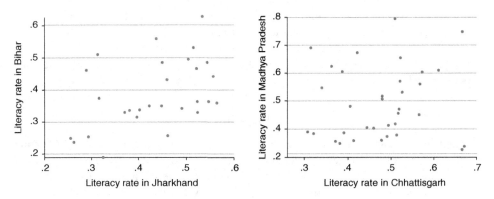

Figure 17.5 Comparison of literacy rates by tribes and state, 2011

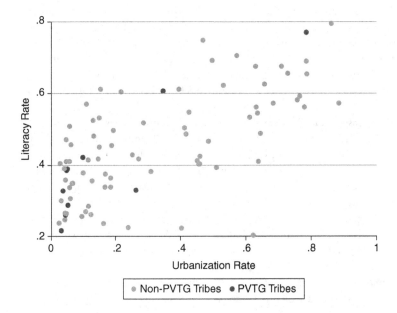

Figure 17.6 Literacy and urbanization rate for PVTG, 2001 and 2011

of Tribal Affairs, 2013b). But it may be that their relative backwardness has changed over time. Thus, Tables 17.5 and 17.6 might show the success of India's policies towards these groups as well as the fact that the PVTG classification is outdated.

Is the solution, then, to just change the definition of what constitutes a PVTG to make sure that only the most backward STs are included? Any classification based on such a distinction would be arbitrary and, ultimately, not do justice to the massive variation in tribal prosperity. Figure 17.6 combines the 2001 and 2011 censuses to show the literacy rates and urbanization rates of all tribes in Madhya Pradesh, distinguishing between PVTG and non-PVTG tribes to illustrate the arguments of this section. Using the data from Figure 17.6, we can make a number of points. First, although PVTGs are primarily clustered around the origin, which reveals them to be backwards in both literacy and urbanization, not all of them are so backward. A number of these tribes actually perform well on one or both of these indicators. Second, there are a large number of non-PVTG tribes that are just as backwards as tribes that are classified as being particularly vulnerable. Third, there is a large variation among these tribes, and while the two indicators are correlated, it is still possible for tribes to lag in one dimension but be ahead on another. A notion of backwards tribes that lag in all dimensions belies the underlying variation.

Conclusion

Despite the constitutional mandate of India's government to minimize income inequality and its efforts since independence with decades of national social policies, STs remain the most deprived social group. Our analysis shows that STs (and SCs) are still more affected by poverty than the rest of the population, though this gap is slowly closing. Nevertheless, almost every second rural ST household has per capita expenditures below the poverty line. Similarly, STs have lower average educational levels and lower health outcomes than the rest of the population. We further find that the Adivasi are mainly in occupations (represented in the agricultural-labourer class) with the highest incidences of poverty. While SC households managed to move from agricultural employment to non-agricultural employment between 1983 and 2009, STs did not, which implies there is a high degree of occupational segregation. We argue that this is due to the geographical isolation of ST villages, which limited the possibilities of agricultural mechanization and commercialization and thus constrained STs' ability to move into non-farm employment.

There are number of reasons for STs' deprivation, such as – among others – generally poor physical access to services, their displacement from their traditional lands and forests (e.g. due to large infrastructure projects, such as dams, or mining activities), the poor enforcement of legislation meant to protect their interests (such as the 2006 Forest Rights Act), their lack of collective voice and political influence (in comparison with the Dalits, whose interests are represented by specific political parties; Gorringe, 2013), and the poor implementation of government programmes (e.g. due to corruption, mismanagement, lack of sufficient funds, and poorly trained staff, etc.) (Das, Hall, Kapoor, & Niktin, 2014). As a response to exploitation, deprivation, marginalization and displacement, India has experienced tribal revolts, rebellions and insurrections since early colonial times (see Xaxa, 2005).[9]

In terms of policymaking, problems arise from the fact that the states classify STs according to a nationally defined list of criteria which is arbitrary at best, leading some Adivasi groups to not being granted ST status and others being granted ST status in one state but not in another. For instance, ST members who migrate to Delhi are not counted as ST members. Moreover, the definition of a ST as applied in the census and official statistical sources is also problematic and, as a result, fails to provide a complete picture of STs and their social and economic situations throughout India.

We have tried to argue that when looking at STs, it is important to take into account the large variation that exists within this group. Attempts to classify tribes as being particularly backwards are likely to fail because tribes do not lag on all indicators in all states. Furthermore, although classifying tribes as PVTG may or may not show the heterogeneity of tribes within states, it does not take into account the fact that the same tribes may perform very differently in another state. Although the Indian government has recognized the heterogeneity of the ST population, most policies still reflect a one-size-fits-all approach and are thus unlikely to be effective. Instead, policies that target STs should take into account the variation among tribes. Static and simplistic concepts, such as the PVTG concept, are incapable of capturing the many facets of heterogeneity among STs as a group.

Notes

1 During colonial rule the British created tribal areas (so-called scheduled areas) with special legal provisions before classifying specific groups as tribes. This resulted in tribes being connected to a specific area. It has to be noted, however, that not all areas with a major share of Adivasi have been classified as scheduled areas.

2 One of the reasons for the rise in the number of groups and the total tribal population is that, earlier, only groups that resided in a respective 'scheduled area' were classified as STs. This area restriction was subsequently removed in 1976 (Maharatna, 2011).

3 Between the 2001 and 2011 censuses, 274 changes were made to the list of STs, including the reclassification of twelve former SCs as STs and the deletion of fifteen groups from the ST list (Census of India, 2013).

4 There is a vast body of anthropological literature that focuses on specific tribes across India, starting with authors like Roy (1925) (for an overview of early anthropological studies, see Vidyarthi & Rai, 1976). The aim of this chapter is to provide a general overview of the situation of STs in India.

5 Separate figures for urban populations and rural populations can be found in Figures 17.1b and 17.1c.

6 Early childhood mortality rates are divided into neonatal, post-neonatal, infant, child, and under-5 mortality rates.

7 The mortality rates (deaths per 1,000 in the five-year period preceding the survey) are 88.1 for SC, 95.7 for ST and 74.3 as the national average. All health statistics used are based on the National Family and Health Survey from 2005/2006. The recent developments in health outcomes over the last years are not covered and therefore not directly comparable with the poverty and education statistics used here.

8 The p-value for this is 1.94.

9 The creation of some of the states in the northeast, such as Nagaland (1963) and Meghalaya (1970), is the outcome of separatist tendencies among STs (the Naga and the Mizo). Later, in 2000 the formation of the states Jharkhand and Chhattisgarh were the result of a political movement for more autonomy led by ST groups. Today, a large number of districts with a larger share of STs are still affected by armed conflicts like the Naxalite insurgency led by Maoist groups (see Singh, 2008).

References

Ananthanarayanan, S. (2010). Scheduled Tribe status for Adivasis in Assam. *South Asia: Journal of South Asian Studies*, *33*(2), 290–303.

Barakat, B. (2015). Education trends in India: Recent results in context. In C. Guilmoto & G. Jones (Eds.), *Contemporary demographic transformations in China, India and Indonesia* (Chapter 11, pp. 177–193). Cham: Springer International Publishing.

Blau, F., & Hendricks, W. (1979). Occupational segregation by sex: Trends and prospects. *Journal of Human Resources*, *14*(2), 197–210.

Census of India. (2013). *Census of India 2011, Primary Census Abstract, Scheduled Castes & Scheduled Tribes*. Government of India, New Delhi.

Das, M., Hall, G., Kapoor, S., & Niktin, D. (2014). India: The Scheduled Tribes. In G. Hall & H. Patrinos (Eds.), *Indigenous peoples, poverty, and development* (pp. 205–248). New York: Cambridge University Press.

Gang, I., Sen, K., & Yun, M. (2008). Poverty in rural India: Caste and tribe. *Review of Income and Wealth*, *54*(1), 50–70.

Gang, I., Sen, K., & Yun, M. (2017). is caste destiny? Occupational diversification among Dalits in rural India. *European Journal of Development Research*, *29*(2), 476–492.

Gorringe, H. (2013). Untouchability, identity, and assertion. In A. Kohli & P. Singh (Eds.), *Routledge handbook of Indian politics* (pp. 119–128). Abingdon: Routledge.

Government of India. (2014). Retrieved 15 December 2015 from www.tribal.nic.in/Content/DefinitionpRrofiles.aspx.

International Institute for Population Sciences (IIPS) and Macro International. (2007). *National Family Health Survey (NFHS-3), 2005–06: India: Volume I*. Mumbai: IIPS.

Jodhka, S. (2004). Sikhism and the caste question: Dalits and their politics in contemporary Punjab. *Contributions to Indian Sociology*, *38*(1–2), 165–192.

Maharatna, A. (2011). How can 'beautiful' be 'backward'? Tribes of India in a long-term demographic perspective. *Economic and Political Weekly*, *46*(4), 42–52.

Ministry of Tribal Affairs. (2013a). *Statistical profile of ST in India 2013*. New Delhi: Government of India.

Ministry of Tribal Affairs. (2013b). *National tribal policy 2013*. New Delhi: Government of India.

Ministry of Tribal Affairs. (2014). *Report of the high level committee on socio-economic, health and educational status of tribal communities of India*. New Delhi: Government of India.

Nongkynrih, A. (2010). Scheduled Tribes and the census: A sociological inquiry. *Economic and Political Weekly, 45*(19), 43–47.

Piang, L. (2014). Moving backwards. Meitei's demand for scheduled tribe status. *Economic and Political Weekly, 49*(15), www.epw.in/reports-states/moving-backwards.html.

Planning Commission. (2013). *Twelfth five-year plan: Volume III, social sectors*. New Delhi: Government of India.

Rathva, A., Rai, D., & Rajaram, N. (2014). Denotification of the Rathvas as Adivasis in Gujarat. *Economic and Political Weekly, 49*(6), 22–24.

Roy, R. (1925). *The Birhors: A little-known jungle tribe of Chota Nagpur*. Ranchi: Man in India Office.

Rycroft, D., & Dasgupta, S. (2011). *The politics of belonging in India*. Abingdon: Routledge.

Singh, K. (2008). The trajectory of the movement. In P.V. Ramana (Ed.), *The Naxal challenge. Causes, linkages, and policy options* (pp. 10–17). New Delhi: Dorling Kindersley.

Spriggs, W., & Williams, R. (1996). A logit decomposition analysis of occupational segregation: Results for the 1970's and 1980's. *Review of Economics and Statistics, 78*(2), 348–355.

Vidyarthi, L., & Rai, B. (1976). *The tribal culture of India*. New Delhi: Concept Publishing Company.

Von Fürer-Haimendorf, C. (1982). *Tribes of India: The struggle for survival*. Berkeley, CA: University of California Press.

Xaxa, V. (1999). Tribes as Indigenous people of India. *Economic and Political Weekly, 34*(51), 3589–3595.

Xaxa, V. (2005). Politics of language, religion and identity: Tribes in India. *Economic and Political Weekly, 40*(13), 1363–1370.

18

MĀORI IDENTITY AND ECONOMIC WELLBEING

Carla A. Houkamau

Introduction

New Zealand (Aotearoa) is a small Pacific country with a population of approximately 4.8 million. Māori (indigenous to New Zealand) were colonized by Pākehā (the Māori name given to the descendants of early European/British settlers) who arrived from the late eighteenth century. Colonization occurred rapidly in New Zealand. By the end of the 1900s, Māori had been politically and physically overwhelmed and lost most of their lands and natural resources in the process (Ministry for Culture and Heritage, 2015). Māori are now a minority in their own country and make up about 15 percent of the total New Zealand population with Pākehā comprising the majority, at around 70 percent (Statistics New Zealand, 2013).

Drawing from diverse strands of literature, this chapter considers the link between Māori culture and economic wellbeing. This is not a comprehensive review. Due to the restrictions of space there are necessary omissions (the reader is directed to Durie, 2002, 2003; Durie & University of Waikato Development Studies Programme, 2000; Te Puni Kōkiri, 2003, 2004a, 2004b, 2005, 2006, 2007a, 2007b, 2008 for deeper insights and Hanson, 1989, for an alternative take on Māori history). It should also be noted that Māori are not culturally homogenous (Greaves, Houkamau, & Sibley, 2015) and the label 'Māori' refers to a culturally and socially diverse population (Durie, 1995, 1997). It can also be stated that a significant proportion of those who identify as Māori today have strong allegiance to Māori culture and continue to express aims, aspirations and perspectives which are different from Pākehā and other non-Māori (Houkamau & Sibley, 2014). In testimony to this, research has found Māori are more likely than any other ethnic group in New Zealand to be involved in cultural arts and activities (Creative New Zealand, 1999). Moreover, government statistics indicate the bulk of Māori still value 'traditional' cultural practices. For example, "Te Kupenga" (Statistics New Zealand's first survey on Māori wellbeing) surveyed 5,549 Māori individuals in 2013 and found that the vast majority (70% of Māori adults) felt Māori culture was important to them and many reported a keen interest in expressing themselves culturally as Māori. This included speaking Te Reo Māori (the Māori language), learning about Māori history and engaging in customary activities (Statistics New Zealand, 2014a, 2014b, 2014c).

The history of Māori–Pākehā relationships provides an important context for understanding Māori economic circumstances as they are now, therefore the chapter starts with an overview of New Zealand's colonial past. Rather than provide a comprehensive portrait of New Zealand history (see King, 2003 for this), I briefly sketch a selection of major historical events. I then outline empirical research related to Māori economic outcomes, including a discussion of outcomes for 'mixed' versus 'sole' Māori. I then turn to the role of Māori values in contemporary Māori economic activity. The chapter concludes with a summary of economic development approaches that meet the cultural needs of Māori people.

Socio-historical context: identity, culture and economic practices

Pre-European Māori social and economic life was communally orientated and organized according to kinship groupings (formed on the basis of *whakapapa*/genealogical descent). *Whānau* (family and extended family) were a vital social unit and usually included three generations of family members who lived together in defined home areas (*kainga*) (Walker, 1990b). Extended *whānau* amalgamated to form larger kinship groups: *hapū* (sub-tribes) and *iwi* (tribes) (Moeke-Pickering, 1996). Although *iwi* occupied distinct geographical locations throughout New Zealand there was no concept of land 'ownership' per se (Barlow, 1991). It was customary for land to be shared between *whānau* and *hapū* and the terms of land usage were negotiated and renegotiated on a regular basis (see Keenan, 2002). Traditional Māori lore required *whānau* and *hapū* to cooperate harmoniously on such matters as tribal survival relied upon symbiotic relationships between group members (Pere, 1982). There were two main reasons for this. First, maintaining an adequate food supply was not easy and all tribal members had to work together to successfully hunt, plant, harvest and gather food. Second, inter-tribal warfare was common and each individual's commitment to their *iwi* provided more protection in times of conflict (Walker, 1990b).

As a reflection of this social system, family interdependence and economic wellbeing were not experienced as separate entities. The practical realities of pre-colonial Māori economic life and culture gave rise to the core cultural values often cited today: respect for *whakapapa* (genealogical ties), *whānaungatanga* (family, relationships and interdependence) and *kōtahitanga* (collective wellbeing and unity) (Harmsworth, 2005; Harmsworth & Awatere, 2013). To uphold these, a complex system of *tikanga Māori* (Māori traditional rules, lore and customs) existed for each tribe and when it came to land, the concept of *kaitiakitanga* (guardianship, responsibility and commitment to land and natural resources) was a particularly important concept (Broughton, 1993; Marsden & Henare, 2003).

The arrival of Pākehā to New Zealand from the seventeenth century brought enormous change. Historical accounts of economic activity prior to 1840 indicate Māori were keen to trade with Pākehā and relations were mainly amicable (Petrie, 2006; Salmond, 1991). However, the economic and political situation of Māori changed rapidly once the Treaty of Waitangi ('The Treaty') was signed in February 1840 (Walker, 1990b). Māori believe that the Treaty guaranteed they would retain all of their lands and their political autonomy as a people (Awatere, 1984). However, that did not occur as, in practice, the Treaty empowered the settler government to establish a system of laws that both Māori and Pākehā were required to follow (Mead, 1985, 1999; Walker, 1990b). After 1840 the European population of New Zealand grew from fewer than 1,000 in 1831 to 500,000 by 1881. Some 400,000 settlers came from Britain, of whom 300,000 stayed permanently (Belich, 1996). The new settler government facilitated large-scale transfer of Māori land to Pākehā ownership (Jackson, 1993). Māori efforts to resist land loss led to open warfare during the 1840s and Māori were eventually subdued. In 1877, the Treaty was nullified by the New Zealand courts and disregarded by the government for over 100 years subsequently (Orange, 1992, 2004).

By the end of the 1900s Māori society was in a state of shock. The population had declined, land loss had undermined 'pre-colonial' economic structures, and Māori were forced to adapt. Some *iwi* worked in *whānau* or *hapū* groups within their own tribal enterprises (Keane, 2015). In reality however, many Māori were left economically vulnerable and sought work from the government, Pākehā entrepreneurs, and Pākehā and farmers (Ministry of Social Development, 1988). Despite considerable integration during the first part of the twentieth century, Māori lived mainly in rural areas and Pākehā in New Zealand towns and cities (King, 1977, 1983, 2003). The maintenance of a distinct Māori culture was possible for Māori in rural environments as they were able to maintain many traditional economic practices (communal gardening, sharing resources and food gathering from the sea as they had for generations) (Biggs, 1960). Although this afforded some protection and stability for Māori in the 1950s when New Zealand's economy boomed, many Māori moved to the cities to seek work. By the 1970s only one in four Māori remained in rural areas (Walker, 1990b).

Urbanization unraveled Māori social and economic structures even further, and over time Māori adapted to a new mode of 'individualistic' economic behaviour, along with a new set of economic priorities. Awatere (1984) suggests that this adjustment was not easy for Māori whose traditional values stood in stark contrast with Pākehā economic imperatives, which championed individual competitiveness and the accumulation of personal wealth. From a Māori perspective these things were a cultural non-priority, second to connectedness and *whānau* commitment. Māori were thrust into an economic structure which was non-Māori in structure and form. This was put bluntly by Sutherland who observed:

> It is fairly safe to say that Māoris [*sic*] will never fully accept European ideas regarding money… their attitude to property is far from being identical with that of the white man… They are not, and probably never will be dominated by the idea that the making and saving of money is the really sacred duty of man and the main means of happiness.
> (Sutherland, 1935, p. 107)

Apart from the challenge of cultural adjustment, it was common for Māori to experience explicit racism in the early years of urbanization (Rangihau, 1975). Beaglehole and Beaglehole (1946) reported a range of negative stereotypes attached to Māori by Pākehā, which included the view that Māori were 'slackers', dirty, lazy and dishonest. Such attitudes seem to have been widely held by Pākehā, which made it difficult for Māori to obtain rental housing in certain areas and find steady employment. In addition, Māori typically lacked the qualifications to secure well-paid work and by the end of the 1970s, Māori were firmly positioned at the lower end of the economic scale (see Walker, 1990b).

The Treaty affirmed

In response to Māori marginalization, Māori leaders and political activists launched a powerful political renaissance in the 1960s and demanded compensation for historical breaches of the rights guaranteed to them as 'Treaty partners' with the New Zealand government (see Poata-Smith, 1997a, 1997b for discussions). As a reflection, the Treaty of Waitangi was given greater recognition after 1975 with the establishment of the Waitangi Tribunal (a forum where Māori could make claims for compensation for breaches of the Treaty). In the mid-1980s the government extended the jurisdiction of the Tribunal to examine Māori grievances retrospective to 1840. Treaty claims, negotiations and settlements have been a significant feature of New Zealand politics since that time. Māori, overall, have achieved a great deal since the 1960s. Not only have Māori reaffirmed the value of Māori culture and identity among their own people, they have gained substantial recognition of their political rights to equality with Pākehā in New Zealand society (Metge, 1990, 1995).

Approximately 30 Acts of Parliament now require government officials to take into account the Treaty or its principles when exercising state powers (New Zealand Constitutional Advisory Panel, 2013). A number of significant long-standing Treaty claims and grievances have also been settled and several large tribal associations throughout New Zealand have received compensation. From the 1990s Māori leaders have worked consistently to advance Māori economic development and this drive continues through Māori organizations throughout New Zealand. There are a number of 'post Treaty-settlement' government entities, Tribal Trust Boards and other mandated tribal organizations which exist to manage Māori assets and deliver social, health and other services to their tribal constituents (see Statistics New Zealand, 2014b). Alongside these, several government and Māori initiatives have also been launched in recent years which continue to play a supportive role for Māori economic progress (for a review of these, see Consedine, 2007 and Māori Economic Development Panel, 2012). At the time of writing, the 'Māori economy' (defined as assets owned and income earned by Māori in collectively owned trusts, incorporations and Māori-owned businesses and privately owned assets) is estimated to be worth over $36 billion (Māori Economic Development Panel, 2012). Some believe Māori stand on the brink of an economic 'Golden Age' (Gibson, 2015).

Although this optimism may seem well placed, at the level of individual Māori households, statistics paint a much darker picture. During the 1980s, economic recessions, policy reforms and structural changes in the New Zealand economy led to widespread unemployment among Māori, many of whom are now in a cycle of benefit dependency (Coleman, Dixon, & Mare, 2005; Kelsey, 1995; Ministry of Social Development, 1988). The benefits of Treaty settlements have not filtered down equally to all Māori who, compared to non-Māori, are still more likely to live in poverty (Cram, 2011; Marriot & Sim, 2014; Mitchell, 2009; Robson, Cormack, & Cram, 2010; Salmond, 2012). In fact, when it comes to economic outcomes and national statistics, the media frequently portray Māori as a 'social problem' and a 'Brown underclass', behind Pākehā in most areas of economic life (Ministry of Business, Innovation and Employment, 2013; Scoop Media, 2011; Statistics New Zealand, 2012; Walker, 1990a).

According to recent government reports, if trends in Māori poverty continue, they have the potential to create significant social and economic problems in New Zealand's future. "Ensuring that Māori are equipped with the skills and education that will enable them to participate in the economy is critical. The country cannot afford for Māori human potential not to be realised – any underperformance in this area is a problem for all New Zealanders" (Te Puni Kōkiri, 2011, p. 6).

Substantial evidence suggests discrimination against Māori remains a very potent factor perpetuating Māori disadvantage (McCreanor, 1997). Recent empirical research which examines the differences in social and economic outcomes between 'mixed-Māori' (Māori who have one non-Māori typically Pākehā parent) and 'sole-Māori' (Māori with two Māori parents) sheds light on the detrimental impact of anti-Māori discrimination.

Mixed and sole Māori: differential outcomes

Converging lines of data suggest that Māori face racist attitudes from non-Māori New Zealanders which acts as a gatekeeper to Māori economic development. Indeed, while the government and New Zealand law may recognize Māori rights to 'equality' with other New

Zealanders, in the general population, Pākehā support for the Treaty of Waitangi has been lukewarm at best. The incidences and impacts of racism against Māori has been documented in numerous publications (Cram & Williams, 2012; McCreanor et al., 2011; Moewaka Barnes, Borell, & McCreanor, 2014; Moewaka Barnes, Taiapa, Borell, & McCreanor, 2013; Rankine et al., 2014). For example, Holmes, Murachver, and Bayard (2001) conducted an interesting exploration of attitudes towards Māori among teenagers and young adults in New Zealand. The researchers showed videotapes of speakers reading an identical short passage to 164 high school students (76% were Pākehā). Speakers who looked Māori and had Māori 'accent' were rated significantly lower on the variables of earnings, education, social class and intelligence, than non-Māori. The authors conclude that "the negative stereotypes of Māori consistently found in research dating back to the 1950's are currently present in New Zealand's youth" (p. 84).

In another line of research, Kukutai (2004) has observed that those of Māori descent who also report having one Pākehā parent ('mixed-Māori') experience social and economic advantage relative to those of Māori descent who identify primarily as Māori ('sole-Māori'; Greaves, Houkamau, & Sibley, 2015). To explain these differences, Gould (1996, cited in Chapple, 2000, p. 6) argues that "intermarriage transfers Western cultural norms to Māori and thus ensures less disparity on the basis of the usual objective measures – based as they are on Western cultural norms – of income, of jobs and of life expectancy and so on". Houkamau and Sibley (2014) disagree with this view and suggest that mixed-Māori experience advantage as they are less likely to experience discrimination based merely on physical appearance. To demonstrate, Houkamau (2006) and Houkamau and Sibley (2014) showed that those who identified as 'mixed-Māori' were less likely to report they appeared Māori to others. In a follow-up study, Houkamau and Sibley (2015) examined differences in rates of home ownership among Māori. Using data drawn from a large national postal sample of 561 Māori, their analyses indicated that self-reported appearance as Māori, significantly predicted decreased rates of home ownership. This association held when adjusting for demographic covariates, such as education, level of deprivation of the immediate area, household income, age, relationship status, region of residence, and so forth. The authors concluded this suggests there is, or at least has been in the recent past, institutional racism against Māori in New Zealand's home lending industry based on merely physical appearance as Māori.

While many complex factors contribute to the poorer economic status for Māori, these studies suggest anti-Māori discrimination contributes to the status quo – and could also partly explain the paradox whereby the Māori 'economy' and businesses report success, while individual Māori households remain in relative poverty. Māori businesses and organizations may provide a haven as they are more likely to recognize Māori language and culture and accept Māori culture among their employees. These data also suggest that the way forward for Māori is through collective action and Māori collaborating with Māori.

Contemporary Māori development

Numerous written accounts have documented the various ways in which Māori leaders throughout New Zealand have worked consistently to restore and strengthen Māori tribal networks and revitalize Māori culture and economic practices in their own tribal areas (e.g. see Belgrave, 2014; Durie, 2000; Ministry for Culture and Heritage, 2014; O'Regan, Palmer, & Langton, 2006; Sorrenson, 2014).

In terms of contemporary developments, the 1984 'Hui Taumata': Māori Economic Development Summit (attended by Māori leaders throughout New Zealand) requires mention, as this Hui stimulated emphasis on Māori economic self-determination, or Tino-Rangatiratanga: "Māori control of all things Māori". From the Hui the Māori Economic Development Commission was established to give practical effect to this aspiration (see Love, 1984, for a discussion of the proceedings and Moon, 2009, for a discussion of the subsequent developments). A more recent Hui Taumata (held in 2005) endorsed Māori self-determination as well as the need for greater collaboration between Māori organizations so that economies of scale can be realized (see Durie, 2005; Hui Taumata Action, 2006; Whitehead & Annesley, 2005).

Although Māori economic aspirations are yet to be fully realized, these Hui demonstrate general consensus among Māori whereby Māori must control their own economic future if they are to thrive. What does this mean in practice? What is a 'Māori business'? Do Māori 'economic drivers' differ from Pākehā and other non-Māori? In the next section I turn my attention to the role of Māori values for economic practices. It is not possible here to discuss the relevance of all Māori values and concepts for contemporary Māori economic activity. Rather here I select some of the key concepts in the literature and link these to Māori well-being (for a thorough review, see Harmsworth, 2005 and The Māori Economic Development Panel, 2012).

In defining what constitutes a Māori business, Durie (2002) described six principles that help shape the Māori business ethic. These principles are: *tuhono* (agreement and alliance), *purotu* (transparency), *whakaritanga* (acknowledge other values and motives), *paiheitia* (integrated multiple goals), *puwaitanga* (seeking best outcomes) and *kōtahitanga* (unity). Several converging lines of research indicate that these cultural values are important drivers of Māori economic activity and they continue to survive even if the social and material circumstances of the Māori world have changed.

Even when individual Māori have been asked to reflect on their economic and career choices, Māori often refer to the implications of their choices for their *whānau, hapū* and *iwi*. For example, Fitzgerald's (1969) study of seventy-five Māori university graduates demonstrated it was common for participants to report that career choice and satisfaction related to communal values and group orientation. Participants also described *whānaungatanga* (family strength and unity), kinship ties (community spirit and cooperation), group identification, pride in *tikanga Māori* as central to their identities and sense of purpose in life. In a study of Tuhoe (a tribe located in the central North Island of New Zealand), Liu and Tamara's (1998) in-depth interviews with sixteen Māori, recorded that older Māori fondly recalled the communal economic activities that characterized their own childhoods. Accordingly, their descriptions of what it meant to be Māori reflected their childhood experiences, that is, they described Māori identity as related to communal activity for collective gain, reciprocity and mutual support. More recently, Haar and Brougham (2013) have demonstrated that collectivist orientations play an important role in Māori career satisfaction at the level of individuals, suggesting that Māori values continue to inspire and motivate Māori work related choices (Māori Economic Development Panel, 2012; Oliver & Love, 2007).

Beyond the individual level, several pieces of research have provided important insights into the role of traditional Māori values in the contemporary New Zealand business environment. While not all Māori businesses operate according to traditional values, the literature reviewed here suggests that when Māori consciously choose to operate according to *tikanga Māori*: culture has a significant role to play. Spiller (2010) demonstrated the crucial importance of Māori values such as *manaakitanga* (respect for hosts or kindness to guests) and *whānaungatanga* (family, relationships) to Māori tourism businesses. She observed that Māori businesses often evaluate their own success according to multiple 'bottom-lines' (i.e. businesses objectives relate to the social, cultural, environmental, spiritual and economic aspirations of Māori).

Harmsworth (2005) closely examined seven successful Māori businesses to clarify the role of Māori values for business activity. Overall, across case studies, Harmsworth found remarkable consistency in the core values that drove Māori businesses. Reflecting the values of *whānaungatanga* and *kōtahitanga* (collective wellbeing and unity), he reported that the majority of successful Māori businesses were collectives (*iwi*, trusts or *whānau* businesses) that existed to provide work and sustenance for their *whānau, hapū* and *iwi*. Consistent with the concept of *rangatiratanga* (empowerment, identity, strength), he found that the businesses were at least partly motivated by the desire to elevate Māori wellbeing and development. Businesses also tended to express a desire to develop and advance resources to benefit future generations (*kaitiakitanga* – guardianship, responsibility; Harmsworth, 1995, 1997; Harmsworth, Barclay-Kerr, & Reedy, 2002).

Harmsworth's findings resonate with Te Puni Kōkiri's (2006) research into the core business characteristics and values of Māori businesses. Their examination of thirty case studies of Māori businesses (mainly Māori Land Incorporations and Trusts) found that Māori see business ventures as a mechanism for supporting *whānau* and tribal development. Views of economic success went beyond financial gain to encompass the business's abilities to contribute to their communities and *iwi* development. Organizations prioritized the use of business practices which were socially and culturally acceptable to Māori people. This also incorporated sustainable processes, which ensured protection of resources for future generations (also see Zygadlo, 2003).

Smith, Tinirau, Gillies, and Warriner (2015) in their analysis of tribal businesses and 'critical success factors' for Māori found that Māori values remain instrumental in defining Māori tribal organizations. In turn, these give rise to cultural and ethical standards that differentiate Māori organizations from non-Māori businesses. Overall, visions and aspirations tended to combine cultural and commercial values so that while financial advancement was seen as important, that should not be at the cost of *tikanga Māori*. Moreover, wealth creation is not seen as an end in itself.

Conclusions

The last 175 years has seen massive changes for Māori, from having full tribal autonomy and control over their lands and natural resources, to social fragmentation and a loss of a socio-economic base. Although Māori have made remarkable advances in the political arena, socio-historical upheaval has created pockets of long-term poverty in Māori society. Anti-Māori discrimination reverberates throughout New Zealand society, further challenging Māori progress in multiple domains. As Durie has observed, there is much potential within a youthful and diverse Māori society (Durie, 2003). It can also be stated that Māori economic prosperity is a key aspect of Māori progress and ultimately is relevant to all New Zealanders. The misalignment between the prosperity of Māori collectives (such as *iwi* groups) in the economic arena and the relative poverty of 'individual' Māori households suggests the way forward for Māori is self-sufficiency and collective activity.

A recurring theme of this chapter is the relational nature of Māori identity (Houkamau & Sibley, 2010). This is distinctive to Māori in New Zealand and is not an abstract concept. For example, data indicate that the vast majority of Māori (nearly 90%) feel whānaungatanga is important to life satisfaction. Moreover, unique among ethnic groups in New Zealand, Te Kupenga found that Māori are happier and more satisfied when they have dependent children in their care (Statistics New Zealand, 2014c).

The centrality of *whānau* to Māori wellbeing provides a starting point for a discussion of Māori 'economic' outcomes at all levels, individual, *whānau, hapū* and *iwi*. Notions of 'wealth' and 'economic' prosperity (and how these things should be achieved) need to be understood in Māori terms – and these are likely to differ from Pākehā perceptions. More work needs to be done to identify new ways of conceptualizing Māori perspectives of financial success that promote Māori wealth accumulation while acknowledging and incorporating uniquely Māori cultural imperatives and values. Better understanding of how Māori balance being financially viable with the social and cultural aspirations may shed light not only on how Māori economic practices are adapting and transforming, but also how all Māori may continue to adapt and move forward as a people.

References

Awatere, D. (1984). *Māori sovereignty.* Auckland: Broadsheet Publications.

Barlow, C. (1991). *Tikanga whakaaro: Key concepts in Māori culture.* Auckland: Oxford University Press.

Beaglehole, E., & Beaglehole, P. (1946). *Some modern Maoris.* Christchurch: New Zealand Council for Education Research.

Belgrave, M. (2014). Beyond the Treaty of Waitangi: Māori tribal aspirations in an era of reform, 1984–2014. *The Journal of Pacific History, 49*(2), 193–213.

Belich, J. (1996). *Making peoples: A history of the New Zealanders: From Polynesian settlement to the end of the nineteenth century.* Auckland: Penguin Press.

Biggs, B. (1960). *Māori marriage: An essay in reconstruction.* Auckland: Reed.

Broughton, J. (1993). Being Maori. *New Zealand Medical Journal, 106*(968), 506–508.

Chapple, S. (2000). *Maori socio-economic disparity.* Paper for the Ministry of Social Policy, Labour Market Policy Group, Department of Labour, Wellington. Retrieved from www.nzcpr.com/wp.../Maori-Economic-Disparity-Simon-Chapple.pdf.

Coleman, A., Dixon, S., & Maré, D.C. (2005). *Māori economic development – Glimpses from statistical sources.* Wellington: Motu Economic and Public Policy Research. Retrieved from http://motu-www.motu.org.nz/wpapers/05_13.pdf.

Consedine, B. (2007). *Historical influences: Māori and the economy.* Wellington: Te Puni Kōkiri.

Cram, F. (2011). Poverty. In T. McIntosh & M. Mulholland (Eds.), *Māori and social issues* (pp. 147–168). Wellington: Huia.

Cram, F., & Williams, L. (2012). A synthesis of literature. In *What works for Māori.* Auckland: Katoa Ltd, Author. Retrieved from www.corrections.govt.nz/__data/assets/pdf_file/0015/700314/What_Works_for_Maori_final.pdf.

Creative New Zealand & Arts Council of New Zealand/Toi Aotearoa. (1999). *Arts every day/Mahi toi ia ra: A survey of arts participation by New Zealand adults, Tirohanga ki te whakauru o nga pakeke o Aotearoa ki nga mahi toi.* Wellington: Creative New Zealand.

Durie, M. (1995). *Ngā Matatini Māori: Diverse Māori realities.* Paper prepared for the Ministry of Health, Massey University Māori Studies Department.

Durie, M. (1997). Identity, nationhood and implications for practice in New Zealand. *New Zealand Journal of Psychology, 26*(2), 32–38.

Durie, M. (2000). *Maori development: Reflections and strategic directions.* A paper presented at Toi Te Kupu, Toi Te Mana, Toi Te Whenua Conference on Maori Development in a Global Society held at Putahi-a-Toi, School of Maori Studies, Massey University, Palmerston North, 4–6 July. He Pukenga Korero, Vol. 5, No. 1.

Durie, M. (2002). *The business ethic and Māori development.* Unpublished paper presented at Maunga Ta Maunga Ora Economic Summit, March, Hawera, New Zealand.

Durie, M. (2003). *Ngā kāhui pou = Launching Māori futures.* Wellington: Huia.

Durie, M. (2005). *Te Tai Tini: Transformation 2025.* Paper presented at Hui Taumata 2005, Wellington, New Zealand. Retrieved from www.whariki.ac.nz/massey/fms/Te%20Mata%20O%20Te%20Tau/Publications%20-%20Mason/M%20Durie%20Te%20Tai%20Tini%20Transformations%202025.pdf.

Durie, M., & University of Waikato Development Studies Programme. (2000). *Contemporary Māori development: Issues and broad directions.* Hamilton: Development Studies Programme, University of Waikato.

Fitzgerald, T.K. (1969). *The social position of the Māori graduate: A reconsideration of some theories of acculturation and identity*. Unpublished doctoral thesis, University of North Carolina, Chapel Hill, USA.

Gibson, A. (2015). Prospects appear even brighter for Maori economic renaissance. *The New Zealand Herald*, 6 February. Retrieved from www.nzherald.co.nz/business/news/article.cfm?c_id=3&objectid=11397182.

Greaves, L.M., Houkamau, C.A., & Sibley, C.G. (2015). Māori identity signatures: A latent profile analysis of the types of Māori identity. *Cultural Diversity and Ethnic Minority Psychology*, *21*(4), 541–549.

Haar, J.M., & Brougham, D.M. (2013). An indigenous model of career satisfaction: Exploring the role of workplace cultural wellbeing. *Social Indicators Research*, *110*(3), 873–890.

Hanson, A. (1989). The making of the Māori: Culture invention and its logic. *American Anthropologist*, *91*(4), 890–902.

Harmsworth, G.R. (1995). *Māori values for land-use planning: Discussion document*. Lincoln, New Zealand: Manaaki Whenua-Landcare Research.

Harmsworth, G.R. (1997). *Māori values and GIS: The New Zealand experience. GIS Asia Pacific: The geographic technology publication for the Asia Pacific region*. Palmerston North: Manaaki Whenua-Landcare Research.

Harmsworth, G., Barclay-Kerr, K., & Reedy, T.M. (2002). Maori sustainable development in the 21st century: The importance of Māori values, strategic planning and information systems. *He Puna Korero: Journal of Maori and Pacific Development*, *3*(2), 40–68.

Harmsworth, G. (2005). *Report on the incorporation of traditional values/tikanga into contemporary Māori business organisation and process*. No. LC/0405/058, Landcare Research New Zealand Ltd. Retrieved from http://citeseerx.ist.psu.edu/viewdoc/download?doi=10.1.1.452.7226&rep=rep1&type=pdf.

Harmsworth, G.R. & Awatere, S. (2013). Indigenous Māori knowledge and perspectives of ecosystems. In J. Dymond (Ed.), *Ecosystem services in New Zealand: Conditions and trends* (pp. 274–286). Lincoln, New Zealand: Manaaki Whenua Press.

Holmes, K., Murachver, T., & Bayard, D. (2001). Accent, appearance, and ethnic stereotypes in New Zealand. *New Zealand Journal of Psychology*, *30*(2), 79–86.

Houkamau, C.A. (2006). *Identity and socio-historical context: Transformations and change among Māori women*. Doctoral dissertation, University of Auckland, Auckland, New Zealand.

Houkamau, C.A., & Sibley, C.G. (2010). The multi-dimensional model of Māori identity and cultural engagement. *New Zealand Journal of Psychology*, *39*(1), 8–28.

Houkamau, C.A., & Sibley, C.G. (2014). Social identity and differences in psychological and economic outcomes for mixed and sole-identified Māori. *International Journal of Intercultural Relations*, *40*, 113–125.

Houkamau, C.A., & Sibley, C.G. (2015). Looking Māori predicts decreased rates of home ownership: Institutional racism in housing based on perceived appearance. *PLOS ONE*, *10*(3), e0118540.

Hui Taumata Action. (2006). *Hui Taumata: Accelerating Maori economic development: Project introductions and overviews*. Wellington: Hui Taumata Action.

Jackson, M. (1993). Land loss and the Treaty of Waitangi. In W. Ihimaera (Ed.), *Te Ao Mārama: Regaining Aotearoa. Māori writers speak out. Vol. 2. He Whakaatanga o te Ao: The reality*. Auckland: Reed.

Keane, B. (2015). *Story: Te Māori i te ohanga – Māori in the economy. Page 7 – Government reforms, 1980s*. Retrieved from www.teara.govt.nz/en/te-maori-i-te-ohanga-maori-in-the-economy/page-7.

Keenan, D. (2002). Bound to the land: Māori retention and assertion of land and identity. In E. Pawson & T. Brooking (Eds.), *Environmental histories of New Zealand* (pp. 246–260). Melbourne: Oxford University Press.

Kelsey, J. (1995). *The New Zealand experiment: A world model for structural adjustment?* London: Pluto Press.

King, M. (1977). *Te Puea: A biography*. Auckland: Hodder and Stoughton.

King, M. (1983). *Māori: A photographic and social history*. Wellington: Reed.

King, M. (2003). *The Penguin history of New Zealand*. Auckland: Penguin.

Kukutai, T. (2004). The problem of defining an ethnic group for public policy: Who is Maaori and why does it matter? *Social Policy Journal of New Zealand*, *23*, 86–108.

Liu, J.H., & Tamara, P. (1998). Leadership, colonisation, and tradition. Identity and economic change in Ruatoki and Ruatahuna. *Journal of Native Education*, *22*(1), 138–145.

Love, R.N. (1984). *Papers, speech notes and submissions presented to the Māori Development Summit Conference*. Maori Economic Development Summit Conference, Wellington, NZ.

Māori Economic Development Panel. (2012). *Strategy to 2040: Māori Economic Development Panel November 2012*. Wellington: Author. Retrieved from www.med.govt.nz/business/economic-development/pdf-docs-library/Māori-economic-development/Strategy.pdf.

Marriot, L., & Sim, D. (2014). *Indicators of inequality for Māori and Pacific people.* Working Paper 09/2014, Working Papers in Finance, Victoria University, Wellington. Retrieved from www.victoria.ac.nz/sacl/centres-and-institutes/cpf/publications/pdfs/2015/WP09_2014_Indicators-of-Inequality.pdf.

Marsden, M., & Henare, Te A. (2003). Kaitiakitanga: A definitive introduction into the holistic worldview of the Māori. In Te A.C. Royal (Ed.), *In the woven universe: Selected writings of Rev. Māori Marsden* (pp. 54–72). Otaki: Estate of Rev. Māori Marsden.

McCreanor, T. (1997). When racism stepped ashore: Antecedents of anti-Maori discourse in Aotearoa. *New Zealand Journal of Psychology, 26*(1), 36–44.

McCreanor, T., Rankine, J., Moewaka Barnes, A., Borell, B., Nairn, R., & McManus, A.L. (2011). The association of crime stories and Māori in Aotearoa New Zealand print media. *Sites: A Journal of Social Anthropology and Cultural Studies, 11*(1), 121–144.

Mead, H.M. (1985). The Treaty of Waitangi and Waitangi, He Korero mo Waitangi (Te Runanga o Waitangi, Auckland). In W. Ihimaera, H. Williams, I. Ramsden, & D.S. Long (Eds.), *Te Ao Marama. Regaining Aotearoa. Māori writers speak out. Volume 2, He Whakaatanga o Te Ao. The reality.* Auckland: Reed.

Mead, H.M. (1999). *Two blankets and a puff of tobacco. The struggle to build bridges of understanding. Landmarks, bridges and visions.* Wellington: Victoria University Press.

Metge, J. (1990). Te Rito o te harakeke: Conceptions of the whaanau. *The Journal of the Polynesian Society, 99*(1), 55–92.

Metge, J. (1995). *The whanau in modern society.* Wellington: Victoria University Press.

Ministry for Culture and Heritage. (2014). Āpirana Ngata. Retrieved from www.nzhistory.net.nz/people/apirana-turupa-ngata.

Ministry for Culture and Heritage. (2015). Māori land loss, 1860–2000. Retrieved from www.nzhistory.net.nz/media/interactive/Māori-land-1860–2000.

Ministry of Business, Innovation and Employment. (2013). *Māori labour market factsheet – March 2013.* Wellington: Author. Retrieved from www.dol.govt.nz/publications/lmr/pdfs/lmr-fs/lmr-fs-maori-mar13.pdf.

Ministry of Social Development. (1988). *Puao-te-ata-tu (Day break): The report of the Ministerial Advisory Committee on a Maori perspective for the Department of Social Welfare.* Wellington: Author. Retrieved from www.msd.govt.nz/documents/about-msd-and-our-work/publications-resources/archive/1988-puaoteatatu.pdf.

Mitchell, L. (2009). *Māori welfare: A study of Māori economic and social progress.* Wellington: New Zealand Business Roundtable.

Moeke-Pickering, T. (1996). *Maori identity within whanau: A review of literature.* Hamilton: University of Waikato.

Moewaka Barnes, A., Taiapa, K., Borell, B., & McCreanor, T. (2013). Māori experiences and responses to racism in Aotearoa New Zealand. *MAI Journal: A New Zealand Journal of Indigenous Scholarship, 2*(2), 63–77.

Moewaka Barnes, H.M., Borell, B., & McCreanor, T. (2014). Theorising the structural dynamics of ethnic privilege in Aotearoa: Unpacking "this breeze at my back". *International Journal of Critical Indigenous Studies, 7*(1).

Moon, P. (2009). A chequered renaissance: The evolution of Māori society, 1984–2004. *Te Kaharoa, 2*(1), 25–41.

New Zealand Constitutional Advisory Panel. (2013). *New Zealand's constitution: A Report on a conversation – He Kōtuinga Kōrero mō Te Kaupapa Ture o Aotearoa.* Wellington: Ministry of Justice.

O'Regan, T., Palmer, L., & Langton, M. (2006). Keep the fires burning: Grievance and aspiration in the Ngāi Tahu Settlement. In M. Langton (Ed.), *Settling with Indigenous people: Modern treaty and agreement-making.* Annadale, NSW: Federation Press.

Oliver, P., & Love, C. (2007). *Mahi Aroha: Māori perspectives on volunteering and cultural obligations.* Wellington: Office for the Community and Voluntary Sector. Retrieved from www.communityresearch.org.nz/wp-content/uploads/formidable/raihania1.pdf.

Orange, C. (1992). *The story of a treaty.* Wellington: Bridget Williams Books.

Orange, C. (2004). *An illustrated history of the Treaty of Waitangi.* Wellington: Bridget Williams Books.

Pere, R. (1982). *Ako: Concepts and learning in the Māori tradition.* Working Paper #17, Department of Sociology, University of Waikato, Hamilton, New Zealand.

Petrie, H. (2006). *Chiefs of industry: Māori tribal enterprise in early colonial New Zealand.* Auckland, New Zealand: Auckland University Press.

Poata-Smith, E. (1997a). Ka Tika a Muri, Ka Tika a Mua? Māori protest politics and the Treaty of Waitangi settlement process. In P. Spoonley, D.G. Pearson, & C. MacPherson (Eds.), *Tangata, Tangata: Changing ethnic contours in Aotearoa New Zealand* (pp. 59–88). Palmerston North: Dunmore Press.

Poata-Smith, E. (1997b). The political economy of inequality between Māori and Pākehā. In C. Rudd & B. Roper (Eds.), *The political economy of New Zealand*. Auckland: Oxford University Press.

Rankine, J., Moewaka Barnes, A., Borell, B., Nairn, R., & McCreanor, T. (2014). Content and source analysis of newspaper items about Māori issues: Silencing the 'natives' in Aotearoa? *Pacific Journalism Review, 20*(1), 213–233.

Rangihau, J. (1975). Being Māori. In M. King (Ed.). *Te Ao Hurihuri: The world moves on. Aspects of Māoritanga*. Wellington: Hicks and Smith.

Robson, B., Cormack, D., & Cram, F. (2010). Social and economic indicators. In B. Robson & R. Harris (Eds.), *Hauora: Māori standards of health IV: A study of the years 2000–2005* (pp. 21–32). Wellington: Te Rōpū Rangahau Hauora a Eru Pōmare.

Salmond, A. (1991). *Two worlds: First meetings between Maori and Europeans, 1642–1772*. Auckland: Viking.

Salmond, A. (2012). New report reveals brown social underclass in New Zealand. *Every Child Counts*, 28 November. Retrieved from www.everychildcounts.org.nz/news/new-report-reveals-brown-social-underclass-in-new-zealand/.

Scoop Media. (2011). New report reveals brown social underclass in New Zealand. *Scoop Media*, 2 September. Retrieved from www.scoop.co.nz/stories/PO1109/S00032/new-report-reveals-brown-socialunderclass-in-new-zealand.htm.

Sibley, C.G., & Houkamau, C.A. (2013). The multi-dimensional model of Māori identity and cultural engagement: Item response theory analysis of scale properties. *Cultural Diversity and Ethnic Minority Psychology, 19*(1), 97–110.

Smith, G.H., Tinirau, R., Gillies, A., & Warriner, V. (2015). *He Mangōpare Amohia: Strategies for Māori economic development*. Wellington: Te Whare Wānanga o Awanuiārangi.

Sorrenson, M.P.K. (2014). *Ko te whenua te utu = Land is the price: Essays on Māori history, land and politics*. Auckland: University of Auckland Press.

Spiller, C. (2010). *How Māori cultural tourism businesses create authentic and sustainable wellbeing*. Unpublished doctoral thesis, University of Auckland, Auckland, New Zealand.

Statistics New Zealand. (2012). *Youth not in employment, education or training: September 2011 quarter*. Wellington: Author.

Statistics New Zealand. (2013). *2013 census quick statistics for Māori*. Wellington: Author.

Statistics New Zealand. (2014a). *2013 census quickstats about income*. Wellington: Author.

Statistics New Zealand. (2014b). *Te Kupenga 2013 (English)*. Wellington: Author.

Statistics New Zealand. (2014c). *Ka mārō te aho tapu, ka tau te korowai: Te reo Māori findings from Te Kupenga 2013*. Wellington: Author.

Statistics New Zealand. (2014d). *Tatauranga Umanga Māori: Statistics on Māori authorities*. Wellington: Author.

Sutherland, L.G. (1935). The Māori situation. In H.H. Tombs (Ed.), *New Zealand texts collection*. Wellington: Tombs. Retrieved from http://nzetc.victoria.ac.nz/tm/scholarly/tei-SutMaor-t1-body-d12.html.

Te Puni Kōkiri. (2003). *Hei Whakatinana i te Tūrua Pō: Business success and Māori organisational governance management study*. Wellington: Ministry of Māori Development and Federation of Māori Authorities Inc.

Te Puni Kōkiri. (2004a). *He Mahi, He Ritenga Hei Whakatinana i te Tūrua Pō. Case studies: Māori organisations business, governance & management practice*. Wellington: Ministry of Māori Development and Federation of Māori Authorities Inc.

Te Puni Kōkiri. (2004b). *Strategic direction – Māori succeeding as Māori*. Wellington: Te Puni Kokiri.

Te Puni Kōkiri. (2005). *Māori business innovation and venture partnerships 2005: Hei Whakatinana i te Tūrua Pō*. Wellington: Ministry of Māori Development and Federation of Māori Authorities Inc.

Te Puni Kōkiri. (2006). *Hei Whakamārama i ngā Āhuatanga o te Tūrua Pō – Investigating key Māori business characteristics for future measures: Thinking paper*. Wellington: Author.

Te Puni Kōkiri. (2007a). *Ngā Kaihanga Hou: For Māori future makers*. Wellington: Ministry of Māori Development.

Te Puni Kōkiri. (2007b). *Statement of Intent – 2007–2010*.

Te Puni Kōkiri. (2008). *Statement of Intent – 2008–09*.

Te Puni Kōkiri. (2011). *Māori Economic Development Panel discussion document*, Wellington. Retrieved from www.cobop.govt.nz/vdb/document/43.

Walker, R. (1990a). The role of the press in defining Pākehā perceptions of the Māori. In P. Spoonley & W. Hirsh (Eds.), *Between the lines: Racism and the New Zealand media* (pp. 38–46). Auckland: Heinemann Reed.

Walker, R. (1990b). *Ka Whawhai Tonu Matou: Struggle without end.* Auckland: Penguin.

Whitehead, J., & Annesley, B. (2005). *Hui Taumata 2005: A brief backgrounder.* Wellington: Hui Taumata.

Zygadlo, F.K., McIntosh, A., Matunga, H.P., Fairweather, J., & Simmons, D.G. (2003). *Maori tourism concepts, characteristics and definition.* Canterbury, New Zealand: Tourism Recreation Research and Education Centre.

PART IV

Cultural and spiritual wellbeing

19

"WE HAVE OUR OWN WAY"

Exploring pathways for wellbeing among Inuit in Nunatsiavut, Labrador, Canada

Alexandra Sawatzky, Ashlee Cunsolo,
Sherilee L. Harper, Inez Shiwak and Michele Wood

Introduction

In recent decades, Inuit have faced some of the most dramatic and rapid changes in ways of life and livelihoods of any Indigenous peoples in Canada (Kirmayer, Fletcher, & Watt, 2009), including ongoing impacts of colonization and processes of sedentarization, land dispossession, and acute climatic and environmental changes that are disrupting their ability to practice and participate in traditional, land-based activities (Cunsolo Willox, Harper, Ford, et al., 2012; Cunsolo Willox et al., 2013; Ford et al., 2014; Ford, Berrang-Ford, King, & Furgal, 2010). Although it is widely understood that Inuit cultures – and associated notions of what it means to be healthy and well – are diverse and vary between and within regions and communities (Pauktuutit Inuit Wowen of Canada, 2006) there is limited understanding of regional perspectives on Inuit-specific pathways for achieving and sustaining good health and wellbeing, which poses challenges when developing Inuit-specific health programming and policies (Durkalec et al., 2015; cf. Richmond, 2009).

To support individual and community health and wellbeing, programming and policies must reflect Inuit cultural values and wisdom (Cameron, 2011). Previously, Inuit in Canada have faced many challenges to acquiring local control over health initiatives, as healthcare was both provincially and federally controlled, creating jurisdictional challenges (Cameron, 2011; Smylie, Kaplan-Myrth, & McShane, 2009). This structure offered few opportunities for Inuit leaders and communities to be involved in defining priorities for health and wellbeing; thus, important cultural, social and environmental relationships and ways of knowing, as well as variations and cultural expressions and practices among communities, were often neglected (Cameron, 2011; Smylie & Anderson, 2006; Smylie et al., 2009). However, with the introduction of Inuit Land Claims Agreements across the North in recent years, Inuit gained self-governance and control over health decision-making, with the power and opportunities to develop new frameworks for the formation, implementation and evaluation of public health strategies with and for Inuit that are grounded in local perspectives, understandings, wisdom, livelihoods and socio-cultural realities (Cameron, 2011; Radu, House, & Pashagumskum, 2014).

To develop these contextually and culturally specific frameworks, more research is needed to reshape and redefine models of practice that resonate with Inuit communities and cultures across Canada. This research must be owned and driven by local and regional community stakeholders and health professionals to ensure Inuit voices and priorities remain at the heart of all discussions, decisions and actions. Indeed, this is the key to strengthening health provisions and programming by embedding them in local autonomy that is firmly rooted in Indigenous knowledge and ways of life (Radu et al., 2014). Further exploring distinct regional perspectives will also reveal what Inuit define as health priorities, highlight what they are already doing to live meaningful, healthy lives, as well as assist in improving the understanding of what they need and want in terms of achieving and sustaining good wellbeing.

In order to explore the various pathways through which Inuit create and pursue a state of good overall wellbeing, and drawing from a regional case study in the Inuit region of Nunatsiavut, Labrador, Canada, this study has three main objectives: (1) characterize conceptualizations of wellbeing and its underlying components from the perspectives of Inuit living in Nunatsiavut; (2) describe pathways through which Inuit in this region achieve and maintain good wellbeing; and (3) compare and contrast protective factors for wellbeing at both individual and community levels across Nunatsiavut. This study contributes to the growing literature on Inuit and Indigenous conceptualizations of wellbeing, while prioritizing regional perspectives that allow for comparisons between and among age groups, gender and communities, in order to inform better healthcare policy, provision and response. Efforts to examine and establish strategies for developing locally appropriate and culturally relevant public health research and policy within an Inuit context may also provide insight for designing stronger health policies and programs when working in partnership with other Indigenous communities.

Methodology

Partner communities: Nunatsiavut, Labrador, Canada

The Inuit Settlement Region of Nunatsiavut (translated to 'Our Beautiful Land' in Labrador Inuttitut) is located on the north coast of Labrador, Canada. Formed in 2005 as a result of the Labrador Inuit Land Claims Agreement, it is the first of the Inuit land regions in Canada to achieve full self-governance. Nunatsiavut comprises five small, remote, fly-in only communities (from north to south): Nain, Hopedale, Postville, Makkovik and Rigolet (Figures 19.1 and 19.2).

Inuit and their ancestors have lived in this region of Labrador for thousands of years, travelling widely in the region to hunt, harvest and fish on the land and sea. In the 1700s, European missionaries and fur traders began to settle in Labrador, beginning a series of rapid changes to Inuit lives, culture and livelihoods, including forced settlement and resettlement, relocation and marginalization throughout the region that is now Nunatsiavut (Natcher, Felt, & Procter, 2012). These changes to lives and livelihoods were compounded by the intergenerational trauma suffered by those who were forced from their homes to attend government-implemented residential schools (Inuit Tapiriit Kanatami, 2014). The ongoing legacies of historical traumas from these experiences continue to resonate with many Inuit in Nunatsiavut who, in more recent years, have had to deal with these enduring physical, mental, emotional and spiritual impacts in the context of rapid climatic, environmental and socioeconomic changes (Cunsolo Willox, Harper, Ford, et al., 2012; Cunsolo Willox et al., 2013; Ford et al., 2014; Harper, Edge, & Cunsolo Willox, 2012). Yet, despite the challenges presented by past and present changes to traditional livelihoods, the Inuit of Nunatsiavut are incredibly resilient and approach wellness from

DEMOGRAPHICS
For communities in Nunatsiavut, Labrador

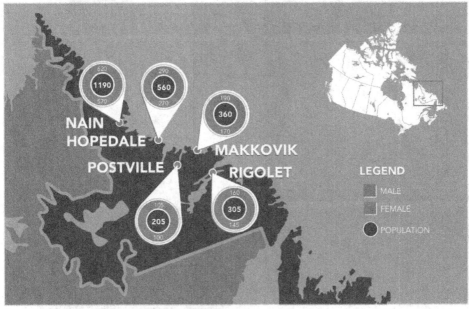

Source: Statistics Canada, 2011 Census of Population

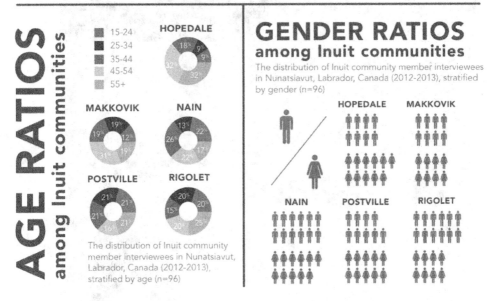

Figure 19.1 Map and demographic composition of Nunatsiavut communities and participating community members, 2012–2013

Figure 19.2   Photo collage of Nunatsiavut communities

a strengths-based approach. This approach involves practicing land-based cultural livelihoods and actively finding innovative and creative ways to adapt to these social and physical changes while preserving their deep and rich cultural history (Cunsolo Willox, Harper, Ford, et al., 2012; Natcher et al., 2012). Indeed, cultural and land-based activities – including hunting, fishing, gathering and trapping – remain central to the livelihoods and wellbeing of many Inuit living in Nunatsiavut. Most individuals support themselves financially through mixed-wage economic structures, with a reliance on semi-subsistence activities to supplement income. Strong preferences for wild, country foods – including seal, caribou, salmon, trout, geese and berries – support the continuation of traditional hunting practices and other land-based activities, and are a key protective factor for physical, mental, emotional and spiritual health and wellbeing (Cunsolo Willox et al., 2013; Petrasek MacDonald et al., 2015; cf. Petrasek MacDonald, Ford, Cunsolo Willox, & Ross, 2013).

Gathering the data

Data were gathered through a multi-year, multi-community, community-led and community-based participatory project (www.lamentfortheland.ca). Led by the Rigolet Inuit Community Government, and working in partnership with the Inuit Community Governments of Nain, Hopedale, Postville and Makkovik, and the Nunatsiavut Government Department of Health and Social Development, this project responded to Inuit-identified needs and priorities for locally specific environment and health research (Cunsolo Willox, 2014a; Cunsolo Willox et al., 2012, 2013; Harper, Edge, & Cunsolo Willox, 2012). Data for this study were drawn from 106 in-depth, semi-structured interviews conducted across Nunatsiavut between November 2012 and May 2013. Over this time period, ninety-two interviews were conducted with ninety-six community members (Figure 19.1) and fourteen interviews were conducted with twenty health professionals (total: n=116 participants).

Local Inuit Research Coordinators were hired in each community to: facilitate and oversee the entire research process; hold community information nights and open houses; recruit interview participants through direct contact, radio announcements, poster and mailbox flyer distribution (in both English and Inuttitut); and act as the first point of contact for this research.

Interviews were conducted conversationally, to allow for participant elaboration and ongoing dialogue (Kvale & Brinkmann, 2009). The questions focused on four main topics: (1) land-based activities; (2) perspectives on community and individual health and wellbeing; (3) perspectives on any social, economic, cultural and environmental changes in the community; and (4) emotional responses to any changes that were mentioned. The interview guide was pre-tested with project leads, community members and health professionals, as well as the Local Inuit Research Coordinators. All interviews were conducted in English, which for many participants was their first language (Statistics Canada, 2014), although a translator was always available should participants choose to conduct their interviews in Inuttitut. The duration of interviews ranged from 60 to 90 minutes and were audio-recorded with permission, and then transcribed.

Data analysis

Given the community-based and community-led participatory approach to this research and data-gathering, analysis was conducted through a multi-step collaborative approach. All interview transcripts were analyzed using an iterative, constant-comparative method (Birks, Chapman, & Francis, 2008), which allowed for emergent themes to be discovered, and for within- and cross-community analysis to be conducted. Weekly meetings were held with members of the research team to establish validity of emerging themes and guide the direction of subsequent analyses, and monthly meetings were held with stakeholders in Nunatsiavut to ensure that the emerging themes continued to reflect the local context (Creswell & Miller, 2010).

All transcripts were entered into the qualitative data management software, Atlas.ti™ Version 1.0.16 (82). An initial list of codes grouped by themes were created, and then expanded, collapsed and solidified. A codebook was then created and stratified by themes (DeCuir-Gunby, Marshall, & McCulloch, 2010). Reflective memos were recorded throughout the entire process to help facilitate the analysis process from the raw data stage to broader themes, and to maintain high levels of continuity and rigor in the research (Birks et al., 2008).

Results

Throughout this research, Inuit throughout Nunatsiavut explained how they created and pursued a variety of pathways that helped both individuals and communities achieve and sustain good health and wellbeing – pathways which spanned physical, mental, emotional, social and spiritual dimensions. Most importantly, all participants identified the land as the underlying determinant for all dimensions of wellbeing, placing emphasis on its roles as a 'healer', 'teacher', 'connector' and 'kin'. As such, the land served to both shape and reinforce pathways for good wellbeing.

These land-based pathways to health and wellbeing identified by participants in this study fell under three main themes: (1) cultural revitalization, through the ongoing practice of traditional activities and through the act of passing on 'traditional knowledge[3]' to younger generations, both in the community and of on the land; (2) relationship-building, through creating supportive networks with family members and friends; and (3) generating a strong sense of community, through collective involvement in formal and informal activities, gatherings, events and programmes, both within the community and on the land. It is important to note that all themes were intrinsically connected to and enhanced by each other, and stemmed from a deep connection to and relationship with the land.

The land is essential to wellness: "it helps people's hearts feel better"

For all Inuit interviewed, the land was "everything," a "traditional and customary way of life." It made people feel "whole" and was foundational to all aspects of Inuit life, culture, livelihoods and overall wellbeing. Indeed, understanding Inuit relationships with the land was essential to discovering and identifying pathways to locally connected health and wellness. While every interviewee described connections to the land, these relationships were very personal and were "kinda hard to define," "it's just a part of you," and "you feel connected to the land, and to the people." Among all the Inuit interviewed, almost everyone had "a story about going off [on the land]."

The land was also identified as a place where people practice, connect with and pass on traditional knowledge and cultural practices. Many participants identified that practicing traditional cultural activities was important for wellbeing because, according to one Inuk, it felt good "to be learning our culture, what our ancestors used to do." Continuing to practice these activities and maintain cultural traditions was essential because "it's our way of life. It's gotta be kept going."

The land was also described as a "saviour," something that "helps people's hearts feel better," and "really, really helps your soul." As a long-time Inuit employee in the health sector explained:

going out on the land is everything to us – it's our heart and our soul. That's real. A lot of people think of spirituality as just a church thing and it's not, that's just one portion of spirituality. For us, going out on the land is a form of spirituality and if you can't get there, then you almost feel like your spirit is dying and then when you get out again, then you feel so much better when you come back. I think it energizes you more and just frees your spirit more by being out on the land.

Almost all interviews described the land as a "healer", "a part of healing", "a treatment in its own self." Individuals said they went off on the land to "get back to proper health." Many people felt that going off on the land did "wonders for your mental health as well as your physical health."

Inuit-identified pathways for achieving and sustaining good wellbeing in Nunatsiavut: "Inuit has been healthy a long time their own way"

Given the holistic conceptions of wellbeing and the many, the land could be "used in different ways" to achieve and sustain good wellbeing. Participants expressed strong desires to get back to their cultural roots and strengthen traditional knowledge systems and, as such, encouraged an intimate kinship with – and connections to – the land. Further, going off on the land to learn traditional skills, or to teach others traditional skills, not only helped people to connect to their cultural roots, but helped them to connect to each other and to their communities. Central to Inuit culture in Nunatsiavut was the need to build strong relationships and networks of support, which was encouraged by participation in both formal and informal community gatherings, programmes, activities and events.

Culture as the cornerstone of Inuit-identified pathways for wellbeing: "culture isn't just a people; it's a way"

The majority of interviewees felt that actively using traditional cultural knowledge and connecting with their heritage was an important pathway for feeling good about themselves and for overall health and wellbeing. There were many ways for individuals to practice traditional cultural skills in their communities or on the land, which many interviewees identified as directly necessary for supporting health and wellbeing. For example, many people enjoyed taking part in traditional cultural activities in their communities, such as "craft projects, going in to learn to sew mittens or moose hides," as they promoted feelings of wellness in a variety of ways through connecting with culture, community and ancestry.

These efforts to connect to culture were reinforced when going off on the land was involved. Going off on the land was commonly mentioned as one of the best ways to develop and use traditional knowledge, while simultaneously fostering health and wellbeing. It was expressed that passing on knowledge surrounding land-based traditions and cultural skills to the younger generations was important because those that who knew how to survive on the land would then be able to "to pass down to the younger ones so they can keep passing it on through every year," supporting a culture of self-sufficiency and cultural wellness.

Building relationships supports wellbeing: "Inuit needs more support peoples… more connectedness to other people"

Relationships with family and friends provided individuals with a network of support that was important for good wellbeing, and that people need to foster this connection through family time and land time. Indeed, many Inuit perceived "healthy" individuals as those that were able to "reach out to others," "keep relationships going over the long term," and "feel connected to those around them, be it family, friends, community." A young female student explained the central role of "support peoples":

> Inuit families are huge and very important... our Inuit people need more support peoples, or they need more connectedness to other people, and that's just stems from history. I mean 'Inuit' means 'people' or 'the people.'

While many people emphasized the need for "a good home life when you're growing up... a family behind you and supporting you," it was also said, "you need friends outside of your family to spend time with." Many people felt that when they were going through a hard time, they wanted to talk to "people that have shared my feelings," which was most often their family and friends. Providing support was something friends and family members could do "without even being aware that's what they're doing." An older male hunter said, "I tend to talk to family more often than I talk with counselors or white people 'cause it's easier talking with family 'cause they know what I'm going through."

The majority of participants identified that going off on the land with friends and family was essential for strengthening relationships. Friends and families who went off on the land together said they were able to connect on a deeper level, and develop healthy, strong relationships while creating memories. A woman who had been born and raised on the land said her family got along better on the land, that families would "help each other more, connect more together." Off on the land, interviewees explained that people were more "honest and open," and "there's a closeness that you feel." One woman who goes off on the land regularly with her family said that these opportunities allowed her to strengthen not only her relationship with her husband, but also their relationships with their children:

> like husband and wife, when they go out on the land together they connect their selves, their relationship gets stronger, they help each other out, it gives them time to be together. Like a father and son when they go out on the land, they're helping each other, they're connecting. Not just to go wooding and collect wood but it makes their relationship stronger helping each other out. So, the land basically, I don't know [pause] heals you, helps you.

A sense of community strengthens collective wellness: "there's a lot of good, strong community support here"

Many individuals felt that community programmes, gatherings and events could positively impact on health and wellbeing by enhancing their sense of belonging, whether in the community or on the land. These programmes were viewed as opportunities to share day-to-day experiences, stories and struggles with fellow community members. One male participant expressed that, "just being able to be more a part of the community than individual minded... I think Inuit people always had this strong need for feeling like they belong to a community and to be able to socialize well with people."

Many community members described how going off on the land with others was another important way to strengthen community support because on the land, "you treat people better; you feel connected to the land, like, and to the people." Emphasis was placed on the benefits of using the land as a space to provide both formal and informal programming to build supportive connections within and between various groups. People from all age groups said they valued land-based programming, but it was said to be particularly beneficial for youth. A mental health and addictions worker who deals primarily with young people said:

> when they're here in the community, they're butting heads; they don't like each other or they're bullying each other. Whereas, when we go out there on the land, after a day they're like… like this [illustrates coming together with interconnected fingers and hands]. They're helping each other; they're supporting each other, and not only that, it's the adults are the same way. There's something about being out there that [pause] I dunno, it's very healing out on the land.

Compared to programmes based in the communities, running programmes on the land – including rehabilitation programmes, youth retreats and other organized outings – was seen to be more beneficial because, according to a number of health professionals, "everybody's different when they're on the land together," and "there's no talk of addictions, there's no talk of violence, there's no talk of suicide… none of those words don't even exist."

Inuit-identified pathways for wellbeing lead to self-determination: "just do what you want to do and be happy doing it"

The independent creation and pursuit of pathways for good wellbeing that were land-based and Inuit-specific helped people realize that they "can choose the way that they live," and that life was "all about making their own choices." This sense of self-determination based on cultural sovereignty was strengthened by "doing things that you want to do instead of doing things that other people want you to do." Across Nunatsiavut, those who actively worked to make their own choices – premised on Inuit culture, histories, livelihoods and ways of knowing – found that they were able to accomplish things they never thought possible.

The land served to reinforce feelings of self-determination in Nunatsiavut, as most individuals felt "a sense of freedom," "no pressures" and "a sense of happiness" when they went off; it was important to "get out and do things that you enjoy." Not only did the land encompass community-wide conceptions of wellbeing that were tied to culture and supportive relationships, it also provided the space for individuals to create and pursue pathways to wellbeing that led to meaningful outcomes that were locally and culturally appropriate and relevant (Figure 19.3). Compared to being in the community, "the big difference is the freedom" when individuals went off on the land. Indeed, there were many individuals who associated the freedom provided by the land with opportunities to practice traditional cultural skills:

> I like to be able to have the freedom to go and collect my food, and the ability get around and do the things I want to do without too much stress – stress free situations – and the ability to be able to exercise my Aboriginal rights.

Discussion

In order to better understand how to improve and support Inuit wellbeing in Canada, health systems, programs and policies must support communities as they define goals that correspond to their specific needs and priorities (Cameron, 2011; Kirmayer et al., 2009; Radu et al., 2014). Many Inuit prioritize relationships with the land as inherently connected to, and essential for, all dimensions of good wellbeing (Cunsolo Willox et al., 2013; Cunsolo Willox, Harper, Ford, et al.,

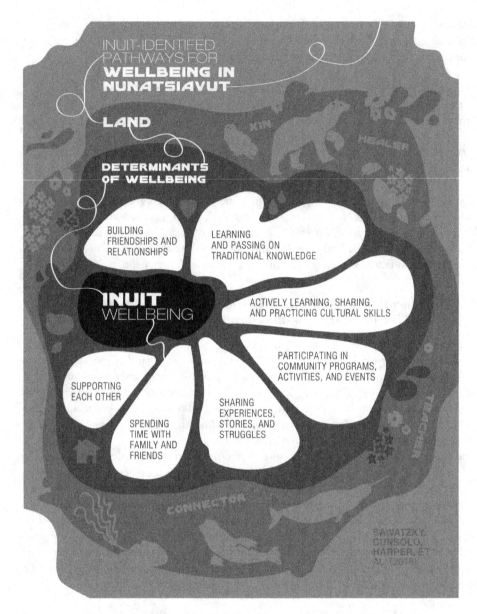

Figure 19.3 Pathways to wellbeing, as identified by Inuit in Nunatsiavut, Labrador

2012; Harper et al., 2015). Policies and programs that neglect to take into account the intricacies of these land-based relationships not only rationalize and perpetuate colonial attitudes and Western norms, but often fail to benefit the communities for whom they are designed (Baba, 2013; Brant Castellano, 2004; Sium, Chandni, & Ritskes, 2012). Working to achieve and sustain good wellbeing is, then, a collective, collaborative process that is constantly being re-negotiated (Radu et al., 2014); placing Inuit knowledge, voices and ways of knowing at the heart of this renegotiation will encourage approaches to public health research, policy and programming, which are grounded in holistic, community-based perspectives (Cameron, 2011; Sium et al., 2012).

This work contributes to establishing a regional perspective on what Inuit in Nunatsiavut are doing to promote and sustain good wellbeing, and presents examples of regional-specific pathways for understanding health and wellbeing from an Inuit perspective in order to better inform health research, policy and programming. By analyzing Inuit approaches to achieving and sustaining wellbeing shared from participants in Nunatsiavut, it is clear that the land, and Inuit relationships with the land, are foundational to many pathways for health and wellness, and are both underlying determinants for all dimensions of wellbeing, as well as determinants in of themselves (Cunsolo Willox, Harper, & Edge, 2012; Cunsolo Willox et al., 2013; Cunsolo Willox, Harper, Ford, et al., 2012; Harper et al., 2015). Indeed, within this context, wellness and wellbeing are centred around the land, resonating with the concept of an ecocentric self (Kirmayer et al., 2009), whereby wellbeing emerges from the complex and continuous interplay between the environment, the individual and the community for physical, emotional and spiritual nourishment (Kirmayer, Dandeneau, Marshall, Kahentonni Phillips, & Jessen Williamson, 2012). This ecocentric understanding highlights the depth and complexity of Inuit relationships with the land as a major pathway to locally connected health and wellness (Cunsolo Willox, Harper, Ford, et al., 2012; Durkalec, Furgal, Skinner, & Sheldon, 2015; Harper et al., 2015; Panelli & Tipa, 2009; Wilson, 2003).

Going further, for participants in this study the land is a place to pass on cultural skills and wisdom, as well as a teacher in and of itself. Simpson (2014) explains how the land is both a process of and place for Indigenous wisdom and how "coming into" this wisdom takes place in the context of family, community, and relationships. When this wisdom is realized collectively, it supports generations of self-determining, interdependent and community-minded individuals, which leads to positive outcomes in overall resilience and wellbeing (Simpson, 2014; cf. Wexler, 2009). The findings of this work also resonate with Cunsolo Willox et al. (2012), who demonstrated how Inuit identities, wellbeing, livelihoods, histories, emotional and spiritual connections are all emergent from the land, as well as with work within a First Nations context, illustrating how communities draw resources from the land and the environment as a way to maintain culture, wellbeing and overall ways of life (Alfred, 2014; Freeland Ballantyne, 2014; Radu, House, & Pashagumskum, 2014; Richmond & Ross, 2009).

These results also indicate the importance of culture and cultural knowledge and activities to support health and wellbeing (Alfred, 2014; Freeland Ballantyne, 2014; Radu et al., 2014). From sewing or crafting to hunting or trapping, Inuit in this study indicated that using cultural skills and knowledge enhanced a person's sense of identity and connection to culture. Indeed, many Inuit communities across Canada recognize the need to actively use traditional knowledge and skills in order to keep their culture strong, and to promote individual and collective health and wellbeing, physically, mentally, emotionally and spiritually, especially when coping with health risks in uncertain futures (Ford et al., 2014; ITK, 2014; Ostapchuk, Harper, Cunsolo Willox, Edge, & Rigolet Inuit Community Government, 2014; Petrasek MacDonald et al., 2013). For interviewees, connecting with culture made people feel good about themselves; this resonates with emotions and experiences shared by Indigenous peoples across Canada when they are learning and practicing traditions that had been around for generations, whether in the community or out on the land (Alfred, 2014; Radu et al., 2014; Richmond & Ross, 2009). A strong sense of cultural identity has also been demonstrated to foster socially defined roles, pathways for resilience and pathways for thriving in present contexts (Wexler, 2009).

Another pathway for wellbeing identified by Inuit involved in this project was the creation and cultivation of relationships with 'support peoples.' Indeed, many individuals expressed a need for connectedness with friends and family – a connection enriched and strengthened by spending time on the land. Being given support, as well as providing support to others, were both ways for individuals in Nunatsiavut to feel valued and needed by those around them. Along these same lines, Kral et al. (2011) investigated meanings of wellbeing, unhappiness, health and social change among Inuit in Nunavut and found the overlap between themes of family and culture reflected an Inuit holistic perspective on wellbeing. Many Inuit interviewed echoed this holistic perspective, and also stressed the importance of a strong sense of community and a complementary network of community-minded individuals, for supporting individual and collective wellness.

Finally, place-based conceptions of physical and mental wellbeing were widely shared by Inuit in this research, resonating with other research (Cunsolo Willox et al., 2013; Cunsolo Willox, Harper, Ford, et al., 2012; Durkalec et al., 2015). Many people expressed that being off on the land made them feel free from struggles of everyday life, and opened up space for achieving greater physical and mental wellbeing – wellbeing that was directly connected to their Inuit identity and ancestry. Furthermore, health-enhancing aspects of this freedom and cultural connections depend on active use of knowledge surrounding how to survive on the land (Durkalec et al., 2015; Durkalec, 2013), because self-worth and value are largely drawn from land-based activities as well as from the knowledge required to practice these activities.

Demonstrating how Inuit in this region are actively creating and pursuing pathways for wellbeing will help to guide future research and policies that aim to enhance wellbeing in relevant and meaningful ways, placing Inuit voices, culture, ways of knowing and conceptualizations of health and wellbeing at the centre of decision-making and action. Reshaping and redefining frameworks for research and policy so that they authentically represent Inuit-identified health and wellbeing definitions and priorities within specific local and regional jurisdictions presents many challenges (Brant Castellano, 2004; Radu et al., 2014; Smylie & Anderson, 2006). Despite these challenges, there are, however, many benefits and opportunities that these locally derived efforts can bring for preserving and promoting Inuit culture, identity and wellbeing within the context of strengthening healthcare provision, programming and policies across the North.

Acknowledgments

Our sincerest gratitude to the five Inuit communities of Nunatsiavut, Labrador – Nain, Hopedale, Postville, Makkovik and Rigolet – and all the participants in this research willing to share their stories, insights, experiences and wisdom. Our deepest thanks to the Inuit Community Governments of Nain, Hopedale, Postville, Makkovik and Rigolet for administrative and project support. Thank you to André Mersereau from Chapter 1 Studios for the graphic design. We are grateful for the funding of this project provided through Health Canada's First Nations and Inuit Health Branch, the Nasivvik Centre for Inuit Health and Changing Environments, the Nunatsiavut Government's Department of Health and Social Development and the Canada Research Chairs program. Ethics approval was received through Cape Breton University, McGill University, the University of Guelph and the Nunatsiavut Research Advisory Committee.

Notes

1 Inuit Mental Health and Adaptation to Climate Change Team: Anthony Andersen and Noah Nochasak, Nain Inuit Community Government; Wayne Piercy and Juliana Flowers, Hopedale Inuit Community Government; Diane Gear and Greg Jacque, Postville Inuit Community Government; Herb Jacque and Myrtle Groves, Makkovik Inuit Community Government; Charlotte Wolfrey and Marilyn Baikie, Rigolet Inuit Community Government.

2   Due to the small number of health professionals who participated in this study, and the small number of health professionals in the region, demographic information has been excluded in order to protect the confidentiality of those individuals.

3   All participants in this study used the term 'traditional knowledge,' which in this context encompasses terms such as 'Inuit knowledge,' 'traditional ecological knowledge', 'local knowledge' and 'cultural knowledge.'

References

Alfred, T. (2014). The Akwesasne cultural restoration program: A Mohawk approach to land-based education. *Decolonization: Indigeneity, Education, and Society, 3*(3), 134–144.

Baba, L. (2013). *Cultural safety in First Nations, Inuit, and Metis public health: Environmental scan of cultural competency and safety in education, training, and health services.* Prince George, BC.

Birks, M., Chapman, Y., & Francis, K. (2008). Memoing in qualitative research: Probing data and processes. *Journal of Research in Nursing, 13*(1), 68–75.

Brant Castellano, M. (2004). Ethics of Aboriginal research. *Journal of Aboriginal Health, Jan.*, 98–114. Retrieved from www.naho.ca/english/pdf/journal_p98-114.pdf.

Cameron, E.S. (2011). *State of the knowledge: Inuit public health, 2011.* Prince George, BC.

Creswell, J.W., & Miller, D.L. (2010). Determining validity in qualitative inquiry. *Theory into Practice, 39*(3), 37–41.

Cunsolo Willox, A., Harper, S.L., & Edge, V.L. (2012). Storytelling in a digital age: Digital storytelling as an emerging narrative method for preserving and promoting Indigenous oral wisdom. *Qualitative Research, 13*(2), 127–147.

Cunsolo Willox, A., Harper, S.L., Edge, V.L., Landman, K., Houle, K., & Ford, J.D. (2013). The land enriches the soul: On climatic and environmental change, affect, and emotional health and well-being in Rigolet, Nunatsiavut, Canada. *Emotion, Space and Society, 6*(1), 14–24.

Cunsolo Willox, A., Harper, S.L., Ford, J.D., Landman, K., Houle, K., & Edge, V.L. (2012). "From this place and of this place": Climate change, sense of place, and health in Nunatsiavut, Canada. *Social Science & Medicine, 75*(3), 538–547.

Cunsolo Willox, A., Stephenson, E., Allen, J., Bourque, F., Drossos, A., Elgarøy, S., Kral, M.J., Mauro, I., Moses, J., Pearce, T., Petrasek MacDonald, J., & Wexler, L. (2014). Examining relationships between climate change and mental health in the Circumpolar North. *Regional Environmental Change, 15*(1), 169–182.

DeCuir-Gunby, J.T., Marshall, P.L., & McCulloch, A.W. (2010). Developing and using a codebook for the analysis of interview data: An example from a professional development research project. *Field Methods, 23*(2), 136–155.

Durkalec, A. (2013). *Understanding the role of environment for Indigenous health: A case study of sea ice as a place of health and risk in the Inuit community of Nain, Nunatsiavut.*

Durkalec, A., Furgal, C., Skinner, M.W., & Sheldon, T. (2015). Climate change influences on environment as a determinant of Indigenous health: Relationships to place, sea ice, and health in an Inuit community. *Social Science & Medicine, 136–137*(1), 17–26.

Ford, J.D., Berrang-Ford, L., King, M., & Furgal, C. (2010). Vulnerability of Aboriginal health systems in Canada to climate change. *Global Environmental Change, 20*(4), 668–680.

Ford, J.D., Cunsolo Willox, A., Chatwood, S., Furgal, C., Harper, S.L., Mauro, I., & Pearce, T. (2014). Adapting to the effects of climate change on Inuit health. *American Journal of Public Health, 104*(S3), e9–e17.

Freeland Ballantyne, E. (2014). Dechinta bush university: Mobilizing a knowledge economy of reciprocity, resurgence, and decolonization. *Decolonization: Indigeneity, Education, and Society, 3*(3), 67–85.

Harper, S.L., Edge, V.L., & Cunsolo Willox, A. (2012). "Changing climate, changing health, changing stories" profile: Using an EcoHealth approach to explore impacts of climate change on Inuit health. *EcoHealth, 9*(1), 89–101.

Harper, S.L., Edge, V.L., Ford, J., Cunsolo Willox, A., Wood, M., & McEwen, S. (2015). Climate-sensitive health priorities in Nunatsiavut, Canada. *BMC Public Health, 15*(1), 605. doi:10.1186/s12889-015-1874-3.

Inuit Tapiriit Kanatami. (2014). *2013–2014 Annual report.* Ontario, Canada.

ITK. (2014). *Social determinants of Inuit health in Canada.* Ottawa: ITK.

Kirmayer, L.J., Dandeneau, S., Marshall, E., Kahentonni Phillips, M., & Jessen Williamson, K. (2012). Toward an ecology of stories: Indigenous perspectives on resilience. In M. Ungar (Ed.), *The social ecology of resilience: A handbook of theory and practice* (pp. 369–386). New York: Springer.

Kirmayer, L.J., Fletcher, C., & Watt, R. (2009). Locating the ecocentric self: Inuit concepts of mental health and illness. In L.J. Kirmayer & G.G. Valaskakis (Eds.), *Healing traditions: The mental health of Aboriginal Peoples in Canada* (pp. 289–314). Vancouver, BC: University of British Columbia Press.

Kral, M.J., Idlout, L., Minore, J.B., Dyck, R.J., & Kirmayer, L.J. (2011). Unikkaartuit: Meanings of well-being, unhappiness, health, and community change among Inuit in Nunavut, Canada. *American Journal of Community Psychology, 48*(3–4), 426–438.

Kvale, S., & Brinkmann, S. (2009). *Interviews: Learning the craft of qualitative research interviewing.* Los Angeles, CA: Sage.

Natcher, D.C., Felt, L., & Procter, A.H. (2012). *Settlement, subsistence, and change among the Labrador Inuit: The Nunatsiavummiut experience* (D.C. Natcher & A.H. Proctor, Eds.). Winnipeg: University of Manitoba Press.

Ostapchuk, J., Harper, S.L., Cunsolo Willox, A., Edge, V.L., & Rigolet Inuit Community Government. (2014). Exploring Elders' and seniors' perceptions of how climate change is impacting health and well-being in Rigolet, Nunatsiavut. *Journal of Aboriginal Health, June*, 5–21.

Panelli, R., & Tipa, G. (2009). Beyond foodscapes: Considering geographies of Indigenous well-being. *Health & Place, 15*(2), 455–465.

Petrasek MacDonald, J., Cunsolo Willox, A., Ford, J.D., Shiwak, I., Wood, M., IMHACC Team, & the Rigolet Inuit Community Government. (2015). Protective factors for mental health and well-being in a changing climate: Perspectives from Inuit youth in Nunatsiavut, Labrador. *Social Science & Medicine, 141*(1), 133–141.

Petrasek MacDonald, J., Ford, J.D., Cunsolo Willox, A., & Ross, N.A. (2013). A review of protective factors and causal mechanisms that enhance the mental health of Indigenous Circumpolar youth. *International Journal of Circumpolar Health, 72*(1), 1–18.

Pauktuutit Inuit Wowen of Canada. (2006). *The Inuit way: A guide to Inuit culture.* Canada, Author.

Radu, I., House, L., & Pashagumskum, E. (2014). Land, life, and knowledge in Chisasibi: Intergenerational healing in the bush. *Decolonization: Indigeneity, Education, and Society, 3*(3), 86–105.

Richmond, C.A.M. (2009). The social determinants of Inuit health: A focus on social support in the Canadian Arctic. *International Journal of Circumpolar Health, 68*, 471–487.

Richmond, C.A.M., & Ross, N.A. (2009). The determinants of First Nation and Inuit health: A critical population health approach. *Health and Place, 15*(2), 403–411.

Simpson, L.B. (2014). Land as pedagogy: Nishnaabeg intelligence and rebellious. *Decolonization: Indigeneity, Education & Society, 3*(3), 1–25.

Sium, A., Chandni, D., & Ritskes, E. (2012). Towards the "tangible unknown": Decolonization and the Indigenous future. *Decolonization: Indigeneity, Education & Society, 1*(1), I–XIII. Retrieved from http://decolonization.org

Smylie, J., & Anderson, M. (2006). Understanding the health of Indigenous peoples in Canada: Key methodological and conceptual challenges. *Canadian Medical Association Journal, 175*(6), 602.

Smylie, J., Kaplan-Myrth, N., & McShane, K. (2009). Indigenous knowledge translation: Baseline findings in a qualitative study of the pathways of health knowledge in three Indigenous communities in Canada. *Health Promotion Practice, 10*(3), 436–446.

Statistics Canada. (2014). *National Household Survey (NHS) Aboriginal Population Profile*, 13 November. Retrieved 25 May 2015 from www12.statcan.gc.ca/nhs-enm/2011/dp-pd/aprof/details/page.cfm?Lang=E&Geo1=BAND&Code1=640001&Data=Count&SearchText=Nunatsiavut&SearchType=Begins&SearchPR=10&A1=All&Custom=&TABID=1.

Wexler, L. (2009). The importance of identity, history, and culture in the wellbeing of Indigenous youth. *The Journal of the History of Childhood and Youth, 2*(2), 267–276.

Wilson, K. (2003). Therapeutic landscapes and First Nations peoples: An exploration of culture, health and place. *Health and Place, 9*(2), 83–93.

20

INDIGENOUS CULTURE-AS-TREATMENT IN THE ERA OF EVIDENCE-BASED MENTAL HEALTH PRACTICE

Andrew Pomerville and Joseph P. Gone

Introduction

The goal of this chapter is to clarify, to the extent current scientific understanding allows, the ways in which traditional cultural-spiritual practices have potential to improve the wellbeing of Indigenous North Americans. Traditional healing is a commonly used term for a number of practices, some employed in contemporary medical care, which are made of cultural teachings and/or spiritual practices that are based in Indigenous historical and contemporary worldviews (Duran, 2006; Gone, 2010). Some research has demonstrated that such teachings and practices may improve wellbeing and psychological health, discussed below, but a full discussion of the use of traditional healing requires that we address the historical context in which such practices take place.

It would be impossible to discuss the wellbeing of Indigenous populations in North America without reference to historical and ongoing colonization, and the impact of such colonization on the spiritual and cultural practices of contemporary Indigenous North Americans. Prior to European contact, hundreds of widely varied spiritual traditions marked the equally numerous and distinct cultural groups now broadly categorized as the Indigenous peoples of the North American continent. Early European contact was marked by mass conversion efforts promoting Christianity that over time built into full-scale campaigns to eliminate Indigenous spiritual practices. Boarding school policies in both nations encouraged or even coerced Indigenous parents to turn their children over to institutions that typically forbade the cultural and spiritual practices of Indigenous groups. In some cases, the effect of such policies was the total extinction of particular Indigenous languages and cultural traditions.

The employment of legal sanctions against certain ceremonial practices in the United States and Canada served to further suppress Indigenous spirituality. In Canada, traditional potlatch ceremonies[1] were outlawed until 1951, for example, while in the United States it took several acts of Congress to restore rights to traditional American Indian spiritual practice, most notably the American Indian Religious Freedom Act of 1978 (Paper, 2007; Pevar, 2012). Even among Indigenous groups whose cultural practices were maintained over generations, the boarding schools nonetheless had deleterious effects on the psychological health and wellbeing of community members (Elias et al., 2012; Evans-Campbell, Walters, Pearson, & Campbell, 2012). Largely as a result of these and other long-standing inequities, Indigenous groups in the United States and Canada face far greater rates of substance dependence, posttraumatic stress disorder (PTSD), and suicidality than the general population of either nation (Gone & Trimble, 2012; Towle, Godolphin, & Alexander, 2006).

This historical backdrop and its legacy have significantly impacted contemporary spiritual and cultural practices. Perhaps surprisingly, given the history of both religious subjugation and suppression of traditional Indigenous spirituality, research indicates that spiritual commitment and participation is especially high among Indigenous North Americans (Garroutte et al., 2014). In a study of over 3,000 American Indians from two regions of the United States, researchers found self-reported rates of participation of about 90 percent for both men and women, with high involvement in three different spiritual traditions that were measured: Aboriginal, Christian and Native American Church (Garroutte et al., 2014). According to this research, blending of Christian and Indigenous spiritual practices is common; approximately three-fourths of participants indicated participating in some form of Christian practice, with rates of two-thirds for Aboriginal practices and one half for the Native American Church.

Given these findings, it makes sense that spiritual approaches and traditional healing are commonly included in Indigenous health service settings (Gone, 2010; Garrett, 2011). Some of the most common spiritual practices used today in Indigenous treatment settings are pan-Indigenous; while they may draw from particular Indigenous traditions, the sweat lodge, medicine wheel and many other practices associated with traditional healing have been distributed broadly to Indigenous contexts far outside their original sources, and have generally been embraced by Indigenous North Americans as acceptable for pan-Indigenous contexts. Native American Church ceremonies, also seen by many as a form of treatment (Calabrese, 1997, 2008), are used more broadly in pan-Indigenous settings, drawing on specific traditions of particular Indigenous groups while also incorporating aspects of Christian spiritual tradition (Garroutte et al., 2014).

Rather than challenging the authenticity of traditional healing practices, these alterations reflect the normal process of cultural reproduction and change. Traditional healing, like any other cultural institution, is subject to shifts and modifications over time in the context of inter-group contact and exchange. In addition to the special relevance of spiritual practices for Indigenous North Americans generally and the relative ubiquity of pan-Indigenous approaches, one takeaway from the spiritual commitment noted in Garroutte et al. (2014)'s findings is that programs designed to promote wellbeing through Indigenous spirituality and traditional healing need to be sensitive to, and respectful of, a number of spiritual traditions, including the Christian faith. Regardless of whether they are pan-Indigenous or specific to local practices, traditional teachings and sacred ceremonies are a major form of treatment in use today in Indigenous communities (Gone & Trimble, 2012; Rowan et al., 2014).

Although often discussed in terms of its spiritual components, much of traditional healing draws on teachings that reflect a holistic conceptualization of health, such as the teaching of the 'four directions' encapsulated by the medicine wheel, which are said to embody mind, emotion, body and spirit (Gone, 2008). Some researchers have found differences in Indigenous conceptualizations of health and wellbeing in comparison to other North American populations, which overlap with an emphasis in traditional healing on holistic understandings of health rather than fractured domains associated with the physical, spiritual and psychological (e.g. Donatuto, Satterfield, & Gregory, 2011; Yurkovich & Lattergrass, 2008). Such conceptualizations are hardly universal, however. For example, Cavanaugh, Taylor, Keim, Clutter, and Geraghty (2008) found that an Indigenous sample presenting for treatment for diabetes made little mention of spirituality or traditional healing in interviews, contrary to these investigators' expectations.

Some Indigenous perspectives on health consider Indigenous and 'Western' illnesses as separate and requiring different forms of treatment, while remaining interested in the treatment of both in their respective contexts (Waldram, 2004). Similarly, although much research has been written on Indigenous populations as 'collectivist' as opposed to 'individualist' in their cultural orientations, Indigenous worldviews prior to European contact would be difficult to designate as solely collectivist, and today are even more likely to be a blend of collectivist and individualist orientations as Indigenous perspectives exist within a (post-)colonial context and have been shaped by cultural interactions (Waldram, 2004). Cultural essentialism would be a serious error; programs which seek to reach a diverse audience of Indigenous peoples need to be flexible and accommodating of numerous perspectives. In addition to building flexibility for differing perspectives on wellbeing into intervention programs, exploring a specific community's understandings of wellbeing is a wise first step prior to the employment of any intervention.

The contemporary use of traditional healing practices

Traditional healing practices are used with relative frequency among American Indians and Alaska Natives. Greensky (2014) found that 90 per cent of American Indian participants employed some form of traditional healing practice to assist with chronic pain. Given the widespread usage of such practices, questions arise about whether they are effective. The basic potential for cultural-spiritual forms of healing for Indigenous North Americans has been fairly well established for some time, but limitations surrounding research efforts have made it impossible to provide the types of evidence typically associated with established 'empirically supported' treatments. Specifically, randomized controlled trials, central to the establishment of an empirically supported treatment (APA Presidential Task Force on Evidence-Based Practice, 2006), have not been undertaken with forms of traditional healing, and numerous barriers to obtaining this kind of evidence remain (Gone, 2010). Despite this, early research generally suggested a connection between Indigenous identity and wellbeing (e.g. Oetting & Beauvais, 1990; Whitbeck, McMorris, Hoyt, Stubben, & LaFromboise, 2002).

Indigenous cultural-spiritual practices have been employed in healthcare settings for a considerable period of time as well; Brady (1995) provides an early discussion of the ongoing use and potential effectiveness of such 'culture as treatment' programs in North America and Australia. More recent research has been more nuanced on the effects of particular Indigenous cultural values, while generally supporting the *potential* for the bolstering of Indigenous identity to improve wellbeing (e.g. Kaufman et al., 2007; Stiffman et al., 2007). Ongoing research into cultural practices and traditional healing as a part of healthcare for Indigenous North Americans has similarly shown potential for such treatments to produce beneficial outcomes (e.g. Gone & Calf Looking, 2015), but thus far has not established the type of 'gold standard' evidence identified by the APA Presidential Task Force (2006). Given how common traditional healing has become, and the lack of any other well-established empirically-supported treatments for Indigenous North Americans (Gone & Alcántara, 2007; Pomerville, Burrage, & Gone, 2016), it is important at this time to delineate what such approaches entail and what evidence supports them, regardless of whether it meets for certain definitions of empirically supported treatments.

Although the term 'traditional healing' is often used in discussing the use of culture-as-treatment within health settings, it would be a mistake to think of the term 'traditional' as harkening to a single, fixed tradition. Numerous ceremonies and traditional teachings have been used as part of contemporary culture-as-treatment, but among these certain traditions and concepts have dominated, particularly those which have become largely pan-Indigenous. Sweat lodges and medicine wheel teachings are two forms of traditional healing that have been used extensively in pan-Indigenous health settings, and the use of each is described briefly below. (Other pan-Indigenous practices have seen use in health services, such as pipe ceremonies [Waldram, 1997] and Native American Church meetings [Calabrese, 2008], but are not covered in detail here for reasons of space; see cited sources for a more in-depth discussion of these specifically.)

In considering likely mechanisms of action for traditional healing as supportive of wellbeing, and possibly as mental health treatment, most advocates have focused on the development of community relations, identity and spiritual selfhood. In addition to promoting healthful and self-affirming values, these cultural practices also harbor potential to revitalize communities and connect individuals to the support that community life can offer. Beyond the recirculation of sacred power proper, some have also suggested that certain ceremonies such as the sweat lodge may be therapeutic due to the creation of states of altered consciousness or the promotion of physical benefits associated with ceremonial practice (e.g. Jilek, 1982; Garrett et al., 2011). Due to their potential for healing in multiple senses, spiritual practices have been advocated in prison settings with Indigenous people, but the atypical nature of Indigenous spiritual practice in comparison to mainstream religions has been a barrier to gaining acceptance as a religion as defined by the United States prison system (Vazzola, 2007). Two traditional healing practices and the existing literature on their potential is outlined below.

The medicine wheel

The medicine wheel as a form of Indigenous cultural teaching has been applied in a large variety of healing contexts, especially addictions treatment. The medicine wheel is a symbol comprising a circle bisected by two perpendicular lines, creating four quadrants within the circle. These quadrants are almost universally associated with the four cardinal directions (east, south, west and north), and in wellness programs are also said to represent the four aspects of the self (spiritual, physical, emotional and mental). The basic concept of the medicine wheel integrates four distinctive components into a unitary totality (Gone, 2008; McCabe, 2008). Thus, the medicine wheel is a visual representation of an Indigenous philosophical outlook that emphasizes integration and holistic balance. It signifies the interrelatedness of all things, in terms of the individual's separate aspects of self but also more broadly in reference to the interrelatedness of communities and of people globally. The symbol of the medicine wheel is widespread in Indigenous North America, and its employment in treatment settings is often used as a metaphor for a broader commitment to Indigenous-centric values and treatment approaches (Gone, 2008).

Beyond these generalities, however, programs designed around the medicine wheel diverge somewhat in what they teach and even in what meanings they ascribe to the four 'directions' (i.e. quadrants). For example, Nabigon (2006) considered north to be associated with caring, east to be associated with feelings, south to be associated with relationships and west to be associated with respect. Coggins (1990) defined the four directions of the circle as "(North) the physical realm, (East) the realm of knowledge and enlightenment, (South) the spiritual realm, (West) the realm of introspective thought" (p. 2). Dapice (2006) explained that north contains the spiritual aspect and is associated with the herbal medicine of sweetgrass, east contains the mental aspect and is associated with the medicine of tobacco, south contains the emotional aspect and is associated with cedar and west contains the physical aspect and is associated with sage. Nabigon

(2006) differed from Dapice (2006) in associating the use of medicines and specifically tobacco, sweetgrass and sage, with the western direction of the medicine wheel. Tafoya and Kouris (2003) offered yet another interpretation of the directions of the medicine wheel which differs from and at points contradicts all of these.

In addition, despite using the circle as a metaphor of holism and continuity, some intervention-focused approaches tend to use the four sections of the medicine wheel as a way of breaking treatment into different steps (e.g. Garner, Bruce, & Stellern, 2011), often borrowing the steps-based approach from Alcoholics Anonymous in the case of tailored addiction interventions (e.g. Coggins, 1990; Coyhis & Simonelli, 2005). As such, the medicine wheel has potential to combine mainstream psychotherapeutic values with Indigenous philosophical trappings in ways that can be fruitful or problematic. Some have even noted similarities between the use of the medicine wheel and parts of contemporary cognitive behavioral therapy (Coffman, 2013).

Despite these seeming challenges to a unified meaning of the medicine wheel, a considerable body of research has demonstrated interest in and appreciation of the medicine wheel by Indigenous North Americans across a large number of contexts. Qualitative reports from clients in treatment settings (Gone, 2008) and from teachers working with Indigenous children (Cherubini, Niemczyk, Hodson, & McGean, 2010) have made note of positive experiences with medicine wheel teachings. Programs making use of the medicine wheel have been created or suggested for use with health treatment (for example, see McCabe, 2008, among many others), adolescent counseling (Garner et al., 2011), childhood resilience (Gilgun, 2002), sexual offender rehabilitation (Dewhurst & Nielsen, 1999), teacher education (Klein, 2008), and end-of-life care (Clarke & Holtslander, 2010), among other instances. Given this proliferation of potential uses of the medicine wheel, there may be ample opportunity to undertake intervention outcome research that might assess the efficacy of this Indigenous-centered philosophy as a contributor to the wellbeing of Indigenous North Americans. To date such research is lacking, but qualitatively analyzed reports gesture to the usefulness of employing medicine wheel teachings in multiple settings where no better evidence for other programs provided for Indigenous North Americans exists.

The sweat lodge

Like any pan-Indigenous ceremony, the details of the sweat lodge as a practice vary according to local traditions as well as the specific healers who are involved in 'putting on a sweat'. One description of a contemporary lodge being constructed follows: "The Anishnabe sweat lodge… is constructed with four pairs of poles, preferably willow, forming four doorways in the cardinal directions… Opposing poles are bent and twisted around each other to form arches… A round pit is dug in the center of the cleared earthen floor… The fire for heating the rocks is laid within" (Paper, 2007, p. 133). Some form of covering is placed over this temporary enclosure to hold in the steam that will be created as part of the ceremony. Within this temporary structure, the ceremony takes place. Water is poured onto prepared heated rocks to create steam; often there is a fire keeper in charge of the rocks and the fire to heat them, as well as a leader who will conduct the ceremony using traditional medicines such as sage and sweetgrass, and leading songs or prayers.

There may be a number of other parts to the ceremony, particular to the purpose of the sweat and the contours of local and healer-specific practice, including but not limited to talking circles and the ceremonial use of tobacco. Feasts are common following a sweat, but the sweat lodge is at times also a precursor to other ceremonies or community events. As expressed by

Bucko (1998), "there is a range of differing but correct procedures that sometimes conflict with each other. Correct procedure is evaluated in light of both historical precedence and contemporary need" (p. 121). More complete descriptions of the sweat lodge ceremony were offered by Bucko (1998), who provided an in-depth description of the complexities of the sweat lodge in historical and contemporary usage, especially among the Lakota, and by Garrett et al. (2011), who presented a more recent discussion of the sweat lodge as a contemporary pan-Indigenous practice taking place in the context of health services.

The sweat lodge as a spiritual and cultural practice has been predominantly associated with Lakota tradition in popular presentations, but there is clear historical evidence for widespread use of some form of this ceremony throughout Native North America (Bucko, 1998; Paper, 2007). Today, the sweat lodge has been well-established as a pan-Indigenous practice (Paper, 2007), and is so common that as of ten years ago half of United States Indian Health Service (IHS) sites made use of it as a part of their health services (Cohen, 2003). A recent survey of Urban Indian Health Organizations in the United States similarly found that half of the surveyed sites made use of the sweat lodge within their behavioral health services (Pomerville & Gone, 2017).

Research into the use of sweat lodges as a form of healing or health promotion has found a number of potential benefits, but experimental research in the form of randomized controlled trials is still lacking. Garrett et al. (2011) made note of a considerable body of literature regarding the health benefits of sweating more generally, though distinctions should be preserved between non-Indigenous forms of sweating (such as saunas) and the spiritual and community-centered nature of the sweat lodge (Bucko, 1998). One empirical study, emphasizing the connection between spirituality and wellbeing for Indigenous Canadians, found a shift in attitudes among participants after taking part in a sweat lodge that appeared to indicate the adoption of more traditional and community-focused Indigenous cultural-spiritual beliefs (Schiff & Moore, 2006). However, as a small pilot study, Schiff and Moore's findings were limited by sample size. In addition, the study did not measure any specific variables which could be more directly related to wellbeing.

Tolman and Reedy (1998) found increases in patient satisfaction among American Indians at a state psychiatric facility following the integration of traditional healing practices, including the sweat lodge, into treatment. This change also sparked an increase in the intake of American Indian patients at this facility, demonstrating that the presence of such practices may make Indigenous North Americans more likely to seek out treatment. Other researchers have noted the similarity of the sweat lodge to group work (e.g. Garrett & Osborne, 1995) and the potential for effectiveness of the sweat lodge as a form of group counseling for Native youth (Colmant & Merta, 1999). Some work has also established potential effects of the sweat lodge for treatment of a wide array of issues for Native people in prison (for example, Gossage et al., 2003, conducted a non-randomized outcome study), but the findings from this work are limited and, as already noted, the existing prison system in the United States presents barriers to the use of Indigenous ceremonies by prisoners (Vazzola, 2007). In a qualitative study of American Indians with chronic pain, Greensky et al. (2014) found that the sweat lodge was one of the traditional healing practices that participants used to help manage their symptoms.

Looking forward

The scientific evidence for assessing the efficacy of Indigenous cultural and spiritual approaches to improving the wellbeing of Indigenous North Americans, as depicted above, is so rudimentary that no clear answer has emerged. Certain forms of traditional healing appear to be associated with improved treatment outcomes and seeking care, and high rates of use and interest in traditional healing continue to point to its value in contemporary health settings despite the lack of a stronger form of evidence for its specific efficacy. The nature of research with Indigenous North Americans makes it difficult to confirm whether specific treatments are effective to skeptical outsiders, and instead many have urged re-traditionalization programs broadly as the best way to support Indigenous wellbeing. Some specific criticisms of evidence-based practice approaches and their relevance for Indigenous North Americans have led to the formation of new approaches to evidence.

Drawing on 'practice-based evidence,' Echo-Hawk et al. (2011) created a compendium of existing approaches and programs for meeting the wellness needs of Indigenous groups today. Such approaches to evidence more explicitly value Indigenous community knowledge and perspectives on what is effective, representing a divergence from other forms of evaluation that allows for the designation of approaches using an evidence-informed approach that better aligns with Indigenous community sensibilities. The compendium includes a list of six 'active ingredients' for behavioral health programs targeted at Indigenous North Americans: "Local Leadership as a Starting Place… Engaging Indigenous Communities… Cultural Foundation of Practices… Spiritual Foundation of Practices… Power of Indigenous Language… Maintaining Local Credibility" (Echo-Hawk et al., 2011, pp. 21–28). As outlined in Table 20.1, the compendium also includes a list of nine programs for American Indians and Alaska Natives which represent 'best practices' (Echo-Hawk et al., 2011), ranging from treatment and prevention services to programs designed to support Indigenous organizations.

Some general guidance can be gleaned from existing research for ongoing efforts to use spiritual-cultural interventions in the promotion of Indigenous wellbeing. Gone (2010) noted that historically there was a significant amount of collaboration between Indigenous traditional healers and mental health professionals, a form of integrated care that could help to improve contemporary treatment for Indigenous North Americans were it to diffuse further. Recent research with Indigenous communities has suggested that remuneration for traditional healers through insurance coverage would be of considerable value for community wellbeing (e.g. Goodkind et al., 2011).

Although the traditional practices are described above in isolation, in reality they are often understood as overlapping or interrelated practices, a part of a broader commitment to

Table 20.1 American Indian and Alaska Native best practices identified in Echo-Hawk et al. (2011)

Name of program	Program goals
Community Readiness Scale	Behavioral Health Prevention
Data Reconnaissance for Native Americans	Increased Service Accessibility, Policy Development
Behavioral Health Financing & Policy Development for Urban Indigenous Americans	Increased Service Accessibility, Policy Development
Historical Trauma & Unresolved Grief Intervention	Behavioral Health Prevention
Oklahoma Tribal State Relations Workgroup	Increased Service Accessibility, Policy Development
Old Minto Family Recovery Group	Behavioral Health Treatment
Project Venture	Behavioral Health Prevention
Therapeutic Village of Care	Behavioral Health Treatment
Two Spirits Gallery	Recovery & Workforce Development

Indigenous cultural-spiritual practice. The sweat lodge is used at times in association with the medicine wheel teachings and can also incorporate pipe ceremonies (McCabe, 2008). It further serves as a precursor to other ceremonies such as the sun dance (Bucko, 1998; Paper, 2007). The embrace of cultural practice is likely to be a more encompassing philosophy (as represented by the medicine wheel) as opposed to a piecemeal modular approach to treatment.

A greater emphasis on family in treatment programs, which may include incorporating whole families as well as allowing those in treatment to have access to their children, has been recommended as a part of wellness programs in studies with Indigenous peoples of Canada (Baskin, Mcpherson, & Strike, 2012). The authors also noted the need for urban Indigenous populations to have greater connections to Indigenous reserve communities in Canada, a recommendation which has also been made for urban Indian populations in the United States. Research has noted that, although there is keen interest among Indigenous North Americans to engage in traditional healing, there is a lack of access to these practices, particularly for those dwelling in urban areas (Greensky, 2014; Hartmann & Gone, 2012; Moghaddam, Momper, & Fong, 2013). Given that the majority of Indigenous North Americans live in urban areas (United States Census Bureau, 2010), this is a serious gap. Efforts which aim to improve the general wellbeing of Indigenous North Americans would do well to focus on exposing urban Indigenous populations to traditional healing practices as a part of these efforts.

Final comments

The state of existing research on programs which might improve the wellbeing of Indigenous North Americans lacks the type of strong empirical evidence often preferred in medical settings, and a better understanding of the effectiveness of interventions is necessary to make more concrete recommendations. Nonetheless, research generally has validated the importance of Indigenous community-building and support for a strong sense of Indigenous identity, which culturally focused programs for Indigenous North Americans should support. Due to the interrelation of culture and spirituality among most Indigenous groups, this likely also includes robust programs of traditional Indigenous spiritual practices such as traditional healing. Although pan-Indigenous traditional healing programs are often appropriate, local Indigenous communities should be consulted regarding their preferences, and local practices should be incorporated when possible at the discretion of the local community. Given the significant health inequities faced by Indigenous North Americans relative to wellbeing, it is important for the research community to help Indigenous communities to better address their particular needs and to support interventions with potential to more effectively meet them.

Note

1 A potlatch involves a community coming together and giving away possessions, particularly by wealthier members of the community, and typically includes numerous ceremonial aspects including feasting, song and dance.

References

APA Presidential Task Force on Evidence-Based Practice. (2006). Evidence-based practice in psychology. *American Psychologist*, 61(4), 271–285.

Baskin, C., McPherson, B., & Strike, C. (2012). Using the Seven Sacred Teachings to improve services for Aboriginal mothers experiencing drug and alcohol misuse problems and involvement with child welfare. In D. Newhouse, K. FitzMaurice, T. McGuire-Adams, & D. Jette (Eds.). *Well-being in the urban Aboriginal community: Fostering Biimaadiziwin, a national research conference on urban Aboriginal peoples.* Toronto: Thompson Educational Publishing.

Brady, M. (1995). Culture in treatment, culture as treatment. A critical appraisal of developments in addictions programs for indigenous North Americans and Australians. *Social Science & Medicine, 41*(11), 1487–1498.

Bucko, R.A. (1998). *The Lakota ritual of the sweat lodge: History and contemporary practice.* Lincoln, NE: University of Nebraska Press (in cooperation with the American Indian Studies Research Institute, Indiana University, Bloomington).

Calabrese, J.D. (1997). Spiritual healing and human development in the Native American Church: Toward a cultural psychiatry of peyote. *Psychoanalytic Review, 84*(2), 237–255.

Calabrese, J.D. (2008). Clinical paradigm clashes: Ethnocentric and political barriers to Native American efforts at self-healing. *Ethos, 36*(3), 334–353.

Cavanaugh, C.L., Taylor, C.A., Keim, K.S., Clutter, J.E., & Geraghty, M.E. (2008). Cultural perceptions of health and diabetes among Native American men. *Journal of Health Care for the Poor and Underserved, 19*(4), 1029–1043.

Cherubini, L., Niemczyk, E., Hodson, J., & McGean, S. (2010). A grounded theory of new Aboriginal teachers' perceptions: The cultural attributions of medicine wheel teachings. *Teachers and Teaching: Theory and Practice, 16*(5), 545–557.

Clarke, V., & Holtslander, L.F. (2010). Finding a balanced approach: Incorporating medicine wheel teachings in the care of Aboriginal people at the end of life. *Journal of Palliative Care, 26*(1), 34–36.

Coffman, S.G. (2013). Cognitive behavioral therapy's mindfulness concepts reflect both Buddhist traditions and Native American medicine. *The Behavior Therapist, 36*(6), 156–157.

Coggins, K. (1990). *Alternative pathways to healing: The recovery medicine wheel.* Deerfield Beach, FL: Health Communications.

Cohen, K. (2003). *Honoring the medicine: The essential guide to Native American healing.* New York: Ballantine Books.

Colmant, S.A., & Merta, R.J. (1999). Using the sweat lodge ceremony as group therapy for Navajo youth. *Journal for Specialists in Group Work, 24*(1), 55–73.

Coyhis, D., & Simonelli, R. (2005). Rebuilding Native American communities. *Child Welfare: Journal of Policy, Practice, and Program, 84*(2), 323–336.

Dapice, A.N. (2006). The medicine wheel. *Journal of Transcultural Nursing, 17*(3), 251–260.

Dewhurst, A.M., & Nielsen, K.M. (1999). A resiliency-based approach to working with sexual offenders. *Sexual Addiction & Compulsivity, 6*(4), 271–279.

Donatuto, J.L., Satterfield, T.A., & Gregory, R. (2011). Poisoning the body to nourish the soul: Prioritising health risks and impacts in a Native American community. *Health, Risk & Society, 13*(2), 103–127.

Duran, E. (2006). *Healing the soul wound: Counseling with American Indians and other native peoples.* New York: Teachers College Press.

Echo-Hawk, H., Erickson, J.S., Naquin, V., Ganju, V., McCutchan-Tupua, K., Benavente, B., King, J.J., & Alonzo, D. (2011). *The compendium of behavioral health best practices for American Indian, Alaska Native, and Pacific Indigenous populations.* Bellingham, WA: First Nations Behavioral Health Association.

Elias, B., Mignone, J., Hall, M., Hong, S. P., Hart, L., & Sareen, J. (2012). Trauma and suicide behaviour histories among a Canadian Indigenous population: An empirical exploration of the potential role of Canada's residential school system. *Social Science & Medicine, 74*(10), 1560–1569.

Evans-Campbell, T., Walters, K.L., Pearson, C.R., & Campbell, C.D. (2012). Indian boarding school experience, substance use, and mental health among urban two-spirit American Indian/Alaska natives. *The American Journal of Drug and Alcohol Abuse, 38*(5), 421–427.

Garner, H., Bruce, M.A., & Stellern, J. (2011). The goal wheel: Adapting Navajo philosophy and the medicine wheel to work with adolescents. *Journal for Specialists in Group Work, 36*(1), 62–77.

Garrett, M.T., Torres-Rivera, E., Brubaker, M., Agahe Portman, T.A., Brotherton, D., West-Olatunji, C., Conwill, W., & Grayshield, L. (2011). Crying for a vision: The Native American sweat lodge ceremony as therapeutic intervention. *Journal of Counseling & Development, 89*(3), 318–325.

Garrett, M.W., & Osborne, W.L. (1995). The Native American sweat lodge as metaphor for group work. *Journal for Specialists in Group Work, 20*(1), 33–39.

Garroutte, E.M., Beals, J., Anderson, H.O., Henderson, J.A., Nez-Henderson, P., Thomas, J., & Manson, S.M. (2014). Religio-spiritual participation in two American Indian populations. *Journal for the Scientific Study of Religion, 53*(1), 17–37.

Gilgun, J.F. (2002). Completing the circle: American Indian medicine wheels and the promotion of resilience of children and youth in care. *Journal of Human Behavior in the Social Environment, 6*(2), 65–84.

Gone, J.P. (2008). The Pisimweyapiy Counselling Centre: Paving the red road to wellness in northern Manitoba. In J.B. Waldram (Ed.), *Aboriginal healing in Canada: Studies in therapeutic meaning and practice* (pp. 131–203). Ottawa: Aboriginal Healing Foundation.

Gone, J.P. (2010). Psychotherapy and traditional healing for American Indians: Exploring the prospects for therapeutic integration. *The Counseling Psychologist, 38*(2), 166–235.

Gone, J.P., & Alcántara, C. (2007). Identifying effective mental health interventions for American Indians and Alaska Natives: A review of the literature. *Cultural Diversity & Ethnic Minority Psychology, 13*(4), 356–363.

Gone, J.P., & Calf Looking, P.E. (2015). The Blackfeet Indian culture camp: Auditioning an alternative Indigenous treatment for substance use disorders. *Psychological Services, 12*(2), 83–91.

Gone, J.P., & Trimble, J.E. (2012). American Indian and Alaska Native mental health: Diverse perspectives on enduring disparities. *Annual Review of Clinical Psychology, 8*(1), 31–60.

Goodkind, J.R., Ross-Toledo, K., John, S., Hall, J.L., Ross, L., Freeland, L., & Lee, C. (2011). Rebuilding trust: A community, multiagency, state, and university partnership to improve behavioral health care for American Indian youth, their families, and communities. *Journal of Community Psychology, 39*(4), 452–477.

Gossage, J.P., Barton, L., Foster, L., Etsitty, L., LoneTree, C., Leonard, C., & May, P.A. (2003). Sweat lodge ceremonies for jail-based treatment. *Journal of Psychoactive Drugs, 35*(1), 33–42.

Greensky, C., Stapleton, M.A., Walsh, K., Gibbs, L., Abrahamson, J., Finnie, D.M., & Hooten, W.M. (2014). A qualitative study of traditional healing practices among American Indians with chronic pain. *Pain Medicine, 15*(10), 1795–1802.

Hartmann, W.E., & Gone, J. P. (2012). Incorporating traditional healing into an Urban American Indian Health Organization: A case study of community member perspectives. *Journal of Counseling Psychology, 59*(4), 542–554.

Jilek, W.G. (1982). Altered states of consciousness in North American Indian ceremonials. *Ethos, 10*(4), 326–343.

Kaufman, C.E., Desserich, J., Crow, C.B., Rock, B.H., Keane, E., & Mitchell, C.M. (2007). Culture, context, and sexual risk among Northern Plains American Indian youth. *Social Science & Medicine, 64*(10), 2152–2164.

Klein, S.R. (2008). Holistic reflection in teacher education: Issues and strategies. *Reflective Practice, 9*(2), 111–121.

McCabe, G. (2008). Mind, body, emotions and spirit: Reaching to the ancestors for healing. *Counselling Psychology Quarterly, 21*(2), 143–152.

Moghaddam, J.F., Momper, S.L., & Fong, T. (2013). Discrimination and participation in traditional healing for American Indians and Alaska Natives. *Journal of Community Health: The Publication for Health Promotion and Disease Prevention, 38*(6), 1115–1123.

Nabigon, H. (2006). *The hollow tree: Fighting addiction with traditional native healing*. Montreal: McGill-Queen's University Press.

Oetting, G.R., & Beauvais, F. (1990). Orthogonal cultural identification theory: The cultural identification of minority adolescents. *International Journal of the Addictions, 25*(5-A-6-A), 655–685.

Paper, J.D. (2007). *Native North American religious traditions: Dancing for life*. Westport, CT: Praeger.

Pevar, S.L. (2012). *The rights of Indians and tribes* (4th ed.). New York: Oxford University Press.

Pomerville, A., Burrage, R.L., & Gone, J. P. (2016). Empirical findings from psychotherapy research with Indigenous populations: A systematic review. *Journal of Consulting and Clinical Psychology, 84*(12), 1023–1038. doi:10.1037/ccp0000150.

Pomerville, A., & Gone, J.P. (2017). Behavioral health services in urban American Indian health organizations: A descriptive portrait. *Psychological Services*.

Rowan, M., Poole, N., Shea, B., Gone, J.P., Mykota, D., Farag, M., & Dell, C. (2014). Cultural interventions to treat addictions in Indigenous populations: Findings from a scoping study. *Substance Abuse Treatment, Prevention, and Policy, 9*(34), 1–26.

Schiff, J.W., & Moore, K. (2006). The impact of the sweat lodge ceremony on dimensions of well-being. *American Indian and Alaska Native Mental Health Research, 13*(3), 48–69.

Stiffman, A.R., Brown, E., Freedenthal, S., House, L., Ostmann, E., & Yu, M.S. (2007). American Indian youth: Personal, familial, and environmental strengths. *Journal of Child and Family Studies, 16*(3), 331–346. doi:10.1007/s10826-006-9089-y.

Tafoya, T., & Kouris, N. (2003). Dancing the circle: Native American concepts of healing. In S.G. Mijares & S.G. Mijares (Eds.), *Modern psychology and ancient wisdom: Psychological healing practices from the world's religious traditions* (pp. 125–146). New York: Haworth Press.

Tolman, A., & Reedy, R. (1998). Implementation of a culture-specific intervention for a Native American community. *Journal of Clinical Psychology in Medical Settings, 5*(3), 381–392.

Towle, A., Godolphin, W., & Alexander, T. (2006). Doctor–patient communications in the Aboriginal community: Towards the development of educational programs. *Patient Education and Counseling, 62*(3), 340–346.

United States Census Bureau. (2010). *The American Indian and Alaska Native population: 2010.* Retrieved 30 August 2015 from www.census.gov/prod/cen2010/briefs/c2010br-10.pdf.

Vezzola, M.A. (2007). Harmony behind bars. *The Prison Journal, 87*(2), 195–210.

Waldram, J.B. (1997). *The way of the pipe: Aboriginal spirituality and symbolic healing in Canadian prisons.* Peterborough, Ont: Broadview Press.

Waldram, J.B. (2004). *Revenge of the Windigo: The construction of the mind and mental health of North American Aboriginal peoples.* Toronto: University of Toronto Press.

Whitbeck, L.B., McMorris, B.J., Hoyt, D.R., Stubben, J.D., & LaFromboise, T. (2002). Perceived discrimination, traditional practices, and depressive symptoms among American Indians in the upper Midwest. *Journal of Health and Social Behavior, 43*(4), 400–418.

Yurkovich, E.E., & Lattergrass, I. (2008). Defining health and unhealthiness: Perceptions held by Native American Indians with persistent mental illness. *Mental Health, Religion & Culture, 11*(5), 437–459.

21

THE RELATIONSHIP BETWEEN CHILD LABOUR, PARTICIPATION IN CULTURAL ACTIVITIES AND THE SCHOOLING OUTCOMES OF CHILDREN

An analysis by Indigenous status

Lilia Arcos Holzinger and Nicholas Biddle

Introduction

Given that exposure to government policies and institutions begins very early in life for most Indigenous people, and that the 'gap' in wellbeing and socioeconomic outcomes between Indigenous and non-Indigenous people not only begins early in life but also accumulates over time, it is crucial to understand how children's education outcomes relate to participation in other activities. In this chapter, we focus on understanding how engaging in activities that help cover household expenditures (i.e. child labour) and in activities of a cultural nature, relate to the educational participation of children and to children's desired level of educational attainment, by Indigenous status.

Although the relationship between child labour, cultural activities and schooling outcomes has been the subject of a substantial body of research in more developed settler-colonial societies such as Australia, New Zealand, Canada and the United States, this is less so for other less developed settler-colonial societies. We focus on the Mexican case for several reasons. First, Mexico is home to the largest total number of Indigenous people, and has been renowned for implementing comprehensive Indigenous-specific policies in recent years (see Chapter 25). Second, the Mexican Family Life Survey (MxFLS) provides us with a rich, nationally representative dataset, which allows us to conduct robust and detailed analysis on objective and subjective schooling outcomes by Indigenous status. Finally, we can conduct comparative analysis of Indigenous and non-Indigenous children, which allows us to pinpoint important differences by Indigenous status, and highlights the need for Indigenous-specific policies. Historically, Indigenous policies across settler-colonial societies have often excluded and suppressed Indigenous cultures with the hope of more easily implementing acculturation aims (Hickling-Hudson & Ahlquist, 2003; Miller, 2004). This is not only reproachable from an ethical standpoint, but also quantifiably detrimental for the wellbeing and socioeconomic progress of Indigenous groups, who benefit from culturally inclusive pedagogies, as will be detailed in the following section.

First, we review the literature on how child labour relates to the schooling outcomes of Indigenous children, and then examine how cultural participation relates to the schooling outcomes of Indigenous children. Second, we summarize our study sample, outcomes of interest, and the individual and household characteristics for which we control in our econometric models. From this stage on, we analyse outcomes disaggregated by age groups – specifically, we consider younger children aged 5–10 years, and older children aged 11–14 years. We do this in order to capture how the relationship between child labour, cultural activities and schooling outcomes changes as children grow older and have more choices on how to spend their time, while arguably also having an increased number of household responsibilities; this is especially true for Indigenous children (Patrinos & Shafiq, 2010). Next, we implement an econometric model to better account for gross average differences in the schooling outcomes of Indigenous and non-Indigenous children, while controlling for a range of other individual and family characteristics. Our results are presented in two sections: one for the younger children group and one for the older children group. Finally, we discuss the implications of our analysis for social policy aimed at boosting schooling outcomes.

Background

The relationship between child labour and the schooling outcomes of Indigenous children

Qualitative studies have long pointed to the importance that Indigenous communities place on child labour as a means to pass on valuable personal qualities. Alcalá et al. (2014) conduct an ethnographic study in an Indigenous Mexican community, documenting the cultural importance that this and other Indigenous communities of the Americas place on the contributions to "family household work, which are valued for children's development… and for preservation of important cultural practices and values such the dignity of work and the importance of reciprocity in relationships" (p. 98). Indeed, studies on community-based work show that children involved in such activities have more prosocial behaviour relative to children who are not involved in such activities (Kartner et al., 2010). In the specific Mexican context, families from an Indigenous-heritage community in Guadalajara more commonly reported that their children provide help as a way to contribute to their family and community, than did non-Indigenous children from a nearby middle-income community (Alcala et al., 2014). There is further ethnographic evidence from Mexico that among Indigenous communities, child labour is strongest in the rural villages of Mexico, although still present among urban Indigenous groups (Lopez et al., 2015).

Similar findings have emerged from recent quantitative work. Patrinos and Shafiq (2010) explain that many Latin American Indigenous families view child labour as a positive activity, especially if the children attend school and the work activity is safe. The authors further explain that qualitative research points to the strong positive stigma of child labour among Indigenous communities, so that children are not only involved in work activities as a means to help their family's subsistence, but rather as a didactic activity that reinforces Indigenous culture and heritage. To complement the qualitative evidence on positive stigma toward child labour, the authors conduct a quantitative study on the stigma related to child labour in a nationally representative sample of Guatemalan families. After controlling for a range of observable characteristics, Indigenous status has a positive and significant effect on being a child labourer, while being Indigenous negatively but only modestly affects the probability of being enrolled in school. The results point to the fact that for a majority of Indigenous households, working does not drastically affect a child's school enrolment. Another study of Guatemalan children explores how child labour and schooling is affected by household shocks, and the authors also find that while child labour increases in response to household shocks, schooling does not decrease substantially, with the results holding for both Indigenous and non-Indigenous families (Vasquez & Bohara, 2009).

The results from the above studies must be interpreted carefully, however, as one of the main reasons for child labour among poor Indigenous households is indeed to help provide income for the family. Bando et al. (2005) examine the impact of the PROGRESA conditional cash transfer for Mexican families with children – the program was specially focused on Indigenous families. The study finds that Indigenous children's probability of working decreased after the implementation of the program, which required families to enrol children in school to receive financial help from the government; specifically, the probability of children working decreased by 6 percentage points over three years, and children's school attainment improved substantially. Similarly, Patrinos and Psacharopoulos (1997) analyse the relationship between family, schooling and child labour in Peru for those children aged 7–18 years, considering effects separately by Indigenous status. They find that being Indigenous and living in rural areas are the strong determinants of child labour. While for the sample of Indigenous children child labour was the most significant determinant of poor schooling performance as measured by age-grade distortion, the effect of child labour on school performance was insignificant for the sample that included non-Indigenous children. There are also variations in the type of work and the ability to balance work and schooling by gender; particularly, Indigenous girls and children living in rural areas of Bolivia were much more likely to work, and much less likely to attend school than were boys or children living in urban areas of Bolivia, respectively (Zapata et al., 2004). These results point to the importance of considering the type of child labour in which children are involved, the existence of national policies that aim to improve Indigenous wellbeing (e.g. PROGRESA), and the level of socioeconomic disadvantage to which a child is exposed, in order to determine the potential impact of child labour on the schooling of Indigenous children.

The relationship between cultural activities participation and schooling for Indigenous children

Most of the quantitative research related to the relationship between participation in cultural activities and the schooling outcomes of Indigenous children comes from more developed settler-colonial societies; findings point to the importance of culturally responsive practices in enhancing the educational engagement and attainment of Indigenous children, and this is a lesson that has international applicability and significance. Importantly, there is evidence that formal education, specially when culturally sensitive and inclusive, can enhance Indigenous-specific measures of wellbeing, so that its benefits are not only constrained to Western notions of development and progress (Dockery, 2011; Miller, 2004).

Incorporating Indigenous knowledge into formal schooling has proven an effective way to minimize the loss of Indigenous skills and local knowledge documented among various Indigenous groups (for an international overview, see Reyes-Garcia et al., 2010; for the case of Mexican Indigenous children, see Ruiz-Mallen et al., 2009). In arguing for the importance of culturally responsive schooling (i.e. teaching based on the cultural competence of teachers and curricula designed for a multicultural audience), Castagno and Bradboy (2008) provide an overview of the positive role that cultural activities play as they help students feel connected to the educational material being taught. Savage et al. (2011) provide evidence from New Zealand, where "a lack of connection between the culture of the school and students has been associated with low engagement in the absence of culturally responsive practices…" for Maori students (p. 183). Similarly, a mixed-methods study on the implementation of culturally inclusive pedagogies showed that schools that properly implemented such programs saw the strongest improvements in the standardized test outcomes of secondary grade students (Bishop et al., 2012); qualitatively similar results on the impact of culturally inclusive programs have also been reached for Australian, American and Latin American Indigenous children (for the Australian and American case, see Hickling-Hudson, 2003; for the case of Peru, see Ames, 2012). The literature on culturally responsive education provides evidence on the importance that cultural activities play in enhancing school engagement and attainment. Hence, for educational systems that do not actively incorporate culturally sensitive practices, Indigenous children could strongly benefit from extracurricular cultural activities that allow them to find a connection with their culture and identity.

The data and the Mexican context

In this chapter, we utilize the Mexican Family Life Survey (MxFLS) to better understand the relationship between child labour, participation in cultural activities and schooling outcomes. The MxFLS is a longitudinal dataset that is nationally representative of Mexico, spanning the years 1999–2004. In Chapter 25, we describe the comprehensive family and individual level information that the MxFLS covers, as well as the broad range of social research in which it has been employed.

Using the MxFLS, we are able to explore determinants of schooling while controlling for participation in child labour and cultural activities, as well as a range of child individual and family characteristics. The MxFLS records the self-reported Indigenous status for children who are over 4 and under 15 years old, so our sample is restricted to Indigenous and non-Indigenous children within this age range. We classify Indigenous Mexican children as those who identify with an Indigenous group and who additionally speak an Indigenous language, as this is a better indicator of Indigeneity in Mexico, a country where most people have a mixed-ethnic background. The outcome variables we analyse are summarized in Tables 21.3 and 21.4 by Indigenous status. Given the small sample of Indigenous children, we present only a binary outcome variable of school attendance. The subjective variable that captures whether a student hopes or does not hope to achieve a college/postgraduate degree, was only asked of children over 10 years of age and in waves 2 and 3, so we present the results for this outcome variable only for the older group of children (i.e. those aged 11–14 years).

In order to overcome the small sample of Indigenous children, our analysis pools the waves of the MxFLS with the total sample size by Indigenous status illustrated in Table 21.1. The number of children by Indigenous status and age are presented in Table 21.2, and show that both Indigenous and non-Indigenous children have similar age distributions, although Indigenous children are slightly older. Most of the children fall in the young children group, while only 34 per cent of the Indigenous and non-Indigenous children fall in the older age group. In order to better understand differences in child labour, participation in cultural activities, and the schooling experience of Indigenous versus non-Indigenous children, we next present summary

Table 21.1 Number of children by Indigenous status and wave (5–14 years)

Wave	1	2	3	All waves
Years	2000	2005–6	2009–12	
Non-Indigenous children	4,102	5,813	4,870	14,785
Indigenous children	559	970	935	2,464
Total	4,661	6,783	5,805	17,249

Table 21.2 Number of children by Indigenous status and years of age (5–14 years)

Age of children (years)	5	6	7	8	9	10	11	12	13	14	5–14
Non-Indigenous children											
Number	1,526	1,530	1,547	1,668	1,724	1,720	1,516	1,209	1,180	1,162	14,782
Percentage	10	10	10	11	12	12	10	8	8	8	100
Indigenous children											
Number	212	247	255	256	279	271	273	214	204	252	2,463
Percentage	9	10	10	10	11	11	11	9	8	10	100
All children (total)											
Number	1,738	1,777	1,802	1,924	2,003	1,991	1,789	1,423	1,384	1,414	17,245
Percentage	10	10	10	11	12	12	10	8	8	8	100

statistics of the outcome variables and controls used separately by young and older age groups, and disaggregate the results by Indigenous status.

Summary statistics and econometric modelling

Summary statistics by Indigenous status and age group

For the younger age group (i.e. 5–10-year-olds), we are only able to examine the schooling outcome measuring whether a child attends or does not attend school. A majority of both Indigenous and non-Indigenous children attend school – respectively 94 per cent and 95 per cent. Analysing child labour and engagement in cultural activities, our two main determinants of interest, we note that non-Indigenous children engage in cultural activities at higher rates than Indigenous children – respectively 18 per cent and 15 per cent. On the other hand, Indigenous children engage in child labour at higher rates than non-Indigenous children – respectively 5 per cent and 3 per cent. There are also notable differences in child and household characteristics; relative to the non-Indigenous population, Indigenous children are about twice as likely to live in communities with less than 2,500 people, and they are slightly more likely to have to care for a sick or elderly household member, as well as to attend a public as opposed to a private school. Indigenous children are also much more likely to live in bigger households with more children, and with lower equivalized household incomes. Evidently, there are large differences by Indigenous status, even when examining gross averages.

Table 21.3 Summary statistics of outcome and control variables for children 5–10 years old, by Indigenous status

	Non-Indigenous children			Indigenous children		
	# of obs.	Mean	Std. Dev.	# of obs.	Mean	Std. Dev.
Outcome variable(s)						
Child attends school	9,714	0.95	0.21	1520	0.94	0.23
Individual characteristics						
Child practises cultural activities	9,712	0.18	0.39	1519	0.15	0.36
Child performs physical labour: work and/or agricultural tasks	9,711	0.03	0.16	1518	0.05	0.22
Age of child	9,715	7.59	1.71	1520	7.63	1.68
Child attends a public school	6,835	0.94	0.23	1062	0.97	0.17
Child takes care of elderly or sick family member	9,713	0.11	0.32	1519	0.14	0.35
Lives in community with <2,500 people	9,713	0.43	0.50	1520	0.70	0.46
Region: North	9,705	0.40	0.49	1520	0.23	0.42
Region: Central	9,705	0.23	0.42	1520	0.10	0.30
Region: East	9,705	0.13	0.34	1520	0.23	0.42
Region: West	9,705	0.14	0.35	1520	0.21	0.41
Region: South	9,705	0.10	0.30	1520	0.24	0.43
Household characteristics						
Log equivalized household income from work	7,825	9.43	1.00	1134	8.81	1.39
Household head is female	9,715	0.17	0.38	1520	0.18	0.38
Number of children in household	9,715	2.89	1.41	1520	3.56	1.82
Household size	9,715	6.03	2.46	1520	7.06	2.83
Number of bedrooms per capita	9,676	0.39	0.29	1516	0.33	0.23
House is owned and paid for	9,684	0.63	0.48	1518	0.64	0.48

For the older age group of children (i.e. 11–14 years old), we are able to consider an additional, subjective schooling outcome – children's desired schooling achievement level. Summary results are presented in Table 21.4 by Indigenous status. Most of the sample children attend school, as was true for the younger age group category – respectively 94 per cent and 93 per cent of non-Indigenous and Indigenous children attend school. However, a large discrepancy is present when considering the subjective schooling outcome: about 52 per cent of non-Indigenous children hope to study to a college or postgraduate level as opposed to a lower educational level (i.e. elementary or secondary school level); on the other hand, only 37 per cent of Indigenous children hope to study to a college or postgraduate level. This divergence is important, as it could point to how different cultural values, objectives and desired lifestyles differ for the Indigenous and non-Indigenous population, as well as to the relatively young age at which these disparities in desired educational attainment begin to appear. In terms of child labour and

Table 21.4 Summary statistics of outcome and control variables for children 11–14 years old, by Indigenous status

	Non-Indigenous children			Indigenous children		
	# of obs.	Mean	Std. Dev.	# of obs.	Mean	Std. Dev.
Outcome variable(s)						
Child attends school	5,070	0.94	0.23	944	0.93	0.26
School level to which child hopes to study: college or postgraduate level	4,506	0.52	0.50	862	0.37	0.48
Individual characteristics						
Child practises cultural activities	5,068	0.30	0.46	944	0.23	0.42
Child performs physical labour: work and/or agricultural tasks	5,067	0.09	0.29	944	0.14	0.34
Age of child	5,067	12.39	1.14	943	12.46	1.17
Child attends a public school	4,899	0.96	0.20	901	0.97	0.16
Child takes care of elderly or sick family member	5,068	0.19	0.39	944	0.22	0.41
Lives in community with <2,500 people	5,068	0.44	0.50	944	0.70	0.46
Region: North	5,065	0.40	0.49	943	0.26	0.44
Region: Central	5,065	0.23	0.42	943	0.08	0.28
Region: East	5,065	0.13	0.33	943	0.24	0.43
Region: West	5,065	0.15	0.36	943	0.22	0.41
Region: South	5,065	0.10	0.30	943	0.19	0.40
Household characteristics						
Log equivalized household income from work	4,041	9.51	0.98	707	8.97	1.26
Household head is female	5,070	0.20	0.40	944	0.20	0.40
Number of children in household	5,070	2.69	1.42	944	3.19	1.85
Household size	5,070	6.31	2.46	944	7.06	2.88
Number of bedrooms per capita	5,039	0.41	0.24	942	0.35	0.23
House is owned and paid for	5,046	0.70	0.46	943	0.70	0.46

cultural activities, we find the same qualitative results that we found for the younger age group, with Indigenous children engaging in more child labour and fewer cultural activities. Similarly, Indigenous children are again much more likely to live in small communities, and slightly more likely to take care of older or sick family members and to attend a public school. Indigenous children are also more likely to live in bigger households with more children, and with lower equivalized household incomes.

It is interesting to note that the gap in cultural and child labour differences by Indigenous status intensify for the older age group of children – older Indigenous children are much less likely to participate in cultural activities, and much more likely to participate in child labour, than the older non-Indigenous children. Furthermore, incorporating a subjective schooling outcome points to potentially differing attitudes to formal schooling between Indigenous and non-Indigenous children. In order to better understand the determinants of the schooling outcomes we have considered, in the next section we analyse the results of econometric models of schooling.

A pooled OLS regression framework for schooling outcomes

We implement a linear regression model, where we pool children across waves and estimate the probability of school attendance for the younger child group. For the older child group, we estimate the probability of school attendance and the probability that the child hopes to achieve college or postgraduate studies. Given the evidence of the differing factors affecting schooling outcomes of Indigenous and non-Indigenous children, we estimate our models separately by Indigenous status. Specifically, the econometric model we are estimating is:

$$\text{Schooling}_i = \alpha + \text{Culture}_i + \text{Work}_i + \beta_i + \varepsilon_i$$

Where Schooling_i is the probability of observing a given schooling outcome for each child i, α is a constant term, β_i is a vector of individual and household level controls for each child i, and ε_i is an error term for each child i. Given our particular interest in how engaging in cultural activities or child labour affects schooling outcomes, we include dummies for these two activities in our models – respectively Culture_i and Work_i.

We choose to present the results using binary OLS models, given the ease of interpreting coefficient estimates, as well as the qualitatively similar results reached when we implement probit models. Our models have no predicted probabilities outside the unit interval, so OLS estimation for our binary dependent variables – as shown by Horrace and Oaxaca (2006) – should yield unbiased and consistent estimates. In the next section, we present our results by young and older age groups, discussing important insights and differences in schooling outcomes once we control more rigorously for the individual and household characteristics of children.

The relationship between cultural activities, child labour participation and the schooling probability of young children (5–10 years)

The results of the pooled OLS regression model of school attendance are presented in Table 21.5 by Indigenous status. There is a significant and positive relationship between participating in cultural activities and attending school for both Indigenous and non-Indigenous children, and the coefficient estimate for the effect of participating in cultural activities on the probability of attending school is slightly larger for Indigenous children. While child labour is an insignificant determinant of the probability of attending school for non-Indigenous children, it is a significant, negative determinant of the probability that Indigenous children attend school. These results provide some evidence that for Indigenous children, child labour is indeed an obstacle to school attendance, while engaging in cultural activities has a positive and significant relationship for both Indigenous and non-Indigenous children's school attendance.

Controlling for other individual and household characteristics yields other important insights. Regional differences have a more consistently significant impact on the schooling probability of Indigenous children; this is perhaps the result of Indigenous people being more concentrated in rural, southern areas of the country. Furthermore, household characteristics have a similar relationship with schooling outcomes for both Indigenous and non-Indigenous children, except for equivalized household income. Specifically, non-Indigenous children living in households with higher equivalized household incomes are more likely to attend school, and this is a statistically significant relationship; in contrast, equivalized household incomes and school attendance have no statistically significant relationship for Indigenous children. This provides some evidence that non-objective socioeconomic factors, such as cultural factors and social norms among Indigenous people, help to explain their schooling decision. On the other

Table 21.5 Pooled OLS regression results for children aged 5–10 years, by Indigenous status

	Probability that child attends school	
	Non-Indigenous	Indigenous
Individual characteristics		
Child practises cultural activities	0.026***	0.038**
Child performs physical labour: work and/or agricultural tasks	0.002	−0.059*
Age of child	0.028***	0.031***
Child takes care of elderly or sick family member	0.011	0.008
Lives in community with <2,500 people	−0.005	0.019
Region: North	−0.003	−0.041*
Region: Central	−0.007	−0.027
Region: East	−0.021**	−0.064***
Region: West	−0.004	−0.069***
Household characteristics		
Log equivalized household income from work	0.009***	0.003
Household head is female	−0.012*	−0.068***
Number of children in household	−0.016***	−0.022***
Household size	0.003***	0.006*
Number of bedrooms per capita	0.022**	0.008
House is owned and paid for	0.009*	0.026*
Constant	0.675***	0.731***
Number of observations	7,797	1,131
Adjusted *R*-squared	0.068	0.081

Notes: *** $p<0.01$, ** $p<0.05$, * $p<0.1$.
Omitted categories are: Child does not practise cultural activities, does not perform physical labour, does not take care of elderly or sick family member, lives in a community with more than 2,500 people, lives in the southern region of the country, lives in a household with a male head, lives in a house that is owned and paid.

hand, objective economic measures such as household incomes, play a potentially less dominant role in the decision to send children to formal Western education.

The relationship between cultural activities, child labour participation and the schooling probability of older children (11–14 years)

Do the above differences by Indigenous status persist for older children? And if so, are there also differences in the determinants of older children's hoped-for school attainment by Indigenous status? The model results for the objective and subjective schooling outcomes of children are presented in Table 21.6. Examining the probability of school attendance we find that for both Indigenous and non-Indigenous children, cultural participation and child labour now have respectively a positive and statistically significant, and a negative and statistically significant relationship to the probability of attending school; the coefficient estimates show that both relationships are stronger for Indigenous children than for non-Indigenous children, as well as for older Indigenous children relative to younger Indigenous children. The size, direction and statistical significance of these relationships highlight how involvement in cultural activities does not conflict with school attendance, particularly for Indigenous children.

Table 21.6 Pooled OLS regression results for children 11–14 years old, by Indigenous status

	Probability that child attends school		Probability that child hopes to study to a college or postgraduate level	
	Non-Indigenous	Indigenous	Non-Indigenous	Indigenous
Individual characteristics				
Child practises cultural activities	0.046***	0.059***	0.068***	0.124***
Child performs physical labour: work and/or agricultural tasks	−0.065***	−0.089***	−0.104***	−0.105*
Age of child	−0.032***	−0.019***	0.024***	0.028*
Child takes care of elderly or sick family member	0.010	0.007	0.050**	0.002
Lives in community with <2,500 people	−0.001	0.044**	−0.111***	−0.175***
Region: North	−0.027**	−0.053*	−0.082***	0.044
Region: Central	−0.043***	−0.048	−0.159***	−0.134*
Region: East	−0.026*	−0.059**	−0.007	0.031
Region: West	−0.079***	−0.055*	−0.197***	−0.152**
Child attends school			0.318***	0.278***
Child attends a public school			−0.144***	−0.179*
Household characteristics				
Log equivalized household income from work	0.008**	0.015*	0.067***	0.050***
Household head is female	−0.014	−0.016	0.010	0.006
Number of children in household	−0.004	−0.010	−0.023***	0.019
Household size	−0.005**	0.003	−0.012***	−0.018*
Number of bedrooms per capita	0.028	0.060	0.183***	0.291**
House is owned and paid for	0.010	0.012	−0.014	0.027
Constant	1.311***	1.046***	−0.381**	−0.431
Number of observations	4,026	704	3,494	634
Adjusted R-squared	0.062	0.045	0.139	0.194

Notes: *** $p<0.01$, ** $p<0.05$, * $p<0.1$.

Omitted categories are the same as in Table 21.5 for both outcome variables. However, additional omitted categories for the 'Probability that child hopes to study to a college or postgraduate level' outcome includes that the chid does not attend school, and that the child attends a private school.

Other individual and household determinants of the probability of school attendance are similar to the results for the group of younger children, with a key difference being that living in small communities now has a positive and statistically significant effect on the school attendance of Indigenous children (while having no effect on the school attendance of non-Indigenous children). Finally, while equivalized household income had a negligible effect on the school attendance of young Indigenous children, it has a positive and significant effect on the school attendance of older Indigenous children, which provides evidence on the changing household roles and responsibilities that Indigenous children face as they age – this also reinforces the claim that child labour among older children is used as a means to help cover household expenditures.

While the gross rate of school attendance was high and comparable between Indigenous and non-Indigenous children of both age groups, we also found that older Indigenous children are much less likely to desire achieving a college or postgraduate degree, relative to older non-Indigenous children. In the last two columns of Table 21.6, we present the results of a pooled OLS model examining this subjective schooling outcome; our controls are the same as for the probability of school attendance, with the only difference being that we are now able to include school attendance and the type of school attended (i.e. public or private) as control variables. The results show the much stronger effect that participating in cultural activities has on Indigenous children's desired educational attainment, relative to non-Indigenous children's desired educational attainment. Furthermore, while child labour has a large and negative relationship for both Indigenous and non-Indigenous children, it is only significant for non-Indigenous children at the 5 per cent level. Indigenous and non-Indigenous children are both less likely to wish to attain tertiary degrees when they live in smaller communities, which points to the potentially different social views toward higher education and more limited study opportunities that children in rural areas experience as they are growing up. Attending school has as expected, a positive and significant relationship with the subjective schooling outcome for both Indigenous and non-Indigenous children. Finally, equivalized household income has a positive and statistically significant effect on the subjective schooling outcome of both Indigenous and non-Indigenous children.

Discussion

This chapter focuses on how the schooling outcomes of Indigenous and non-Indigenous Mexican children relate to engagement in child labour and cultural activities. We disaggregate our analysis by a younger (5–10 years) and older (11–14 years) age group, in order to better understand how the determinants of schooling outcomes differ, as children grow older. Analysing gross averages, we find that an overwhelming majority of young and older children attend school, and these rates are very similar for Indigenous and non-Indigenous children. We also find that relative to Indigenous children, non-Indigenous children are more like to engage in cultural activities and are less likely to engage in child labour, and these ethnic disparities grow as children age. For older children, we are able to analyse their hoped-for level of educational attainment, and find large discrepancies by Indigenous status: non-Indigenous children are much more likely to hope to achieve tertiary qualifications than are Indigenous children.

In order to better account for these differences by Indigenous status, we implemented a regression framework. For the younger group of children, we find evidence that cultural activities have a positive and significant effect on the probability that both Indigenous and non-Indigenous children attend school, while child labour has an insignificant effect for both Indigenous and non-Indigenous children. For the older group of children, we find that although cultural and labour activities have a significant positive and negative effect on the probability of attending school respectively, the size of the effects is much stronger for Indigenous children. Finally, when analysing the determinants of the outcome capturing whether a child hoped to achieve tertiary qualifications, we find that cultural participation has a positive and significant relationship with the outcome variable for both Indigenous and non-Indigenous children. In contrast, child labour has a large and negative relationship with the outcome variable for non-Indigenous and Indigenous children (although the relationship is statistically insignificant).

Our results provide evidence on the important relationship that participating in cultural activities has on the objective and subjective schooling outcomes of younger and older Mexican children, especially Indigenous ones. Hence, incorporating such practices into the schooling curriculum from an early age could be especially helpful in boosting the schooling engagement of Indigenous children. On the other hand, since child labour has a negative relationship with school attendance for both Indigenous and non-Indigenous older children, policies to help restrict the spread of child labour (by providing financial help to families) are likely to boost school attendance in the Mexican context.

Since participating in child labour has an insignificant but large negative relationship with the probability that an Indigenous child hopes to achieve a tertiary degree, Indigenous children likely face economic impediments that act to diminish their hopes of tertiary education. This claim is further reinforced by the large and significant relationship that having a higher equivalized household income has with the probability that Indigenous and non-Indigenous children want to achieve a tertiary degree. Hence, social policies aimed at boosting the schooling outcomes of Indigenous children would benefit from analysing subjective measures of student engagement, as these measures are likely to reveal attitudes and financial barriers that could act to impede the schooling attainment of Indigenous children later in life.

References

Alcalá, L., Rogoff, B., Mejía-Arauz, R., Coppens, A.D., & Dexter, A.L. (2014). Children's initiative in contributions to family work in indigenous-heritage and cosmopolitan communities in Mexico. *Human Development, 57*(2–3), 96–115.

Ames, P. (2012). Language, culture and identity in the transition to primary school: Challenges to indigenous children's rights to education in Peru. *International Journal of Educational Development, 32*(3), 454–462.

Bando, R., López-Calva, L., & Patrinos, H. (2005). *Child labor, school attendance, and indigenous households: Evidence from Mexico.* Working Paper No. 3487.

Bishop, A.R., Berryman, M.A., Wearmouth, J.B., & Peter, M. (2012). Developing an effective education reform model for indigenous and other minoritized students. *School Effectiveness and School Improvement, 23*(1), 49–70.

Castagno, A.E., & Brayboy, B.M.J. (2008). Culturally responsive schooling for Indigenous youth: A review of the literature. *Review of Educational Research, 78*(4), 941–993.

Dockery, A. M., et al. (2011). *Traditional culture and the wellbeing of Indigenous Australians: An analysis of the 2008 NATSISS.* Centre for Labour Market Research, Curtin University.

Hickling-Hudson, A., & Ahlquist, R. (2003). Contesting the curriculum in the schooling of Indigenous children in Australia and the United States: From Eurocentrism to culturally powerful pedagogies. *Comparative Education Review, 47*(1), 64–89.

Horrace, W.C., & Oaxaca, R.L. (2006). Results on the bias and inconsistency of ordinary least squares for the linear probability model. *Economics Letters, 90*(3), 321–327.

Kärtner, J., Keller, H., & Chaudhary, N. (2010). Cognitive and social influences on early prosocial behavior in two sociocultural contexts. *Developmental Psychology, 46*(4), 905.

López, A., Ruvalcaba, O., & Rogoff, B. (2015). Attentive helping as a cultural practice of Mexican-heritage families. In *Mexican American children and families: Multidisciplinary perspectives* (pp. 150–161). New York: Routledge.

Miller, M. (2004). *Ensuring the rights of indigenous children.* Washington, DC: UNICEF Innocenti Research Centre.

Patrinos, H.A., & Psacharopoulos, G. (1997). Family size, schooling and child labor in Peru: An empirical analysis. *Journal of Population Economics, 10*(4), 387–405.

Patrinos, H.A., & Shafiq, N. (2010). An empirical illustration of positive stigma towards child labor. *Economics Bulletin, 30*(1), 799–807.

Reyes-García, V., Kightley, E., Ruiz-Mallén, I., Fuentes-Peláez, N., Demps, K., Huanca, T., & Martínez-Rodríguez, M.R. (2010). Schooling and local environmental knowledge: Do they complement or substitute each other? *International Journal of Educational Development, 30*(3), 305–313.

Ruiz-Mallen, I., Barraza, L., Bodenhorn, B., & Reyes-García, V. (2009). Evaluating the impact of an environmental education programme: An empirical study in Mexico. *Environmental Education Research, 15*(3), 371–387.

Savage, C., Hindle, R., Meyer, L.H., Hynds, A., Penetito, W., & Sleeter, C.E. (2011). Culturally responsive pedagogies in the classroom: Indigenous student experiences across the curriculum. *Asia-Pacific Journal of Teacher Education, 39*(3), 183–198.

Vásquez, W.F., & Bohara, A.K. (2009). Household shocks, child labor, and child schooling: Evidence from Guatemala. *Latin American Research Review, 45*(3), 165–186.

Zapata, D., Contreras, D., et al. (2004). *Child labor in Bolivia: Schooling, gender and ethnic groups*. Econometric Society 2004 Latin American Meetings. Econometric Society.

22

MABU LIYAN

The Yawuru way

Mandy Yap and Eunice Yu[1]

Introduction

The literature on wellbeing has grown exponentially in the last four decades. Historically, interest in wellbeing was primarily contained within the fields of philosophy and theology; today it includes a wide range of disciplines such as psychology, politics, sociology, anthropology and economics (Frey & Stutzer, 2002; Diener & Seligman, 2004; Tiberius, 2006; Mathews & Izquierdo, 2009; Thin, 2009; Graham, 2012; Haybron, 2015; Bache & Reardon, 2016). *Prima facie*, it appears that the term wellbeing is often used synonymously with happiness, life satisfaction, health and quality of life. However, there are subtle and distinct ideological differences that stem from disciplinary, historical and philosophical underpinnings.

Nobel Prize-winning economist Amartya Sen's 1986 Stanner Lecture, *Standard of Living*, is an important reference point for navigating through the commonalities and divergence in understandings of wellbeing. In the lecture, Sen made several notable points which demonstrate the challenges of measuring wellbeing. Sen (1987, p. 3) described the complexities of understanding and measuring standard of living when he stated:

> You could be *well* off, without being *well*. You could be *well*, without being able to lead the life you *wanted*. You could have got the life you *wanted*, without being *happy*. You could be *happy*, without having much *freedom*. You could have a good deal of *freedom* without *achieving* much. We can go on.
>
> (Emphasis in original)

The inherent subjectivity and multidimensionality of conceptualizing living standards captured in the quote above is further complicated by the operationalization of these concepts into measures for evaluating wellbeing. Despite the widespread recognition that wellbeing is multidimensional, with both subjective and objective aspects, and also context- and population-specific, the tendency in development discourse has been to establish universal criteria and indicators for the measurement of progress towards wellbeing (OECD, 2015). One problem with such universal application is that different peoples hold different meanings and understandings of what constitutes wellbeing, and these differences can sometimes be subsumed by the dominant, universalist paradigm (White, 2016).

In tandem with this global agenda is a growing body of literature which serves to deconstruct the normative way in which wellbeing is conceptualized and characterized. There are two substantial bodies of literature in this space. The first is primarily driven from developing countries or the global South (Escobar, 1995; White & Blackmore, 2016). The second is occurring within the Indigenous movement of conceptualizing and measuring wellbeing according to the worldviews of Indigenous peoples[2] (Richmond et al., 2005; Adelson, 2009; Heil, 2009; Izquierdo, 2009; Merino, 2016; Watene, 2016a; Yap and Yu, 2016a).

In challenging the discourse of wellbeing, Indigenous peoples have mobilized a self-determination movement which is centred on their worldviews and priorities from the international levels down to more localized levels (Grieves, 2007; Taylor et al., 2012; Rigney and Hemming, 2014; Taylor et al., 2014; Kukutai and Walter, 2015; Kukutai and Taylor, 2016; Watene, 2016b). This wellbeing agenda starts from a relational view where the centrality of a collective sense of wellbeing, not just individual wellbeing, and the importance of sustaining one's relationship to the natural world and environment are promoted (Ruttenberg, 2013; Waldmüller, 2014; Merino, 2016).

To meaningfully embed wellbeing in policy requires an understanding of wellbeing concepts, measures and evaluation tools. The fundamental tasks include deciding '*what objects (dimensions and indicators) are of value*' and the '*importance attached to the object or objects*' (Sen, 1987). These two questions are deceptively straightforward but are critically dependent on how wellbeing is conceptualized, by whom and through what process. In this chapter, the current approaches to understanding and measuring Indigenous wellbeing are outlined. Following that, an approach starting from Indigenous perspectives working with the Yawuru community in Broome, Western Australia is described. Using participatory sequential mixed-methods approach, this chapter will explore how conceptions and measures of *mabu liyan* can lay the foundation for measuring wellbeing from a relational perspective. The stories will be interwoven with findings from the Yawuru Wellbeing Survey to elucidate how *mabu liyan* conceptions overlap and differ from orthodox wellbeing frameworks and measures.

Wellbeing concepts and measurement

In the edited volume titled 'Culture, Place and Methods', the four faces of wellbeing—evaluative, substantive, subjective and objective—are introduced as a way of navigating the various wellbeing approaches in public policy across multiple schools of thought (White, 2016, pp. 6–7). Much of the literature on wellbeing can be broadly grouped into 'substantive' aspects of wellbeing and 'evaluative' aspects of wellbeing. Scholars interested in substantive wellbeing are primarily concerned with the complexity and diversity of wellbeing experiences and conceptions. The other body of literature attempts to cast a spotlight on the evaluative aspect of wellbeing using indicators or measures as the object of interest, and exploring what facilitates improvements in wellbeing across the objective and subjective domains (White, 2016). In the rest of this chapter, the literature on Indigenous wellbeing will be summarized from these two perspectives.

Approaches to understanding indigenous wellbeing

In the substantive space, qualitative approaches have primarily been used to enable a more nuanced understanding of wellbeing across different locations. For example, ethnography has been employed to understand how wellbeing is conceptualized by Indigenous peoples in Peru and Canada (Adelson, 2009; Izquierdo, 2009). The use of interviews and focus groups to identify and generate themes of Indigenous wellbeing has also been employed in Australia. The relatedness between 'country' and wellbeing has been explored with the Nywaigi peoples in Queensland (Greiner, Larson, Herr, & Bligh, 2005) and with Aboriginal people living in Victoria (Kingsley et al., 2013). Grieves (2007) and Priest et al. (2012) respectively have looked at definitions and constructs of Indigenous wellbeing in urban settings, with the former undertaken in Sydney and the latter with child care workers and children in Victoria. More recently, Altman (2015) explored what is perceived as and constitutes a good life for the Kuninjku people in Maningrida in a remote living context using interviews. The literature suggest that wellbeing is comprehensive, context-specific and culturally constructed, not dissimilar to the broader literature. There are however, specificities within those common themes which are unique and critical to the understanding and framing of Indigenous wellbeing such as context, distinctiveness and the importance of the collective.

Indigenous context

Conceptualizations of wellbeing cannot be meaningfully separated from context and this includes 'place' as context. 'Place' extends beyond just the physical geographical space to include the deeper spiritual connection that many Indigenous peoples have to their ancestral land (Panelli & Tipa, 2007). From an Indigenous perspective, context also requires an understanding of how a history of colonization and marginalization has impacted on the ways that Indigenous health and wellbeing is conceptualized and understood (Gee, Dudgeon, Schultz, Hart, & Kelly, 2014; Axelsson, Kukutai, & Kippen, 2016).

Context is also about recognizing the social and political circumstances and struggle of Indigenous peoples for recognition (Deneulin, 2008). Many Indigenous groups today remain invisible in official statistics and are located within nation states which may not be embracing the United Nations Declaration of the Rights of Indigenous Peoples (UNDRIP) in their policies even if they are signatories. This has significant implications for how wellbeing is experienced, constructed and pursued within those contexts.

Distinctiveness

A recurring central theme in the literature is the importance of having strong identity. That in turn is tied to one's connection to culture and country (Ganesharajah, 2009; Biddle & Swee, 2012; Willeto, 2012; Watene, 2016a; Nguyen & Cairney, 2013). The understanding of country or land as an extension of the individual is something unique to Indigenous populations worldwide (Panelli & Tipa, 2007). This is a theme which has not featured prominently in the broader literature on wellbeing. The importance of the environment and sustainable development more broadly in the universal wellbeing frameworks do not reflect the spiritual connection between Indigenous peoples and their land and sea country.

Connection to country is multidimensional in nature and permeates how Indigenous people manage, access and live, and learn through their connection to country, culture and their environment (Bird Rose, 1996). The connection to country and culture for many Indigenous people is strongly linked to other aspects of their wellbeing, including health, spirituality, identity, economic development and standard of living (McDermott, O'Dea, Rowley, Knight, & Burgess, 1998; Jorgensen & Taylor, 2000; Greiner et al., 2005; Hunt, 2010; Altman & Kerins, 2012). As a result, Indigenous peoples have described the devastating spiritual impacts resulting from the misuse and disturbance of the health and vitality of their land and waters to their sense of wellbeing (Richmond, Elliott, Matthews, & Elliot, 2005; Yawuru RNTBC, 2013; Kerins & Green, 2016).

Collective wellbeing

The central importance of family and kinship for the wellbeing of Indigenous peoples is evident in the literature (Greiner et al., 2005; Durie, 2006; Grieves, 2007; Kral, Idlout, Minore, Dyck, & Kirmayer, 2011; Calestani, 2013). As such, the importance of the collective and relational sense of wellbeing instead of just the individual is a recurring theme in the literature (Deneulin, 2008; McCubbin, McCubbin, Zhang, Kehl, & Strom, 2013; Cram, 2014; Murphy, 2014). The concept of family transcends the boundaries of immediate blood relations to those of skin group[3] names and kinship and social structures. It is these structures which govern what social and cultural exchange occurs between the giver and receiver and these exchanges occur both in everyday living, reinforcing Indigenous peoples' connection to country and culture (Martin, 1995; Schwab, 1995). The importance of family in Indigenous wellbeing has resulted in many wellbeing frameworks using the family as the unit of analysis or the starting point of thinking about Indigenous wellbeing policies and programs (McGregor, Matsuoka, Rodenhurst, Kohn, & Spencer, 2003; Lawson-Te, 2010; Cram, 2014).

Self-determination and autonomy

The importance of autonomy and self-determination for indigenous peoples overarches all aspects of Indigenous wellbeing. A central aspect of autonomy relates to the collective right to self-determination and a collective sense of wellbeing, which are inextricably linked to the ability to be self-determining at the individual level. Indigenous autonomy and self-determination are basic human rights which carry intrinsic value in themselves but they are also instrumental in the pathways towards achieving other aspects of wellbeing (Tsey, Whiteside, Deemal, & Gibson, 2003; Gooda, 2010; Murphy, 2014; Bainbridge, McCalman, Clifford, & Tsey, 2015).

Important for research relating to issues facing Indigenous peoples is the value of self-determination that arises from the transforming of the power relations in research paradigms. This can enable Indigenous peoples to fully participate in the research process, methodology and dissemination of findings to empower change and action in their communities. This has to occur alongside mutual capacity building and a co-production of knowledge where Indigenous peoples are not seen as passive recipients of research outcomes, but instead active co-producers of knowledge on their wellbeing and worldviews (Smith, 1999, 2012; Cairney, Abbott, & Yamaguchi, 2015; Cairney et al., 2017).

Evaluative wellbeing

The literature on evaluative Indigenous wellbeing has primarily been through two avenues – the construction of composite measures to represent Indigenous wellbeing and looking at factors which enable Indigenous wellbeing.

Composite measures of Indigenous wellbeing

The Human Development Index has been calculated for Indigenous populations in Canada, USA, Aotearoa New Zealand and Australia to articulate the failure of country level measures such as the HDI in showing the heterogeneity within different sub-population groups (Cooke, Mitrou, Lawrence, Guimond, & Beavon, 2007; Yap & Biddle, 2010; Mitrou et al., 2014). There have also been efforts toward constructing composite measures to better contextualize the variations within Indigenous populations in these countries. In Canada, the HDI has been calculated for Registered Indians On- and Off-Reserve, for Aboriginal youth, by gender as well as for Inuit and Métis populations (Cooke, 2007; Cooke & Beavon, 2007; Sénécal, O'Sullivan, Guimond, & Uppal, 2008). In the United States, HDI has been constructed for all sub-populations including Asian Americans, Native Americans, Latinos and African Americans (Lewis & Burds-Sharps, 2010).

To highlight a greater level of geographical diversity within indigenous populations, composite indices have also been constructed at a more disaggregated spatial unit of analysis. In Canada, the Community Wellbeing Index (CWB) has been constructed at the census subdivisions level to compare how First Nations, non-Aboriginal and Inuit communities fare against a set of socioeconomic characteristics (O'Sullivan, 2011; Aboriginal Affairs and Northern Development Canada, 2015). Since 1986, composite measures summarizing the social and economic outcomes of the Australian Indigenous population at the area level based on an Indigenous geographical framework have been constructed for every census (Tesfaghiorghis, 1991; Altman & Liu, 1994; Gray & Auld, 2000; Biddle, 2009; Yap & Biddle, 2010; Biddle, 2013).

What factors support Indigenous wellbeing

Several authors have examined determinants of subjective wellbeing in Australia more broadly and found that Indigenous Australians were more likely to report higher life satisfaction compared to non-Indigenous Australians (Shields, Wheatley, & Wooden, 2009; Ambrey & Fleming, 2014). An alternative approach is to estimate an Indigenous only sample and a non-Indigenous sample using the same explanatory variables to investigate whether the relationships are different in varying contexts (e.g. whether the relationship between unemployment and subjective wellbeing is the same for both the Indigenous and non-Indigenous population). Building on the literature on life satisfaction determinations in Australia, Manning, Ambrey, and Fleming (2015) found that the relationship between life satisfaction and age, unemployment, health and partnership status is similar across both population groups. However, there were some notable differences. Indigenous Australians who reported having poor spoken English skills were more likely to report higher life satisfaction and income was not positively associated with life satisfaction in the Indigenous context (Manning et al., 2015).

Indigenous subjective wellbeing

The availability of a suite of questions around different aspects of Indigenous wellbeing in the National Aboriginal and Torres Strait Islander Social Survey (NATSISS) provided the beginnings of an examination of Indigenous wellbeing within the broader literature on wellbeing. More importantly, it also allowed for some aspects of Indigenous worldviews and experiences to be understood within broader wellbeing determinants. Dockery (2009) pioneered the examination of associations between culture and socioeconomic wellbeing in Australia. His findings established that there remained significant associations between cultural attachment and socioeconomic wellbeing after controlling for age, marital status, gender and whether the individual experienced the historical legacy of separation first hand or had members of their family who were separated from their natural family (Dockery, 2009).

Biddle (2014), using the HILDA and NATSISS, found that Indigenous peoples were less likely to report frequent periods of happiness and more likely to report periods of extreme sadness than their non-Indigenous counterparts. However, Indigenous Australians were significantly more likely to report above average satisfaction with their life than non-Indigenous

Australians. Using some of the previous correlates identified in the literature, the author found that age, geography, mobility, labour force status and education were associated with self-reported happiness among the Indigenous population.

The release of the *Te Kupenga*, the first Māori social survey, in 2013 allows for the examination of Māori wellbeing within Māori worldviews and lived experiences. The survey design aimed to reflect Māori worldviews and conceptions of wellbeing. The analysis of life satisfaction of Māori using *Te Kupenga* demonstrated that relationships, health status, standard of living and trust are important contributions to overall life satisfaction. Cultural attachments such as perceived importance of Māori culture and proficiency in Māori language were also important correlates, but had a much weaker association (Statistics NZ, 2015).

Indigenous social and emotional wellbeing (SEWB)

The concept of social and emotional wellbeing recognizes the Australian Aboriginal worldviews of health and wellbeing as being holistic and encompasses mental, health, cultural, spiritual and social wellbeing. It also acknowledges the trauma and grief resulting from colonization. As such, it has particular resonance with Aboriginal and Torres Strait Islander peoples (Garvey, 2008; AIHW, 2009; Kelly et al., 2009; Gee et al., 2014; Dudgeon & Walker, 2015). Researchers have noted that the poor social and emotional wellbeing of Indigenous peoples stems from ongoing consequences of colonization (Swan & Raphael, 1995; Garvey, 2008).

Psychological distress is one measure by which social and emotional wellbeing of Indigenous peoples can and have been evaluated. Many of the factors noted as enablers of subjective wellbeing more broadly are also noted in the literature on Indigenous SEWB in Australia. Health status, family breakdown, racism, substance abuse and socioeconomic status are some factors associated with Indigenous SEWB (Paradies et al., 2008). However, the themes canvassed as being central to Indigenous wellbeing as a whole earlier in this chapter are also important factors. They include self-determination, community governance, connectedness to country, strength of identity, family relationships and cultural continuity (Chandler & Lalonde, 2008; Gee et al., 2014; Parker & Milroy, 2014; Zubrick et al., 2014; Dudgeon & Walker, 2015).

Empirical research undertaken by Cunningham and Paradies (2012) using the 2004–05 National Aboriginal and Torres Strait Islander Health Survey demonstrated that food security, marital status, education, employment, income, home ownership and area-level disadvantage were associated with psychological distress. However, the authors noted that findings related to traditional indicators of socioeconomic status were not statistically significant in remote areas for Indigenous Australians. More recently, Marwick and colleagues (2015) found that in Victoria, being female, unmarried or a lone parent was associated with higher psychological distress. Socioeconomic status, social support and contact and age were also important determinants of psychological distress.

Challenges of understanding Indigenous wellbeing

In an ideal world, conceptions of wellbeing would inform the development of measures used to evaluate wellbeing in an iterative and interactive process. However, evaluating wellbeing using quantitative methods are constrained by the use of existing secondary data which may not adequately capture the breadth and depth of wellbeing accounts. Scholars in the substantive domain argue for the importance of localized particularities and illuminate the power struggles occurring against the backdrop of Indigenous affairs. Scholars in the evaluative domain highlight findings that are nationally representative and true on average. The substantive and evaluative literature appears to have developed in isolation, with little interaction, instead of conversing to enrich our understandings of Indigenous wellbeing.

Despite the voluminous data on the 'Indigenous population' of Australia, there is a sense there is still a lack of knowledge on what living well means for 'Indigenous people'. While useful at some level, the existing tools and datasets described above are restricted in terms of their functionality for Indigenous communities and polities to understand and monitor their own wellbeing (Morphy, 2007, 2016; Taylor, 2008, 2009; Walter, 2010; Prout, 2011; Yu, 2012; Walter & Andersen, 2013; Kukutai & Walter, 2015). There are several reasons for this state of affairs – the usefulness of existing wellbeing concepts, the distinction between population and peoples and the importance of process in conceptualizing wellbeing.

Usefulness of existing wellbeing concepts

Despite the growing consensus that wellbeing and happiness vary across cultures, there is still a tendency to use existing tools or surveys to reflect the reality of wellbeing cross-culturally rather than to question the appropriateness of these tools, despite their seeming inability to capture underlying cultural differences (Mathews, 2012, p. 301). Much of the literature presented above on evaluating Indigenous wellbeing utilizes existing tools such as happiness and life satisfaction. While the usefulness of happiness as a metric for evaluating wellbeing has been debated on both philosophical grounds as well as in its conceptual operations (Mathews, 2012), an important consideration here is whether these tools have cross-cultural validity and are appropriate for understanding and evaluating Indigenous wellbeing.

Even when there are surveys specifically designed to capture Indigenous worldviews such as the NATSISS, a large part of these surveys is still intended for comparative purposes with the general population and to meet government needs (Taylor, 2008; Walter, 2013). The defined spatial and geographical classifications mask the diversity of the hundreds of language groups and nations that make up Australia's First Peoples, and as a result limit the usability of the data to inform the wellbeing and aspirations of collective groups such as the Ngunnawal, Noongar, Torres Strait or the Yawuru, just to name a few. This brings us to the second issue, the distinction between peoples and population.

Population versus peoples

In Australia, a survey of the literature, information databases and national statistical collection agencies points to a common thread of the production of population binaries of Indigenous and non-indigenous through the inclusion of Indigenous self-identification questions (Rowse, 2012; Taylor, 2013; Walter & Andersen, 2013). However, these population binaries collected through a post-colonial framework is not of geographical, social or cultural relevance to Indigenous people and communities on the ground (Morphy, 2007; Kukutai, 2011; Kukutai & Taylor, 2013; Yu, 2012). Furthermore, the production and representation of the lives of Indigenous peoples through the binary of Indigenous and non-Indigenous populations reduces Indigenous peoples, their unique history, affiliation to country and cultural identity to a statistical creation based on aggregated individual-level data (Walter, 2013; Rowse, 2012). The distinction between 'peoples' and 'population' is a significant one. As Rowse (2012, pp. 4–5) notes, when we refer to Aboriginal and Torres Strait Islanders as a 'peoples', we are thinking about them as collectives with self-governing capabilities and rights as opposed to referring to them as a 'population'.

Conceptualizing wellbeing: a process and outcome of wellbeing

The 2007 United Nations Declaration on the Rights of Indigenous Peoples (UNDRIP) provides an international standard to support Indigenous peoples' right for development. Specifically, articles 3, 43 and 44[4] of the UNDRIP assert that Indigenous peoples want to become agents of their own development and to determine and develop priorities and strategies for development (UN, 2007). The principles of self-determination, participation, cultural rights, land rights, ownership and free prior and informed consent all form the basis for supporting Indigenous groups in their efforts to set an agenda for improving their wellbeing (UN, 2007).

While achieving Indigenous wellbeing is a goal in itself, involving Indigenous peoples to achieve a better understanding of what defines 'wellbeing' is also crucial to the development of frameworks used to measure progress towards wellbeing goals (Gooda, 2010). This brings us to the last key issue relating to methodologies, in particular, the recognition that to date there have been few attempts at developing appropriate methodologies for understanding and measuring Indigenous wellbeing which prioritize Indigenous worldviews, highlight local priorities and represent Indigenous collectives (Walter, 2013, 2016).

Mabu liyan: Indigenizing wellbeing from the group up

Yawuru's participation: a necessary and critical element

Kukutai and Walter (2015) identify five research principles that should inform the conduct of research involving Indigenous peoples – recognizing geographical diversity, recognizing cultural diversity, recognizing other ways of knowing, mutual capability-building and Indigenous decision-making. The case study in this chapter demonstrates how these research principles are invoked to ensure that Yawuru participate meaningfully in the research process by bringing Yawuru notions of wellbeing into the measurement space and co-producing knowledge on Yawuru wellbeing. Yawuru's own agenda to measure wellbeing according to their worldviews, together with a PhD research proposal which aimed to develop a methodology for deriving culturally relevant measures of wellbeing, provided common ground for this collaborative partnership between the two authors (Yap & Yu, 2016a, 2016b). Yawuru's participation is interwoven throughout the process, from research content to survey design and collection. The grounding of the measures of wellbeing from the community voices serves to increase statistical functionality of the measures and associated data generated for the community on the ground, but also to aid in the development of a more policy-relevant concept of wellbeing (Kukutai & Walter, 2015; McGregor, 2015).

Who and what perspectives matter?

Working with the Yawuru community as opposed to working broadly with Indigenous peoples living in remote areas is recognizing the importance of Yawuru as a collective but also the importance that Yawuru attaches to 'place'. Following Yawuru practice, this includes the relational aspect of community, one that is premised on Yawuru's connection to country and the *bugarrigarra*,[5] yet it is also locational as the connection is tied to the physical locality of Broome in remote Western Australia. Composition of community also includes Yawuru individuals who may not be living in Broome but are still part of the Yawuru community through their relational, historical and cultural ties to Broome and to Yawuru families. The definition of the Yawuru community also recognizes Yawuru as native title holders, with rights, interest and responsibilities over Broome and the surroundings. The purpose of developing and constructing indicators of wellbeing for Yawuru therefore is to determine how Yawuru are faring according to their own benchmarks and standards.

Mabu liyan: *a different way of knowing Yawuru's philosophy of wellbeing*

Understanding wellbeing requires the use of multiple knowledge systems which can capture the complexity and diversity of human experience. Starting with *liyan* as the philosophy of how Yawuru relate to, understand and define wellbeing is recognizing there are different ways of understanding Indigenous wellbeing. Following that, the framing of questions around Yawuru ways of knowing, being and doing reflects the cultural specificities of wellbeing within the Indigenous context, and can further validate the appropriateness of existing measures of Indigenous wellbeing.

Liyan is a Yawuru philosophy of being, which is shared with other Indigenous groups using variant words for the same idea. *Mabu liyan* (good *liyan*) reflects Yawuru's sense of belonging and being, emotional strength, dignity and pride. Expressions of *liyan* are articulated based on collective structures: it is a model of living well in connection with country, culture, others and with oneself (Yap & Yu, 2016a, 2016b). McKenna and Anderson (2011, p. 4) explain, "*liyan* is the center of our being and emotions. It is a very important characteristic that forms our wellbeing, keeping us grounded in our identity and our connection to country, to our family, our community and it is linked to the way we care for our emotions and ourselves."

How: *conceptualizing and measuring Yawuru wellbeing*

In the Yawuru case study, process is a priority. A process where wellbeing measures are created, from the bottom up in partnership with those who are experts on their own lives and knowledge. As Smith (2012, p. 196) argues, "When indigenous peoples become the researchers and not merely the researched, the activity of research is transformed. Questions are framed differently, priorities are ranked differently, problems are defined differently and people participate on different terms." This necessitates a fundamentally different starting point from what is considered the norm in the academy, to one that privileges Indigenous worldviews, recognizes the existence of a different way of understanding Indigenous wellbeing and reveals the cultural, geographical and context diversity of Indigenous conceptions of wellbeing. This requires Yawuru's participation to be interwoven throughout the entire process.

There are several ways in which Yawuru's participation has been exercised beyond the collaborative partnership between the authors of this chapter. A Yawuru Guidance and Reference Committee was formed consisting of Yawuru women and men to ensure that the information generated through the research reflected local aspirations and values, and more importantly, was functional for community purposes. The Committee provided and continues to provide cultural and local knowledge to facilitate the conduct of the research and ensure that the information was relevant for community purposes and for the service delivery organizations based in Broome more broadly. Most importantly, Yawuru's participation was embedded throughout the process, from research content to survey design and collection as is evident in the next section of this chapter (Yap & Yu, 2016a).

Mutual capacity-building is a critical and necessary component of research with a transformative agenda. For example, the preparation and management of the project itself provided for mutual capacity-building between the two authors, particularly in terms of communication and relationship building in this cross-cultural space. There was also a larger capacity-building

Table 22.1 The development of indicators relating to sense of *liyan*

Examples of interview	Indicators	Selected/not selected by focus groups	Translated to survey question or statement
Liyan has many components to it such as the physical, mental, emotional and spiritual elements. All these elements have to be balanced in order to have a good, strong liyan. To many Yawuru people, it is a spiritual word.	Having a strong balanced spiritual centre Knowing how to return to centre when things are difficult	Picked by Yawuru women Picked by Yawuru men	My inner spirit felt strong, balanced and clear most or all of the time
I try and get back into country in the afternoons. With my liyan I go back and I sit down on the rocks, get out on country and go fishing and that makes my liyan good.	Spending time on country	Picked by Yawuru women Picked by Yawuru men	I felt deeply connected to my country and surrounds

component built in at the quantitative phase of the research. To enable this to be undertaken, additional funds were obtained through the Bankwest Research Grants Stream 2014 to employ ten local research assistants during the data collection process and for the purchase of iPads for data collection (Yap & Yu, 2016a).

From stories to indicators, from indicators to survey questions

A participatory mixed-methods approach in a sequential manner through two interconnected phases was used to conceptualize and measure Yawuru wellbeing.[6] The first phase of the study is qualitative in nature, exploring how wellbeing is understood, experienced and defined by the Yawuru community through semi-structured interviews and focus group exercises and discussions. The qualitative information in the first phase of the research was transformed in a manner which helps guide the quantitative phase. The qualitative phase therefore provided the foundation for the development of the Yawuru Wellbeing Survey and provided a pool of potential attributes for inclusion in an exercise to determine Yawuru priorities and weights. For a more detailed description of both phases, please see Yap and Yu (2016a, 2016b).

Underpinning Yawuru's wellbeing is the notion of *liyan*. There were several key themes arising from narratives of *mabu liyan* by Yawuru. They include relatedness, holism and balance. These concepts lay the foundation of grounding of indicators and survey questions according to Yawuru's worldviews. The grounding of the indicators from the stories by Yawuru women and men further created a sense of 'ownership' in what measures of wellbeing should be constructed allowing for expressions of self-determination by Yawuru (see Table 22.1).

The many dimensions of *mabu liyan*

Liyan *as holistic wellbeing*

Yawuru women and men describe *liyan* as a *feeling*, not just in one sense but all senses. Yawuru derive good *liyan* from feeling, being, doing and relating. As such, *liyan* as a sense is linked strongly with one's way of being. As this Yawuru male describes:

It's [*Liyan*] not just a description of emotions. It is a state of being. It influences not just your day, it influences your life. *Liyan* for country, strong *liyan* for country, that connectedness, the strength, the spirituality.

(Yawuru male, 49 years)

Most of the participants saw a link between *liyan* and wellbeing although they are not one and the same. Many Yawuru individuals noted that how one's *liyan* was feeling very much related to one's interaction with others. It is therefore important for the Indigenous and non-Indigenous people that Yawuru individuals interact to understand the importance of *liyan* to Yawuru wellbeing.

Bad *liyan* can spread from bad to worse. It might start with two person and they bring more people and family get involved. Your *liyan* is connected to other people's *liyan*. It catches and it spreads.

(Yawuru female, 70 years)

Liyan has always been there. Like the soul when you are born… I get pain in my belly then I know someone is affecting my *liyan*. I have to make that right first before communicating with others.

(Yawuru female, 56 years)

Absolutely *liyan* has to do with a good life. Doesn't matter where we are, and it doesn't matter even in the non-Indigenous context, if we are talking to people, if our *liyan* is not good, or if we don't feel right, we explain that.

(Yawuru female, 32 years)

Liyan *as balance*

Mabu liyan is in essence a balance of all the emotions and is achieved when one is in balance with one's self, one's relationship with others and one's relationship to country. The importance of balance is also about one's feelings and spiritual centre, which consist of not only the body and the mind but also the spirit. Wellbeing therefore is seen as being interconnected, consisting of cultural, spiritual, physical and emotional wellbeing. As this Yawuru female eloquently describes:

Liyan is the connection between your emotional and spiritual centre rolled into one. That spiritual centre is linked to identity and identity is linked to kinship, family. *Liyan* has many components to it such as the physical, mental, emotional and spiritual elements. All these elements have to be balanced in order to have a good, strong *liyan*. To many Yawuru people, it is a spiritual word.

(Yawuru female, 34 years)

Perhaps unsurprisingly, some Yawuru individuals describe happiness as one of the ways in which *liyan* is expressed. This is not unexpected given that linguistically *liyan* is feelings. However, the descriptions and stories arising from a Yawuru's conception of *liyan* and wellbeing did not always signify positive feelings. More often than not, *liyan* is described as finding that balance in feelings and negotiating the positive and negative events. There are instances, such as disruptions to country, where *liyan* will be bad as this Yawuru male notes:

To see the landscape cleared from what it previously was… a lot of Yawuru people feel… we feel… our *liyan* no good. Yawuru people and the land are intrinsically connected… and wellbeing are intrinsically connected. Anything done to the land, it's like hurting them because of that connection to the land.

(Yawuru male, 41 years)

However, a comfortable medium might be achieved, not necessarily positive or happy feelings, but a balance if there are actions taken to counter the bad *liyan* as described below:

Others have their own ideas of how to live and we need to enforce our way and through education, get into good government areas so that they can push those issues and make it balance.

(Yawuru male, 63 years)

Liyan *as relatedness*

Relatedness or connectedness is a strong foundation for Yawuru wellbeing. The stories in this chapter alongside the literature on Indigenous wellbeing highlight the relational wellbeing of Indigenous peoples to their country and culture, the reciprocity of that relatedness and how it is shaped by the *bugarrigarra* and with that the obligations and responsibilities as Yawuru.

A major source of attaining good *liyan* is relatedness with family. The importance of family includes being a source of support and giving one a sense of belonging. The kinship structures which underpin the social and cultural exchanges in many Indigenous communities including Yawuru serve to fulfil a person's sense of belonging and affirm their identity and place within the family. As a Yawuru female articulates:

Usually being around family. Being at a family gathering, on country with family, at my grandmother's house with family. Times like that make my *liyan* feel good. When it doesn't feel good, I resort to those things to make it better.

(Yawuru female, 28 years)

How one relates and connects to country and culture is a further element of *liyan*. Relatedness to country and culture is both physical and spiritual relatedness. Several Yawuru individuals, both younger and older, highlight the importance of being on country not just spiritually but physically as well:

Part of that connection to country that contributes to *liyan* is actually being physically here not just about speaking the language. Mind you, if I am away from Broome and I am finding it difficult, if I see family or see something that resembles Broome… that makes me connect… remind me… it is still a sense.

(Yawuru female, 28 years)

Relatedness and sense of *liyan* also manifests through the practice of traditional culture, the transmission of knowledge and mutual reciprocity and obligation to that the broader kinship system. In addition,

I try and get back into country in the afternoons. With my *liyan* I go back and I sit down on the rocks, get out on country and go fishing and that makes my *liyan* good.

(Yawuru female, 52 years)

My *liyan* feels good when I link in with country, when I feel the breeze, feel the fire. I find a spot and feel cleansed and I feel good. The more times I do that, the more times I feel good… when I am getting out fishing and practising cultural things that I have learnt.

(Yawuru male, 49 years)

A strong sense of connection means that interruptions and interferences to country are often seen and described by Yawuru individuals as not only affecting them physically but also spiritually, thereby contributing to the loss of *mabu liyan* as described by the Yawuru male in the previous section.

What we measure matters

At this juncture, it is perhaps useful to consider whether the different conceptions and approaches of understanding wellbeing give rise to different conclusions. Using the more common measures of subjective wellbeing in the literature, we find that of the total sampled 156 Yawuru women and men aged 18 years and over, almost 75 per cent reported feeling satisfied or very satisfied with their life on a whole most or all of the time. On the other hand, 67.5 per cent of Yawuru women and men reported feeling happy most or all of the time in the last four weeks. Taking a broader health perspective to consider social and emotional wellbeing using the Kessler Psychological Distress Scale (K-5), we find that about three in every four Yawuru men and women reported experiencing low psychological distress.

In an attempt to capture a more nuanced understanding of wellbeing through Yawuru's philosophy of *liyan*, a series of statement drawing on narratives from Yawuru women and men were developed including 'My inner spirit felt strong, balanced and clear' (Yap & Yu, 2016a).[7] In the survey, Yawuru women and men were asked how often their inner spirit felt strong, balanced and clear. Using that measure as one way of capturing Yawuru's wellbeing, the results suggest that a lower share of Yawuru women and men report strong wellbeing (62.5%).

Table 22.2 shows the share of Yawuru women and men who may report having positive and high wellbeing on a particular measure or concept while also reporting negative or low wellbeing on a separate measure. About 22 per cent of Yawuru women and men reported being happy most or all of the time yet their inner spirit did not feel strong, balanced and clear all or most of the time. Similarly, one quarter of those experiencing low psychological distress reported not feeling happy all or most of the time.

Concluding remarks

The question of universality in conceptions of wellbeing has implications for both the selection of dimensions of wellbeing and the associated indicators to quantify and measure wellbeing. The narratives by Yawuru women and men suggest that Yawuru conceptions of wellbeing both intersect with and diverge from the broader wellbeing literature. Conceptions of *liyan* suggest that subjective measures such as happiness is one aspect of wellbeing for Yawuru. However, the broader themes of connectedness, holism and balance are also key characteristics of Yawuru wellbeing.

The narratives by Yawuru provide evidence of socio-historical circumstances being a significant aspect of the evaluative space for achieving wellbeing from Yawuru perspectives. The intergenerational impacts of colonization mean that social and emotional wellbeing is an important aspect of Indigenous health and wellbeing. The use of K-5 rather than the K-10 pointed to an approach of ensuring cultural appropriateness in assessing social and emotional

Table 22.2 Overlap and differences between the different measures of Yawuru wellbeing

Measures of wellbeing	Number	%
Feeling happy most or all of the time (a)	102	67.5
Satisfied or very satisfied with life as a whole most or all of the time (b)	111	73.0
Experiencing low psychological distress as measured by the K-5 (c)	106	72.6
Inner spirit felt strong, balanced and clear most or all of the time (d)	95	62.5
For those who reported feeling happy most or all of the time (*n*=102)		
Happy but not satisfied	15	14.7
Happy but high psychological distress	13	12.7
Happy but inner spirit felt weak, unbalanced	23	22.5
For those who reported feeling satisfied or very satisfied with life as a whole most or all of the time (*n*=111)		
Satisfied but not happy	23	20.7
Satisfied but high psychological distress	19	17.1
Satisfied but inner spirit felt weak, unbalanced	31	27.9
For those who reported experiencing low psychological distress (*n*=106)		
Low psychological distress but not happy	27	25.5
Low psychological distress but not satisfied	17	16.0
Low psychological distress but inner spirit felt weak, unbalanced	23	21.7
For those who reported their inner spirit felt strong balanced and clear most or all of the time (*n*=95)		
Spirit felt strong, balanced and clear but not happy	16	16.8
Spirit felt strong, balanced and clear but not satisfied	15	15.8
Spirit felt strong, balanced and clear but high psychological distress	17	17.9

Notes: Non-response or refusal to answer is not included in the calculation. Non-response for questions on life satisfaction, feeling happy and spirit feeling strong and balanced (*n*=4). Non-response for question on psychological distress (*n*=10).

Source: Yawuru Wellbeing Survey 2015. The total sample of the survey was 156 individuals.

wellbeing for Indigenous Australians (Jorm, Bourchier, Cvetkovski, & Stewart, 2012). However, the use of K-5 does not go far enough to capture the spiritual and cultural aspects of SEWB.

The innovative use of a participatory sequential mixed-methods approach starting with a different way of knowing, challenges existing paradigms in relation to what matters for Indigenous wellbeing, moving from a deficit discourse to one of strength and cultural relevance. The Yawuru case study demonstrates how qualitative and quantitative methods can be brought together to develop potential measures of wellbeing. Starting with *mabu liyan*, and interweaving Yawuru articulations in to the process of developing and validating wellbeing measures, ensured that the measures that were developed in the quantitative phase were strengthened. The capacity-building component of employing Yawuru women as research assistants in the quantitative phase further ensured that knowledge was co-produced from the ground up, bringing together different ways of knowing. This has the potential to transform the way that measures and information on Indigenous wellbeing are represented and collected, by actively involving those who know their lives best.

Notes

1 The authors would like to acknowledge that this work was undertaken on Yawuru country and extend their gratitude to all the Yawuru women and men who have generously given their time to share their ideas, views and thoughts for advancing the research, in particular the Yawuru Reference and Guidance

Committee who have been a guiding compass to ensure the research is fit for purpose for community needs and aspirations. We would also like to acknowledge the Yawuru Wellbeing Survey 2015 team of research assistants without whom the findings in Table 22.2 would not be possible. The research received both financial and in-kind support from the following organizations to which the authors are very grateful: Centre for Aboriginal Economic Policy Research (Australian National University), Kimberley Institute Limited, Bankwest Curtin Economics Centre, Nulungu Institute (University of Notre Dame), Nyamba Buru Yawuru, Nagula Jarndu, Bottles of Australia and Yawuru Prescribed Body Corporate.

2 Throughout this chapter, the use of an upper case 'Indigenous' refers to the First Peoples of Australia and the Torres Strait Islands, while a lower case 'indigenous' refers generally to the First Peoples, aboriginal peoples, native peoples, or autochthonous peoples of the world.

3 Classificatory kinship systems.

4 Article 3 states that Indigenous peoples have the right to self-determination. By virtue of that right they freely determine their political status and freely pursue their economic, social and cultural development. Article 43 and 44 states the rights recognized herein constitute the minimum standards for the survival, dignity and wellbeing of the Indigenous peoples of the world and that the rights and freedom are equally guaranteed to male and female individuals.

5 *Bugarrigarra* is the core of Yawuru cosmology. *Bugarrigarra* is the time before time, when the creative forces shaped and gave meaning and form to the landscape, putting the languages to the people within those landscapes and creating the protocol and laws for living within this environment Yawuru RNTBC (2011, p. 13).

6 The research activities received formal approval from the Human Research Ethics Committee at the Australian National University (Protocol Number: 2013/249) for the first stage. A variation was submitted and accepted in May 2015 for the quantitative phase.

7 For a list of other statements developed by Yawuru, please see Yap and Yu (2016a).

Bibliography

Aboriginal Affairs and Northern Development Canada. (2015). *The Community Well-Being Index: Well-Being in First Nations communities, 1981–2011.* HM the Queen in Right of Canada, represented by the Minister of Aboriginal Affairs and Northern Development, Ottawa.

Adelson, N. (2009). The shifting landscape of Cree well-being. In G. Mathews & C. Izquierdo (Eds.), *Pursuits of happiness: Well-being in anthropological perspective* (pp. 109–126). London: Berghahn.

Adler, A., & Seligman, M.E. (2016). Using wellbeing for public policy: Theory, measurement, and recommendations measurement and recommendations. *International Journal of Wellbeing, 6*(1), 1–35.

AIHW. (2009). *Measuring the social and emotional wellbeing of Aboriginal and Torres Strait Islander peoples.* Cat. no. IHW 24, Australian Institute of Health and Welfare, Canberra.

Altman, J.C., & Liu, J. (1994). *Socioeconomic status at the ATSIC regional level, 1986 and 1991: Data for regional planning.* CAEPR Discussion Paper 76, ANU, Canberra.

Altman, J., & Kerins, S. (2012). *People on country: Vital landscapes, indigenous futures.* Sydney: The Federation Press.

Altman, J. (2015). The quest for the good life: Kuninjku perspectives opinion. *Land Rights News Northern Edition,* 10–11.

Ambrey, C.L., & Fleming, C.M. (2014). Life satisfaction in Australia: Evidence from ten years of the HILDA survey. *Social Indicators Research, 115*(2), 691–714.

Andersen, C. (2008). From nation to population: The racialisation of 'Metis' in the Canadian census. *Nations and Nationalism, 14*(2), 347–368.

Andersen, C. (2014a). Ethnic or categorical mobility: Challenging conventional demographic explanation of Métis population growth. In F. Trovato & A. Romaniuk (Eds.), *Aboriginal populations: Social, demographic and epidemiological perspectives* (pp. 276–298). Edmonton: The University of Alberta Press.

Andersen, C. (2014b). *Metis: Race, recognition and the struggle for Indigenous peoplehood.* Vancouver: University of British Columbia Press.

Axelsson, P., Kukutai, T., & Kippen, R. (2016). The field of Indigenous health and the role of colonisation and history. *Journal of Population Research, 33*(1), 1–7.

Axelsson, P., Sköld, P., Ziker, J., & Anderson, D. (2011). From indigenous demographics to an indigenous demography. In P. Axelsson & P. Sköld, (Eds.), *Indigenous peoples and demography: The complex relation between identity and statistics* (pp. 295–305). Oxford: Berghahn.

Bache, I., & Reardon, L. (2016). *The politics and policy of wellbeing: Understanding the rise and significance of a new agenda.* Cheltenham: Edward Elgar Publishing.

Bainbridge, R., McCalman, J., Clifford, A., & Tsey, K. (2015). Cultural competency in the delivery of health services for Indigenous people. Issues Paper 13, Closing the Gap Clearinghouse.

Biddle, N. (2009). Ranking regions: Revisiting an index of relative socio-economic outcomes. *Australasian Journal of Regional Studies, 15*(3), 329–354.

Biddle, N. (2013). *Socioeconomic outcomes.* 2011 Census Paper 13, CAEPR, ANU, Canberra.

Biddle, N. (2014). Measuring and analysing the wellbeing of Australia's Indigenous population. *Social Indicators Research, 116*(3), 713–729.

Biddle, N., & Swee, H. (2012). The relationship between wellbeing and indigenous land, language and culture in Australia. *Australian Geographer, 43*(3), 215–232.

Bird Rose, D. (1996). *Nourishing terrains: Australian Aboriginal views of landscape and wilderness.* Canberra: Australian Heritage Commission.

Cairney, S., Abbott, T., Quinn, S., Yamaguchi, J., Wilson, B., & Wakerman, J. (2017). Interplay wellbeing framework: A collaborative methodology 'bringing together stories and numbers' to quantify Aboriginal cultural values in remote Australia. *International Journal for Equity in Health, 16*(68). doi: 10.1186/s12939-017-0563-5.

Cairney, S., Abbott, T., & Yamaguchi, J. (2015). *Study protocol: The Interplay Wellbeing Framework and methodology to assess wellbeing in Aboriginal and Torres Strait Islander people in remote Australia.* CRC-Rep Working Paper CW024, Ninti One Limited, Alice Springs.

Calestani, M. (2013). *An anthropological journey into well-being: Insights from Bolivia.* Dordrecht: Springer Netherlands.

Canadian Index of Wellbeing. (2016). *How are Canadians really doing? The 2016 CIW National Report.* Waterloo, ON: Canadian Index of Wellbeing and University of Waterloo.

Chandler, M.J., & Lalonde, C.E. (2008). Cultural continuity as a protective factor against suicide in First Nations youth. *Horizons, 10*(10), 68–72.

Chandler, M., & Lalonde, C. (1998). Cultural continuity as a hedge against suicide in Canada's First Nations. *Transcultural Psychiatry, 35*, 191–219.

Cooke, M. (2007). The Registered Indian Human Development Indices: Conceptual and methodological issues. In J. White, D. Beavon, & N. Spence (Eds.), *Aboriginal well-being: Canada's continuing challenge* (pp. 25–47). Toronto: Thompson Educational Publishing.

Cooke, M., & Beavon, D. (2007). The Registered Indian Human Development Index, 1981–2001. In J. White, D. Beavon, & N. Spence (Eds.), *Aboriginal well-being: Canada's continuing challenge* (pp. 51–68). Toronto: Thompson Educational Publishing.

Cooke, M., Mitrou, F., Lawrence, D., Guimond, E., & Beavon, D. (2007). Indigenous well-being in four countries: An application of the UNDP's Human Development Index to indigenous peoples in Australia, Canada, New Zealand, and the United States. *BMC International Health and Human Rights, 7*, 9-9.

Cram, F. (2014). Measuring Māori wellbeing: A commentary. *MAI Journal, 3*(1), 18–32.

Cunningham, J., & Paradies, Y.C. (2012). Socio-demographic factors and psychological distress in Indigenous and non-Indigenous Australian adults aged 18–64 years: Analysis of national survey data. *BMC Public Health, 12*(1), 95.

Deneulin, S. (2008). Beyond individual freedom and agency: Structures of living together in the capability approach. In F. Comim, M. Qizilbash, & S. Alkire, (Eds.), *Capability approach: Concepts, measures and applications* (pp. 105–124). New York: Cambridge University Press.

Diener, E., & Seligman, E.P. (2004). Beyond money: Toward an economy of well-being. *Psychological Science in the Public Interest, 5*(1), 1–31.

Dockery, A.M. (2009). *Culture and wellbeing: The case of Indigenous Australians.* CLMR Discussion Paper Series 09/01, Centre for Labour Market Research.

Dodge, R., Daly, A.P., Huyton, J., & Sanders, L.D. (2012). The challenge of defining wellbeing. *International Journal of Wellbeing, 2*, 222–235.

Dudgeon, P., & Walker, R. (2015). Decolonising Australian psychology: Discourses, strategies, and practice. *Journal of Social and Political Psychology, 3*(1), 276–297.

Durie, M. (2006). *Measuring Māori wellbeing.* Treasury guest lecture series, August, 1–16.

Escobar, A. (1995). *Encountering development.* Princeton, NJ: Princeton University Press.

Frey, B., & Stutzer, A. (2002). The economics of happiness. *World Economics, 3*(1), 1–17.

Ganesharajah, C. (2009). *Indigenous health and wellbeing: The importance of country.* Native Title Research Report 1, Australian Institute of Aboriginal and Torres Strait Islander Studies AIATSIS, Canberra.

Garvey, D. (2008). A review of the social and emotional wellbeing of indigenous Australian peoples. *Australian Indigenous Health Reviews*, 1–22.

Gee, G., Dudgeon, P., Schultz, C., Hart, A., & Kelly, K. (2014). Aboriginal and Torres Strait Islander social and emotional wellbeing. In P. Dudgeon, H. Milroy, & R. Walker (Eds.), *Working together: Aboriginal and Torres Strait Islander mental health and wellbeing principles and practice* (2nd ed., pp. 55–68). Canberra: Department of The Prime Minister and Cabinet.

Gooda, M. (2010). *Social justice and wellbeing*. AIATSIS Seminar Series 2010: Indigenous Wellbeing, Canberra.

Graham, C. (2012). *The pursuit of happiness: An economy of well-being*. Washington, DC: Brookings Institution Press.

Gray, M., & Auld, A. (2000). *Towards an index of relative Indigenous socioeconomic disadvantage*. CAEPR Discussion Paper 196, CAEPR, ANU, Canberra.

Greiner, R., Larson, S., Herr, A., & Bligh, V. (2005). *Wellbeing of Nywaigi Traditional Owners: The contribution of country to wellbeing and the role of natural resource management*. CSIRO Sustainable Ecosystems, Townsville.

Grieves, V. (2007). *Indigenous well-being: A framework for governments' Aboriginal cultural heritage activities*. NSW Department of Environment and Conservation, Sydney.

Haybron, D.M. (2015). Mental state approaches to well-being. In M. Adler & M. Fleurbaey (Eds.), *Oxford handbook of well-being and public policy* (pp. 347–378). Oxford: Oxford University Press.

Heil, D. (2009). Embodied selves and social selves: Aboriginal well-being in rural New South Wales, Australia. In G. Mathews & C. Izquierdo (Eds.), *Pursuits of happiness: Well-being in anthropological perspective* (pp. 88–108). London: Berghahn.

Hunt, J. (2010). *Looking after country in New South Wales: Two case studies of socioeconomic benefits for Aboriginal people*. CAEPR Working Paper 75, CAEPR, ANU, Canberra.

Izquierdo, C. (2009). Well-being among the Matsigenka of the Peruvian Amazon: Health, missions, oil, and "progress". In G. Mathews & C. Izquierdo (Eds.), *Pursuits of happiness: Well-being in anthropological perspective* (pp. 67–87). London: Berghahn.

Jorgensen, M., & Taylor, J. (2000). *What determines Indian economic success? Evidence from tribal and individual Indian enterprises*. John F. Kennedy School of Government, Harvard University.

Jorm, A.F., Bourchier, S.J., Cvetkovski, S., & Stewart, G. (2012). Mental health of Indigenous Australians: A review of findings from community surveys. *Medical Journal of Australia*, *196*(2), 118–121.

Kelly, K., Dudgeon, P., Gee, G., & Glaskin, B. (2009). *Living on the edge: Social and emotional wellbeing and risk and protective factors for serious psychological distress among Aboriginal and Torres Strait Islander people*. Discussion Paper 10, Cooperative Research Centre for Aboriginal Health, Darwin.

Kerins, S., & Green, J. (2016). Jacky Green: Desecrating the rainbow serpent. *Artlink*, 90–93.

Kingsley, J., Townsend, M., Henderson-Wilson, C., & Bolam, B. (2013). Developing an exploratory framework linking Australian Aboriginal peoples' connection to country and concepts of wellbeing. *International Journal of Environment Research and Public Health*, *10*, 678–698.

Kral, M., Idlout, L., Minore, B., Dyck, R., & Kirmayer, L. (2011). Unikkaartuit: Meanings of well-being, unhappiness, health and community change among Inuit in Nunavut, Canada. *American Journal of Community Psychology*, *48*, 426–438.

Kukutai, T. (2011). Contemporary issues in Māori demography. In T. McIntosh & M. Mullholland (Eds.), *Māori and social issues* (pp. 11–48). Wellington: Huia.

Kukutai, T., & Taylor, J. (2013). Postcolonial profiling of indigenous populations: Limitations and responses in Australia and New Zealand. *Espace-Populations-Societes*, *1*, 13–27.

Kukutai, T., & Taylor, J. (2016). Data sovereignty for indigenous peoples: Current practice and future needs. In T. Kukutai & J. Taylor (Eds.), *Indigenous data sovereignty: Towards an agenda* (pp. 1–22). Canberra: ANU Press.

Kukutai, T., & Walter, M. (2015). Recognition and indigenizing official statistics: Reflections from Aotearoa New Zealand and Australia. *Statistical Journal of the IAOS*, *31*(2), 317–326.

Lawson-Te, A. (2010). *Definitions of whānau: A review of selected literature*. Family Commissions Report, April, New Zealand.

Lewis, K., & Burds-Sharps, S. (2010). *A century apart: New measures of well-being for U.S. racial and ethnic groups*. New York: American Human Development Project.

Manning, M., Ambrey, C., & Fleming, C. (2015). *Indigenous wellbeing in Australia: Evidence from the HILDA*. CAEPR Working Paper 101, CAEPR, ANU, Canberra.

Markwick, A., Ansari, Z., Sullivan, M., & McNeil, J. (2015). Social determinants and psychological distress among Aboriginal and Torres Strait islander adults in the Australian state of Victoria: A cross-sectional population based study. *Social Science & Medicine*, *128*, 178–187.

Martin, D. (1995). *Money, business and culture: Issues for aboriginal economic policy*. CAEPR Discussion Paper 101, CAEPR, ANU, Canberra.

Mathews, G. (2012). Happiness, culture, and context. *International Journal of Wellbeing, 2*(4), 299–312.

Mathews, G., & Izquierdo, C. (2009). Anthropology, happiness and well-being. In G. Mathews & C. Izquierdo (Eds.), *Pursuits of happiness: Well-being in anthropological perspective* (pp. 1–19). London: Berghahn.

McCubbin, L.D., McCubbin, H.I., Zhang, W., Kehl, L., & Strom, I. (2013). Relational well-being: An indigenous perspective and measure. *Family Relations, 62*(2), 354–365.

McDermott, R., O'Dea, K., Rowley, K., Knight, S., & Burgess, P. (1998). Beneficial impact of the Homeland Movement on health outcomes in central Australian Aborigines. *Australian and New Zealand Journal of Public Health, 22*(6), 653–658.

McGregor, D., Morelli, P., Matsuoka, J., Rodenhurst, R., Konh, N., & Spencer, M. (2003). An ecological model of native Hawaiian well-being. *Pacific Health Dialogue, 10*(2), 106–128.

McGregor, J.A. (2015). *Global initiatives in measuring human wellbeing: Convergence and difference*. CWiPP Working Paper No. 2, Center for Wellbeing in Public Policy, University of Sheffield.

McKenna, V., & Anderson, K. (2011). *Kimberley dreaming: Old law, new ways: Finding new meaning*. World Congress for Psychotherapy, Sydney.

Merino, R. (2016). An alternative to 'alternative development'? *Buen vivir* and human development in Andean countries. *Oxford Development Studies, 44*(3), 271–286.

Mitrou, F., Cooke, M., Lawrence, D., Povah, D., Mobilia, E., Guimond, E., & Zubrick, S.R. (2014). Gaps in Indigenous disadvantage not closing: A census cohort study of social determinants of health in Australia, Canada, and New Zealand from 1981–2006. *BMC Public Health, 14*(201), 1–9.

Morphy, F. (2007). Uncontained subjects: 'Population' and 'household' in remote Aboriginal Australia. *Journal of Population Research, 24*(2), 163–184.

Morphy, F. (2016). Indigenising demographic categories: A prolegomenon to indigenous data sovereignty. In T. Kukutai & J. Taylor (Eds.), *Indigenous data sovereignty: Towards an agenda* (pp. 99–115). Canberra: ANU Press.

Murphy, M. (2014). Self-determination as a collective capability: The case of Indigenous peoples. *Journal of Human Development and Capabilities, 15*(4), 320–334.

Nguyen, O., & Cairney, S. (2013). *Literature review of the interplay between education, employment, health and wellbeing for Aboriginal and Torres Strait Islander people in remote areas: Working towards an Aboriginal and Torres Strait Islander wellbeing framework*. CRC-REP Working Paper CW013, Ninti One Limited, Alice Springs.

O'Sullivan, E. (2011). *The Community Well-being Index (CWB): Measuring well-being in First Nations and non-Aboriginal communities, 1981–2006*. Strategic Research Directorate, Aboriginal Affairs and Northern Development Canada, Ottawa.

OECD. (2015). *How's life? 2015: Measuring Well-being*. Paris: OECD Publishing.

Panelli, R., & Tipa, G. (2007). Placing well-being: A Māori case study of cultural and environmental specificity. *EcoHealth, 4*(4), 445–460.

Paradies, Y., Harris, R., & Anderson, I. (2008). *The impact of racism on Indigenous health in Australia and Aotearoa: Towards a research agenda*. Discussion Paper Series 4, Cooperative Research Centre for Aboriginal Health, Darwin.

Parker, R., & Milroy, H. (2014). Aboriginal and Torres Strait Islander mental health: An overview. In P. Dudgeon, H. Milroy, & R. Walker (Eds.), *Working together: Aboriginal and Torres Strait Islander mental health and wellbeing principles and practice* (2nd ed., pp. 25–38). Canberra: Department of the Prime Minister and Cabinet.

Priest, N., Mackean, T., Davis, E., Briggs, L., & Waters, E. (2012). Aboriginal perspectives of child health and wellbeing in an urban setting: Developing a conceptual framework. *Health Sociological Review, 21*(2), 180–195.

Priest, N., Paradies, Y., Gunthorpe, W., Cairney, S., & Mayers, S. (2011). Racism as a determinant of social and emotional wellbeing for Aboriginal Australian youth. *Medical Journal of Australia, 194*, 546–550.

Prout, S. (2011). Indigenous wellbeing frameworks in Australia and the quest for quantification. *Social Indicators Research, 109*(2), 317–336.

Richmond, C., Elliott, S.J., Matthews, R., & Elliott, B. (2005). The political ecology of health: Perceptions of environment, economy, health and well-being among 'Namgis First Nation. *Health and Place, 11*(4), 349–365.

Rigney, D., & Hemming, S. (2014). Is 'closing the gap' enough? Ngarrindjeri ontologies, reconciliation and caring for country. *Educational Philosophy & Theory, 46*(5), 536–545.

Rowse, T. (2012). *Rethinking social justice: From 'peoples' to 'populations'*. Canberra: Aboriginal Studies Press.

Ruttenberg, T. (2013). Wellbeing economics and buen vivir: Development alternatives for inclusive human security. *The Fletcher Journal of Human Security, VXXXIII,* 68–93.

Ryan, R., & Deci, E. (2001). On happiness and human potentials: A review of research on hedonic and eudaimonic well-being. *Annual Review of Psychology, 52,* 141–166.

Schwab, J. (1995). *The calculus of reciprocity: Principles and implications of Aboriginal sharing.* CAEPR Discussion Paper 100, ANU, Canberra.

Sen, A. (1987). *The standard of living: The Tanner lectures on human values.* Cambridge: Cambridge University Press.

Sénécal, S., O'Sullivan, E., Guimond, E., & Uppal, S. (2008). Applying the community well-being index and the human development index to Inuit in Canada. In J. White, D. Beavon, & N. Spence (Eds.), *Aboriginal well-being: Canada's continuing challenge* (pp. 149–172). Toronto: Thompson Educational Publisher.

Shields, M.A., Wheatley Price, S., & Wooden, M. (2009). Life satisfaction and the economic and social characteristics of neighbourhoods. *Journal of Population Economics, 22*(2), 421–443.

Smith, L.T. (1999). *Decolonizing methodologies: Research and Indigenous peoples.* London: Zed Books.

Smith, L.T. (2012). *Decolonizing methodologies: Research and indigenous peoples* (2nd ed.). London: Zed Books.

Statistics New Zealand. (2015). *Ngā tohu o te ora: The determinants of life satisfaction for Māori 2013.* Wellington: Statistics New Zealand Tatauranga Aotearoa.

O'Sullivan, E., & McHardy, M. (2013). The Community Well-being Index (CWB): Well-being in First Nations communities, present, past, and future. In J. White, D. Beavon, & N. Spence (Eds.), *Aboriginal well-being: Canada's continuing challenge* (pp. 111–148). Toronto: Thompson Educational Publishing.

Swan, P., & Raphael, B. (1995). *Ways forward: Aboriginal and Torres Strait Islander mental health policy National Consultancy Report.* Canberra: Australian Government Publishing Service.

Taylor, J. (2008). Indigenous peoples and indicators of well-being: Australian perspectives on United Nations global frameworks. *Social Indicators Research, 87*(1), 111–126.

Taylor, J. (2009). Indigenous demography and public policy in Australia: Population or peoples? *Journal of Population Research, 26*(2), 115–130.

Taylor, J. (2013). Data for better Indigenous policy evaluation: Achievements, constraints and opportunities. In Productivity Commission (Ed.), *Better Indigenous policies: The role of evaluation, Roundtable Proceedings* (pp. 119–130). Canberra: Productivity Commission.

Taylor, J., Doran, B., Parriman, M., & Yu, E. (2012). *Statistics for community governance: The Yawuru Indigenous population survey of Broome.* CAEPR Working Paper 82, CAEPR, ANU, Canberra.

Taylor, J., Doran, B., Parriman, M., & Yu, E. (2014). Statistics for community governance: The Yawuru Indigenous population survey. *International Indigenous Policy Journal, 5*(2), 1–31.

Te Aho, L. (2010). Indigenous challenges to enhance freshwater governance and management in Aotearoa-New Zealand: The Waikato River settlement. *The Journal of Water Law, 20*(5), 285–292.

Tesfaghiorghis, H. (1991). *Geographic variations in the economic status of Aboriginal people: A preliminary investigation.* CAEPR Discussion Paper 2, CAEPR, ANU, Canberra.

Thin, N. (2009). Why anthropology can ill afford to ignore well-being. In G. Mathews & C. Izquierdo (Eds.), *Pursuits of happiness: Well-being in anthropological perspective* (pp. 23–44). London: Berghahn.

Thin, N. (2012). Counting and recounting happiness and culture: On happiness surveys and prudential ethnobiography. *International Journal of Wellbeing, 2*(4), 313–332.

Tiberius, V. (2006). Well-being: Psychological research for philosophers. *Philosophy Compass, 1*(5), 493–505.

Tsey, K., Whiteside, M., Deemal, A., & Gibson, T. (2003). Social determinants of health, the 'control factor' and the Family Wellbeing Empowerment Program. *Australasian Psychiatry, 11*(s1), 34–39.

UN. (2007). *United Nations Declaration on the Rights of Indigenous Peoples.* United Nations, New York.

Waldmüller, J. (2014). Buen vivir, sumak kawsay, good living: An introduction and overview. *Alternautas, 1*(1), 17–28.

Walter, M. (2010). The politics of the data: How the Australian statistical indigene is constructed. *International Journal of Critical Indigenous Studies, 3*(2), 45–56.

Walter, M. (2013). The 2014 National Aboriginal and Torres Strait Islander Social Survey is an anachronism. *Online Opinion,* 6 August.

Walter, M. (2016). Data politics and Indigenous representation in Australian statistics. In T. Kukutai & J. Taylor (Eds.), *Indigenous data sovereignty: Towards an agenda* (pp. 79–98). Canberra: ANU Press.

Walter, M., & Andersen, C. (2013). *Indigenous statistics: A quantitative research methodology,* Walnut Creek, CA: West Coast Press.

Watene, K. (2016a). Valuing nature: Māori philosophy and the capability approach. *Oxford Development Studies, 44*(3), 287–296.

Watene, K. (2016b). Indigenous peoples and justice. In K. Watene & J. Drydyk (Eds.), *Theorising justice: Novel insights and future directions* (pp. 133–152). London: Rowman and Littlefield International.

White, S.C. (2016). Introduction: The many faces of wellbeing. In S.C. White & C. Blackmore (Eds.), *Culture of wellbeing: Method, place and policy* (pp. 1–44). Basingstoke: Palgrave Macmillan.

White, S., & Blackmore, C. (2016). *Culture of wellbeing: Method, place and policy.* Basingstoke: Palgrave Macmillan.

Willeto, A. (2012). Happiness in Navajos (Dine BA Hozho). In H. Selin & G. Davey (Eds.), *Happiness across cultures: View of happiness and quality of life in non-Western cultures* (pp. 377–386). Dordrecht: Springer.

Yap, M., & Biddle, N. (2009). *Towards a gender-related index for Indigenous Australians.* CAEPR Working Paper 52, CAEPR, ANU, Canberra.

Yap, M., & Biddle, N. (2010). Gender gaps in Indigenous socioeconomic outcomes: Australian regional comparisons and international possibilities. *International Indigenous Policy Journal, 1*(2), 1–27.

Yap, M., & Yu, E. (2016a). *Community wellbeing from the ground-up: A Yawuru example.* BCEC Report 3.

Yap, M., & Yu, E. (2016b). Operationalising the capability approach: Developing culturally relevant indicators of indigenous wellbeing – an Australian example. *Oxford Development Studies, 44*(3), 315–331.

Yawuru RNTBC. (2011). *Walyjala-jala buru jayida jarringgun Nyamba Yawuru ngan-ga mirlimirli: Planning for the future: Yawuru Cultural Management Plan.* Broome, WA: Pindan Printing Pty Ltd.

Yawuru RNTBC. (2013). Submission to the Standing Committee on Environment and Public Affairs: Inquiry into the implications for Western Australia of Hydraulic Fracturing for Unconventional Gas.

Yu, P. (2012). *The power of data in Aboriginal hands.* CAEPR Topical Issue 4, CAEPR, ANU, Canberra.

Zubrick, S.R., Shepherd, C.C.J., Dudgeon, P., Gee, G., Paradies, Y., Scrine, C., & Walker, R. (2014). Social determinants of social and emotional wellbeing. In P. Dudgeon, H. Milroy, & R. Walker (Eds.), *Working together: Aboriginal and Torres Strait Islander mental health and wellbeing principles and practice* (pp. 93–112). Canberra: Department of The Prime Minister and Cabinet.

PART V

Subjective wellbeing

23

SUBJECTIVE WELLBEING OF ABORIGINAL PEOPLES OF CANADA

Shashi Kant, Ilan Vertinsky and Bin Zheng

Introduction

Aboriginal peoples of Canada include Indians or First Nations, Inuit and Métis. First Nations and Inuit are indigenous people of Canada while the Métis have mixed ancestry of First Nations and European peoples. Inuit are from Arctic areas of North America while First Nations historically lived below the Arctic region. As per the 2011 census, there were about 1.4 million (about 4.3% of the Canadian population) Aboriginal people. First Nations, Métis, and Inuit peoples constitute about 60.8 percent, 32.3 percent and 4.2 percent respectively of the Aboriginal population of Canada (Statistics Canada, 2013).

Legislation known as the Indian Act was first introduced in 1876 to superimpose European culture over First Nations culture. This is the principal statue to govern the Indian status, First Nations governments and the management of reserve land – land set aside by the Canadian government for use by First Nations people. The Act has been amended many times, most recently in 1984. The Act pertains to First Nations people only and Inuit and Métis are not covered under the Act. The Indians who are registered under the Indian Act are known as Status Indians and these people may or may not live on designated Indian reserves. Non-status Indians identify themselves with Indian people but are not registered under the Indian Act. As per 2011 census, about 74.9 percent First Nations people were Registered Indians, and nearly one-half of them lived on Indian reserves while other First Nations peoples live in urban areas (Statistics Canada, 2013).

The Inuit and Metis are considered 'nations' in themselves but under the First Nations umbrella there are numerous nations. Six hundred and seventeen First Nations communities represent more than 50 cultural groups (Aboriginal Affairs and Northern Development Canada, 2013). The Royal Commission on Aboriginal Peoples (1996) defined Aboriginal peoples as nations because "they are political and cultural groups with values and lifeways distinct from those of other Canadians." These are known as nations because "they were nations when they forged military and trade alliances with [*the colonizing*] European nations. They were nations when they signed treaties to share their lands and resources. And they are nations today – in their coherence, their distinctiveness and their understanding of themselves" (Aboriginal Affairs and Northern Development Canada, 2013b, p. 15).

The historical relationship of Aboriginal people is enshrined in Section 35 of the Constitution of Canada. The United Nations Declaration on the Rights of Indigenous Peoples, adopted on 13 September 2007, also recognized a wide range of individual and collective rights of Aboriginal peoples. However, various historical events, such as colonization, treaty negotiations, infringement on Aboriginal land rights and the residential school system, have had a significant negative impact on the wellbeing of Aboriginal people (King et al., 2009), and as a consequence a developing or underdeveloped world of Aboriginal people exists within the developed world of Canada. The dominant reason for this disastrous outcome is the continuous belief of various governments of Canada in the supremacy of Western culture over Indigenous cultures. The current prime minister of Canada, Justin Trudeau, on 8 December 2015, articulated the need for new relationships with First Nations peoples based on nation-to-nation relationships and a sacred obligation to uphold the constitutionally guaranteed rights of First Nations in Canada (Mas, 2015). The necessary and critical element, however, for building successful and respectful relationships with Aboriginal people is to develop an understanding of the basic differences between the worldviews of Aboriginal and European peoples, and to respect and incorporate the Aboriginal worldviews in the policies designed for their welfare (Morgan et al., 1997; Mussell et al., 2005). The Aboriginal worldview is based on respecting and living in harmony with nature, non-possession, collectivism and seeing all things as interconnected to each other, while the European worldview is based on control over nature, materialism, individualism and deductive methods of learning (Mussell et al., 2005).

In Aboriginal worldviews, human wellbeing is a holistic concept in which physical, mental, emotional and spiritual dimensions are balanced, and Mother Earth plays a critical role in their wellbeing. However, most efforts of measurement of Aboriginal wellbeing have been focused on conventional objective single measures of economic prosperity such as income, employment and education (The National Aboriginal Economic Development Board, 2015) or standard composite indices based on objective measures such as the Human Development Index and the Community Wellbeing Index (Cooke, Beavon, & McHardy, 2004; McHardy & O'Sullivan, 2004, 2006; Sacha et al., 2008). These measures focus on the physical dimension of wellbeing and are unable to measure the multiple dimensions of Aboriginal wellbeing, ignoring the foundations of Aboriginal worldviews.

In recent years, Aboriginal peoples have articulated their concept of wellbeing in terms of Holistic Lifelong Learning Models while researchers working on Aboriginal wellbeing have included measurements of subjective wellbeing in their tool kit to measure and analyze the wellbeing of Canadian Aboriginal peoples. This chapter provides the current state of research on the subjective wellbeing of Aboriginal peoples of Canada, and suggests future research directions.

In the next section, we provide an overview of Aboriginal peoples' conceptualization of wellbeing in terms of lifelong learning. It is followed by a discussion of the current state of research on subjective wellbeing of Aboriginal peoples of Canada; we divide our discussion into three categories – subjective wellbeing expressed in terms of some indicators such as psychological distress and self-esteem; subjective wellbeing measured by the concept of overall wellbeing or general life satisfaction; and subjective wellbeing represented by a composite of satisfaction with different domains of life. Finally, we discuss the current state of research, draw conclusions and make recommendations for future research.

Aboriginal conceptualization of learning and wellbeing

In 2007, the Canadian Council on Learning (CCL) with the Aboriginal Education Research Centre at the University of Saskatchewan and the First Nations Adult Higher Education

Consortium in collaboration with Aboriginal learning experts and the National Aboriginal Organizations in Canada developed three Holistic Life-Long Learning Models – one each for First Nations, Metis and Inuit. Each model uses a graphical representation to capture the power of holistic lifelong learning and its relationships to wellbeing. These models are living documents to be updated and revised as the respective communities, organizations, researchers and governments continue to explore and learn from the use of these models. The basic foundations of all three models are similar – holistic approach to lifelong learning and its relations to wellbeing, but the graphics and terminology used are slightly different. Hence, next we discuss The First Nations Holistic Lifelong Learning Model (FNHLLM) with some detail on the Metis and the Inuit models more briefly. This discussion is based on chapter 4 of Canadian Council on Learning (2007) and readers can refer to this document for further details regarding the models.

In the First Nations worldview, learning is holistic and a lifelong process that develops knowledge, skills, values and wisdom required to respect and protect nature and to ensure sustainability of life forever. The holistic nature of learning contributes to individual as well as community wellbeing. The FNHLLM (Figure 23.1) has four components captured in a stylized graphic of a living tree: (i) the sources and domains of knowledge represented by the roots; (ii) the individual's learning cycle represented by the rings; (iii) the individual's personal development process represented by the branches; and (iv) the community's wellbeing represented by the leaves. The model captures the circular, cumulative, experiential and holistic nature of the First Nations learning and wellbeing.

The FNHLLM represents the sources and domains of knowledge by ten roots that support the learner (the tree). These roots represent the foundations of First Nations peoples' learning based on an individual's relations with nature and people. Relations with people include self, family, ancestors, clan, community, nation and other nations, as well as experiences with languages, traditions and ceremonies. The representation of the sources and domains of knowledge by

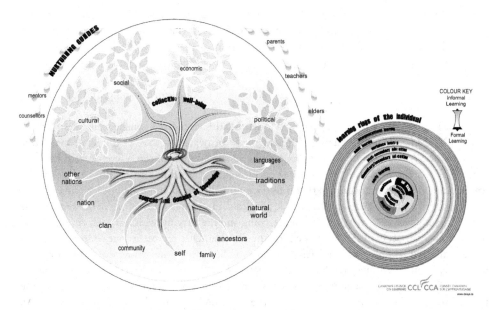

Figure 23.1 First Nations' Holistic Lifelong Learning Model
Source: CCL (2007).

roots indicates that First Nations people draw their nourishment from a rich heritage of beliefs, values, traditions and practices of balanced relations with all living and deceased members of the community and nation as well as with nature.

Seven Learning Rings of an individual are depicted by the cross-sectional view of the trunk of the tree. Indigenous and Western knowledge are at the core of the tree representing complementarity of two learning approaches. The core is surrounded by the four dimensions of personal development: spiritual, emotional, physical and mental; learning is experienced through these dimensions. The rings portray a lifelong learning process that begins at birth with early childhood learning and progresses through elementary, secondary and post-secondary education, to adult skills training and employment. The rings also affirm the role of formal and informal learning settings such as in the home, on the land or in the school, and this range of learning opportunities facilitates intergenerational transmission of knowledge; the seven rings depict that each generation is responsible to ensure the survival of seven generations.

The FNHLLM depicts four dimensions of their being/personal development – physical, emotional, mental and spiritual – as radiating upward from the trunk into the four branches – each branch representing one dimension of personal development. The individual learns to balance the four dimensions of personal development to experience harmony/life satisfaction. From each branch grows a cluster of leaves representing the four branches of collective well-being — cultural, economic, political and social. Nurturing guides such as elders, teachers, parents, mentors and counsellors are depicted by raindrops, and these guides offer opportunities for mental, spiritual, emotional and physical development throughout the lifespan. Vibrant colors represent well-developed aspects of collective wellbeing. Similar to fallen leaves providing nourishment to the roots to support the tree, community's wellbeing rejuvenates the individual's learning and wellbeing.

The premise of the FNHLLM is that:

> the First Nation learner dwells in a world of continual reformation, where interactive cycles, rather than disconnected events, occur. In this world, nothing is simply a cause or an effect, but is instead the expression of the interconnectedness of life. These relationships are circular, rather than linear, holistic and cumulative, instead of compartmentalized.
>
> (Canadian Council on Learning, 2007, p. 19)

The Métis Holistic Lifelong Learning Model (MHLLM) follows similar principles to those of the FNHLLM but uses a slightly different mode of depiction though the same living tree model. In the Métis worldview, learning is done in the context of the 'Sacred Act of Living a Good Life'. In the MHLLM: (i) the tree's roots depicts the economic, health, physical, political, social and spiritual conditions that influence individual and community wellbeing; (ii) the trunk's core includes the emotional, mental, physical and spiritual dimensions of the self; (iii) the outer rings illustrate the stages of lifelong learning and the varying width of each ring indicates that learning can occur at different rates; (iv) the four branches represent four sources of knowledge – the self, people, land and language and traditions; (v) the clusters of leaves on each branch represent the domains of knowledge, such as knowledge of languages and understanding of the land; and (vi) the integration of Western and Métis learning approaches is captured by the iconic image of the red Métis sash. In brief, the MHLLM captures the Metis worldview: "All life – and all learning – is interconnected through relationships that involve contributing to and benefitting from the well-being of each living entity… By respecting the physical and spiritual laws that govern the Natural Order, individual and collective balance and harmony are maintained" (Canadian Council on Learning, 2007, p. 22).

The Inuit Holistic Lifelong Learning Model (IHLLM) is also based on cyclical and holistic learning, different stages of learning, learning experiences in formal and informal settings, and complementarity of Inuit and Western learning approaches. However, it uses a stylized graphic of an Inuit blanket toss (a common game of Inuit people) and a circular path, and it has its roots in *Inuit Qaujimajatuqangit* (IQ) meaning Inuit Values and Beliefs. The model portrays thirty-eight community members, each representing an Inuit value and belief, holding up a learning blanket. The ancestors' acknowledgement of the role of naming a scared tradition that fosters identity, kinship relations and intergenerational transmission of knowledge is captured. The sources and domains of knowledge and their sub-domains are also included within the learning blanket and illustrated by images of Inuit life. The circular shape of the blanket reflects interconnectedness of all life and therefore links between the past, present and future.

In summary, all three models identify emotional, mental, physical and spiritual dimensions of the self, and learning and wellbeing being rooted in relations with other people and nature. Hence, as per the Aboriginal peoples' worldview depicted through these learning models, Aboriginal peoples' wellbeing cannot be measured by one-dimensional measures of economic prosperity. The measures of Aboriginal peoples' wellbeing should incorporate emotional, mental, physical and spiritual dimensions of the self, and their relations with nature and other people; this may be possible only through comprehensive subjective measures of wellbeing. In the next section, we discuss briefly the objective measures of Aboriginal wellbeing and their limitations, and after that we return to subjective measures.

Aboriginal peoples' subjective wellbeing

The multidimensional nature of human wellbeing has been well accepted (McGillivray, 2007), and its measurement approaches have been grouped in two broad categories (Conceição & Bandura, 2008): objective indicators, such as the Physical Quality of Life Index (PQLI) and the Human Development Index (HDI), to complement or replace single economic measures of GDP or income, and subjective measures such as self-reported life satisfaction, which is usually called subjective wellbeing – an expression for the perceived quality of life and the positive emotions that an individual experiences. Diener (1984) identified the affective and the cognitive components of subjective wellbeing. The affective component is an instantaneous feeling while the cognitive part is an ex-post and retrospective assessment of the quality of life (Sumner, 1996). Subjective wellbeing is based on purely subjective evaluations and measures of subjective wellbeing are self-reported and self-evaluative, which are solicited through a survey using an ordinal scale. Usually the cognitive component in subjective wellbeing is called 'life satisfaction' or 'happiness' (Andrews & Whitey, 1976). Some scholars differentiate between life satisfaction – reflecting individuals' perceived distance from their aspirations – and happiness – a balance between positive and negative effect – but economists have used these two terms interchangeably as a measure of subjective wellbeing (Easterlin, 2004).

In this chapter, our focus is on subjective wellbeing elicited from individuals on a satisfaction scale. Most scholars have used a single measure of subjective wellbeing – the overall or general wellbeing or satisfaction or happiness, and have used various social, economic and demographic factors, such as income, employment, education, gender, family-level social capital, faith, community involvement and friends and neighbors, to explain the variations across individuals and nations (Helliwell & Putnam, 2004). For example, some studies, using cross-country and panel data, have found that the average satisfaction remains relatively constant over time in spite of a large increase in income per capita, called the Easterlin paradox (Easterlin, 1974). In contrast, other studies, using within country cross-sectional and panel data, have found a positive correlation between individual income and individual measures of subjective wellbeing (Blanchflower & Oswald, 2004; Clark et al., 2008; Deaton, 2008). More importantly, research has found evidence of diminishing returns in income at both the individual and national levels, so increases in income have a larger effect on subjective wellbeing among low income groups (Diener & Biswas-Diener, 2002). The effects of education are stronger among individuals with low incomes and those living in poorer nations (Diener et al., 1999). Kapteyn et al. (2010) have reported a high association between health and life satisfaction.

Another stream of scholars have recognized the multidimensional nature of subjective wellbeing encompassing all aspects of human life, and have used satisfaction with multiple domains of life as a measure of subjective wellbeing. Multiple domains used by various scholars include leisure, marriage, work, standard of living, friendships, sex life and health domains (Heady & Wearing, 1992); material, health, productivity, intimacy, safety, community and emotional domains (Cummins, 1996); and money, health, work, social relationships, leisure, housing and education domains (Argyle, 2001). Van Praag and Ferrer-I-Carbonell (2004) used satisfaction from six domains of life (financial, job, housing, leisure, environment and health) to explain the differences in overall satisfaction using data from the UK and Germany.

Scholars that study the wellbeing of Aboriginal peoples of Canada have used the subjective wellbeing approach sparingly, but these scholars have used both approaches of subjective wellbeing. There are also some studies that have not used these two approaches, but rather have used the concept of subjective wellbeing to evaluate the contributions of some factors to Aboriginal peoples' wellbeing or tried to compare the subjective wellbeing among different groups/sections of Aboriginal people. These studies have used some indicators of subjective wellbeing such as psychological distress and self-esteem. Next, we discuss studies from these three categories separately.

Aboriginal peoples' subjective wellbeing studies that used some indicators of subjective wellbeing

A number of isolated studies that use multidimensional and inter-disciplinary approaches to understand and analyze different aspects of First Nations wellbeing have included various elements/components of the holistic model discussed in the previous section. For example, psychological distress, part of mental and emotional wellbeing, among the Cree of James Bay was analyzed by Kirmayer et al. (2000). The authors used the data for 1,136 Cree (aged 15–85) from a general population health survey in 1991 conducted by Santé Québec. Psychological distress was measured by a fourteen-item index adapted by Santé Québec from the Ilfeld Psychiatric Symptom Index (Ilfeld, 1976). Using multivariate analysis, the authors found that a good relationship with others in the community and spending more time in the bush reduced psychological stress while having fewer than five friends increased psychological stress.

Schiff and Moore (2006) analyzed the impact of sweat lodge ceremony on physical, mental, emotional and spiritual domains of wellbeing. The authors used two questionnaires – SF-36[R] (Ware et al. 1998) and the Heroic Myth Index (Pearson, 1991). The SF-36[R] consists of thirty-six items and provides a generic measure of physical and mental health. Similarly, in the absence of any specific Aboriginal-specific measurement instrument of spiritual and emotional wellbeing, the Heroic Myth Index (HMI) was used to measure these two aspects of spirituality. The HMI consists of seventy-two items constructed into twelve scales representing personality types; the twelve scales are grouped into three sets of four scales each, which measure aspects of ego, soul and the self. The participants were asked to complete both surveys before and after the ceremony; thirty-nine complete sets of responses were collected by researchers. Among respondents, 59 percent were Aboriginal and 41 percent non-Aboriginal. The authors found that participants were more similar in spiritual and emotional dimensions after the ceremony than before.

The role of cultural identity clarity in personal identity, self-esteem and subjective wellbeing was analyzed by Usborne and Taylor (2010). The study covered the samples of undergraduate students, anglophone Quebecers, francophone Québécois, Chinese North Americans and Aboriginal Canadians. The sample of Aboriginal Canadian included members of the Yellowknives Dene First Nation from the Northwest Territories. A questionnaire was used to collect data. The questionnaire included three questions on cultural identity (derived from the Cultural Identity Clarity Scale developed by the authors), four questions on personal identity (derived from the Self-Concept Clarity Scale; Campbell et al., 1996), five questions on self-esteem (derived from the Rosenberg Self-Esteem Scale; Rosenberg, 1965) and a mood scale asking participants how often in the past week they felt depressed, confident, tired, hopeful, worried and happy. A ten-point Likert scale was used for all questions. A total of seventy-six members (fifty-six women and twenty men) participated in the research. The relationship between cultural identity clarity and personal identity clarity was significant at the 5% significance level, while between cultural identity clarity and positivity was significant at the 10% level. In the test of self-identity as a mediator, there was no significant direct effect of cultural identity clarity on self-esteem and self-identity clarity significantly predicted self-esteem. However, the indirect effect of cultural identity clarity on self-esteem via self-identity clarity was significant. Similar effects were obtained after controlling for the age and gender of participants.

These three studies provide just a few examples of the studies that fall in this category of studies. The main feature of this group is their focus on factors such as language, religion and gender on subjective wellbeing or some indicator of subjective wellbeing such as psychological distress of Aboriginal peoples of Canada. Generally, in secondary data-based studies, Aboriginal sample is one of the samples covered in the studies; and in primary data-based studies, the sample size is very small – normally restricted to one First Nation or one location.

Aboriginal peoples' wellbeing based on overall/general life satisfaction

Generally, Aboriginal peoples living on-reserve are not included in most general-purpose surveys organized by government agencies such as Statistics Canada. Hence, there are very few data sources on life satisfaction of Aboriginal people, specifically data sources that cover all three groups of Aboriginal people of Canada. Scholars, therefore, have used some special purpose surveys as their data sources to study subjective wellbeing of Aboriginal peoples. Due to this data limitation, the number of studies based on overall wellbeing is quite limited.

The role of ethnicity, including Aboriginal background, in life satisfaction of the Canadian people was analyzed by Fernando (2002) using data from 1997 National Survey of Giving, Volunteering and Participating. In this survey, life satisfaction was measured on a four-point Likert scale (1 – very dissatisfied, 2 – somewhat dissatisfied, 3 – somewhat satisfied, 4 – very satisfied). These data included the sample of 17,109 individuals aged 15 and older, but the sample excluded the residents of Yukon and Northwest Territories, and persons living on Indian Reserves. Hence, the sample, in a way, included only those Aboriginal people who were living within non-Aboriginal populations. The author found that the average satisfaction of Aboriginal people was 3.15 against the sample average of 3.35; the proportion of dissatisfied (either very or somewhat) people was 13 percent among Aboriginal people against 7 percent among the total sample, and this proportion was highest among all ethnic groups; and among younger and older people, Aboriginal people were least satisfied. Multivariate analysis indicated that variations in life satisfaction are mostly attributable to demographic, social, economic, attitudinal and residential factors and ethnic background did not have much predictive power. However, in the multivariate model that included ethnic and other covariates, the coefficient of the Aboriginal dummy variable was -0.18 and significant at 5% level, which was the highest negative coefficient among all ethnic dummy variables. Hence, the study provides some evidence of lower life satisfaction of Aboriginal people living as a minority within largely non-Aboriginal populations and does not cover the majority of the Aboriginal people in Canada.

Overall quality of life and health status of Aboriginal residential schools survivors, Aboriginals who did not attend residential schools and non-Aboriginals living in Bella Coola valley in British Columbia were compared by Barton et al. (2005). They used data from the Determinants of Health and Quality of Life Survey 2001 (Michalos et al., 2005). The survey had one question on overall quality of life that used a seven-point Likert scale (1 – very dissatisfied and 7 – very satisfied). The dataset includes forty-seven Aboriginal residential school survivors, sixty Aboriginal non-residential school attendees and ninety-four non-Aboriginal people. The mean values for the response to the question on overall quality of life (Q.18) were 4.9, 5.5 and 5.7 for Aboriginal residential school survivors, Aboriginal no-residential school attendees and non-Aboriginals, respectively. The mean value for residential school survivors was significantly (at 1% level) lower than the mean value for non-Aboriginals as well as non-residential school attendees. The authors also analyzed the differences in health status and chronic disease prevalence rates among these three groups of residents.

Overall life satisfaction among Aboriginal peoples in the Canadian prairies was examined by Barrington-Leigh and Sloman (2016). The authors used data from two components of the Equality, Security and Community Survey (ESC) Project of the Institute for Social Research at York University, Toronto, Canada, and the General Social Survey, Cycle 24 (GSS24), conducted by Statistics Canada. Wave 2 of the ESC, the General ESC survey, was completed during 2002 and 2003, and included 5,654 respondents from all ten provinces. In 2004 and 2005, a modified ESC questionnaire to reflect Aboriginal context was used to collect data from 6,084 self-identified Aboriginal respondents from Aboriginal reserves as well as Aboriginal urban populations from Manitoba, Saskatchewan and Alberta; the data from this survey are referred to as the Aboriginal ESC survey. The GSS 24 data are from the year 2010, and this sample consists of randomly selected Canadian households (n=15,390). The authors constructed an Aboriginal subsample (n=579) from GSS 24 data using an Aboriginal identification indicator in the dataset; this sub-sample is referred to as the Aboriginal GSS sample. The ESC and GSS surveys use the same life satisfaction question and used a ten-point (1 – dissatisfied and 10 – satisfied) Likert scale.

The authors found mean values of Satisfied with Life (SWL) scores of 8.2, 7.9, 7.6 and 7.4 for the respondents of ESC General, ESC Aboriginal, GSS General and GSS Aboriginal, respectively, which indicate that the mean self-reported SWL scores in the Aboriginal ESC sample is closer to the mean score in the general ESC sample, and the same is true with the General GSS and Aboriginal GSS. However, socioeconomic variables such as income and employment are not the same for general and Aboriginal ESC samples. For example, household income for the General ESC sample is $57,000 and for the Aboriginal ESC sample it is $34,000; the unemployment rate in the General ESC sample is 5.9 percent compared to 19 percent in the Aboriginal ESC sample; and the high school completion rate of the general ESC sample is 84 percent compared to 50 percent of the Aboriginal ESC sample.

The authors also calculated the point estimates of the effects of several variables on SWL scores, and found that the effects of family, friends, gender and number of children on SWL in the Aboriginal ESC sample are as much as double compared to their magnitudes in the general population. The most interesting finding was a negative association between household income and SWL among on-reserve Aboriginal respondents in stark contrast to the positive coefficient estimated for the general Canadian population sample and also coefficients reported in the literature based on samples from different countries. The results also did not provide any evidence of the expected positive association between income and SWL score of the off-reserve Aboriginal peoples in the GSS and ESC samples.

The authors argued that for such discrepancies (i.e. similar SWL score for Aboriginal and general respondents and negative relationship between income and SWL scores for Aboriginal people), there might be two alternative explanations. The first is that there is a problem with SWL measures and thus the SWL scores should not be trusted. The second suggests that the importance of different life-supporting factors varies with context. Their conclusion is that basing policy decisions on SWL scores is either wrong or, in the best case, very difficult.

We contend that what was explained by the authors as a discrepancy resulting from a flawed measurement is a true reflection of fundamental differences between Aboriginals and the European worldviews with respect to the weights placed on different domains of life – differences unaccounted by the authors. For example, the authors did not include, in their regression, variables related to land and/or nature and thus could not capture the role of relationship with nature in Aboriginal being. Other evidence for the need for a better understanding of the impact of the deep differences between the Aboriginal and European worldviews is related to the impacts of seeing family and friends on SWL. These were almost double in the Aboriginal ESC sample compared to the general population, highlighting the importance of relationships with people (family and friends) in Aboriginal wellbeing.

Aboriginal peoples' subjective wellbeing based on satisfaction with multiple domains of life

All three Holistic Learning Models, previously discussed, clearly stipulated multiple domains associated with Aboriginal peoples' wellbeing. If one accepts the proposition that the framework for assessment of wellbeing is endogenous, the concept of satisfaction with multiple domains of life is the one that is aligned more with Canada's aboriginal peoples' culture and worldview. Furthermore, the definitions of domains, the satisfaction with domains, the interrelationships between satisfactions of various domains and the view of those factors, which drive the level of satisfaction within each domain, should reflect the perceptions, beliefs and judgment of the peoples of the community being assessed.

Kant, Vertinsky, Zheng, and Smith (2014) and Kant, Vertinsky, and Zheng (2016) used the concept of multiple domains of satisfaction to assess First Nations peoples' wellbeing in Canada. These papers focus on the wellbeing of On-Reserve First Nations (ORFN) people in Ontario and British Columbia. The two papers analyze different aspects of wellbeing using the same dataset that was generated through the unique participatory approach rooted in Aboriginal culture. We first describe data collection methods, followed by important findings.

The authors collected data using a three-step participatory approach, and Aboriginal peoples actively participated in all three steps. The first step involved open-ended discussions with members of band office and elders regarding cultural perspectives and wellbeing of First Nations people. Each discussion started with the researchers' explanation of the objectives of the project and the main purpose of discussion. After introduction, the researchers were mainly listeners and recorders. In the second step, semi-structured interviews were conducted with elders and focus groups. These were organized to identify domains of First Nations peoples' wellbeing and contributing factors to each domain. Following the introduction of the project and process, participant(s) were requested to suggest domains of wellbeing important to satisfaction with their lives. Once the list of domains was complete, the participant(s) were requested to identify factors and their measurement units that may contribute to the satisfaction with each domain. In the final step, a preliminary questionnaire was designed using the domains and their contributing factors that were identified in the second step; the questionnaire included questions on: (i) social, economic and demographic variables; (ii) satisfaction with each domain as well as overall satisfaction with life in general; and (iii) factors that contribute to the satisfaction with each of the different domains. The questionnaire was finalized after incorporating the inputs from the people who participated in the identification of domains and potential contributing factors, and the results of a pre-testing exercise.

On the basis of discussions and suggestions by participants, a household, and not an individual, was used as the unit of analysis. Life and domain satisfaction questions were about household's satisfaction, and all satisfaction questions used a seven-point (1 – worst possible satisfaction and 7 – best possible satisfaction) Likert scale. The question to measure overall household satisfaction with life was:

> *After evaluation of your satisfaction with different domains of life, where on the ladder below do you rate your household's satisfaction with life as a whole for a period of one year preceding this survey?*

Domain's satisfaction questions were similar to the overall life satisfaction question. The state of influencing factors was measured during the same period of one year. Three types of measurement scales were used to measure factors: (i) actual units such as years and dollars, (ii) binary (yes/no) response and (iii) rating on Likert scale; details of all factors and their measurement units are provided in Table 23.1.

The final questionnaire was hand delivered by a postdoctoral fellow to all households where an adult was available. Completed questionnaires were collected one week later. The response rate was 90 percent. Some 315 questionnaires with complete information were collected (167 completed by males and 148 by females). To note, the survey was designed to measure a household's satisfaction, not individual-person satisfaction.

The First Nations participants identified seven domains – land use, social and cultural, education, income, employment, health and housing; the inclusion of land use activities as a domain is a clear departure from the existing literature, and indicator of differences between First Nations and European worldviews. Similarly, identification of various land use, social and cultural factors (such as factors related to gathering, trapping, traditional diets, ceremonies, cultural sites and spiritual activities) and unique factors related to health (such as frequent and occasional occurrence of problems related to internal organs, external organs and mental state) confirm the distinctive features of First Nations worldviews and cultures.

Using First Nations peoples' inputs, Kant, Vertinsky, Zheng, and Smith (2014) conceptualized a multi-domain life satisfaction model that included six domains – social, cultural and land use (SCLU), income, education, employment, health and housing. It should be noted that, in the analysis, the domains of social and cultural activities and land use activities were combined (social, cultural and land use domain) due to very high correlations in the satisfaction scores of these two domains. Path analysis models were estimated for overall wellbeing and each domain of wellbeing.

The mean values of overall wellbeing and domains' wellbeing for men and women respondents from Ontario and British Columbia (BC) First Nations are provided in

Table 23.1 Explanation and measurement of influencing factors of different domains

	Details of factor	Measurement units
AcceCultu	Access to First Nation's cultural sites	LS1[a]
Age	Age of the head of household	Year
BreWinPay	Satisfaction with breadwinner's total pay	LS1
BreWorkdays	Breadwinner's work days per week	Hours
Ceremony	Frequency of household participation in cultural ceremonies	LS2[b]
Children	Number of children younger than 16 years in household	#
ChildEdu	Perception of transmission of traditional knowledge in children education	LS1
Gatherhrs	Average hours per day spent on gathering	Hours
GatherQualit	Quality of time spent on gathering	LS1
Gathers	Numbers of people in household that gather wild produce	#
ExtOrgFreq	Frequent occurrence of external organ illnesses in household	Yes/No
HealServ	Satisfaction with government health services	LS1
HousTitle	Ownership of house	Yes/No
HousSpac	Satisfaction with space in house	LS1
HousLoc	Satisfaction with the location of house	LS1
HousMaint	Satisfaction with house maintenance	LS1
IntOrgFreq	Frequent occurrence of internal organ illnesses in household	Yes/No
LawLanduse	Satisfaction with the government laws that influence household's land use activities	LS1
LawCultu	Satisfaction with the government laws that influence household's cultural and social life	LS1
Logbrinc	Log of breadwinner's total income	
MaritalStatus	Respondent's marital status	Yes/No
MentalFreq	Frequent occurrence of mental and psychological problems in household	Yes/No
MentalOc	Occasional occurrence of mental and psychological problems in household	Yes/No
SocTies	Sense of belonging to local community and social ties	LS1
SpouUnemFull	Spouse of breadwinner is full time unemployed	Yes/No
SpouEdu	Education level of spouse	LS1
Spiritual	Household freedom to participate in spiritual activities	LS1
StatCSAreas	State of areas of cultural significance	LS1
TradDiets	Percentage of typical household meal that comes from traditional foods (diets obtained from land use activities such as hunting, fishing, gathering, etc.)	%
TrapInc	The percentage of income attributable to trapping	%
Trappers	Number of trappers in household	#
Traphrs	Average number of hours per day spent on trapping	Hours
Unemplfull	Breadwinner is full-time unemployed	Yes/No

Notes:

a LS1: Likert Scale 1 (four-point scale, 1 = very low, 4 = very high).

b LS2: Likert Scale 2 (three-point scale, 0 = never, 1 = occasionally, 2 = often).

Source: Kant et al. (2014).

Table 23.2. The overall wellbeing for both communities was higher than 5.0, and all domain's satisfaction levels, except health, were between 4 and 5, while the health domain's satisfaction was higher than 5 for all groups. The satisfaction levels of Ontario's First Nations peoples were higher than BC First Nation peoples in all domains, and the differences were statistically significant at the 1% level for overall wellbeing and the housing domain, and at 10% for health and the education domains. The satisfaction levels of female respondents were higher with their households' health domain than those of males (significant at the 5% level), but lower than those of men with the SCLU and employment domains (significant at the 1% and 10% levels, respectively).

The path coefficients of the overall wellbeing model indicate that in addition to the direct contributions to overall wellbeing, the SCLU domain contributed indirectly to the overall wellbeing through the health domain. The education and employment domains contributed indirectly through the income domain. The ranking of domains for their total contributions (in terms of their unstandardized path coefficients) to the overall wellbeing for females was: (i) SCLU; (ii) education; (iii) income; (iv) health; (v) housing; and (vi) employment; and for males the ranking was (i) SCLU and income; (iii) health; (iv) housing; (v) employment; and (vi) education. The total contribution of the employment, health, housing and income domains to overall wellbeing was not significantly different between the male and female models. Results were consistent with the ORFN peoples' worldview that emphasizes the strong inter-relations between different domains.

The path coefficients indicate that the SCLU domain was the most important domain and the health domain was as important as the income domain for both males and females. The unstandardized path coefficients indicate that an increase of 1 unit in the SCLU domain increases overall satisfaction by 0.228 units (0.192 units directly and 0.036 units indirectly through the health domain) for the female model, and 0.136 units (0.100 unit directly and 0.036 units indirectly through health domain) for the male model. The unstandardized path coefficients from the education domain to overall wellbeing were 0.138 and 0.026 for females

Table 23.2 Average levels and standard deviations of overall wellbeing and domains' satisfaction

	Average for all households N=315	*Average for Ontario's people* N=203	*Average for BC's people* N=112	*Average for all female responses* N=148	*Average for all male responses* N=167
Overall wellbeing	5.12 (0.86)	5.30*** (0.94)	5.02*** (0.81)	5.21 (0.97)	5.11 (0.82)
SCLU domain	4.50 (1.22)	4.62 (1.30)	4.44 (1.17)	4.24*** (1.32)	4.54*** (1.25)
Income domain	4.57 (1.16)	4.70 (1.38)	4.49 (1.02)	4.50 (1.34)	4.68 (1.25)
Employment domain	4.72 (1.49)	4.79 (1.82)	4.67 (1.29)	4.30* (1.88)	4.78* (1.53)
Education domain	4.52 (1.32)	4.71* (1.67)	4.42* (1.06)	4.59 (1.64)	4.42 (1.00)
Housing domain	4.61 (1.53)	5.18*** (1.66)	4.31*** (1.36)	4.61 (1.74)	4.65 (1.34)
Health domain	5.18 (1.11)	5.32* (1.18)	5.10* (1.07)	5.28** (1.16)	5.10** (1.13)

Notes:
A two-group *t*-test was conducted between ON and BC group, and Female and Male group.
* Indicate statistical significance at the 10% significance levels.
** Indicate statistical significance at the 5% significance levels.
*** Indicate statistical significance at the 1% significance levels
Source: Kant et al. (2014).

and males models, respectively; indicating the big difference in the role of education domain for females and males.

The results of overall and domains' wellbeing models confirmed the ORFN peoples' view about the critical role of SCLU factors in First Nations peoples' wellbeing. The SCLU domain was the most important determinant of overall wellbeing and SCLU factors made significant contributions to all other domains. A summary of the contributions of different SCLU factors through different domains is provided in Table 23.3. Household's freedom to participate in spiritual activities contributed to the overall wellbeing through five domains and therefore seems the most important factor.

Satisfaction with government laws that impact land use activities and the satisfaction with access to cultural sites contributed to the overall wellbeing through the SCLU domain and three other domains. In addition, five SCLU activities contributed to overall wellbeing through two domains each: gathering hours (education and employment domains), number of gatherers (education and housing domains), trapping income (SCLU and housing domains), state of areas of cultural significance (housing and income domains), and satisfaction with government laws that impact social and cultural activities (health and education domains). Two SCLU activities, number of trappers and social ties, contributed to the overall wellbeing through the SCLU domain, and three other SCLU activities contributed to the overall wellbeing through one domain only – gathering quality through the housing domain; and trapping hours through the employment domain, and participation in cultural ceremonies through the education domain. These results confirm the multidimensional contribution of SCLU activities in First Nations peoples' lives.

The valuation of SCLU activities was the focus of Kant, Vertinsky, and Zheng (2016). The authors argue that the standard market-oriented valuation methods such as the replacement cost method, the hedonic wage method and choice experiments are not appropriate for the valuation of SCLU activities due to their inability to account for non-substitutability of these

Table 23.3 The standardized total effect of SCLU factors to different domains' satisfaction

SCLU factors	Standardized total effect for female/male					
	SCLU domain	Health domain	Education domain	Housing domain	Employment domain	Income domain
AcceCultu	0.116	0.030/0.028		−0.106/0.235	−0.032/−0.010	
Ceremony			0.023			
Gatherhrs			−0.059/−0.022		0.009/0.025	
GatherQualit				0.049		
Gathers			0.015	−0.026		
LawCultu		0.022/0.002	0.032/0.020			
LawLanduse	0.291		0.053/0.012	0.018	0.003/0.026	
SocTies	0.191					
Spiritual		−0.029/0.033	−0.040	−0.019	0.002/0.009	0.027
StatCSAreas				−0.013		0.020
TradDiets	0.311/0.461					−0.034
TrapInc	0.090			0.004/−0.025		
Trappers	0.051/0.035					
Traphrs					−0.013/−0.009	

Source: Kant et al. (2014).

activities with market commodities (see discussion in Adamowicz et al., 1998). In addition, assigning a dollar value to these activities is not acceptable as per the Aboriginal worldview. The authors suggested a multi-domain life satisfaction model consisting of a General Satisfaction (GS) equation and one equation for each domain's satisfaction (DS). In their final model, they included four domains – SCLU, income, health and housing, and estimated the model as a system of five equations using 3SLS instead of estimating each equation independently. Hence, this paper extended the analysis presented in the path analysis paper, and contributed a different perspective about the important of different SCLU activities in First Nations peoples' subjective wellbeing.

The coefficients of the GS equation indicate that a one unit change in the SCLU domain, the health domain and the housing domain satisfaction result into 2.29, 2.28 and 2.05 times change in GS as compared to change in GS resulting from a one unit change in the financial domain satisfaction. The authors used a unit-less measure of elasticity to compare values of different domains, SCLU activities and other factors. Mean values of elasticities are provided in Table 23.4.

The elasticities of GS with respect to the financial, the housing, the SCLU and the health domains are 0.09, 0.19, 0.20 and 0.23, respectively, and therefore the GS is inelastic with respect to domain's satisfaction. Hence, for the same change in GS, the financial domain satisfaction has to be increased by more than double of the percentage change in the SCLU/health/ housing domain satisfaction. The GS is also inelastic with respect to all the SCLU activities, and elasticities with respect to all SCLU activities, except gathering days, are higher than the elasticity with respect to breadwinner's income. The GS elasticity with respect to gathering days is lowest and with respect to gathering quality is highest. The ratios of mean GSEF (GS elasticity with respect to a factor) and mean GSEIF (GS elasticity with respect to breadwinner's income) indicate that for the same incremental change in GS: for a 1% increase in gathering quality, social ties and the traditional diets, breadwinner's income has to be increased by 31.32 percent, 7.97 percent and 5.41 percent, respectively. The GS is also inelastic with respect to all housing factors and health services. Among these factors, the elasticity is lowest with respect to housing maintenance and highest with respect to housing utilities. The ratios of Mean GSEF and Mean GSEIF indicate that to achieve the same change in GS as the one generated by a 1% increase in the satisfaction with health services, housing maintenance, housing space and housing utilities breadwinner's income has to be increased by 10.58 percent, 5.68 percent, 9.64 percent and 15.11 percent, respectively.

The authors did not assign dollar values to SCLU activities but gave an example to demonstrate the use of their valuation approach to assign dollar values. As per this example, the value of one trapping day per month is $945, the value of one gathering day per month is $1,600 and the value of a 1% increase of traditional foods in the total diet is $1,257.

These studies, which focused on multiple domains of life satisfaction, have brought Aboriginal peoples' subjective wellbeing research closer to the holistic conceptualization of wellbeing by the Aboriginal people of Canada, and captured some important aspects of relations with land and other people being important contributors to Aboriginal wellbeing. However, these studies are limited to First Nations and Métis – Inuit nations were not included. In addition, the studies did not cover all aspects of the three holistic models but did reflect the intensive contributions of members of the two nations to the development and estimation of the models. While the study covered only two First Nations, and thus generalizations of results are speculative, it should be noted that results uncover a strong similarity in the conceptual frameworks developed separately in each First Nation. This was despite the large geographical distances between the two nations as well as significant differences in other important factors such as forest environments and languages.

Table 23.4 General satisfaction elasticity with respect to different domains and factors

General satisfaction elasticities with respect to domain

	Financial domain	SCLU domain	Health domain	Housing domain
Mean GSED	0.09	0.20	0.23	0.19
Mean GSED/ Mean GSEFD	1.00	2.22	2.55	2.11

General satisfaction elasticities with respect to SCLU factors

	Breadwinner's income	Traditional diet	Social ties	Law land use	Gathering quality	Gathering days
Mean GSEF	0.0034	0.0184	0.0271	0.0318	0.1065	0.0028
Mean GSEF/ Mean GSEIF	1.00	5.41	7.97	9.35	31.32	0.82

General satisfaction elasticities with respect to health and housing factors

	Breadwinner's income	Housing space	Housing utility	Housing maintenance	Health services
Mean GSEF	0.0034	0.0328	0.0514	0.0193	0.0360
Mean GSEF/ Mean GSEIF	1.00	9.64	15.11	5.68	10.58

Source: Kant, Vertinsky, and Zheng (2016).

Discussion and conclusion

Similar to the research on subjective wellbeing in general, the subjective wellbeing of Aboriginal peoples of Canada has also attracted scholars from various fields including anthropology, economics, psychology, political science and Native Aboriginal scholars. However, there is no study that covers subjective wellbeing of all Aboriginal peoples of Canada. Comparatively, subjective wellbeing of First Nations peoples has attracted more attention of researchers than the subjective wellbeing of Métis and Inuit peoples. The lack of Canada-wide studies on the subjective wellbeing of Aboriginal peoples may be due to the exclusion of First Nations peoples living on reserves and sometimes exclusion of some geographical regions dominated by Inuit and First Nations peoples. The choice of the population studied reflects, in part, priorities of funding agencies, cost and budget considerations as well as issues of ease of access to the populations.

The main focus of researchers has been on the first category of studies discussed in this chapter – the studies that use some indicators of subjective wellbeing and do not use two standard approaches of subjective wellbeing. Most of these studies are focused in cultural attributes such as sweat lodge ceremony, cultural identity, land use and bush activities, and make an important contribution in understanding the role these attributes play in determining the level of subjective wellbeing. From the lens of Aboriginal worldview, these studies ignore the holistic nature of wellbeing and follow the European tradition of compartmentalization. As a result, these types of studies cannot capture the linkages between different domains of wellbeing and their contributing factors. Future research should focus on the synthesis of these studies to develop a holistic picture of subjective wellbeing of all three groups of Aboriginal peoples of Canada.

The focus of studies based on overall wellbeing or general satisfaction with life has been to compare Aboriginal wellbeing with the wellbeing of non-Aboriginal groups, and explain Aboriginal wellbeing in terms of the same factors that have been used to explain subjective wellbeing of non-Aboriginal populations. These aspects ignore the differences between Aboriginal and European worldviews in general and specific wellbeing. One of the main driving forces behind the popularization of the concept of subjective wellbeing has been the Easterlin paradox – the higher levels of per capita income do not correlate with the self-reported scores of life satisfaction/happiness. Given this paradox, income may have a positive correlation with life satisfaction in some cases while in others it may not have any correlation or it may have even negative correlation; and given the conceptualization of Holistic Lifelong Learning Models, income may not be a very important contributing factor to Aboriginal peoples' life satisfaction. Hence, such findings should not be surprising in the case of Aboriginal peoples' subjective wellbeing.

The use of life satisfaction scores to compare subjective wellbeing of Aboriginal peoples with non-Aboriginal peoples is also questionable. Such comparative studies treat subjective measures of wellbeing as objective measures. These studies ignore the essence of subjective measures. The fundamental reason why subjective measures were introduced in the first place was to correct for the inadequacy of so-called objective measures. In the case of subjective measures, a respondent's answer depends on his/her reference group, which he/she uses for comparison purposes. The reference groups of Aboriginal peoples living on reserves or Inuit peoples living in the far north are quite different than non-Aboriginal groups living in southern Canada. Hence, the life satisfaction scores should not be treated as similar to objective measures such as income and wages, and the comparative outcomes from Aboriginal and non-Aboriginal groups' subjective wellbeing should not be used for any policy decisions relating to Aboriginal welfare. Similarly, applying the same explanatory variables, used to explain non-Aboriginal peoples' wellbeing, to explain Aboriginal peoples' wellbeing is not only conceptually flawed but can be (and often is) seen by the Aboriginals as another attempt by non-Aboriginals to demonstrate superiority of Western thought over Aboriginal thought. The three Holistic Lifelong Learning models have clearly demonstrated the differences in conceptualization of subjective wellbeing by Aboriginal people and European people. In the case of Aboriginal people, relationships with nature and other people are the key to wellbeing while in European worldviews these relationships hardly have any role in wellbeing. Given such contrasting views, how can the factors that are used to explain wellbeing of non-Aboriginal peoples meaningfully explain Aboriginal peoples' subjective wellbeing?

In terms of future work, there is a need for the development of a solid understanding of the overall wellbeing of all Aboriginal peoples of Canada. This may require additional questions on overall wellbeing and Aboriginal-peoples-specific factors that may contribute to overall wellbeing – these factors should be identified with the assistance of Holistic Lifelong Learning Models. Data from surveys can then be used to develop a good understanding of the overall wellbeing of First Nations peoples living on reserves, Métis and Inuit. Similarly, models to explain overall wellbeing should be developed and analyzed using the overall wellbeing and Aboriginal-peoples-specific factors from these surveys.

The studies based on satisfaction of multiple domains, specifically domains identified by Aboriginal peoples themselves and the inclusion of SCLU domain, and the inclusion of SCLU activities as contributing factors is a step in the right direction. However, these studies are in their infancy stage and much more work is required. First, the two studies discussed in this chapter include seven domains identified by participants, but these domains may not cover, at least fully, spiritual, emotional and mental domains of wellbeing. Some factors included are related to spiritual and mental domains, and in the estimated models these factors may be contributing to overall wellbeing through other domains, but without explicit inclusion of all four domains identified in the Holistic Lifelong Learning models, overall subjective wellbeing cannot be fully understood. Second, Holistic Lifelong Learning models should be used as the foundation of the design of future multi-domain studies. Third, future studies should cover a sufficient proportion of First Nations, Métis and Inuit peoples to provide a comprehensive picture of the subjective wellbeing of the Aboriginal peoples of Canada.

Acknowledgments

We would like to express our sincere thanks to the Canadian Council on Learning (CCL) and all First Nations, Inuit and Métis organizations, professionals and researchers who contributed to the development of three Holistic Lifelong Learning Models originally presented in CCL (2007).

References

Aboriginal Affairs and Northern Development Canada. (2013). *Aboriginal peoples and communities*, 10 November. Retrieved from www.aadnc-aandc.gc.ca/eng/1100100013785/1304467449155.

Adamowicz, W., Boxall, P., Williams, M., & Louviere, J. (1998). Stated preference approaches for measuring passive use values: Choice experiments and contingent valuation. *American Journal of Agricultural Economics, 80*(1), 64–75.

Andrews, F.M., & Withey, S.B. (1976). *Social indicators of wellbeing: Americans' perception of life quality*. New York: Plenum Press.

Argyle, M. (2001). *The psychology of happiness*. New York: Routledge.

Barrington-Leigh, C.P., & Sloman, S. (2016). Life satisfaction among Aboriginal peoples in the Canadian prairies: Evidence from the equality, security and community survey. *The International Indigenous Policy Journal, 7*(2), Article 2.

Barton, S.S., Thommasen, H.V., Tallio, B., Zhang, W., & Michalos, A.C. (2005). Health and quality of life of Aboriginal residential school survivors, Bella Coola Valley, 2001. *Social Indicators Research, 73*(2), 295–312.

Blanchfower, D.G., & Oswald, A.J. (2004). Wellbeing over time in Britain and the USA. *Journal of Public Economics, 88*(7–8), 1359–1386.

Campbell, J.D., Trapnell, P.D., Heine, S.J., Katz, I.M., Lavallee, L.F., & Lehman, D.R. (1996). Self-concept clarity: Measurement, personality correlates, and cultural boundaries. *Journal of Personality and Social Psychology, 70*, 141–156.

Canadian Council on Learning (CCL). (2007). *Redefining how success is measured in First Nations, Inuit and Métis learning: Report on learning in Canada 2007.* Ottawa: Canada.

Clark, A.E., Frijters, P., & Shields, M. (2008). Relative income, happiness, and utility: An explanation for the Easterlin paradox and other puzzles. *Journal of Economics Literature, 46*(1), 95–144.

Conceição, P., & Bandura, R. (2008). *Measuring subjective wellbeing: A summary review of the literature.* Retrieved 19 March 2012, from web.undp.org/developmentstudies/docs/subjective_wellbeing_conceicao_bandura.pdf.

Cooke, M., Beavon, D., & McHardy, M. (2004). *Measuring the well-being of Aboriginal people: An application of the United Nations Human Development Index to registered Indians in Canada, 1981–2001.* Aboriginal Policy Research Consortium International (APRCi), paper 158.

Cummins, R.A. (1996). The domains of life satisfaction: An attempt to order chaos. *Social Indicators Research, 38*, 303–332.

Deaton, A. (2008). Income, aging, health and wellbeing around the world: Evidence from the Gallup World Poll. *Journal of Economic Perspectives, 22*(2), 53–72.

Diener, E. (1984). Subjective wellbeing. *Psychological Bulletin, 95*, 542–575.

Diener, E., & Biswas-Diener, R. (2002). Will money increase subjective wellbeing? A literature review and guide to needed research. *Social Indicators Research, 57*(2), 119–169.

Diener, E., Suh, E.M., Lucas, R.E., & Smith, H.L. (1999). Subjective wellbeing: Three decades of progress. *Psychological Bulletin, 125*(2), 276–302.

Easterlin, R.A. (1974). Does economic growth improve the human lot? Some empirical evidence. In P.A. David & M.W. Reder (Eds.), *Nations and households in economic growth: Essays in honor of Moses Abramovitz* (pp. 89–125). New York: Academic Press.

Easterlin, R.A. (2004). The economics of happiness. *Daedalus, 133*(2), 26–33.

Fernando. M. (2002). A Look at life satisfaction and ethnicity in Canada. *Canadian Ethnic Studies, XXXIV*(I), 51–64.

Headey, B., & Wearing, A. (1992). *Understanding happiness: A theory of subjective wellbeing.* Melbourne: Australia Longman Cheshire.

Helliwell, J.F., & Putnam, R.D. (2004). The social context of wellbeing. *Philosophical Transactions of the Royal Society London B, 359*, 1435–1446.

Ilfeld, F.W. (1976). Further validation of a psychiatric symptom index in a normal population. *Psychological Reports, 39*, 1215–1228.

Kant, S., Vertinsky, I., & Zheng, B. (2016). Valuation of ecosystem services using the life satisfaction approach: The case of land use activities of the First Nations peoples of Canada. *Forest Policy and Economics, 72*, 46–55.

Kant, S., Vertinsky, I., Zheng, B., & Smith, P. (2014). Multi-domain subjective wellbeing of two Canadian First Nations communities. *World Development, 64*, 140–157.

Kapteyn, A., Smith, J.P., & van Soest, A. (2010). Life satisfaction. In E. Diener, J.F. Helliwell, & D. Kahneman (Eds.), *International differences in wellbeing* (pp. 70–104). New York: Oxford University Press.

King, M., Smith, A., & Gracey, M. (2009). Indigenous health part 2: The underlying causes of the health gap. *The Lancet, 374*(9683), 76–85.

Kirmayer, L.J., Boothroyd, L.J., Tanner, A., Adelson, N., Robinson, E., & Oblin, C. (2000). Psychological distress among the Cree of James Bay. *Transcultural Psychiatry, 37*(1), 35–56.

Mas, S. (2015). Trudeau lays out plan for new relationship with indigenous people. *CBC News.* Retrieved 18 August 2017 from www.cbc.ca/news/politics/justin-trudeau-afn-indigenous-aboriginal-people-1.3354747.

McHardy, M., & O'Sullivan, E. (2004). *First Nations community well-being in Canada: The Community Well-Being Index (CWB), 2001.* Published under the authority of the Minister of Indian Affairs and Northern Development, Ottawa. Retrieved 22 August 2017 from http://epe.lac-bac.gc.ca/100/200/301/inac-ainc/ first_nations_comm_e/ cwb_e.pdf.

McGillivray, M. (2007). Human wellbeing: Issues, concepts and measures. In M. McGillivray (Ed.), *Human wellbeing: Concept and measurement.* Basingstoke: Palgrave Macmillan.

Michalos, A.C., Thommasen, H.V., Read, R., Anderson, N., & Zumbo, B.D. (2005). Determinants of health and the quality of life in the Bella Coola Valley. *Social Indicators Research, 72*(10), 1–50.

Morgan, D.L., Slade, M.D., & Morgan, C.M. (1997). Aboriginal philosophy and its impact on health care outcomes. *Australian and New Zealand Journal of Public Health, 21*(6), 597–601.

Mussell, W.J. (2005). *Warrior-caregivers: Understanding the challenges and healing of First Nations men: A guide prepared for the Aboriginal Healing Foundation.* Ottawa: Aboriginal Healing Foundation.

O'Sullivan, E. (2006). *The Community Wellbeing (CWB) Index: Wellbeing in First Nations communities, 1981– 2001 and onto the future.* Ottawa: Strategic Research and Analysis Directorate, Indian and Northern Affairs Canada.

Pearson, C. (1991). *Awakening the heroes within: Twelve archetypes to help us find ourselves and transform our world.* New York: Harper Collins Publishers.

Rosenberg, M. (1965). *Society and the adolescent self-image.* Princeton, NJ: Princeton University Press.

Royal Commission on Aboriginal Peoples. (1996). *People to people, nation to nation: Highlights from the Report of the Royal Commission on Aboriginal Peoples.* Ottawa: Minister of Supply and Services Canada.

Sacha, S., O'Sullivan, E, Guimond, E., & Uppal, S, (2008). *Applying the Community Well-being Index and the Human Development Index to Inuit in Canada.* Aboriginal Policy Research Consortium International (APRCi), paper 4, http://ir.lib.uwo.ca/aprci/4.

Schiff, J.W., & Moore, K. (2006). The impact of the sweat lodge ceremony on dimensions of wellbeing. *American Indian Alaska Native Mental Health Research, 13*(3), 48–69.

Statistics Canada. (2013). *Aboriginal peoples in Canada: First Nations people, Metis and Inuit – National household survey, 2011.* Catalogue No. 99, 011-X2011001.

Sumner, W. (1996). *Welfare, happiness, and ethics.* Oxford: Clarendon Press.

The National Aboriginal Economic Development Board. (2015). *The Aboriginal economic progress report.* Retrieved 22 August 2017 from www.naedb-cndea.com/reports/NAEDB-progress-report-june-2015.pdf.

Usborne, E., & Taylor, D.M. (2010). The role of cultural identity clarity for self-concept clarity, self-esteem, and subjective wellbeing. *Personality and Social Psychology Bulletin, 36*(7), 883–897.

van Praag, B., & Ferrer-I-Carbonell, A. (2004). *Happiness quantified: A satisfaction calculus approach.* New York: Oxford University Press.

Ware, J., Kosinski, M., Gandek, B., Aaronson, N., Alonso, J., & Apolone, G. (1998). The factor structure of the SF-36® health survey in 10 countries: Results from the International Quality of Life Assessment (IQOLA) project. *Journal of Clinical Epidemiology, 51*(11), 1159–1165.

24

SUBJECTIVE WELLBEING OF INDIGENOUS LATIN AMERICANS

Regional trends and the case of Mexico's Indigenous people

Lilia Arcos Holzinger and Nicholas Biddle

Introduction and overview

Latin American countries, which we take to be the Spanish- or Portuguese-speaking countries from Mexico in the north to Argentina and Chile in the south, are outliers from a global relationship between subjective wellbeing and GDP per capita. Based on the global relationship and the GDP per capita of Latin American countries, one would predict substantially lower levels of subjective wellbeing (self-reported life satisfaction and happiness) than are actually observed across the region.

In a cross-national study of subjective wellbeing, including dummy variables for Latin American nations and ex-Communist countries (which collectively report far below expected subjective wellbeing given their GDP per capita levels) leads to a substantial increase in the explained cross-country variations of subjective wellbeing, and points to plausible country-specific or cultural factors (e.g. nationalism and religiosity) that enhance subjective wellbeing yet are not captured by standard economic outcomes (Ingleheart et al., 2008). It is however misleading to conclude that there is a shared national culture for countries as vastly heterogeneous in ethnicity – and thereby culture – as are those of Latin America, and even more so to claim that higher than expected subjective wellbeing holds across the ethnic sub-populations of the region.

Indigenous groups in Latin America have been historically deprived of the burgeoning economic prosperity of the region. Although there have been improvements in socioeconomic development for Indigenous people in recent times, they are still lagging behind their non-Indigenous counterparts. This claim is supported by evidence from a wide range of outcomes indicating ethnic disparities in average household incomes and assets, human capital levels (in terms of education and health), and access to public goods and services (Patrinos & Skoufias, 2007). Moreover, these disparities hold across the region despite the proportion of Indigenous people to total national population ranging from 6 per cent to 62 per cent across countries (Hall & Patrinos, 2006). Most importantly, Indigenous Latin Americans also show the clearest diversion of ethnic sub-groups in terms of cultural values and standard socioeconomic outcomes, warranting an Indigenous-specific focus of the determinants of subjective wellbeing and its relationship with orthodox economic outcomes. Given Indigenous cultures' emphasis on unorthodox and hard-to-quantify factors such as well-established social networks, skills for indigenous-specific activities, closeness to land and involvement in cultural and religious activities, subjective wellbeing is a promising approximation of unobservable overall human wellbeing in that it can capture factors valuable to Indigenous peoples in ways that standard economic outcomes cannot (Hall & Patrinos, 2012).

With the prospect that subjective wellbeing provides a good approximation for the overall human wellbeing of Latin America's Indigenous peoples, we take a multi-level approach to build a better understanding of the subjective wellbeing determinants and outcomes across the region. We first present national cross-country comparisons of subjective wellbeing trends over recent times, as well as trends by Indigenous status and age groups. We then focus on a case study of Mexico's Indigenous people (collectively the most populous Indigenous group of any Latin American country), and again analyse trends in subjective wellbeing over time and by age groups. Finally, we present a modelling framework and regression analysis that aims at better understanding the determinants of subjective wellbeing outcomes, and which explores the link between perceptions of safety and life improvements.

Subjective wellbeing in Latin America by country and indigenous status

Latin American trends in current subjective wellbeing by country

Using the World Value Survey longitudinal data (WVS), we map subjective wellbeing (happiness, health, life satisfaction and feelings of safety) across eight large Latin American nations by age groups and time periods. The WVS carries out nationally representative surveys across the world using a standardized questionnaire on a range of values as well as social, economic and political outcomes (Fleche et al., 2011). The aim of this exercise is to better understand the variability of subjective wellbeing by country and to then benchmark subjective wellbeing outcomes for later comparison with the Mexican study case. To do this, we utilize the last three available waves of the WVS, which correspond to the period of 1999–2004, 2005–2009 and 2010–2014. The subjective wellbeing outcomes examined are presented in detail in Table 24.1,

Table 24.1 World Value Survey: subjective wellbeing outcome measures and adjusted scales

Outcome	Question	Scale
Feeling of unhappiness	Taking all things together, would you say you are:	1 – Very happy or quite happy 0 – Not very happy or not at all happy
Subjective state of morbidity	All in all, how would you describe your state of health these days?	1 – Very good, good or fair 0 – Poor or very poor
Satisfaction with your life	All things considered, how satisfied are you with your life as a whole these days on a scale of 1–10, with 1 being very dissatisfied and 10 being very satisfied?	1 – Satisfaction level falls between 7–10 0 – Satisfaction level falls between 1–6
Unsafe from crime in own home	Frequency you and your family felt unsafe from crime in your own home (past 12 months)	1 – Often or sometimes 0 – Rarely or never

and the total numbers of observations by country are presented in Table 24.2. We have modified some of the categorical questions of the data used to be binary, as this allows an easier comparison across the outcomes while remaining insightful; later, this more parsimonious specification allows us to conduct detailed regression analysis for Mexico's indigenous people that may have been unviable with the original categorical specifications.

Average subjective wellbeing trends by country and over time are presented in Figure 24.1. In terms of sadness, there is a modest variability by country with a range of about 5 per cent to 35 per cent average sadness, and Mexico and Peru report respectively the lowest and highest average levels of sadness. Subjective morbidity is consistently low across waves and countries, with the average probability of reporting morbidity occurring below 10 per cent for all countries and waves. The largest variability by country and over time occurs for the life satisfaction measure, where averages range between 50 per cent and 90 per cent of the population. From the first to the third wave, there is a slight increase in the average number of people reporting being satisfied with life for all countries – recall that life satisfaction is defined here as responses of 7 or higher on the 0–10 scale of life satisfaction. Surprisingly, it is not the Latin American countries with higher GDP per capita that score highest on life satisfaction but Colombia and Mexico; Peru consistently lags behind on average life satisfaction at each wave.

The last subjective wellbeing measure we analyse from the WVS is feelings of unsafety, but due to data unavailability, we are only able to plot outcomes for the latest survey wave. Given the high levels of crime that occur throughout much of the region (Ayres, 1998), this is a highly relevant subjective outcome measure. The average number of respondents who feel unsafe from crime by country ranges between 25 per cent and 50 per cent, so there are very large variations across countries, as is true with objective crime statistics across the region.

Overall, these international comparisons show that Latin American nations place quite well on the subjective wellbeing outcomes related to health, happiness and overall life satisfaction, although there are large variations across countries on the life satisfaction outcome. In terms of fear from crime however, not only are there large variations across countries, but those with the highest averages also have a sizable proportion of the population (e.g. about 50% in Peru) who live in fear from crime even when at home.

Latin American trends in current subjective wellbeing by Indigenous status

While there is an ethnicity indicator in the WVS, the number of Indigenous people is very low by country, precluding any cross-country comparisons. Given that the WVS is a nationally representative sample and that the questionnaires are standardized, we are however able to pool Indigenous respondents across countries to get a general idea of how Indigenous Latin Americans' subjective wellbeing maps relative to that of the non-Indigenous. Table 24.2 presents the number of respondents by country and Indigenous status across the three waves of the WVS. Note that with the exception of Bolivia, we are able to analyse trends for those countries with the largest proportion of Indigenous people to total population: Peru, Mexico, Guatemala and Ecuador (Hall & Patrinos, 2006). By pooling respondents across WVS waves and countries, we obtain a total of 838 Indigenous observations and 22,593 non-Indigenous observations, which we next utilize to explore trends of subjective wellbeing by age groups and Indigenous status.

Figure 24.2 presents the same subjective wellbeing outcomes discussed in the previous section, this time averaged by Indigenous status and three age groups: 18–34, 35–54 and 55+ years. The first graph presents the probability of feeling sad. It is clear that across all three age groups Indigenous people are more likely to experience sadness, and that the gap with the

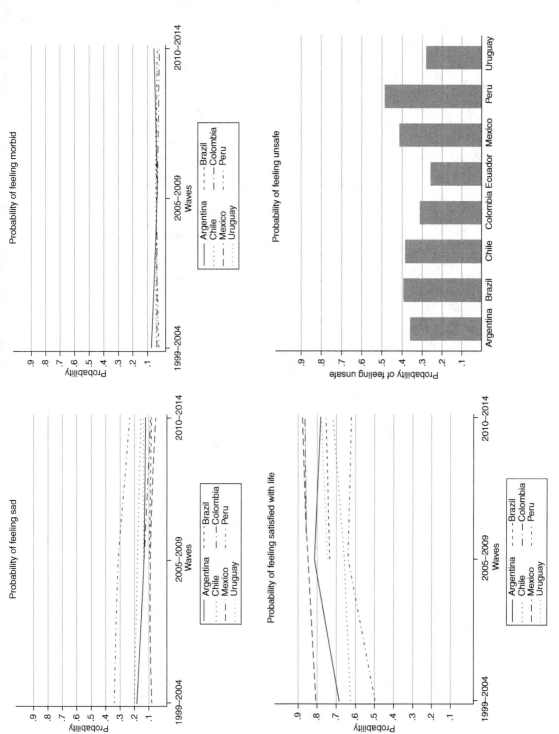

Figure 24.1 Subjective wellbeing outcomes in Latin America by country and WVS wave

Table 24.2 WVS: Individuals by indigenous status and country (3 waves: 1999–2014)

Latin American country	Indigenous	Non-Indigenous
Brazil	16	2,970
Chile	20	3,180
Colombia	48	4,489
Ecuador	10	1,192
Guatemala	287	713
Mexico	49	5,046
Peru	402	3,809
Venezuela	6	1,194
Total	838	22,593

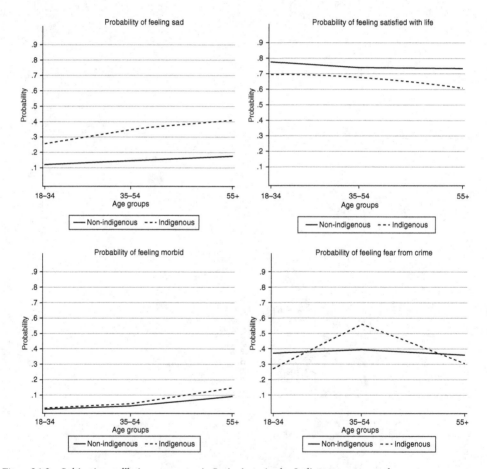

Figure 24.2   Subjective wellbeing outcomes in Latin America by Indigenous status and age groups

non-Indigenous widens as age increases: at the age of 55+, about 20 per cent of the non-Indigenous experience feeling sad, while the Indigenous average is about 40 per cent. In terms of subjective morbidity, there is essentially no gap on the average level of morbidity by Indigenous status for young respondents, yet a difference appears at the 35–54 age group with Indigenous people being more likely to experience morbidity, and this difference widens further for the 55+ age group, reaching about a 5 percentage-point difference in averages by ethnicity. In terms of life satisfaction, while the majority of both ethnicities self-assess as being highly satisfied with life (a range of about 60–80%), Indigenous people consistently have averages about 10 percentage points lower than those of the non-Indigenous at all age groups. For the last subjective wellbeing, fear from crime, there are large differences by Indigenous status: while the non-Indigenous trend is constant across age groups with about 40 per cent of people reporting fear from crime, the Indigenous trend lies below·the non-Indigenous trend at the 18–34 and 55+ age groups (the Indigenous average is about 30% at both age groups), there is a large spike in the probability of Indigenous people fearing crime at the 35–54 age group with about 60 per cent of people fearing crime – this is about 20 percentage points higher than the non-Indigenous average at this age group. Overall, these trends point to the consistently lower subjective wellbeing of Indigenous people compared to non-Indigenous Latin Americans. However, the movements of the trends across age groups, particularly that of fear of crime, also point to complex and possibly different determinants of subjective wellbeing not only by Indigenous status, but also across the life course, which we later explore through a more rigorous approach.

Subjective wellbeing trends of Mexico by Indigenous status

The geographic distribution of Mexicans by Indigenous status

Indigenous Mexicans present an important study case of the subjective wellbeing of Latin American Indigenous groups. First, they collectively make up the largest number of Indigenous people in all of Latin America, yet of the five countries with the largest total number of Indigenous people – Mexico, Peru, Guatemala, Peru and Ecuador – Mexico has the lowest percentage of Indigenous to total population. Second, although there are over sixty different Indigenous groups in Mexico, over 80 per cent live in the Southern region (made up of the states of Campeche, Chiapas, Guerrero, Hidalgo, Oaxaca, Puebla, Quintana Roo, Tabasco, Tlaxcala, Veracruz and Yucatán – see Figure 24.3 for a labelled map of Mexican states) (Hall & Patrinos, 2006). Figures 24.4 and 24.5 show the population density of non-Indigenous and Indigenous Mexicans in 2010; we have omitted the figures for 1990 and 2000 as population densities of states were almost identical to the 2010 figures, which shows that inter-state mobility by Indigenous status has overall had a stable trend over this period. Not only is the Indigenous population densely established in the Southern states, but this distribution is also very different from the non-Indigenous population who is more densely concentrated to the north, particularly the Central region. Third, since the 1990s Indigenous Mexicans have experienced rising political importance through initiatives such as the Zapatista (ELZN) movement in the state of Chiapas, which has strengthened their say in public policy issues that affect their wellbeing (Linares, 2010). Finally, given that Mexico as a whole presents one of the strongest positive outliers of subjective wellbeing given its GDP per capita, it is important understand how Indigenous Mexicans compare with the national trend, and the extent to which ethnic socioeconomic disparities and different cultural values impact subjective wellbeing outcomes.

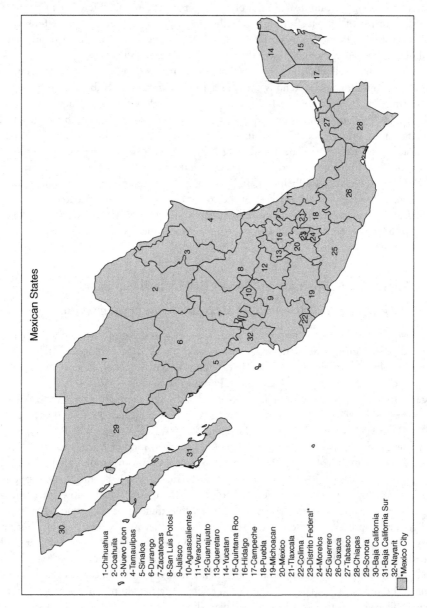

Mexican States

1-Chihuahua
2-Coahuila
3-Nuevo Leon
4-Tamaulipas
5-Sinaloa
6-Durango
7-Zacatecas
8-San Luis Potosi
9-Jalisco
10-Aguascalientes
11-Veracruz
12-Guanajuato
13-Queretaro
14-Yucatan
15-Quintana Roo
16-Hidalgo
17-Campeche
18-Puebla
19-Michoacan
20-Mexico
21-Tlaxcala
22-Colima
23-Distrito Federal*
24-Morelos
25-Guerrero
26-Oaxaca
27-Tabasco
28-Chiapas
29-Sonora
30-Baja California
31-Baja California Sur
32-Nayarit
*Mexico City

Figure 24.3   Labelled map of Mexican states

Source: Own depiction.

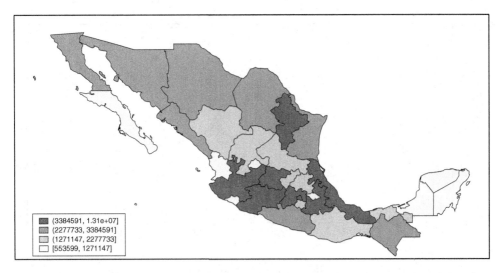

Figure 24.4 Population densities of non-Indigenous Mexicans by state, 2010
Source: Own depiction from INEGI data.

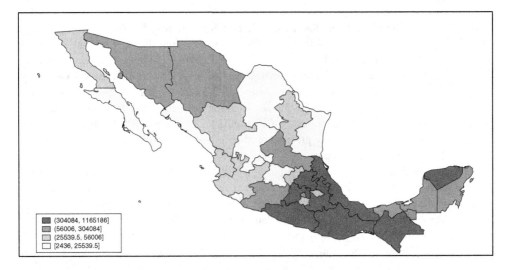

Figure 24.5 Population densities of Indigenous Mexicans by state, 2010
Source: Own depiction from INEGI data.

An overview of violence and crime in Mexico

Before presenting subjective wellbeing trends in Mexico and a regression framework that more rigorously examines these outcomes, we present an overview of Mexico's violence problem with the objective that the reader better understand the magnitude of this issue and the increasing risk it poses to the wellbeing of Mexicans.

Although the number of homicides per annum is only one measure of violence in Mexico, it provides a window into the social and economic costs of the problem, which has been primarily

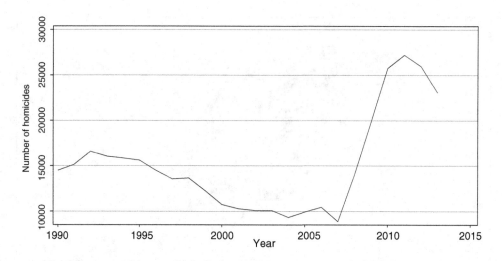

Figure 24.6 Number of homicides in Mexico per annum, 1990–2013
Source: Own depiction from INEGI data.

triggered by drug-related illicit activities. Figure 24.6 shows a steady decrease in the number of homicides between 1990 and 2007, with the number of homicides surging from 5,000 to about 27,000 in just three years following 2007, and then falling slightly to about 23,000 by 2014. Figure 24.7 presents homicide rates per 100,000 people by state in the year 2000, and Figure 24.8 does the same for the year 2010. Over this ten-year period, there is a clear geographic change in homicide rates, as more homicides began to occur in the Northern region of Mexico. There is also a clear change in the rates themselves: in 2000, the states with the greatest number of homicides had a rate of between 15 and 31 homicides per 100,000 people; in comparison, by 2010 the states with the greatest number of homicides had a rate of between 31 and 218 homicides per 100,000 people.

Despite governmental attempts to suppress the drug trade and the violence it generates, drug-related violence is still an ongoing problem in Mexico, even as total homicides have begun to fall. In recent years, violence has spread from a few states and major cities to other parts of the country, including Southern states that previously had low rates of homicides. The violence has increasingly targeted vulnerable civilian groups (including women, children and journalists) and governmental authorities (Molzahn et al., 2012). Besides homicides, drug-related violence includes a rise in kidnappings, extortions and torture, which have been met by a poor judicial system and government officials caught up in corruption cases (International Crisis Group, 2013). The impact of Mexico's violence also expands beyond objective crime statistics to include negative socioeconomic and health effects. Brown and Velásquez (2015) show that the drug-related violence has led children aged 14–17 to lower their educational attainment, score worse on cognitive assessments, and work at higher rates. Similarly, Michaelsen (2012) finds that for the working-age population, the surge in violence has led to less labour being supplied as a result of poorer mental health and higher anxiety levels in the adult population. The MxFLS waves occur at 2002, 2005–2006 and 2009–2012. Hence in our regression framework, the first two waves serve as important time controls of the period before the strong increase in violence, while the third wave captures the current period characterized by high violence and crime.

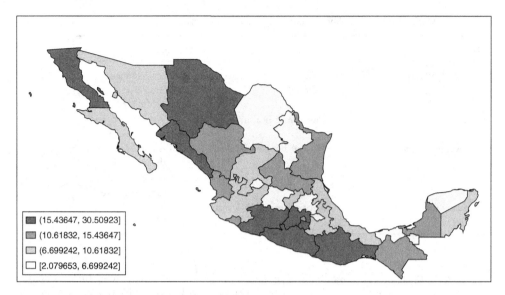

Figure 24.7 Number of homicides in Mexico per annum, 2000
Source: Own depiction from INEGI data.

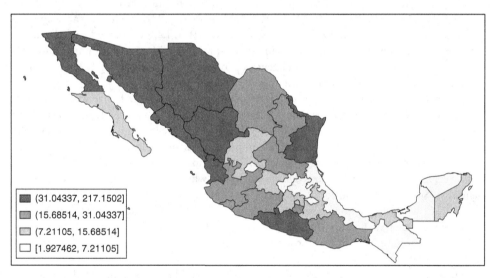

Figure 24.8 Number of homicides in Mexico per annum, 2010
Source: Own depiction from INEGI data.

The Mexican Family Life Survey (MxFLS) and subjective wellbeing trends

The MxFLS is a longitudinal study of Mexico's population covering the years 2002–2012, and for which almost 90 per cent of individuals were successfully recontacted in waves 2 and 3. It is a nationally representative sample of Mexico and comprehensively covers individual socioeconomic characteristics as well as a range of subjective wellbeing outcomes. Moreover, the survey records family-level characteristics, providing valuable information on household

Table 24.3 MxFLS subjective wellbeing outcome measures and scales

Outcome	Question	Scale
Feeling of sadness	In the last 4 weeks, have you felt sad?	1 –Yes, sometimes; yes, a lot of times; yes, all the time 0 – No
Subjective state of morbidity	How is your health?	1 –Very good, good, or fair 0 – Poor or very poor
Improvements in your life	Has your life gotten better?	1 – Become a lot worse; become a little worse 0 – Stayed the same; improved a little; improved a lot
Increasing unsafety over 5 past years	Safety compared to 5 years ago?	1 – Less safe 0 – Safe or safer

factors that affect subjective wellbeing. The survey has been utilized in a broad range of demographic, social, economic and health analyses.[1] Relevant works that utilize the MxFLS include analysis of the longer-term impact of the *Progresa* conditional cash transfer program that is primarily aimed at Indigenous people (see respectively, Farfán et al., 2011; McKee & Todd, 2011); the consequences of violence on human capital accumulation, labour supply and mental health (see respectively, Brown & Velásquez, 2015; Michaelsen, 2012); and the ways migration affects families (Silver, 2014). Only Servan-Mori et al. (2014) have conducted an Indigenous-specific analysis using the MxFLS. They find that although health and development measures have improved over 2000–2010 for Indigenous people, they are still lagging behind the non-Indigenous population, and this disparity has not decreased over time.

The rest of this section explores trends of subjective wellbeing by Indigenous status over the three waves of the survey and for different age groups. Using the three waves of the MxFLS (1999–2014), we can explore a range of subjective wellbeing outcomes. Specifically, we analyse trends in self-assessed sadness, life improvements, morbidity, and unsafety. The outcome measures used are detailed in Table 24.3. It is important to distinguish between those who feel as part of an Indigenous group, and those who additionally speak an Indigenous language. Speaking an Indigenous language is a stricter and arguably a better self-reported measure of being Indigenous given that a large majority of the Mexican population is of mixed-race ancestry, and that Indigenous status is self-reported. Hence, our analysis below classifies Indigenous Mexicans as those who identify with an Indigenous group and speak an Indigenous language.

Figure 24.9 presents subjective wellbeing trends by MxFLS wave. Although the trends for sadness and morbidity lie close together and move in similar directions over time for Indigenous and non-Indigenous Mexicans, the average Indigenous Mexican consistently has slightly higher feelings of sadness and morbidity. Indigenous Mexicans also have a lower sense of recent life improvements, which is about 10 percentage points lower than that of the non-Indigenous, and this disparity hasn't narrowed for more recent waves. The one measure where Indigenous Mexicans place better than non-Indigenous Mexicans is in feelings of safety; Indigenous people are less likely to feel that unsafety has increased than non-Indigenous Mexicans at all waves, and this gap widens by wave 3, when the average for the non-Indigenous increases by 15 percentage points relative to the previous wave while the average of Indigenous Mexicans stays constant over time.

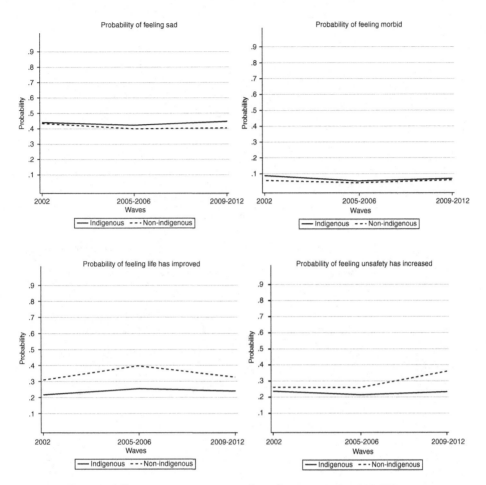

Figure 24.9 Subjective wellbeing outcomes in Mexico by Indigenous status and MxFLS wave

Figure 24.10 shows trends on the same subjective wellbeing outcomes presented before, this time by Indigenous status and age groups. The probability of feeling sad is very similar for Indigenous and non-Indigenous people between the ages of 35 and 70. However, young (aged 18–34) and older (aged 70+) Indigenous people have a much higher propensity to feel sad than do the non-Indigenous under the same age groups. In contrast, self-assessed morbidity is on average about the same for both Indigenous and non-Indigenous respondents, and actually lower for older Indigenous than non-Indigenous respondents by about 5 percentage points; the opposite trend was found using the WVS for the pooled Indigenous Latin Americans, and provides evidence that the health status of Indigenous Mexicans is overall better than for other Latin American Indigenous groups. In terms of life improvements, both Indigenous and non-Indigenous Mexicans tend to feel life has improved at lower rates as age increases, yet the trend for the Indigenous falls below that of the non-Indigenous at all age groups, with an especially large ethnic gap of about 15 percentage points for the youngest age group. Finally, the trend for feelings of unsafety is constant across the life course for both Indigenous and non-Indigenous groups, and the Indigenous trend constantly falls below that of the non-Indigenous.

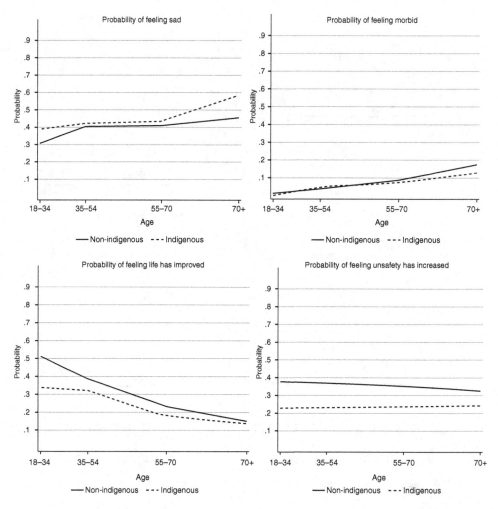

Figure 24.10 Subjective wellbeing outcomes in Mexico by Indigenous status and age groups

The trends for the Mexican population by Indigenous status are roughly consistent with the findings from the WVS for the pooled group of Latin American Indigenous groups for subjective sadness and life satisfaction/improvements, with Indigenous people being consistently more likely to feel sad, less likely to be satisfied with life and less likely to feel that their lives have improved. However, while subjective morbidity is higher for Indigenous people across Latin America than for non-Indigenous Latin Americans, it is very similar between Indigenous and non-Indigenous Mexicans. Finally, fear from crime and feelings of unsafety are lower for Indigenous Latin Americans, including those in Mexico, than they are for the non-Indigenous. These ethnic divergences regarding feelings of unsafety may be explained by differing salient determinants, differing socioeconomic characteristics, and/or differing community characteristics for Indigenous and non-Indigenous people. Next, we specify and implement a modelling framework to more rigorously account for these differences in subjective wellbeing by ethnicity.

A regression framework using the MxFLS: subjective wellbeing outcomes by Indigenous status

Modelling the relationship between overall human wellbeing and subjective wellbeing

Overall human wellbeing is a latent variable, meaning that it cannot be measured or observed and that its value must be inferred using other observable outcomes. While the proxies of choice for this latent variable have overwhelmingly fallen within standard socio-economic outcomes (e.g. income levels), there is a strong imperative for, and an increasing number of works utilizing self-assessed measures of wellbeing as proxies. The first reason why subjective wellbeing outcomes make good approximations for overall wellbeing is that wellbeing is determined by many different factors, some which are hard to quantify in terms of mainstream economic variables; hence, when self-assessing through subjective well-being, individuals are able to better incorporate these factors. Second, a key component of economic theory is the idea that individuals are the best judges of their preferences and their wellbeing, and so self-assessed measures provide a promising complement to positive economic theories that rely on objective individual choices to proxy individual wellbeing (Stutzer & Frey, 2004).

The challenge of a subjective approach to estimating wellbeing lies is creating a theoretic framework that properly captures the determinants of subjective wellbeing outcomes and the way in which these interact. This framework is particularly important given that subjective wellbeing measures are often correlated, and that some of them are determinants of other sub-jective wellbeing variables. As a result, empirical studies that are not properly specified may suffer from omitted variable bias and reverse causality problems.

Using insights from psychology, the OECD guidelines on measuring subjective wellbeing distinguish among three classes of subjective wellbeing outcomes, namely positive or negative affect (i.e. feelings and emotional states), life evaluation (i.e. a reflection on one's life as a whole) and eudaimonia (i.e. proper psychological functioning). The modelling framework presented in OECD (2013) and reproduced in Figure 24.11 states that within the three classes of subjective wellbeing outcomes there are sub-components, and that these sub-components are related to other sub-components within the same and the other two classes. So for example, happiness is related to worry, and both happiness and worry are related to health satisfaction. Besides the sub-components and their interactions, there exist other demographic factors, personality traits and social influences that can be important determinants of subjective wellbeing outcomes and should be accounted for in empirical analysis.

Important determinants and interactions have been tested widely in empirical studies.[2] For our first set of regression analysis, then, we include demographic characteristics at the individual and household level that have been found to be empirically significant determinants of similar subjective wellbeing outcomes, while we later justify the inclusion of different controls for our second set of regression analysis concerning life improvements and feelings of unsafety.[3]

The MxFLS sample

As discussed before, the MxFLS is representative of the Mexican population in urban and rural areas, and has a strong retention rate throughout the three waves of the survey. Nonetheless, in order to properly analyse the determinants of subjective wellbeing through time, we require

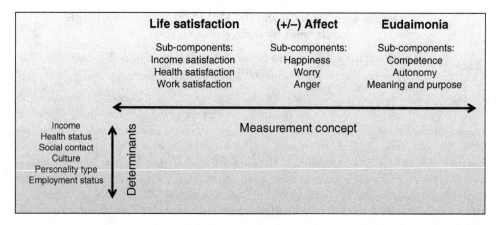

Figure 24.11 Reproduction: model of subjective wellbeing presented in OECD (2013)

both individual and household characteristics to be present throughout the three waves, so after dropping non-panel observations (both those who were dropped and those who joined in later waves), children under 18 years of age, and those with missing information on essential outcomes and controls, our usable sample consists of 34,452 pooled observations; the sample size in subsequent analysis varies according to the outcome measure analysed. Of the overall usable sample, 4,667 time-person observations identify as part of an Indigenous group, and of these, 3,397 time-person observations additionally speak an Indigenous language. Table 24.4 summarizes by ethnicity the outcome variables and controls that will be used in subsequent regression analysis, with the purpose of providing a better understanding of the characteristics of the usable sub-sample of the MxFLS. As before, we choose to identify Indigenous people by whether they speak an Indigenous language, given that this stricter condition minimizes some of the potential errors of utilizing self-reported ethnicity measures, as is the case with the MxFLS.

The summary statistics reinforce the findings from the trends presented in the previous section, as well as of the geographic distribution by ethnicity presented using official statistics from INEGI. We also find that relative to the non-Indigenous, Indigenous people tend to be married more often, have lower educational attainment, live in smaller communities (15,000 or less), participate in government transfer programs at higher rates, have medical insurance, savings and debts at lower rates, and live in places with lower police presence. At the household level, the results are similar for the Indigenous and non-Indigenous, with Indigenous families being slightly less likely to have a female head of household, more likely to have more children and bigger household sizes, as well as fewer bedrooms per capita.

Pooled regression analysis for subjective wellbeing outcomes

The modelling framework described above can be estimated for the subjective wellbeing outcomes of the MxFLS related to the probability of feeling sad, morbid or that life has improved (see Table 24.4). Specifically, the econometric model we are estimating is:

$$SW_{it} = \alpha + I_i + \beta_{it} + w1 + w2 + \varepsilon_{it}$$

where SW_{it} is the probability of observing a subjective-wellbeing state for each person i at time period t, α is a constant term, I_i is a dummy variable equal to one if an individual is Indigenous,

Table 24.4 Summary of outcomes and controls by Indigenous status

	Non-Indigenous Mexicans			Indigenous Mexicans		
	# of obs.	Mean	Std. Dev.	# of obs.	Mean	Std. Dev.
Subjective wellbeing outcomes						
Probability of feeling sadness	30,124	1.481	0.642	3385	1.507	0.645
Probability of feeling morbid	30,120	2.522	0.694	3385	2.637	0.669
Probability of feeling life has improved in the last 5 years	30,072	3.278	0.785	3391	3.127	0.648
Probability of feeling unsafety has increased in the last 5 years	30,080	0.295	0.456	3390	0.229	0.420
Individual characteristics						
Female	30,039	0.613	0.487	3350	0.599	0.490
Region: Central	30,444	0.218	0.413	3384	0.036	0.187
Region: North	30,444	0.434	0.496	3384	0.085	0.280
Region: South	30,444	0.082	0.275	3384	0.407	0.491
Region: East	30,444	0.133	0.340	3384	0.306	0.461
Region: West	30,444	0.132	0.339	3384	0.165	0.371
Age	30,484	43.611	15.484	3385	48.402	15.977
Married or in union	30,481	0.720	0.449	3386	0.783	0.412
Education: elementary	24,461	0.557	0.497	2274	0.775	0.417
Education: secondary	26,960	0.387	0.487	2365	0.198	0.398
Education: higher than secondary	26,960	0.108	0.310	2365	0.057	0.231
Not working	29,951	0.506	0.500	3377	0.533	0.499
Lives in community with <15,000 people	30,653	0.539	0.498	3396	0.891	0.311
Lives in community with >15,000 people	30,653	0.356	0.479	3396	0.079	0.270
Receives income from Progresa	30,658	0.014	0.118	3397	0.536	0.225
Receives income from Procampo	30,658	0.015	0.121	3397	0.044	0.205
Participates in community savings program (Tanda)	30,658	0.113	0.316	3397	0.028	0.165
Has relatives in USA^	30,116	0.363	0.481	3383	0.272	0.445
Has medical insurance^	30,118	0.536	0.499	3382	0.349	0.477
Has savings	29,910	0.113	0.316	3372	0.049	0.216
Has debts	29,577	0.772	0.419	3320	0.709	0.454
Police present in neighbourhood in the last month ★	30,084	0.605	0.489	3390	0.442	0.497
Carries valuables ★	30,083	0.284	0.451	3389	0.192	0.394
Household characteristics						
Household head is female	30,658	0.190	0.392	3397	0.169	0.375
Number of children in household	30,658	1.455	1.455	3397	1.844	1.828
Household size	30,658	5.139	2.446	3397	5.886	3.000
Number of bedrooms per capita	30,553	0.527	0.394	3385	0.419	0.353
House is owned and paid for	30,580	0.737	0.440	3392	0.744	0.436
Log equivalized household income from work	23,720	9.570	1.036	2532	8.730	1.194

Note: The ^ and ★ are used to indicate controls that are used only in some regressions, as will be explained when relevant.

β_{it} is a vector of individual and household level controls for each person i at time period t, and ε_{it} is an error term for each person i at time period t. We control for time-period effects by including dummy variables for wave 1 and wave 2 ($w1$ and $w2$, respectively). Given that our outcome variables are binary, we choose to present the results using binary OLS models, although the results were qualitatively the same for all regressions when estimated using probit models. We choose the OLS model given that it is more straightforward to interpret coefficients and implement the instrumental variable technique that will be discussed. Horrace and Oaxaca (2006) show that if only a few or no predicted probabilities lie outside the unit interval – none of the predicted probabilities lie outside the unit interval for any of the regressions we estimate, then OLS estimation for a binary dependent variable should yield unbiased and consistent estimates. Hence, this drawback of using OLS with a binary dependent variable is not applicable in our analysis.

Using all the controls described in Table 24.4 (except those with the ★ next to the variable name), we test the determinants of subjective wellbeing outcomes for the pooled sample of males and females, and Indigenous and non-Indigenous groups over the three survey waves. Table 24.5 shows whether speaking an Indigenous language was a statistically significant determinant of a subjective wellbeing outcome (the full regression results can be found in the Appendix Tables 24A.1–24A.6). After controlling for other covariates, speaking an Indigenous language had no impact on the sad or morbidity outcomes, and only had a statistically significant negative effect on the probability of feeling that life had improved.

We also estimate an OLS model for the probability of feeling that unsafety has increased compared to five years before, but this time include some controls that differ from those used for the other three subjective wellbeing outcomes, as they are more relevant for this crime-related measure (i.e. we include all the controls in Table 24.4 without a ^ symbol next to the variable name). We find that for the life improvement variable, being Indigenous leads to a statistically significant lower chance of reporting feeling that unsafety has increased. This is consistent with the average trends by Indigenous status discussed before, and shows that even after controlling for relevant observable individual characteristics including region of inhabitance, Indigenous people feel less exposed to the crime and violence, even after its rapid rise in recent years. The two wave dummies are also significantly negative for both population sub-groups, showing that relative to wave 3 individuals were much less likely to report feeling unsafety had increased in wave 1 and wave 2.

Given the rise in violence that Mexico has been exposed to in recent years and the negative impacts that it has had on several socioeconomic and psychological outcomes as previously discussed, the difference in feelings of unsafety by ethnicity is an important finding. As shown in the modelling framework of Figure 24.11, subjective wellbeing sub-components can influence other subjective wellbeing outcomes. Feelings of unsafety and of life improvements

Table 24.5 Statistically significant Indigenous status controls and respective subjective wellbeing outcomes

Subjective wellbeing outcomes	*Indigenous language*
Probability of feeling life has improved	Negative
Probability of feeling unsafety has increased compared to 5 years before	Negative
Probability of feeling sadness sometimes or often in past month	Insignificant
Probability feeling morbid	Insignificant

are two important sub-components of affect and life evaluations, respectively. It is sensible to think that they could be related, as increased feelings of unsafety can lead to increased feelings that life – amid more violence and crime – has not improved. Particularly, living in an unsafe or deprived community has been linked with lower outcomes in life satisfaction (see Dolan et al., 2008, for a review of empirical findings), and subjective measures of safety have been linked more strongly to subjective wellbeing than objective measures (Helliwell & Wang, 2010). Wills-Herrera et al. (2011) find a significant effect of subjective perceptions of insecurity on a subjective-wellbeing index, and explain how individual's subjective wellbeing "is influenced by contextual and social variables [such as]... community connectedness and social capital". In this way, subjective-wellbeing outcomes go beyond being an affect sub-component, to capturing eudaimonic information on the psychological state of individuals (Forero-Pinena et al., 2014).

When we estimate the determinants of feeling that unsafety has increased for Indigenous and non-Indigenous people separately (see Table 24.4), we find that determinants differ widely by Indigenous status. For the non-Indigenous, most of the controls have a significant effect on feelings of safety and the expected sign, yet this is not true for the Indigenous sub-population: many of the controls are insignificant; regional dummies show different signs and significance compared to the non-Indigenous; less educated Indigenous people report feeling more unsafe than do more educated ones, while the opposite holds for the non-Indigenous. Similarities exist for the two sub-populations in that people were less likely to report that unsafety had increased in the first and second waves, having debts lead to a higher probability of reporting that unsafety had increased, and people in smaller communities were less likely to report that unsafety had increased. Clearly, even under a framework that controls for geographic, personal and household characteristics, subjective feelings of unsafety in Mexico differ widely by Indigenous status, and point to the different culture, values and overall social experiences that Indigenous Mexicans are exposed to relative to the non-Indigenous population.

Regression specification and results for the relationship between subjective feelings of unsafety and subjective life improvements

As has been shown, there is a strong link between subjective insecurity and self-assessed life evaluations, as well as strong differences by ethnic identity, so the next set of regression analysis investigates how feelings of unsafety affect life improvements by Indigenous status. Before specifying the models, we use to estimate this relationship, there is one more crucial modelling issue to discuss: reverse causality. While including measures of subjective wellbeing as predictors of other subjective wellbeing measures can improve the predictability of models and capture important correlations, it is hard to argue that causality flows from one subjective outcome to the other, and not vice versa. In our particular case, it is sensible to think that if a person feels unsafety has increased, this feeling of insecurity and vulnerability has a negative impact on the probability that a person feels their life has improved. We cannot however rule out *a priori* the possibility that feeling your life has not improved due to other factors unrelated to crime and violence, will not impact your subjective perception of whether unsafety has increased. Because both subjective wellbeing outcomes could be co-determined, we have a potential endogeneity problem, and so our OLS estimates could be inconsistent and biased (Angrist & Pischke, 2008). To ensure that our model and conclusions do not suffer from a reverse causality problem, we estimate the model using an instrumental variable – the presence of police in the community.

This instrument is strongly related to feelings of unsafety, and we have no reason to believe that it directly affects the probability of feeling life has improved.

We estimate the following equations by OLS separately for Indigenous and non-Indigenous respondents in order to better capture any differences in important determinants by Indigenous status:

$$\text{LifeImprov}_{it} = \alpha + \text{Unsafety}_{it} + \beta_{it} + w1 + w2 + \varepsilon_{it}$$

We then use 'presence of police in the community' as an instrumental variable (IV) for feelings of unsafety, and estimate the following simultaneous equation model using two-stage least squares:[4]

$$\text{Unsafety}_{it} = \gamma + \text{Police}_{it} + v_{it}$$

$$\text{LifeImprov}_{it} = \alpha + \text{Unsafety}_{it} + \beta_{it} + w1 + w2 + \varepsilon_{it}$$

Table 24A.1 in the Appendix presents the OLS and IV results by Indigenous status. Once again, the determinants of life improvements are similar only for a few of the variables; for the most part the statistical significance of controls is different across the two sub-groups, and for some of the controls, so are the signs of the effects. Both estimation techniques (i.e. OLS and IV) consistently yield qualitatively equivalent results with the exception of the time dummies, as will be discussed. For both sub-groups, females tend to report life improvements more than men, more education leads to higher reported life improvements, and having higher savings, household income and being part of a community savings group also lead to higher chances of reporting that life has improved. Nonetheless, many of the determinants are quite different by ethnicity. Particularly, bigger households have a positive effect on the life improvement outcome for Indigenous people, and a negative effect for non-Indigenous people; on the other hand, the number of bedrooms per capita has an insignificant effect on life improvements for Indigenous respondents, but a positive effect for the non-Indigenous.

The key purpose of this exercise was however, to see how subjective perceptions of unsafety affect the probability that the respondent feels life has improved. We find that using both OLS and IV estimations (although the marginal effects are much larger when the IV estimation is used), the associations for non-Indigenous people are as expected: negative and statistically significant. On the other hand, the association for Indigenous people while negative, is statistically insignificant using both OLS and IV estimations. Hence, being part of an Indigenous group, even after controlling for a wide range of individual and household characteristics, affects subjective wellbeing assessments on unsafety and life improvements in different ways to the non-Indigenous population.

Finally, while unsafety has objectively increased over the most recent two waves at a national level, life improvements for the first two waves are negative and significant (using IV regression) relative to the third wave, while they are statistically insignificant for Indigenous people using both OLS and IV. This points to the possibility that while violence and unsafety have spiked in Mexico in recent years, other time-specific changes have moderated the negative impact of violence.

Discussion

While Latin American countries as a whole exhibit unusually high levels of subjective wellbeing given their average level of per capita GDP, this anomaly does not seem to hold to the same extent for the region's Indigenous people. Analysing the pooled sample of Indigenous people for eight large countries in the region, we found consistent disparities in subjective health, sadness and perceptions of life improvement, across the life course and for the period of 1999–2014. Except for morbidity, which is very similar for both sub-groups, these broad regional results also held qualitatively for Mexico's indigenous groups. Given the levels of crime that characterize much of Latin America and the vulnerable economic status of many Indigenous people across the region, we also examined the probability that people across eight Latin American countries fear crime, and for Mexico, we analysed the probability of feeling that unsafety had increased. Surprisingly, while across the region Indigenous people tend to fear crime to a greater extent than the non-Indigenous population, the same does not hold for Mexico's Indigenous group across the life course or over recent years.

To more rigorously explore these differences by ethnicity within Mexico as well as the way in which subjective feelings of unsafety relate to other subjective wellbeing outcomes, we use a modelling framework. We estimated OLS regressions by Indigenous status, controlling for individual, household and community characteristics, and found that after controlling for these covariates, Indigenous status only significantly affects feelings of life improvements and of feelings of unsafety, which point to potential cultural factors that shape how individuals perceive and assess these two outcome variables. Finally, when we explored the effect of feelings of unsafety on the probability of feeling that life had improved (while controlling for the possibility of reverse causality through IV estimations), we found that feelings of unsafety are significant determinants for the non-Indigenous, but not so for Indigenous people. Collectively, these results support the importance of accounting for Indigenous-specific factors that affect subjective wellbeing, as important determinants of subjective wellbeing outcomes differ greatly between Indigenous and non-Indigenous people. A recent study on Mexicans' life satisfaction by Dugain and Olaberriá (2015) claims that most of the difference in life satisfaction by Indigenous status disappears once education and income are controlled for, yet our separate analysis by ethnicity shows that there are significantly different determinants outcomes by ethnicity, even after controlling for socioeconomic characteristics.

Our analysis yields insights into the determinants by Indigenous status for life improvements and feelings of unsafety, and explores the causal relationship between these two outcomes by ethnicity, yet it is unable to pinpoint the particular cultural values that affect the sizable differences of these outcomes. Doing so is a particularly difficult task given the numerous cultural factors that would need to be considered, as well as the fact that incorporating these factors into subjective wellbeing models as controls could potentially lead to reverse causality problems, as it is difficult to establish causal flows with certainty. Nonetheless, subjective wellbeing analysis has the potential to better proxy unobserved human wellbeing than one-dimensional economic outcomes – specially for Indigenous people whose wellbeing is more strongly linked to non-economic and hard-to-quantify influences – and should be a fundamental component of designing policies aimed at increasing wellbeing in ways more equitable across the vastly heterogeneous societies of Latin America.

Appendix: Full regression results

Table 24A.1 Pooled OLS estimates: probability respondent has felt sad often or sometimes during the past four weeks

Indigenous	0.010
Female	0.188***
Region: Central	0.043***
Region: South	−0.004
Region: East	0.024**
Region: West	0.042***
Age	0.003***
Married or in union	−0.007
Education: elementary	0.062**
Education: secondary	0.047*
Not working	0.031***
Lives in community with <15,000 people	−0.036***
Receives income from Progresa	−0.047*
Receives income from Procampo	0.007
Participates in community savings program (Tanda)	0.060***
Has relatives in USA	0.049***
Has medical insurance	−0.003
Has savings	−0.004
Has debts	0.120***
Household head is female	0.018*
Number of children in household	0.006*
Household size	−0.005**
Number of bedrooms per capita	−0.000
House is owned and paid for	−0.004
Log equivalized household income from work	−0.028***
Wave 1	−0.037***
Wave 2	−0.072***
Constant	0.310***
	Number of observations: 19,847
	Adjusted *R*-squared: 0.063

Notes: *** $p<0.01$, ** $p<0.05$, * $p<0.1$.
Omitted categories are: non-Indigenous; male; region: Northern; not married or in union; education: higher than secondary; working; lives in community with >15,000 people; doesn't receive income from Progresa or Procampo; doesn't participate in Tanda; doesn't have relatives in the USA, medical insurance, savings or debts; household head is male; house is not owned and paid; wave 3.

Table 24A.2 Pooled OLS estimates: probability respondent feels his/her life has improved

Indigenous	−0.026**
Female	0.040***
Region: Central	−0.001
Region: South	−0.013
Region: East	0.033***
Region: West	−0.011
Age	−0.005***
Married or in union	0.036***
Education: elementary	−0.135***
Education: secondary	−0.057**
Not working	−0.013
Lives in community with <15,000 people	−0.026***
Receives income from Progresa	0.073***
Receives income from Procampo	0.011
Participates in community savings program (Tanda)	0.053***
Has relatives in USA	−0.001
Has medical insurance	0.060***
Has savings	0.123***
Has debts	−0.004
Household head is female	−0.003
Number of children in household	0.003
Household size	−0.003
Number of bedrooms per capita	0.013
House is owned and paid for	0.010
Log equivalized household income from work	0.022***
Wave 1	−0.038***
Wave 2	0.068***
Constant	0.339***
	Number of observations: 19,849
	Adjusted R-squared: 0.071

Notes: *** $p<0.01$, ** $p<0.05$, * $p<0.1$.
Omitted categories are: non-Indigenous; male; region: Northern; not married or in union; education: higher than secondary; working; lives in community with >15,000 people; doesn't receive income from Progresa or Procampo; doesn't participate in Tanda; doesn't have relatives in the USA, medical insurance, savings or debts; household head is male; house is not owned and paid; wave 3.

Table 24A.3 Pooled OLS estimates: probability respondent feels morbid

Indigenous	−0.003
Female	0.011★★★
Region: Central	0.010★★
Region: South	−0.006
Region: East	−0.002
Region: West	0.017★★★
Age	0.002★★★
Married or in union	−0.002
Education: elementary	0.033★★★
Education: secondary	0.018
Not working	0.016★★★
Lives in community with <15,000 people	0.005
Receives income from Progresa	−0.002
Receives income from Procampo	0.012
Participates in community savings program (Tanda)	−0.001
Has relatives in USA	0.007★★
Has medical insurance	0.0001
Has savings	−0.004
Has debts	0.015★★
Household head is female	0.006
Number of children in household	−0.004★★★
Household size	0.0002
Number of bedrooms per capita	−0.005
House is owned and paid	−0.005
Log equivalized household income from work	−0.005★★★
Wave 1	0.002
Wave 2	−0.014★★
Constant	−0.030
	Number of observations: 19,847
	Adjusted R-squared: 0.027

Notes: ★★★ $p<0.01$, ★★ $p<0.05$, ★ $p<0.1$.

Omitted categories are: non-Indigenous; male; region: Northern; not married or in union; education: higher than secondary; working; lives in community with >15,000 people; doesn't receive income from Progresa or Procampo; doesn't participate in Tanda; doesn't have relatives in the USA, medical insurance, savings or debts; household head is male; house is not owned and paid; wave 3.

Table 24A.4 Pooled OLS estimates: probability respondent thinks unsafety has increased compared to five years before

Indigenous	−0.021★
Female	0.043★★★
Region: Central	0.076★★★
Region: South	0.001
Region: East	−0.040★★★
Region: West	0.028★★★
Age	0.001★★★
Married or in union	0.029★★★
Education: elementary	−0.066★★★
Education: secondary	−0.033
Not working	−0.018★★
Lives in community with <15,000 people	−0.061★★★
Receives income from Progresa	−0.018
Receives income from Procampo	0.004
Participates in community savings program (Tanda)	0.015
Has savings	0.007
Has debts	0.102★★★
Police present in neighbourhood in the last month	−0.044★★★
Carries valuables	−0.034★★★
Household head is female	−0.020★★
Number of children in household	0.003
Household size	−0.001
Number of bedrooms per capita	0.023★★
House is owned and paid for	−0.001
Log equivalized household income from work	−0.001
Wave 1 dummy	−0.149★★★
Wave 2 dummy	−0.157★★★
Constant	0.327★★★
	Number of observations: 19,853
	Adjusted R-squared: 0.032

Notes: ★★★ $p<0.01$, ★★ $p<0.05$, ★ $p<0.1$.
Omitted categories are: non–Indigenous; male; region: Northern; not married or in union; education: higher than secondary; working; lives in community with >15,000 people; doesn't receive income from Progresa or Procampo; doesn't participate in Tanda; doesn't have savings or debts; police not present in neighbourhood in last month; does not carry valuables outside home; household head is male; house is not owned and paid; wave 3.

Table 24A.5 OLS estimates by ethnicity: probability respondent thinks unsafety has increased compared to five years before

	Indigenous	Non-Indigenous
Female	−0.013	0.047***
Region: Central	−0.037	0.078***
Region: South	0.032	0.005
Region: East	0.012	−0.045***
Region: West	0.121***	0.021*
Age	0.0002	0.001***
Married or in union	0.024	0.029***
Education: elementary	0.127*	−0.086***
Education: secondary	0.157**	−0.053**
Not working	0.029	−0.021**
Lives in community with <15,000 people	−0.111***	−0.059***
Receives income from Progresa	−0.016	−0.028
Receives income from Procampo	−0.008	0.006
Participates in community savings program (Tanda)	0.020	0.015
Has savings	−0.040	0.011
Has debts	0.099**	0.099***
Police present in neighbourhood in the last month	−0.083***	−0.039***
Carries valuables	0.004	−0.037***
Household head is female	0.011	−0.022**
Number of children in household	0.005	0.002
Household size	0.007	−0.001
Number of bedrooms per capita	0.108**	0.018*
House is owned and paid for	0.002	−0.0003
Log equivalized household income from work	−0.016*	0.001
Wave 1 dummy	−0.055	−0.154***
Wave 2 dummy	−0.094**	−0.160***
Constant	0.191	0.332***
	Number of observations: 1,672	Number of observations: 18,181
	Adjusted R-squared: 0.023	Adjusted R-squared: 0.033

Notes: *** $p<0.01$, ** $p<0.05$, * $p<0.1$.
Omitted categories are the same as in Table 24A.4 except for Indigenous status.

Table 24A.6 OLS and IV estimates: probability respondent feels his/her life has improved

	OLS estimates		IV estimates	
	Indigenous	*Non-Indigenous*	*Indigenous*	*Non-Indigenous*
Unsafety has increased	−0.033	−0.036★★★	−0.462	−0.948★★★
Female	0.046	0.042★★★	0.045	0.087★★★
Region: Central	−0.007	0.001	−0.023	0.074★★★
Region: South	0.064★	−0.027★★	0.083★	−0.021
Region: East	0.087★★	0.029★★★	0.097★★	−0.010
Region: West	−0.033	−0.001	0.023	0.014
Age	−0.002★	−0.005★★★	−0.001	−0.004★★★
Married or in union	0.027	0.037★★★	0.040	0.065★★★
Education: elementary	−0.147★	−0.139★★★	−0.111	−0.215★★★
Education: secondary	−0.027	−0.063★★	0.024	−0.111★★★
Not working	−0.048★	−0.011	−0.036	−0.031★★
Lives in community with <15,000 people	−0.042	−0.028★★★	−0.093★	−0.078★★★
Receives income from Progresa	0.046	0.081★★★	0.036	0.055
Receives income from Procampo	−0.095★	0.030	−0.097	0.035
Participates in community savings program (Tanda)	0.099★	0.051★★★	0.105★	0.063★★★
Has relatives in USA	−0.011	−0.002	−0.025	−0.006
Has medical insurance	0.038	0.060★★★	0.007	0.052★★★
Has savings	0.127★★★	0.122★★★	0.113★★	0.131★★★
Has debts	0.010	−0.001	0.054	0.090★★★
Household head is female	−0.011	−0.003	−0.008	−0.022
Number of children in household	−0.011	0.004	−0.009	0.007
Household size	0.008	−0.004★	0.011★	−0.005★
Number of bedrooms per capita	0.038	0.013	0.083	0.029★
House is owned and paid for	−0.005	0.012	−0.003	0.011
Log equivalized household income from work	0.020★	0.023★★★	0.013	0.023★★★
Wave 1	0.0002	−0.047★★★	−0.033	−0.189★★★
Wave 2	0.047	0.063★★★	−0.003	−0.089★★
Constant	0.165	0.361★★★	0.259	0.639★★★
	Number of observations: 1,671	Number of observations: 18,172	Number of observations: 1,671	Number of observations: 18,172
	Adjusted R−squared: 0.0513	Adjusted R−squared: 0.072		

Notes: ★★★ $p<0.01$, ★★ $p<0.05$, ★ $p<0.1$.
Omitted categories are same as in Table 24A.2 except for Indigenous status.

Notes

1 For a comprehensive list of publications using the MxFLS, see www.ennvih-mxfls.org/english/working-papers.html.
2 There are moderate to high correlations among the three classes of subjective wellbeing. For a review of empirical evidence on the interactions among the three classes of subjective-wellbeing classes, see chapter 1 in OECD (2013).
3 Reviewing the empirical works on important determinants of subjective wellbeing not only falls outside the direct focus of this chapter, but would also be too lengthy. We encourage readers to read Boarini et al. (2012), and chapter 3 of OECD (2013) for a thorough review of relevant works.
4 Testing for instrument relevance, we find that police presence and feelings of unsafety are strongly correlated: F-statistic of 13.3 and 33.2 for Indigenous and non-Indigenous groups respectively.

We also use the Durbin-Wu-Hausman test of endogeneity, and find that while we can reject the null hypothesis that feelings of unsafety is an endogenous variable, we cannot reject the null for the Indigenous group. This provides evidence of the importance of correcting for reverse causality through IV estimation.

References

Angrist, J.D., & Pischke, J.S. (2008). *Mostly harmless econometrics: An empiricist's companion.* Princeton, NJ: Princeton University Press.

Ayres, R.L. (1998). *Crime and violence as development issues in Latin America and the Caribbean.* Washington, DC: World Bank Publications.

Boarini, R., Comola, M., Smith, C., Manchin, R., & De Keulenaer, F. (2012). *What makes for a better life? The determinants of subjective well-being in OECD countries–Evidence from the Gallup World Poll* (No. 2012/3). Paris: OECD Publishing. http://dx.doi.org/10.1787/5k9b9ltjm937-en.

Brown, R., & Velásquez, A. (2015). The *effect of violent conflict on the human capital accumulation of young adults.* Working paper, Duke University.

Dolan, P., Peasgood, T., & White, M. (2008). Do we really know what makes us happy? A review of the economic literature on the factors associated with subjective well-being. *Journal of Economic Psychology, 29*(1), 94–122.

Dugain, V., & Olaberriá, E. (2015). *What makes Mexicans happy?* OECD Economics Department Working Papers (No. 1196). Paris: OECD Publishing. http://dx.doi.org/10.1787/5js4h5qp6l0w-en.

Farfán, G., Genoni, M. E., Rubalcava, L., Teruel, G., & Thomas, D. (2011). *Oportunidades and its impact on child nutrition.* Working paper, Duke University.

Fleche, S., Smith, C., & Sorsa, P. (2011). *Exploring determinants of subjective wellbeing in OECD countries: Evidence from the World Value Survey* (No. 921). Paris: OECD Publishing.

Forero-Pineda, C., Wills Herrera, E., Andonova, V., Orozco Collazos, L.E., & Pardo, O. (2014). Violence, insecurity and hybrid organisational forms: A study in conflict-ridden zones in Colombia. *Journal of Development Studies, 50*(6), 789–802.

Hall, G., & Patrinos, H.A. (Eds.). (2006). *Indigenous peoples, poverty, and human development in Latin America.* New York: Palgrave Macmillan.

Hall, G.H., & Patrinos, H. A. (2012). *Indigenous peoples, poverty, and development.* Cambridge: Cambridge University Press.

Helliwell, J.F., & Wang, S. (2010). *Trust and well-being* (No. w15911). Working paper, National Bureau of Economic Research.

Horrace, W.C., & Oaxaca, R.L. (2006). Results on the bias and inconsistency of ordinary least squares for the linear probability model. *Economics Letters, 90*(3), 321–327.

Inglehart, R., Foa, R., Peterson, C., & Welzel, C. (2008). Development, freedom, and rising happiness: A global perspective (1981–2007). *Perspectives on Psychological Science, 3*(4), 264–285.

International Crisis Group. (2013). *Pena Nieto's challenge: Criminal cartels and rule of law in Mexico.* International Crisis Group.

Linares, F.N. (2010). *Los pueblos indígenas de México: Pueblos indígenas del México contemporáneo.* México, DF: Monografía Nacional, 20.

McKee, D., & Todd, P.E. (2011). The longer-term effects of human capital enrichment programs on poverty and inequality: Oportunidades in Mexico. *Estudios de economía, 38*(1), 68.

Michaelsen, M.M. (2012). *Mental health and labour supply: Evidence from Mexico's ongoing violent conflicts.* Ruhr Economic Paper, 378.

Molzahn, C., Ríos, V., & Shirk, D.A. (2012). *Drug violence in Mexico: Data and analysis through 2011.* Trans-Border Institute, University of San Diego, San Diego, CA.

OECD. (2013). *OECD guidelines on measuring subjective well-being.* Paris: OECD Publishing. http://dx.doi.org/10.1787/9789264191655-en.

Patrinos, H.A., & Skoufias, E. (2007). *Economic opportunities for Indigenous peoples in Latin America.* Conference Edition.

Servan-Mori, E., Torres-Pereda, P., Orozco, E., & Sosa-Rubí, S.G. (2014). An explanatory analysis of economic and health inequality changes among Mexican indigenous people, 2000–2010. *Children, 15,* 16.

Silver, A. (2014). Families across borders: The emotional impacts of migration on origin families. *International Migration, 52*(3), 194–220.

Stutzer, A., & Frey, B.S. (2004). Reported subjective well-being: A challenge for economic theory and economic policy. *Schmollers Jahrbuch, 124*(2), 1–41.

Wills-Herrera, E., Orozco, L.E., Forero-Pineda, C., Pardo, O., & Andonova, V. (2011). The relationship between perceptions of insecurity, social capital and subjective well-being: Empirical evidences from areas of rural conflict in Colombia. *The Journal of Socio-Economics, 40*(1), 88–96.

25

SUBJECTIVE WELLBEING OF THE P'URHÉPECHA PEOPLE

Between tradition and modernity

Mariano Rojas and Paz Chávez

Introduction

This chapter studies the explanatory structure of the P'urhépecha people's wellbeing. For centuries the P'urhépecha people were relatively isolated from the rest of the world and they lived according to their own values, norms and beliefs, as specified by the *P'indékua* (customs). The P'urhépecha's ancestral tradition emphasizes a cosmovision where the family and the spiritual understanding of their relationship with nature play a central role in their daily life and, as expected, in their wellbeing. However, during the past decades some P'urhépecha communities have experienced a process of modernization and of integration into a market-driven economy. Thus, their culture has been affected by these socioeconomic changes, which are likely to modify their subjective wellbeing explanatory structure.

This chapter advances two main arguments. First, that culture plays an important role in the explanation of people's wellbeing. Values, traditions and perspectives influence what is relevant in people's lives and, consequently, the relevant factors that explain the experience of being well. It is important to be precise about this argument: it is in the human condition to experience wellbeing and, thus, the human experiences of being well are comparable across people independently of their ethnic and cultural background; however, the factors that give rise to these experiences may change across people and across cultures. Second, culture is not static. Large socioeconomic transformations may lead to changes in people's values and beliefs, some traditions may disappear and new values may emerge. These transformations lead to modifications in the explanatory structure of people's wellbeing.

This chapter presents the main findings from a study of culture, modernization and subjective wellbeing in the P'urhépecha people. The study focuses on understanding the explanatory structure of wellbeing of the P'urhépecha people, as well as on investigating how it was affected by the process of socioeconomic modernization some groups of the community have been exposed to. The empirical research takes advantage of a survey applied in two P'urhépecha communities, Comachuén and Sevina, which have been asymmetrically exposed to the process of modernization and integration into a market-driven economy. The spoken language is used as the main criterion to segment the sample and to distinguish between those P'urhépecha people who remain relatively isolated from the modernization process and those who have, at least partially, been integrated into modern society and a market-driven economy.

A domains-of-life approach is used to explain people's wellbeing. Life satisfaction is explained based on satisfaction in five domains of life: health, economic, occupational, family and spiritual. The main findings from the investigation show that those who are closely attached to P'urhépecha customs have an explanatory structure of life satisfaction that depends heavily on satisfaction in the family, spiritual and health domains of life, whereas satisfaction in the economic and occupational domains play no role in explaining life satisfaction. In contrast, those who no longer speak P'urhépecha largely base their life satisfaction on the economic and occupational domains, with no importance at all placed on the family and spiritual domains of life.

The P'urhépecha people

Historical background

The P'urhépecha people are part of a larger Indigenous group that has inhabited the current Mexican territory since the twelfth century. By the fourteenth century, the P'urhépecha people had established a vast state in what is now the Mexican state of Michoacán. Like all Indigenous groups in the region, they were conquered by the Spaniards during the sixteenth century and later became vassals of the Spanish empire. In present time, the P'urhépecha people live in the north-central region of the state of Michoacán.

The P'urhépecha people have gone through important historical events, such as: the Spanish arrival and military conquest in the sixteenth century; the spiritual conquest by the Catholic church in the sixteenth and seventeenth centuries; and their integration into the centralized construction of the Mexican state, which took place in the nineteenth and early twentieth centuries. These developments have transformed the original P'urhépecha culture; however, several elements of the ancient civilization are still present. For example, current religious ceremonies reflect a process of syncretism between Catholic rituals and ancient P'urhépecha beliefs (Cipriani, 2009; Jacinto, 1988).

During the beginning of the twentieth century, and as a consequence of the Mexican revolution, the country advanced a strategy to strengthen its national identity and to foster economic development. The progress of the country required the implementation of economic, social and educative programs aimed at integrating all peoples into the construction of the Mexican nation (Vasconcelos, 2007). In addition, the modernization ideas were in vogue at the time and it was understood that traditional values were an obstacle to the big social transformations that were required in the name of progress (Inkeles & Smith, 1974). Consequently, the values and beliefs of Indigenous communities were considered a hindrance to be overcome, rather than as a valuable inheritance to preserve. That is to say that the modernization of the country required the 'Westernization' of its Indigenous peoples, implying significant modifications in their social organization and in their identity (Bonfil, 1990; Sebastián, 2006). The success of the acculturation campaign, however, was not regionally homogeneous and, consequently, it is still possible to find, in many communities, the predominance of their original beliefs, values, social organization and way of life.

The *P'indékua*

The *P'indékua* literally means 'customs', and it refers to the traditions, practices, norms and conventions of the P'urhépecha people. These customs have been transmitted from generation to generation and they play an important role in the social organization and way of life in the P'urhépecha communities. These norms involve many aspects of life in the community, such as the importance of solidarity, collective work and local festivities; the norms introduce social, economic, political and religious order into the daily lives of the P'urhépecha people. The agricultural and life cycles, the rituals and dances, the system of weights and measures, the rites of passage, and even the ownership of land are regulated by the *P'indékua*. Compliance to these norms is supervised by all community members (García, 2013; Jacinto, 1988; Muñoz, 2009).

García (2013) states that the *P'indékua* has facilitated life in the community, which has been central to the identity and sense of membership of the P'urhépecha people. The *P'indékua* remains important to the P'urhépecha people, however, greater exposure to the modernization process during the twentieth century has diminished its relevance in many P'urhépecha communities.

Some key elements of the *P'indékua*, which are central to this study, are discussed below.

The community

There is a strong sense of community in the P'urhépecha people. Adult members of the community participate in the construction of facilities such as schools and health centers. The P'urhépecha word *tánjatsikuni*, which makes reference to these communal chores, can be translated as 'taking while you are giving'. This word clearly reflects the idea of everybody benefiting by giving to others (García, 2013; Villanueva, 2009). Activities such as farming, sowing, fixing roads and building family houses involve the cooperation of all members of the community. The organization of festivities is also an opportunity to engage the community (Aguirre, 1969). In general, daily life in the P'urhépecha communities is not understood in an individual sense, but rather in a community one. Cipriani (2009) states that the socio-political and religious system of the P'urhépecha people can be synthesized into two main principles: *jats'ipeni* (serving others) and *marhuatspeni* (serving societies). Land and natural resources are collectively owned; the P'urhépecha people were not enthusiastic about external efforts seeking to introduce the private property concept in both the nineteenth century (as a consequence of the Mexican liberal movement) and the twentieth century (as a consequence of the modernization movement) (Aguirre, 1995; Sebastián, 2006).

The family

The extended family is central in the social organization of the P'urhépecha people; the strength of the family is at the base of the organization of the community (Villanueva, 2009). The term used by the P'urhépecha people to refer to the extended family is *k'umanchekua*, which can be translated as house or home. Marriage celebrations involve the participation of the whole community and recently married people are not expected to live in a separate house; during the first years of marriage, they are expected to live with the parents of either the groom or the bride.

Family relationships are very important to the P'urhépecha people; their houses are designed in such a way as to favor extended family interactions. For example, houses have common areas for the extended family to meet and collectively cook their meals. Members of the extended family share some domestic chores, such as preparing meals, cleaning the house and nurturing children. Having children and forming a family is an important goal in the life of most P'urhépecha people (Villanueva, 2009).

Neighbors are also important; visits among neighbors are frequent, and their support and help is expected and given as part of daily life. The institution of *compadrazgo* (godparents) is also central to the P'urhépecha people; it creates bonds that go beyond the extended family. The *compadrazgo* is an institution that emerges from the responsibilities that godparents accept at the child's baptism in raising the child and contributing to his/her success in life.

In practice, the *compadrazgo* creates strong and formal bonds between the parents and the godparents of a child.

Nature and the spiritual cosmovision

The Catholic religion is predominant among the P'urhépecha people; however, there is a high degree of syncretism between Catholic rituals and the old spiritual beliefs of the P'urhépecha. Argueta (2008) states that in the spiritual cosmovision of the P'urhépecha people the gods reveal themselves not through sacred scriptures but through daily events, dreams and omens. Hence within the P'urhépecha cosmovision there is a close relationship between spirituality and surrounding nature. Like many other Indigenous cultures, the P'urhépecha understand themselves as being part of nature. Hence, they do not aim to master nature and they do not approach it as an economic resource (Alarcón-Cháires, 2009; Chávez, 1997). Consequently, there are strong bonds between the P'urhépecha community and nature, which emerge from their understanding of nature as revealing signs and messages from their gods. Nature is, literally, sacred and the P'urhépecha people learn to live within it, rather than above it (Alarcón-Cháires, 2009; Argueta, 2008). The modernization process, however, has deteriorated the sacred and lively character of nature, with some communities now viewing forests as a natural resource and land as having a market value. Integration into a market economy has implied a transformation of the P'urhépecha peoples' relationship with nature; with some communities understanding this transformation as a rupture of their sacred covenant (Aguirre, 1953; Muñoz, 2009).

Festivities

Festivities have been central to P'urhépecha culture since pre-Hispanic times. Religious celebrations such as weddings, baptisms and the many feasts honoring the patron saints in every neighborhood, as well as ancestral celebrations (such as the day of the death) are opportunities for the P'urhépecha people to share their experiences and joys with all members of the community. All community members accept different responsibilities in the organization of these celebrations (Topete, 2009). From a Western perspective (and in particular a Western economic calculus, which is based on individualistic and materialistic values) the expenditures the community makes in organizing these festivities could be considered a waste of resources. However, from the P'urhépecha perspective, festivities constitute an opportunity to collectively share wealth and experiences (Cipriani, 2009; Jacinto, 1988). The resources invested in festivities not only provide high status within the community for the givers (Aguirre, 1995), but they are also considered a social, religious and personal duty that people have to their community (Topete, 2009).

In short, the *P'indékua* stresses the importance of family, community and the sacred relationship with nature, while it disregards a materialistic and individualistic calculus based on treating nature as a natural resource and on emphasizing private, rather than communal, gains.

Subjective wellbeing

Life satisfaction: a wellbeing synthesis

Subjective wellbeing refers to the experience of being well. There are at least three kinds of wellbeing experiences: (1) evaluative experiences – experiences associated with assessments of failure and success in attaining one's goals and aspirations; (2) affective experiences – experiences associated with emotions and moods, usually classified as positive or negative; and (3) sensorial experiences – experiences associated with pain and pleasure. Human beings are also capable of making a general synthesis based on these experiences so that they can make an overall assessment of their life, which is often expressed as: 'my life is going well', 'I am happy with my life', 'I am satisfied with my life' (Rojas, 2014). Reported life satisfaction is commonly used in the subjective wellbeing literature as an overall synthesis for the experience of being well people have (Rojas & Veenhoven, 2013).

It is important not to confuse the experiences of being well and the synthesis people make with the many potential causes of these experiences. The human condition makes these experiences and synthesis universal; however, the relevance of the potential causes may differ among people and across countries due to differences in personality traits, values, surrounding conditions, circumstances and culture. Hence, the experience of being well and the overall synthesis can be considered as universal, while the explanatory structure is contingent on many factors and may differ across individuals and across cultures.

Domains of life: a first level of explanation

The domains-of-life literature states that life can be approached as an aggregate construct of many specific domains. The domains of life refer to human activities and spheres of being that constitute the essence of being human (Rojas, 2007a). Thus, rather than working with an abstract and out-of-context notion of human beings, the domains-of-life literature approaches human beings as concrete persons whose wellbeing emerges from the many activities they do. These activities include: interacting with family members; getting married and having children; taking economically related decisions regarding production, consumption and expenditures; having an occupation and taking responsibilities; taking care of others; and performing leisure activities and hobbies. Essential experiences of being well are generated through these activities, and human beings can assess how satisfied they are with them.

The domains-of-life approach understands life satisfaction as an overall assessment of life that emerges from satisfaction in the domains of life (Cummins, 1996; Rojas, 2006). The enumeration and demarcation of life domains is arbitrary; it can range from a small number to an almost infinite recount of human activities and spheres of being. However, any partitioning of life domains must satisfy the criteria of: parsimony (the number of domains must be manageable and each domain should refer to a clearly separable sphere of being); meaning (the life domains must correspond to how people understand their lives, they must not be sophisticated academic constructs); and usefulness (the delimitation of the life domains must contribute to the understanding of life satisfaction) (Rojas, 2007a).

Culture and subjective wellbeing

Culture refers to values, norms and beliefs that differ across social groups. Culture also implies that the drivers of wellbeing will differ across these social groups; however, this does not imply that wellbeing itself is not comparable across people and cultures. It is possible to make wellbeing comparisons across people and social groups because the experience of being well is in the human condition. Evaluative experiences (such as failure and attainment), affective experiences (such as fear, love, anxiety and many more) and sensorial experiences (such as pain and pleasure) are common to all human beings. It is the drivers of wellbeing which are expected to differ across cultures. It is due to this reason that wellbeing comparisons across cultures should not be made based on lists of (objective) drivers, but on the reports people make.

There is a vast literature pointing to the importance that culture plays in the explanatory structure of wellbeing. Differences between materialistic-oriented and relational-oriented values are emphasized by Kral and Idlout (2012) and by Rojas (2005, 2007b, 2012, 2016). The idea of a culturally determined hierarchy of needs has been stressed by Yamamoto (2011) and by Yamamoto, Feijoo, and Lazarte (2008). The difference between individualistic-oriented and collectivistic-oriented societies is studied by Luo and Gilmour (2004) and by Luo, Gilmour, and Kao (2001). The degree of social comparisons and the object of comparisons itself is mentioned by Taiaiake and Corntassel (2005). The literature on religious beliefs and the role of religion in determining values is large (Moore, Heather, & Lavis, 2005; Joshanloo, 2014). Authors such as Ingersoll-Dayton and Saengtienchai (2001) point towards differences in social and power distance.

Two volumes dealing with the importance culture plays in explaining wellbeing are Diener and Suh (2000) and Selin and Davey (2012), the latter focusing on 'non-Western cultures'.

The empirical study

The survey

The survey instrument was randomly implemented in houses in the communities of Comachuén and Sevina during May and June 2014. The survey was applied to people who were born in these communities or who have lived there for more than eight years. The survey was stratified by neighborhood and balanced by gender. The design of the questionnaire incorporated a block of subjective wellbeing questions designed based on an emic study (Kottak, 2006) previously applied in the communities. The emic exercise took three days; many informal talks were carried out with people in Comachuén and Sevina in order to incorporate their perspectives and understandings into the study.

In total, 301 persons were interviewed – 151 in Comachuén and 150 in Sevina. Forty-four percent of people in the survey are men, the average age is 41.5 years old and the age range goes from 16 to 87 years old.

The two communities: Comachuén and Sevina

Comachuén and Sevina are located in the municipality of Nahuatzen (Michoacan state, Mexico). The two communities are located in what is called the P'urhépecha plateau, at 2,400 and 2,600 meters above sea level, respectively.

The two communities share a common historical background and are geographically close. However, during the past decades they have experienced different socioeconomic processes. The two communities were relatively isolated until the late 1980s, when a new main road connecting the cities of Cherán and Patzcuaro allowed for the integration of Sevina into social and economic activities in the region (Nuño, 1996). A secondary road connecting Comachuén and Sevina was built during the mid-1990s. Currently, Comachuén is considered a community where the P'urhépecha values, tradition and culture are well preserved, while Sevina is highly exposed to the modernization process and has become more integrated into the market-driven economy (Muñoz, 2009; Garibay & Bocco, 2007). Based on the Mexican socioeconomic classification system, Sevina is classified as a highly marginalized community, while Comachuén is classified as a very highly marginalized community.

Authors such as Cipriani (2009), Jacinto (1988) and Muñoz (2009) express their doubts about whether the quality of life of the P'urhépecha people has been improved as a consequence of this process of integration into the national and global economy. These researchers recognize the enhancement in some indicators of education, health and communications, but they also point to the deterioration of some factors which are relevant to the P'urhépecha due to their values and traditions. They specifically mention the loss of collective values, the decline of solidarity, the disunion of communities, the deterioration of family bonds and the abandonment of language. It can be said that the P'urhépecha's ancestral way of life is threatened by their incorporation into the region, generating the well-known conflict between modernity and tradition.

Main variables

Life satisfaction was measured on the basis of the following question: 'How satisfied are you with your life on a 0 to 10 scale?' 0 constituted the lowest value and 10 the highest.

The following question format was used to get information about satisfaction in domains of life: 'On a 0 to 10 scale, how satisfied are you with…?' The block of questions asks about satisfaction in the following domains: the health situation you have; the economic situation in your household; the occupation or domestic activity you practice; family relationships (with spouse, children, parents, rest of family); and spiritual life (whatever your beliefs).

Table 25.1 presents descriptive statistics for life satisfaction and satisfaction in domains of life. It is observed that mean life satisfaction is close to 8 (on a scale from 0 to 10) and, as expected, mean scores are very high for satisfaction in the family domain, reaching values close to 9 for satisfaction with relationships with parents, children and spouse. Satisfaction is relatively low for the economic and occupational domains.

It is also observed in Table 25.1 that satisfaction with life and with domains of life tends to be slightly higher for those who do not speak P'urhépecha than for those who do speak it. However, statistically significant differences in mean values are observed only in the health and occupational domains of life; thus, in general, life satisfaction and satisfaction in the economic, family and spiritual domains of life do not differ between those who do speak P'urhépecha and those who do not.

Table 25.1 Life satisfaction and satisfaction in domains of life, average values

	Total	Do not speak P'urhépecha	Speak P'urhépecha	Ratio Do_not_ speak/speak
Life satisfaction	7.98	8.09	7.91	1.02
Domains of life				
Health satisfaction	7.89	8.14	7.73	1.05
Economic satisfaction	6.51	6.67	6.41	1.04
Occupational satisfaction	7.64	8.04	7.40	1.09
Spouse relationship	8.59	8.81	8.45	1.04
Children relationship	8.97	9.13	8.88	1.03
Parents relationship	9.08	9.28	8.95	1.04
Rest of family relationship	8.39	8.52	8.30	1.03
Average family domain	8.70	8.90	8.58	1.04
Spiritual life	8.37	8.32	8.40	0.99
Number of observations	301	111	184	

Source: Own survey.

The survey also gathered information regarding monthly household income. In general, these are low to extremely low income households; average monthly household income is about 2,600 pesos (approximately US$200) for a household of 5.5 members. There is a substantial household income difference between those who speak P'urhépecha (about US$170 per month) and those who do not speak P'urhépecha (about US$250). As expected, the more integrated to the economy people are the higher their income.

Life satisfaction, domains of life and modernization

Differences in the explanatory structure of wellbeing

The main argument advanced in this chapter is that the explanatory structure of wellbeing is contingent on people's culture. Culture determines what people value – those aspects that are relevant to people and that make life worth living. This section studies the wellbeing structure of people who have a similar cultural background but who have been exposed in different degrees to the process of modernization and to a market-oriented society. Spoken language is used as the main criterion to segment the sample: 183 people in the sample speak P'urhépecha while 112 do not. The following regression was run to study how satisfaction in domains of life relates to life satisfaction in the two populations; an ordinary least squares technique was used.

$$LS_i = \alpha_0 + \alpha_1 HS_i + \alpha_2 ES_i + \alpha_3 OS_i + \alpha_4 FS_i + \alpha_5 SS_i + \mu_i \qquad (1)$$

where *LS* refers to life satisfaction, *HS* to health satisfaction, *ES* to economic satisfaction, *OS* to occupational satisfaction, *FS* to family satisfaction (average of the available information for the questions regarding satisfaction in the relationship with spouse, children, parents and rest of family), and *SS* to the spiritual satisfaction of person *i*.

Table 25.2 presents the results from the econometric exercise that was applied to the two populations under study.

The *R*-squared coefficient indicates the percentage of the variability in life satisfaction that is explained by satisfaction in the domains of life under consideration. It is observed in Table 25.2 that this coefficient is between 0.37 for people who speak P'urhépecha and 0.39 for those

Table 25.2 Explaining life satisfaction: a domains of life approach OLS regression

	Do not speak P'urhépecha		Speak P'urhépecha		*Difference* *speak/do not speak*	*Statistical significance of difference*
	Coefficient	*P>t*	*Coefficient*	*P>t*		
Health	0.167	0.09	0.325	0.00	0.16	★★★
Economic	0.200	0.01	0.000	1.00	−0.20	★★★
Occupational	0.304	0.00	0.065	0.28	−0.24	★★★
Family	0.179	0.22	0.322	0.00	0.14	★
Spiritual	0.061	0.41	0.172	0.01	0.11	★
Intercept	0.850	0.45	0.694	0.39	−0.16	
R-squared	0.39		0.37			
N	106		183			

Note: Statistical significance: ★★★ 1%, ★ 10%.

Source: Based on information from own survey.

who do not. Thus, about 40 percent of the variability in life satisfaction is explained by the five domains of life; this can be considered a relatively high explanatory capability.

It is also observed in Table 25.2 that the explanatory structure of life satisfaction substantially differs between those who speak P'urhépecha and those who do not. For those who do not speak P'urhépecha, the most important domains of life are occupational and economic; health satisfaction is only slightly significant, while the family and spiritual domains of life are not statistically significant. Thus, it is possible to state that those who do not speak P'urhépecha base their life satisfaction mostly on the economic and occupational domains of life. These findings contrast with the situation of those who do speak P'urhépecha; they base their life satisfaction on the health, family and spiritual domains of life, while satisfaction in the occupational and economic domains are not important.

The results support two main arguments advanced in this chapter. First, the explanatory structure of wellbeing is contingent on culture. Second, the P'urhépecha people have ancestral values that emphasize human relations, extended family and a close relationship with nature and their spirituality, and that this is revealed in the explanatory structure of their wellbeing. In addition, the P'urhépecha people hold non-materialistic values and this is revealed in the negligible importance that the economic domain has in explaining life satisfaction. In contrast, those members of the P'urhépecha community who no longer speak their autochthonous language show a modified explanatory structure of wellbeing, where the economic and occupational domains become more important, with a complete decline in the importance of the family and spiritual domains.

Tests of differences in the estimated coefficients for those who speak and do not speak P'urhépecha were performed. These differences are statistically significant, which corroborates the hypothesis that the explanatory structure of wellbeing is different between the two groups.

Explanatory structure of people with P'urhépecha background

It could be argued that those people who do not speak P'urhépecha do not necessarily have a P'urhépecha background and that, consequently, they do not share an ancestral tradition with those who do speak P'urhépecha. This possibility would not affect the first argument of this chapter – that culture plays an important role in the explanatory structure of wellbeing, but it could undermine the second argument – that exposure to the modernization process has modified the explanatory structure of wellbeing of the P'urhépecha people. Thus, a regression analysis similar to Equation (1) was performed only on those people with a clear P'urhépecha background in order to further study the impact of modernization. We concentrate only on those people who report having at least one parent who speaks (or spoke) P'urhépecha. Sixty-two percent of people in the survey speak P'urhépecha, while 82 percent report having at least one parent who speaks (or spoke) P'urhépecha.

In the new sample we have fifty-nine persons who do not speak P'urhépecha but who have at least one parent who speaks (or spoke) P'urhépecha. Most of them (56) live in Sevina, which is the town that has been highly integrated into the market-oriented economy and exposed to the modernization process due to the construction of a main inter-city road in the late 1980s.

Table 25.3 presents the results from this econometric exercise. The results are consistent with those from the previous exercise. Satisfaction in the economic and occupational domains of life is very important for the life satisfaction of those P'urhépecha people who no longer speak their native language. Furthermore, satisfaction in the family and spiritual domains is not important for their life satisfaction. In contrast, those people who have a P'urhépecha background and

Table 25.3 Explaining life satisfaction: a domains of life approach, only for people whose parents spoke P'urhépecha OLS regression

	Do not speak P'urhépecha		Speak P'urhépecha		Difference speak / do not speak	Statistical significance of difference
	Coefficient	P>t	Coefficient	P>t		
Health	0.271	0.09	0.316	0.00	0.046	★
Economic	0.216	0.07	0.006	0.90	−0.210	★★★
Occupational	0.369	0.00	0.062	0.29	−0.308	★★★
Family	−0.104	0.65	0.246	0.02	0.351	★★★
Spiritual	0.008	0.94	0.197	0.00	0.188	★★★
Intercept	2.331	0.30	1.209	0.14	−1.122	
R-squared	0.38		0.36			
N	59		180			

Note: Statistical significance: ★★★ 1%, ★ 10%.

Source: Based on information from own survey.

who still speak P'urhépecha have an explanatory structure of wellbeing where satisfaction in the family, spiritual and health domains is central for their life satisfaction.

The transformation of the explanatory structure of wellbeing that is observed in those who have a P'urhépecha background but who no longer speak the language of their ancestors can be attributed to their exposure to the market-oriented economy and to the modernization process. Most of them live in Sevina and it is clear that their ancestral values have been modified.

Final considerations

Some groups of the P'urhépecha people have gone through a process of modernization and integration into a market-driven economy. This process implies a transformation of their ancestral customs, beliefs and values and, as a consequence, a modification in the explanatory structure of their wellbeing. Those P'urhépecha groups who have remained closely attached to the ancestral customs, as stated by the *P'indékua* and as measured by their ability to speak the native language, have an explanatory structure of life satisfaction that depends heavily on satisfaction with family relations, spiritual life and health, and where satisfaction in the economic and occupational domains of life play a negligible role. However, those P'urhépecha groups that have experienced a process of acculturation and modernization show a modification in their explanatory structure of wellbeing: their life satisfaction depends heavily on the economic and occupational domains, with no importance at all placed on the family and spiritual domains of life.

This research shows that the explanatory structure of wellbeing is contingent on the values, beliefs and customs people have. It has also shown that relevant socioeconomic transformations can modify the explanatory structure of wellbeing. Modernization has not necessarily altered the reported level of overall life satisfaction for the P'urhépecha people, but it has transformed their values and, consequently, has promoted important behavioral changes in their pursuit of happiness. Modernization promotes a pursuit of happiness, which is based on economic and occupational concerns rather than on spiritual and relational ones. Thus, greater production and income is observed in those communities that are highly exposed to the market-driven economy; however, this greater production is not associated with greater wellbeing. On the other hand, those communities that base their wellbeing on spiritual and relational concerns may show lower production and income indicators, but this does not mean that their subjective wellbeing is lower. Hence, differences in values across peoples do imply differences in their explanatory structure of wellbeing and, in consequence, it makes it impossible to judge the wellbeing of people based on their income or production indicators. Furthermore, it is important to remark that this lack of universality in explanatory factors of wellbeing makes it inappropriate to measure social progress based on indicators such as gross domestic product and Human Development Index, which assume homogeneity across regions and cultures.

References

Aguirre, G. (1953). *Formas de Gobierno Indígena*. México: Imprenta Universitaria.

Aguirre, G. (1969). Las características de las culturas indígenas. In L. Zea, A. Warman, G. Aguirre, C. Monsiváis, & A. Alatorre (Eds.), *Características de la cultura nacional* (pp. 33–56). México: Instituto de Investigaciones Sociales-UNAM.

Aguirre, G. (1995). *Obra antropológica. Problemas de la población indígena de la Cuenca de Tepalcatepec*. México. Universidad Veracruzana, FCE, INI, Gobierno del Estado de Veracruz.

Alarcón-Cháires, P. (2009). *Etnoecología de los Indígenas P'urhépecha. Una Guía para el análisis de la apropiación de la naturaleza*. UNAM-CIECO.

Argueta, A. (2008). *Los Saberes P'urhépecha. Los animales y el diálogo con la naturaleza*. México: UMSNH, PUMNC-UNAM, Gobierno del estado de Michoacán, Universidad Intercultural Indígena de Michoacán, PNUMA.

Bonfil, G. (1990). *México profundo. Una civilización negada*. México: Grijalbo.

Chávez, F. (1997). Naturaleza, recursos naturales y cosmovisión P'urhépecha: Notas etnográficas para su estudio. In C. Paredes Martínez (Ed.), *Lengua y Etnohistoria Purépecha* (pp. 257–263). México: Instituto de Investigaciones Históricas-UMSNH.

Cipriani, R. (2009). *El pueblo solidario. Nahuatzen: De la cultura P'urépecha a la modernización* (V. Roldán, Trans.). México: El Colegio Mexiquense.

Cummins, R. (1996). The domains of life satisfaction: An attempt to order chaos. *Social Indicators Research, 38*, 303–332.

Diener, E., & E. Suh (Eds.). (2000). *Culture and subjective wellbeing*. Cambridge, MA: The MIT Press.

García, C. (2013). *El orden social Purépecha*. Retrieved August 2013 from www.purhepecha.com.mx/files/el-entramado-social-purepecha.pdf.

Garibay, C., & Bocco, G. (2007). *Situación actual en el uso del suelo en las comunidades indígenas de la región P'urhépecha 1976–2005*. México: CDI.

Inkeles, A., & Smith, D. (1974). *Becoming modern: Individual change in six developing countries*. Cambridge, MA: Harvard University Press.

Ingersoll-Dayton, B., & Saengtienchai, C. (2001). Psychological wellbeing Asian style: The perspective of Thai elders. *Journal of Cross-Cultural Gerontology, 16*(3), 283–302.

Jacinto, A. (1988). *Mitología y modernización*. México: Colmich; Gobierno del Estado de Michoacán.

Joshanloo, M. (2014). Eastern conceptualizations of happiness. Fundamental differences with Western views. *Journal of Happiness Studies, 15*(2), 475–493.

Kottak, C. (2006). *Mirror for humanity*. New York: McGraw-Hill.

Kral, M.J., & Idlout, L. (2012). It's all in the family: Wellbeing among Inuit in artic Canada. In H. Selin & G. Davey (Eds.), *Happiness across cultures. Views of happiness and quality of life in non-Western cultures* (pp. 387–398). New York: Springer.

Luo, L., & Gilmour, R. (2004). Culture and conceptions of happiness. Individual oriented and social oriented subjective wellbeing. *Journal of Happiness Studies, 5*(3), 269–291.

Luo, L., Gilmour, R., & Kao, S. (2001). Cultural values and happiness: An East–West dialogue. *Journal of Social Psychology, 141*(4), 477–493.

Moore, S.E., Heather Young, L., & Lavis, C.A. (2005). Subjective wellbeing and life satisfaction in the Kingdom of Tonga. *Social Indicators Research, 70*(3), 287–311.

Muñoz, O. (2009). Historia y tiempo histórico en una comunidad purépecha: El más antes, el antes y el antes... ahorita. *Revista Española de Antropología Americana, 39*(2), 115–137.

Nuño, M.R. (1996). La relación naturaleza-cultura en una comunidad Purépecha a través de sus expresiones orales. In L. Paré & M. J. Sánchez (Eds.), *El Ropaje de la tierra. Naturaleza y cultura en cinco zonas rurales* (pp. 29–82). México: Plaza y Valdés; Instituto de Investigaciones Sociales-UNAM.

Rojas, M. (2005). A conceptual-referent theory of happiness: Heterogeneity and its consequences. *Social Indicators Research, 74*(2), 261–294.

Rojas, M. (2006). Life satisfaction and satisfaction in domains of life: Is it a simple relationship? *Journal of Happiness Studies, 7*(4), 467–497.

Rojas, M. (2007a). The complexity of wellbeing: A life-satisfaction conception and a domains-of-life approach. In I. Gough & J.A. McGregor (Eds.). *Researching wellbeing in developing countries: From theory to research* (pp. 259–280). Cambridge: Cambridge University Press.

Rojas, M. (2007b). Heterogeneity in the relationship between income and happiness: A conceptual-referent-theory explanation. *Journal of Economic Psychology, 28*(1), 1–14.

Rojas, M. (2012). Happiness in Mexico: The importance of human relations. In H. Selin & G. Davey (Eds.), *Happiness across cultures. Views of happiness and quality of life in non-Western cultures* (pp. 241–252). New York: Springer.

Rojas, M. (2014). *El estudio científico de la felicidad.* México D.F.: Fondo de Cultura Económica.

Rojas, M. (Ed.). (2016). *Handbook of happiness research in Latin America.* New York: Springer.

Rojas, M., & Veenhoven, R. (2013). Contentment and affect in the estimation of happiness. *Social Indicators Research, 110*(2), 415–431.

Sebastián, P. (2006). *Meseta tarasca y las políticas de aculturación 1917–1940.* Unpublished UMSNH, Morelia, Michoacán.

Selin, H., & Davey, G. (Eds.). (2012). *Happiness across cultures. Views of happiness and quality of life in non-Western cultures.* New York: Springer.

Taiaiake, A., & Corntassel, J. (2005). Being indigenous. Resurgences against contemporary colonialism. *Government Opposition, 40*(4), 597–614.

Topete, H. (2009). El gusto, el cargo, la deuda, las normas y sus alrededores. Meseta purépecha, México. *Diálogo Andino, 33,* 91–104.

Vasconcelos, J. (2007). *La raza cósmica* (4th ed.). México: Porrúa.

Villanueva, R. (2009). *Sistema de instituciones indígenas de la comunidad P'urhépecha de Comachuén, municipio de Nahuátzen: Propuestas para un desarrollo local con identidad.* UMSNH, Morelia.

Yamamoto, J. (2011). Necesidades universales, su concreción cultural y el desarrollo en su contexto. Hacia una ciencia del desarrollo. In M. Rojas (Ed.), *La medición del progreso y del bienestar. Propuestas desde América Latina* (pp. 93–102). México: Foro Consultivo Científico y Tecnológico.

Yamamoto, J., Feijoo, A.R., & Lazarte, A. (2008). Subjective wellbeing: An alternative approach. In J. Copestake (Ed.), *Wellbeing and development in Peru. Local and universal views confronted.* New York: Palgrave Macmillan.

26

SUBJECTIVE WELLBEING OF THE ABORIGINAL AND TORRES STRAIT ISLAND PEOPLE OF AUSTRALIA

Christopher L. Ambrey, Christopher Fleming and Matthew Manning

Introduction

Indigenous populations in countries such as Australia, Canada, New Zealand and the US are severely disadvantaged according to a range of socioeconomic indicators (Kimmel, 1997; Kuhn & Sweetman, 2002; Maani, 2004). In Australia, according to the 2017 *Closing the Gap Prime Minister's Report*, Indigenous Australians' outcomes were either not improving or were deteriorating across six out of seven health, education and employment measures. For example, in comparison to non-Indigenous Australians, Indigenous Australians are expected to die ten years younger, are approximately three to four times more likely to be unemployed, and are less likely to have completed year 12 or higher. Indigenous Australian children and teenagers are twenty-four times more likely to be incarcerated (Commonwealth of Australia, 2017).

To place these figures in a global context, in 2011 Australia ranked second out of 187 countries on the United Nations' Human Development Index (HDI), with an index value of 0.928. The index value for Indigenous Australians, however, was markedly lower (0.745) (Manning et al., 2016), a value similar to the HDI scores for Serbia (0.744), Jordan (0.744), Sri Lanka (0.740), Brazil (0.740) and Iran (0.733) (United Nations Development Programme, 2014).

In response to this disadvantage, successive Australian governments have introduced a wide range of policies and programs in order to 'close the gap' between Indigenous and non-Indigenous Australians. Examples include the Council of Australian Governments' Closing the Gap in Indigenous Disadvantage framework and, more recently, the Commonwealth Government's Indigenous Advancement Strategy (Australian Government, 2014; Council of Australian Governments, 2014). In all policy responses 'progress' is measured against objective criteria such as life expectancy, rates of literacy and levels of unemployment. Wellbeing, however, is necessarily a subjective concept. While there is an increasing body of literature on using subjective wellbeing (i.e. wellbeing indicators based on personal opinions, interpretations, points of view, emotions and judgment) for economic and social policy (e.g. Dolan & White,

2007; Kahneman & Sugden, 2005; Layard, 2006), subjectivity has been largely absent from the Indigenous policy domain. This is problematic because many things that matter to Indigenous peoples cannot be measured objectively, such as family stability, community life, cultural identity and connectedness with country.

The purpose of this chapter is to move beyond objective measures and explore the subjective wellbeing of Indigenous Australians. Specifically, we focus on the self-reported life satisfaction of Indigenous Australians, reporting: (1) mean levels of self-reported life satisfaction; (2) trends in these means; and (3) differences in the determinants of life satisfaction between Indigenous and non-Indigenous Australians. Our aim is to make a significant contribution to the understanding of Indigenous wellbeing, with the overall goal of assisting in the development of stronger and more effective Indigenous policy.

Subjective wellbeing and Indigenous Australians

While much is known about the relative performance of Indigenous and non-Indigenous Australians against objective criteria, far less is known about their relative performance on sub-jective grounds. Further, the evidence that is available is often inconclusive or counterintuitive. For example, in stark contrast to the objective measures of wellbeing reported above, sev-eral studies find that, on average, Indigenous Australians report higher levels of life satisfaction than non-Indigenous Australians (*ceteris paribus*). This result was first highlighted by Shields and Wooden (2003), who note:

> One unexpected finding is the coefficient on the indigenous identifier. Other things held constant, Aboriginal and Torres Strait Islander men score higher on the life sat-isfaction scale than non-indigenous men. Moreover, the size of the effect is relatively large. Among indigenous women, the size of the differential is smaller, and statistically insignificant.
>
> (p. 11)

Similar results are reported by Shields et al. (2009) and Ambrey and Fleming (2011, 2012, 2014b, 2014c). Even among adolescents defined as 'at-risk' of not completing their schooling, Indigenous students score higher on subjective wellbeing than non-Indigenous students (Tomyn et al., 2014).

In one of the most comprehensive assessments of the subjective wellbeing of Indigenous Australians undertaken to date, Biddle (2014) confirms that Indigenous Australians, on average, report higher levels of life satisfaction than non-Indigenous Australians. Biddle (2014) suggests that it may be the case that Indigenous Australians interpret the questions differently to non-Indigenous Australians due to language differences – however, the result holds when focusing on those who only speak English. Further, Biddle suggests that Indigenous Australians may have a different baseline against which they evaluate their own life. It is also likely that there are other dimensions of life uniquely experienced by Indigenous Australians; these potentially play an important role in Indigenous life satisfaction. He also finds that Indigenous Australians are sig-nificantly more likely to report both above and below average satisfaction with their lives. It may be the case, therefore, that the full spectrum of subjective self-reports requires attention. Such an approach would be in line with the growing recognition that positive and negative wellbeing are more than opposite ends of the same phenomenon, and that factors which increase satisfac-tion may not necessarily decrease dissatisfaction (Boes & Winkelmann, 2010). In contrast to the finding of higher levels of life satisfaction, Biddle (2014) notes that Indigenous Australians are less likely to report frequent periods of happiness and more likely to report periods of extreme sadness than non-Indigenous Australians.

Indigenous-specific determinants of wellbeing

Much of the existing literature on the measurement of subjective wellbeing focuses on the determinants of wellbeing, independent of whether or not a person is Indigenous. Ambrey and Fleming (2014b) provide a comprehensive overview in an Australian context. There clearly remains considerable scope to discover more about the Indigenous-specific determinants of wellbeing. The notion that the determinants of life satisfaction may differ systemically due to cultural differences (Uchida et al., 2004) deserves further attention. Exploring likely heterogeneity in the determinants of life satisfaction between Indigenous and non-Indigenous Australians will advance our knowledge.

Early evidence, much of which does not permit easy comparison between Indigenous and non-Indigenous populations, suggests a number of different Indigenous-specific determinants of subjectively measured wellbeing. For example, Browne-Yung et al. (2013) suggest that cultural identity has a unique impact on Indigenous wellbeing. Furthermore, while assimilation may improve objectively measured labour market or educational outcomes (Bradley et al., 2007; Kuhn & Sweetman, 2002), it may concomitantly reduce wellbeing if assimilation requires sacrificing elements of culture (Dockery, 2010). Dockery finds that for Indigenous Australian's stronger cultural attachment is associated with: (1) a greater level of self-assessed health; (2) a lower likelihood of engaging in risky alcohol consumption; (3) an increased probability of being employed; and (4) a greater number of years of post-primary education. Conversely, weaker cultural attachment is found to be associated with an increased probability of having been arrested in the last five years and a reduced chance of being employed. The author argues that the level of life satisfaction of Indigenous Australians may be determined by Indigenous cultural attachment functioning through factors such as self-esteem, self-efficacy and a positive sense of self-identity (Dockery, 2010).

Cultural identity among Indigenous Australians also supports, and is supported by, social capital, with positive and negative implications for health and wellbeing. Browne-Yung et al. (2013) suggest that a shared cultural identity strengthens social networks and mediates the health impact of disadvantage. Further, shared values, social networks and volunteering in Aboriginal health organizations facilitates greater access to medical and dental care, in addition to activities that address drug and alcohol dependency. In contrast, a lack of reciprocation or virtuous behaviour adversely impacts wellbeing; an outcome that is compounded by existing economic disadvantage. These findings are corroborated by Brough et al. (2004), Dietsch et al. (2011) and Waterworth et al. (2014).

Most recently, for Indigenous Australians subjective wellbeing evidence is emerging which is counter to conventional economic and policy thinking; that is, a negative association between income and subjective wellbeing for Indigenous Australians. The association between wellbeing and the natural log transformed income measure has been described as not statistically significant elsewhere (Biddle, 2014), although a linear functional form reveals a small negative coefficient, which is statistically significant at conventional levels (Manning et al., 2016). Biddle (2015) sought to address this issue, focusing on the link between income and happiness and sadness. Biddle reports a positive association for Indigenous males living in non-remote locations, an association which is weaker for non-remote Indigenous females and virtually non-existent for Indigenous males and females living in remote locations. It is worth noting though that these results are found without holding other factors constant. The candidate explanations offered for the paucity of a relationship between income and wellbeing include the sharing of resources, the prices of commodities where Indigenous people live, and the ability of many Indigenous people in remote and regional Australia to supplement their income with resources from hunting, fishing and gathering (Biddle, 2015).

Data

The measure of self-reported life satisfaction, and the socioeconomic and demographic characteristics of respondents, are obtained from Waves 1 (2001) to 15 (2015) of the Household, Income and Labour Dynamics in Australia (HILDA) survey. The use of panel datasets such as HILDA allow the examination of determinants of wellbeing while controlling for time-invariant individual specific confounders such as stable personality traits. In this respect, the HILDA survey is particularly useful for this study and is the only source of data that accommodates our research design.

The life satisfaction variable is obtained from individuals' responses to the question: 'All things considered, how satisfied are you with your life?' The variable is ordinal, the individual choosing a number between 0 (totally dissatisfied with life) and 10 (totally satisfied with life).

Presenting data from Wave 15, Figure 26.1 illustrates the distribution of responses and Figure 26.2 shows the proportion of Indigenous and non-Indigenous Australians that fall in different categories. Figure 26.1 shows that the distribution of the responses is negatively skewed, with more than half of the respondents reporting an 8 or higher. A life satisfaction score

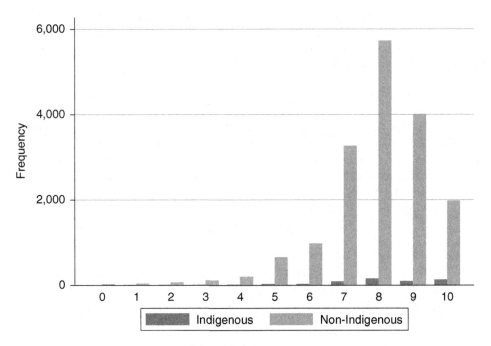

Figure 26.1 Frequency distribution of life satisfaction scores, 2015
Source: Derived from HILDA survey.

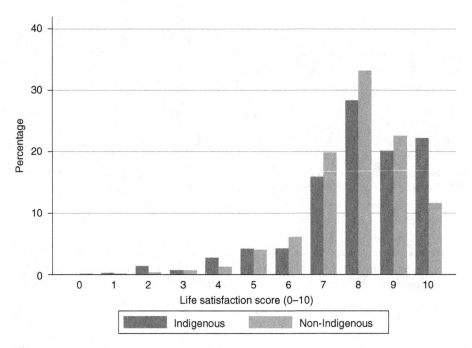

Figure 26.2 Percentage of Indigenous or non–Indigenous reporting life satisfaction scores, 2015
Source: Derived from HILDA survey.

of 8 is both the median and the mode. The mean life satisfaction score is 7.92. Figure 26.2 indicates that Indigenous Australians are more likely than non-Indigenous Australians to report a score of 10 (totally satisfied with their life), are less likely to report scores of 7, 8 or 9, and are more likely to report a score of 6 or below.

Empirical analysis

Figure 26.3 illustrates mean life satisfaction scores for Indigenous and non-Indigenous Australians over the period 2001 to 2015. Adjusted Wald tests, which appreciate the complex survey design of the HILDA dataset, indicate that (over the period 2001 to 2015) there is no statistically significant change in the life satisfaction of Indigenous or non-Indigenous Australians. For both groups, life satisfaction peaked in 2003.

Trends in life satisfaction

To examine the nature of any general change in life satisfaction, we estimate a fixed effects model for individual i at time t, as follows:

$$LS_{i,t} = \sum_{j=1}^{k} \alpha_i\, x_{i,t} + \eta\, \text{Indigenous Trend}_t + \rho\, \text{non-Indigenous Trend}_t + \iota_i + \varepsilon_{i,t} \qquad (1)$$

where $LS_{i,t}$ is the self-reported life satisfaction of individual i, at time t; $x_{i,t}$ is a vector of socio-economic and demographic characteristics including income, marital status, employment status,

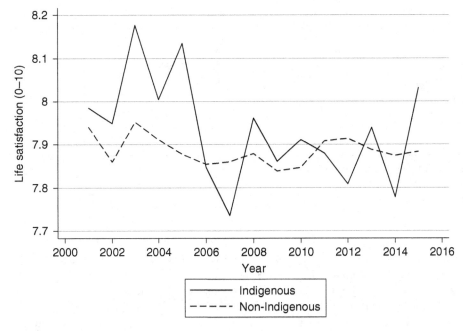

Figure 26.3   Life satisfaction, 2001–2015
Source: Derived from HILDA survey.

health, education, number of children and so forth; IndigenousTrend$_i$ is an Indigenous specific time trend (Indigenous$_i$ × (Year$_t$ − 2000) / 100)); non-IndigenousTrend$_i$ is a non-Indigenous specific time trend (non-Indigenous$_i$ × (Year$_t$ − 2000) / 100)). Finally, ι_i is the individual specific fixed effect and $\varepsilon_{i,t}$ the error term. Equation (1) is estimated using the 'blow up and cluster' (BUC) estimator, which appreciates the ordinal nature of the dependent variable while concomitantly controlling for unobserved individual specific fixed effects (Baetschmann et al., 2013). The BUC estimator replaces every observation in the sample with $K − 1$ copies of itself (where K is the number of ordered outcomes in the dependent variable) and dichotomizes each of the $K − 1$ copies of the individual at a different cut-off point. The estimates are obtained by conditional maximum likelihood estimation using the entire sample. The standard errors are adjusted for clustering as observations are dependent by construction.

Table 26.1 presents the estimates for the trend terms. The results indicate that, *ceteris paribus*, both coefficient estimates are not statistically significant and are not statistically significantly different from one another.

Determinants of life satisfaction

To investigate differences in the determinants of life satisfaction between Indigenous and non-Indigenous Australians, the Indigenous identifier is interacted with all socioeconomic and demographic characteristics, and then estimated via maximum likelihood estimation in an ordered probit model. A Chow test of the interaction terms and the Indigenous identifier is strongly statistically significant ($F(46, 612) = 5.6300$, p-value = 0.0000). This indicates that the determinants of life satisfaction are not the same and, therefore, it is not appropriate to pool the two groups. Hence, we estimate two separate models. This allows the parameter estimates to

Table 26.1 Trends in Indigenous and non-Indigenous life satisfaction

Variable	Calculation
Indigenous trend	0.1165 (1.3940)
Non-Indigenous trend	0.2500 (0.5470)
Summary statistics	
Observations	561,935
Individuals	22,102
Pseudo R^2	0.0188

Note: Standard errors are given in parentheses.
* $p<0.10$, ** $p<0.05$, *** $p<0.01$.
Includes independent variables in Table 26.2.

vary uniquely for Indigenous and non-Indigenous Australians. The Breusch-Pagan Lagrangian multiplier test for random effects is then applied to determine whether a random effects model is appropriate or a simple ordinary least squares model can be used. Results reveal a strong rejection ($\chi^2(48) = 407.8100$, p-value $= 0.0000$) of the null hypothesis for both groups, pointing towards the need to employ a random effects model.

However, the use of a random effects model relies on the assumption that the individual-specific fixed effects are not correlated with the regressors in the model, which if invalid would produce inconsistent estimates. The results reveal strong evidence against this assumption; a test of overidentifying restrictions (asymptotically equivalent to the usual Hausman fixed versus random effects test) yields a strong rejection of the null hypothesis (Sargan-Hansen statistic $\chi^2(44) = 137.0940$, p-value $= 0.0000$) (Schaffer & Stillman, 2010). As such, for both Indigenous Australians and non-Indigenous Australians, separate fixed effects life satisfaction models, as shown in Equation (2), are estimated using the BUC estimator:

$$LS_{i,t} = \sum_{j=1}^{k} \alpha_j x_{i,t} + \sum_{l}^{t} d_t \tau_t + \iota_i + \varepsilon_{i,t}$$

(2)

The variables are as previously defined in Equation (1). τ_t is a vector of time (year) dummy variables. Results are reported in Table 26.2.

In terms of how Indigenous (column 1 of Table 26.2) and non-Indigenous (column 2 of Table 26.2) estimates compare, life satisfaction is found to have the usual U-shape in age for non-Indigenous Australians, however, no such effect is found for the Indigenous sample. Surprisingly, for Indigenous Australians poor English is associated with higher levels of life satisfaction, while the reverse is true for non-Indigenous Australians. With regards to marital status, being married is only positive and statistically significant for non-Indigenous Australians. For both groups it appears being in a *de facto* relationship is positively associated with life satisfaction and being separated negatively associated with life satisfaction. Being a widow is much more negative for Indigenous Australians, although this result is not statistically significant.

Being a lone parent has no statistically significant association with life satisfaction for either group. The number of children in the household is not statistically significant for Indigenous Australians, while for non-Indigenous Australians it is statistically significant and negative. For both groups, poor health is associated with lower levels of life satisfaction. However, for Indigenous Australians the coefficient for having a severe health condition is markedly higher than for the non-Indigenous population. Higher levels of education are associated with

Table 26.2 BUC estimates for Indigenous and non-Indigenous

	(1)		(2)	
	Indigenous		*Non-Indigenous*	
Age (15–19)	0.1704	(0.2704)	0.3686***	(0.0558)
Age (20–29)	−0.1585	(0.1754)	0.0001	(0.0366)
Age (40–49)	−0.0193	(0.2213)	−0.0312	(0.0350)
Age (50–59)	0.0740	(0.3753)	0.0639	(0.0529)
Age (60 or greater)	0.4755	(0.4983)	0.4370***	(0.0708)
Poor English	1.7265***	(0.3342)	−0.2100**	(0.0892)
Married	0.1252	(0.2344)	0.4707***	(0.0466)
De facto	0.4499***	(0.1422)	0.4893***	(0.0361)
Separated	−0.9675**	(0.4379)	−0.5567***	(0.0669)
Divorced	0.0186	(0.3972)	−0.0802	(0.0667)
Widow	−1.2139	(0.8817)	−0.0765	(0.0893)
Lone parent	−0.1047	(0.2508)	−0.0429	(0.0583)
Number of children	0.0330	(0.0708)	−0.0999***	(0.0139)
Severe health condition	−1.4058***	(0.3045)	−0.8189***	(0.0583)
Moderate health condition	−0.7593***	(0.1289)	−0.6235***	(0.0236)
Mild health condition	−0.0986	(0.1380)	−0.1628***	(0.0218)
Bachelor's degree or higher	−0.7364	(0.6844)	−0.3242***	(0.0983)
Certificate or diploma	0.1187	(0.3364)	−0.2499***	(0.0598)
Year 12	−0.5352**	(0.2670)	−0.3136***	(0.0494)
Employed part-time	−0.0605	(0.1483)	0.1007***	(0.0222)
Unemployed	−0.2930*	(0.1605)	−0.2893***	(0.0365)
Non-participant	−0.0454	(0.1553)	0.0248	(0.0288)
Disposable income (ln)	−0.0041	(0.0483)	0.0461***	(0.0101)
Comparison income (ln)	0.0192	(1.1362)	0.1962	(0.1681)
Richer	0.0051	(0.0108)	0.0088***	(0.0016)
Others present	−0.0513	(0.0810)	0.0986***	(0.0137)
Years interviewed[-1]	−0.2416	(0.2770)	0.3021***	(0.0548)
Inner regional	0.0974	(0.2096)	0.1266***	(0.0398)
Outer regional	−0.1766	(0.2321)	0.0940*	(0.0569)
Remote areas	0.1861	(0.3215)	−0.0192	(0.0976)
Summary statistics				
Observations	15,346		546,589	
Individuals	615		21,487	
Pseudo R^2	0.0347		0.0195	

Note: Standard errors in parentheses.
* $p<0.10$, ** $p<0.05$, *** $p<0.01$.
Includes controls for time (year) fixed effects.

lower levels of life satisfaction for both groups. Being employed part-time is positive for non-Indigenous Australians only. Being unemployed is associated with lower levels of life satisfaction for both groups beyond any change in income.

Surprisingly, for Indigenous Australians, the natural log of equivalized disposable household income is negatively associated with life satisfaction (although this is not statistically significant). Naive pooled ordered logit model results, not reported here, show a negative and statistically significant income coefficient. This result is not hard to find. In contrast, the same measure is positively linked to life satisfaction for non-Indigenous Australians. Others being present during the interview is associated with higher levels of life satisfaction for non-Indigenous Australians only, suggesting some degree of social desirability bias for this group. The estimated coefficients for the inverse of years interviewed (a control for panel conditioning effects) take different signs for the Indigenous and non-Indigenous samples. Noting that in a fixed effects model we can only explore the influence of location on life satisfaction if people move between different regions over time, we find that living in an inner regional area is associated with higher levels of life satisfaction compared to living in a major city for non-Indigenous Australians.

Broadly speaking, the results for non-Indigenous Australians are consistent with existing evidence and *a priori* expectations. However, the results for Indigenous Australians differ in many respects, thus offering opportunities for further research.

Discussion

This chapter set out to explore Indigenous wellbeing in Australia using data from the HILDA survey. In particular, this chapter focuses on: (1) mean levels of self-reported life satisfaction; (2) trends in these means; and (3) differences in the determinants of life satisfaction between Indigenous and non-Indigenous Australians.

Mean levels of life satisfaction and trends in these levels provide a picture of stagnant wellbeing for both Indigenous and non-Indigenous Australians. On one hand, earlier evidence suggests that life satisfaction for Indigenous Australians may be higher than that of non-Indigenous Australians. This seems inconsistent with the current evidence on progress towards meeting the objective targets set out in the 'Closing the gap' framework. On closer inspection, however, it is evident that life satisfaction for both Indigenous and non-Indigenous Australians peaked in 2003, and Indigenous life satisfaction declined sharply between 2003 and 2012 (Manning et al., 2016). For both groups between 2003 and 2015 there was no change. This is despite significant investment by all levels of Australian government in addressing Indigenous disadvantage and suggests that existing policies are having little effect.

Focusing on the distribution of life satisfaction scores, Indigenous Australians are more likely to report being totally satisfied with their life (i.e. report a score of 10), are less likely to report scores of 7, 8 or 9, and are more likely to report a score of 6 or below. This suggests there may be a polarized experience in terms of the life satisfaction of Indigenous Australians.

Results for the determinants of life satisfaction reveal some interesting differences between the two groups. For example, speaking English either not well or not at all is associated with higher life satisfaction for Indigenous Australians, whereas the reverse is true for non-Indigenous Australians. The curious result for Indigenous Australians may reflect the fact that those reporting lower English speaking ability are more closely connected with their culture and community. This close connection acts as a protective factor against psychological distress (Kelly et al., 2009) and, therefore, is plausibly positively associated with life satisfaction. It may also reflect the urban and rural differences between Indigenous Australians experiences.

We also find that being a widow is almost sixteen times more detrimental to life satisfaction for Indigenous than non-Indigenous, although not statistically significant. Candidate explanations for this result include: (1) the fact that Indigenous women have more children than non-Indigenous women (Australian Indigenous HealthInfoNet, 2013), and thus widowhood imposes a larger burden in terms of child rearing responsibilities; (2) job opportunities are limited by socioeconomic status, and therefore, Indigenous people whose partner has died are less likely to be able to find employment to support themselves and their family; and (3) Indigenous men die approximately 11.5 years younger than non-Indigenous men (Australian Bureau of Statistics, 2011) and, therefore, do not accumulate as much superannuation or other financial assets for their beneficiaries.

For Indigenous Australians the negative effect of a severe (long-term) health condition that prevents them from working is almost double that of non-Indigenous Australians. A plausible explanation for this result is inequality in access to healthcare between the two groups. It may be the case that non-Indigenous Australians are more easily able to access healthcare and thus receive treatment to relieve the symptoms of the condition. This result, however, deserves further research.

Perhaps the most intriguing result is that income is not positively associated with life satisfaction for Indigenous Australians (in fact, the coefficient estimate is negative – although not statistically significant). This is in stark contrast to overwhelming evidence in the life satisfaction literature of the positive (albeit diminishing) effects of income on life satisfaction (Frijters et al., 2004). As with the result for poor English speaking ability and consistent with the arguments put forward by Dockery (2010), a possible explanation may be that activities that disconnect the individual from their community and culture (e.g. living in an urban centre attracted by the prospect of gainful employment) have the potential to reduce life satisfaction; a reduction that is not adequately compensated for in terms of higher income. Future research into the association between income and life satisfaction for Indigenous Australians may benefit from employing a more plausibly exogenous measure of income, such as a subset of windfall income (Ambrey & Fleming, 2014a; Ambrey et al., 2017a, 2017b) or alternatively the use of quantile regression methods to a larger sample of Indigenous Australians in order to identify some potential non-linearity in the relationship between income and life satisfaction. Biddle (2015) focuses on this issue specifically and alludes to the potential role of lack of control of income among Indigenous Australians. This is a particularly appropriate explanation for Indigenous Australians in the Northern Territory where social security benefits are generally income managed. That is, the government ensures that income is put aside to pay for essential items (Department of Human Services, 2017). What this may mean for objective and subjective wellbeing represents an area worthy of future research.

Final comments

Despite considerable investment from all levels of government, many indicators show that outcomes for Indigenous Australians are not improving and there is still a considerable way to go to achieve the Council of Australian Governments' commitment to 'close the gap' in Indigenous disadvantage. As noted by Dockery (2010):

> From the arrival of the 'First Fleet' in Australia in 1788… policy towards the Indigenous population has oscillated through a number of stages. It remains an issue of intense debate among Indigenous and non-Indigenous Australians alike. The one point of consensus is that our past efforts have been a failure.
>
> (p. 315)

The United Nations Permanent Forum on Indigenous Issues (2006) declaration states:

> Indigenous peoples will define their own understandings and visions of wellbeing from which indicators will be identified, and include the full participation of Indigenous peoples in the development of these indicators.
>
> (p. 15)

Despite such declarations, in many countries (including Australia) policy development and application remains deeply rooted in improving Indigenous wellbeing, as it is perceived by the dominant (Western) non-Indigenous culture. This position is most clearly articulated in the framework underpinning the 'Closing the Gap' suite of policies, where Indigenous outcomes are benchmarked against outcomes achieved by the non-Indigenous population (Australian Government, 2013). The use of a non-Indigenous perspective of wellbeing in the design and application of Indigenous policy may be problematic, as it does not account for traditional Indigenous ways of life. What is needed is an appreciation of Indigenous wellbeing, as perceived by the Indigenous population itself.

This is particularly important if one considers the pursuit of pleasure implicitly motivates behaviour. A point which underpins much of economics (Hands, 2009, 2010). In light of these results (especially for education and income), *a posteriori* it is reasonable to conclude that these results may explain the lack of 'progress' in terms of closing the gap on key indicators among Indigenous Australians. That is, despite the well-intended efforts to improve objective Indigenous Australians' outcomes and the focus on objective indicators, it may be that the pathway or the achievement of these apparently desirable objective outcomes; given the current circumstances (and preferences) of Indigenous Australians, serves to reduce their life satisfaction. A similar line of reasoning could also be applied to other disadvantaged groups (e.g. those on low-income, women – e.g. Ambrey et al., 2017c – and people from culturally and linguistically diverse backgrounds). Greater appreciation needs to be given to the current conditions people experience and how this may translate into potentially insurmountable barriers, for even the most conscientious person, in terms of the hedonistic cost on the pathway to the achievement of outcomes deemed desirable by scholars and policymakers, notwithstanding endorsement by the broader public.

On this point, as noted by Biddle (2015, p. 148):

> Ultimately though, the weaker relationship between income and wellbeing needs to be factored into the design of policy and, more importantly, in the evaluation of what works and what does not work to achieve long-term changes in outcomes.

While some of the insights from our research apply to disadvantaged groups more broadly, with a clearer understanding of Indigenous wellbeing and its determinants, more appropriate policy and ultimately better outcomes, will be able to be achieved for this population. The introduction of subjective measures into the policy discourse will go some way to achieving this goal. Further research in this area requires that additional funding be directed towards those scholars who have a track record of high-quality research.

It is hoped that the results presented in this chapter will provide policymakers with a barometer of the state of Indigenous wellbeing in Australia, highlight the importance of subjective measures of wellbeing and illustrate the opportunity offered by such measures to enrich policy discussion and promote public debate.

References

Ambrey, C., & Fleming, C. (2011). Valuing scenic amenity using life satisfaction data. *Ecological Economics, 72*(1), 106–115.

Ambrey, C., & Fleming, C. (2012). Valuing Australia's protected areas: A life satisfaction approach. *New Zealand Economic Papers, 46*(3), 191–209.

Ambrey, C., & Fleming, C. (2014a). The causal effect of income on life satisfaction and the implications for valuing non-market goods. *Economics Letters, 123*(2), 131–134.

Ambrey, C., & Fleming, C. (2014b). Life satisfaction in Australia: Evidence from ten years of the HILDA survey. *Social Indicators Research, 115*(2), 691–714.

Ambrey, C., & Fleming, C. (2014c). Valuing ecosystem diversity in South East Queensland: A life satisfaction approach. *Social Indicators Research, 115*(1), 45–65.

Ambrey, C., Fleming, C., & Manning, M. (2017a). Forest fire danger, life satisfaction and feelings of safety: Evidence from Australia. *International Journal of Wildland Fire, 26*(3), 240–248.

Ambrey, C., Fleming, C., & Manning, M. (2017b). The social cost of the Black Saturday bushfires. *Australian Journal of Social Issues, 52*(4), 298–312.

Ambrey, C., Ulichny, J., & Fleming, C. (2017c). The social connectedness and life satisfaction nexus: A panel data analysis of women in Australia. *Feminist Economics, 23*(2), 1–32.

Australian Bureau of Statistics. (2011). *Life expectancy trends – Australia*. 4102.0 – Australian Social Trends. Retrieved 30 October 2014 from http://abs.gov.au/AUSSTATS/abs@.nsf/Lookup/4102.0Main+Features10Mar+2011.

Australian Government. (2013). *Closing the gap: The Indigenous reform agenda*. Retrieved 21 August 2014 from www.dss.gov.au/our-responsibilities/indigenous-australians/programs-services/closing-the-gap.

Australian Government. (2014). *Indigenous Affairs*. Department of Prime Minister and Cabinet, Canberra.

Australian Indigenous HealthInfoNet. (2013). *Summary of Australian Indigenous health*. Retrieved 30 October 2014 from www.healthinfonet.ecu.edu.au/health-facts/summary.

Baetschmann, G., Staub, K., & Winkelmann, R. (2013). *Consistent estimation of the fixed effects ordered logit model*. IZA Working Paper, Bonn, Germany.

Biddle, N. (2014). Measuring and analysing the wellbeing of Australia's indigenous population. *Social Indicators Research, 116*(3), 713–729.

Biddle, N. (2015). Indigenous income, wellbeing and behaviour: Some policy complications. *Economic Papers: A Journal of Applied Economics and Policy, 34*(3), 139–149.

Boes, S., & Winkelmann, R. (2010). The effect of income on general life satisfaction and dissatisfaction. *Social Indicators Research, 95*(1), 111–128.

Bradley, S., Draca, M., Green, C., & Leeves, G. (2007). The magnitude of educational disadvantage of indigenous minority groups in Australia. *Journal of Population Economics, 20*(3), 547–569.

Brough, M., Bond, C., & Hunt, J. (2004). Strong in the city: Towards a strength-based approach in Indigenous health promotion. *Health Promotion Journal of Australia, 15*(3), 215–220.

Browne-Yung, K., Ziersch, A., Baum, F., & Gallaher, G. (2013). Aboriginal Australians' experience of social capital and its relevance to health and wellbeing in urban settings. *Social Science & Medicine, 97*(1), 20–28.

Commonwealth of Australia. (2017). *Closing the gap: Prime minister's report 2017*. Retrieved 15 September 2017 from https://closingthegap.pmc.gov.au/sites/default/files/ctg-report-2017.pdf.

Council of Australian Governments. (2014). *Closing the gap in Indigenous disadvantage*. Retrieved 4 October 2014 from www.coag.gov.au/closing_the_gap_in_indigenous_disadvantage.

Department of Human Services. (2017). *About income management*. Retrieved 17 September 2017 from www.humanservices.gov.au/organisations/business/enablers/about-income-management.

Dietsch, E., Martin, T., Shackleton, P., Davies, C., McLeod, M., & Alston, M. (2011). Australian Aboriginal kinship: A means to enhance maternal well-being. *Women and Birth, 24*(2), 58–64.

Dockery, A. (2010). Culture and wellbeing: The case of Indigenous Australians. *Social Indicators Research, 99*(2), 315–332.

Dolan, P., & White, M. (2007). How can measures of subjective well-being be used to inform public policy? *Perspectives on Psychological Science, 2*(1), 71–85.

Frijters, P., Haisken-DeNew, J., & Shields, M. (2004). Money does matter! Evidence from increasing real income and life satisfaction in East Germany following reunification. *American Economic Review, 94*(3), 730–740.

Hands, D. (2009). Effective tension in Robbins' economic methodology. *Economica, 76*(s1), 831–844.

Hands, D. (2010). Economics, psychology and the history of consumer choice theory. *Cambridge Journal of Economics, 34*(4), 633–648.

Kahneman, D., & Sugden, R. (2005). Experienced utility as a standard of policy evaluation. *Environmental and Resource Economics, 32*(1), 161–181.

Kelly, K., Dudgeon, P., Gee, G., & Glaskin, B. (2009). *Living on the edge: Social and emotional wellbeing and risk and protective factors for serious psychological distress among Aboriginal and Torres Strait Islander people*. Australian Indigenous Psychologists Association and Cooperative Research Centre for Aboriginal Health Discussion Paper No. 10, Cooperative Research Centre for Aboriginal Health, Casuarina, Northern Territory.

Kimmel, J. (1997). Rural wages and returns to education: Differences between whites, blacks, and American Indians. *Economics of Education Review, 16*(1), 81–96.

Kuhn, P., & Sweetman, A. (2002). Aboriginals as unwilling immigrants: Contact, assimilation and labour market outcomes. *Journal of Population Economics, 15*(2), 331–355.

Layard, R. (2006). Happiness and public policy: A challenge to the profession. *Economic Journal, 116*(510), c24–c33.

Maani, S. (2004). Why have Maori relative income levels deteriorated over time? *Economic Record, 80*(248), 101–124.

Manning, M., Ambrey, C., & Fleming, C. (2016). A longitudinal study of Indigenous wellbeing in Australia. *Journal of Happiness Studies, 17*(6), 2503–2525.

Schaffer, M., & Stillman, S. (2010). *Xtoverid: Stata module to calculate tests of overidentifying restrictions after xtreg, xtivreg, xtivreg2 and xthtaylor.* Retrieved 10 September 2014 from http://ideas.repec.org/c/boc/bocode/s456779.html.

Shields, M., Price, S., & Wooden, M. (2009). Life satisfaction and the economic and social characteristics of neighbourhoods. *Journal of Population Economics, 22*(2), 421–443.

Shields, M., & Wooden, M. (2003). *Investigating the role of neighbourhood characteristics in determining life satisfaction.* Paper prepared for the Department of Family and Community Services, Canberra.

Tomyn, A., Cummins, R., & Norrish, J. (2014). The subjective wellbeing of 'at-risk' Indigenous and Non-Indigenous Australian adolescents. *Journal of Happiness Studies, 16*(4), 813–837.

Uchida, Y., Norasakkunkit, V., & Kitayama, S. (2004). Cultural constructions of happiness: Theory and empirical evidence. *Journal of Happiness Studies, 5*(3), 223–239.

United Nations Development Programme. (2014). *Table 2: Human Development Index trends, 1980–2013.* Human Development Reports. Retrieved 4 October 2014 from http://hdr.undp.org/en/content/table-2-human-development-index-trends-1980–2013.

United Nations Permanent Forum on Indigenous Issues. (2006). *Report of the Meeting on Indigenous Peoples and Indicators of Wellbeing.* United Nations, New York.

Waterworth, P., Rosenberg, M., Braham, R., Pescud, M., & Dimmock, J. (2014). The effect of social support on the health of Indigenous Australians in a metropolitan community. *Social Science & Medicine, 119*(1), 139–146.

27

INDIGENOUS WELLBEING AND FUTURE CHALLENGES

Matthew Manning and Christopher Fleming

The contributions made in this handbook by our authors have shone a light on how Indigenous populations around the world fare with regards to wellbeing. They have shown us what works and what doesn't. But importantly, they have provided guidance on what we can do to improve the lives of Indigenous people. The news is not always bad and there is much to be learnt from the good things that people and governments do. Sometimes, the news is not as positive, but here we need to take stock of the lessons and rather than engage in more overblown rhetoric, we need to research, understand, reflect and take decisive collaborative action. Below, we provide a summary of the respective domains of wellbeing by region. We hope that this will give you both a picture of how Indigenous people are faring, but also what actions are being undertaken or should be undertaken to improve the lives of the Indigenous people of that region.

Europe and the Circumpolar North

Physical wellbeing: Per Axelsson and Christina Storm Mienna

The Sámi people in general live longer and healthier lives than most other Indigenous people, with no or little difference in life expectancy between Sámi and non-Sámi people living in the same region. Specific causes of death are also similar. Nevertheless, there remain pronounced challenges and threats to Sámi people and their health – including increasing reports of suicide, depression and anxiety among young Sámi reindeer herders. Further, despite signing the United Nations Declaration on the Rights of Indigenous Peoples and other international declarations, the Nordic countries lack a long-term strategy and commitment for supporting Sámi health research, although Norway is leading discussions on ethical guidelines for Sámi health research, an important step in further supporting relevant research in the field. A major future challenge for Sámi health is connected to understanding the effects of colonization on the people affected, a phenomenon that is often poorly articulated in health research not only for the Sámi, but for Indigenous people more generally.

Social and emotional wellbeing: Susanne Garvis and Lotta Omma

Young Sámi people and children are proud to be Sámi; they have great respect for their culture and take an active responsibility to ensure the preservation of their language and traditions.

Discrimination within the education system, however, is prevalent and leads to increased stress and worry – and consequently a deterioration in mental health and wellbeing. Six recommendations are put forward to promote the wellbeing of Sámi children and young people's wellbeing in Sweden. These include the development of Sámi-focused health programs, education programs for all Swedish people on the importance of eliminating discrimination, a revision of the Swedish educational curriculum, training and professional development for teachers with a focus on Sámi culture, perspective and wellbeing, and a review of Sámi language provision.

Cultural and spiritual wellbeing: Alexandra Sawatzky, Ashlee Cunsolo, Sherilee L. Harper, Inez Shiwak and Michele Wood

The Inuit in Canada have faced dramatic and rapid changes in ways of life and livelihoods, including (but not limited to) land dispossession, and environmental changes that are disrupting their ability to practice and participate in traditional, land-based activities. This is of great importance, as relationship with the land is inherently connected to the wellbeing of many Inuit. Policies and programs that neglect to consider this both rationalize and perpetuate colonial attitudes and Western norms, and often fail. Place-based conceptions of physical and mental wellbeing were widely shared by Inuit participants of this study. Many expressed that being on the land freed them from the struggles of everyday life, and opened up space for achieving greater physical and mental wellbeing – wellbeing that was directly connected to their Inuit identity and ancestry. These health and wellbeing benefits were viewed as dependent on active use of the knowledge needed to survive on the land, as self-worth and value are drawn from land-based activities as well as from the knowledge required to practice these activities. The authors conclude that demonstrating how Inuit are actively creating and pursuing pathways for wellbeing will help to guide future research and policies that aim to enhance wellbeing in relevant and meaningful ways, placing Inuit voices, culture, ways of knowing, and conceptualizations of health and wellbeing at the centre of decision-making and action.

North America

Physical wellbeing: Leslie Redmond and Joel Gittelsohn

Native North Americans (NNA) have emerged as disproportionately affected by chronic disease since the mid-twentieth century. The conditions include diabetes, obesity and heart disease, and are believed to be influenced by traditional factors as well as subjection to colonialism and historical traumas. Partnerships between tribal communities and public academic institutions remains a priority for further education on NNA health and wellbeing. Health organizations also contribute essential support in the development of prevention and intervention, as well as the funding of projects and grants that create opportunities for active living and support of healthy food. Intervention programs are of critical importance as they aim to target the augmentation of the traditional environment to promote healthier living within the traditional and cultural practices of the NNA population. Further policy initiatives may be taken to restrict the adverse food products available in these environments in order to complement and enhance the effect of interventions.

Social and emotional wellbeing: Lyle J. Noisy Hawk and Joseph E. Trimble

A study of traditional wellbeing conducted among Lakota healers demonstrates a lack of research in the conceptual processes and cultural determinants of psychological illness and wellness. The integration of Western psychological principles to the Lakota determinants of living within cultural laws, the family and the tribe have the potential to provide an appropriate counselling approach and improve the results of these strategies in American Indian and Alaskan Native ethnic groups. Further research into areas such as cultural anthropology, linguistics and internal medicine are required to understand how Western psychological practice can supplement traditional healing rituals and spiritual practice in order to improve wellbeing among the population.

Economic wellbeing: Belayet Hossain and Laura Lamb

Research conducted on the employment income of Canadas Indigenous peoples demonstrates the explanatory significance of human and social capital as measures of wellbeing. Individual health and education factors have positive and significant effects on Indigenous employment income as Indigenous peoples with good health generally earn higher incomes than those in poor health. Education levels are believed to play a significant role in the disparity of median incomes measured between Native American communities, however this may be subject to the costs associated with urban residency. The research undertaken by the authors emphasizes the need for culturally sensitive policy development. This is required in order to respond to the varied needs of Indigenous Canadians as those residing in remote communities require a higher level of employment income to achieve the equivalent economic wellbeing as those in urban settings. Further research needs to be conducted on more comprehensive and refined data in order to obtain a more nuanced understanding of the effects of human and social capital, controlling for geographic influence on different costs of living.

Cultural and spiritual wellbeing: Andrew Pomerville and Joseph P. Gone

The limited access to traditional healing practices for Indigenous North American peoples living in urban areas of Canada and the US remains an issue in regard to measuring its effectiveness. Evidence indicates that particular forms of traditional healing are associated with improved treatment outcomes, and Indigenous people often seek these traditional methods. In spite of this success and uptake, some traditional practices have been suppressed by legal frameworks and there is continued contention between enhancing tradition and delivering synthesized programs. Practice-based evidence demonstrates the success of behavioural health programs that address a number of cultural and traditional elements among Indigenous North American populations including, but not limited to, spiritual foundations and the power of Indigenous language. Ongoing use of spiritual-cultural interventions are empirically supported to have positive outcomes on Indigenous wellbeing, but further research is required to understand the effects of family and community settings, and accessibility to traditional healing opportunities.

Subjective wellbeing: Shashi Kant, Ilan Vertinsky and Bin Zheng

A review on the measurement of subjective wellbeing among Aboriginal peoples of Canada demonstrated an underdeveloped and restricted understanding of the perceptions of life satisfaction and happiness in these Native populations. A limited analysis of cultural attributes relating to land use and cultural identity fails to recognize the holistic nature of Aboriginal perceptions on wellbeing and its diverse contributing factors. Similarly, the use of income as a determinate of wellbeing has demonstrated inconsistency and inaccuracy in the scoring of Aboriginal peoples' wellbeing, especially in contrast to non-Aboriginal populations. The proposed Holistic

Lifelong Learning model is a progressive step in stabilizing the conceptual framework of subjective wellbeing to account for the differences in explanatory elements perceived by Aboriginal and non-Aboriginal peoples. Studies that consider satisfaction measurements in a number of domains, as supported and recognized by Indigenous peoples, have substantiated the importance of including spiritual, emotional and mental domains, and having these measured by a greater variety of Aboriginal peoples comprising Native North America.

South and Central America

Economic wellbeing: Ana Maria Peredo

Community-based enterprises (CBEs) have emerged as mechanisms to boost the wellbeing and health of the community through market participation in South America. Wealth creation in these cases is not the goal in and of itself. Rather, self-reliance and improvement of life in the community through income opportunities, access to social services and support for cultural activities are the aims. These goals, in turn, reduce the drive for migration due to economic circumstances. The formation and functioning of CBEs is affected by the ability of a community to combine and adapt in an innovative way – ancestral and new skills, experiences, cooperative practices and values to meet the challenges and engage in a global market.

Typically, CBEs are triggered by social, economic and political stress. They draw on cultural heritage, experience of collective action and values toward protection of common patrimony for the common good. Communities that have engaged the market economy in their own collective ways have been able to gain some control over their lives. They have been able to increase food security, create and direct jobs, build a social infrastructure, increase security and achieve civic democracy. The Andean Indigenous cases studied in this region reinforce the possibilities of Indigenous, endogenous forms of development that have potential to generate a multifaceted wellbeing.

Cultural and spiritual wellbeing: Lilia Arcos Holzinger and Nicholas Biddle

Participation in cultural activities has been shown to have a positive and significant effect on the attendance of younger Indigenous and non-Indigenous children in school, as well as the determination of child desire to achieve tertiary qualifications. Policy restrictions on child labour in cooperation with cultural practice in the school environment is suggested to counter the negative relationship between child labour and school attendance. The cultural programs proposed by the authors are envisaged to improve school engagement especially for Mexican children and generally improve Indigenous-specific aspects of wellbeing. As an alternative or addition to systemically adopted programs, Indigenous children should be given opportunities to engage in extracurricular cultural activities that can enhance the positive effects of improved wellbeing on academic engagement and performance.

Subjective wellbeing: Lilia Arcos Holzinger and Nicholas Biddle

Latin American countries generally show high levels of subjectively perceived wellbeing despite their low average Gross Domestic Product per capita rating. This result, however, does not adequately account for the region's Indigenous population. Cultural factors are believed to significantly influence the perception of an Indigenous person's feelings of life improvement and feelings of unsafety after controlling for socioeconomic characteristics in an ordinary least squares regression. The particular cultural values that influence the relationship between ethnicity and the perceptions of wellbeing require further research, but clearly indicate the importance of considering non-economic factors during policy design in South America.

Subjective wellbeing: Mariano Rojas and Paz Chávez

Research conducted on the effect of modernization among the P'urhépecha people of Mexico demonstrated the influence of structural conditions such as values, beliefs and customs on individual perceptions of subjective wellbeing. Communities that base their measure of wellbeing on the modernized structures driven by more economic and occupational concerns demonstrate greater productivity (e.g. more employment) and higher individual income. Communities that endorsed traditional structures more aligned with spiritual and relational concerns demonstrated lower productivity and lower incomes than those exposed to the market-driven economy. In light of this finding however, those that did endorse traditional structures did not express lower subjective wellbeing. The lack of universality in wellbeing and its explanatory factors makes the measurement of subjective wellbeing extremely difficult. From an Indigenous policy perspective, the authors note the importance of considering an individual's subjective perceptions without overreliance on economic indicators alone.

Africa

Physical wellbeing: Rebecca Gearhart Mafazy and Munib Said Mafazy

A case study of the Swahili peoples of Lamu Town in Africa demonstrates the importance of further research in understanding the complex cultural frameworks within which African societies conceptualize illness and wellness. The unique interpretation and practice of general wellbeing and the traditional strategies of healing, such as herbal remedies, ritual and biomedicine, need to be synthesized to ensure healthcare is applicable and functional in the region. A great emphasis on pluralistic approaches is proposed for both general health and improvement of wellbeing, as exposure to modern medical knowledge has better informed the management of increasingly prevalent chronic diseases through supplement of traditional practice with biomedical training. Local healthcare providers play a critical role in the initiation of dialogue surrounding traditional customary frameworks and how current practice within the various communities may be enhanced to adequately address the cultural and medical requirements of the Indigenous population.

Social and emotional wellbeing: Keitseope Nthomang and Pelotshweu Moepeng

The experiences of the Basarwa people of Botswana is indicative of the critical requirement for culture and tradition to be given greater regard. The failure of the Remote Area Development Programme (RADP) is evident through its exposure of the native population to poverty, unemployment, poor healthcare and restricted income opportunities. Displacement of the Indigenous peoples to new territory with which they are culturally unfamiliar and historically disconnected leads to the alienation of traditional way-of-life and the subsequent damage to social and emotional wellbeing. Reviews of the implemented program found that discount of land rights and self-identity were significant contributors to the marginalization of the Basarwa and their vulnerability to decreased socioeconomic conditions impacting their wellbeing. Findings recommend a greater recognition of cultural individuality across the various Indigenous communities of Africa in the development and implementation stages of intervention programs. The consideration of such factors should recognize issues such as geographic heritage and the ritualism of cultural practices that may be affected and should be preserved during and after the intervention.

Economic wellbeing: Robert K. Hitchcock and Maria Sapignoli

The San people of Botswana are an underprivileged minority of southern Africa recording high rates of poverty, low rates of employment, low health standards and restricted access to land and resources compared to other population groups in the region. Programs introduced by the Botswana government are largely ineffective in addressing these problems as the reach fails to include remote, rural or peri-urban areas, and places within the country where the government has failed to implement these programs. General assessments of wellbeing find insufficient levels of medical aid, including staff and resources for the many Indigenous San people dwelling in the country, as well as below average levels of education for San children and many San adults who have never been to school. Despite these general data, life satisfaction levels and remoteness are positively correlated for San people. The impetus behind this was the measurement of quality of life by an indicator of perceived livelihood security, which was higher for those who did not fear eviction or issues with alcohol and drug abuse which were serious issues in the urban setting. The grave concerns for economic wellbeing and its collateral effects on general wellbeing intensify as the government intend to relocate Indigenous San from their traditional dwellings and make way for private companies who are ill-equipped to address the cultural and economic needs of the population.

Asia Pacific

Physical wellbeing: Joseph Keawe'aimoku Kaholokula, Andrea H. Hermosura and Mapuana C.K. Antonio

Despite the implementation of US Federal Legislation in 1988 that aimed to address the higher rates of chronic disease and mortality among Native Hawaiians, they continue to remain disproportionately affected by these problems. The Native Hawaiian Health Care Improvement Act currently appears best practice moving forward, but requires further commitment through funding and accessibility. The authors note the importance of tailoring the program to address health inequality by paying attention to the social and cultural determinants that are experienced by the population on their modernizing ancestral lands. Despite concerns for overrepresentation of chronic disease among the population, Native Hawaiians report generally good levels of subjective wellbeing. This result indicates that there are other contributing factors that drive and shape individual wellbeing.

Economic wellbeing: Rick Colbourne and Robert B. Anderson

An ongoing challenge for the Indigenous peoples of the Asia Pacific region is the exercise of their agency in the demand that governments, corporations and international bodies recognize and respect their identity and wellbeing. The economic wellbeing of the Indigenous populations includes historical, cultural and linguistic factors that are embedded in the traditional territories of the communities, and make their belief in how the land is used of great importance. Decisions of whether or not lands will be exposed to resource-driven or tourist-based ventures should include a greater voice of the Indigenous people, and where the exposure is rejected greater respect extended to the Indigenous people and their rights to preserve and sustain the traditions of the land. Frameworks for future economic ventures that require land procurement throughout the Asia Pacific should pay closer attention to the processes of these ventures that are both considerate and sustainable towards the economic and cultural wellbeing of the Indigenous people of those territories.

Economic wellbeing: Daniel Neff, Cornelis W. Haasnoot, Sebastian Renner and Kunal Sen

There is an inherently complex dynamic between the tribes dependent on their integration into the Hindu social hierarchy and subjective recognition by subsequent states across India. Scheduled Tribes (ST) are generally understood to encompass the 'backward tribes' among the Adivasi groups that demonstrate more primitive traits and shyness toward community contact, with approximately 90 percent residing in rural areas of India. The STs remain the most deprived social group across India with lower than average educational outcomes and average household expenditure per capita below the poverty line. A number of factors contributing to the continued deprivation of this group is the displacement of people from their traditional lands, lack of representation and political influence, and their restricted access to inadequately designed government programmes. The research demonstrates a clear structural disadvantage to those identifying as ST and a poorly developed treatment and response to their participation in society. A more comprehensive understanding of what cultural and traditional elements define the identity of ST members is required in order to develop more appropriate policy that successfully addresses the economic wellbeing of these communities.

Oceania

Physical wellbeing: Annabel Ahuriri-Driscoll and Amohia Boulton

Despite the influences of colonialism, the holistic healing system of *rongoā* is still practised throughout New Zealand. The traditional and customary system uses herbal remedies and prayer rituals among other native practices during their healing interventions, which benefits physical wellbeing on a psychological and biological level. Although the current practice of *rongoā* is supported by existing policy infrastructure, Māori healthcare more generally continues to struggle with limited resources and funding, and a restricted autonomy due to inflexible contracting. To enhance the *rongoā* practices and Māori healthcare there should be an adjustment of how contract developments account for the unique and varying cultural contexts of the practices that are involved, and how the accountability of their implementation extends beyond the practitioner.

Physical wellbeing: Denise Wilson, Amohia Boulton and Isaac Warbrick

Māori wellbeing comprises physical, psychological, spiritual and social factors that each contribute to an individual's perception of their health. It is apparent that the multifaceted nature of wellbeing among these Indigenous communities needs to be addressed through an adjustment of the role of healthy lifestyle practices within the culture. The development of several physically active events within the Māori communities has further shown the collective orientation of wellbeing among the community and why group initiatives are an effective approach. The undeniable effects of colonialism on the psychological determinants of Māori physical wellbeing should also be considered and addressed in the development of health promotion which considers cultural identity and promotes the contemporary Māori worldview.

Social and emotional wellbeing: Matthew Gray and Boyd Hunter

Indigenous Australians fare worse relative to non-Indigenous Australians than Māori fare relative to non-Māori populations with regard to employment, income, health and incarceration. Although discrepancies in employment factors can be generally attributed to fluctuations in the market economy, discrepancies in other measures such as income and health prove to be a serious problem in Australia. However, in New Zealand there appears to be less tension between economic and non-economic wellbeing outcomes for Māori. Further, both Māori and Indigenous Australians' suicide rates have increased substantially relative to non-Indigenous populations in their respective countries. In addition, Indigenous Australians are more likely to experience high or very high psychological distress compared to their non-Indigenous counterparts. Although the result is similar in the New Zealand context, the relative difference is smaller. Combined, these results can be potentially linked to relative differences among the Indigenous and non-Indigenous populations with regards to social and emotional wellbeing.

Responses that focus on enhancing the opportunities for Indigenous peoples in the market economy are limited and only truly effect those individuals that already have access to those services. Such a response does not achieve a broadening of the opportunity for Indigenous peoples to have greater access to the market economy and as a consequence improved employment opportunity. This research demonstrates the need for Indigenous contributions during the policy design process so that interventions are more attuned to the cultural and social contexts of the disadvantage that is being experienced.

Economic wellbeing: Carla Houkamau

In order to properly evaluate Māori economic wellbeing there needs to be a greater understanding of the multifaceted and complex nature of Māori identity. The transition from tribal autonomy to colonial acclimatization created problems for the socioeconomic stability of the Māori people who continue to struggle with discrimination. The perception that collective prosperity is representative of household economic stability is especially misleading in the assessment of Māori poverty as well as undermining the importance of individual identity. Socio-cultural factors such as the role of caregiver to dependent children contribute to the perception of self-wellbeing in Māori communities, in conjunction with Indigenous values such as hospitality (*manaakitanga*) and relationships (*whānaungatanga*). In light of this knowledge many business structures have adapted collective systems of operation to mobilize these cultural values and enhance the success of the business which is often measured according to its relative social, cultural and spiritual purposes as well as the economic results. Further development of business models that are considerate of Māori perceptions of identity and cultural values are important to ensure the success of economic opportunity in spite of the historic experiences that have impacted their holistic and therefore economic wellbeing.

Cultural and spiritual wellbeing: Mandy Yap and Eunice Yu

The Yawuru people of Broome in Western Australia have a complex and multifaceted perception of wellbeing. Their lives are characterized by operating within a collective framework and in consequence place much significance on relationships and connectivity, both among the people and between themselves and their territory, culture and self-identity. This phenomenon is understood within the community as *mabu liyan* and can be conceptualized as a holistic and fluid evaluation of one's wellbeing. Applying the Kessler Psychological Distress Scale (K-5), the authors revealed a number of the emotional and psychological elements that contribute to this concept of wellbeing, but K-5 failed to recognize a number of the deeper spiritual and cultural influences. The mixed-methods approach used by the authors proved to be the most effective method of analysis that represents the multifaceted understanding of wellbeing both qualitatively and quantitatively. Another critical element to ensuring the appropriate analysis and consequent understanding of *mabu liyan* is the inclusion of Indigenous peoples that can subjectively explore the meanings and dynamics presented by each participant in the research. The Yawuru people are an essential representation in the complex and contextual nature of developing knowledge and understanding in cultural and spiritual wellbeing of Indigenous peoples.

Subjective wellbeing: Christopher L. Ambrey, Christopher Fleming and Matthew Manning

Indigenous Australians experience a considerable disadvantage from their non-Indigenous counterparts across a number of determinant factors in wellbeing measurement. Despite generally reporting higher levels of life satisfaction, Indigenous Australians continue to demonstrate stagnation or non-improvement in areas such as life expectancy, literacy and unemployment. The ineffectiveness of the various policy measures and programs introduced by the Australian government throughout the years can be generally attributed to the subjective approach of these institutions developing frameworks that are aligned with Western non-Indigenous perceptions of wellbeing. Although these policy initiatives are implemented with the intention of 'closing the gap' between Indigenous and non-Indigenous measures of wellbeing, they often fail to fully appreciate those subjective cultural and traditional perceptions of wellbeing that are held among the Indigenous peoples.

Future directions

A number of consistent themes surfaced across all chapters with regard to factors that have, to varying degrees, shaped policies that attempt to improve the lives of Indigenous people while at the same time eliminate the relative disparity on domains of wellbeing between Indigenous and non-Indigenous populations. What we have learnt is that context matters and attempting to make broad statements with regard to those factors that affect the wellbeing of Indigenous people anywhere would be a mistake. Rather, each country/community must be a study unto itself. Instead of asking the question, 'what factors shape the current state of wellbeing of all Indigenous populations?', the question should be, 'what factors influence the wellbeing of a given Indigenous population in the area in which they live?' Our contributors have, in our eyes, done a wonderful job of attempting to synthesize and answer such a large question with a focus on a given domain of wellbeing in which they have a very good understanding.

However, in saying that the one central theme that does emerge is the need to understand the unique relationship that exists between land, history, culture and a whole range of other factors – mentioned throughout the book – and wellbeing. In short, Indigenous people around the world possess a holistic vision of wellbeing that incorporates the physical, spiritual, mental, emotional, social, economic and environmental. The focus is not solely on the individual but also on the wellbeing of the community. Thus, to fully appreciate the many ways that society can facilitate the healing of Indigenous people, we must first understand the Indigenous view of wellbeing and understand that it is different to that of Western culture.

We gain incredible insights into facilitating Indigenous wellbeing by looking at risks and protective factors. But we must note, that these risk and protective factors are dynamic and at times very different to those which have been creatively examined by scholars across the decades with regards to non-Indigenous populations. The nature of risk and protective factors within Indigenous communities, and the many developmental and situational pathways that affect these factors, cannot be understood in isolation. Here history is critical. History is not always strongly associated with poor wellbeing, but it plays a role in understanding where people have come from, where they are now, and shapes through lessons learnt, where they are going. We also cannot disassociate ourselves from the often fractious relations that have created a dominant Western paradigm that has marginalized Indigenous populations across the world. Unfortunately, this paradigm has, at times, dislocated the Indigenous population from those protective factors that have for centuries or more safeguarded their way of life and ultimate wellbeing. As described by our authors, Indigenous populations possess many traditional protective factors and we should be building upon these strengths.

This leads us to question why we are not building upon these strengths. Apart from the many historical and institutional injustices that have affected Indigenous populations around the world, one clear finding that emerges from this handbook is that we all need to better understand the influences of wellbeing across all domains. This requires further research. To date, much research has been lacking in both quality and substance, this can be remedied by the growing cadre of highly qualified researchers who are focusing their efforts on eliminating relative disparities between Indigenous and non-Indigenous populations. Future research should be conducted in the context of specific prevention programs that are designed and controlled by local Indigenous people, with the assistance (where requested) from the scientific community. Quality of research matters. We cannot continue to flippantly waste resources on poor research, irrespective of race, gender or indigeneity that inevitably leads to no improvement or, in some cases, detrimental outcomes.

We encourage the reader to fully explore the wonderful contributions that have been made by the authors of this handbook. What they have done is synthesize their knowledge into a succinct piece of literary work. We hope this book provides a gateway to the interesting work our authors have undertaken to improve the lives of Indigenous peoples and we encourage you to fully engage with this by not only reading their work but also by using this knowledge to act as ambassadors of change.

INDEX

Printed in the United States
by Baker & Taylor Publisher Services